Guide

FLORIDA
TAXES

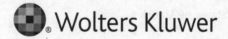

Wolters Kluwer

Wolters Kluwer Editorial Staff Publication

Editors . . . . Timothy Bjur, Carol Kokinis-Graves
Production Coordinator . . . . Govardhan. L
Production Editors . . . . Ravikishore. M,
Shashikant G

This publication is designed to provide accurate and authoritative information in regard to the subject matter covered. It is sold with the understanding that the publisher is not engaged in rendering legal, accounting or other professional service. If legal advice or other expert assistance is required, the services of a competent professional person should be sought.

ISBN: 978-0-8080-5757-4

This publication is designed to provide accurate and authoritative information in regard to the subject matter covered. It is sold with the understanding that the publisher is not engaged in rendering legal, accounting or other professional service. If legal advice or other expert assistance is required, the services of a competent professional person should be sought.

Printed in the United States of America

MIX
From responsible sources
FSC® C099992
FSC
www.fsc.org

PREFACE

This *Guidebook* gives a general picture of the taxes imposed by the state of Florida and the general property tax levied by the local governments. All 2022 legislative amendments received as of press time are reflected, and references to Florida and federal laws are to the laws as of the date of publication of this book.

The emphasis is on the law applicable to the filing of income tax returns in 2023 for the 2022 tax year. However, if legislation has made changes effective after 2022, we have tried to note this also, with an indication of the effective date to avoid confusion.

The taxes of major interest—income and sales and use—are discussed in detail. Other Florida taxes, including intangibles taxes, are summarized, with particular emphasis on application, exemptions, returns, and payment.

Throughout the *Guidebook,* tax tips are highlighted to help practitioners avoid pitfalls and use the tax laws to their best advantage.

The *Guidebook* is designed as a quick reference work, describing the general provisions of the various tax laws, rules, and administrative practices. It is useful to tax practitioners, business persons, and others who prepare or file Florida returns or who are required to deal with Florida taxes.

The *Guidebook* is not designed to eliminate the necessity of referring to the law and rules for answers to complicated problems, nor is it intended to take the place of detailed reference works, such as the CCH FLORIDA TAX REPORTS. With this in mind, specific references to the publisher's Florida and federal tax products are inserted in most paragraphs. By assuming some knowledge of federal taxes, the *Guidebook* is able to provide a concise, readable treatment of Florida taxes that will supply a complete answer to most questions and will serve as a time-saving aid where it does not provide the complete answer.

SCOPE OF THE BOOK

This *Guidebook* is designed to do three things:

1. Give a general picture of the impact and pattern of all taxes levied by the state of Florida and the general property tax levied by local governmental units.

2. Provide a readable, quick reference work for the tax on corporate income. As such, it explains briefly what the Florida law provides and indicates whether the Florida provision is the same as federal law.

3. Analyze and explain the differences, in most cases, between Florida and federal law.

HIGHLIGHTS OF 2022 FLORIDA TAX CHANGES

The most important 2022 Florida tax changes received by press time are noted in the "Highlights of 2022 Florida Tax Changes" section of the *Guidebook,* beginning on page 7 This useful reference gives the practitioner up-to-the-minute information on changes in tax legislation.

FINDERS

The practitioner may find information by consulting the general Table of Contents at the beginning of the *Guidebook,*.

October 2022

CONTENTS

HIGHLIGHTS OF 2022 FLORIDA TAX CHANGES

The most important 2022 tax changes and new developments are noted below.

Corporation Income Tax

• *Florida updates IRC conformity tie-in date*

Florida updated its IRC conformity tie-in date for computing corporate income tax liability. (Ch. 97 (H.B. 7071), Laws 2022) (¶ 10-515)

• *Florida creates railroad construction and infrastructure maintenance credit*

Florida created a corporate income tax credit for railroad construction and infrastructure maintenance expenditures. Eligible taxpayers can claim the credit for tax years beginning on or after January 1, 2023. The credit equals 50% of the taxpayer's qualifying expenditures in Florida during the tax year. Florida limits the credit each tax year to $3,500 for each mile of railroad track owned or leased in the state at the close of the tax year. (Ch. 97 (H.B. 7071), Laws 2022) (¶ 12-001)

• *Florida enacts changes to Strong Families, New Worlds Reading Initiative, other credits*

Florida enacted legislation that changes the eligibility dates for claiming credits under the New Worlds Reading Initiative and Strong Families Credit Programs from January 1, 2022 to January 1, 2021. The legislation also increased the annual caps for the community contributions credit, the Strong Families credit, and the New Worlds Reading Initiative credit. (Ch. 97 (H.B. 7071), Laws 2022) (¶ 12-001)

Sales and Use Taxes

• *Exemption for boiler fuels expanded to include hydrogen*

Effective July 1, 2022, the sales and use tax exemption for purchases of machinery and equipment necessary to produce electrical or steam energy by burning boiler fuels is expanded to include purchases of machinery and equipment that burns hydrogen. (Ch. 2022-97 (H.B. 7071), Laws 2022; *Tax Information Publication, No. 22A01-14*, Florida Department of Revenue, June 30, 2022, CCH FLORIDA TAX REPORTS, ¶ 206-585) (¶ 60-510)

• *Exemption enacted for machinery and equipment related to the production or use of green hydrogen*

Effective July 1, 2022, certain purchases of machinery or equipment for use at a fixed location in Florida are exempt from sales and use tax when the machinery or equipment will be used to produce or use green hydrogen. (Ch. 2022-97 (H.B. 7071), Laws 2022; *Tax Information Publication, No. 22A01-14*, Florida Department of Revenue, June 30, 2022, CCH FLORIDA TAX REPORTS, ¶ 206-585) (¶ 60-620)

• *Exemptions enacted for fencing and trailers used in agricultural production*

Effective July 1, 2022, sales and use tax exemptions for fencing and trailers used in agricultural production are enacted. (Ch. 2022-97 (H.B. 7071), Laws 2022; *Tax Information Publication, No. 22A01-15*, Florida Department of Revenue, June 29, 2022, CCH FLORIDA TAX REPORTS, ¶ 206-584) (¶ 60-250)

• *Temporary exemption enacted for impact-resistant doors, garage doors, and windows*

A temporary Florida sales and use tax exemption applies to impact-resistant doors, impact-resistant garage doors, and impact-resistant windows purchased for commercial or non-commercial use beginning July 1, 2022, and ending June 30, 2024.

(Ch. 2022-97 (H.B. 7071), Laws 2022; *Tax Information Publication, No. 22A01-07*, Florida Department of Revenue, May 6, 2022, CCH FLORIDA TAX REPORTS, ¶ 206-564) (¶ 60-330)

- *Temporary exemption enacted for children's diapers, clothing, and shoes*

A temporary Florida sales and use tax exemption applies to children's diapers and baby and toddler clothing, apparel, and shoes beginning July 1, 2022, and ending June 30, 2023. (Ch. 2022-97 (H.B. 7071), Laws 2022; *Tax Information Publication, No. 22A01-06*, Florida Department of Revenue, May 6, 2022, CCH FLORIDA TAX REPORTS, ¶ 206-565) (¶ 60-290)

- *Temporary exemption enacted for new Energy Star appliances*

Florida provides a temporary sales and use tax exemption on new Energy Star appliances purchased for noncommercial use beginning July 1, 2022, and ending June 30, 2023. (Ch. 2022-97 (H.B. 7071), Laws 2022; *Tax Information Publication, No. 22A01-05*, Florida Department of Revenue, May 6, 2022, CCH FLORIDA TAX REPORTS, ¶ 206-566) (¶ 60-770)

- *Indexed tax rate on asphalt announced*

The indexed tax rate for the calculation of Florida use tax due on asphalt manufactured by a contractor for the contractor's own use effective July 1, 2022, through June 30, 2023, is announced. (*Tax Information Publication, No. 22A01-10*, Florida Department of Revenue, June 9, 2022, CCH FLORIDA TAX REPORTS, ¶ 206-576) (¶ 60-110)

Severance Taxes

- *Severance tax rates on gas and sulfur modified*

Florida has issued the severance tax rates for the production of gas and sulfur effective July 1, 2022, through June 30, 2023. (*Tax Information Publication, No. 22B07-02*, Florida Department of Revenue, May 10, 2022, CCH FLORIDA TAX REPORTS, ¶ 206-570) (¶ 37-301)

- *Solid mineral tax rates announced*

Florida has released the severance tax rates on the production of heavy minerals and other solid minerals for tax year 2022. (*Tax Information Publication, No. 22B07-01*, Florida Department of Revenue, March 21, 2022, CCH FLORIDA TAX REPORTS, ¶ 206-555) (¶ 37-301)

Practice and Procedure

- *Electronic filing and payment threshold reduced*

Florida legislation reduced the electronic return filing (¶ 89-106) and tax payment threshold (¶ 89-108) effective beginning January 1, 2023. Taxpayers must file returns and pay taxes electronically if the amount of taxes paid in the previous state fiscal year was $5,000. The threshold was $20,000. (*Tax Information Publication, No. 22ADM-06*, Florida Department of Revenue, June 24, 2022, CCH FLORIDA TAX REPORTS, ¶ 206-582) (¶ 89-106)

[¶10-050]

FEDERAL/MULTISTATE ISSUES

[¶10-055] Comparison of Federal/State Key Features

The following is a comparison of key features of federal income tax laws that have been enacted as of August 16, 2022 and Florida corporate income tax laws. Florida corporate income tax liability is based on a federal taxable income starting point. Federal taxable income is modified by Florida addition and subtraction adjustments.

• *Foreign Tax Credit (IRC Sec. 27)*

Florida has no equivalent to the federal foreign tax credit (IRC Sec. 27). It allows a subtraction from federal taxable income for certain foreign taxes.

• *Alcohol Fuels Credit (IRC Sec. 40)*

Florida has no equivalent to the federal alcohol fuels credit (IRC Sec. 40).

• *Incremental Research Expenditures Credit (IRC Sec. 41)*

Florida allows a credit to targeted industry businesses for qualified research and development expenses. Taxpayers must qualify for and claim the federal credit (IRC Sec. 41). Taxpayers can also exclude certain payroll and property related to research and development activities from their Florida apportionment formula.

• *Low-Income Housing Credit (IRC Sec. 42)*

Florida provides a credit similar to the federal low-income housing credit (IRC Sec. 42) for construction and renovation of low-income housing in urban areas.

• *Disabled Access Credit (IRC Sec. 44)*

Florida has no equivalent to the federal disabled access credit (IRC Sec. 44).

• *Indian Employment Credit (IRC Sec. 45A)*

Florida has no equivalent to the federal Indian employment credit (IRC Sec. 45A).

• *Employer Social Security Credit (IRC Sec. 45B)*

Florida has no equivalent to the federal employer social security credit (IRC Sec. 45B).

• *Orphan Drug Credit (IRC Sec. 45C)*

Florida has no equivalent to the federal orphan drug credit (IRC Sec. 45C).

• *New Markets Credit (IRC Sec. 45D)*

Florida has a credit similar to the federal new markets credit (IRC Sec. 45D). It also allows a credit for contributions to public development organizations that sponsor community development and housing projects for low-income individuals.

• *Small Employer Pension Plan Start-Up Costs (IRC Sec. 45E)*

Florida has no equivalent to the federal small business pension start-up costs credit (IRC Sec. 45E).

• *Employer-Provided Child Care Credit (IRC Sec. 45F)*

Florida has no equivalent to the federal employer-provided child care credit (IRC Sec. 45F).

• *Fuel from Nonconventional Source Credit (IRC Sec. 45K)*

Florida has no equivalent to the federal fuel from nonconventional source credit (IRC Sec. 45K).

• *New Energy-Efficient Homes Credit (IRC Sec. 45L)*

Florida has no equivalent to the federal new energy-efficient homes credit (IRC Sec. 45L).

• *Energy Efficient Appliance Credit (IRC Sec. 45M)*

Florida has no equivalent to the federal energy efficient appliance credit (IRC Sec. 45M).

• *Investment Credit (IRC Sec. 46 — IRC Sec. 49)*

Florida has no equivalent to the federal investment credits (IRC Sec. 46, IRC Sec. 47, IRC Sec. 48, IRC Sec. 48A, IRC Sec. 48B,IRC Sec. 48C, IRC Sec. 48D, IRC Sec. 48E). It allows a credit for capital investments that create jobs in certain high impact industries, including solar panel manufacturing.

• *Wage Credits (IRC Secs. 51 — 52 and IRC Sec. 1396)*

Florida has no equivalent to the federal work opportunity credit (IRC Sec. 51— IRC Sec. 52) or empowerment zone employment credit (IRC Sec. 1396). It allows a subtraction from federal taxable income for wages and salaries disallowed under IRC Sec. 280C to taxpayers that claimed the federal credit. It also has an urban high crime area jobs tax credit and a rural jobs tax credit.

• *Alternative Minimum Tax (IRC Sec. 55 — IRC Sec. 59)*

Florida no longer imposes an alternative minimum tax based on the federal alternative minimum tax on corporations (IRC Sec. 55—IRC Sec. 59).

• *Base Erosion and Anti-Abuse Tax (IRC Sec. 59A)*

Florida has no equivalent to the base erosion and anti-abuse tax (BEAT) (IRC Sec. 59A).

• *Deemed Dividends (IRC Sec. 78)*

Florida allows a subtraction for any amount included in federal taxable income as foreign dividend "gross-up" income (IRC Sec. 78). The does subtraction cannot include related expenses.

• *Interest on Federal Obligations*

Florida taxes interest on U.S. obligations because the starting point for computing corporate net income is federal taxable income. Florida does not allow a subtraction adjustment for the interest.

• *Interest on State Obligations (IRC Sec. 103)*

Florida requires an addition to federal taxable income for exempt interest from state obligations (IRC Sec. 103(a)). The addition adjustment does not include expenses disallowed for federal income tax purposes under IRC Sec. 265.

• *Discharge of Indebtedness (IRC Sec. 108)*

Generally, the same as federal (IRC Sec. 108) , because the starting point for determining Florida corporate income tax liability is federal taxable income This

¶10-055

includes the federal exclusion for income from the forgiveness of Payment Protection Program (PPP) loans and the federal deduction for business expenses paid with those loans.

Florida did not allow taxpayers to defer the recognition of income from the cancellation of certain debt instruments in 2009 and 2010. It required an addition to federal taxable income for the amount of the deferred income. It allows a subtraction from federal taxable income when taxpayers must recognize the deferred income for federal tax purposes.

• *Contributions to the Capital of a Corporation (IRC Sec. 118)*

The same as federal (IRC Sec. 118), because the starting point for determining Florida corporate income tax liability is federal taxable income.

• *Certain Excessive Employee Remuneration (IRC Sec. 162(m))*

The same as federal (IRC Sec. 162(m)), because the starting point for determining Florida corporate income tax liability is federal taxable income.

• *Interest on Indebtedness (IRC Sec. 163)*

Generally, the same as federal (IRC Sec. 163, because the starting point for determining Florida corporate income tax liability is federal taxable income. Florida requires an addition to federal taxable income for part of the business interest expense deduction (IRC Sec. 163(j)).

• *Income and Franchise Tax Deductions (IRC Sec. 164)*

Florida requires an addition to federal taxable income for income taxes paid to any state or the District of Columbia.

• *Losses (IRC Sec. 165)*

The same as federal (IRC Sec. 165), because the starting point for determining Florida corporate income tax liability is federal taxable income.

• *Bad Debts (IRC Sec. 166)*

The same as federal (IRC Sec. 166), because the starting point for determining Florida corporate income tax liability is federal taxable income.

• *Depreciation (IRC Secs. 167 and 168)*

Generally, treated the same as federal (IRC Sec. 167 and IRC Sec. 168) because the starting point for determining Florida corporate income tax liability is federal taxable income. Florida requires an addition to federal taxable income for IRC Sec. 168(k) bonus depreciation and depreciation of qualified improvement property. Taxpayers can subtract part of the bonus depreciation addback amount in later tax years.

• *Safe Harbor Leasing (Pre-1984 Leases) (IRC Sec. 168(f))*

Florida recognized safe harbor leases under former IRC Sec. 168(f).

• *Pollution Control Facilities Amortization (IRC Sec. 169)*

The same as federal (IRC Sec. 169), because the starting point for determining Florida corporate income tax liability is federal taxable income.

• *Charitable Contributions (IRC Sec. 170)*

The same as federal (IRC Sec. 170), because the starting point for determining Florida corporate income tax liability is federal taxable income. Florida requires an addition to federal taxable income for charitable contribution carryover. It allows a subtraction from federal taxable income for charitable contribution carryover apportioned to the state.

• *Amortizable Bond Premium (IRC Sec. 171)*

The same as federal (IRC Sec. 171), because the starting point for determining Florida corporate income tax liability is federal taxable income.

• *Net Operating Loss (IRC Sec. 172)*

Florida requires an addition to federal taxable income for the amount of any federal net operating loss (NOL) deduction (IRC Sec. 172). Taxpayers can claim a NOL carryforward deduction from a loss year that is based on the amount allowed under IRC Sec. 172. The carryforward period is also the same as the period allowed under IRC Sec. 172. Florida does not allow NOL carrybacks.

• *Research and Experimental Expenditures (IRC Sec. 174)*

The same as federal (IRC Sec. 174), because the starting point for determining Florida corporate income tax liability is federal taxable income.

• *Asset Expense Election (IRC Sec. 179)*

Generally, the same as federal (IRC Sec. 179), because the starting point for determining Florida corporate income tax liability is federal taxable income. Florida required an addition to federal taxable income in tax years beginning after 2007 and before 2015 for taxpayers that claimed the enhanced federal deduction. Taxpayers can subtract part of the addback amount in later tax years.

• *Energy Efficient Commercial Buildings Deduction (IRC Sec. 179D)*

The same as federal (IRC Sec. 179D), because the starting point for determining Florida corporate income tax liability is federal taxable income.

• *Deduction for Qualified Film and Television and Live Theatrical Productions (IRC Sec. 181)*

Florida requires an addition to federal taxable income for the deduction of film, television, and live theater production expenses (IRC Sec. 181).

• *Deduction for Barriers Removal (IRC Sec. 190)*

The same as federal (IRC Sec. 190), because the starting point for determining Florida corporate income tax liability is federal taxable income.

• *Start-Up Expenditures (IRC Sec. 195)*

The same as federal (IRC Sec. 195), because the starting point for determining Florida corporate income tax liability is federal taxable income.

• *Amortization of Intangibles (IRC Sec. 197)*

The same as federal (IRC Sec. 197), because the starting point for determining Florida corporate income tax liability is federal taxable income.

• *Domestic Production Activities (IRC Sec. 199)*

The same as federal (IRC Sec. 199), because the starting point for determining Florida corporate income tax liability is federal taxable income. Florida follows the repeal of the federal domestic production activities deduction (DPAD) for tax years beginning after 2017.

•*Pass-Through Deduction (IRC Sec. 199A)*

Florida does not have reporting requirements for the pass-through deduction (IRC Sec. 199A), because the state does not impose a personal income tax.

¶10-055

• *Dividends Received Deduction (IRC Sec. 243 — IRC Sec. 245)*

The same as federal (IRC Sec. 243—IRC Sec. 245), because the starting point for determining Florida corporate income tax liability is federal taxable income after the special dividends received deductions.

• *Participation Dividends Received Deduction (IRC Sec. 245A)*

The same as federal (IRC Sec. 245A), because the starting point for determining Florida corporate income tax liability is federal taxable income after the special dividends received deductions.

• *Organizational Expenditures (IRC Sec. 248)*

The same as federal (IRC Sec. 248), because the starting point for determining Florida corporate income tax liability is federal taxable income.

• *Foreign-Derived Intangible Income and Global Intangible Low-Taxed Income (IRC Sec. 250)*

The same as federal (IRC Sec. 250), because the starting point for determining Florida corporate income tax liability is federal taxable income after the special dividends received deductions. But, taxpayers must reduce any Florida subtraction from federal taxable income for global intangible low-taxed income (GILTI) by amounts deducted under IRC Sec. 250.

• *Disallowance of Certain Entertainment Expenses (IRC Sec. 274)*

Florida requires an addition to federal taxable income for part of any business meal expense deduction (IRC Sec. 274).

• *Corporate Distributions and Adjustments (IRC Sec. 301 — IRC Sec. 385)*

The same as federal (IRC Sec. 301—IRC Sec. 385), because the starting point for determining Florida corporate income tax liability is federal taxable income.

• *Accounting Periods and Methods (IRC Sec. 441 — IRC Sec. 483)*

Generally, the same as federal (IRC Sec. 441—IRC Sec. 483), because the starting point for determining Florida corporate income tax liability is federal taxable income. Florida has a provision similar to IRC Sec. 482 that authorizes adjustments to income, deductions, or exclusions if necessary to clearly reflect a taxpayer's income.

• *Exempt Organizations (IRC Sec. 501 — IRC 530)*

Corporations that are exempt under IRC Sec. 501 are also exempt from the Florida corporate income tax. Exempt organizations must pay tax on unrelated business income to the same extent as under federal law. This includes the federal rule that exempt organizations with more than one unrelated business must calculate unrelated business taxable income separately for each unrelated trade or business.

• *Corporations Used to Avoid Shareholder Taxation (IRC Sec. 531 — IRC Sec. 547)*

Florida has no provisions regarding corporations used to avoid shareholder taxation (IRC Sec. 531—IRC Sec. 547). Florida does not impose a tax on accumulated earnings or an additional tax on the undistributed income of personal holding companies (IRC Sec. 541).

• *Banking Institutions (IRC Sec. 581 — IRC Sec. 597)*

Florida has no equivalent to the federal provisions on financial institutions (IRC Sec. 581—IRC Sec. 597). Banks and savings associations must pay Florida a franchise tax instead of the corporate income tax.

- *Natural Resources (IRC Sec. 611 — IRC Sec. 638)*

The same as federal (IRC Sec. 611—IRC Sec. 638), because the starting point for determining Florida corporate income tax liability is federal taxable income.

- *Insurance Companies (IRC Sec. 801 — IRC Sec. 848)*

Florida has no equivalent to the federal provisions on insurance companies (IRC Sec. 801—IRC Sec. 848). Insurance companies must pay both the Florida corporate income tax and an insurance gross premiums tax.

- *RICs, REITs, REMICs, and FASITs (IRC Sec. 851 — IRC Sec. 860L)*

Florida's treatment of RICs, REITs, and REMICs is generally the same as federal treatment (IRC Sec. 851—IRC Sec. 860L). It requires an addition to federal taxable income by RICs and REITs for undistributed net long-term capital gains. Generally, FASITs were repealed for tax years after 2004.

- *Foreign Source Income (IRC Sec. 861 — IRC Sec. 865)*

Florida does not follow the federal foreign sourcing rules (IRC Sec. 861—IRC Sec. 865). Multistate and international businesses that conduct business both in and outside Florida must use the state's allocation and apportionment rules for determining whether income is from state sources.

Florida allows a subtraction from federal taxable income for IRC Sec. 862 foreign source income.

- *Foreign Tax Credit (IRC Sec. 901 — IRC Sec. 908)*

Florida allows a subtraction by certain corporations for certain foreign taxes allowable as credits under IRC Sec. 901.

- *Global Intangible Low-Taxed Income (GILTI) (IRC Sec. 951A)*

Florida allows a subtraction from federal taxable income (IRC Sec. 951A).

- *Transition (Repatriation) Tax (IRC Sec. 965)*

Florida does not require an addition to federal taxable income for transition (repatriation) income (IRC Sec. 965). If this income flows through to federal taxable income, Florida allows a subtraction from federal taxable income.

- *Gain or Loss on Disposition of Property (IRC Sec. 1001 — IRC Sec. 1092)*

The same as federal (IRC Sec. 1001—IRC Sec. 1092) because the starting point for determining Florida corporate income tax liability is federal taxable income. Florida does not recognize gain or loss on the exchange of property qualifying for like-kind exchange treatment. A taxpayer can defer the gain or loss until it sells the property.

- *Alternative Capital Gains Tax (IRC Sec. 1201)*

Florida does not provide for an alternative tax rate on capital gains.

- *Capital Losses (IRC Secs. 1211 and 1212)*

Generally the same as federal (IRC Sec. 1211 and IRC Sec. 1212). Florida requires an addition to federal taxable income for net capital loss carryforward. It allows a subtraction from federal taxable income for net capital loss carryforward apportioned to the state. Taxpayers cannot carryback net capital losses).

- *Determining Capital Gains and Losses (IRC Sec. 1221 — IRC Sec. 1260)*

The same as federal (IRC Sec. 1221—IRC Sec. 1260), because the starting point for determining Florida corporate income tax liability is federal taxable income.

- *S Corporations (IRC Sec. 1361 — IRC Sec. 1379)*

Florida generally adopts the federal income tax treatment of S corporations (IRC Sec. 1361—IRC Sec. 1379). It exempts S corporations from the corporate income tax, except on income taxable under IRC Sec. 1374 or IRC Sec. 1375. Florida does not have a personal income tax, so S corporation income does not pass-through to shareholders.

- *Empowerment Zones and Renewal Communities (IRC Secs. 1391 — 1397F and IRC Secs. 1400E — 1400J)*

Florida has no equivalent to the federal provisions on empowerment zones and renewal communities (IRC Sec. 1391—IRC Sec. 1400J). The starting point for determining Florida corporate income tax liability is federal taxable income, so taxpayers can treat certain empowerment zone tax incentives the same as federal. Florida allows a subtraction from federal taxable income for wages and salaries disallowed under IRC Sec. 280C to taxpayers that claimed the federal empowerment zone employment credit. It also has an urban high crime area jobs tax credit and a rural jobs tax credit.

- *Consolidated Returns (IRC Sec. 1501 — IRC Sec. 1504)*

An affiliated group that files a federal consolidated return (IRC Sec. 1501—IRC Sec. 1504) can elect to file a Florida consolidated income tax return. Florida can require a consolidated return if it determines that separate returns will not accurately reflect the taxable income of affiliated corporations.

[¶10-075] Nexus--P.L. 86-272--Doing Business in State

What is the Florida nexus standard?

Florida follows an economic presence income tax nexus standard. Florida imposes its corporate income tax on foreign corporations and other entities for the privilege of doing business or gaining income in Florida. (Sec. 220.11, F.S.)

"Doing business" means actively engaging in any transaction for financial gain. Income gained from or attributed to sources in Florida includes income from tangible or intangible property located in Florida and income from any activities carried on in Florida. (Rule 12C-1.003)

What activities create nexus in Florida? Nexus-creating activities may include:

— incorporating in Florida;

— maintaining an office or other place of business;

— owning or leasing real or tangible personal property;

— maintaining a research facility for the exclusive use of a company in Florida;

— maintaining an inventory or merchandise or material for sale, distribution or manufacture in Florida;

— maintaining an inventory of tangible personal property on consignment to dealers or agents for sale or display in Florida;

— displaying a corporation's merchandise in leased space on a prolonged or recurring basis in Florida;

— agents or employees assembling, installing, servicing or repairing products in Florida;

— employees accepting orders in Florida;

— selling goods through mobile stores;

— making sales that are approved in Florida by independent contractors who do not hold themselves out to be engaged in selling, or soliciting orders for the sale of more than one principal;

— making sales through representatives in Florida if the activities exceed P.L. 86-272 protection;

— having employees in Florida that perform functions other than the solicitation of sales there;

— performing any service in Florida;

— having corporate officers who have permanent or extended temporary residency (3 months out of a 12 month period) in Florida who make management decisions while in Florida;

— selling or licensing the use of intangible property in Florida;

— conducting seminars;

— conducting management training courses for franchisees or affiliated corporations in Florida or regularly or systematically visiting franchisees or affiliated corporations in Florida to advise on business matters; or

— a financial organization earning or receiving interest from loans secured by real or tangible property in Florida regardless of place of receipt. (Rule 12C-1.011)

Also, selling, managing or providing consulting services for intangible assets in Florida may create nexus. This does not include out-of-state corporations that only manage out-of-state assets in the state. For example, a New York investment company that continues to manage investments for someone who is now a Florida resident will not have Florida nexus because of this limited connection with the state. (Rule 12C-1.011)

Operating professional sports teams. Out-of-state corporations engaged in professional sports activities are conducting a business or deriving income from such activities, and therefore creating nexus, if they:

— provide preseason training for athletes coaches, and staff, at Florida facilities, including exhibition games;

— play games in Florida during the regular playing season;

— participate in playoff or championship games in Florida;

— own or rent real and tangible property in Florida for the training or other activities;

— share in gate receipts from games played in Florida; and

— share in radio and television receipts from local stations and from networks under league contracts, a some of which are attributable to games played in Florida. (Rule 12C-1.011(1)(t))

Transportation companies traveling in Florida. Transportation companies that deliver or pick up goods in Florida are subject to Florida corporate income tax if they have revenue miles in Florida. This also applies to corporations that do not have a point of origin or termination in the state but have Florida revenue miles. (Rule 12C-1.011(1)(u))

Partnerships or joint ventures. Foreign corporations that are partners or members of Florida partnerships or joint ventures may have nexus because of their membership in the partnerships or joint ventures. Florida partnerships are partnerships doing business, gaining income, or existing in Florida. A partnership exists in

Florida if an active partner who participates in management decisions has permanent or extended temporary residency (3 months out of a 12 month period) in the state. If an active partner is residing in Florida, management of the partnership is presumed to be occurring in the state. (Rule 12C-1.011(1)(v))

Insurers. Nexus creating activities for insurers include:

— issuing insurance policies or annuity contracts under a certificate of authority issued by the Florida Department of Insurance, if the policies or contracts will be performed in Florida or if the policies insure or cover persons, property, subjects or risks in Florida;

— collecting premiums on insurance policies or annuity contracts on persons, property, subjects, or risks if the policies were initially issued by an insurer with a certificate of authority issued by the Florida Department of Insurance;

— issuing insurance policies or annuity contracts or collecting premiums without possessing a certificate of authority issued by the Florida Department of Insurance, if the issuing or collecting insurer would have been required to obtain a certificate of authority to perform those activities;

— entering into reinsurance contracts if the contracts are placed with an approved reinsurer by a ceding insurer domiciled or resident in Florida, or by either an artificial entity domiciled or resident in this state or a political subdivision of this state where either the artificial entity or political subdivision are engaged in self insurance; or

— surplus lines insurers with an office or employees located in this state. (Rule 12C-1.011(1)(w))

What activities do not create nexus in Florida? The following activities in Florida will not, in themselves, create Florida nexus for out-of-state corporations:

— maintaining an account in a Florida bank or savings association;

— holding stock in a Florida corporation or in a Florida corporate income taxpayer;

— having an independent Florida accountant, attorney, or bookkeeper maintain accounting records, audit, or do tax preparation;

— having resident salespersons soliciting sales of tangible personal property in Florida;

— having salespersons maintain samples to demonstrate the product or give free samples to a customer as long as the samples are not sold; or

— providing company cars to salespersons. (Rule 12C-1.011)

[¶10-200]

BUSINESS ENTITIES

[¶10-210] C Corporations

Florida follows the federal income tax treatment of C corporations, as set out in IRC Sec. 301—IRC Sec. 385, because federal taxable income is the starting point for computing Florida net income.

A tax measured by net income is imposed on every taxpayer for the privilege of conducting business, earning income or receiving income in Florida, or being a resident or citizen of Florida. (Sec. 220.11, F.S.)

The term "taxpayer" means any corporation subject to the Florida income tax, including all corporations for whom a consolidated return is filed and includes all successors and assigns. (Sec. 220.03(1)(aa), F.S.; Sec. 220.03(2)(a), F.S.)

A corporation that is a partner of a natural person must include in its net income its share of the partnership income. (Sec. 220.02, F.S.)

The term "corporation" includes all domestic corporations and foreign corporations qualified to do business in Florida or actually doing business in Florida, joint-stock companies, limited liability companies, common-law declarations of trust, corporations not for profit, agricultural cooperative marketing associations, professional service corporations, foreign unincorporated associations, private school corporations, foreign corporations not for profit that are carrying on their activities in Florida, and all other organizations, associations, legal entities, and artificial persons created by or pursuant to the statutes of Florida, the United States, or any other state, territory, possession, or jurisdiction. (Sec. 220.03(1)(e), F.S.)

An emergency excise tax is imposed on corporations that have elected not to be governed by 1980 federal and Florida law concerning depreciation. (Sec. 221.01(1), F.S.) The emergency excise tax is repealed effective January 1, 2012.

• *Federal income tax provisions*

Every corporation that is taxed under subchapter C of the tax code is called a C corporation. A C corporation is a separate taxpaying entity independent from its shareholders. It is organized under state law by filing a corporate charter with the competent state authorities. The corporation must also comply with other state law formalities such as the holding of an organizational meeting and issuance of stock. Individuals, corporations or non-corporate business entities may become shareholders in a corporation by contributing money or other property to the corporation's capital in exchange for its stock. There is no limitation on the number of shareholders, and any changes in the type or the number of shareholders do not affect the existence of the corporation. The liability of the shareholders for the corporation's debts is limited to their investment in the corporation's capital.

Federal tax law rather than state law determines if a corporation exists for tax purposes. State law determines if relationships essential to the federal tax concept of a corporation exist. An entity that qualifies as a corporation under state law is usually taxed as a corporation, unless it is a sham, inactive or organized solely for tax avoidance purposes. On the other hand, a business entity that fails to comply with some of the corporate organization formalities under state law may be treated as a corporation for federal tax purposes.

A C corporation pays a corporate income tax on its annual taxable income at specified corporate tax rates. The shareholders are taxed if and when the corporation's earned income is distributed in the form of dividends. Thus, the distributed corporate income of a C corporation may be subject to double taxation, first at a corporate level and then at a shareholder level. The corporation may also be subject to additional taxes, such as the accumulated earnings tax and the personal holding company tax.

[¶10-215] S Corporations

S corporations are not subject to Florida income tax, except on income taxable under IRC Sec. 1374 (built-in gains) or IRC Sec. 1375 (net passive investment income). (Sec. 220.13(2)(i), F.S.) There is no pass through of S corporation income or losses to individual shareholders for Florida income tax purposes, because individuals are not subject to income tax in Florida.

Except as otherwise provided under the IRC, a qualified subchapter S subsidiary is not treated under Florida law as a separate corporation or entity from the S corporation parent to which the subsidiary's assets, liabilities, income, deductions, and credits are attributed. (Sec. 220.02(11), F.S.)

• *Federal income tax provisions*

An S corporation is a small business corporation that satisfies the requirements of Subchapter S of the tax code and has elected to be taxed under those rules. In order to qualify as a small business corporation, the corporation must be a domestic corporation and is restricted on the number and types of shareholders it can have and on the type of stock that it can issue.

The difference between an S corporation and a regular corporation is that the S corporation has elected to be taxed similarly to a partnership for federal tax purposes. After making the S election, the income, losses, tax credits, and other tax items of the corporation flow through the corporation to the shareholders. Thus, income is only taxed once, at the shareholder level. However, an S corporation that was formerly a C corporation may be subject to taxes at the corporate level for LIFO recapture, excessive net passive income, and built-in gains.

[¶10-220] General Partnerships

How does Florida treat general partnerships?

Florida adopts the federal treatment of general partnerships and their partners under IRC Sec. 701–IRC Sec. 761. Any term used under the Florida income tax code has the same meaning when used in a similar context under the Internal Revenue Code and other federal income tax laws. (Sec. 220.03(2)(c), F.S.)

Under Florida income tax law, the term "partnership" includes a syndicate, group, pool, joint venture, or other unincorporated organization carrying on any business, financial operation, or venture in the state. The term "partner" includes a member having a capital or profits interest in a partnership. (Sec. 220.03(1)(s), F.S.)

Florida does not tax individuals who engage in a trade, business, or profession in the state as a partner in a partnership. But, a corporation or other or other taxable entity that is or becomes a partner in a partnership cannot exclude its share of the partnership's income from Florida taxable income. (Sec. 220.02(1), F.S.)

Are partnerships subject to reporting requirements? Every Florida partnership that has any partner subject to the state corporate income tax must file an information return for the tax year. (Instructions, Form F-1065, Florida Partnership Information Return)

Does Florida require estimated tax payments for corporate partners? Florida does not require estimated tax payments by partnerships for corporate partners. (Instructions, Form F-1065, Florida Partnership Information Return)

Does Florida require withholding for corporate partners? Florida does not require income tax withholding by partnerships for corporate partners. (Instructions, Form F-1065, Florida Partnership Information Return)

Does Florida allow composite returns or payments for corporate partners? Florida does not allow composite income tax returns or payments for corporate partners. (Instructions, Form F-1065, Florida Partnership Information Return)

How does federal law treat general partnerships?

Federal income tax law treats a general partnership as a pass-through entity that does not pay tax on its income. Instead, the partnership passes along its income or loss, gains, deductions, and credits to the partners. Each partner reports a percentage of the partnership income and other items on the partner's own tax return.

A partnership does not pay tax, but it does compute income, deductions and credits on an annual basis. It must report information about the business on federal Form 1065 and to the individual partners on separate Schedules K-1. The partners report the partnership income on their own returns and pay any taxes due based on their own tax rates.

[¶10-225] Limited Partnerships; Limited Liability Partnerships

Florida authorizes the formation of limited partnerships (Sec. 620.108, F.S.) and limited liability partnerships (LLPs). (Sec. 620.9001, F.S.) As under federal law, limited partnerships and LLPs are not taxable entities for Florida corporate income tax purposes. There is no pass through of limited partnership or LLP income to individual partners for Florida income tax purposes, because individuals are not subject to income tax in Florida. However, the partnership income of a partner that is a corporation or other taxable entity is taxable. Income and losses, including net operating losses (NOLs), of a partnership pass through to partners that are not individuals. (Sec. 220.02(1), F.S.)

Limited partnerships may be formed by executing a certificate of limited partnership (Sec. 620.108, F.S.) and paying a filing fee based upon the anticipated amount of capital contributions of the limited partners. (Sec. 620.182, F.S.) A limited partnership must file an annual report in the office of the Secretary of State between January 1 and May 1 of each year. (Sec. 620.177, F.S.) , along with a filing fee based upon the amount of capital contributions of the limited partners. (Sec. 620.182, F.S.)

LLPs may be formed in Florida by filing a statement of qualification (Sec. 620.9001, F.S.) and paying a $50 filing fee. (Sec. 620.81055, F.S.) An LLP must file an annual report in the office of the Secretary of State between January 1 and May 1 of each year (Sec. 620.9003, F.S.) , along with a $25 filing fee. (Sec. 620.81055, F.S.)

Limited partnerships may also become LLPs. (Sec. 620.187, F.S.)

Foreign LLPs must file a statement of foreign qualification and pay a $25 filing fee. (Sec. 620.9102, F.S.) Foreign LLPs must file an annual report in the office of the Secretary of State between January 1 and May 1 of each year (Sec. 620.9003, F.S.), along with a $25 filing fee. (Sec. 620.81055, F.S.)

Limited partnerships do not provide the same level of protection from liability as the LLC and S corporation forms, and pose obstacles to management participation. Limited partners of limited partnerships risk exposure to personal liability for the debts of the partnership if they participate in management of the enterprise (Sec. 620.129, F.S.) and general partners remain liable for partnership debts. (Sec. 620.125, F.S.)

• *Federal income tax provisions*

The state laws regulating limited liability partnerships (LLPs) vary widely. Accordingly, it is difficult to generalize about the requirements and state law consequences of obtaining LLP status.

LLPs are general partnerships in which each individual partner is liable for the partnership's general contractual obligations, his or her own individual business liability, and the tort liabilities deriving from the acts of those over whom the partner had supervisory duties. By complying with a prescribed registration requirement, the partner is otherwise insulated from the malpractice, negligence and similar liabilities of the other partners in excess of the value of the partner's interest in the partnership. The classification and tax treatment of LLPs is not affected by the check-the-box entity selection rules. The federal income tax status of an LLP depends on the provisions of the state law under which the partnership is formed.

[¶10-240] Limited Liability Companies (LLCs)

How does Florida treat LLCs?

Florida follows a limited liability company's classification for federal income tax purposes. It treats limited liability companies (LLCs) formed in the state or authorized to transact business in the state as partnerships, unless classified otherwise for federal income tax purposes. (Sec. 605.1103(2), F.S.; Rule 12C-1.013(1)(e); *Tax Information Publication, No. 98(C)1-05*, Florida Department of Revenue, July 1, 1998)

Florida does not impose the corporate income tax on LLCs classified as a partnership for federal income tax purposes. (Sec. 220.02(1), F.S.; Sec. 605.1103(1), F.S.) However, an LLC with 1 or more corporate owners must file a Florida partnership return. (*Tax Information Publication, No. 98(C)1-05*, Florida Department of Revenue, July 1, 1998; Instructions, Form F-1065, Partnership Information Return; Instructions, Form F-1120, Corporate Income/Franchise Tax Return) In addition, the corporate owner must file a Florida corporate income tax return to report its share of the LLC's distributive income. (Sec. 220.02(1), F.S.; Instructions, Form F-1120, Corporate Income/Franchise Tax Return)

How does Florida treat SMLLCs?

Florida follows a single member limited liability company's classification for federal income tax purposes. It treats single member limited liability companies (SMLLCs) as disregarded entities, unless classified otherwise for federal income tax purposes. (Sec. 605.1103(2), F.S.; *Tax Information Publication, No. 98(C)1-05*, Florida Department of Revenue, July 1, 1998)

Florida does not impose the corporate income tax on SMLLCs classified as disregarded entities for federal income tax purposes. It treats the SMLLC's activities in the same manner as a sole proprietorship, branch, or division of the owner. (Sec. 605.1103(1), F.S.)

If a corporation directly or indirectly owns a SMLLC, it must report the SMLLC's income on the corporation's return. The corporation must file a Florida income tax return reporting its own income and the SMLLC's income, even if the corporation's only activity in Florida is ownership of the SMLLC. (Instructions, Form F-1120, Corporate Income/Franchise Tax Return)

How does federal law treat LLCs?

Depending on elections made by the LLC and the number of members, the IRS treats an LLC as:

- a corporation;
- a partnership; or
- disregarded as an entity separate from its owner.

Specifically, the IRC classifies a domestic LLC with at least two members as a partnership for federal income tax purposes. The default classification applies unless the LLC files Form 8832 and affirmatively elects to be treated as a corporation.

Special check-the-box election timing requirements apply.

[¶10-245] Exempt Organizations

The Florida IRC conformity tie-in provision adopts the federal income tax treatment of exempt organizations under IRC Sec. 501—IRC Sec. 530. Exempt organizations must pay Florida corporate income tax on unrelated business income. (Sec. 220.13(2)(h), F.S.)

• *Federal income tax provisions*

Organizations may qualify for tax-exempt status if they are organized and operated exclusively for religious, charitable, scientific, testing for public safety, literary, or educational purposes, promotion of amateur sports, or the prevention of cruelty to animals or children (Section 501(c)(3) organizations). Any corporation, community chest, fund, trust, or foundation may qualify for this exemption. Private foundations and organizations that are not public charities are exempt from tax if they are not organized for profit and their earnings do not benefit any individual. Each type of organization must meet specific requirements for exemption. Organizations that are granted exemption will still be taxed on their unrelated business income. In general, an organization must apply for exemption.

[¶10-325]

REGULATED INDUSTRIES

[¶10-335] Insurance Companies

Florida insurance companies are subject to both the Florida corporate income tax and an insurance gross premiums tax. A credit is allowed against the gross premiums tax for the amount of corporate income tax paid. (Sec. 624.509, F.S.; Sec. 624.510, F.S.) For corporate income tax purposes, insurance companies are generally treated the same as under federal law (IRC Sec. 801—IRC Sec. 848) because the starting point for Florida net income is federal taxable income. However, special apportionment provisions apply to insurance companies that are doing business in Florida and another state or states.

• *Federal income tax provisions*

Insurance companies are generally subject to income tax computed at the normal corporate tax rates. However, the taxable income of insurance companies is determined under special rules. A company qualifies as an insurance company if more than half of its business during the tax year is the issuing of insurance or annuity contracts, or the reinsuring of risks underwritten by insurance companies. If an insurance company's net written premiums or direct written premiums (whichever is greater) for the tax year do not exceed a specified amount, the company may elect to be taxed only on its taxable investment income. Very small property and casualty (non-life) insurance companies may be exempt from tax if they meet certain requirements.

[¶10-340] Banks--Financial Corporations

Florida has no provisions comparable to IRC Sec. 581—IRC Sec. 597. Banks and savings associations are exempt from the corporate income tax, but are subject to a franchise tax measured by net income. (Sec. 220.65, F.S.; Sec. 220.63(1), F.S.) Banks may subtract from their net income base the "eligible net income" of an international banking facility.

For purposes of the tax on banks and savings associations, "bank" means a registered bank holding company, or a bank or trust company, incorporated and doing business under the laws of the United States, of any state, or of any territory, a substantial part of whose business consists of receiving deposits and making loans and discounts, or of exercising fiduciary powers similar to those permitted to national banks under authority of the Comptroller of the Currency, and that is subject by law to supervision and examination by state, territorial, or federal authorities having supervision over banking institutions. The term "bank" also includes any banking association, corporation, Florida Industrial Development Corporation, or other similar organization organized and operated under the laws of any foreign country that is also operating in Florida. (Sec. 220.62, F.S.)

"Savings association" means a savings association holding company registered under the Homeowner's Loan Act (HOLA) of 1933, 12 U.S.C. 1467a, or any savings association, building association, building and loan association, savings and loan association, or mutual savings bank that does not have capital stock. (Sec. 220.62, F.S.)

"International banking facility" means a set of asset and liability accounts segregated on the books and records of a banking organization that includes only international banking deposits, borrowings, and extensions of credit. (Sec. 220.62(3), F.S.)

"Banking organization" means:

— a bank organized and existing under the laws of any state;

— a national bank organized and existing as a national banking association pursuant to the Federal National Bank Act;

— an Edge Act corporation;

— an international banking facility;

— a federal agency licensed pursuant to sections 4 and 5 of the International Banking Act of 1978;

— a savings association organized and existing under the laws of any state; or

— a federal association organized and existing pursuant to the provisions of the Federal Home Owners' Loan Act of 1933.

For purposes of this definition, "foreign" and "domestic" have the same meaning as set forth in IRC Sec. 7701. (Sec. 220.62(4), F.S.)

• *Federal income tax provisions*

A "bank" for federal tax purposes is a corporation that receives deposits and makes loans or that exercises fiduciary powers as a trust company, and that is subject to banking regulatory supervision by a state or federal government. Banks are subject to the same federal income tax rates that apply to other corporations. Banking institutions are categorized as either commercial or non-commercial institutions. Non-commercial banking institutions include mutual savings banks, savings and loan associations, and credit unions. While similar in many respects to commercial banks, they are controlled by different sets of organizational, operational and regulatory rules, as well as by different sections of the Internal Revenue Code (IRC). Special tax treatment applies to insolvent banks and common trust funds. The definition of "bank" applies specifically under the IRC to bad debts, losses and securities gains, common trust funds, and bad debt reserves.

[¶10-375]
RATES

[¶10-380] Rates of Tax

What is the Florida corporate income tax rate?

The Florida corporate income tax rate is:

- 3.535% of net income for tax years beginning on or after January 1, 2021 and before January 1, 2022; (*Tax Information Publication, No. 21C01-02*, Florida Department of Revenue, September 14, 2021)

- 4.458% of net income for tax years beginning on or after January 1, 2019 and before January 1, 2021; (*Tax Information Publication, No. 19C01-04*, Florida Department of Revenue, September 12, 2019) and

- 5.5% of net income for tax years beginning before 2019 and on or after January 1, 2022. (Sec. 220.11(2), F.S.)

Effective for tax years before 2018, taxpayers had to pay the larger of the corporate income tax or the alternative minimum tax.

Exemption amount. Florida exempts up to $50,000 of net income from the corporate income tax. (Sec. 220.14(1), F.S.; Instructions, Form F-1120, Corporate Income/Franchise Tax Return) The exemption is the smaller of:

- $50,000; or

- the sum of adjusted federal income apportioned to Florida plus nonbusiness income allocated to the state. (Sec. 220.14(1), F.S.; Instructions, Form F-1120, Corporate Income/Franchise Tax Return)

DEPARTMENT OF REVENUE COMMENT: Companies that haven't been in business for a full year or have changed their fiscal year end are not entitled to the full exemption. Ineligible companies claiming the full exemption on their return are likely to draw the Florida Department of Revenue's attention, and that could trigger an audit.

Peter Steffens, Revenue Program Administrator, and David Bruns, DOR spokesperson, Florida Department of Revenue, Tallahassee, FL

Florida allows only one exemption to:

- taxpayers that file a consolidated return; (Sec. 220.14(3), F.S.) and

- members of a controlled group of corporations, as defined under IRC Sec. 1563, that file separate returns. (Sec. 220.14(4), F.S.)

Members of the controlled must divide the exemption equally, unless each member agrees to an unequal allocation. (Sec. 220.14(4), F.S.)

Bank franchise tax. Florida imposes a separate franchise tax on banks and savings associations (Sec. 220.65, F.S.) at the same rate and with the same exemption amount as the corporate income tax. (Sec. 220.63(2), F.S.)

Automatic rate adjustment and refund. Florida provides automatic rate reductions and refunds if net collections for the corporate income tax exceed forecasts in the:

- 2018-2019 fiscal year; and

- 2020-2021 fiscal year. (Sec. 220.1105(2), F.S.)

"Net collections" means the sum of:

- the total amount of income taxes collected, including interest and penalties, minus

- the total amount of refunds in that fiscal year. (Sec. 220.1105(1), F.S.)

If net collections exceed forecasted collections, Florida must adjust the tax rate on or after January 1 following the end of the fiscal year. (Sec. 220.1105(2), F.S.) The adjustment formula is the tax rate for the previous tax year multiplied by the sum of:

- the adjusted forecasted collections divided by

- the net collections. (Sec. 220.1105(2), F.S.)

"Adjusted forecasted collections" means forecasted net collections for a fiscal year multiplied by 1.07. (Sec. 220.1105(1), F.S.)

Taxpayers can claim a refund if their final tax liability is greater than $0 and their tax year begins between:

- April 1, 2018, and March 31, 2019; or

- April 1, 2019, and March 31, 2020. (Sec. 220.1105(4), F.S.)

Florida must determine a taxpayer's tax liability and refund share by April 15 after the fiscal year. It must issue a refund by May 1 after the fiscal year. (Sec. 220.1105(4), F.S.)

[¶10-500]

TAXABLE INCOME COMPUTATION

[¶10-505] Overview of Taxable Income Computation

Florida imposes a tax measured by net income on all corporations for the privilege of conducting business, receiving income, or existing in the state. (Sec. 220.02(1), F.S.; Sec. 220.11(1), F.S.) The tax is in addition to all other occupation, excise, privilege, and property taxes imposed by the state and any of its local governments. (Sec. 220.11(1), F.S.)

A taxpayer computes Florida corporate income tax liability by:

- starting with federal taxable income;

- making Florida addition and subtraction adjustments;

- multiplying base income by the taxpayer's apportionment fraction;

- allocating nonbusiness income to the state;

- subtracting a state exemption amount;

- multiplying net income by the state income tax rate; and

- applying any income tax credits.

For related information on determining corporate income tax liability, see:

- federal conformity; and

- rules for special industries and entities.

[¶10-510] Starting Point for Computation

What is the starting point for computation of the Florida corporate income tax?

A taxpayer's Florida net income is:

- its adjusted federal income or share of its adjusted federal income apportioned to the state, plus
- its nonbusiness income allocated to Florida, minus
- an exemption. (Sec. 220.12, F.S.)

"Adjusted federal income" (Sec. 220.13(1), F.S.) is the taxpayer's federal taxable income determined under IRC Sec. 63 (Sec. 220.13(2), F.S.) and reported on line 30 of its federal income tax return. (Instructions, Florida Form F-1120N, Corporate Income and Franchise Tax Return)

[¶10-515] Federal Conformity

Florida adopts the Internal Revenue Code (IRC) in effect on a specific tie-in date for computing corporate income tax liability.

What is the Florida conformity tie-in date?

Florida defines the "Internal Revenue Code" to mean the IRC as amended and in effect on January 1, 2022. (Sec. 220.03(1)(n)) It also gives effect to any IRC amendment taken into account in the computation of net income subject to tax. (Sec. 220.03(3), F.S.)

Does Florida provide any other conformity provisions?

Florida intends that the state income tax laws use, to the greatest extent possible, legal concepts which have been developed under federal income tax laws. (Sec. 220.03(3), F.S.)

COMMENT: Florida required information reporting for certain federal items affected by the Tax Cuts and Jobs Act (TCJA). Taxpayers required to file a Florida return for tax years 2018 and 2019 had to submit information to the state on:

- IRC Sec. 951A global intangible low-taxed income (GILTI) included in the taxpayer's federal taxable income;
- foreign-derived intangible income (FDII) included in the taxpayer's federal taxable income;
- the taxpayer's GILTI and FDII deduction under IRC Sec. 250;
- the taxpayer's IRC Sec. 163 business interest expense deduction and the amount that was not deducted due to TCJA limits; and
- the taxpayer's IRC Sec. 172 net operating loss (NOL) deduction and the amount that was not deducted due to TCJA limits. (Sec. 220.27(1)(a), F.S.)

A taxpayer also had to submit information on:

- the taxpayer's North American Industry Classification System (NAICS) code for business activity that generates the greatest proportion of its gross receipts;
- the taxpayer's Florida taxable income and apportionment fraction for the tax year;
- the total state net operating loss carryover available after the filing of the return for the tax year; and
- the total the state alternative minimum tax credit carryover available after the filing of the return for the tax year. (Sec. 220.27(1)(a), F.S.)

The certified information report was due by the earlier of:

- 10 days after the extended due date of the Florida return; or
- 10 days after the date the state return is filed. (Sec. 220.27(1)(c), F.S.)

A penalty applies to taxpayers who failed to provide the information report based on the larger of:

- $1,000; or
- 1% of the tax liability reported on a Florida return for the most recent tax year. (Sec. 220.27(1)(e), F.S.)

For additional information on Florida conformity with key provisions of the IRC, see Comparison of Federal/State Key Features.

[¶10-525] Special Industries or Entities

How do banks and savings associations compute taxable income?

The Florida franchise tax base for a bank or savings association is:

- its adjusted federal income apportioned to the state, plus
- its nonbusiness income allocated to Florida, minus
- eligible net income of an international banking facility and a $50,000 exemption. (Sec. 220.63(3), F.S.)

"Adjusted federal income" (Sec. 220.13(1), F.S.) is the taxpayer's federal taxable income determined under IRC Sec. 63 (Sec. 220.13(2), F.S.) and reported on line 30 of its federal income tax return. (Instructions, Florida Form F-1120N, Corporate Income and Franchise Tax Return)

The "eligible net income of an international banking facility" is the amount remaining after subtracting from the eligible gross income the applicable expenses. (Sec. 220.63(5), F.S.) The "eligible gross income" is the international banking facility's gross income from:

- foreign loans in which substantially all the proceeds are for use outside the U.S.;
- foreign deposits; and
- foreign trading or hedging transactions. (Sec. 220.63(5), F.S.)

The "applicable expenses" are any expenses or other deductions attributable to the eligible gross income. (Sec. 220.63(5), F.S.)

How do insurance companies compute taxable income?

The starting point for computing Florida corporate income tax liability is:

- federal taxable income under IRC Sec. 801 for life insurance companies; and
- federal taxable income under IRC Sec. 831 for other insurance companies. (Sec. 220.13(2)(a)-(c), F.S.)

How do regulated investment companies and real estate investment trusts compute taxable income?

The starting point for computing Florida corporate income tax liability is:

- federal taxable income under IRC Sec. 852 for regulated investment companies (RICs); and
- federal taxable income under IRC Sec. 857 for real estate investment trusts (REITs). (Sec. 220.13(2)(d) and (e), F.S.)

Florida requires an addition to federal taxable for the excess of a RIC's or REIT's net long-term capital gain over the amount of the capital gain dividends for the tax year. (Sec. 220.13(1), F.S.)

How do cooperatives compute taxable income?

The starting point for cooperatives computing Florida corporate income tax liability is federal taxable income under IRC Secs. 1381-1388. (Sec. 220.13(2)(g), F.S.) If a nonprofit corporation holds a parimutuel permit and is exempt from federal income tax as a farmers' cooperative, Florida requires an addition to federal taxable income for the excess of the gross income from the parimutuel operations over expenses for the tax year. (Sec. 220.13(1), F.S.)

[¶10-600] Additions to Taxable Income Base

Florida requires certain additions to the federal taxable income starting point that taxpayers must use to compute state corporate income tax liability.

Florida also allows certain subtraction adjustments from the federal taxable income base.

What are the Florida corporate income tax addition adjustments?

Florida requires additions to the federal taxable income base for a taxpayer's federal exclusion or deduction of:

- net operating losses (NOLs);
- interest;
- state income tax;
- net capital loss carryover;
- business interest and meal expenses;
- film, television, and live theatrical production expenses;
- excess charitable contribution carryover;
- excess employee benefit plan contribution carryover;
- bonus depreciation; and
- depreciation of qualified improvement property.

Florida also requires addition adjustments to the federal taxable income base for:

- state credits;
- partnership income or loss;
- consolidated income; and
- certain depreciation elections.

How do taxpayers report Florida corporate income tax addition adjustments?

Taxpayers report additions to federal taxable income on the taxpayer's Florida corporate income and franchise tax return, Form F-1120. (Instructions, Form F-1120N, Corporate Income and Franchise Tax Return)

[¶10-605] Additions--Net Operating Loss

The starting point for computing Florida corporate income tax liability is federal taxable income after net operating losses (NOLs). Florida requires an addition to federal taxable income for the amount of taxpayer's federal NOL deduction. (Instructions, Form F-1120N, Corporate Income and Franchise Tax Return)

The state allows a subtraction from taxable income for NOL carryovers. (Rule 12C-1.013(13); The two-step computation process is necessary because the amounts allowed for federal and Florida purposes can differ due to:

- application of the Florida apportionment ratio in the loss year; or

- Florida adjustments to federal taxable income that can increase or decrease the Florida NOL carryover. (Rule 12C-1.013(13); Instructions, Form F-1120N, Corporate Income and Franchise Tax Return)

For a list of other Florida addition adjustments, see Additions to Taxable Income Base.

[¶10-610] Additions--Federally Exempt Interest

Florida requires an addition to federal taxable income for all interest from state, local, and other obligations exempt from income tax by:

- IRC Sec. 103(a) or other federal law;

- state law; or

- the terms of issue. (Sec. 220.13(1)(a), F.S.; Rule 12C-1.013(4))

The addback is net of expenses disallowed in the computation of federal taxable income under IRC Sec. 265. (Sec. 220.13(1)(a), F.S.; Rule 12C-1.013(4))

The addback also applies to original issue discount (OID) on state or local obligations. (Rule 12C-1.013(4)) It does not apply to market discounts or premiums paid on municipal bonds. (Rule 12C-1.013(4))

Florida allowed taxpayers that paid alternative minimum tax (AMT) for tax years before 2018 to exclude 60% of any interest income included in the taxpayer's federal AMT under IRC Sec. 55(b)(2). (Sec. 220.13(1)(a), F.S.; Rule 12C-1.013(4))

For a list of other Florida addition adjustments, see Additions to Taxable Income Base.

[¶10-615] Additions--Taxes

Does Florida require an addback for taxes paid?

Yes, Florida requires an addback to federal taxable income for taxes measured by income and deducted under IRC Sec. 164. (Sec. 220.13(1)(a)(1), F.S.; Rule 12C-1.013(5)) The addback applies to income taxes paid to:

- any state; or

- the District of Columbia. (Sec. 220.13(1)(a)(1), F.S.; Rule 12C-1.013(5))

The addback does not apply to taxpayers paid to:

- city, county, or other local municipality;

- the Commonwealth of Puerto Rico;

- any U.S. territory or possession; or

- any foreign country. (Sec. 220.13(1)(a)(1), F.S.; Rule 12C-1.013(5))

It also does not apply to value added taxes. (Sec. 220.13(1)(a)(1), F.S.; Rule 12C-1.013(5))

For a list of other Florida addition adjustments, see Additions to Taxable Income Base.

[¶10-635] Additions--Losses

The net capital loss carryover pursuant to IRC Sec. 1212 deducted from capital gains in computing federal taxable income is added (Instructions, Form F-1120N, Corporate Income and Franchise Tax Return).

The Florida corporate income tax return provides for the addition of net operating losses and net capital losses on one return line, together with the amount of federal excess charitable contributions deduction and excess employee benefit plan deductions. The taxpayer must attach a statement identifying each amount included in the total. A two-step computation process, with an addition, and subtractions for each of these items, is provided because the amounts reportable for federal and Florida purposes may differ. Differences could occur due to the apportionment ratio in the loss year, or the use of the loss when either federal or Florida income was greater than the other. (Rule 12C-1.013(13); Sec. 220.13(2), F.S.; Instructions, Form F-1120N, Corporate Income and Franchise Tax Return)

[¶10-645] Additions--Expense Items

Does Florida require an addback for business interest expenses?

Effective for tax years beginning after 2017, IRC Sec. 163(j) limits the business interest expense deduction for the tax year to:

- the taxpayer's business interest;
- 30% of the taxpayer's adjusted taxable income (ATI); and
- the taxpayer's floor planning financing interest.

The ATI limit is 50% for the 2019 and 2020 tax years. Taxpayers can carryforward the amount that is not deductible indefinitely to later tax years.

Florida does not adopt the increase in the business interest expense deduction limit. Effective for tax years beginning after December 31, 2018 and before January 1, 2021, corporate income taxpayers must addback the amount that exceeds the 30% limit. Taxpayers can carryforward and subtract the unused business interest expenses in later tax years. (Sec. 220.13(1)(e), F.S.)

Does Florida require an addback for business meal expenses?

IRC Sec. 274 limits the federal deduction for most business meal expenses to 50% of those expenses for tax years after 2017. There is an exception for business meals provided by restaurants in 2021 and 2022. Taxpayers can deduct 100% of those expenses.

The 100% business meal expense deduction does not apply to taxpayers computing Florida corporate income tax liability. Taxpayers must addback the amount that exceeds the 50% limit. (Sec. 220.13(1)(e), F.S.)

Does Florida require an addback for other expenses?

Taxpayers can claim a federal deduction under IRC Sec. 181 for up to $15 million in qualified film, television, and live theater production expenses. Florida does not adopt the federal extension of the sunset date for the deduction from December 31, 2020 to December 31, 2025. Effective for tax years beginning after December 31, 2020 and before January 1, 2026, it requires an addition to federal taxable income by taxpayers that claim the deduction. (Sec. 220.13(1)(e), F.S.)

For a list of other Florida addition adjustments, see Additions to Taxable Income Base.

[¶10-650] Additions--Charitable Contributions

Florida requires corporate income taxpayers to add to federal taxable income both:

• the federal deduction for excess charitable contribution carryover under IRC Sec. 170(d)(2); (Sec. 220.13(2), F.S.; Rule 12C-1.013(13); Instructions, Form F-1120N, Corporate Income and Franchise Tax Return) and

• the credit for contributions to nonprofit scholarship funding organizations (SFOs). (Sec. 220.13(1)(a)(11), F.S.)

Florida allows a subtraction from taxable income for excess charitable contribution carryovers apportioned to the state.

The addition for the scholarship contribution credit is intended to ensure that the same amount is not allowed as both a deduction from income and a credit against the tax. This addition is not intended to result in adding the same amount back to income more than once. (Sec. 220.13(1)(a)(11), F.S.) Florida also created an exception to the addback, effective beginning July 1, 2018, if a taxpayer:

• added the credit to taxable income in a previous tax year; and

• claimed the SFO contribution as a federal charitable carryover deduction in the current tax year. (Sec. 220.13(1)(a)(1), F.S.)

Florida does not require an addition for the amount of that federal charitable deduction. The exception is intended to ensure that the credit addback does not result in a duplicate addition in a later tax year. (Sec. 220.13(1)(a)(1), F.S.)

For a list of other Florida addition adjustments, see Additions to Taxable Income Base.

[¶10-660] Additions--Items Related to Federal Deductions or Credits

Taxpayers can claim a federal deduction under IRC Sec. 181 for up to $15 million in qualified film, television, and live theater production expenses. Florida does not adopt the federal extension of the sunset date for the deduction from December 31, 2020 to December 31, 2025. Effective for tax years beginning after December 31, 2020 and before January 1, 2026, it requires an addition to federal taxable income by taxpayers that claim the deduction. (Sec. 220.13(1)(e), F.S.))

Florida also requires an addition to federal taxable income by employers that claim a deduction for the carryover of excess contributions to:

• qualified pension plans under IRC Sec. 404(a)(1)(E); and

• qualified stock bonus or profit-sharing plans under IRC Sec. 404(a)(3)(A)(ii). (Sec. 220.13(2), F.S.)

It allows a corresponding subtraction from federal taxable income for the excess employer contributions apportioned to Florida. (Rule 12C-1.013(13))

For a list of other Florida addition adjustments, see Additions to Taxable Income Base.

[¶10-670] Additions--Depreciation

Does Florida require an addback of federal bonus depreciation?

Florida requires an addback for all federal bonus depreciation allowed under IRC Sec. 168(k). (Sec. 220.13(1)(e), F.S.; Rule 12C-1.013(14)) The addition adjustment applies to:

- property placed in service in tax years beginning after 2007 and before 2027; and

- the 100% bonus depreciation deduction enacted by the federal Tax Cuts and Jobs Act of 2017 (TCJA) (P.L. 115-97). (Sec. 220.13(1)(e), F.S..)

Florida allows a subtraction for a portion of the amounts of bonus depreciation that have been added back to Florida taxable income.

Does Florida require an addback of federal deduction taken for depreciation other than bonus depreciation?

The Coronavirus Aid, Relief, and Economic Security Act (CARES Act) changed the depreciation recovery period for qualified improvement property (QIP) from 39 years to:

- 15 years under the general depreciation system; and

- 20 years under the IRC Sec. 168(g) alternative depreciation system.

The change in the recovery period made QIP eligible for federal bonus depreciation under IRC Sec. 168(k).

Effective for QIP placed in service on or after January 1, 2018, Florida requires an addition to federal taxable income for 100% of a taxpayer's federal depreciation deduction for the property. (Sec. 220.13(1)(e), F.S.)

Does Florida require an addback of Sec. 179 asset expense deduction amounts?

Florida does not require an addback of IRC Sec. 179 asset expense deduction amounts for tax years beginning on or after January 1, 2015. Florida required taxpayers to add back all Sec. 179 asset expense deduction amounts in excess of $128,000 for taxable years beginning after December 31, 2007, and before January 1, 2015 and any amount in excess of $250,000 for the 2010 taxable year. (Sec. 220.13(1)(e)(2), F.S.; Rule 12C-1.013(14))

Florida allows a subtraction for a portion of the federal expense deduction added back to Florida taxable income in tax years before 2015.

For a list of other Florida addition adjustments, see Additions to Taxable Income Base.

[¶10-695] Additions--Florida Credits

Florida requires additions to federal taxable income by taxpayers that claim:

- the enterprise zone jobs credit; (Sec. 220.13(1)(a), F.S.; Rule 12C-1.013(6))

- the enterprise zone property tax credit; (Sec. 220.13(1)(a), F.S.; Rule 12C-1.013(7))

- the insurance guaranty association and health maintenance organization consumer assistance assessment credits; Sec. 220.13(1)(a), F.S.; Rule 12C-1.013(9))

- the rural and urban high crime area job credits; (Sec. 220.13(1)(a), F.S.)

- the state housing tax credit; (Sec. 220.13(1)(a), F.S.)

- the scholarship, strong families, or New Worlds Reading Initiative program credits; (Sec. 220.13(1)(a), F.S.)

- the renewable energy production credit; (Sec. 220.13(1)(a), F.S.)

- the new markets credit; (Sec. 220.13(1)(a), F.S.)

- the entertainment industry tax credit; (Sec. 220.13(1)(a), F.S.)

- the research and development credit; (Sec. 220.13(1)(a), F.S.) or

- the student internship program credit. (Sec. 220.13(1)(a), F.S.; Instructions, Form F-1120, Florida Corporate Income/Franchise Tax Return)

For a list of other Florida addition adjustments, see Additions to Taxable Income Base.

[¶10-696] Additions--Other Additions

Additions may be required for which no specific line is provided on the Florida return.

Schedule I of the Florida Form F-1120, Corporate Income and Franchise Tax Return, provides a line for other additions that may be needed in the computation of Florida tax. The instructions discuss, as examples, a partnership adjustment, a consolidated income adjustment (if a specified election was made within 90 days of December 20, 1984, or upon the filing of the taxpayer's first return after that date), and an adjustment for depreciation (if specific elections were made for depreciable assets placed in service during 1981, or during 1981 through 1986) (Instructions, Form F-1120N, Corporate Income and Franchise Tax Return).

[¶10-701] Additions--Discharge of Indebtedness

Florida did not allow taxpayers to defer the recognition of income from the cancellation of certain debt instruments in 2009 and 2010. It required an addition to federal taxable income for the amount of the deferred income. (Sec. 220.13(1)(e)(3), F.S.) It allows a subtraction from federal taxable income when taxpayers must recognize the deferred income for federal tax purposes.

For a list of other Florida addition adjustments, see Additions to Taxable Income Base.

[¶10-800] Subtractions from Taxable Income Base

Florida allows certain subtractions from the federal taxable income starting point that taxpayers must use to compute state corporate income tax liability. The state also requires certain addition adjustments to the federal taxable income base.

What are the Florida corporate income tax subtraction adjustments?

Florida subtractions from the federal taxable income base include:

- net operating losses;
- dividends;
- foreign gross-up income;
- Subpart F income;
- global intangible low-taxed income (GILTI);
- net capital losses;
- film, television, and live theatrical production expenses;
- nonbusiness income;
- expenses related to federal employment credits;
- foreign taxes allowed as federal credit;
- excess charitable contributions;
- excess employee benefit plan contributions;
- bonus depreciation;
- depreciation of qualified improvement property;
- IRC Sec. 179 asset expenses; and
- deferred income from the discharge of indebtedness.

Taxpayers cannot subtract from federal taxable income Social Security and Medicare taxes paid on certain employee tip income if those taxes are taken as a federal credit under IRC Sec. 45B. Florida does not have provide a similar credit or subtraction from federal taxable income for those taxes. (Instructions, Form F-1120N, Corporate Income and Franchise Tax Return)

How do taxpayers report Florida corporate income tax addition adjustments?

Taxpayers report subtractions from federal taxable income on the taxpayer's Florida corporate income and franchise tax return, Form F-1120. (Instructions, Form F-1120N, Corporate Income and Franchise Tax Return)

[¶10-805] Subtractions--Net Operating Loss

Does Florida allow a net operating loss (NOL) deduction?

Florida allows taxpayers computing corporate income tax liability to deduct net operating losses (NOLs). (Sec. 220.13(1)(b), F.S.; Rule 12C-1.013(13)) Taxpayers generally compute the NOL deduction based on IRC Sec. 172 (Sec. 220.13(1)(b), F.S.; Rule 12C-1.013(15))

A taxpayer determines its Florida NOL by applying the apportionment factor in effect for the loss year. (Rule 12C-1.013(15)(c)) The NOL deduction applies to a taxpayer's adjusted and apportioned income in later tax years. (Rule 12C-1.013(15)(b))

To support a deduction, the taxpayer must attach a schedule showing its:

- tax year;
- adjusted federal loss;
- apportionment fraction for the loss year;
- Florida apportioned income or loss;
- NOL carryover applied;
- Florida portion of adjusted federal income; and
- NOL carryforward to the next year. (Instructions, Form F-1120, Corporate Income and Franchise Tax Return

Does Florida require adjustments for debt cancellation income? IRC Sec. 108 limits any NOL or NOL carryover in a year in which there has been a discharge of a taxpayer's indebtedness. Florida piggybacks the IRC Sec. 108 limitation. A Florida taxpayer must recalculate its NOL to reflect the reduction for any discharge of indebtedness. (Rule 12C-1.013(15))

How does Florida treat NOLs following mergers and acquisitions? Florida follows federal rules that govern the use of NOLs following corporate mergers and acquisitions. It incorporates by reference:

- IRC Sec. 381 carryover rules; (Rule 12C-1.013(15)(h); Rule 12C-1.0511(1)(e)) and

- IRC Sec. 382 loss limitation rules. (Rule 12C-1.013(15)(i); Rule 12C-1.0511(f))

It otherwise follows the IRC for the computation and handling of NOLs, including:

- IRC Sec. 269 anti-abuse rules; and
- IRC Sec. 384 built-in loss limitation rules. (Rule 12C-1.013(15)(a))

How does Florida treat farm losses? Florida follows the IRC Sec. 172 treatment of farm losses, except the carryback period for NOLs. (Sec. 220.13(1)(b), F.S.; Rule 12C-1.013(15))

How does Florida treat S corporation losses? Florida follows IRC Sec. 1371(b), which prohibits S corporations from using NOL carryback or carryforward from C corporation years. (Rule 12C-1.013(15); *Unofficial Department Guidance*, Florida Department of Revenue, May 12, 2011)

Does Florida allow net operating loss (NOL) carryback and or carryforward adjustments?

Florida follows IRC Sec. 172 NOL carryforward periods, including:

- the 20 year carryforward period for NOLs sustained in tax years before 2018; and

- the indefinite carryforward period for NOLs sustained in 2018 and future tax years. (Sec. 220.13(1)(b), F.S.; Rule 12C-1.013(15))

Taxpayers cannot carryback Florida NOLs to previous tax years. (Sec. 220.13(1)(b), F.S.; Rule 12C-1.013(15))

For a list of other subtractions from the taxable income base, see Subtractions from Taxable Income Base.

[¶10-810] Subtractions--Dividends

Florida allows corporate income taxpayers subtractions from federal taxable income for certain dividend and other income they report on Schedule C of their federal Form 1120. Taxpayers must reduce these subtractions by any federal expense deduction directly or indirectly related to the income. (Sec. 220.13(1)(b), F.S.; Rule 12C-1.013(10))

Does Florida allow a subtraction for dividends from foreign corporations?

Florida allows a subtraction from federal taxable income for dividends treated as received from IRC Sec. 862 foreign source income. (Sec. 220.13(1)(b), F.S.; Rule 12C-1.013(10))

Does Florida allow a subtraction for foreign gross-up dividends?

Florida allows a subtraction from federal taxable income for IRC Sec. 78 foreign gross-up dividends. (Sec. 220.13(1)(b), F.S.; Rule 12C-1.013(10))

Does Florida allow a subtraction for Subpart F income?

Florida allows a subtraction from federal taxable income for IRC Sec. 951 Subpart F income. (Sec. 220.13(1)(b), F.S.; Rule 12C-1.013(10))

COMPLIANCE ALERT: The Tax Cuts and Jobs Act (P.L. 115-97) made numerous changes to federal income tax provisions. The changes include the IRC Sec. 965 transition (repatriation) tax on untaxed earnings and profits of certain foreign corporations. If IRC Sec. 965 income flows through to federal taxable income, like REIT flow-through income, Florida allows a subtraction from federal taxable income. (*Tax Information Publication*, No. 18C01-01, Florida Department of Revenue, April 27, 2018)

Does Florida allow a deduction for global intangible low-taxed income?

Florida allows a subtraction from federal taxable income for IRC Sec. 951A global intangible low-taxed income (GILTI). The GILTI subtraction is effective retroactively to tax years beginning on or after January 1, 2018. (Sec. 220.13(1)(b), F.S.)

For a list of other Florida subtraction adjustments, see Subtractions from Taxable Income Base.

[¶10-820] Subtractions--Losses

A subtraction is made on the Florida return for amounts derived from federal net capital losses. The subtraction is the second part of a two-step computation process, with additions and subtractions, because the amounts reportable for federal and Florida purposes may differ. Differences could occur due to the apportionment ratio in the loss year, or the use of the loss when either federal or Florida income was greater than the other. (Rule 12C-1.013(13); Instructions, Form F-1120N, Corporate Income and Franchise Tax Return)

• *Loss carrybacks disallowed*

Net capital losses may not be carried back in Florida as a deduction to a prior taxable year. However, such losses are considered carryovers and are treated in the same manner, to the same extent and for the same time periods, as prescribed by IRC Sec. 1212 (capital loss carrybacks and carryovers). (Sec. 220.13(1)(b), F.S.)

A deduction for net capital losses that has been allowed for Florida purposes in a prior year is not allowed again, even if the deduction has not been fully utilized for federal purposes. (Sec. 220.13(1)(d), F.S.)

• *Carryover loss apportionment and computation rules*

Corporations enter as a subtraction the entire Florida amount of the net capital losses, if the corporation does all of its business in Florida. However, if a corporation does business outside of Florida, the Florida subtraction for these federal loss items is limited to the portion of the carryforward for that item apportioned to Florida, determined by using the apportionment fraction for the year in which the loss occurred. The subtraction then is taken on the return after the current year apportionment factor has been applied to activities in the current year. (Sec. 220.13(1)(b)(1), F.S.; Rule 12C-1.013(14); Rule 12C-1.013(15); Instructions, Form F-1120N, Corporate Income and Franchise Tax Return)

A capital loss carryover is allowed for Florida purposes to the extent that it is allowed for federal tax purposes. Thus, a loss is allowed to the extent of federal capital gains, if the deduction does not exceed the available Florida carryover. (Rule 12C-1.013(15))

[¶10-830] Subtractions--Expense Items

Florida allows a subtraction from federal taxable income by taxpayers required to addback the deduction for film, television, and live theatrical production expenses under IRC Sec. 181. It limits the subtraction adjustment to any federal deduction allowed for those expenses without application of IRC Sec. 181. (Sec. 220.13(1)(e), F.S.; Instructions, Form F-1120, Florida Corporate Income/Franchise Tax Return)

A taxpayer must include a schedule with its Florida income tax return showing the amount of the original addition and the subtraction adjustment by tax year (Instructions, Form F-1120, Florida Corporate Income/Franchise Tax Return)

For a list of other subtractions from the taxable income base, see Subtractions from Taxable Income Base.

[¶10-835] Subtractions--Corporate Transactions

A subtraction is provided for the amount of nonbusiness income included in federal taxable income (Sec. 220.13(1)(b)(4), F.S.; Rule 12C-1.013(11)). Corporations doing business entirely within Florida are not eligible for this subtraction. Other corporations subtract their total nonbusiness income. The separate amounts of nonbusiness income allocated to Florida and elsewhere, which together equal the amount eligible for subtraction, must be reported on Schedule R (Instructions, Form F-1120N, Corporate Income and Franchise Tax Return).

[¶ 10-855] Subtractions--Items Related to Federal Deductions or Credits

Subtractions may be required on the Florida return to account for Florida differences with Internal Revenue Code provisions concerning employment credits, employee benefit plan deductions, and foreign taxes taken as a federal credit.

• *Federal employment credits*

A subtraction is allowed for the amount of wages and salaries paid or incurred within Florida for which no federal deduction is allowed, pursuant to IRC Sec. 280C(a) (relating to federal employment credits). (Sec. 220.13(1)(b)(3), F.S.; Rule 12C-1.013(12)) Florida Form F-1120, Corporate Income and Franchise Tax Return, does not provide a specific line for this subtraction. However, a line is provided for "other subtractions" to be made on the return, including any required subtraction. (Instructions, Form F-1120N, Corporate Income and Franchise Tax Return)

• *Foreign taxes allowed as federal credits*

Florida allows a subtraction from federal taxable income for foreign taxes that are allowed as credits under IRC Sec. 901 to any corporation that derived less than 20% of its gross income or loss for its tax year ending in 1984 from sources within the U.S. Excluded from this subtraction are credits allowed under IRC Secs. 902 and 960, withholding taxes on dividends treated under IRC Sec. 862, and withholding taxes on royalties, interest, technical service fees, and capital gains. (Sec. 220.13(b)(5), F.S.) Form F-1120 does not provide a specific line for this subtraction. However, a line is provided for "other subtractions" to be made on the return, and this subtraction is used as one of the examples for that return line. (Instructions, Form F-1120N, Corporate Income and Franchise Tax Return)

• *Excess retirement and charitable contributions*

An addition is required for the amount of excess employee benefit plan deductions under IRC Sec. 404(a)(1)(E) pertaining to qualified pension plans, and under IRC Sec. 404(a)(3)(A)(ii) pertaining to qualified stock bonus or profit-sharing plans, when carried forward and deducted for federal purposes in the taxable year (Instructions, Form F-1120N, Corporate Income and Franchise Tax Return).

This amount and the amount of excess charitable contribution deductions is aggregated with the corporation's net operating loss deduction and net capital loss carryover and reported on one line on Schedule I of the Form F-1120, Corporate Income and Franchise Tax Return. This is required as part of a two-step computation process with additions and subtractions for these federal items to account for any Florida differences. (Sec. 220.13(2), F.S.; Rule 12C-1.013(13); Instructions, Form F-1120N, Corporate Income and Franchise Tax Return)

[¶ 10-880] Subtractions--Charitable Items

As the second part of a two-step computation process requiring additions and subtractions to account for possible Florida differences from federal amounts, corporations subtract the Florida amount of the excess charitable contributions deduction under IRC Sec. 170(d)(2) allowable for federal purposes in the taxable year. (Sec. 220.13(1)(b)(1), F.S.; Rule 12C-1.013(13))

In general, corporations subtract the amount of excess charitable contribution deductions allowable for federal income tax purposes for the taxable year, if the corporation does all of its business in Florida. However, if a corporation does business outside of Florida, the Florida subtraction is limited to the portion of the carryforward for that item apportioned to Florida, determined by using the apportionment fraction for the year in which the excess occurred. The subtraction then is taken on the return after the current year apportionment factor has been applied to activities in the current year. (Sec. 220.13(1)(b)(1), F.S.; Rule 12C-1.013(16); Rule 12C-1.013(17); Instructions, Form F-1120N, Corporate Income and Franchise Tax Return)

The apportioned amount determined is the Florida excess contribution carryover for the taxable year. A deduction would be allowed for Florida purposes to the extent claimed for federal purposes, as long as the deduction did not exceed the total amount of the Florida carryover to the taxable year. Also, the deduction for the excess contributions may not create or increase a net operating loss in Florida. (Sec. 220.13(1)(b)(1), F.S.; Rule 12C-1.013(16); Rule 12C-1.013(17); Instructions, Form F-1120N, Corporate Income and Franchise Tax Return)

A deduction for excess contributions that has been allowed for Florida purposes in a prior year is not allowed again, even if the deduction has not been fully utilized for federal purposes. (Sec. 220.13(1)(d), F.S.)

[¶10-890] Subtractions--Jobs Programs or Employee Benefits

As the second part of a two-step computation process requiring additions and subtractions to account for possible Florida differences from federal amounts, corporations subtract the Florida amount of excess employee benefit plan contribution deductions allowable under IRC Sec. 404 (pertaining to qualified pension plans and qualified stock bonus or profit-sharing plans) for federal purposes in the taxable year. (Sec. 220.13(1)(b)(1), F.S.; Rule 12C-1.013(13))

In general, corporations subtract the amount of excess employee benefit plan contribution deductions allowable for federal income tax purposes for the taxable year, if the corporation does all of its business in Florida. However, if a corporation does business outside of Florida, the Florida subtraction is limited to the portion of the carryforward for that item apportioned to Florida, determined by using the apportionment fraction for the year in which the excess occurred. The subtraction then is taken on the return after the current year apportionment factor has been applied to activities in the current year. (Sec. 220.13(1)(b)(1), F.S.; Rule 12C-1.013(16); Rule 12C-1.013(17); Instructions, Form F-1120N, Corporate Income and Franchise Tax Return)

The apportioned amount determined is the Florida excess contribution carryover for the taxable year. A deduction would be allowed for Florida purposes to the extent claimed for federal purposes, as long as the deduction did not exceed the total amount of the Florida carryover to the taxable year. Also, the deduction for the excess contributions may not create or increase a net operating loss in Florida. (Sec. 220.13(1)(b)(1), F.S.; Rule 12C-1.013(16); Rule 12C-1.013(17); Instructions, Form F-1120N, Corporate Income and Franchise Tax Return)

A deduction for excess contributions that has been allowed for Florida purposes in a prior year is not allowed again, even if the deduction has not been fully utilized for federal purposes. (Sec. 220.13(1)(d), F.S.)

[¶10-900] Subtractions--Depreciation

Does Florida allow a subtraction for bonus depreciation?

Yes, Florida allows a subtraction from federal taxable income by taxpayers required to addback IRC Sec. 168(k) federal bonus depreciation. Taxpayers can claim the subtraction from federal taxable income equally over a 7-year period, beginning with the year that the addition occurs. (Sec. 220.13(1)(e), F.S.; Rule 12C-1.013(14))

The surviving company after a merger or acquisition can claim the subtraction adjustment. Otherwise, a taxpayer that ceases to do business during the 7-year period cannot accelerate, transfer, or use the subtraction. (Rule 12C-1.013(14))

A taxpayer must include a schedule with its Florida income tax return showing the amount of the original addition and the subtraction adjustment by tax year (Rule 12C-1.013(14); Instructions, Form F-1120, Florida Corporate Income/Franchise Tax Return)

Does Florida allow an IRC Sec. 179 asset expense deduction?

Yes, Florida allows a subtraction from federal taxable income by taxpayers required to addback the federal IRC Sec. 179 asset expense deduction before January 1, 2015. (Sec. 220.13(1)(e)(2), F.S.; Rule 12C-1.013(14)) The rules for the subtraction adjustment are the same as those that apply to the bonus depreciation adjustment, including:

- the 7-year recovery period; (Sec. 220.13(1)(e)(2), F.S.; Rule 12C-1.013(14))

- use of the adjustment after a merger or acquisition; (Rule 12C-1.013(14)) and

- documentation requirements. (Rule 12C-1.013(14); Instructions, Form F-1120, Florida Corporate Income/Franchise Tax Return)

Does Florida allow a subtraction for other depreciation?

Yes, Florida allows a subtraction from federal taxable income by taxpayers required to addback the federal deduction for qualified improvement property (QIP) placed in service on or after January 1, 2018. (Sec. 220.13(1)(e), F.S.) A taxpayer must compute the subtraction:

- under IRC Sec. 167 in effect on January 1, 2020 before the changes to the depreciation recovery period for QIP made by the Coronavirus Aid, Relief, and Economic Security Act (CARES Act); and

- without taking into account any sale or other disposition of the property. (Sec. 220.13(1)(e), F.S.)

For a list of other subtractions from the taxable income base, see Subtractions from Taxable Income Base.

[¶10-911] Subtractions--Discharge of Indebtedness

Florida did not allow taxpayers to defer the recognition of income from the cancellation of certain debt instruments in 2009 and 2010. It required an addition to federal taxable income for the amount of the deferred income. It allows a subtraction from federal taxable income when taxpayers must recognize the deferred income for federal tax purposes. (Sec. 220.13(1)(e)(3), F.S.) The subtraction cannot exceed the amount of income addback. (Instructions, Form F-1120N, Florida Corporate Income/Franchise Tax Return)

For a list of other subtractions from the taxable income base, see Subtractions from Taxable Income Base.

[¶10-915] Subtractions--Other Subtractions

Schedule I of the Form F-1120, Corporate Income and Franchise Tax Return, provides a line for other subtractions that may be needed in the computation of Florida tax. The instructions provide as examples a partnership adjustment, and an adjustment for certain corporations that take foreign taxes as a federal credit. A specific line is provided for the deduction of eligible net income of an international banking facility that has not otherwise been deducted (Instructions, Form F-1120N, Corporate Income and Franchise Tax Return).

[¶11-500]
ALLOCATION AND APPORTIONMENT

[¶11-505] Allocation and Apportionment

Florida corporations that have income from business activity that is taxable both within and without Florida must allocate and apportion their income among the taxing states. Nonbusiness income is subject to allocation. Business income is subject to apportionment on the basis of a three-factor formula consisting of a sales factor, a property factor, and a payroll factor.

If the standard apportionment formula does not fairly represent the extent of the taxpayer's tax base attributable to Florida, the taxpayer may petition for, or the Florida Department of Revenue may require, the use of an alternative apportionment method.

Insurance companies, transportation service companies, financial organizations, and citrus growers are subject to special apportionment provisions.

Affiliated group members may file consolidated returns.

[¶11-510] Income Subject to Allocation and Apportionment

Florida has not adopted the UDITPA provision, but has similar provisions that divide income into business income, which is subject to formula apportionment, and nonbusiness income, which is subject to allocation.

• *Business income*

Florida follows the UDITPA approach, utilizing the transactional and functional tests in determining whether corporate income may be apportioned to the state as business income. (Rule 12C-1.003)

Transactional test.—"Business income" means income arising from transactions and activity in the regular course of the taxpayer's trade or business. (Rule 12C-1.003)

Functional test.—"Business income" also includes income from tangible and intangible property if the acquisition, management, and disposition of the property constitute integral parts of the taxpayer's regular trade or business operations. (Rule 12C-1.003)

Functionally related dividends are presumed to be business income. Dividends are considered "functionally related dividends" if they are:

— are received from a subsidiary of which the voting stock is more than 50% owned or controlled by the taxpayer or members of its affiliated group and that is engaged in the same general line of business;

— are received from any corporation that is either a significant (15% or more) source of supply for the taxpayer or its affiliated group or a significant purchaser of the output of the taxpayer or its affiliated group, or that sells a significant part of its raw materials or input from the taxpayer or its affiliated group; or

— result from the investment of working capital or some other purpose in furtherance of the taxpayer or its affiliated group.

(Sec. 220.03(1)(bb), F.S.)

A regulation provides examples of business income and nonbusiness income. (Rule 12C-1.016)

• *Nonbusiness Income*

"Nonbusiness income" means all income other than business income. (Rule 12C-1.016) "Nonbusiness income" includes rents and royalties from real or tangible personal property, capital gains, interest, dividends, and patent and copyright royalties, to the extent that they do not arise from transactions and activities in the regular course of the taxpayer's trade or business. "Nonbusiness income" does not include income from tangible and intangible property if the acquisition, management, and disposition of the property constitute integral parts of the taxpayer's regular trade or business operations, nor any amounts that could be included in apportionable income without violating the due process clause of the United States Constitution. (Sec. 220.03(1)(r), F.S.)

• *Specific types of income or activities*

All income at the partnership level is classified by Florida as business income subject to formula apportionment, unless proven otherwise. The business income determination is made at the partnership level. (Rule 12C-1.016)

[¶11-515] Allocation

Nonbusiness income must be allocated as discussed below. Allocated income is reported on Form F-1120, Schedule R, Florida Corporate Income and Franchise Tax Return.

• *Net rents and royalties*

Net rents and royalties from real property located in Florida are allocable to Florida. (Sec. 220.16(1), F.S.)

Net rents and royalties from tangible personal property are allocable to Florida as follows:

— if and to the extent that the property is utilized in Florida; or

— in their entirety if the taxpayer's commercial domicile is in Florida and the taxpayer is not organized under the laws of or taxable in the state in which the property is utilized.

(Sec. 220.16(1), F.S.)

• *Capital gains and losses*

Capital gains and losses from sales of real property located in Florida are allocable to Florida. (Sec. 220.16(2), F.S.)

Capital gains and losses from sales of tangible personal property are allocable to Florida if:

— the property had a situs in Florida at the time of the sale; or

— the taxpayer's commercial domicile is in Florida and the taxpayer is not taxable in the state in which the property had a situs.

(Sec. 220.16(2), F.S.)

Capital gains and losses from sales of intangible personal property are allocable to Florida if the taxpayer's commercial domicile is in Florida. (Sec. 220.16(2), F.S.)

• *Interest and dividends*

Interest and dividends are allocable to Florida if the taxpayer's commercial domicile is in Florida. (Sec. 220.16(3), F.S.)

• *Patent and copyright royalties*

Patent and copyright royalties are allocable to Florida if and to the extent that the patent or copyright is:

— utilized by the payor in Florida; or

— utilized by the payor in a state in which the taxpayer is not taxable and the taxpayer's commercial domicile is in Florida.

(Sec. 220.16(4), F.S.)

[¶11-520] Apportionment

What is the standard Florida apportionment formula?

A corporation doing business in and outside Florida uses a standard three factor apportionment formula to determine corporate income tax liability from its activities in the state. (Sec. 220.15(1), F.S.) The formula consists of a:

• 25% property factor;

• 25% payroll factor; and

• 50% (double-weighted) sales factor. (Sec. 220.15(1), F.S.)

The formula measures Florida's share of adjusted federal income by ratios of the taxpayer's property, payroll, and sales in Florida to total property, payroll, and sales everywhere. (Instructions, Form F-1120N, Corporate Income and Franchise Tax Return)

Taxpayers compute the apportionment formula on the taxpayer's Florida corporate income and franchise tax return, Form F-1120. (Instructions, Form F-1120N, Corporate Income and Franchise Tax Return)

Florida also uses special apportionment factors for specific industries.

COMPLIANCE ALERT: The Tax Cuts and Jobs Act (P.L. 115-97) made numerous changes to federal income tax provisions. The changes include the IRC Sec. 965 transition (repatriation) tax on untaxed earnings and profits of certain foreign corporations. The tax applies at a reduced rate to earnings and profits accumulated after 1986 and before 2018. Florida's conformity provision adopts the federal tax treatment of IRC Sec. 965 income. Generally, IRC Sec. 965 income does not flow into federal taxable income. Therefore, Florida excludes this income from the apportionment formula computation. (*Tax Information Publication*, No. 18C01-01, Florida Department of Revenue, April 27, 2018)

Does Florida allow optional apportionment formulas? Florida allows certain taxpayers to apportion business income using a single sales factor formula. The optional formula applies to taxpayers that invest $250 million or more in qualified capital expenditures over a 2 year period. Eligible taxpayers do not include financial and banking organizations. (Sec. 220.153(2), F.S.)

A taxpayer notifies the Department of Economic Opportunity (DEO) of its intent to qualify for the optional formula. The taxpayer must apply for the optional formula within 2 years after notifying the DEO. (Sec. 220.153(3), F.S.)

Florida authorizes the DEO to revoke a taxpayer's eligibility for the optional formula if it determines that the taxpayer submitted materially false information. If the DEO revokes the optional formula, the taxpayer pays additional taxes and interest on the difference between the tax that would have been due under the standard apportionment method. The DEO also imposes a 100% penalty on the additional tax liability. (Sec. 220.153(4)(b), F.S.)

How do pass-through entities apportion income? S corporations, partnerships, and limited liability companies (LLCs) classified as partnerships for income tax purposes use the same standard apportionment formula as C corporations. (Instructions, Form F-1120N, Corporate Income and Franchise Tax Return; Instructions, Form F-1065, Partnership Information Return)

A partnership or LLC completes the apportionment part of its Florida return, Form F-1065, if either:

- the partnership or LLC does business outside Florida; or

- any of its corporate partners or members do business outside Florida.

How do pass-through entity owners apportion distributive income? A partnership's or LLC's Florida payroll, property, and sales factors flow through to its corporate partners or members. A corporate partner doing business in Florida combines its own Florida factors with its distributive share of the partnership's factors. (Rule 12C-1.015(10); Instructions, Form F-1065, Partnership Information Return)

Partnerships and LLCs use Form F-1065 to distribute to each corporate partner or member its share of the partnership's or LLC's apportionment factors. (Rule 12C-1.015(10); Instructions, Form F-1065, Partnership Information Return)

Does Florida allow alternative apportionment methods?

Florida allows or requires an alternative apportionment method if:

- the standard apportionment formula does not fairly represent the taxpayer's business activity in Florida; (Sec. 220.152, F.S.; Rule 12C-1.0152(1))

- the standard apportionment formula leads to a grossly distorted result in a particular case; (Rule 12C-1.0152(1)) or

- the standard apportionment formula produces a result inconsistent with results from previous tax years. (Rule 12C-1.0152(3))

Neither the taxpayer nor the Florida Department of Revenue (DOR) can seek an alternative apportionment method merely because it reaches a different result than the standard formula. (Rule 12C-1.0152(1))

What alternative apportionment methods does Florida allow? Florida alternative apportionment methods include:

- separate accounting;

- excluding any one or more factors;

- including one or more additional factors that fairly represent the taxpayer's business activity in Florida; or

- employing any other method that will produce a fair apportionment. (Sec. 220.152, F.S.)

Who carries the burden of proof? The party seeking to use an alternative formula must prove that the formula fairly and accurately apportions income to Florida based on the taxpayer's business in the state. (Rule 12C-1.0152(2))

What is the standard of proof? A taxpayer seeking to use an alternative apportionment method must show by clear and cogent evidence that the standard formula results in taxation of extraterritorial values. A taxpayer meets this standard of proof only if it demonstrates that the standard formula unreasonably and arbitrarily apportions income to Florida far out of proportion to the taxpayer's business in the state. (Rule 12C-1.0152(1))

How does a taxpayer apply for alternative apportionment? A taxpayer requests a departure from the standard formula by filing with the DOR either:

- a written request for a technical assistance advisement; or
- a petition for a declaratory statement. (Rule 12C-1.0152(4))

A taxpayer must file the request by the original due date of its Florida corporate income and franchise tax return. The taxpayer's request or petition must include a summary of the evidence to show it meets its burden and standard of proof. (Rule 12C-1.0152(4))

[¶11-525] Sales Factor

What is the Florida sales factor?

The sales factor of the apportionment formula for multistate taxpayers that derive business income from Florida is a fraction. The numerator is the total sales of the taxpayer in Florida during the taxable year or period, and the denominator is the total sales of the taxpayer everywhere during the taxable year or period. (Sec. 220.15(5), F.S.; Rule 12C-1.0155) Sales are reported on Form F-1120, Schedule III-C, Florida Corporate Income and Franchise Tax Return.

What sales or receipts are included in the Florida sales factor? The term "sales" means all gross receipts of the taxpayer from transactions and activities in the regular course of its trade or business. (Sec. 220.15(5), F.S.; Rule 12C-1.0155)

The Florida definition of sales includes gross receipts from the following:

— sales of tangible personal property of taxpayers engaged in manufacturing and selling or purchasing and reselling goods or products including all interest income, service charges, carrying charges, or time-price differential charges incidental to those sales;

— federal or state taxes, like federal manufacturers' excise taxes, if those taxes are a part of the selling price except where the taxpayer is required to add the taxes as a separate item to the selling price and collect the tax from the purchaser; (Rule 12C-1.0155(1)(a))

— sales of business assets; (Rule 12C-1.0155(1)(b))

— installment sales, including interest associated with the sale; (Rule 12C-1.0155(1)(c))

— rental income, if at least 10 percent of the taxpayer's total income reported on the federal tax return consists of leasing or renting real or tangible personal property; (Rule 12C-1.0155(1)(d))

— the disposition of a partnership interest; (Rule 12C-1.0155 (1)(g))

— the performance of services including fees, commissions, and similar items; (Rule 12C-1.0155(1)(h))

— intercompany sales, which may be included in the sales factor of a consolidated return; (Rule 12C-1.0155(1)(j))

— the sale, assignment, or licensing of intangible personal property like patents and copyrights; (Rule 12C-1.0155(1)(f)3)

— interest and dividend income that can be readily identified; (Rule 12C-1.0155)

— income from intangible personal property. (Rule 12C-1.0155(1)(f))

If the income producing activity generating business income from intangible personal property can be easily identified, then that income must be included in the denominator of the sales factor. If the income producing activity occurs in Florida, then the income must also be included in the numerator of the sales factor. For example, the income producing activity can usually be easily identified in the case of interest income received on deferred payments on sales of tangible personal property and income from the sale, licensing, or other use of intangible personal property. The sale or licensing of the use of a trade name, trademark, or patent will be attributable to the state in which the trade name, trademark, or patent is used. (Rule 12C-1.0155(1)(f)1) If business income from intangible property cannot easily be attributed to any particular income producing activity of the taxpayer, that income cannot be assigned to the numerator of the sales factor for any state. The income must be excluded from the denominator of the sales factor. For example, if business income in the form of dividends received on stock, royalties received on patents or copyrights, or interest received on bonds, debentures or government securities results from the mere holding of the intangible personal property by the taxpayer, those dividends and interest will be excluded from the denominator of the sales factor. (Rule 12C-1.0155(1)(f)2) In the case of a taxpayer selling, assigning, or licensing intangible personal property like patents and copyrights, "sales" includes the gross receipts from. (Rule 12C-1.0155(1)(f)3)

What sales or receipts are excluded from the Florida sales factor? Interest, dividends, rents, royalties, and gross receipts from the sale, exchange, maturity, redemption, or other disposition of securities are excluded from the sales factor. (Sec. 220.15(5), F.S.; Rule 12C-1.0155)

Management fees charged by a parent corporation to a subsidiary are generally excluded from the sales factor. If the fees are just a pass-through of corporate overhead expenditures, the fees will not be included in sales. However, if the parent is not a vendor of tangible personal property or a "financial organization" and the preponderance of its gross receipts are management fees, these may be included in the sales factor. In the case of a parent holding company, management fees are clearly in "its trade or business" and, therefore, includable in the sales factor. (Rule 12C-1.0155(1)(i))

What are the Florida sourcing rules for sales of tangible property?

Florida follows the destination test for determining the sales factor of the general apportionment formula. (Sec. 220.15(5), F.S.) Sales of tangible personal property are sourced to Florida if the property is delivered or shipped to a purchaser in Florida, regardless of the F.O.B. point, other conditions of the sale, or ultimate destination of the property, unless shipment is made via a common or contract carrier. However, for industries in NAICS National Number 311411, if the ultimate destination of the product is to a location outside Florida, the sale will not be considered to occur in Florida, regardless of the method of shipment or F.O.B. point. (Sec. 220.15(5)(b)1, F.S.) Reimbursement of expenses under an agency contract between a cooperative, a grower-member of a cooperative, or a grower and a processor is not considered a sale within Florida. (Sec. 220.15(5)(b)3, F.S.)

What are the sourcing rules in Florida for sales other than tangible property?

Gross receipts from sales of other than tangible property are attributable to Florida if the income producing activity that gave rise to the receipts is performed entirely in Florida. Also, gross receipts must be attributed to Florida if the income producing activity is performed in and outside Florida but the greater proportion of the income producing activity is performed in Florida, based on cost of performance. (Rule 12C-1.0155(2)(l))

Definition of income producing activity. The term "income producing activity" applies to each separate item of income and means the transactions and activity the taxpayer directly engages in for the ultimate purpose of obtaining gains or profits. (Rule 12C-1.0155(2)(l))

If independent contractors are used to complete a contract, then the term "income producing activity" includes amounts paid to the independent contractors. (Rule 12C-1.0155(2)(l))

Simply holding intangible personal property is not, by itself, an income producing activity. (Rule 12C-1.0155(2)(f)1)

Definition of costs of performance. The term "costs of performance" means direct costs determined in a manner consistent with generally accepted accounting principles and according to accepted conditions or practices in the taxpayer's trade or business. If independent contractors are used to complete a contract, then "costs of performance" includes amounts paid to the independent contractors. (Rule 12C-1.0155(2)(e))

What are the Florida sourcing rules for the rental, leasing, or licensing of property?

Gross receipts from the rental, lease, or licensing of tangible personal property are sourced to Florida if the property is located in Florida. The rental, lease, licensing, or other use of tangible personal property in Florida is a separate income producing activity from the rental, lease, licensing, or other use of the same property while located in another state. Thus, if property is in and outside Florida during the rental, lease or licensing period, gross receipts attributable to Florida must be measured by the ratio that the time the property was physically present or was used in Florida bears to the total time or use of the property everywhere during such period. (Rule 12C-1.0155(2)(b))

Sales, lease, rental, or licensing of real property. Gross receipts from the sale, lease, rental, or licensing of real property are in Florida if the real property is located in Florida. (Rule 12C-1.0155(2)(c))

What are the Florida sourcing rules for services?

Gross receipts for the performance of personal services are attributable to Florida if the services are performed in Florida. If services relating to a single item of income are performed partly in and partly outside Florida, the gross receipts for the performance of the services must be attributable to Florida only if a greater portion of the services were performed in Florida, based on costs of performance. (Rule 12C-1.0155(2)(e))

If services are performed partly in and partly outside Florida, then the services performed in each state may constitute a separate income producing activity, even though the client is billed a lump sum amount. In these cases, the gross receipts for the performance of services attributable to Florida will be measured by the ratio that the time spent in performing the services in the state bears to the total time spent in performing such services everywhere. Time spent in performing services includes the amount of time spent in the performance of a contract or other obligation that gives rise to the gross receipts. Personal services not directly connected with the performance of the contract or other obligation, for example, time expended in negotiating the contract, are excluded from the computations. (Rule 12C-1.0155(2))

A special formula applies to growers of citrus fruit. If citrus fruit is delivered by a cooperative for a grower-member, by a grower-member to a cooperative, or by a grower-participant to a Florida processor, then the sales factor for the growers for the citrus fruit delivered to the processor is the same as the sales factor for the most recent taxable year of that processor. That sales factor, expressed only as a percentage and not in terms of the dollar volume of sales, in order to protect the confidentiality of the sales of the processor, must be furnished on the request of the grower promptly after it has been determined for that taxable year. (Sec. 220.15(5)(b)2, F.S.)

Does Florida have a throwback or throwout rule?

Florida does not have a throwback or throwout rule for sales of tangible personal property. (Rule 12C-1.015(1)(d))

However, if business income from intangible property cannot readily be attributed to any particular income producing activity of the taxpayer, then the income cannot be assigned to the numerator of the sales factor for any state and is excluded from the denominator of the sales factor. (Rule 12C-1.0155)

[¶11-530] Property Factor

The property factor of the apportionment formula is a fraction, the numerator of which is the average value of the taxpayer's real and tangible personal property owned or rented and used in Florida during the tax period, and the denominator of which is the average value of all of the taxpayer's real and tangible personal property owned or rented and used everywhere during the tax period. (Sec. 220.15(2), F.S.; Rule 12C-1.0153)

Property and rent are reported on Form F-1120, Schedule III-B, Florida Corporate Income and Franchise Tax Return.

• *Construction in progress*

Property or equipment under construction during the tax period (except inventoriable goods in-process) are excluded from the factor until the property is actually used for the production of income. If the property is partially used for the production of income while under construction, the value of the property to the extent used is included in the property factor. However, construction companies must include property under construction in the property factor. Regardless of the method of accounting used, the costs of construction-in-progress are included in the property factor to the extent the costs exceed progress billings. (Rule 12C-1.0153(b))

• *Leasehold improvements*

Leasehold improvements are, for the purposes of the property factor, treated as property owned by the taxpayer regardless or whether the taxpayer is entitled to remove the improvements or the improvements revert to the lessor upon expiration of the lease. Therefore, the original cost of leasehold improvements must be included in the factor. (Rule 12C-1.0153(8))

• *Method of averaging property values*

The average value of all real and tangible personal property is determined by averaging the value at the beginning and at the end of the taxable year or period, unless the Florida Department of Revenue determines that an averaging of monthly values during the taxable year or period is reasonably required to reflect properly the average value of the taxpayer's real and tangible personal property. (Sec. 220.15(2), F.S.)

• *Owned property*

Real and tangible personal property owned by the taxpayer is valued at original cost. (Sec. 220.15(2), F.S.)

As a general rule "original cost" is deemed to be the basis of real and tangible personal property at the time of acquisition by the taxpayer and adjusted by subsequent capital additions or improvements thereto and partial disposition thereof, by reason of sale, exchange, or abandonment, etc. Depreciation is not taken into account in determining the value of the property. (Rule 12C-1.0153(5)(a))

If the original cost of property is unascertainable, the property is included in the factor at its fair market value as of the date of acquisition by the taxpayer. (Rule 12C-1.0153(5)(e))

Florida law excludes from the property factor of the apportionment formula property attributed to Florida that is dedicated exclusively to research and development activities performed pursuant to sponsored research contracts with a state university or certain nonpublic universities. To be excluded, real or tangible personal property must be located in Florida, and it must be certified to the Department of Revenue that such property is dedicated exclusively to the applicable research and development activities. No contract in existence prior to July 1, 1998, is eligible to participate in this exclusion. Furthermore, the property is eliminated from the factor only for the duration of the contractual period for the conduct of the sponsored research, and the reduction in tax due to the exclusion may not exceed the amount paid to the university for the conduct of the sponsored research. (Sec. 220.15(2), F.S.; Sec. 220.15(8), F.S.)

• *Rented property*

Real and tangible personal property rented by the taxpayer is valued at eight times the net annual rental rate paid by the taxpayer less any annual rental rate received from subrentals. (Sec. 220.15(2), F.S.)

If property owned by others is used by the taxpayer at no charge or rented by the taxpayer for a nominal rate, the net annual rental rate for such property shall be determined on the basis of a reasonable market rental rate for such property. (Rule 12C-1.0153(6))

Florida law excludes from the property factor of the apportionment formula property attributed to Florida that is dedicated exclusively to research and development activities performed pursuant to sponsored research contracts with a state university or certain nonpublic universities. To be excluded, real or tangible personal property must be located in Florida, and it must be certified to the Department of Revenue that such property is dedicated exclusively to the applicable research and development activities. No contract in existence prior to July 1, 1998, is eligible to participate in this exclusion. Furthermore, the property is eliminated from the factor only for the duration of the contractual period for the conduct of the sponsored research, and the reduction in tax due to the exclusion may not exceed the amount paid to the university for the conduct of the sponsored research. (Sec. 220.15(2), F.S.; Sec. 220.15(8), F.S.)

• *Standby or idle property*

Property held as reserves or standby facilities or property held as a reserve source of materials is included in the property factor. For example, a plant temporarily idle or raw material reserves not currently being processed are includible in the factor. Property that is held for the production of income must remain in the property factor until its permanent withdrawal is established by an identifiable event such as its sale or the lapse of five years during which time the property was held for sale. (Rule 12C-1.0153(2)(a), (c))

• *Inventory*

Inventory of stock of goods must be included in the factor in accordance with the valuation method used for federal income tax purposes. (Rule 12C-1.0153(5)(f))

• *Mobile property*

The value of mobile or movable property such as construction equipment, trucks, or leased electronic equipment which is located within and without Florida during the tax period is determined for the purposes of the numerator of the factor on the basis of total time within Florida during the tax period. (Rule 12C-1.0153(4))

• *Property in transit*

Property in transit between locations of the taxpayer to which it belongs is considered to be at the destination for purposes of the property factor. (Rule 12C-1.0153(3)(a))

Property in transit between a buyer and a seller which is included in the denominator of the property factor in accordance with regular accounting practices must be included in the numerator of the state of destination. (Rule 12C-1.0153(3)(b))

[¶11-535] Payroll Factor

The payroll factor of the apportionment formula is a fraction, the numerator of which is the total amount paid in Florida during the taxable year or period by the taxpayer for compensation, and the denominator of which is the total compensation paid everywhere during the taxable year or period. (Sec. 220.15(4), F.S.; Rule 12C-1.0154) Payroll is reported on Form F-1120, Schedule III, Florida Corporate Income and Franchise Tax Return.

The term "compensation" means wages, salaries, commissions and any other form of remuneration paid to employees for personal services. (Sec. 220.15(4), F.S.) Amounts considered compensation include deferred compensation, value of board, rent, housing, lodging, and other benefits or services furnished to employees by the taxpayer in return for personal services, provided that such amounts constitute income to the recipient under the Internal Revenue Code. (Rule 12C-1.0154(2)(b))

The term "everywhere" means in all states of the United States, the District of Columbia, the Commonwealth of Puerto Rico, any territory or possession of the United States, any foreign country, or any political subdivision of the foregoing. (Sec. 220.15(7), F.S.)

Compensation is considered to be paid in Florida if:

— the employee's service is performed entirely within Florida;

— the employee's service is performed both within and without Florida, but the service performed outside Florida is incidental to the employee's service within Florida; or

— some of the employee's service is performed in Florida and (a) the base of operations or, if there is no base of operations, the place from which the service is directed or controlled is in Florida or (b) the employee's residence is in Florida and the base of operations or the place from which the service is directed or controlled is not in any state in which some part of the service is performed.

(Sec. 220.15(4), F.S.; Rule 12C-1.0154(2)(b))

Partnership employees.—Compensation paid to employees of a partnership is included in the denominator of the taxpayer's payroll factor to the extent of the taxpayer's interest in the partnership and the amount paid to Florida employees is included in the numerator of the taxpayer's payroll factor to the extent of the taxpayer's interest in the partnership. Partnership payroll should be allocated to each partner based on the partner's interest in the partnership or as designated in the partnership agreement for inclusion in the Florida payroll factor. (Rule 12C-1.0154(6))

Compensation related to research and development activities.—Florida law excludes from the payroll factor of the apportionment formula compensation attributed to Florida that is dedicated exclusively to research and development activities performed pursuant to sponsored research contracts with a state university or certain nonpublic universities. To be excluded from the payroll factor, compensation must be paid to an employee located in Florida, and it must be certified to the Florida Department of Revenue that such compensation was paid to employees dedicated exclusively to the applicable research and development activities. No contract in existence prior to July 1, 1998, is eligible to participate in this exclusion. Furthermore, the payroll is eliminated from the factor only for the duration of the contractual period for the conduct of the sponsored research and the reduction in tax due to the exclusion may not exceed the amount paid to the university for the conduct of the sponsored research. (Sec. 220.15(4), F.S.; Sec. 220.15(8), F.S.)

• *Director compensation*

A director not acting in the capacity of an employee would exclude compensation from the payroll factor. However, Florida includes officer compensation in the payroll factor as all officers are defined as employees. (Sec. 220.15(4), F.S.; Rule 12C-1.0154(3)(a))

• *Leased employee compensation*

Compensation for leased employees is included in the payroll factor if the employee is a common law employee. (Sec. 220.15(4), F.S.; Rule 12C-1.0154(2); *Unofficial Guidance*, Florida Department of Revenue, May 19, 2014)

• *Stock options*

Stock options are included in the payroll factor. (Sec. 220.15(4), F.S.; Rule 12C-1.0154(2))

• *General sourcing rules*

Compensation is sourced to Florida if:

— the employee's service is performed entirely within Florida; or

— the employee's service is performed both within and without Florida, but the service performed without the state is incidental to the employee's service within Florida; or

— some of the employee's service is performed in Florida, and the base of operations or, if there is no base of operations, the place from which the service is directed or controlled is in the state, or

— the base of operations or the place from which the service is directed or controlled is not in any state in which some part of the service is performed and the employee's residence is in Florida. (Sec. 220.15(4)(a), F.S.; Rule 12C-1.0154(2))

[¶11-540] Apportionment Factors for Specific Industries

What special industry apportionment formula does Florida use?

Florida has special apportionment formulas for insurance companies, transportation service companies, financial organizations, and citrus growers.

Insurance companies. Insurance companies use a one-factor apportionment formula based on direct premiums. (Sec. 220.151, F.S.) Insurance companies whose principal source of written premiums is premiums for reinsurance use a fraction. The numerator is the sum of direct premiums written for insurance on properties and risks in Florida plus premiums written for reinsurance and accepted by the company on properties and risks in Florida. The denominator is the sum of direct premiums and premiums for reinsurance accepted by the company on properties and risks everywhere. (Sec. 220.151(1)(b), F.S.)

All other insurance companies use a different fraction. The numerator is the direct premiums written for insurance on properties and risks in Florida and the denominator is the direct premiums written for insurance on properties and risks everywhere. (Sec. 220.151(1)(a), F.S.)

Transportation service companies. Transportation companies use a one-factor apportionment formula based on revenue miles. (Sec. 220.151, F.S.) This formula is a fraction. The numerator is the taxpayer's revenue miles in Florida and the denominator is the taxpayer's revenue miles everywhere. (Sec. 220.151(2), F.S.)

For transportation services other than pipeline companies, a "revenue mile" is transportation of one passenger or one net ton of freight the distance of one mile for a consideration. (Sec. 220.151(2)(a), F.S.)

If a taxpayer is transporting both passengers and freight, the apportionment fraction is determined by the weighted average of the taxpayer's passenger revenue mile fraction and its freight revenue mile fraction. Railroads weight the fraction to reflect the taxpayer's relative railway operating income from freight and passenger service as reported to the Interstate Commerce Commission. Other transportation services weight the fraction to reflect the relative gross receipts from passenger and freight transportation. (Sec. 220.151(2)(a), F.S.)

Air and sea transportation services that offer transportation service from or to a point in the continental U.S. but outside Florida, compute "revenue miles in the state" according to specific latitudinal and longitudinal points. (Sec. 220.151(2)(c), F.S.)

Pipeline companies. Pipeline companies use a one-factor apportionment formula based on revenue miles. (Sec. 220.151, F.S.) This formula is expressed as a fraction. The numerator is the revenue miles of the taxpayer in Florida and the denominator is the revenue miles of the taxpayer everywhere. (Sec. 220.151(2), F.S.) For pipeline companies, a "revenue mile" is transportation by pipeline of one barrel of oil, 1,000 cubic feet of gas, or any specified quantity of any other substance, the distance of one mile for a consideration. (Sec. 220.151(2)(b), F.S.)

Financial organizations. Financial organizations use the general apportionment formula, but financial institution's have special rules for computing sales and property factors. (Sec. 220.15, F.S.)

Sales of a financial organization are considered to be in Florida for sales factor purposes if derived from any of the following:

— fees, commissions, or other compensation for financial services rendered in Florida;

— gross profits from trading in stocks, bonds, or other securities managed in Florida;

— interest, other than interest from loans secured by mortgages, deeds of trust, or other liens upon real or tangible personal property located outside Florida, and dividends received in Florida;

— interest charged to customers at places of business maintained in Florida for carrying debit balances of margin accounts, without deduction of any costs incurred in carrying such accounts;

— interest, fees, commissions, or other charges or gains from loans secured by mortgages, deeds of trust, or other liens on real or tangible personal property in Florida or from installment sale agreements originally executed by a taxpayer or his agent to sell real or tangible personal property in Florida;

— rents from real or tangible personal property in Florida; or

— any other gross income, including other interest, resulting from operation as a financial organization in Florida. (Sec. 220.15(5), F.S.)

A financial organization's property factor must include intangible personal property, other than goodwill, that is owned and used in the business, valued at its tax basis for federal income tax purposes. Intangible personal property is considered to be in Florida for property factor purposes if it consists of any of the following:

— coin or currency in Florida;

— assets in the nature of loans in Florida or deeds of trust or other liens on real or tangible personal property in Florida;

— a portion of a participation loan if the office that enters into the participation is in Florida;

— credit card receivables from customers who reside or are commercially domiciled in Florida;

— investments in securities that generate business income if the taxpayer's commercial domicile is in Florida, unless the securities have acquired a business situs elsewhere;

— securities used to maintain reserves against deposits to meet federal or state deposit requirements, based on the ratio that total deposits in Florida compared to total deposits everywhere;

— securities held by a state treasurer or other public official or pledged to secure funds or trust funds deposited with the taxpayer if the office that the secured deposit is maintained is in Florida;

— leases of tangible personal property if the taxpayer's commercial domicile is in Florida;

— installment sale agreements a taxpayer or its agent originally executes to sell real or tangible personal property in Florida; or

— any other intangible personal property in Florida that is used to generate business income. (Sec. 220.15(3), F.S.)

Citrus growers. Citrus fruit growers use a single sales factor apportionment formula. When citrus fruit is delivered by a cooperative for a grower-member, by a grower-member to a cooperative, or by a grower-participant to a Florida processor, the sales factor for the grower is the same as the sales factor for the most recent taxable year of the processor. That sales factor is expressed as a percentage of the dollar volume of sales. (Sec. 220.15(5)(b)2, F.S.)

[¶11-545] Consolidated Returns

Does Florida allow consolidated returns?

A parent company of an affiliated group of corporations can elect to file a Florida consolidated income tax return using Form F-1120 if:

- the parent has taxable nexus with the state
- each member consents to the election on Form F-1122;
- the group filed a federal consolidated income tax return for the tax year; and

- the group members are identical to the members that filed the federal consolidated return. (Sec. 220.131(1), F.S.; Rule 12C-1.0131)

Florida adopts the definition of "affiliated group of corporations" under IRC Sec. 1504. (Sec. 220.03(1)(b), F.S.) A consolidated return can include 1 or more affiliated banks or savings associations. (Sec. 220.64, F.S.)

The parent corporation must attach to the return either:

- Florida Form F-851;

- or a copy of federal Form 851. (Rule 12C-1.0131(1))

The election is binding on the affiliated group for all future tax years. (Sec. 220.131(3), F.S.; Rule 12C-1.0131(3)) The affiliated group can get permission to discontinue filing consolidated returns based on changes in law or business circumstances resulting in:

- a substantial adverse effect on the group's consolidated tax liability for the tax year compared to the aggregate tax liability if the group members filed separate returns; or

- a substantial reduction in the consolidated net operating loss (NOL) for the tax year compared to the aggregate NOLs if the group members filed separate returns. (Rule 12C-1.0131(3))

The group cannot break its consolidated election because the parent company no longer has nexus with Florida. (Rule 12C-1.0131(3))

Can Florida require consolidated returns?

Florida can require a consolidated return for members of an affiliated group to:

- prevent the material distortion of income apportioned to the state; and

- fairly reflect the taxable income of the group members. (Sec. 220.131(2), F.S.; Rule 12C-1.0131(2))

How is income tax liability for affiliated group members computed?

Florida follows the federal rules and procedures for computing the state consolidated taxable income of affiliated group members, (Sec. 220.131(4), F.S.; Rule 12C-1.0131(4)) including:

- the taxable year of group members; (Rule 12C-1.0131(3)) and

- intercompany adjustments and eliminations. (Sec. 220.131(4), F.S.; Rule 12C-1.0131(4))

Each group member must apportion its income using the same apportionment factors and rules as general business corporations. (Sec. 220.131(5), F.S.; Rule 12C-1.015(7)) The property, payroll, and sales factors include the property, payroll, and sales for all consolidated group members. The affiliated group members cannot determine separate apportionment factors to apply to their portion of the consolidated adjusted federal income. The apportionment factors do not just include the members that are doing business in Florida. The consolidated adjusted federal income is then multiplied by the consolidated apportionment factor to determine the adjusted federal income apportioned to Florida.(Rule 12C-1.015(7))

An affiliated group can include members that use a special industry apportionment formula. The general apportionment rules apply in determining the denominators of the property, payroll, and sales factors for those members. (Rule 12C-1.015(7)) But each special industry member must determine the numerators of its sales, property, and payroll factors by multiplying the denominator of each factor by its single factor apportionment ratio. (Sec. 220.131(5), F.S.; Rule 12C-1.015(7)) The numerators for each of the factors are then added to the numerators of the other group members to determine the apportionment factor used by the affiliated group. (Rule 12C-1.015(7))

[¶11-550] Combined Reports

Does Florida allow elective combined reporting?

Florida law does not permit the filing of combined reports. Separate reporting is required unless an election is made to file a consolidated return. (Sec. 220.22, F.S.; Corporate Income/Franchise Tax Return Instructions)

Does Florida require combined reporting for unitary business groups?

Florida law does not require or permit the filing of combined reports by members of a unitary business. Separate reporting is required unless an election is made to file a consolidated return. (Sec. 220.22, F.S.; Corporate Income/Franchise Tax Return Instructions)

Does Florida authorize or require affiliated group combined reporting?

Florida does not authorize or require affiliated group combined reporting. Separate reporting is required unless an election is made to file a consolidated return. (Sec. 220.22, F.S.; Corporate Income/Franchise Tax Return Instructions)

[¶12-000]

CREDITS

[¶12-001] Overview of Credits

Florida allows taxpayers to claim credits against corporate income tax liability for variety of activities.

- *Education credits*

    Tax credit scholarship program

    New Worlds Reading Initiative credit

- *Community development and neighborhood assistance credits*

    Community contributions credit

- *Investment credits*

    Railroad construction and maintenance credit

    New markets credit

- *Enterprise zone credits*

    Enterprise zone jobs credit

    Enterprise zone property tax credit

- *Research credits*

    Research and development credit

- *Job creation/hiring credits*

    Urban job credit

    Rural job credit

    Student internship credit program

- *Environmental credits*

    Hazardous waste facility credit

    Voluntary cleanup tax credit

- *Capital investment credits*

    Capital investments credit

- *Housing credits*

    State housing tax credit

- *Family credits*

    Strong families credit program

- *Other credits*

    Health maintenance organization consumer assistance assessment credit

    Insurance guaranty association assessment credit

- *Estimated tax*

    All payments made as estimated tax may be applied as a credit toward corporate income tax liability. (Sec. 220.31(2), F.S.)

- *Overpayments of tax*

    Overpayments of tax can be applied as a credit toward corporate income tax liability. (Sec. 220.31(2), F.S.)

- *Credit carryforward*

    Florida does not have a general credit carryforward provision. Carryforward provisions are specifically provided for each credit.

- *Credit restrictions*

    Corporations, partnerships, associations and other entities that travel to, or do business with, any country located in the Western Hemisphere that lacks diplomatic relations with the U.S. is not eligible to claim a credit against Florida corporate income tax liability. (Sec. 110.1155, F.S.)

- *Repealed and expired credits*

    Florida has several repealed and expired credits, some of which have an open carryforward period.

PROPERTY

[¶20-100]
TAXABILITY OF PROPERTY AND PERSONS

[¶20-105] Classification of Property

When preparing the real property rolls, real property is classified based on 10 major groups. (Rule 12D-8.008, F.A.C.) Residential property is subclassified into one category for homestead property and one for nonhomestead property. (Sec. 195.073, F.S.)

Each year, the county assessor classifies all lands within the county as either agricultural or nonagricultural. (Sec. 193.461(1), F.S.)

The real property is classified as one of the following: (Rule 12D-8.008, F.A.C.)

— residential (homestead or non-homestead;

— commercial and industrial;

— agricultural;

— exempt, wholly or partially;

— leasehold Interest (government owned);

— other;

— centrally assessed;

— non-agricultural acreage;

— timeshare property; and

— high water recharge.

Classifications are used to create categories of property that are entitled to exemptions, assessments at present use value, or other special treatment.

[¶20-115] Agriculture

The Florida Constitution provides that agricultural land may be classified by general law and assessed solely on the basis of character or use. (Sec. 4(a), Art. VII, Fla. Const.) The homestead portion of agricultural land is assessed separately.

• *Aquaculture products*

Effective January 1, 2023, land used in the production of aquaculture products is assessed based solely on its agricultural use. For purposes of the income methodology approach to assessment, structures and equipment on the property used for producing aquaculture products are considered a part of the average yield per acre and carry no separately contributory (taxable) value. In addition, when utilizing the income methodology approach, the property appraiser must rely on five-year moving average data. (Sec. 193.4613, F.S.)

Once a request for assessment is approved, the property must be assessed for 10 years unless the ownership or use of the property changes. The property appraiser may require the property owner to submit audited financial statements, but may not require an annual application. (Sec. 193.4613, F.S.)

• *Annual crops, nonbearing fruit trees, nursery stock*

Growing annual agricultural crops, nonbearing fruit trees, nursery stock and aquacultural crops are considered to have no ascertainable value and are not taxable until they have reached maturity or a stage of marketability, and have passed from the hands of the producer or are offered for sale. (Sec. 193.451, F.S.)

Personal property leased or subleased by the Department of Agriculture and Consumer Services and utilized in the inspection, grading, or classification of citrus fruit is deemed to have value for purposes of assessment no greater than its market value as salvage. (Sec. 193.451(3), F.S.)

• *Classification of agricultural land*

Each year, the county assessor classifies all lands within the county as either agricultural or nonagricultural. (Sec. 193.461(1), F.S.) Automatic renewal of agricultural classification is not allowed. In order for the classification to be renewed, the owner of land classified as agricultural land must annually certify in writing that neither the ownership nor the use of the land has changed. The property appraiser must, no later than January 31 of each year, provide notice to the owner of land that was classified agricultural in the previous year informing the owner of the requirements of classification and certification. However, a county may waive the requirement that an annual application be made for property that was previously classified as agricultural and may waive the notice and certification requirements for reclassification. The county may revoke both these waivers. (Sec. 193.461, F.S.; *Informational Bulletin No. PTA-02-26*, Florida Department of Revenue, November 21, 2002)

Natural disaster.—Lands classified for Florida property tax purposes as agricultural lands, that are not being used for agricultural production as a result of a natural disaster for which a state of emergency is declared, when such disaster results in the halting of agricultural production, must continue to be classified as agricultural lands for five years after termination of the emergency declaration. However, if such lands are diverted from agricultural use to nonagricultural use during or after the five-year recovery period, such lands must be assessed. (Sec. 193.461, F.S.)

Classified use assessment post-Hurricane Michael clarified.—Florida clarifies classified use assessment post-Hurricane Michael for property tax purposes. Hurricane Michael caused significant damage to agriculturally-classified properties. Lands classified for assessment purposes as agricultural lands:

- that are not being used for agricultural production as a result of a natural disaster for which a state of emergency is declared;

- when such disaster results in the halting of agricultural production;

- must continue to be classified as agricultural lands for five years after termination of the emergency declaration.

(*Technical Bulletin PTO 19-01*, Florida Department of Revenue, March 21 2019)

However, if such lands are diverted from agricultural use to nonagricultural use during or after the five-year recovery period, such lands must be assessed at a just valuation. (*Technical Bulletin PTO 19-01*, Florida Department of Revenue, March 21 2019)

This applies retroactively to natural disasters that occurred on or after July 1, 2017. This applies to all damaged agriculturally-classified properties, including timber parcels. (*Technical Bulletin PTO 19-01*, Florida Department of Revenue, March 21 2019)

Screened enclosed structures.—In addition, screened enclosed structures used in horticulture production for pest exclusion, when consistent with state or federal eradication or compliance agreements, have no separately assessable value for purposes of ad valorem taxation. (Sec. 193.461, F.S.)

Application for agricultural zoning.—In order for land to be considered agricultural, an application for agricultural zoning must be filed with the county property appraiser by March 1. An applicant who is qualified to receive an agricultural classification but fails to file an application for that classification by the March 1 deadline may pay a $15 nonrefundable fee and file a late application with the property appraiser and a petition with the value adjustment board requesting that the agricultural classification be granted. The application and petition may be filed at any time during the taxable year through the 25th day following the property appraiser's mailing of the assessment notice. Agricultural classification may be granted if the property appraiser or value adjustment board, upon review of the petition, decides that the applicant is qualified and has demonstrated particular extenuating circumstances to warrant granting that classification. (Sec. 193.461(3), F.S.; *Turner v. Lusk*, Florida Court of Appeal, Second District, No. 2D00-5348, June 28, 2002)

Bona fide agricultural purposes.—Only land that is used primarily for bona fide agricultural purposes (that is, "good faith commercial agricultural use of the land") can be so classified. (Sec. 193.461(3), F.S.) "Agricultural purposes" includes horticulture, floriculture, viticulture, forestry, dairy, livestock, poultry, bee, pisciculture for production of tropical fish, aquaculture (including algaculture) and all forms of farm production. (Sec. 193.461(5), F.S.)

In determining whether the agricultural use is bona fide, the appraiser may take into consideration:

— the length of time the property has been used as agricultural land;

— whether the use has been continuous;

— the purchase price paid;

— size as it related to specific agricultural use, but in no even will a minimum acreage be required for agricultural assessment;

— whether an effort has been made to care for the land in accordance with accepted commercial agricultural practices, including fertilizing, liming, tilling, mowing, and reforesting; and

— whether the land is under lease and, if so, the length, terms, and conditions of the lease.

(Sec. 193.461(3), F.S.)

Offering property for sale does not constitute a primary use of land and may not be the basis for denying an agricultural classification if the land continues to be used primarily for bona fide agricultural purposes while it is being offered for sale. This change is remedial and clarifying in nature. This change applies retroactively to all parcels for which a final court order has not yet been entered. (Sec. 193.461(3)(b)(2), F.S.)

Effect of classification.—If agricultural classification is granted, the assessor may consider only the following factors in the assessment:

— quantity and size of the property;

— condition of the property;

— present market value of the property as agricultural land;

— income produced by the property;

— productivity of the land in its present use;

— economic merchantability of the agricultural product; and

— other agricultural factors that may become applicable, which are reflective of the standard present practices of agricultural use and production.

County property appraisers must rely on five-year moving average data when using the income methodology approach in an assessment of agricultural property. This is designed to remedy the extreme fluctuations in the year-to-year property tax assessments of agricultural lands. When the income methodology approach is applied to the assessment of agricultural property, any irrigation systems, including pumps and motors, physically attached to the land must be treated as part of the average yields per acre and as having no separately assessable contributory value. (Sec. 193.461(6), F.S.)

Effect of change in use.—Generally, when property classified as agricultural is no longer used for agriculture, it is reclassified as nonagricultural. (Sec. 193.461(4), F.S.)

However, agricultural lands mandatorily taken out of production by any state or federal eradication or quarantine program, including the Citrus Health Response Program, continues to be classified as agricultural lands for five years after the date of execution of a compliance agreement between the landowner and the Department of Agriculture and Consumer Services or a federal agency pursuant to such program or successor programs. (Sec. 193.461(7)(a), F.S.)

If such lands are left in a fallow or other non-income producing state, these lands will be assessed at a de minimis value of no more than $50 per acre. Lands that are replanted in citrus pursuant to a compliance agreement shall continue to be classified as agricultural lands and shall be assessed at a de minimis value of up to $50 acre, on a single-year methodology. If these lands are converted to permissible income-producing agricultural uses under the programs, the lands will be assessed similarly to other agricultural lands. If the lands are diverted from an agricultural to a nonagricultural use, the lands will be assessed as any other nonagricultural lands. (Sec. 193.461(7)(a), F.S.)

• *Obsolete agricultural equipment*

Agricultural equipment that is located on property classified as agricultural and that no longer is usable for its intended purpose is deemed to have a market value no greater than its value for salvage. (Sec. 193.4615, F.S.)

• *Agricultural privilege taxes*

Florida imposes an annual Everglades agricultural privilege tax for the privilege of conducting an agricultural trade or business on each acre of real property. The state also imposes an annual C-139 agricultural privilege tax for the privilege of conducting an agricultural trade or business on:

— all real property located within the C-139 Basin that is classified as agricultural property; and

— all leasehold or other interests in real property located within the C-139 Basin owned by the United States, the state, or any agency of the state permitting the property to be used for agricultural purposes in a manner that would result in the property being classified as agricultural if not governmentally owned, whether or not such property is actually classified as agricultural.

(Sec. 373.4592, F.S.)

Rates.—The annual Everglades agricultural privilege tax is imposed in the amount of:

— $25 per acre for tax notices mailed from November 2014 through November 2026;

— $20 per acre for tax notices mailed from November 2027 through 2029;

— $15 per acre for tax notices mailed from November 2030 through November 2035; and

— $10 per acre for tax notices mailed during or after November 2036.

(Sec. 373.4592, F.S.)

¶20-115

[¶20-135] Computer Hardware and Software

Florida has no specific property tax statutory provisions regarding taxability of computer hardware, although a regulation assigns a code reference and property classifications in its requirements for tangible personal property assessment roll. (Rule 12D-8.009, F.A.C.) However, there is a statutory provision for software.

Prior to installation, computer software constitutes personal property only to the extent of the value of the unmounted or uninstalled medium on or in which the information, program, or routine is stored or transmitted. After installation or mounting, computer software does not increase the value of the computer or computer-related peripheral equipment, or any combination thereof. (Sec. 192.001(19), F.S.)

The above definition of "computer software" does not apply to embedded software that resides permanently in the internal memory of a computer or computer-related peripheral equipment and that is not removable without terminating the operation of the computer or equipment. (Sec. 192.001(19), F.S.)

The Florida Circuit Court has ruled that software used in wireless telephone switching devices was not embedded software, and therefore, was not subject to Florida property tax. The software was stored in the random access memory (RAM) section of the computer's memory, and by definition memory stored in RAM was not permanently embedded. If the software was removed, the computer would not terminate its operation. (*Primeco Personal Communications, L.P. v. Markham*, Florida Circuit Court, Seventh Judicial Circuit, Broward County, December 19, 2005)

[¶20-145] Construction Work in Progress

Real property is assessed on January 1 of each year. Any improvement to real property that is not substantially completed on January 1 has no value placed on it. "Substantially completed" means that the improvement or some self-sufficient unit within it can be used for its intended purpose. (Sec. 192.042, F.S.)

• *Constitutionality*

The constitutionality of the no value assessment provision has been the subject of several court cases in recent years. However, the Florida Supreme Court upheld the constitutionality of the provision in 2005 and reversed a 2003 lower appellate opinion to the contrary.

The statutory provision that precluded valuation of real property for years in which improvements were not substantially completed on January 1 did not violate the state constitution's "just valuation" requirement, it merely temporarily postponed valuation, the Florida Supreme Court held. (*Sunset Harbour Condominium Association v. Robbins*, No. SC03-520, July 7, 2005; reversing and remanding *Sunset Harbour North Condominium Association v. Robbins*, 837 So2d 1181 (Fla. 3d DCA 2003)) Although the constitution had been amended after Florida Supreme Court precedent that established that rule, both the pre-amendment and post-amendment constitutions mandated a just valuation for all property. There was no reason to believe that the amendments were intended to invalidate the "substantial completion" statute.

The statute implements the constitutional just valuation provision in such a way as to provide predictability in the assessment rolls that serve as the basis for revenue projections in the local government budget-making process, the Florida Supreme Court explained. The statute prescribes reasonable guidelines for valuation of incomplete improvements that infuse uniformity and certain into ad valorem taxation. The absence of the statute would promote uncertainty and encourage litigation.

County fee.—The Florida Supreme Court in May of 1999 held that a county's proposed fee on real property improvements substantially completed after January 1 unconstitutionally conflicted with the state no value provision. The method and timing of the assessment was set out unambiguously in the state's constitutionally required general law on ad valorem taxation of real property, the Supreme Court held. (*Collier County v. State of Florida, et al.*, No. 93,802, 733 So2d 1012, May 6, 1999)

[¶20-165] Energy Systems or Facilities

The legislature may prohibit the consideration of the installation of a renewable energy source device or a solar renewable energy device in the determination of the assessed value of real property used for residential purposes. (Sec. 4(i), Art. VII, Fla. Const.) "Renewable energy source devices" include solar energy collectors, storage tanks, rockbeds, thermostats, heat exchange devices, pumps, fans, roof ponds, and windmills, and pipes, ducts, and other equipment used to interconnect such systems. (Sec. 193.624, F.S.)

• *Exemption*

In determining the assessed value of real property used for residential purposes for both new and existing property, a property appraiser may not consider the increase in the just value attributed to the installation of a renewable energy source device. (Sec. 193.624, F.S.) The Legislature can apply the same restriction on solar devices. (Sec. 4(i), Art. VII, Fla. Const.)

[¶20-170] Enterprise Zones and Other Redevelopment Areas

Florida law provides for several tax credits for qualifying businesses located in state-designated enterprise zones. For example, both sales tax credits and income tax credits are authorized for jobs creation in enterprise zones. New businesses locating in enterprise zones also may be eligible for an income tax credit measured by their property taxes paid.

• *Economic development property tax exemption*

Subject to voter approval, any county or municipality can exempt up to 100% of property taxes for new businesses and expansions of businesses that are located in an enterprise zone, under certain circumstances, or in a brownfield area. For enterprise zone businesses, the exemption can be granted only if the local government has adopted an appropriate ordinance by December 30, 2015. However, the exemption applies only to the taxes levied by the unit of government granting the exemption. Local governments are allowed to extend economic development property tax exemptions for a subsequent period of 10 years after an initial 10 year period if each 10 year renewal is approved in a referendum. (Sec. 196.1995, F.S.)

All data center equipment in a data center is exempt for the term of an approved exemption. The exemption will remain in effect for up to 20 years regardless of either any change in local authority to grant such exemptions or the expiration of the Enterprise Zone Act. (Sec. 196.1995, F.S.)

[¶20-195] Health Care Facilities and Equipment

Health care facilities are exempt from property tax. However, leasehold interests in health care facilities operated for profit are subject to tax. (Sec. 154.2331(1), F.S.)

Life care communities, however designated, that are financed through the sale of health facilities authority bonds, whether on a sale-leaseback arrangement, a sale-repurchase arrangement, or other financing arrangement, are exempt from tax. (Sec. 154.2331(2), F.S.)

[¶20-205] Homestead

Florida property tax exemptions are governed in the first instance by the state constitution. (Sec. 6, Art. VII, Fla. Const.) There are a variety of exemptions, some of which are discussed elsewhere.

• *Constitutional provisions*

Constitutionally authorized provisions relating to homestead exemptions or other property tax relief include:

— an exemption of up to $25,000 for qualifying permanent residences and another $25,000 for residences with assessed valuations greater than $50,000 and up to $75,000;

— a limit of one homestead exemption for any individual or family, and only one exemption on any residential unit;

— ad valorem tax relief for renters;

— alternative exemptions for senior citizens who are 65 years or older and who meet certain income limitations of (1) $25,000 for maintaining a permanent residence and (2) up to $250,000 if the owners have resided on the property for at least 25 years;

— an exemption for veterans with service-connected disabilities in an amount based on the percentage of the disability;;

— extension of exemptions to the surviving spouses of veterans who died from service-connected causes and first responders who died in the line of duty; and

— an extension of the timeframe during which a property owner may transfer accrued save-our-homes benefits pursuant to Constitutional Amendment 5 approved by voters in the November 3, 2020, general election.

(Sec. 6, Art. VII, Fla. Const.)

Additional homestead exemption for certain critical public service employees.— Legislation is enacted that implements the proposed constitutional amendment in H.J.R. 1 by providing an additional homestead exemption on the assessed value between $100,000 and $150,000 for all Florida property tax taxes, other than school district taxes, for certain critical public service employees. (Sec. 196.077, F.S.)

The exemption, if the constitutional amendment to the Florida Constitution is approved, will apply to the following critical public service employees:

— classroom teachers;

— law enforcement officers;

— correctional officers;

— firefighters;

— emergency medical technicians;

— paramedics;

— child welfare services professionals;

— active duty members of the United States Armed Forces; and

— members of the Florida National Guard.

(Sec. 196.077, F.S.)

This provision will take effect on the effective date of the amendment to the Florida Constitution proposed by H.J.R. 1, or a similar joint resolution having substantially the same specific intent and purpose, if such amendment to the Florida Constitution is approved at the next general election or at an earlier special election specifically authorized by law for that purpose. (Sec. 196.077, F.S.; Ch. 219 (H.B. 1563), Laws 2022)

• *Qualifications*

An individual who, on January 1, has legal or beneficial title in equity to real property in Florida, and who in good faith makes the property his or her permanent residence or the permanent residence of a legal or natural dependent, is entitled to a homestead exemption, except for assessments for special benefits, for up to $25,000 of assessed value on the property. The exemption will not be granted unless the deed or instrument is recorded in the official records of the county where the property is located. The property appraiser may also request the applicant to provide additional ownership documents to establish title. (Sec. 196.031(1)(a), F.S.)

Every person who qualifies for the homestead exemption is entitled to an additional exemption of up to $25,000 on the assessed valuation greater than $50,000 and up to $75,000 for all levies other than school district levies. (Sec. 196.031(1)(b), F.S.)

Property rented for more than six months is presumed to be used for commercial purposes, and thus does not constitute "real estate used and owned as a homestead." Additionally, the homestead exemption can be lost through abandonment if the owner rents all or substantially all of the dwelling. However, the owner can retain the exemption if the property is rented for less than 30 days per calendar year, not to exceed two consecutive years. (Sec. 196.061, F.S.)

A person who is receiving a property tax exemption or credit in another state that requires permanent residence in that state may not claim a homestead exemption, unless the taxpayer's Florida property is used as the permanent residence of a person who is legally or naturally dependent on the taxpayer. (Sec. 196.031, F.S.)

• *Damaged or destroyed property*

When homestead property is damaged or destroyed by misfortune or calamity and deemed uninhabitable on January 1 after the damage occurs, the homestead exemption may be granted if the property is otherwise qualified and if the property owner notifies the property appraiser that the property will be repaired and rebuilt for use as the owner's primary residence afterwards. The owner may not claim a homestead exemption on another property. Failure to commence repair or rebuilding within three years after January 1 will constitute abandonment. The expiration, lapse, nonrenewal, or revocation of a building permit after the three-year period also constitutes abandonment. (Sec. 196.031, F.S.)

An owner of a homestead property that was significantly damaged or destroyed as a result of a named tropical storm or hurricane can elect, in the calendar year following the storm or hurricane, to have the homestead deemed to have been abandoned as of the date of the named tropical storm or hurricane even though the owner received a homestead exemption on the property as of January 1 of the year immediately following the named tropical storm or hurricane. Such an election is available only if the owner establishes a new homestead as of January 1 of the third year immediately following the storm or hurricane. This provision applies to homestead property damaged or destroyed on or after January 1, 2017. (Sec. 193.155(8)(m), F.S.)

• *Change in ownership*

Real property is assessed as of January 1 of the year following any change of ownership. (Sec. 193.155, F.S.)

• *Application process*

An annual application for the homestead exemption must be filed with the county tax appraiser on or before March 1. (Sec. 196.011, F.S.)

A property appraiser may mail notices after February 5 to persons entitled to the exemption for the preceding year who have not applied by February 1 for the current year. A taxpayer who is qualified to receive a homestead exemption and who fails to file an application by March 1 must file an application for the exemption with the property appraiser on or before the 25th day following the mailing by the property appraiser of the notice. The applicant must provide sufficient evidence to show why the applicant failed to apply for the exemption in a timely manner. (Sec. 196.011, F.S.)

● *Portability*

A qualifying person with a homestead exemption who establishes a new homestead can have the new homestead assessed at less than just value by transferring some or all of the difference between the assessed value and market value (assessment limitation difference) of the previous homestead when establishing a new homestead. (Sec. 193.155(8), F.S.) In determining the assessment limitation difference, the assessed value refers to the value of the homestead property as limited by the "Save Our Homes" assessment increase limitations. Under the "Save Our Homes" assessment increase limitation, the growth in the assessed value of the homestead property cannot exceed the lower of 3% or the percentage change in the Consumer Price Index, with assessments never being able to exceed just value. (Sec. 4(c), Art. VII, Fla. Const.) The transfer of the assessment limitations difference is generally referred to as portability.

A qualifying taxpayer will be able to transfer some or all of the assessment limitation difference of a prior homestead when establishing a new homestead. A person having had a homestead exemption at one residence may apply for transfer of an assessment difference to another residence if, among other things, the previous property was timely abandoned as a homestead. The maximum assessment difference that can be transferred is $500,000. (Sec. 193.155(8), F.S.)

● *Living quarters for senior parents*

A county may provide a property tax exemption for increases in the assessed value of homestead property resulting from the construction of living quarters for the property owner's parent or grandparent who is age 62 or older. The exemption applies only during taxable years in which at least one qualifying parent or grandparent maintains the constructed living quarters as his or her primary place of residence. The amount of the exemption is limited to the lesser of the increase in assessed value resulting from the construction or 20% of the total assessed value of the property as improved. (Sec. 193.703, F.S.)

● *Condominiums, leased property*

The homestead exemption is available to owners of condominiums and cooperative apartments as well as to owners of single-family homes and mobile homes. (Sec. 196.031, F.S.) Lessees owning the leasehold interest in a bona fide lease with an original term of 98 years or more in a residential parcel are deemed to have legal or beneficial and equitable title to the property for purposes of the homestead exemption. (Sec. 196.041(1), F.S.)

● *Homestead property probated in another state*

If the estate of a person who claimed a homestead exemption in Florida is probated in another state, with the decedent treated as a resident of that state, the county in which the homestead is located may, within three years of the death, record a tax lien against the property for the exempted taxes for ten years before the death. The lien may include 15% interest per year on the exempted taxes. (Sec. 196.161, F.S.)

● *Tax deferral*

A person entitled to a homestead tax exemption may apply to defer payment of a portion of the combined total of the property taxes, non-ad valorem assessments, and interest accumulated on a tax certificate. Approval of an application will defer the combined total that exceeds:

— 5% of the applicant's household income for the prior calendar year if the applicant is younger than 65 years old;

— 3% of the applicant's household income for the prior calendar year if the applicant is 65 years or older; or

— in its entirety if the applicant's household income for the previous calendar year is less than $10,000 or is less than the designated amount for the additional homestead exemption and the applicant is over 65 years of age.

(Sec. 197.252, F.S.)

• *Deployed servicemen*

Eligible servicemembers who receive a homestead exemption may receive an additional Florida property tax exemption on the homestead property if the servicemember was deployed during the calendar year on active duty outside of the United States in support of designated military operations. The amount of the exemption is equal to the taxable value of the homestead on January 1 of the year in which the exemption is sought multiplied by the number of days that the servicemember was on a qualifying deployment in the preceding calendar year and divided by the number of days in that year. (Sec. 196.173(2), F.S.)

[¶20-215] Housing

Florida property used to provide affordable housing for low-income or very low-income persons and natural persons or families that meet certain income limits may be entitled to a property tax exemption as property owned by an exempt entity and used for a charitable purpose. To qualify, the property must be owned entirely by a nonprofit entity that is a corporation not for profit. The corporation must qualify as charitable under IRC Sec. 501(c)(3) and also comply with *Rev. Proc. 96-32*, 1996-1 C.B. 717. (Sec. 196.196, F.S.; Sec. 196.1978, F.S.)

Affordable housing ad valorem property tax exemption.—For purposes of the exemption, a property owned by a limited liability company that has a single owner and is disregarded as an entity separate from its owner for federal income tax purposes must be treated as owned by its sole member. (Sec. 196.1978, F.S.)

Effective January 1, 2021, if the sole member of the limited liability company that owns the property is also a limited liability company that is disregarded as an entity for federal income tax purposes (pursuant to Treasury Regulation 301.7701-3(b)(1)(ii)), the legislature intends that the property be treated as owned by the sole member of the limited liability company that owns the limited liability company that owns the property. In effect, an affordable housing project owned by a limited liability company, which is also owned by a limited liability company, is exempt from property tax as long as the owner of the second limited liability company is a qualifying 501(c)(3) entity. (Sec. 196.1978, F.S.)

Effective July 1, 2021, those portions of property in a multifamily project that provide housing to extremely-low-income, very-low-income, or low-income families are fully exempt. Until that date, a discount of 50% of property tax is provided for properties that offer affordable housing to specified low-income persons and families in qualifying multifamily projects. A qualified applicant must submit the application by March 1. The property appraiser shall apply the discount by reducing the taxable value on those portions of the affordable housing property that provide housing to natural persons or families meeting certain low-income limits. (Sec. 196.1978, F.S.)

For a discussion relating to assessment of property used for affordable housing, community land trust, and subject to a low-income housing tax credit.

• *Tax deferral program*

A tax deferral program is available for affordable rental housing property if the owners are engaged in the operation, rehabilitation, or renovation of certain properties. (Sec. 197.2524, F.S.)

The tax deferral applies only on a pro rata basis to the property taxes levied on residential units within a property for where units for which the monthly rent along with taxes, insurances, and utilities does not exceed 30% of the median adjusted gross annual income for households occupied by extremely-low-income, very-low-income, low income, or moderate-income persons. Tax deferral procedures have been consolidated. (Sec. 197.2526, F.S.)

[¶20-230] Intangible Property

Taxpayers that own intangible personal property such as stocks, bonds, mutual funds, money market funds, and unsecured notes are not required to file an intangible personal property tax return. Florida repealed its annual tax on such intangible personal property. (Ch. 312 (H.B. 209), Laws 2006) However, the repeal does not include:

— the nonrecurring tax on a note, bond, or other obligation for payment of money that is secured by a mortgage deed or other lien of real property, (Sec. 199.133, F.S.) or

— the recurring tax is due at the same time as a rental payment for leased real property owned by a government and leased to a nongovernmental entity that does not serve or provide a governmental, municipal, or public purpose/function. (Sec. 196.199, F.S.)

(*Tax Information Publication No. 07C02-01*, Florida Department of Revenue, January 2, 2007)

• *Nonrecurring tax*

A onetime nonrecurring tax of $2 per $1,000 of the principal amount of indebtedness is imposed on the just valuation of all notes, bonds, and other obligations for payment of money that are secured by mortgage, deed of trust, or other lien on real property located in Florida. (Sec. 199.133, F.S.) The taxpayer is solely liable for payment of the nonrecurring tax, but may pass on the amount of the nonrecurring tax to borrowers and mortgagors. (Sec. 199.135, F.S.) Each taxpayer shall retain all books and other records necessary to identify the taxpayer's intangible personal property. (Sec. 199.218, F.S.)

If the instruments are secured partially inside and partially outside the state, the tax will apply to that portion of the note, bond, or other obligation that bears the same ratio to the entire principal balance of the note, bond, or other obligation as the value of the real property located in the state bears to the value of all of the security. (Sec. 199.133, F.S.)

If the security is made up entirely of personal and real property in the state, the taxpayer can elect to apportion the taxes based upon the value of the collateral, if any, to which the taxpayer by contract or law must look first for collection. In no event should the portion of the instrument or obligation which is subject to the nonrecurring tax exceed in value the value of the real property located in Florida which is the security. (Sec. 199.133, F.S.)

Where a note, bond, or other obligation upon which a nonrecurring tax has previously been paid is refinanced with the original obligee or its assignee, no additional nonrecurring tax would be due if the principal balance of the new obligation is less than or equal to the unpaid principal balance of the original obligation, plus accrued but unpaid interest, as of the date of the refinancing. However, an additional nonrecurring tax would be due if the principal balance of the new obligation exceeds the principal balance of the original obligation, plus accrued but unpaid interest, as of the date of the refinancing. (Sec. 199.145, F.S.)

If a mortgage, deed of trust, or other lien secures:

— future advances, the nonrecurring tax is paid on the initial obligation secured, excluding future advances. Each time a future advance is made, an additional nonrecurring tax will be paid on the amount of the advance. (Sec. 199.143, F.S)

— a line of credit, the nonrecurring tax is paid on the maximum amount of the line of credit. No further nonrecurring tax is due on borrowing under the line of credit. (Sec. 199.143, F.S)

— an identical original note, or an obligation that covers the identical real property that was covered by an original mortgage, deed of trust, or other lien, which was defective, an additional nonrecurring tax will not be paid upon proof of payment of the tax on the original recording. (Sec. 199.145, F.S.)

No additional nonrecurring tax is due upon the assignment by the obligee of a note, bond, or other obligation for the payment of money upon which a nonrecurring tax had previously been paid. (Sec. 199.145, F.S.)

No additional nonrecurring tax will be due upon the assumption of a note, bond, or other obligation for the payment of money if a nonrecurring tax has previously been paid and the amount of the indebtedness remains the same, whether or not the original obligor is released from liability. (Sec. 199.145, F.S.)

All notes, bonds, and other obligations for payment of money subject to the nonrecurring tax shall be valued at the principal amount of indebtedness evidenced by such obligation. (Sec. 199.155, F.S.)

Collection of tax.—The nonrecurring tax that is payable upon recordation is collected from the person recording the obligation. The clerk of the circuit court collects the tax. Where an instrument is being recorded in more than one county, the tax can be paid to the clerk of any of the counties where it is being recorded. If the instrument is not recorded, the tax is payable directly to the Department of Revenue. (Sec. 199.135, F.S.)

The nonrecurring tax on obligations secured by real property in Florida is assessed on the value of the principal amount of indebtedness and is due either on presentation for recording or, if there is no recording, within 30 days following the creation of the obligation. (Sec. 199.135, F.S.)

Assessment and collection procedures.—The Department of Revenue administers and enforces assessment and collection of nonrecurring intangibles taxes and any related interest and penalties. It has the power to conduct an audit, and it can assess a tax deficiency based on the best information available to it under certain circumstances. The assessment by the Department is considered prima facie correct, and the taxpayer has the burden of proving it incorrect. (Sec. 199.232, F.S.)

The Department of Revenue will credit or refund any overpayment of tax when the overpayment is revealed in an audit or when a claim for refund is filed. Claims for refunds, other than those regarding adjustments due to changes in federal income tax liability, must be filed within three years after the date on which the tax was paid. (Sec. 199.232(5), F.S.; Sec. 215.26(2), F.S.) The application must be filed by the taxpayer, his heirs, personal representatives, successors, or assigns. The claim must include the information required by the Department. (Sec. 199.232(5), F.S.) The Department must refund any overpayment whether or not the taxpayer had filed a written claim for refund, but may require the taxpayer to file a statement affirming that he or she made the overpayment. (Sec. 199.232(7), F.S.)

Delinquencies and penalties.—The nonrecurring tax is considered to be delinquent if not paid by the due date. A penalty of 10% of the delinquent tax is imposed for each calendar month or portion of a month from the due date until the tax is paid. The penalty may not exceed 50% of the total unpaid tax. (Sec. 199.282, F.S.) If any nonrecurring tax is not paid by the statutory due date, then despite any extension, interest will run on the unpaid balance from such due date until paid at the rate of 12% per year. (Sec. 199.282, F.S.)

If property is undervalued on or omitted from a return, a specific penalty of 30% of the tax attributable to each undervaluation is charged. No delinquency or late filing penalty is charged with respect to an undervaluation. (Sec. 199.282, F.S.)

When tax becomes delinquent or is in jeopardy, the Department of Revenue can issue a warrant for the full amount of tax due or estimated to be due, together with any interest, penalties, and collection costs. The warrant is addressed to sheriffs in the state and must be recorded with the clerk of the circuit court in the county where the delinquent taxpayer's property is located. Once it has been recorded, the amount of the warrant will become a lien upon the taxpayer's real and personal property. When the warrant is paid, the Department has 30 days to satisfy the lien of record, and any interested person can thereafter compel the Department to satisfy the lien of record. (Sec. 199.262, F.S.)

A late-reporting penalty of at least $100 is imposed on any corporation that does not timely file the written notice to stockholders due on June 30, with a separate penalty for each delinquent notice. The $100 minimum penalty is also imposed upon any security broker who does not timely file the required position statements. (Sec. 199.282, F.S.)

Any person who willfully fails or refuses to comply with the intangibles tax law or violates the provisions of the intangibles tax law will be guilty of a third degree felony. (Sec. 199.282, F.S.)

[¶20-245] Leased Property

Leasehold interests in property of the United States, the State of Florida, or any political subdivision, municipality, agency, authority, or other public body of the state are taxable. (Sec. 196.001, F.S.)

A leasehold interest of a nongovernmental lessee in federal, state, or locally owned government property is exempt from ad valorem taxation only when the lessee performs a governmental, municipal, or public purpose function. (Sec. 196.199, F.S.) However, a leasehold interest in state property may not be exempted when the nongovernmental lessee uses the property for the operation of a multipurpose hazardous waste treatment facility.

Spaceport lessees.—An exemption from Florida property tax is granted to non-governmental lessees of real property used for aerospace activities at a spaceport governed by the Florida Space Authority. (Sec. 196.012(6), F.S.)

[¶20-260] Manufactured and Mobile Homes

The Florida Constitution provides that trailers, trailer coaches, and mobile homes are generally not subject to ad valorem taxes and are subject to license taxes for operation within the state. (Sec. 1(b), Art. VII, Fla. Const.) Unlicensed mobile homes are presumed to be taxable. (Rule 12D-6.002(2)(c), F.A.C.)

Florida taxes mobile homes in three ways: an annual license tax, assessed and taxed as real property, or assessed and taxed as tangible personal property.

License tax.—Mobile homes are generally subject only to a license tax. (Sec. 320.015, F.S.) The owner of a mobile home who does not own the lot or land on which the mobile home is situated must pay the annual license tax by purchasing an MH (mobile home) series sticker from the local county tax collector's office. (*Taxation of Mobile Homes in Florida*, Florida Department of Revenue, June 2009)

Real property tax.—Mobile homes are considered real property and are subject to property tax only when the owner of the mobile home is also the owner of the land on which the mobile home is situated and said mobile home is permanently affixed to the land. (Sec. 320.015, F.S.) The owner must buy an RP (real property) series sticker from the local county tax collector. This is a one-time purchase. If the property appraiser lists a mobile home as real property, the owner pays only the real property tax and not the annual license tax. (*Taxation of Mobile Homes in Florida*, Florida Department of Revenue, June 2009)

A prefabricated or modular housing unit that is not manufactured on an integral chassis or undercarriage for travel over the highways is taxed as real property once it is permanently affixed to real property. (Sec. 320.015, F.S.)

Tangible personal property tax.—A mobile home without a current license sticker is presumed to be tangible personal property. (Rule 12D-6.002, F.A.C.) Mobile homes which meet the criteria for an MH series sticker which do not have a current MH sticker will be taxed as tangible personal property. An owner cannot cancel the assessment for tangible personal property tax by paying the previous year's annual license tax and purchasing the MH series sticker. (*Taxation of Mobile Homes in Florida*, Florida Department of Revenue, June 2009)

A mobile home classified as personal property at the time a security interest is granted continues to be classified as personal property for the purposes of the loan. Classification as personal property by a seller or lender does not, however, prohibit the owner from having the mobile home classified and taxed as real property. (Sec. 320.015, F.S.)

Real property or tangible personal property.—A mobile home is considered to be real property if the owner of the mobile home is also the owner of the land on which the mobile home is permanently affixed and the mobile home has a current sticker affixed, regardless of the series ("MH" or "RP"). (Rule 12D-6.002, F.A.C.) Permanently affixed mobile homes and appurtenances that are held for display by a licensed mobile home dealer or a licensed mobile home manufacturer are considered tangible personal property and inventory not subject to the property tax if the following conditions are met (Sec. 193.075, F.S.; Rule 12D-6.002, F.A.C.) : (1) The mobile home and any appurtenance is being held strictly for resale as tangible personal property and is not rented, occupied, or otherwise used; (2) The mobile home is not used as a sales office by the mobile home dealer or mobile home manufacturer; and (3) The mobile home does not bear an "RP" series sticker. Any item of tangible personal property or any improvement to real property that is appurtenant to a mobile home and that is not held strictly for resale is subject to ad valorem tax. (Rule 12D-6.002, F.A.C.) A mobile home without a current license sticker is presumed to be tangible personal property. (Rule 12D-6.002, F.A.C.)

[¶20-265] Manufacturing and Industrial Property

Generally, Florida provides no specific property tax exemptions for manufacturing and industrial property.

• *Tools*

Unless expressly exempted from tax, personal property is subject to tax. (Sec. 196.001, F.S.)

Personal effects.—Personal effects, including certain tools, are exempt from Florida property tax. (Sec. 196.181, F.S.; Sec. 3(b), Art. VII, Florida Const.) "Personal effects" includes such items as clothing, jewelry, tools, and hobby equipment. (Rule 12D-8.001 F.A.C.) Only personal effects of the taxpayer which are actually employed in the use of serving the creature comforts of the owner and not held for commercial purposes are entitled to the exemption. "Creature comforts" are things which give bodily comfort, such as food, clothing and shelter. "Commercial purposes" includes owning personal effects as stock in trade or as furnishings in rental dwelling units. (Rule 12D-7.002, F.A.C.)

Farming machinery and equipment.—Certain farming machinery and equipment is classified as tangible person property and may be subject to tax. (Rule 12D-8.009, F.A.C.) However, farming tools that qualify as personal effects would be exempt from tax. (Sec. 196.181, F.S.; Sec. 3(b), Art. VII, Florida Const.)

[¶20-270] Mining, Oil, and Gas Properties

Minerals, oil, and gas are generally not taxed as real property until they have been severed from the land.

• *Mineral and subsurface rights*

When the mineral, oil, gas, or other subsurface rights in real property have been severed by being sold or otherwise transferred, or by being retained when the real property is sold, the rights are treated as an interest in real property subject to taxation separate and apart from the fee interest or ownership. (Sec. 193.481, F.S.)

The owner of the real property can request assessment of the subsurface rights and the remainder of the property as separate items on the tax roll. (Sec. 193.481, F.S.)

Taxation of the subsurface rights is not against the owner of the real property. Tax certificates and tax liens encumbering subsurface rights are enforced as they would be against real property. (Sec. 193.481, F.S.)

• *Oil and gas production machinery and equipment*

Property used for oil and gas exploration and production is subject to Florida property tax, unless a specific exemption applies. (Sec. 196.001, F.S.) The presence of any producing oil or gas equipment or machinery does not increase land's value for ad valorem taxation if the equipment is actually used in the operation of an oil well or a gas well on the land. In addition, the value is not increased because there may be taxable products under the surface of the land. (Sec. 211.13, F.S.)

[¶20-275] Motor Vehicles

The Florida Constitution exempts motor vehicles from ad valorem taxation, making them subject to license taxes instead. (Sec. 1(b), Art. VII, Fla. Const.) For registration purposes, "motor vehicle" means an automobile, motorcycle, truck, trailer, semitrailer, truck tractor and semitrailer combination, or any other vehicle operated on Florida roads, used to transport persons or property, and propelled by power other than muscular power, excluding traction engines, road rollers, vehicles that run only on a track, bicycles, or mopeds. (Sec. 320.01(1)(a), F.S.)

• *Automobile trailers*

The Florida Constitution classifies automobile trailers with other motor vehicles and exempts them from ad valorem taxation. They are subject to license fees. (Sec. 1(b), Art. VII, Fla. Const.) Unlicensed mobile homes are, however, presumed to be taxable.

Licensing and registration of automobile trailers are governed by Chapter 320 of the Florida Statutes.

[¶20-285] Nonprofit, Religious, Charitable, Scientific, and Educational Organizations

The Florida Constitution provides that portions of property used predominantly for educational, literary, scientific, religious, or charitable purposes may be exempted by general law. (Sec. 3, Art. VII, Fla. Const.)

• *Charitable, religious, scientific, or literary use*

Portions of property used predominantly for charitable, religious, scientific, or literary purposes is exempt. Portions of property not predominantly used for those purposes are not exempt. (Sec. 196.196(2), F.S.) An application for exemption may not be granted until the applicant is determined to be nonprofit. (Sec. 196.195(5), F.S.) However, qualified Florida nonprofit organizations with a valid consumer certificate of exemption from sales and use tax and an exemption from federal income tax under IRC Sec. 501(c)(3) require no further proof of their nonprofit status. (Sec. 196.195(4), F.S.)

The criteria used to determine if the exempt use is the predominant use of the property are:

— the nature and extent of the charitable, religious, scientific, or literary activity as compared with other activities;

— the extent to which the property and services are made available to exempt groups and to persons at or below the cost of providing the facilities or services; and

— the extent to which the property is used to conduct activities that cause a corporation to qualify for a consumer certificate of exemption.

(Sec. 196.196(1), F.S.)

Only portions of the property used for exempt purposes are exempt. Incidental use of the property does not qualify the property for exemption, nor does it impair exemption of an otherwise exempt property. (Sec. 196.196(2), F.S.)

Property claimed as exempt is taxable if it is used for profit-making purposes. Functions that do not require a business license, specifically including bingo, are not considered profit-making if the revenue is used wholly for exempt purposes. (Sec. 196.196(3), F.S.)

Qualifying property used by an owner organization to display different historical aspects of the Bible is exempt from Florida property tax. In order for the property to qualify for the exemption, the organization must be exempt from federal income tax under IRC Sec. 501(c)(3), and the Bible-related use of the property must be open to the public for no admission charge at least one day each calendar year. Designated activities that constitute exempt religious use of property include:

— exhibition, illustration, and interpretation of Biblical manuscripts, codices, stone tablets, and other Biblical archives;

— live and recorded demonstrations, explanations, reenactments, and illustrations of Biblical history and Biblical worship; and

— exhibition of times, places, and events of Biblical history and significance.

The organization must have written correspondence from the IRS stating that the conduct of the organization activities does not adversely affect the federal exemption. In addition, any portion of the property that is used for nonexempt purposes may be valued and placed upon the tax rolls. (Sec. 196.1987, F.S.)

• *Scientific research in space*

A module, pallet, rack, locker, and any necessary associated hardware and subsystem owned by any person and intended to be used to transport or store cargo used for a space laboratory for the primary purpose of conducting scientific research in space is deemed to carry out a scientific purpose and is exempt from ad valorem taxation. (Sec. 196.1999, F.S.)

• *Community centers*

A single general-purpose structure used as a community center is exempt from property taxes if it is owned and operated by a private, nonprofit organization and is used predominantly for educational, literary, scientific, religious, or charitable purposes. The exemption does not apply if alcoholic beverages are served or consumed on the premises in conjunction with the use of the building or if the building is not generally open and available for use by the general public. The exemption does not apply to condominium common elements. (Sec. 196.1986, F.S.)

• *Educational use*

Educational institutions in Florida and their property used by them or by any other exempt entity or educational institution exclusively for educational purposes are exempt from taxation. Sheltered workshops that provide rehabilitation and retraining for disabled individuals, if they are exempted by certificate under the federal Fair Labor Standards Act of 1938, are considered wholly educational. Child care facilities which have been granted Gold Seal Quality Status by the state of Florida and are either licensed by the state of Florida or are exempt from licensing requirements under Florida law are considered educational institutions. In addition, institutions of higher education that participate in the Higher Education Facilities Financing Act are considered educational institutions. (Rule 12D-7.015, F.A.C)

Property is deemed to be used for an educational purpose if the institution has taken affirmative steps to prepare the property for educational use. Property used exclusively for educational purposes is deemed owned by the educational institution if the entity owning 100% of the educational institution is owned by identical persons who own the property or if the entity owning 100% of the education institution and the entity owning the property are owned by the identical natural persons. If the title to land is held by the trustee of an irrevocable inter vivos trust and the trust grantor owns 100% of the entity that owns an educational institution that is using the land exclusively for educational purposes, the land is deemed to be property owned by the educational institution. (Sec. 196.198, F.S.)

The exemption is extended to include nonprofit entities that own 100% of land, buildings, and other improvements used by an educational institution pursuant to a ground lease or other contractual agreement for educational purposes. To qualify, the education institution must have IRC 501(c)(3) status and only provide education to prekindergarten through grade 8 students. (Sec. 196.198, F.S.)

Any portion of a facility used for a public charter school-in-the-workplace is exempt from Florida property taxes for the duration of its use as a public school. A charter school-in-the-workplace may be established when a business provides the facility, enrolls students based upon a random lottery involving all of the children of employees seeking enrollment, and enrolls students according to racial/ethnic balance provisions. (Sec. 1002.33, F.S.)

Also, any facility or portion of a facility used to house a charter school whose charter is approved by its sponsor and governing board is exempt from ad valorem tax. (Sec. 196.1983, F.S.)

Those portions of property of college fraternities and sororities certified by the college or university as being essential to the educational process are exempt.

The use of property by public fairs and exhibitions chartered by Chapter 616 of the Florida Statutes is presumed to be educational and is exempt.

If legal title to property is held by a government agency that leases that property, that property is considered to be owned by the agency and used exclusively for educational purposes if the agency continues to use the property exclusively for educational purposes pursuant to a sublease or other contractual agreement with the lessee. (Sec. 196.198, F.S.)

• *Hospitals, nursing homes, homes for the aged, homes for special services*

Exemption may be claimed by any Florida corporation operating as a hospital, nursing home, or home for special services that is exempt from federal taxation under Sec. 501(c)(3) of the Internal Revenue Code (IRC). (Sec. 196.197(1), F.S.) Court decisions have found unconstitutional the requirement that the applicant be a Florida corporation. (*Miller, as Executive Director of the Department of Revenue, and Muckenfuss, as Property Appraiser of Marion County v. The Board of Pensions of the United Presbyterian Church in the United States of America*, FlaDistCtApp, May 20, 1983) The exemption also applies to certain property used for a nonprofit home for the aged and leased to a Florida limited partnership for purposes of allocating the federal low-income housing credit under IRC Sec. 42(h)(5). The sole general partner of the partnership must be a nonprofit corporation, and the home for the aged must have been in existence or under construction on or before April 1, 1995. (Sec. 196.1975(1), F.S.)

Nonprofit housing projects financed by loans from the U.S. Department of Housing and Urban Development under the National Housing Act are exempt, subject to income limitations established by the Department of Revenue. (Sec. 196.1975(5), F.S.)

Parking facilities.—In the determination of the extent of exemption for an institution licensed as a hospital, nursing home, or home for special services, any portion of the property leased as a parking lot or garage operated by private enterprise is not exempt. Property or facilities leased to nonprofit corporations that provide direct medical services to patients and qualify as charitable are exempt. (Sec. 196.197(2), F.S.)

Homes for the aged.—Nonprofit homes for the aged that are not for profit corporations or Florida limited partnerships (the sole general partner of which is a not for profit corporation) and that were qualified as not for profit corporation was as of January 1 of the year for which exemption is being sought are exempt to the extent that:

— any portion of the home is devoted exclusively to the conduct of religious services, nursing services, or medical services and;

— residency in the home is restricted to or occupied by persons who have resided in the home and made Florida their permanent state of residence by January 1 and:

• have a gross income of $7,200 or less per year and are 62 years of age or older;

• are permanently and totally disabled and who have a gross income of $7,200 or less per year;

• are couples, one of whom is 62 years of age or older, and have a combined income of $8,000 or less per year;

• are couples, one of whom is totally and permanently disabled, and have a combined income of $8000 or less per year; and

• are surviving spouses of a qualifying couple and who lived with the deceased at the time of the deceased's death in the home for the aged.

(Sec. 196.1975, F.S.)

A nonprofit applying for an exemption as a home for the aged generally must provide an affidavit from each person who occupies an apartment that states the person's income. However, an affidavit is not required for a resident who is a totally and permanently disabled veteran. (Sec. 196.1975(4)(c), F.S.)

If any provision of the statute creating an exemption for property used by nonprofit homes for the aged is held to be invalid, it is the legislative intent that the invalidity not affect other provisions or applications of the statute that can be given effect without the invalid portion. (Sec. 196.1976, F.S.)

Florida law sets income tests for residents of tax-exempt homes for the aged in Sec. 196.1975, F.S.. In the past, the Florida Supreme Court has found that similar age and income provisions violated the Florida Constitution. (*Presbyterian Homes of the*

Synod of Florida v. Wood et al. (FlaSCt 1974), 297 So2d 556; *Markham, etc. et al. v. Evangelical Covenant Church of America et al.*, FlaSCt, February 26, 1987)

Continuing care facilities.—Apartments in certified continuing care facilities, that do not qualify for any other exemption, are exempt to the extent of $25,000 of assessed valuation for each apartment which is occupied on January 1 of the year in which the exemption is requested by a person holding a continuing care contract. The facility itself must not qualify for a similar exemption and the individual must not be eligible for the homestead exemption. When applying for the exemption, a facility must file with the annual application an affidavit from each person stating that the person resides in the apartment and in good faith makes it his or her permanent residence. Any portion of the facility used for nonexempt purposes may be valued and placed upon the tax rolls separately from any exempt portion. The resident must receive the full benefit derived from this exemption in either an annual or monthly credit to his or her unit's monthly maintenance fee. (Sec. 196.1977, F.S.)

• *Investment Fraud Restoration Financing Corporation*

The Investment Fraud Restoration Financing Corporation is a nonprofit public benefit corporation financing the remedial measures instituted by the legislature with respect to victims of GIC Governmental Securities, Inc., and the payment of approved claims. It is exempt from taxation and assessments of any type on its income and any property, assets, or revenues acquired or received in pursuance of its stated purpose. Upon the dissolution of the corporation (July 1, 2021, or upon fulfillment of the purposes for which it was created, whichever is earlier), the title to all property owned by it will revert to the Securities Guaranty Fund. (Sec. 517.1204, F.S.)

• *Labor organizations*

Real property owned by any labor organization, chartered by a state or national organization, and used predominantly for educational purposes is considered exempt from ad valorem taxation to the extent of its exempt use. Any portion of the property used for nonexempt purposes may be valued and placed on the tax rolls separate from any exempt portion. (Sec. 196.1985, F.S.)

• *Municipal exemptions*

Property owned or occupied by a religious institution and used as a place of worship or education; by a public or private elementary, middle, or high school; or by a governmentally financed, insured, or subsidized housing facility that is used primarily for persons who are elderly or disabled will be exempt from any special assessment levied by a municipality to fund any service if the municipality so desires. (Sec. 170.201, F.S.)

• *Religious exemptions*

Property owned by an exempt organization is used for a religious purpose if the institution has taken affirmative steps to prepare the property for use as a house of public worship. The term "affirmative steps" means environmental or land use permitting activities, creation of architectural plans or schematic drawings, land clearing or site preparation, construction or renovation activities, or other similar activities that demonstrate a commitment of the property to a religious use as a house of public worship. "Public worship" means religious worship services and those other activities that are incidental to religious worship services, such as educational activities, parking, recreation, partaking of meals, and fellowship. (Sec. 196.196)

• *Affordable housing*

Property owned by a qualified exempt organization is used for a charitable purpose if the organization has taken affirmative steps to prepare the property to provide affordable housing to persons or families that meet the extremely-low income, very-low income, low-income, or moderate-income limits. (Sec. 196.196)

[¶20-295] Personal Property

Each tangible personal property tax return is eligible for an exemption from ad valorem taxation of up to $25,000 of assessed value. (Sec. 3(f), Art. VII, Fla. Const.; Sec. 196.183(1), F.S.) Otherwise, all personal property in Florida and all personal property belonging to residents of Florida is subject to ad valorem taxes, unless specifically exempted. (Sec. 196.001, F.S.)

Tangible personal property is defined as "all goods, chattels, and other articles of value capable of manual possession and whose chief value is intrinsic to the article itself". (Sec. 192.001(11)(d), F.S.) Inventories and household goods are expressly excluded from the definition. Also excluded are vehicles subject to license taxes, as enumerated in Sec. 1(b), Art. VII, Fla. Const., of the Florida Constitution.

A single return must be filed for each site in the county where the owner of tangible personal property transacts business. (Sec. 196.183(1), F.S.) Such sites include facilities where the business ships or receives goods, where employees are located, and where goods or equipment are stored, produced manufactured, or developed. (Sec. 196.183(2), F.S.)

The $25,000 exemption for freestanding property placed at multiple locations and for centrally assessed property will be allocated to each taxing authority based on the proportion of just value of such property located in the taxing authority. (Sec. 196.183(1), F.S.)

Tangible personal property reports must be filed by the property owner with the county property appraiser by April 1 of each year and must reflect the owner's estimate of the true value of the property covered by the return. (Sec. 193.062, F.S.; Sec. 193.052, F.S.) However, the annual filing requirement will be waived for taxpayers owning taxable personal property, the value of which does not exceed the $25,000 exemption, provided that the taxpayer has filed an initial return showing the value of the property and on which the taxpayer takes the exemption. In any subsequent year in which the value of the taxpayer's taxable personal property exceeds the exemption amount, the taxpayer must file a return. (Sec. 196.183(2), F.S.)

The exemption does not apply in any year a taxpayer fails to file a return that is not properly waived. If a taxpayer has a return waiver for a year but exceeds the $25,000 exemption limitation in a later year and does not file a return for the later year, the taxpayer will be subject to a penalty calculated without the benefit of the exemption. Any taxpayer claiming more exemptions than allowed is subject to the taxes exempted as a result of the wrongful claims, interest on those taxes in the amount of 15% per annum, and a penalty in the amount of 50% of the taxes exempted. (Sec. 196.183(3), F.S.)

The personal property exemption does not apply to a mobile home that is presumed to be tangible personal property. (Sec. 196.183(4), F.S.)

• *Computer software*

Computer software is considered personal property only to the extent of the value of the unmounted or uninstalled medium on which the information, program, or routine is stored or transmitted. Computer software does not increase the value of the computer or computer-related peripheral equipment. (Sec. 192.001(19), F.S.) Computer software is intangible rather than tangible personal property and the tax applies only to tangible personal property. Computer software constitutes personal property only to the extent of the value of the disk or tape itself. The information, program, or routine does not constitute tangible personal property. (*Gilreath v. General Electric Company*, Florida District Court of Appeal, No. 5D99-64, February 11, 2000)

¶20-295

[¶20-310] Real Property

All real property in Florida is subject to ad valorem taxes, unless the property is specifically exempted. (Sec. 196.001, F.S.)

Real property is defined as "land, buildings, fixtures, and all other improvements to land." The terms "land," "real estate," "realty," and "real property" may be used interchangeably. (Sec. 192.001(12), F.S.)

Nonresidential real property is defined as any real property not subject to the assessment limitations for:

— agricultural land,

— land producing high water recharge to Florida's aquifers,

— land used exclusively for noncommercial recreational purposes,

— tangible personal property held for sale as stock,

— livestock,

— the homestead exemptions under Sec. 6, Art. VII, Fla. Const, and

— residential real property containing nine or fewer units.

(Sec. 193.1555, F.S.)

Nonhomestead residential property is defined as residential real property containing nine or fewer dwelling units, including vacant properties zoned for residential use, that did not receive the homestead exemption under Sec. 196.031, F.S.. (Sec. 193.1554, F.S.)

[¶20-330] Utilities

Property of a nonprofit sewer and water company is exempt if the income from it exempt from federal income tax under IRC Sec. 115(a) and the company serves a public purpose for which public funds would have to be spent in the absence of the sewer and water company. The following additional conditions must be met:

— the net income does not inure to any private shareholder or individual;

— the gross receipts do not constitute gross income for federal income tax purposes;

— the board members are not compensated;

— rates are regulated by the governing board of the county or by the Public Service Commission; and

— ownership reverts to the county upon retirement of all outstanding indebtedness.

(Sec. 196.2001, F.S.)

• *Nonprofit water and wastewater systems*

Property of a nonprofit water or wastewater corporation is exempt from tax if:

— the corporation is exempt from federal income tax under IRC Sec. 501(c)(12); and

— the sole or primary function of the corporation is to construct, maintain, or operate a water and/or wastewater system in Florida.

(Sec. 196.2002, F.S.)

[¶20-400]
RATES

[¶20-405] Rates of Tax

The process of establishing property tax rates begins when property values are certified by the county tax appraiser to the various taxing units—county commissioners, school districts, municipalities, and special taxing districts.

The governing body of each taxing unit is instructed by the county appraiser to compute a millage rate that provides the prior year's revenue, less any amount paid to a redevelopment trust fund, paid to fund a qualifying project, or paid to finance essential infrastructure (dedicated increment value). This rate is the "rolled-back rate". This millage rate is exclusive of:

— new construction,

— additions,

— deletions,

— property added by boundary changes,

— increases in the value of improvements that have undergone a substantial rehabilitation that increased the assessed value of the improvements by at least 100%,

— total taxable value of tangible personal property in excess of 115% of the previous year's total taxable value, and

— any dedicated increment value.

(Sec. 200.065(1), F.S.)

The maximum millage rate that a governing body may levy is the rolled-back rate based on the amount of taxes that would have been levied in the prior year if the maximum millage rate had been applied, adjusted for change in per capita Florida personal income, unless a higher rate is adopted by the governing body, in which case the maximum is the adopted rate. (Sec. 200.065(5), F.S.)

If the taxing unit proposes a higher rate, it must give public notice and hold hearings. (Sec. 200.065(3), F.S.) A higher rate may be adopted only under the following conditions:

— a rate of not more than 110% of the rolled-back rate based on the previous year's maximum millage rate may be adopted if approved by a two-thirds vote of the governing body; or

— a rate in excess of 110% may be adopted if approved by (1) a unanimous vote of the governing body of fewer than nine members, (2) three-fourths vote of a governing body having at least nine members, or (3) a referendum.

(Sec. 200.065(5)(a), F.S.)

•*County levy*

The county commissioners determine the amount to be raised for all county purposes other than school purposes and the rates to be levied for each fund, recorded with the rates certified by taxing units for which the county commissioners are required to levy taxes. The commissioners ascertain the aggregate rate necessary to cover all such taxes and certify the rate to the county property appraiser. (Sec. 200.011, F.S.)

Generally, the county may not levy an aggregate ad valorem tax millage in excess of 10 mills, except for voted levies. (Sec. 200.071(1), F.S.) If the proposed millage exceeds the 10-mill limitation, the commissioners must reduce the millage to be levied for county officers, departments, divisions, commissions, authorities, and dependent special districts. (Sec. 200.071(2), F.S.)

Referendum requirement.—The 10-mill limitation authorized for county purposes, including dependent special districts, may be increased by referendum. The additional millage may be levied for no more than two years. (Sec. 200.091, F.S.)

Additional county levies.—Any county that has a municipal services unit that provides services or facilities of the type usually provided my municipalities can levy an additional ad valorem tax millage not in excess of 10 mills to pay for the services or facilities. The additional tax is levied only on property within the municipal service taxing unit. (Sec. 200.071(3), F.S.)

Certain additional levies are allowed to counties based upon population for specific purposes, such as beautifying public highways and publicity. These special provisions are not codified in the Florida Statutes. The additional levies are reflected in the total rate for county purposes.

• *City and county consolidation*

Any city or county that provides both municipal and county services has the right to levy up to 20 mills for county, district, and municipal services. However, for each increase in county millage above 10 mills attributable to assumption of municipal services by a county having home rule (or for each increase in municipal millage above 10 mills attributable to assumption of county services by a city having home rule), there must be an equivalent decrease in the millage levied by each municipality or county whose services have been assumed. (Sec. 200.141, F.S.)

• *Municipal taxes*

A municipality tax is limited to 10 mills, absent voter approval of a greater levy. (Sec. 200.081, F.S.) Voters can pass a referendum to increase the millage for up to two years. (Sec. 200.101, F.S.)

• *School districts*

In addition to voted levies, a school district may levy a millage up to the minimum rate certified by the Commissioner of Education as the minimum millage rate necessary to provide the district required local effort for the current year. A school district may also levy up to 1.5 mills for new construction, remodeling, maintenance, renovation, repair of existing school plants or leased facilities; purchase, lease-purchase, or lease of equipment (including school buses, drivers education vehicles, motor vehicles used for the maintenance or operation of plants and equipment, security vehicles, and vehicles used in storing or distributing materials and equipment); payment of the cost of premiums for property and casualty insurance necessary to insure school district educational and ancillary plants; payments for educational facilities and sites due under a lease-purchase agreement; payment of loans, payment of costs for complying with state and federal environmental statutes and regulations, and payment of costs of renting or leasing educational facilities and sites; and leasing relocatable educational facilities. (Sec. 1011.71, F.S.)

• *Local rates*

County and municipal property tax data is available at the Florida Department of Revenue: http://floridarevenue.com/dor/property/resources/data.html.

[¶20-500]
EXEMPTIONS

[¶20-505] Exemptions in General

Every person or organization whose property qualifies for exemption, with the exceptions noted below, must file an application for exemption with the county property appraiser on or before March 1 each year. Failure to make application constitutes a waiver of the exemption privilege for the year, except for a homestead exemption if the applicant can document that the failure to apply was due to a postal error.

Application forms are prescribed by the Department of Revenue and are available from the county property appraiser.

• *Public property*

Application is not required for property of the state, any county, any municipality, any school district, or any community college district. Neither is application required for public roads, rights-of-way, and borrow pits owned, leased, or held for exclusive governmental use.

• *Religious property*

Annual application is not required for certain property owned by religious organizations, including houses of worship, the land on which they are located, parsonages, burial grounds and tombs, and other property not rented out for other than religious or educational purposes.

Owners of religious property who fail to timely file an application for exemption and who, because of a misidentification of property ownership on the property tax roll, are not notified of the tax obligations by the property appraiser and the tax collector are permitted to file a late application for exemption. If the property appraiser determines that the property owner would have been entitled to the exemption had the application been timely filed, any taxes assessed on the property will be canceled, and if paid, refunded.

• *Household goods*

No application is required for exemption of household goods and personal effects of permanent residents of Florida.

• *Procedure*

When an application is not required, an annual return must be filed with the county property appraiser. If property has been determined to be fully exempt from taxation because of its exclusive use for religious, literary, scientific, or charitable purposes, the property appraiser may accept, in lieu of the annual application, a sworn statement that there has been no change in the ownership and use of the property.

Once an original application for exemption has been granted, the property appraiser will mail a renewal application to the applicant by February 1, of subsequent years. If an exemption is granted for real property dedicated in perpetuity for conservation purposes, no renewal application is required so long as use of the property complies with the restrictions and requirements for the exemption.

• *Short form*

After the first year of an exemption, or when an exemption has been denied solely because the application was not filed by March 1, the applicant may use a short form. The short form requires affirmation that the use of the property and the applicant's status as a permanent resident have not changed since the initial application. Once the initial application and reapplication has been granted, the property may qualify for exemption in each succeeding year.

• *Denial of application*

The property appraiser may deny an application for exemption if the use of the property is not clear or if the property is being held for speculative purposes. The applicant must be notified of the denial by July 1. Appeal of the denial may be made to the property appraisal adjustment board.

• *Partial exempt use*

All property used exclusively for exempt purposes is exempt from ad valorem taxes. Property used predominantly for exempt purposes is exempt to the extent of the ratio of the exempt use to the nonexempt use. Property owned by a limited liability company, the sole member of which is an exempt entity, will be treated as if the property were owned directly by the exempt entity.

"Exclusive use" means that the property is used for exempt purposes 100% of the time. "Predominant use" means that the property is used for exempt purposes more than 50% of the time.

[¶20-600]
VALUATION, ASSESSMENT, AND EQUALIZATION

[¶20-610] Valuation Procedures

The Florida Constitution requires that all real and personal property be assessed at a just valuation. (Sec. 4, Art. VII, Fla. Const.)

Property appraisers are allowed to consider a number of factors. (Sec. 193.011, F.S.)

If an assessment of tangible personal property for the preceding year is adjusted by the Value Adjustment Board and unsuccessfully appealed by the property appraiser, the appraiser must consider the reduced values determined by the board in assessing the property for the current year. If the appraiser nonetheless adjusts the board-reduced values upward, then the appraiser must assert the additional basic and underlying facts not properly considered by the board that were utilized as the basis for the increased valuation.

Returns must be filed by April 1 each year for tangible personal property and any property specifically named by statute. (Sec. 193.052(1), F.S.; Sec. 193.062, F.S.) A return must be filed in each county where the property has tax situs. (Sec. 193.052(3), F.S.) No return is required for real property unless otherwise specified by law. (Sec. 193.052(2), F.S.)

A return must reflect the owner's estimate of the true value of the property covered by the return. (Sec. 193.052(4), F.S.) The return is filed with the county property appraiser for each county in which the property has tax situs. (Sec. 193.052(3), F.S.) All returns are to be completed by the taxpayer. (Sec. 193.052(4), F.S.)

In making a return for tangible personal property, the owner must include any exemptions. Failure to claim an exemption on the return constitutes waiver of the exemption and any subsequent claim will not be allowed for that tax year. (Sec. 196.021, F.S.)

• *Valuation dates*

Property is assessed for each calendar year according to its value on January 1. (Sec. 192.042, F.S.) Improvements or construction work in progress that is not substantially completed on January 1 has no value placed on it. "Substantially completed" is defined as "can be used for the purpose for which it was constructed."

However, the District Court of Appeal, Third District, has ruled that setting the value of property under construction at zero is unconstitutional for failing to provide a just valuation of the property for Florida real property tax. (*Sunset Harbour North Condominium Association v. Robbins*, No. 3D02-2258, February 26, 2003; *Klein v. Robbins*, Florida Court of Appeal, Third District, No. 3D03-1571, May 26, 2004)

The property appraiser must complete the assessment of the value of all property no later than July 1 of each year. An extension may be granted for good cause. (Sec. 193.023(1), F.S.)

The property appraiser is required to inspect all property every five years. The owner or taxpayer may request an inspection before the required time. (Sec. 193.023(2), F.S.)

• *Application of assessment percentage*

Assessment, in the property tax scheme, is the application of a percentage to the appraised valuation to calculate the assessed value. The term may cause some confusion because, for other taxes, the word "assess" generally means to determine the tax. And in Florida, the term is often used to mean valuation. Some states, California, for example, assess all property at its full cash value with the result that appraised value is the same as assessed value. Other states apply the same percentage to all property to determine the assessed value.

• *Due dates*

Returns for tangible personal property, railroad property, and any returns or applications whose due dates are not specified by statute are due on April 1. Property appraisers are authorized to grant an extension for the filing of tangible personal property tax returns for up to 45 days, when such requests are timely submitted and can be acted upon before the regular return due date. Due dates for returns for real property are determined by specific provisions of general law. (Sec. 193.063, F.S.; Sec. 193.062, F.S.)

An official postmark of the U. S. Postal Service is considered the date of filing a return. When the deadline for filing a return falls on Saturday, Sunday, or a legal holiday, the deadline is extended through the next working day immediately following the statutory deadline. For property tax exemption applications, special assessment classification applications, or returns mailed via a commercial delivery service, the postmark on the commercial parcel will be treated the same as a U.S. Postal Service postmark. (Sec. 192.047, F.S.)

[¶20-620] Income Method of Valuation

The income method of valuation, which is one of the methods an appraiser may consider in valuing property involves somewhat of a deductive process. Several factors are known, and from their interaction, the value of a given property is deduced. What is known is the potential net operating income (usually equated to rental income) from the property and the prevailing cost of money. When the income is divided by the investor rate of return, the resulting figure is the value of the property. (Sec. 193.011, F.S.)

For example, assume that a small bookstore is leased for $425 per month or $5,100 annually and that the prevailing rate of interest for borrowing business funds is 9%. Under a simple application of the income method, the bookstore would be valued at $56,666 ($5,100 divided by 9%). In practice, this simple example would be complicated by such issues as (1) whether the actual rent is representative of the property's income potential; (2) how much of an offset for operating expenses would be allowed against the rental income; and (3) what is the appropriate capitalization rate. (Sec. 193.011, F.S.)

¶20-620

As is the case with the cost method, the lease figure could be an actual figure, as in the above example, or it could be a statistical average compiled from recent rentals of comparable properties. Similarly, the interest rate to be used for capitalizing property is usually statutorily pegged to a federal or state standard rate or is otherwise prescribed. (Sec. 193.011, F.S.)

• *Advantages and disadvantages*

The income method lends itself to the valuation of properties for which replacement value does not correspond to market value. In the example above, for instance, $425 is low rent for a building adequate for a bookstore. Presumably the low rent reflects a poor location for book sales, for whatever reason. The building itself, however, may be of excellent and expensive construction, which would cost $125,000 to reproduce. (Sec. 193.011, F.S.)

The indirectness of the method may be considered to be a disadvantage in that it is not as readily understood as the cost or market data methods. (Sec. 193.011, F.S.)

The income method may be used to foster certain uses of land, such as agriculture, forestry, or open space. Under the income method, such land is valued at a smaller figure than if it were used for industrial centers or shopping malls, for example. (Sec. 193.011, F.S.)

[¶20-625] Sales Method of Valuation

The market data method, also called the sales comparison method, is a common valuation technique whose use has been enhanced by the wholesale use of computerized transactions. The market data method is used to value property by comparing it to the prices at which comparable properties have recently been sold. The value brought by computer use is in multiplying the number of transactions available for comparison.

In some simple situations, the sales comparison method is virtually foolproof. For example, if there were several sales in a subdivision where the houses are identical except for number of bedrooms and the community amenities such as schools, taxes, and traffic are the same, the value could be determined by finding a recent sale of a house with the same number of bedrooms.

Seldom, however, is the situation so simple. Adjustments must be made for the inevitable differences that exist in most comparable sales. Differences in location, size, quality of construction, time of sale, financing and numerous other subtle differences must be taken into consideration.

The net proceeds of the sale of the property, after deduction of all reasonable fees and costs and allowing for unconventional financing arrangements are considered by the appraiser when valuing property. (Sec. 193.011, F.S.) The determination of net proceeds excludes payments for household furnishings or other personal property included in the sale.

The Department of Revenue publication, *Standard Measures of Value: Tangible Personal Property Appraisal Guidelines*, adds that the location of the property is relevant to considering which freight and installation costs should be included in an appraisal. In addition, adjustment of sales prices may be required to account for any special conditions, such as forced sales, lease cancellations, value attributed to trade names, and goodwill. The *Guidelines* list potential sources of market data relating to personal property, such as leasing companies, commercial bankers, new and used equipment dealers, trade and sales journals, newspaper advertisements, and auction sales.

• *Advantages and disadvantages*

An advantage of this method is that it is grounded in common sense; it is the way that most individuals estimate the value of their own properties: by noticing the sales prices of nearby homes. On the other hand, seldom are properties exactly the same. Even in a subdivision, one house is on a corner and has a deeper lot; another is closer to schools, etc. The greater the number of differences, the more difficult it is to evaluate them.

Taxpayers probably have more scope for challenge with this method than with others. Because the method is based upon comparison by taxing authorities, taxpayers are equally able to offer in evidence examples favorable to their claims.

The method may also be difficult to apply in the case of unusual properties for which there are few or no comparable sales.

[¶20-630] Cost Method of Valuation

The cost of the property and the present replacement value of any improvements on the property are factors that the appraiser considers when valuing property. (Sec. 193.011, F.S.) The Department of Revenue publication, *Standard Measures of Value: Tangible Personal Property Appraisal Guidelines*, states that the historical or original cost is sometimes used as a starting point to the calculation of value. The value of property is reduced by deterioration and obsolescence.

• *Advantages and disadvantages*

The cost method lends itself to implementation by computer. Cost figures of materials and varying types of construction can be entered and accessed automatically, with great speed, and with very few errors. On the negative side, market conditions are not reflected. Consequently, property may not in fact be saleable at its replacement cost in a down market.

Depreciation and obsolescence.—Because the cost method relies upon statistical averages, property owners who can offer evidence that their property differs from the average may wish to protest a valuation or classification. Depreciation and obsolescence are often argued in this method. For example, a warehouse near a high school that has undergone excessive damage from vandalism might gain by questioning the amount of depreciation allowed on the appraisal.

[¶20-635] Unit Method of Valuation

Unit valuation is applied to property in certain highly regulated industries that cross jurisdictions. When unit valuation was first developed, the U.S. Supreme Court recognized that the true value of a railroad line was something more than an aggregation of the values of the separate parts of it, because there was a value arising from the combined operation of all of the parts as one continuous line. (*Cleveland, Cincinnati, Chicago & St. Louis Rwy Co. v. Backus*, 154 U.S. 439 (1894 US SCt)) Commonly, the aggregate property will be valued, then the value will be apportioned among the jurisdictions. States adopted unit valuation for certain industries, such as airlines, telegraph and telephone companies, pipelines, and electric companies. When an industry is deregulated and becomes subject to market forces, experts recommend that the states stop using unit valuation.

Florida defines the unit rule method of valuation as an appraising method used to value an entire operating property, considered as a whole with minimal consideration being given to the aggregation of the values of separate parts. (Rule 12D-2.001, F.A.C.) The rights, franchises, and property essential to the continued business and purpose of the entire property being treated as one thing having but one value in use.

The Department of Revenue is authorized to promulgate rules and regulations to insure that all property of railroads and utilities is properly returned in the appropriate county. (Sec. 193.052(6), F.S.).

All operating property within the state as of January 1 of the assessment year is subject to annual assessment by The Department of Revenue in accordance with the unit rule method of valuation. (Rule 12D-2.002, F.A.C.) Operating property is all property owned by or leased to railroad and railroad terminal companies and directly related to the operation of railroads. (Rule 12D-2.001, F.A.C.)

The rolling stock of all private car and freight line and equipment companies operating in the state is subject to assessment by the Department of Revenue based on the total value of the average number of cars which are habitually present within this State. (Rule 12D-2.003, F.A.C.)

[¶20-640] Real Property Valuation

The Florida Constitution requires that all real property be assessed at just valuation. (Sec. 4, Art. VII, Fla. Const.) Generally, there are specific laws and regulations for three types of property: homestead property, nonhomestead property, and nonresidential real property.

• *Multiple parcel buildings*

The value of land upon which a multiple parcel building is located, regardless of ownership, may not be separately assessed and must be allocated among and included in the just value of all the parcels in the multiple parcel building. The property appraiser, for assessment purposes, must allocate all of the just value of the land among the parcels in a multiple parcel building in the same proportion that the just value of the improvements in each parcel bears to the total just value of all the improvements in the entire multiple parcel building. (Sec. 193.0237, F.S.)

"Multiple parcel building" means a building, other than a building that consists entirely of a single condominium, timeshare, or cooperative, which contains separate parcels that are vertically located, in whole or in part, on or over the same land. (Sec. 193.0237, F.S.)

For non-ad valorem special assessments based on the size or area of the land containing a multiple parcel building, regardless of ownership, the special assessment must be levied on and allocated among all the parcels in the multiple parcel building on the same basis that the land value is allocated among the parcels as indicated above. For non-ad valorem assessments not based on the size or area of the land, each parcel in the multiple parcel building will be subject to a separate assessment. (Sec. 197.3631)

• *Homestead property*

Florida has specific assessment laws and rules for homestead properties. A homestead property is the property where a person has legal or equitable title to real estate and where they maintain their permanent residence. The real estate may be held by the entirety, jointly, in common, as a condominium, or indirectly by stock ownership or membership representing the owner's or member's proprietary interest in corporation owning a fee or a leasehold initially in excess of 98 years. Homestead properties are exempt from taxation up to the assessed valuation of $25,000 and, for all levies other than school district levies, an additional $25,000 on the assessed valuation greater than $50,000 and up to $75,000. (Sec. 196.031, F.S.; Sec. 6, Art. VII, Fla. Const.)

Unless portability rules apply, property receiving the homestead exemption will be assessed at just value as of January 1 of the year in which the property receives the exemption, or of the year following a change in ownership. (Sec. 193.155, F.S.; Sec. 4(c), Art. VII, Fla. Const.)

Changes, additions, or improvements to homestead property will be assessed at just value as of the first January 1 after substantial completion. Replacement of all or a portion of homestead property damaged or destroyed by misfortune or calamity will not increase the homestead property's assessed value when the square footage of the improved homestead property does not exceed:

— 110% of the square footage of the homestead property before the damage, or

— 1,500 square feet.

The improved property's assessed value will be increased by the just value of any portion of the improved property in excess of the 110% or the 1,500 square feet. These criteria apply to changes, additions, or improvements commenced within three years after January 1 of the year following the damage or destruction of the homestead. (Sec. 193.155(4), F.S.)

Additionally, when property is destroyed or removed and not replaced, the assessed value of the parcel shall be reduced by the assessed value attributable to the destroyed or removed property. (Sec. 193.155(5), F.S.)

When damaged homestead property is uninhabitable, the homestead exemption may be granted if:

— the property otherwise is qualified,

— the owner notifies the property appraiser that he or she intends to repair or rebuild the property and live there as the primary residence, and

— the owner does not claim a homestead exemption on any other property.

The owner's failure to commence repair or rebuilding of the property within three years after January 1 following the year of the destruction constitutes abandonment of the property as a homestead. (Sec. 196.031(6), F.S.)

"Save Our Homes" assessment limitation.—Any change in just value resulting from a reassessment of property that has been granted a homestead exemption may not exceed the lower of the following:

— 3% of the assessed value of the property for the prior year; or

— the percentage change in the Consumer Price Index for all urban consumers, U.S. City Average, all items 1967=100, or successor reports for the preceding calendar year as initially reported by the U.S. Department of Labor, Bureau of Labor Statistics.

(Sec. 4(c), Art. VII, Fla. Const.)

Taxpayers must actually be granted a homestead exemption in the year at issue in order for the assessment cap to apply. Taxpayers who qualify for or who are entitled to the exemption but who do not timely file for the exemption are not entitled to the limitation. (*Zingale v. Powell*, Florida Supreme Court, September 15, 2004)

Constitutional Amendment 5.—Effective January 1, 2021, the timeframe during which a property owner may transfer accrued save-our-homes benefits from a prior homestead to a new homestead has been increased from two to three years. This change is the result of the voters' approval of Constitutional Amendment 5 in the November 3, 2020, general election. (*Property Tax Informational Bulletin: PTO 20-11*, Florida Department of Revenue, November 24, 2020)

Change in ownership.—A "change of ownership" means any sale, foreclosure, or transfer of legal title or beneficial title in equity to any person except in certain circumstances. (Sec. 193.155(3), F.S.)

A leasehold interest that qualifies for the homestead exemption will be treated as an equitable interest in the property. (Sec. 193.155(3), F.S.)

• *Nonhomestead residential property*

Florida has assessment laws and rules for nonhomestead residential property. Nonhomestead residential property is residential real property containing nine or fewer dwelling units, including vacant properties zoned for residential use, that did not receive the homestead exemption under Sec. 196.031, F.S.. (Sec. 193.1554, F.S.)

Starting with the year following the year nonhomestead residential property becomes eligible for assessment, the property shall be reassessed annually on January 1. Any change resulting from a reassessment may not exceed 10% of the assessed value of the property for the prior year. (Sec. 193.1554, F.S.)

Nonhomestead residential property will be assessed at just value as of January 1 of the year following a change of ownership or control. Change of ownership is:

— any sale,

— any foreclosure,

— any transfer of legal title or beneficial title in equity to any person, or

— the cumulative transfer of control or of more than 50% of the ownership of the legal entity that owned the property when it was most recently assessed at just value.

(Sec. 193.1554(5), F.S.)

Any person or entity that owns a nonhomestead property must notify the property appraiser promptly of any change of ownership or control. (Sec. 193.1556, F.S.)

Changes, additions, or improvements that replace all or a portion of nonhomestead residential property that was damaged or destroyed will not increase the property's assessed value when the square footage of the property as changed or improved does not exceed:

— 110% of the square footage of the property before the damage or destruction, or

— 1,500 square feet.

Under this provision, the properties will be reassessed annually on January 1 and the reassessment will not exceed 10% of the assessed value of the property for the prior year. These criteria apply to changes, additions, or improvements commenced within three years after January 1 of the year following the damage or destruction of the homestead. (Sec. 193.1554(6), F.S.)

Any increase in the value of the property attributable to combining or dividing parcels will be assessed at just value. The just value will be apportioned among the parcels created:

— For divided parcels, the amount by which the sum of the just values of the divided parcels exceeds what the just value of the parcel would be if undivided shall be attributable to the division. This amount shall be apportioned to the parcels pro rata based on their relative just values.

— For combined parcels, the amount by which the just value of the combined parcel exceeds what the sum of the just values of the component parcels would be if they had not been combined shall be attributable to the combination.

— A parcel that is combined or divided after January 1 and included as a combined or divided parcel on the tax notice is not considered to be a combined or divided parcel until the January 1 on which it is first assessed as a combined or divided parcel.

(Sec. 193.1554(7), F.S.)

Nonhomestead residential property damaged or destroyed, which has a square footage of less than 100% of the property's total square footage before the damage, or if the property has been removed and not replaced, will have assessments that are reduced by the assessed value attributable to the destroyed or removed property. (Sec. 193.1554(8), F.S.)

Change in ownership.—Any change of ownership means any sale, foreclosure, or transfer of legal title or beneficial title in equity to any person, or the cumulative transfer of control or of more than 50% of the ownership of the legal entity that owned the property when it was most recently assessed at just value. There is no change of ownership if:

— the transfer of title is to correct an error;

— the transfer is between legal and equitable title;

— the transfer is between husband and wife, including a transfer to a surviving spouse or a transfer due to a dissolution of marriage; or

— for a publicly traded company, the cumulative transfer of more than 50% of the ownership of the entity that owns the property occurs through the buying and selling of shares of the company on a public exchange. However, this exception does not apply to a transfer made through a merger with or an acquisition by another company.

(Sec. 193.1554(5), F.S.)

Additionally, any person or entity that owns nonhomestead residential property must notify the property appraiser promptly of any change of ownership or control. If the change of ownership is recorded by a deed or other county public record instrument, the recorded deed or instrument will serve as notice. (Sec. 193.1556)

• *Nonresidential real property*

Florida has assessment laws and rules for nonresidential real property. Nonresidential real property is any real property not subject to the assessment limitations for:

— agricultural land,

— land producing high water recharge to Florida's aquifers,

— land used exclusively for noncommercial recreational purposes,

— tangible personal property held for sale as stock,

— livestock,

— the homestead exemptions under Sec. 6, Art. VII, Fla. Const, and

— residential real property containing nine or fewer units.

(Sec. 193.1555, F.S.)

Starting with the year following the year nonresidential real property becomes eligible for assessment, the property shall be reassessed annually on January 1. Any change resulting from a reassessment may not exceed 10% of the assessed value of the property for the prior year. (Sec. 193.1555, F.S.)

Nonresidential real property will be assessed at just value as of January 1 of the year following a qualifying improvement or change of ownership or control. Qualifying improvement means any substantially completed improvement that increased the just value of the property by at least 25%. Changes of ownership means:

— any sale,

— any foreclosure,

— any transfer of legal title or beneficial title in equity to any person, or

— the cumulative transfer of control or of more than 50% of the ownership of the legal entity that owned the property when it was most recently assessed at just value.

(Sec. 193.1555(5), F.S.)

¶20-640

Any person or entity that owns a nonresidential real property must notify the property appraiser promptly of any change of ownership or control. (Sec. 193.1556, F.S.)

Changes, additions, or improvements to nonresidential real property will be assessed at just value as of the first January 1 after the changes, additions, or improvements are substantially completed.

Changes, additions, or improvements that replace all or a portion of nonresidential real property that was damaged or destroyed will not increase the property's assessed value when the square footage of the property as changed or improved does not exceed 110% of the square footage of the property before the damage or destruction. Additionally, the changes, additions, or improvements may not change the property's character or use.

The damaged or destroyed properties will be reassessed annually on January 1. The reassessment may not exceed 10% of the assessed value of the property for the prior year. These criteria apply to changes, additions, or improvements commenced within three years after January 1 of the year following the damage or destruction of the homestead. (Sec. 193.1555(6), F.S.)

Any increase in the value of the property attributable to combining or dividing parcels will be assessed at just value. The just value will be apportioned among the parcels created:

— For divided parcels, the amount by which the sum of the just values of the divided parcels exceeds what the just value of the parcel would be if undivided shall be attributable to the division. This amount shall be apportioned to the parcels pro rata based on their relative just values.

— For combined parcels, the amount by which the just value of the combined parcel exceeds what the sum of the just values of the component parcels would be if they had not been combined shall be attributable to the combination.

— A parcel that is combined or divided after January 1 and included as a combined or divided parcel on the tax notice is not considered to be a combined or divided parcel until the January 1 on which it is first assessed as a combined or divided parcel.

(Sec. 193.1555(7), F.S.)

Nonresidential real property damaged or destroyed, which has a square footage of less than 100% of the property's total square footage before the damage, or if the property has been removed and not replaced, will have assessments that are reduced by the assessed value attributable to the destroyed or removed property. (Sec. 193.1555(8), F.S.)

Change in ownership.—Any change of ownership means any sale, foreclosure, or transfer of legal title or beneficial title in equity to any person, or the cumulative transfer of control or of more than 50% of the ownership of the legal entity that owned the property when it was most recently assessed at just value. There is no change of ownership if:

— the transfer of title is to correct an error;

— the transfer is between legal and equitable title;

— for a publicly traded company, the cumulative transfer of more than 50% of the ownership of the entity that owns the property occurs through the buying and selling of shares of the company on a public exchange. However, this exception does not apply to a transfer made through a merger with or an acquisition by another company.

(Sec. 193.1555(5), F.S.)

Additionally, any person or entity that owns nonresidential real property must notify the property appraiser promptly of any change of ownership or control. If the change of ownership is recorded by a deed or other county public record instrument, the recorded deed or instrument will serve as notice. (Sec. 193.1556 F.S.)

• *Wind damage equipment*

The legislature may prohibit the consideration of any change or improvement made for the purpose of improving the property's resistance to wind damage in the determination of the assessed value of real property used for residential purposes. (Sec. 4, Art. VII, Fla. Const.)

[¶20-645] Personal Property Valuation

The property tax appraiser is authorized to estimate, from the best information available, the assessment of the tangible personal property of taxpayers who have not properly and timely filed their tax returns. (Sec. 193.073, F.S.) Such assessments are deemed to be prima facie correct, and may be included on the tax roll.

Supplies.—When using the cost approach to value tangible personal property, sales tax and other external costs of sale should be included in the purchase price. External costs of sale are items like sales tax, transportation costs, handling, and installation charges that are paid at the time of purchase. (*Mazourek v. Wal-Mart Stores, Inc.*, Supreme Court of Florida, No. SC01-663, June 13, 2002) The property appraiser properly considered all the factors to consider in deriving just valuation enumerated in Sec. 193.011, F.S..

[¶20-750]
PAYMENT, COLLECTION OF TAXES

[¶20-752] Interest

Delinquent real property taxes are subject to a maximum annual interest rate of 18% from the date of delinquency until a tax certificate is sold. The minimum charge for delinquent taxes paid prior to the sale of a certificate is 3%. Delinquent personal property taxes also are subject to a maximum annual interest rate of 18% from the date of delinquency until the taxes are paid or are barred by the seven-year limitation. Interest is calculated from the first day of each month. (Sec. 197.172, F.S.)

Any annual or nonrecurring intangible personal property tax not timely paid is subject to an annual interest rate of 12%, any extension of filing notwithstanding. (Sec. 199.282, F.S.)

Value adjustment board.—If the value adjustment board or the property appraiser determines that a petitioner owes property taxes in excess of the amount paid, the unpaid amount accrues interest at an annual percentage rate equal to the bank prime loan rate on July 1 until the amount is paid. If the value adjustment board determines that a refund is due, the overpaid amount accrues interest at the same rate. Interest does not accrue on amounts paid in excess of 100% of the current taxes due. (Sec. 194.014(2), F.S.)

[¶20-756] Payment of Tax

Property taxes are due and payable on November 1 of each year, or as soon thereafter as the certified tax roll is received by the tax collector. (Sec. 197.333, F.S.)

Within 20 days of receipt of the certified roll, the tax collector must send a notice of current taxes due to each taxpayer on the roll whose address is known. The notice may be sent electronically or by postal mail. Electronic transmission, however, may only be used with the express consent of the property owner. The electronic transmission may be sent earlier than postal mailings, but will not be sent later. The notice is accompanied by a statement of any back taxes due and information on the discounts allowed for early payment. Previously, the tax collector could only mail the notice. (Sec. 197.322, F.S.) Any additional notices of property taxes due must be mailed by the tax collector by April 30. The board of county commissioners of a county may, at the recommendation of the tax collector, adopt a resolution instructing the collector not to mail tax notices when the tax due is less than $30. (Rule 12D-13.037, F.A.C.)

The collector publishes a notice in a local newspaper that the tax roll is open for collection. This notice appears on November 1 or as soon as the assessment roll is open. (Sec. 197.322, F.S.)

Payment of county and municipal property taxes is made to the county tax collector. The tax collector is elected by the qualified voters of the county every four years. (Sec. 100.041, F.S.)

Payment prior to certification of roll.—Taxpayers must pay county and municipal property taxes on or before November 1 of each year (or as soon thereafter as the certified tax roll is received by the tax collector). (Sec. 197.333, F.S.) Taxpayers can receive discounts for early payment as shown below. However, there are provisions for voluntary payment of estimated taxes when the roll is not certified in time to allow payment prior to January 1 of the tax year. The estimated payment cannot take any discount into consideration, although discounts will be considered in the final assessment. (Sec. 197.2301, F.S.)

Tax discount payment period.—For all taxes assessed on the county tax rolls and collected by the county tax collector, discounts for payments made before delinquency depending on when the payment is made.

If paid in	Discount
November	4
December	3
January	2
February	1

The early payment discount rate applicable at the time that a request for correction of a tax notice is made will apply for 30 days after the sending of the corrected tax notice, and a four percent discount rate will apply for 30 days after the mailing of a tax notice resulting from the action of a value adjustment board. (Sec. 197.162, F.S.; Rule 12D-13.002, F.A.C.) A discount period may not be extended due to a tax bill being returned as undeliverable electronically or by postal mail. (Sec. 197.322, F.S.)

• *Installment payments*

Ad valorem taxes on real property, if the amount due is over $100, can be prepaid in quarterly installments. Real property taxes can be prepaid in installments for each tax notice. The payments are based on the actual taxes assessed in the previous year. (Sec. 197.222, F.S.)

The due date and allowed discount for each installment are shown below. (Sec. 197.222, F.S.)

If paid by	Discount
June 30	6
September 30	4.5
December 31	3
March 31	None

Payment of portion of taxes.—The tax collector of the county is authorized to allow the payment of a part of a tax notice when:

— the part to be paid can be ascertained by legal description,

— the part is under a contract for sale or has been transferred to a new owner, and

— the request is made by the person purchasing the property, the new owner, or someone acting on behalf of the purchaser or owner.

(Sec. 197.373, F.S.)

The request must be made at least 45 days before the tax certificate sale. (Sec. 197.373, F.S.)

Partial payment of current years taxes.—The tax collector may accept one or more partial payments of any amount per parcel for payment of current taxes and assessments on real property or tangible personal property as long as such payment is made prior to the date of delinquency. The remaining amount of tax due, when paid, must be paid in full. Any remaining balance that is not paid before April 1 or the date of delinquency becomes delinquent. (Sec. 197.374, F.S.)

Extension of time.—Taxpayers who pay on an installment basis may pay the first installment within 30 days of its June 30 due date, provided a 5 penalty is paid. (Sec. 197.222, F.S.) If original tax notices are mailed after January 31 (60 days before the statutory delinquency date of April 1), all other dates or time periods related to collection of or administrative procedures regarding delinquent taxes are extended the same number of days. (Sec. 197.333, F.S.) Taxpayers can request payment on an installment basis.

• *Adverse possession*

A tax collector is required to determine whether a duplicate Florida property tax payment has been made by an adverse possessor. A priority has also been established if a person claiming adverse possession pays an annual tax assessment on a parcel of property before the assessment is paid by the owner of record and the owner of record subsequently makes a payment of that same annual tax assessment before April 1 following the year in which the tax is assessed. In such an instance, the tax collector must accept the payment made by the owner of record and refund within 60 days any payment made by the person claiming adverse possession. (Sec. 197.3335, F.S.)

• *Property tax deferral programs*

If a property owner applies for a property tax deferral and meets the established criteria for the deferral, the tax collector must approve the deferral of the property taxes and non-ad valorem assessments. Currently, the authorized property tax deferral programs are:

— the homestead tax deferral;

— the recreational and commercial working waterfront deferral; and

— the affordable rental housing deferral.

(Sec. 197.2421, F.S.)

A property owner is responsible for submitting an annual application for tax deferral with the county tax collector on or before March 31 following the year in which the taxes and non-ad valorem assessments are assessed. The application must be made on a form prescribed by the Department of Revenue and provided by the tax collection. However, the tax collector may require additional evidence and documentation in considering the application. (Sec. 197.2423, F.S.)

A tax deferral may not be granted if the total amount of deferred taxes, non-ad valorem assessments, and interest, plus the total amount of all other unsatisfied liens on the property exceeds 85% of the just value of the property or the primary mortgage financing on the property is for an amount that exceeds 70% of the just value of the property. (Sec. 197.2423(9), F.S.)

¶20-756

An applicant who is not entitled to a deferral will be sent a notice of disapproval within 45 days after the date the application is filed, citing the reason for disapproval. (Sec. 197.2423(10), F.S.) An appeal of a denied tax deferral must be made by the property owner to the value adjustment board. The appeal must be filed with the value adjustment board within 30 days after the mailing of the notice of disapproval. (Sec. 197.2425, F.S.)

• *Tangible personal property*

Taxpayers must file tangible personal property tax returns by April 1 each year in each county where the property has taxable situs. (Sec. 193.052(1), F.S.; Sec. 193.062, F.S.; Sec. 193.052(3), F.S.) A return must reflect the owner's estimate of the true value of the property covered by the return. (Sec. 193.052(4), F.S.)

Property appraisers can grant an extension for the filing of tangible personal property tax returns for up to 45 days. (Sec. 193.063, F.S.)

Installment payments.—A county tax collector may implement a payment program for the payment of delinquent personal property taxes. If implemented, the tax collector will require each taxpayer who requests to participate in the program to submit and application. The taxpayer must pay all amounts due within three years to repay their debt. Upon application by the taxpayer, the county tax collector must prescribe a written installment payment plan providing for the full satisfaction of all amounts owed by no later than three years after the due date of the first payment. (Sec. 197.4155, F.S.)

[¶20-758] Assessment of Delinquent Tax

Property taxes are delinquent if not paid by the later of April 1 following the year in which they were assessed or 60 days after the mailing of the original tax notice. (Sec. 197.333, F.S.)

Notice of delinquent property tax is mailed by the Department by April 30 of each year. The notice must include a description of the property and a statement notifying the taxpayer that if the taxes are not paid in full, a tax certificate will be sold for the delinquent taxes and a tax sale may be held for the property. (Sec. 197.343, F.S.; Rule 12D-13.042, F.A.C.)

If the Department does issue a tax deed for sale of the property after a tax certificate is issued, it must send notice that an application for a tax deed sale has been made by certified mail to the taxpayer and other interested parties at least 20 days prior to the date of sale; if no address is available, no notice is required. (Sec. 197.522, F.S.) The notice must include a description of the property, the names in which it was assessed, and the date and time of the sale. (Rule 12D-13.062, F.A.C.) The notice must be published once a week for four consecutive weeks in a local newspaper; the sale may not be held until 30 days after the first publication of notice. (Sec. 197.512, F.S.)

When requested in writing, property tax notices may be mailed to mortgagees, lienholders, or vendees. (Sec. 197.344, F.S.)

Tangible personal property.—Prior to May 1 of each year following the year of assessment, the tax collector prepares a list of unpaid tangible personal property taxes, showing the names and addresses of the taxpayers and the property involved. (Sec. 197.413, F.S.)

[¶20-762] Agreements in Compromise of Tax Due

There are no provisions for agreements in compromise of property tax specifically.

[¶20-768] Audits

The Department of Revenue must examine tax returns to determine the correct amount of tax as soon as practicable after the returns are filed. (Sec. 220.709, F.S.)

Except in criminal and internal investigations, the Department must conduct its audits, inspections of records, and interviews at reasonable times and places. (Sec. 213.025, F.S.)

Within the appropriate limitations period, the Department may audit and examine the accounts, books, or records of a taxpayer to ascertain that taxpayer's compliance with tax laws. (Sec. 213.34, F.S.; Sec. 95.091(3), F.S.) The audit authority of the Department includes the power to investigate accounts, books, and records of persons who may not be subject to the revenue laws but are otherwise placed under the control and administration of the Department. (Sec. 213.34(1), F.S.)

Discussed below are audit provisions specific to property tax.

• *Limitations period*

If real or tangible personal property escapes taxation, the authorized officers can back-assess the property only for three years preceding the year in which it was discovered that the tax has not been assessed, levied, or collected. The basis of valuation is that used in the year the tax should have been assessed, levied, or collected, not the year in which the assessment is later made. (Sec. 193.092, F.S.)

The property is subject to the arrears of taxation regardless of whose hands or possession it is in when found. However, personal property acquired in good faith by purchase is not subject to assessment for taxes prior to the time of purchase, but the individual or corporation liable for the assessment continues personally liable. (Sec. 193.092, F.S.)

If a delay occurs because of litigation and an assessment is then declared invalid, the re-assessment may be made within the statutory period after the litigation ends. (Sec. 193.092, F.S.)

Bona fide purchasers.—Property acquired by a bona fide purchaser who was without knowledge of the escaped taxation is not subject to assessment for taxes for any time prior to the time of purchase. However, taxes will be assessed against the previous owner and the property appraiser must serve the previous owner with a notice of intent to record a notice of tax lien against any property owned by that person in the county. (Sec. 193.092, F.S.; Rule 12D-8.006, F.A.C.; Rule 12D-13.011, F.A.C.)

Property not previously assessed.—The retroactive assessment and collection of property taxes is not applicable if:

— the owner of a building, structure, or other improvement to land that has not been previously assessed complied with all necessary permitting requirements when the improvement was completed; or

— the owner of the property that has not been previously assessed voluntarily discloses to the property appraiser the existence of such property before January 1 of the year the property is first assessed.

(Sec. 193.092(3), F.S.)

• *Intangibles tax*

The Department may audit books and records of any person to determine whether intangible personal property taxes have been properly paid. The audit powers of the Department include the right to inspect the books and records of any person, to issue third-party subpoenas, and to administer oaths and affirmations. The period during which an audit must be commenced is the same for both the annual and nonrecurring intangibles taxes. (Sec. 199.232, F.S.)

An audit by the Department is officially commenced by service of a written notice of intent to audit upon the taxpayer, either in person or by certified mail. (Sec. 199.232(1)(b), F.S.)

An audit consists of an inspection of the books, documents, and other records of the person who filed the return and is under investigation, or the records of any other person. The Department may issue subpoenas for the following two purposes:

— to compel the attendance of witnesses; and

— to compel the production of records and other evidence.

(Sec. 199.232(2), F.S.)

Oaths and affirmations may be administered by authorized Department members. (Sec. 199.232(2), F.S.)

[¶20-770] Penalties

Penalties may be imposed for noncompliance with property tax laws and regulations.

• *Civil penalties*

For failing to file a return, the penalty is 25% of the total tax levied against the property for the year. For filing a return after the due date, the penalty is 5% of the total tax levied against the property for each month or partial month the return is filed after the due date, up to 25% of the total tax. For not listing property on a return, the penalty is 15% of the tax attributable to the unlisted property. (Sec. 193.072, F.S.)

A late penalty of 5% applies to taxpayers who pay their first installment of ad valorem property tax between June 30 and July 30 of the tax year. (Rule 12D-13.027, F.A.C.)

For incomplete returns by railroad, private car, and freight line companies, the penalty is 2% per month of the assessed value apportioned to the county for which the return is incomplete, up to 10% of the assessed value. A return is not deemed to be incomplete until 15 days after notice of incompleteness is provided to the taxpayer. All penalties are determined from the total of all ad valorem personal property taxes, penalties, and interest levied on the property, and the penalties are a lien on the property. (Sec. 193.072, F.S.)

For good cause and upon finding that the failure to list property or to file returns on time was not intentional or made with intent to evade the taxes, the property appraiser may reduce or waive any of the penalties. (Sec. 193.072, F.S.)

Intangible property tax.—Combined penalties for failure to file or to timely pay intangible personal property tax shall not exceed 10% monthly of the amount of taxes due or 50% of that amount in the aggregate. If an annual return is filed and property is either omitted or undervalued, each omitted or undervalued items is subject to a 10% penalty. (Sec. 199.282, F.S.)

• *Criminal penalties*

Any person who knowingly and willfully gives false information for the purpose of claiming homestead exemption is guilty of a misdemeanor of the first degree, punishable as provided in Sec. 775.082, F.S., or by fine not exceeding $5,000, or both. (Sec. 196.131, F.S.)

[¶20-800]
CREDITS, ABATEMENTS, REFUNDS, INCENTIVES

[¶20-805] Credits

Florida does not have any provisions regarding property tax credits.

[¶20-810] Abatements

There are no provisions authorizing the abatement of taxes, generally. However, abatements or refunds are authorized in certain instances.

[¶20-815] Refunds

The Florida Department of Revenue can order refunds of voluntary or involuntary ad valorem property tax payments pursuant to:

— an overpayment;

— a payment when no tax was due;

— a bona fide controversy between the tax collector and the taxpayer, payment of the amount claimed by the tax collector, and a court judgment for the taxpayer;

— an erroneous payment for a delinquent tax if, within 12 months of the payment and before the property is sold, the taxpayer demands reimbursement from the owner and does not receive reimbursement within 45 days of the demand;

— an erroneous payment for a payment of tax which has not become delinquent if, within 18 months of the payment and before the property is sold, the taxpayer demands reimbursement from the owner and does not receive reimbursement within 45 days of the demand; or

— a payment for tax certificates that are subsequently corrected or determined to be void.

Court-ordered refunds and refunds that do not result from assessed value changes on the tax roll are made directly by the tax collector, without an order from the Department, from undistributed funds. (Sec. 197.182, F.S.) In addition, tax collectors will directly process and pay claims for property tax refunds of $400 or less. Claims for refunds of more than that amount will be submitted to the Department of Revenue for processing. (Rule 12D-13.009, F.A.C.)

If a taxpayer pays in error because of an error in the tax notice, the tax collector must either pay a refund to the taxpayer or, at the taxpayer's request, apply the payment in error towards the taxpayer's actual tax liability. The tax collector does not need the approval of the Department of Revenue to take action. (Sec. 197.182, F.S.)

Generally, property taxpayers are entitled to a refund within 100 days of filing the claim. The Department must approve or deny all refunds within 30 days after receiving the claim. Both of these limits may be extended by 60 days for good cause. An action to contest the denial of a refund may not be brought after the later of 60 days after the date the tax collector issues the denial to the taxpayer, or four years after January 1 of the year for which the taxes were paid. (Sec. 197.182, F.S.; Rule 12D-13.009, F.A.C.)

Claim procedure.—Pursuant to ad valorem assessment errors by property appraisers, a tax collector refund action is authorized only after the property appraiser has issued a certificate of correction. With respect to non-ad valorem assessment errors, a tax collector refund action is authorized only after the local governing board has issued a certificate of correction. For either kind of assessment error, tax collectors must first submit to the Department refund claims resulting from:

- agricultural classifications;
- collector-taxpayer controversies;
- certain tax certificate corrections;
- void or corrected tax certificates;
- void tax deed applications; and
- material mistakes of fact.

(Sec. 197.182, F.S.; Rule 12D-13.009, F.A.C.)

Department approval is not required with respect to:

- overpayments;
- payments on properties immune or exempt from, or not subject to, tax;
- payments erroneously remitted to tax collectors;
- court ordered refunds;
- refunds not resulting from assessed value changes on certified tax rolls;
- interim assessment roll statute refunds; or
- refunds resulting from tax roll extensions before value adjustment board hearings end; and changes and corrections limited to millage.

(Rule 12D-13.009, F.A.C.)

Time limitations.—Refund claims must be filed within four years of January 1 of the tax year for which the taxes were paid. The four-year limitations period does not apply to, or bar refunds resulting from, cancellation of void or corrected tax certificates and release of tax deeds. Otherwise proper refunds may be made for void and corrected tax certificates where a claim for refund is made during the seven-year life of the certificate. (Rule 12D-13.009, F.A.C.)

Refund claims for unclaimed redemption funds and for unclaimed proceeds of tax deed sales must be filed with the clerk of the circuit court within two years from the date such funds were paid to the board of county commissioners. With respect to taxes paid in error, the taxpayer also must have requested reimbursement from the property owner in writing within two years of the erroneous payment, or before the property is transferred to a third party for consideration, whichever is earlier. After receiving the Department's written refund denial, tax collectors must issue a written denial to the taxpayer. (Rule 12D-13.009, F.A.C.)

[¶20-820] Incentives

Many states take positive action to lure new business and industry. Even states that do not aggressively seek to entice new firms are often receptive to bargaining efforts by business principals who offer to locate factories or administrative facilities in the state. The types of incentives that a state can provide are wide-ranging and can involve many taxes in addition to the property tax. In the simplest example, states can reduce property tax, or waive it for a given number of years. Credits can be given, based upon the number of new employees to be hired in an area. Favorable valuation of properties, both real and personal, can be negotiated. In some cases, grants by the state have enabled new business to add the infrastructure—roads, drainage, overpasses, and utilities—needed to serve the business.

Most often these incentives are not statutory, or, often, even publicized, but rather are negotiated by state or county officials and the principals of the business, including corporate counsel. Meetings are most effective when the corporate representatives bring factual detail to the table: expected investment, number of employees, anticipated gross receipts, etc., together with a suggested package of the incentives sought by the business.

[¶20-900]

TAXPAYER RIGHTS AND REMEDIES

[¶20-904] Overview of Appeal Process

Florida taxpayers who want to appeal an assessment of property tax have a variety of options. However, there are time limits for appeals. Appeals can be made locally to the Value Adjustment Board, at which stage taxpayers are entitled to representation. Finally, taxpayers can appeal to courts.

[¶20-906] Protest and Appeal of Assessments

Discussed here in relation to the assessment appeals are:

— representation of taxpayers,

— limitations periods for appeals,

— informal conferences,

— local administrative hearings,

— state administrative hearings, and

— judicial appeals and remedies.

• *Representation of taxpayer*

Taxpayers are expressly granted the right, in Value Adjustment Board (VAB) proceedings, to be represented an employee of the taxpayer, by an attorney who is a member of the Florida Bar, a qualifying real estate broker, or a qualifying certified public accountant. In addition, a petitioner before the VAB may be represented by a person with a power of attorney or an uncompensated person with written to act on the taxpayer's behalf. (Sec. 192.0105(2)(f), F.S.; Sec. 194.034, F.S.)

• *Limitations periods for appeals*

The calendar below lists the limitation periods for Florida property taxpayers who seek an abatement, reduction in tax liability, or other ameliorating change.

Petition for review of valuation may be filed	25 days after notice of assessment mailed
Taxpayer bring action in court	within 60 days after certification of tax roll
Taxpayer bring action in court	within 60 days after decision of Value Adjustment Board
Municipality may bring suit	after 2 years from date of tax certificate
Municipality may bring suit	after 2 years from date municipal tax delinquent
Municipality may bring suit	after 1 year from date municipal special assessment delinquent
Tax collector's warrant to levy and seize property valid	7 years
Latest Tax collector's warrant to levy and seize property may be requested	May 1 each year after year of assessment
Holder of tax certificate may request deed on property	after 2 years from April 1 of the year the certificate was issued and within 7 years from issuance of certificate
Escape assessment may be levied	3 years after non-assessment of property discovered
Homeowner's association member may opt out of joint petition	20 days
Value Adjustment Board meets	30-60 days after mailing of notice and approval of assessment rolls

• *Informal conferences*

Any taxpayer who objects to the assessment may request an informal conference with the property appraiser or a member of the appraiser's staff. This informal exchange is not a prerequisite to formal administrative or judicial review. (Sec. 194.011, F.S.)

• *Local administrative hearings*

A taxpayer who objects to an assessment of property tax may file a petition requesting review by the Value Adjustment Board of the county in which the property is located. (Sec. 194.015, F.S.; Sec. 194.011, F.S.) The Board is created by law to review property assessments in each county. (Sec. 194.015, F.S.)

In an administrative or judicial action, the burden of proof in on the party initiating the challenge. If the challenge is to the assessed value of the property, the party initiating the challenge has the burden of proving by the preponderance of the evidence that the assessed value:

— does not represent the just value of the property,

— does not represent the classified use value if the property is required to be assessed based on character or use, or

— is arbitrarily based on appraisal practices that are different from the appraisal practices generally applied by the property appraiser to comparable properties within the same county.

(Sec. 194.301(2), F.S.)

Value Adjustment Board.—The Value Adjustment Board for each county will consist of:

— two members of the governing body of the county as elected from the membership of the governing body's board (one of whom will be elected chairperson),

— one member of the school board as elected from the membership of the school board,

— one citizen member who will be appointed by the governing body of the county and must own homestead property within the county, and

— one citizen member who will be appointed by the school board and must own a business occupying commercial space located within the school district.

(Sec. 194.015, F.S.)

Rules establish uniform procedures for hearings on property tax matters before the value adjustment boards ("VAB") and their special magistrates. (Rule 12D-9.001, F.A.C., *et al.*)

The citizen members of the Board may not be members or employees of any taxing authority. Additionally, the citizen members may not be persons who represent property owners in any administrative or judicial review of property taxes. (Sec. 194.015, F.S.)

Filing a petition.—The taxpayer's petition is presented on a form prescribed by the Department of Revenue and available from the property appraiser. The petition must include the parcel number of the property involved and an estimate of the time the taxpayer will require to present arguments to the Board. (Sec. 194.011, F.S.; Rule 12D-9.015, F.A.C.)

The petition is filed with the clerk of the Value Adjustment Board of the county, who must acknowledge receipt and promptly furnish a copy to the property appraiser. (Sec. 194.011, F.S.; Rule 12D-9.015, F.A.C.) The property appraisal adjustment board is authorized to charge a fee for filing the petition. The fee cannot exceed $15.

The fee will no longer be refunded should the taxpayer prevail at the Value Adjustment Board hearing or at a conference with the property appraiser. (Sec. 194.013, F.S.; Rule 12D-9.015, F.A.C.)

A petition for review of valuation issues must be filed no later than the 25th day following mailing of the notice of assessment. A petition for review of denial of an exemption, an application for agricultural or high-water recharge classification, or deferral must be filed no later than the 30th day following notice. (Sec. 194.011, F.S.; Rule 12D-9.015, F.A.C.)

A condominium or cooperative association or mobile homeowners' association, with approval of its administrative board or board of directors, may file a single joint petition on behalf of any association members who own parcels that the property appraiser determines are substantially similar with respect to location, proximity to amenities, number of rooms, living area, and condition. An association member must be given notice of the association's intent to file a single joint petition and must be given at least 20 days to notify the association in writing if he does not wish his unit to be included in the petition. An owner of contiguous, undeveloped parcels may also file a single joint petition if the property appraiser determines that the parcels are substantially similar. The individual, agent, or legal entity that signs a petition before the Value Adjustment Board protesting an assessment becomes an agent of the taxpayer for the purpose of serving process to obtain personal jurisdiction over the taxpayer for the entire Board proceedings, including any appeals of a Board decision by the property appraiser. (Sec. 194.011, F.S.; Rule 12D-9.015, F.A.C.)

Partial payments.—A petitioner who challenges the assessed value of property must pay all of the nonad valorem assessments and make a partial payment of at least 75% of the property tax, minus any applicable discounts, before the tax becomes delinquent. A petitioner who challenges an assessment based on an argument that the property was not substantially complete as of January 1 must pay all of the non-ad valorem assessments and the amount of tax that the owner admits in good faith to owe, minus any applicable discount, before the taxes become delinquent. However, the tax collector must collect a penalty of 10% of the deficiency per year from the date the taxes became delinquent if the value adjustment board determines that the amount of the tax the owner admitted to owe was made not in good faith and is grossly disproportionate to the amount found to be due. (Sec. 194.014, F.S.)

Hearing procedures.—The Value Adjustment Board meets not earlier than 30 days and not later than 60 days after the mailing of notice and after the approval of the assessment rolls by the Department of Revenue. The Board hears petitions relating to:

— assessments;

— homestead exemptions;

— appeals from exemptions denied or disputes arising from exemptions granted;

— appeals concerning ad valorem tax deferrals and classifications; and

— determinations that certain changes in ownership or qualifying improvements have occurred.

(Sec. 194.032(1)(a), F.S.; Rule 12D-9.005, F.A.C.)

The clerk of the governing board of the county prepares a schedule of appearances based on timely filed petitions and original applications for ad valorem tax exemptions. A petitioner is allowed to request a copy of the record card containing information used in computing his current assessment. The clerk of a county's governing body must notify each petitioner of the scheduled time of his or her hearing before the Board no less than 25 days prior to the scheduled date. The notice will indicate if the petition has been scheduled to be heard at a particular time or during a block of time. Additionally, the notice will include a copy of the record card if it was requested by the petitioner in their application. Moreover, petitioners are not required to wait more than two hours after the start of their assigned block of time for their hearing to commence. If a petitioner waits more than two hours, they can inform the chairperson their intention to leave and if they do leave the clerk will reschedule a rehearing. This rescheduled rehearing will not count as the petitioners right to request a rehearing once. (Sec. 194.032, F.S.(2)(a); Rule 12D-9.007, F.A.C.)

At least 15 days before the hearing before the Board, the taxpayer must provide the appraiser with a list of evidence to be presented at the hearing, copies of documents, and a summary of evidence to be presented by witnesses. The appraiser must provide the taxpayer with the same material no more than seven days before the hearing, if the taxpayer has already provided the required information and has requested the information from the appraiser in writing. Failure of the property appraiser to timely comply with these notice requirements will result in a rescheduling of the hearing. (Sec. 194.011(4), F.S.)

A taxpayer before the Board may be represented by an attorney who is a member of the Florida Bar, a licensed or certified real estate appraiser, a licensed real estate broker, or a licensed certified public accountant. (Rule 12D-9.018, F.A.C.) A verbatim record of the proceedings is kept. (Sec. 194.034(1), F.S.)

The Board is authorized to appoint special magistrates to take testimony and make recommendations to the Board. (Sec. 194.034(2), F.S.; Rule 12D-9.010, F.A.C.)

The Value Adjustment Board has the power to hear disputed or appealed applications for exemptions, to grant the exemptions in whole or in part, and to review exemptions on its own motion or upon motion of the property appraiser. The Board must give an applicant five days' notice of its intent to review an application. (Sec. 196.194(1), F.S.; Rule 12D-9.027, F.A.C.)

Protest and appeal of "Portability" assessments.—Applicable to petitions concerning the assessment of homestead property at less than just value, the taxpayer may petition the Value Adjustment Board in the county where the new homestead is located. If a taxpayer does not agree with the assessment limitation difference amount stated by the property appraiser in the county where the previous homestead property was located, the Value Adjustment Board in the county where the new homestead is located will send notice to the Value Adjustment Board in the county where the previous homestead was located. However, the taxpayer may not petition to have the just, assessed, or taxable value of the previous homestead changed. (Sec. 194.011(6), F.S.; Rule 12D-9.028, F.A.C.)

• *State administrative hearings*

There are no provisions for state administrative hearings with respect to property tax appeals.

• *Judicial appeals and remedies*

The circuit court of the county in which the property is located has original jurisdiction over all matters relating to property taxation. (Sec. 194.171(1), F.S.)

The taxpayer must pay the amount in good faith admitted to be owing before maintaining a suit contesting the assessment. Timely filing of an action contesting a property tax assessment in the circuit court and payment of all noncontested property taxes suspend all procedures for the collection of taxes prior to final disposition of the action. (Sec. 194.171(3), F.S.)

In a taxpayer court challenge, the appraiser's assessment is presumed correct.

Relief from illegal taxes.—The Florida Constitution provides that no court may grant relief from the payment of any illegal or illegally assessed tax until payment is made of all legally assessed taxes on property of the same owner. (Sec. 13, Art. VII, Fla Const.)

When an assessment is made and payment is refused on an allegation of illegality, the taxpayer may file an action in chancery. The court has jurisdiction to decide the matter and may declare the assessment illegal. (Sec. 68.01, F.S.)

Injunctive relief.—In any tax suit, the court may issue injunctions to restrain the sale of real or personal property for any tax that appears to be contrary to law or equity. A bill cannot be dismissed because the injunction requested involves personal property only. (Sec. 194.211, F.S.)

Statute of limitations.—No action can be brought to contest a tax assessment after 60 days from the date the assessment roll is certified for collection, or 60 days from the rendering of a decision by the value adjustment board if the board's action is taken after extension of the assessment roll. (Sec. 194.171(2), F.S.) This requirement does not apply to a claim involving property owned by the state and used by it for a governmental purpose. (*Florida Department of Management Services v. Cason*, Florida Court of Appeal, First District, No. 1D04-4836, August 4, 2005)

The Florida Supreme Court has held that the 60-day filing requirement applies broadly to taxpayer actions challenging the assessment of taxes against their property regardless of the legal basis of the challenge. In its decision, the Court rejected the taxpayers' argument that "classification" challenges resulting in a denial of a tax exemption are entitled to a four-year statute of limitations period while other claims are not. The Court stated that such a rule would be contrary to the spirit and purpose of the tax assessment statutes, including the explicit provisions of the statute implementing the 60-day filing requirement. Regardless of the terminology used, taxpayers that challenge a property appraiser's judgment to deny them an exemption are subject to the 60-day time limit. (*Ward v. Brown*, Florida Supreme Court, No. SC03-783, October 21, 2004)

Parties.—The plaintiff in any tax suit is either the property appraiser or the taxpayer who is responsible for payment of the tax being contested. (Sec. 194.181(1), F.S.)

When the taxpayer files suit contesting an assessment, the county property appraiser is party defendant. In any suit involving the collection of property taxes or questions related to tax certificates and tax deeds, the tax collector is the defendant. (Sec. 194.181, F.S.)

In a suit that alleges violation of the Florida Constitution, the state official responsible for overall supervision of the assessment and collection of the contested tax is party defendant. (Sec. 194.181(5), F.S.)

The Florida Supreme Court found that county property appraisers did not have standing, in either their official or unofficial capacities, to seek a declaratory ruling concerning the taxability of household goods and personal effects of nonresident taxpayers, since there was no genuine controversy affecting nonresidents actually aggrieved. (*Department of Revenue v. Markham, as Broward County Property Appraiser*, FlaSCt, March 12, 1981)

Florida District Court's were split on whether a county appraiser may institute a legal proceeding challenging the validity of exemptions. In *Turner v. Hillsborough County Aviation Authority*, FlaDistCtApp, 2ndDist, No. 98-03123, September 3, 1999, the District Court of Appeal, Second District, found that a county appraiser did not have standing to challenge the constitutionality of a Florida real property tax exemption for government property that was leased to a sports authority and used by a professional baseball team as a sports facility. In *Fuchs v. Robbins*, FlaDistCtApp, 3rdDist, No. 98-275, June 30, 1999, the District Court of Appeal, Third District, allowed a county property appraiser to challenge a statute which sets the valuation of any building that is not substantially completed at zero. However, in its review of the *Turner* and *Fuchs* decisions, the Florida Supreme Court held that county property appraisers do not have standing to challenge the constitutionality of state statutes. (*Fuchs v. Robbins*, Florida Supreme Court, Nos. SC96182, SC96183, SC96674, April 4, 2002)

Costs, interest, and penalties.—The court assesses all costs related to a tax suit. (Sec. 194.192(1), F.S.)

If the court finds that the amount owed by the taxpayer is more than what the taxpayer has in good faith admitted and paid, it enters a judgment against the taxpayer for interest on the deficiency as well as the deficiency itself. Interest is calculated at the rate of 12 per year from the date the tax became delinquent. (Sec. 194.192(2), F.S.)

If the court finds that the amount the taxpayer has admitted and paid is grossly disproportionate to the amount of tax found to be owed, it may assess a penalty at the rate of 10% per year from the date the tax became delinquent. This penalty is in addition to the interest due on the deficiency. (Sec. 194.192(2), F.S.)

Federal court actions.—An assessment may be appealed to a federal court if there is a question involving the U.S. Constitution or a federal statute. However, the right to bring a federal suit is limited by the Tax Injunction Act and the fundamental principle of comity. The Tax Injunction Act prohibits injunctions in federal district courts against the assessment, levy, or collection of any state tax when there is a "plain, speedy, and efficient remedy" in state courts. (28 U.S.C. 1341) Because this federal provision has been the subject of considerable litigation, the case law interpreting this provision should be researched if a federal action is contemplated.

In addition, any appeal of a state tax case to a federal court would be subject to established principles of federal jurisdiction and abstention.

[¶35-000]

CITRUS FRUIT TAXES

[¶35-001] Citrus Fruit Taxes

Florida imposes two taxes or assessments on citrus fruits, a citrus fruit assessment and a fruit equalizing tax.

• *Citrus fruit assessment*

A citrus fruit assessment is imposed upon each standard-packed box of citrus fruit grown and placed into the primary channel of trade in Florida. The term "assessment" was substituted for the words "excise tax" effective July 1, 2012, in what was formerly known as the "Florida citrus fruit excise tax." Maximum assessment rates are provided but the rates may be set at any lower rate in any year, as specified. The assessment rate on fresh fruit is expressed per 4/5 bushel box or "bu box." The assessment rate on processed fruit is expressed per 1-3/5 bu box (i.e., a "field box"). Two 4/5 bu boxes equal 1-3/5 bu box. However, the citrus fruit assessment rates for each season indicated below are expressed per each standard packed box of citrus fruit grown and placed into the channels of trade. The assessment rates are not determined until the USDA crop estimate (citrus forecast) is released. (Sec. 601.15(3)(a), F.S.)

Persons liable for the periodic payments of assessments must submit a letter of credit from an issuing financial institution located in the United States, a cash bond, an appropriate certificate of deposit, or an approved surety bond in an amount and manner as prescribed by the department, to guarantee payment. (Sec. 601.15(6)(b), F.S.)

The Florida Citrus Commission, as head of the Department of Citrus, upon an affirmative vote of a majority of its members and by an order entered by it prior to November 1 of any year, may set the citrus fruit assessment rates up to the maximum rates specified. The assessment rates apply only to the citrus season that begins on August 1 of the same calendar year. (Sec. 601.15, F.S.; *Florida Citrus Commission Summary*, Florida Citrus Commission, October 22, 2008; *Telephone Discussion*, Florida Citrus Commission, December 8, 2008)

Citrus fruit assessment rates for 2022-2023.—Although the rate is effective from August 1 through July 31 of the following year, rate approval by the Florida Citrus Commission is usually delayed until late October or November of each year. The Florida citrus fruit assessment rates per each standard packed box of citrus fruit grown and placed into the channels of trade effective August 1, 2022, through July 31, 2023, are as follows:

—processed oranges: 12¢;

—fresh oranges: 5¢;

—processed grapefruit: 7¢;

—fresh grapefruit: 7¢;

—fresh tangerines and hybrids: 7¢; and

—processed tangerines and hybrids: 7¢

(Sec. 601.15(3)(a), F.S.; Sec. 601.155(2), F.S.; *Email*, Florida Department of Citrus, October 26, 2022)

Assessment of citrus fruit packing and processing equipment rendered unused due to Hurricane Irma or citrus greening.—For ad valorem taxation purposes and applicable to the 2018 tax roll only, tangible personal property that a citrus fruit packing or processing facility owns and operates will have a market value no greater than its value for salvage, provided the facility no longer uses the tangible personal property in its operation because of Hurricane Irma or citrus greening. (Sec. 193.4516, F.S.; *Property Tax Oversight Bulletin: PTO 18-02*, Florida Department of Revenue, June 1, 2018)

To facilitate reporting this one-year ad valorem assessment reduction, the department has added a temporary exemption code "Z" to the NAP assessment roll for the 2018 roll submission cycle. The value to report with this code will be the difference between the market value and the salvage value of the eligible tangible personal property. Taxpayers are also instructed to include the assessment reduction on Form DR-489V, 2018 Preliminary Recapitulation of the Ad Valorem Assessment Roll, and DR-403V, 2018 Revised Recapitulation of the Ad Valorem Assessment Roll. Report the total just value of the eligible tangible personal property on line 5, column II, and report the total assessed value on line 18, column II. (*Property Tax Oversight Bulletin: PTO 18-02*, Florida Department of Revenue, June 1, 2018)

CCH COMMENT: Challenge to citrus fruit excise tax. In *Department of Citrus v. Graves Brothers Co.*, the Florida Second District Court of Appeal held that Florida's citrus fruit excise tax violated the free speech provisions of the First Amendment by compelling commercial speech. However, in a similar case concerning beef advertising, the U.S. Supreme Court ruled in May of 2005 that the advertising in that case represented "government speech" that was immune from First Amendment challenges. (*Johanns v. Livestock Marketing*, 125 S.Ct. 2055 (2005)). In an order issued September 8, 2005, the Florida Supreme Court quashed the decision by the Second District Court of Appeal and remanded the case for consideration in light of the *Johanns* decision. All parties to the citrus excise tax case have agreed to accept the decision by the U.S. Supreme Court as controlling and have agreed that both the Florida appellate and trial courts should enter orders reversing their earlier decisions. These orders would constitute a final adjudication. (*Department of Citrus v. Graves Brothers Co.*, Florida Second District Court of Appeal, No. 2D03-2276, October 20, 2004)

The assessment is due at the time the citrus fruit is first handled in the primary channels of trade. (Sec. 601.15(6)(a), F.S.) The assessment does not apply to citrus fruit used for noncommercial domestic consumption on the premises where produced. (Sec. 601.15(3)(c), F.S.)

Maximum assessments.—The maximum assessment for grapefruit that enter the primary channel of trade for use in fresh or processed form is set at 36¢ per box, and the maximum assessment for oranges that enter the primary channel of trade for use in the fresh form is 7¢ per box and 25¢ per box in the processed form. The actual assessment levied each year on tangerines and citrus hybrids regulated by the Florida Department of Citrus that enter the primary channel of trade for use in processed form cannot exceed 25¢ per box or 16¢ per box in the fresh form. (Sec. 601.15, F.S.)

• *Citrus fruit equalizing tax*

A citrus fruit equalizing tax is imposed on the first person who exercises in Florida the privilege of:

— processing, reprocessing, blending, or mixing processed orange products or processed grapefruit products,

— packaging or repackaging processed orange products or processed grapefruit products into retail or institutional size containers, or

— storing any processed orange product or any processed grapefruit product or removing any portion of the product from the original container in which it arrived for purposes other than official inspection or direct consumption by the consumer. (Sec. 601.155(1), F.S.)

Products made in whole or in part from citrus fruit on which the citrus fruit assessment is levied are wholly or partially exempt from the equalizing tax. (Sec. 601.155(5), F.S.)

The equalizing tax is imposed at the same rate per box of oranges or grapefruit utilized in the initial production of the processed citrus products as that imposed, at the time of exercise of the taxable privilege, by the citrus fruit assessment. The tax is due within 61 days after the taxable privilege giving rise to its imposition is exercised in Florida. (Sec. 601.155(2) and (8), F.S.)

When the tax is imposed on any processed orange or grapefruit product that is stored or removed from its original container and that is subsequently shipped out of Florida, the taxpayer is entitled to a refund of any tax paid on the product. (Sec. 601.155(9), F.S.)

Any person liable for the equalizing tax may annually object to payment of the tax and must be granted the immediate right to elect not to pay two-thirds of the applicable tax rate. (Sec. 601.155(10), F.S.)

[¶37-000]
ALCOHOLIC BEVERAGES

[¶37-001] Alcoholic Beverages

Florida's Alcoholic Beverage Tax is covered in the Florida Statutes, Title XXXIV Alcoholic Beverages and Tobacco, Chapter 565 Liquor, Section 12 Excise tax on liquors and beverages. Current tax rates per gallon are:

— Wines, wine coolers and other beverages with 0.5% to less than 17.259% alcohol by volume $2.25

— Wines with 17.259% or more alcohol by volume $3.00

— Natural sparkling wines $3.50

— Ciders $0.89

— Other beverages with 17.259% to 55.780% alcohol by volume $6.50

— Other beverages with more than 55.780% alcohol by volume $9.53

— Malt beverages $0.48

(http://www.myfloridalicense.com/dbpr/abt/rules_statutes/tax_rate_info.html)

Comprehensive coverage of taxation of alcohol, as well as licensing and distribution information is provided in Wolters Kluwer, CCH Liquor Control Law Reporter.

[¶37-050]
DOCUMENT RECORDING TAX

[¶37-051] Document Recording Tax

The document recording tax in Florida is known as the documentary stamp tax. The documentary stamp tax is imposed on bonds, debentures, deeds and conveyances, and other documents and instruments of writing. Contracts of sale and purchase are not taxable under the provision "written obligations to pay money." In general, the law is limited to transfers of property and to those instruments given primarily for the payment of money loaned. The tax on documents that convey realty is levied at a higher rate than the tax on other instruments.

Discussed below:

— documents subject to tax,

— exemptions,

— basis of tax,

— rate of tax,

— payment of tax,

— reports,

— assessment, revision, and appeals,

— collection of tax,

— refunds and remedies,

— payment of tax, and

— penalties.

• *Documents subject to tax*

The documentary stamp tax is levied on those instruments whose primary purpose is the payment or repayment of money, and transfers of property. (Sec. 201.01, F.S.) Documents include:

— Bonds, Debentures, and Certificates of Indebtedness

— Notes, Assignment of Wages, and Mortgages

— Supplements or Amendments

— Deeds and Conveyances

— Conveyance to a Partner from a Partnership

— Uniform Commercial Code Transactions—Financial Statements

Bonds.—The documentary stamp tax is imposed on all bonds, debentures, and certificates of indebtedness issued in Florida by any person, and all instruments and documents issued by a corporation with interest coupons or in registered form, provided that only that part of the value of the bonds, debentures, or certificates of indebtedness, the property of which is within Florida bears to the whole value of the property described in the instrument, is taxed. (Sec. 201.07, F.S.)

Notes, Assignment of Wages, and Mortgages.—The documentary stamp tax is imposed on promissory notes, non-negotiable notes, written obligations to pay money, and assignments of salaries, wages, or other compensation made, executed, delivered, sold, transferred, or assigned in Florida, and for each renewal of such an instrument. The tax applies to mortgages, trust deeds, security agreements, and other evidences of indebtedness filed or recorded in Florida, and for each renewal of such an instrument. A written promise to pay money that is not fixed and absolute at the time of execution is not subject to tax. (Sec. 201.08(1), F.S.; Rule 12B-4.054(4), F.A.C.) The tax is also due upon the assignment of a beneficial interest in a land trust, based upon the consideration paid for the assignment. (Rule 12B-4.013(29), F.A.C.) However, no tax is due on a mortgage when title to property is taken subject to the mortgage, and the grantee is not responsible to the holder of the promissory note for the payment of any tax. (Rule 12B-4.053(19), F.A.C.)

If the mortgage, trust deed, security agreement, or other evidence of indebtedness secures future advances, the tax is paid at the time of recordation on the initial debt secured, excluding future advances. At the time any future advance is made, the tax is paid on the sum advanced. Any increase in the amount of original indebtedness caused by interest accruing under an adjustable rate note or mortgage with an initial adjustment interval of at least six months and secured by a one- to four-family structure is taxable as a future advance only to the extent that the increase is computable when the document is executed. (Sec. 201.08(1), F.S.)

The documentary stamp tax is imposed on promissory notes, non-negotiable notes, written obligations to pay money, or other compensation made in Florida in connection with sales made under retail charge account services incident to sales that are not conditional and that are not secured by mortgage or other pledge of the purchaser. (Sec. 201.08(2), F.S.) The phrase "written obligations to pay money" has been construed by the Florida Supreme Court not to include contracts of sale or purchase where the payment of money is only incidental to the contract. (*Metropolis Publishing Co. et al. v. Lee* (1936), 126 Fla. 107, 170 So. 442)

Receipts, charge slips and other records of transactions effected with the use of a credit card, charge cards, and debit cards are exempt from the documentary stamp tax. (Sec. 201.08(2), F.S.)

Renewals only include modifications of an original document which change the terms of the indebtedness evidenced by the original document by adding one or more obligors, increasing the principal balance, or changing the interest rate maturity date or payment terms. Other modifications to documents are not renewals and the tax does not apply. (Sec. 201.08(5), F.S.)

Taxability of a document is determined solely from the face of the document and any separate document expressly incorporated into the document. (Sec. 201.08(6), F.S.) When multiple documents evidence, secure, or form part of the same primary debt, tax will not be imposed more than once on the total indebtedness evidenced.

A mortgage, trust deed, or security agreement filed or recorded in Florida which is given by a taxpayer different than or in addition to the prior obligated taxpayer is not a separate obligation. Instead, it secures the obligated taxpayer's primary note, certificate of indebtedness, or obligation. (Sec. 201.08(7), F.S.) To the extent that tax is paid on any document evidencing or securing the primary note, certificate of indebtedness, or obligation, the tax will be paid once, notwithstanding that more than one mortgage, trust deed, or security agreement is recorded.

If a tax was imposed by Sec. 201.08, F.S., prior to July 1, 1997, and was not actually collected on documents exempted by or otherwise not subject to tax pursuant to Sec. 201.08(6), F.S., then no tax is due. (Sec. 2(2), Ch. 97-123, Laws 1997, footnote 1)

The documentary stamp tax is not imposed on promissory notes executed for students to receive financial aid from federal or state educational assistance programs, from loans guaranteed by the federal or state government when federal regulations prohibit assessment of the tax, or from any financial aid program administered by a state university or community college. (Sec. 201.08(3), F.S.)

Also exempt are all promissory notes, nonnegotiable notes, and other written obligations to pay money bearing dates after July 1, 1957, when the maker is a security dealer and when they are for a 30-day or less duration and secured by pledge or deposit, as collateral security for the payment of notes and other obligations, provided all documentary stamp taxes have been paid on the collateral security. (Sec. 517.32, F.S.)

Supplements or amendments.—A supplement or amendment to a mortgage, deed, indenture, or security agreement filed or recorded in connection with a new issue of bonds is subject to the documentary stamp tax only to the extent of the aggregate amount of the new issue of bonds or other evidence of indebtedness, not to the extent of the aggregate amount previously issued under the instrument being supplemented or amended. In order to qualify for this tax treatment, the document that evidences the increase in indebtedness must show the official records book page number and county where the original obligation and any prior increase in that obligation are recorded. (Sec. 201.08(4), F.S.)

Deeds and Conveyances.—The documentary stamp tax is imposed on deeds, instruments, or writings that grant, assign, transfer, or otherwise convey to or vest in the purchaser any lands, tenements, or other real property, or any interest in such property. Any document that conveys a beneficial interest in real property is subject to tax, even if the interest is designated as personal property.

Any document that grants the right to a tenant-stockholder to occupy an apartment in a building owned by a cooperative apartment corporation or in a dwelling on real property owned by any other form of cooperative association is subject to the documentary stamp tax. Marital property transferred between spouses or ex-spouses during an action for dissolution of marriage is exempt. (Sec. 201.02, F.S.)

The documentary stamp tax does not apply to a deed or other instrument that transfers or conveys homestead property or any interest in homestead property between spouses, if the only consideration for the transfer or conveyance is the amount of a mortgage or other lien encumbering the homestead property at the time of the transfer or conveyance. This provision applies to transfers or conveyances from one spouse to another, from one spouse to both spouses, or from both spouses to one spouse. (Sec. 201.02, F.S.)

The tax is to be paid by the purchaser and the document recorded in the office of the clerk of the Circuit Court as evidence of ownership. (Sec. 201.02, F.S.)

The tax applies when real property is conveyed to a conduit entity. A "conduit entity" is a legal entity to which real property is conveyed without full consideration by a grantor who owns a direct or indirect interest in the entity, or a successor entity. (Sec. 201.02, F.S.; Rule 12B-4.060, F.A.C.)

This tax does not apply to a contract to sell the residence of an employee relocating at his or her employer's direction or to documents related to the contract between the employee and the employer or between the employee and a person in the business of providing employee relocation services. The tax will apply only to the transfer of the real property by deed that vests legal title in a named grantee. (Sec. 201.02, F.S.)

The conveyance of property from a nonexempt party to an entity with the power of eminent domain as part of an out-of-court settlement of condemnation proceedings, or under threat of condemnation, is exempt from the documentary stamp tax. (*Technical Assistance Advisement No. 01B4-008*, Florida Department of Revenue, September 11, 2001)

Consideration for a document that transfers an interest in real property under a short sale does not include the amount of an indebtedness forgiven or released by a mortgagee holding a mortgage on the grantor's interest in the property. (Sec. 201.02(11), F.S.; *Tax Information Publication 10B04-01*, Florida Department of Revenue, June 17, 2010) To be classified as a "short sale," a purchase and sale of real property must include all of the following conditions:

— the grantor's interest is encumbered by a mortgage or mortgages in an aggregate amount greater than the purchase price paid by the grantee,

— a mortgagee releases the real property from its mortgage in exchange for a partial payment of less than the total of the outstanding mortgage indebtedness,

— the releasing mortgagee does not receive any interest in the property transferred, and

— the releasing mortgagee is not controlled by or related to the grantor or the grantee.

(Sec. 201.02(11), F.S.)

¶37-051

Conveyance to a partner from a partnership.—Unless the taxpayer establishes that the conveyance is for purposes other than the avoidance of the tax, all conveyances of real property to a partner from a partnership after July 1, 1986, that meet either of the following conditions are taxable:

(1) The partner receiving the real property from the partnership is a partner other than the partner who conveyed the real property to the partnership; or

(2) The partner receiving the real property from the partnership is the partner who conveyed the real property to the partnership and there is a mortgage or other debt secured by the real property and for which the partner was not personally liable prior to conveying the real property to the partnership. (Sec. 201.02, F.S.)

The value of the consideration paid for the conveyance to the partner is the amount of any outstanding mortgage debt or other debt that the partner pays or agrees to pay in exchange for the real property, regardless of whether the partner was personally liable for the debts of the partnership prior to the conveyance to the partner from the partnership. (Sec. 201.02, F.S.)

Uniform Commercial Code transactions—Financial statements.—The excise tax on documents applies to transactions covered by the Uniform Commercial Code to the same extent that it would if the UCC had not been enacted. The clerk or filing officer will not accept for filing and recording any financing statement unless it has the notation that the required documentary tax stamps have been placed on the promissory instruments secured by the financing statement. (Sec. 201.22, F.S.)

• *Exemptions*

The exemptions provided from the documentary stamp tax by statute are detailed below, including exemptions for:

— Business entity mergers and conversions

— Renewal of Original Promissory Notes

— Renewal of Adjustable Rate Note or Mortgage

— Certificates of Deposit

— Marital Property in Actions for Dissolution

— Principal Obligations Pursuant to Wholesale Warehouse Mortgage Agreement

— Promissory Notes and Other Written Obligations of Security Dealers

— Deferred Payment of Student Fees

— Credit Card Transaction Records

— Foreign Notes

— Municipalities, Political Subdivisions and Agencies of the State

— Certain Federal Mortgage Institutions

— Certain loans made by the Florida Small Business Emergency Bridge Loan Program and any loans made by the Agricultural Economic Development Program

Business entity mergers and conversions.—The documentary stamp tax will not be due on deeds or other instruments that purport to convey interests in Florida real property and instruments purporting to assume notes and other written obligations to pay money that are executed or delivered as a result of the mergers or conversions described as follows:

— a domestic corporation converting into another business entity;

— another business entity converting into a domestic business corporation;

— a domestic limited liability company converting into another business entity;

— an organization other than a limited partnership converting into a limited partnership and a limited partnership converting into an organization other than a limited partnership;

— a limited partnership merging with one or more constituent organizations;

— an organization other than a partnership converting into a partnership and a partnership converting into another organization; and

— a partnership merging with one or more other constituent organizations.

In each of those mergers or conversions, title to all real property is conveyed to the surviving or converted entity by operation of law, and all debts and liabilities of the merging or converting entity become the debts and liabilities of the surviving or converted entity by operation of law. (*Tax Information Publication, No. 05ADM-03*, Florida Department of Revenue, August 10, 2005)

Renewal of original promissory notes.—The documentary stamp tax is not imposed on a promissory note given in renewal of an existing promissory note if the renewal only extends or continues the identical contractual obligations of the original note and evidences part or all of the original indebtedness. To qualify for the exemption, the renewal note evidencing a term obligation must not enlarge the original contract and obligation in any way and must be executed by the original obligor and renew and extend only the unpaid balance of the original contract and obligation. (Sec. 201.09, F.S.) A renewal note evidencing a revolving obligation, in order to qualify for the exemption, must be executed by the original obligor and must renew and extend no more than the original face amount of the original contract and obligation.

If a renewal note that qualifies for the exemption is evidenced by a mortgage, trust deed, security agreement, or other evidence of indebtedness, the evidence of indebtedness is also exempt. (Sec. 201.09, F.S.)

If the only reason a document is not exempt is the nonpayment or underpayment of tax on the document evidencing the original contract and obligation or the original primary debt or mortgage, then payment of the tax deficiency, plus interest and penalties, will cause the renewal to qualify for the exemption.

A renewal note evidencing a term obligation that increases the unpaid balance of the original contract and obligation, but that otherwise would be exempt, is taxable only on the face amount of the increase. Similarly, a renewal note evidencing a revolving obligation that increases the original face amount of the original contract and obligation, but that otherwise would be exempt, is taxable only on the face amount of the increase. (Sec. 201.09, F.S.)

Renewal of adjustable rate note or mortgage.—The documentary stamp tax does not apply to a note given in renewal of an adjustable rate note or mortgage that has an initial interest rate adjustment interval of at least six months. Tax must be paid, however, on any accrued interest upon which the tax has not previously been paid. (Sec. 201.09, F.S.)

Certificates of deposit.—All certificates of deposit issued by any bank, banking association, or trust company are exempt from the documentary stamp tax. (Sec. 201.10, F.S.)

Marital property in actions for dissolution.—Deeds, transfers, or conveyances (conveyances) of marital homes between spouses or former spouses in the course of an action for dissolution are not subject to Florida's documentary stamp tax. Taxes paid for conveyances within one year before a dissolution shall be refunded, although the exemption does not apply to any actions executed before July 1, 1997. (Sec. 201.02(7), F.S.)

Wholesale warehouse mortgages.—The documentary stamp tax does not apply to promissory notes, nonnegotiable notes, and other written obligations to pay, referred to as "principal obligations," that the maker pledges or deposits, pursuant to a wholesale warehouse mortgage agreement, any collateral obligation with the payee or holder of the principal obligation, provided that the tax has been paid on the collateral obligation. The exemption does not apply to any indebtedness in excess of the amount evidenced by the collateral obligation. (Sec. 201.21, F.S.)

The temporary removal of the documents that represent the collateral obligation for a reasonable commercial purpose does not invalidate the exemption, as long as the documents are not removed for more than 60 days. (Sec. 201.21, F.S.)

Promissory notes and other written obligations of security dealers.—All promissory notes, nonnegotiable notes, and other written obligations to pay money bearing dates after July 1, 1957, are exempt from the documentary stamp tax when the maker is a security dealer and when they are for a 30-day or less duration and secured by pledge or deposit, as collateral security for the payment of notes and other obligations, provided all documentary stamp taxes have been paid on the collateral security. (Sec. 517.32, F.S.)

Deferred payment of student fees.—The documentary stamp tax is not imposed on promissory notes executed for students to receive financial aid from federal or state educational assistance programs, from loans guaranteed by the federal or state government when federal regulations prohibit assessment of the tax, or from any financial aid program administered by a state university or community college. This provision includes a note executed by a student to defer student fees to institutions within the state university or community college system. (Sec. 201.08(3), F.S.)

Credit card transaction record.—Receipts, charge slips and other records of transactions effected with the use of a credit card are exempted from the documentary stamp tax. (Sec. 201.08(2)(b), F.S.)

Foreign notes.—The documentary stamp tax is not imposed on promissory notes, nonnegotiable notes, and other written obligations to pay money made by individuals residing outside the United States or businesses located outside the United States at the time the obligations are executed. The exemption also applies to drafts or bills of exchange drawn upon and accepted by a Florida bank that arise out of the importation or exportation of goods or the storage of goods abroad, or that are drawn by foreign banks for the purpose of furnishing dollar exchange required for trade, provided that the drawer of the draft or bill of exchange resides outside the United States on the date of acceptance. (Sec. 201.23(1), F.S.)

Also exempt are notes and obligations, executed outside Florida and secured by a mortgage, deed of trust, or similar security agreement on property outside the state, if they are:

(1) brought into Florida as collateral security under a wholesale warehouse mortgage agreement,

(2) deposited with a custodian as security for obligations issued by a federal agency, or

(3) included in a pool of mortgages to be serviced by a licensed mortgage lender.

(Sec. 201.23(1), F.S.)

International banking transactions are also exempt. (Sec. 201.23(4), F.S.)

Not exempt from the tax are mortgages and other evidences of indebtedness relating to the purchase of real property in Florida, and instruments of any business organization unless a majority of its equity securities are owned by persons located outside the United States. (Sec. 201.23(2), F.S.)

These provisions do not apply to any instrument entered into before July 1, 1977. (Sec. 201.23(3), F.S.)

Municipalities, political subdivisions, and agencies of the state.—Exempt from the documentary stamp tax are any obligations to pay money issued by a municipality, political subdivision, or agency of the state. Also exempt are assignments, transfers, dispositions or documents arising out of rentals, leases or lease-purchases of educational facilities and sites by a federal, state, county or municipal government agency or any public nonprofit agency. (Sec. 201.24, F.S.)

Certain federal mortgage institutions.—Although several federal mortgage institutions are exempt from the state's document stamp tax the underlying document transferring an interest in real property remains subject to tax and that the nonexempt party to the transfer is liable for the tax. The exempt institutions are the Federal National Mortgage Association, the Government National Mortgage Association, and the Federal Home Loan Mortgage Company. (*Tax Information Publication, No. 12B04-01,* Florida Department of Revenue, May 10, 2012)

Certain loans made by the Florida Small Business Emergency Bridge Loan Program.—Any loan made by the Florida Small Business Emergency Bridge Loan Program in response to a disaster that results in a state of emergency declared by executive order or proclamation of the Governor is exempt from the documentary stamp tax. (Sec. 201.25, F.S.)

Loans made by the Agricultural Economic Development Program.—Any loan made by the Agricultural Economic Development Program is exempt from the documentary stamp tax. (Sec. 201.25, F.S.)

• *Basis of tax*

The documentary stamp tax is based on the value of the instrument. Bonds are taxed on their face value; stock with a par value is taxed on that value; no par stock, notes, and obligations to pay money are taxed on their actual value. for an agreement to sell or a memorandum of sale, the tax is based on the character of the object covered by the agreement or memorandum.

• *Rate of tax*

The documentary stamps tax rate depends on the type of document.

Bonds, Debentures and Certificates of Indebtedness.—On bonds, debentures, and certificates of indebtedness issued by any person, and on instruments and documents with interest coupons or in registered form issued by any corporation, the tax is 35¢ on each $100 of value. Only that part of the value of the instrument represented by property located within Florida is taxable. (Sec. 201.07, F.S.)

Notes, Assignment of Wages and Mortgages.—On promissory notes, nonnegotiable notes, written obligations to pay money, and assignments of salaries, wages, or other compensation, and for each renewal of such an instrument, the documentary stamp tax is levied at the rate of 35¢ per $100 of value. However, the tax on any of these documents may not exceed $2,450. (Sec. 201.08, F.S.)

Charge Accounts.—On promissory notes, nonnegotiable notes, and written obligations to pay money executed in connection with sales made under retail charge account services, the documentary stamp tax is levied at the rate of 35¢ per $100 of value. However, the tax on any of these documents may not exceed $2,450. (Sec. 201.08(2), F.S.)

¶37-051

Deeds and Conveyances.—The documentary stamp tax on any instrument that conveys an interest in realty is levied at the rate of 70¢ per $100 of the consideration. However, the tax is 60¢ per $100 of the consideration for deeds and other taxable instruments relating to realty in any Florida county that imposes a surtax on documents. If the full amount of consideration is not shown on the instrument, the tax is nevertheless on the full amount. If the consideration is expressed in terms other than money, the tax is based on the reasonable value of the property. (Sec. 201.02, F.S.)

When real property is conveyed to a conduit entity and all or a portion of the grantor's direct or indirect ownership interest in the conduit entity is subsequently transferred for consideration within three years of such conveyance, a tax is imposed on each such transfer of an interest in the conduit entity for the consideration at a rate of 70 cents for each $100 of the consideration paid. (Sec. 201.02, F.S.)

• *Payment of Taxes*

The documentary stamp tax is paid at the time of the transfer or sale of each bond, share of stock, or instrument subject to the tax. Once the tax is paid on a specific transaction, it is not paid again until another transfer or sale is undertaken.

• *Reports*

The documentary stamp tax on instruments related to retail charge account services is payable quarterly on forms issued by the Department of Revenue. (Sec. 201.08(2), F.S.) In addition, circuit court clerks must report to the department the names and addresses of any individual, firm, or corporation that fails to affix the required stamps or notation on any taxable document recorded in the circuit court. (Sec. 201.12, F.S.)

For taxes collected on certain instruments to which stamps are not affixed, reports must be filed with the Department of Revenue by the comptroller, clerk of courts, or registered agent no later than seven working days after the end of the week in which collected. (Sec. 201.132, F.S.; Sec. 201.133, F.S.)

• *Assessment, Revision, and Appeals*

The statutes do not contain specific provisions relating to the assessment, revision, or appeal of documentary stamp taxes. However, the law does say that all revenue laws relating to the assessment of taxes are extended to the documentary stamp tax for the purpose of collecting stamp taxes omitted through mistake or fraud. (Sec. 201.16, F.S.) Apparently, this provision refers only to the state and does not operate to the benefit of the taxpayer.

In other statutes, the circuit court is given jurisdiction to hear cases involving the legality of taxes, assessments, and tolls. (Sec. 194.171, F.S.) In addition, the taxpayer is given the right to refuse an assessment by alleging its illegality and may apply to the chancery court for a determination of the question. (Sec. 68.01, F.S.)

Several regulations provide for conferences and protest procedures for taxes in general. (Rule 12-6.0033, F.A.C.)

• *Collection of Tax*

The revenue laws relating to the assessment and collection of taxes apply to the documentary stamp tax for the purpose of collecting taxes omitted through mistake or fraud. (Sec. 201.16, F.S.)

The tax required on promissory notes, nonnegotiable notes, and written obligations to pay money made in connection with retail charge account services is paid quarterly. (Sec. 201.08(2), F.S.)

Affixing and Cancelling of Stamps.—When an agent affixes documentary tax stamps, he writes or stamps on them the initials of his or its name and the date, so that the stamps cannot be used again. The stamps must be affixed in a way that their removal requires the continued application of water or steam, or as otherwise prescribed by the Department of Revenue. (Sec. 201.14, F.S.)

Exception for Recorded Document.—The country comptroller or clerk of the circuit court may collect the documentary stamp tax without affixing the stamps to the document to be recorded under the following conditions.

(1) A notation must be placed on the document showing the amount of tax paid and the county in which it was paid. The notation must be signed, initialed, or stamped with the name or initials of the comptroller, clerk, or designated agent.

(2) The taxes collected during any month, less the collection allowance, must be transmitted to the Department of Revenue no later than seven working days after the end of the week in which collected. A report certifying the amount of tax payable must be submitted with the remittance on forms furnished by the department.

(3) A register approved by the department must be maintained listing all recorded documents according to the agent's filing number assigned to each document.

Agents who use this procedure are subject to audit and must make all records available for inspection by the Department of Revenue. A bond posted at the agent's expense may be required. (Sec. 201.132, F.S.)

Any person who averages at least five taxable transactions per month must register with the Department of Revenue and remit tax due on documents which are not to be recorded. Prior to April 1, 1997, any person who uses an average of $150 in stamps or more per month or who engages in at least 50 transactions per month for six months may apply for permission to collect the tax in any transaction not recorded, without affixing any documentary tax stamps. The application is filed with the Department of Revenue for each place of business. The department issues certificates of registration to qualified applicants (Sec. 201.133, F.S.)

Exception for unrecorded document.—Persons who use this procedure must file a report by the 20th of each month showing the taxes collected for the preceding month. Payment must be remitted with the report. (Sec. 201.133, F.S.) The Department of Revenue may vary the number of returns and payments based on the amount of tax remitted for the preceding four calendar quarters, as follows: tax not exceeding $100, annual returns and payments; tax of at least $100 but not more than $500, semiannual returns and payments; and tax of at least $500 but not more than $1,000, quarterly returns and payments. Adequate records must be kept, and the certificate of registration can be revoked on certain grounds. (Sec. 201.133, F.S.)

• *Refunds and Remedies*

The statutes make no specific provision for a refund of documentary stamp taxes erroneously paid. However, the State Comptroller may make refunds of overpayments or erroneous payments of any tax, license, or account due. (Sec. 215.26(1), F.S.) Applications for refunds must generally be filed within three years after the date on which the tax was paid. The Comptroller may delegate the authority to accept refund applications to certain state agencies. (Sec. 215.26(2), F.S.)

The circuit courts have exclusive original jurisdiction over matters relating to property taxation. The court may refuse to hear a case unless the plaintiff pays the full amount of the assessed tax when the complaint is filed or before. (Sec. 194.171, F.S.)

Quasi-credits.—Though not characterized as credits, taxpayers that create new jobs under specific conditions are eligible for tax refunds from multiple tax types (including document stamp tax). The refunds are available to qualified defense contractors/space flight businesses, qualified target industry businesses, and qualified target industry businesses redeveloping a brownfield.

Economic Development Trust Fund refunds to qualified defense contractors and space flight business.—Qualified applicants may apply by January 31 of each fiscal year to the Department of Economic Opportunity for a refund from the Economic Development Trust Fund for the corporate income, sales and use, excise, property, documentary stamp, and communications services taxes due and paid by them, beginning with the applicant's first taxable year commencing after entering into a tax refund agreement. The amount of the refund is based on the number of jobs created by the taxpayer's activities. (Sec. 288.1045, F.S.).

Refunds for qualified target industry businesses.—Qualified target industry businesses, after entering into tax refund agreements with the Department of Economic Opportunity, are entitled to apply by January 31 of each fiscal year for refunds from the Economic Development Incentives Account for the corporate income, insurance premium, sales and use, intangible personal property, excise, and property taxes due and paid by them after entering into the agreement. The amount of the refund is based on the number of jobs created by the taxpayer's activities. (Sec. 288.106, F.S.).

Brownfield redevelopment bonus refund.—A bonus refund of property tax, sales and use tax, documentary stamp tax, corporate income tax, intangible personal property tax, emergency excise tax, or insurance premium tax is available to any qualified target industry business or "other eligible business" for each new Florida job created in a brownfield that is claimed on the business's annual tax refund claim. The amount of the refund is based on the number of jobs created by the taxpayer's activities. (Sec. 288.107, F.S.).

• *Payment of Tax*

County comptrollers or clerks of the circuit courts are authorized to collect documentary stamp tax on documents to be recorded. (Sec. 201.132, F.S.) Persons averaging at least five taxable transactions per month must register and pay tax directly to the Department of Revenue for documents subject to tax which are not required to be recorded. (Sec. 201.133, F.S.)

For bonds, shares, mortgages, and other taxable instruments, the documentary stamp tax is due at the time of transfer or sale. (Sec. 201.08(1), F.S.) For notes and wage assignments executed in connection with retail charge account services, the tax is paid quarterly and stamps are not required. (Sec. 201.08(2), F.S.)

Sales of timeshare interests in timeshare plans.—In recognition of the special escrow requirements that apply to sales of timeshare interests in timeshare plans by a developer, provisions are enacted to designate the time that certain tax payments are due.

For purposes of Florida documentary stamp tax on deeds and instruments on real property, the tax is due on the earlier of the date on which

(1) the deed or other instrument conveying the interest in Florida real property is recorded, or

(2) all conditions precedent to the release of the purchaser's escrowed funds or other qualifying property have been met.

(Sec. 201.02(10), F.S.)

Florida documentary stamp tax on promissory or nonnegotiable notes is due on the earlier of the date on which

(1) the note, other written obligation, mortgage, or other evidence of indebtedness is recorded or filed in Florida, or

(2) all conditions precedent to the release of the purchaser's escrowed funds or other qualifying property have been met.

(Sec. 201.08(08), F.S.)

In each of these instances, the second due date applies regardless of whether the developer has posted an alternative assurance. The tax is due on or before the 20th day of the month following the month in which the conditions were met.

• *Penalties*

Florida imposes several penalties to taxpayers who fail to pay documentary stamps taxes or fails to follow the administrative procedures set forth by the Department of Revenue in regards to the documentary stamp tax.

Failure to Allow Inspection of Books and Records.—Anyone subject to the documentary stamp tax who makes it difficult to enforce its provisions by refusing to allow full inspection of the books, records, documents, or premises that relate in any way to the taxpayer's liability is guilty of a second-degree misdemeanor. (Sec. 201.11, F.S.)

Making, Issuing or Accepting Documents on Which Tax Has Not Been Paid.— Anyone who makes, signs, issues, or accepts any taxable document without the full amount of documentary stamp tax having been paid is guilty of a first-degree misdemeanor. (Sec. 201.17(1), F.S.)

Failure to Cancel Stamps.—Anyone who uses adhesive stamps to denote payment of the documentary stamp tax without canceling or obliterating the stamps as required is guilty of a first-degree misdemeanor. (Sec. 201.17(1), F.S.)

Counterfeiting and Restoring.—Anyone who uses on any taxable document an adhesive stamp that has been removed from another document, is of insufficient value, or is forged or counterfeited is guilty of a first-degree misdemeanor. Anyone who willfully removes or alters the cancellation marks on a stamp or otherwise prepares or counterfeits an adhesive stamp with the intent to use it to avoid the documentary stamp tax, or who knowingly buys or sells a washed, restored, altered, or counterfeit stamp, is guilty of a third-degree felony. (Sec. 201.18, F.S.)

Additional penalties.—If any taxable document is found upon audit or at the time of recording not to show payment of the proper amount of tax or if the tax was not timely reported and paid, the person liable for the tax is subject to:

(1) Payment of the unpaid tax.

(2) A specific penalty added to the tax in the amount of 10% of any unpaid tax if the failure is for not more than 30 days, with an additional 10% of any unpaid tax for each additional 30 days, or fraction thereof, not to exceed a total penalty of 50%. In no event is the penalty less than $10.

(3) Payment of interest accruing from the date the tax is due until payment at the rate of 1% per month on the unpaid tax.

(Sec. 201.17(2), F.S.)

The Department of Revenue has the authority to settle or compromise any assessed interest or penalties that do not arise from fraud. (Sec. 213.21, F.S.)

Reports of clerks of circuit courts.—The clerk of the circuit court is required to report to the Department of Revenue any and all individuals, firms, and corporations who fail to affix the required documentary tax stamps, or a notation that the taxes have been paid directly to the department, on any taxable documents that are presented to the clerk for recording. (Sec. 201.12, F.S.)

¶37-051

[¶37-100]
MOTOR VEHICLES

[¶37-101] Motor Vehicles

Property taxation of motor vehicles is discussed at ¶20-275 Motor Vehicles and ¶20-325 Transportation Equipment. Sales taxation of motor vehicles is discussed at ¶60-570 Motor Vehicles.

[¶37-150]
ENVIRONMENTAL TAXES AND FEES

[¶37-151] Environmental taxes and fees

Discussed below are the various environmental taxes and fees collected by the Florida Department of Revenue.

Florida imposes several environmental taxes and fees, including the:

— dry cleaning gross receipts tax,

— perchloroethylene tax.

— inland protection tax,

— coastal protection tax,

— water quality tax, and

— commercial hazardous waste facilities gross receipt tax.

• *Dry cleaning gross receipts tax*

A gross receipts tax is levied on every person who engages in the business of laundering and dry cleaning clothing or other fabrics in Florida. A gross receipts tax is also levied on persons who run a drop-off service for laundering and dry cleaning clothing or other fabrics in Florida. (Sec. 376.70(1), F.S.; Rule 12B-11.0011)

Rate of Tax.—The tax is imposed at the rate of 2% of all charges imposed for the dry cleaning, laundering, or uniform rental or linen supply services. (Sec. 376.70(1), F.S.; Rule 12B-11.0011)

Exemptions.—An exemption from tax is provided for gross receipts from:

— coin-operated laundry machines;

— laundry done on a wash, dry, and fold basis;

— coin-operated dry cleaning machines, unless operated at an establishment primarily engaged in the business of dry cleaning clothing and other fabrics;

— uniform rental companies; and

— linen supply companies.

(Sec. 376.70(1), F.S.; Rule 12B-11.0011)

Gross receipts arising from charges for taxable laundry and dry cleaning services to persons who also impose charges to others for the same services are exempt. The Florida Department of Revenue must refund any tax remitted by such companies. (Sec. 376.70(5), F.S.; Rule 12B-11.0011)

Reports and payments.—The tax is due on the first day of the month succeeding the month in which the charge is imposed. The tax must be reported and paid on or before the 20th day of each month. The tax is to be reported on forms prescribed by the department. (Sec. 376.70(3), F.S.)

Collection and administration.—The department will administer, collect, and enforce the tax under the state sales tax procedures. Such procedures include those regarding the filing of consolidated returns, the granting of sale for resale exemptions, and interest and penalties on delinquent taxes. (Sec. 376.70(6)(a), F.S.)

The dry cleaning gross receipts tax is not to be included in the computation of estimated taxes. The dealer's credit for collecting taxes and fees does not apply to the dry cleaning gross receipts tax, nor does the provision prohibiting the absorption of tax. (Sec. 376.70(6)(b), F.S.)

The department is authorized to establish audit procedures and to assess delinquent taxes. (Sec. 376.70(6)(c), F.S.)

The department may not deny eligibility in the dry cleaning solvent cleanup program because of failure to submit gross receipts tax unless the department:

    (1) ascertains the amount of delinquent tax due and notifies the dry cleaning cleanup program applicant and the real property owner of that amount in writing, and

    (2) provides a method of payment for the facility owner, facility operator, and the real property owner.

Once the department has fulfilled these requirements, the delinquent taxpayer must prove that the failure to pay was not due to willful and overt actions in order to be eligible for the dry cleaning solvent cleanup program. (Sec. 376.70(7), F.S.)

• *Perchloroethylene tax*

The perchloroethylene tax is imposed on the sale of perchloroethylene (tetrachloroethylene) to dry cleaning facilities within Florida or the importation of the product into the state by dry cleaning facilities. (Sec. 376.75(1), F.S.) Persons subject to the perchloroethylene tax or who sell tax-paid perchloroethylene, other than retail dealers, must separately state the amount of the tax paid on any charge ticket, sales slip, invoice, or other tangible evidence of the sale or must certify on the sales document that the tax has been paid. (Sec. 376.75(4), F.S.) All perchloroethylene imported, produced, or sold in Florida is presumed to be subject to the tax. Persons who have purchased perchloroethylene for use in their dry cleaning facility within Florida must document that the tax has been paid or must pay the tax directly to the Department of Revenue. (Sec. 376.75(5), F.S.; Rule 12B-12.0031)

The perchloroethylene tax is not subject to sales and use tax. (Sec. 376.75(1), F.S.)

Basis, rate of tax.—A tax of $5 per gallon is levied on the sale of perchloroethylene in Florida to a dry cleaning facility located in the state or the import of such product into the state by a dry cleaning facility. (Sec. 376.75(1), F.S.)

Credits and refunds.—If a taxpayer has paid tax on perchloroethylene and the product is exported from Florida, or is acquired for a purpose other than use in a dry cleaning facility within the state, or for sale, resale, or other transfer for such use, the taxpayer is entitled to take a credit for the amount of tax paid or to apply to the department for a refund, after refunding the tax to the person who incurred the tax burden. (Sec. 376.75(11), F.S.; Rule 12B-12.007)

Records and payments.—The tax is due on the first day of the month succeeding the month of sale. (Sec. 376.75(3), F.S.) The tax must be reported and paid on or before the 20th day of each month. (Sec. 376.75(3), F.S.; Rule 12B-12.006) The tax is to be reported on forms prescribed by the department.

Returns other than monthly: The department may authorize a quarterly return and payment when the tax remitted by the licensee for the preceding quarter did not exceed $100. (Sec. 376.75(7), F.S.) A semiannual return and payment may be authorized when the tax remitted by the licensee for the preceding six months did not exceed $200. An annual return and payment may be authorized when the tax remitted by the licensee for the preceding 12 months did not exceed $400.

Registered producers, importers, sellers, and other transferors of perchloroethylene who have not made any taxable sales or taxable transfers during the year must file a form with the department stating the quantity of perchloroethylene sold or transferred and indicating that all sales were tax-exempt from tax, and any other information prescribed by the department (Sec. 376.75(6), F.S.) A claim that the perchloroethylene was not sold or transferred to a dry cleaning facility for eventual use in a dry cleaning facility in Florida may be substantiated with a certificate, signed by a transferee of the product and signed under the penalty of perjury, stating that the transferee does not own or operate a dry cleaning facility and will not use the product in a dry cleaning facility in Florida and signed under penalty of perjury.

Collection and administration.—The department will administer, collect, and enforce the tax under the general state sales tax procedures (Sec. 376.75(9)(a), F.S.) The provisions regarding the authority to audit and make assessments, the keeping of books and records, and interest and penalties on delinquent taxes are made specifically applicable.

The perchloroethylene tax is not to be included in the computation of estimated taxes. The dealer's credit for collecting taxes and fees does not apply to the perchloroethylene tax, nor does the provision prohibiting the absorption of tax.

The department is authorized to establish audit procedures and to assess delinquent taxes. (Sec. 376.75(9)(c), F.S.)

• *Inland protection tax*

The Inland Protection tax is one of four taxes (including the perchloroethylene tax, coastal protection tax, and water quality tax) collectively known as the pollutants tax.

Rate.—The rates of tax, which depends on the balance in the Inland Protection Trust Fund, are:

— 30¢ when the unobligated balance is between $100 million and $150 million.

— 60¢ when the unobligated balance is above $50 million, but below $100 million.

— 80¢ when the unobligated balance is $50 million or less.

Any change in the tax rate is effective for a minimum of six months, unless the unobligated balance of the fund requires that a higher rate be levied. When the unobligated balance exceeds $150 million, the tax is discontinued until the unobligated balance reaches $100 million. (Sec. 206.9935(3), F.S.)

Application.—The inland protection tax does not apply to:

(1) American Society for Testing and Materials grades no. 5 and no. 6 residual oils; intermediate fuel oils used by the taxpayer for bunkering with a viscosity of 30 and higher; asphalt oil; petrochemical feedstocks; and pesticides, ammonia, chlorine, and derivatives thereof;

(2) petroleum products exported from the first storage facility at which they are held in the state by the licensed refiner who first imported the products; and

(3) crude oil produced at a regulated well site and exported from that site by the producer exclusively by pipeline, truck, or rail to beyond the jurisdiction of the state without intermediate storage or stoppage.

(Sec. 206.9941, F.S.)

A licensed refiner who has purchased tax-paid petroleum products from another licensed refiner and who exports such products from the state may deduct the amount of inland protection tax paid from the amount of petroleum taxes owed to the state. Any licensed importer or wholesaler who has purchased tax-paid petroleum products from a licensed refiner and who exports such products from the state may apply for a refund of the amount of inland protection tax paid. Any licensed importer who has directly remitted the inland protection tax and subsequently exports the petroleum product from the state may deduct the tax paid from any amount of petroleum tax subsequently owed to the state. (Sec. 206.9942, F.S.)

• *Coastal protection tax*

The coastal protection tax is one of four taxes (including the perchloroethylene tax, inland protection tax, and water quality tax) collectively known as the pollutants tax.

Rate.—The tax rate is 2¢ per barrel. The 2¢ per barrel rate is a base rate, and may be increased to a rate not to exceed 10¢ per barrel if a discharge of catastrophic proportions significantly reduces the balance in the Coastal Protection Fund. The tax may be suspended depending on the balance in the Fund. (Sec. 206.9935(1), F.S.)

Excluding natural gas drilling activities, if offshore oil drilling activity is approved by the U. S. Department of the Interior for the waters off the coast of Florida in the Atlantic Ocean, Gulf of Mexico or Straits of Florida, the excise tax is 2¢ per barrel of pollutant produced or imported into Florida with the proceeds deposited into the Coastal Protection Trust Fund with a $100 million cap. If a discharge of catastrophic proportions occurs, the excise tax may be increased to an amount not to exceed 10¢ per barrel of pollutants for a period of time sufficient to pay any proven claim against the Fund and restore a $50 million balance to the Fund. For any fiscal year following the year in which the Fund is equal to or exceeds $50 million, the excise tax is 2¢ to be deposited into the Fund with a $100 million cap. (Sec. 206.9935(1), F.S.)

• *Water quality tax*

The water quality tax is one of four taxes (including the perchloroethylene tax, coastal protection tax, and inland protection tax) collectively known as the pollutants tax.

Rate.—The rate of tax depends on the balance in the Water Quality Assurance Trust Fund, and may be increased, decreased or suspended. (Sec. 206.9935(2)(a), F.S.)

When the unobligated balance is below $3 million, the rates are:

— 5.9¢ per gallon of solvents,

— 2.5¢ per gallon of motor oil or other lubricants,

— 2¢ per barrel of ammonia, and

— 5¢ per barrel of petroleum products, pesticides, and chlorine.

(Sec. 206.9935(2)(b), F.S.)

When the unobligated balance of the fund exceeds $12 million, the rates are:

— 2.36¢ per gallon of solvents,

— 1¢ per gallon of motor oil or other lubricants, and

— 2¢ per barrel of petroleum products, pesticides, ammonia, and chlorine.

(Sec. 206.9935(2)(b), F.S.)

Changes in the rate take effect on the first day of the month after 30 days' notification to the Department of Revenue that the fund balance has changed to a limit that necessitates a rate change. (Sec. 206.9935(2)(b), F.S.)

¶37-151

• *Commercial hazardous waste facilities gross receipt tax*

A 3-percent tax is hereby levied on the annual gross receipts of commercial hazardous waste facilities. The tax is payable on or before July 1 by the owner of the facility to the local government. The owner or operator of each commercial hazardous waste facility must file a statement, which indicates the gross receipts from all imposed charges during the preceding calendar year before or no January 25 of each year. The charges are for the storage, treatment, or disposal of hazardous waste at the facility. (Sec. 403.7215, F.S.)

[¶37-300]

SEVERANCE TAXES

[¶37-301] Severance Taxes

Excise taxes are imposed on the severance of sulfur and solid minerals, and the severance and production of gas and oil, in Florida. The tax on oil is imposed generally at a rate of 5% of gross value for small-well and tertiary oil and 8% for all other oil. The gas and sulfur tax rates will be determined by the Department of Revenue.

Additional levies are imposed for the conservation of oil and gas, not as taxes but as fees paid for all permits. A fee is charged for any application for a permit to drill an oil or gas well.

The excise tax on the severance of solid materials is imposed on every person engaged in the business of severing solid minerals from the soil and waters of Florida for commercial use. The tax is 8% of the value of the solid minerals severed, except that the tax on severing phosphate rock and heavy minerals is a base rate adjusted for inflation.

Permits are required of all owners wanting to drill or abandon wells or dry holes. No licenses are required for production or severance of oil or gas. (Sec. 377.24, F.S.)

Discussed below are the excise taxes on:

— oil,

— gas,

— sulfur, and

— minerals, including solid minerals, phosphate rock, Lake Belt area limerock and sand, and heavy minerals.

Also discussed are the following administrative topics:

— constitutional issues,

— assessment, revision, and appeal,

— penalties and interest,

— refunds and credits, and

— forms.

• *Constitutional issues*

In *Michigan-Wisconsin Pipe Line Co. v. Calvert*, a 1954 Texas case, 347 U.S. 157, 74 S.Ct. 396, it was held that a tax on the occupation of "gathering gas" measured by the entire volume of gas "taken", as applied to an interstate natural gas pipeline company, where the taxable incident is the taking of gas from the outlet of an independent gasoline plant within the state for the purpose of immediate interstate transmission, violated the commerce clause of the Constitution and was invalid.

In *Oklahoma Tax Commission v. The Texas Company, et al.*, a 1949 Oklahoma case, 336 U.S. 342, 69 S.Ct. 561, it was held that lessees of mineral rights in allotted and restricted Indian lands are not exempted by the Constitution from payment to Oklahoma of nondiscriminatory gross production and excise taxes on petroleum produced from such lands. The taxes imposed on the operations of the lessees constitute nothing but a theoretical interference with governmental functions. Private persons claiming immunity for their ordinary business operations, although the same may be conducted in connection with governmental activities, have no implied constitutional immunity from taxation based on asserted hypothetical interference with governmental functions. Such immunity may be granted only by action of Congress.

State constitution.—According to the Florida constitution, no tax will be levied except pursuant to law. Additionally, state ad valorem taxes will not be levied on real estate or tangible personal property. All other forms of taxation will be preempted to the state except as provided by general law. (Sec. 1, Article VII, Fla. Const.)

• *Oil*

An excise tax is imposed on each person who severs oil in the state for commercial purposes. The tax is imposed on the basis of the entire production of oil in the state, including royalty interest. (Sec. 211.02, F.S.) Gas-phase hydrocarbons that are transported into the state, injected in the gaseous phase into a permitted natural gas storage facility, and later recovered as a liquid hydrocarbon are excluding from the definition of "oil."(Sec. 211.02(7), F.S.)

The tax is imposed on the producer of the product in proportion to the producer's ownership of the taxable product at the time of the severance. The operator is required to collect the tax by deducting the proportionate amount of tax due from amounts due each producer and withholding the amount deducted from any payments made to producers. Any operator selling taxable products on the open market is required to deduct the amount of tax imposed from any amounts due interest owners and to withhold the amount deducted from any payments made to interest owners. If taxable products have been sold under a contract that requires the purchaser to pay the owners directly, the operator is not required to deduct tax. The purchaser is required to collect the tax by deducting it from the amount due the owners and withholding it from payments made to each of the owners. (Sec. 211.09, F.S.)

A person wishing to drill a well is required to apply for a permit before any drilling begins. (Sec. 377.24(1), F.S.) A fee of $2,000 must be paid with each application. (Reg. Sec. 16C-26.003(9)) The owner of an abandoned well or a dry hole is required to pay a fee, as set by the Department of Environmental Protection, and plug each hole. (Sec. 377.24(3), F.S.)

Exemptions.—Other than the severance tax, no other excise or license taxes will be imposed upon the production of oil by removal from the earth or water in Florida. (Sec. 211.13, F.S.)

An exemption is provided for oil production used for lease operations on the lease or unit where produced. (Sec. 211.027(1), F.S.; Rule 12B-7.006, F.A.C.)

Although not explicitly exempt from tax, gas-phase hydrocarbons that are transported into the state, injected in the gaseous phase into a permitted natural gas storage facility, and later recovered as a liquid hydrocarbon are excluding from the definition of "oil."(Sec. 211.02(7), F.S.)

Basis of tax.—The tax is measured by the value of the oil produced and saved or sold during a month. In this context, "value" is defined as the sale or market price of oil at the mouth of the well in its natural, unrefined condition. (Sec. 211.02, F.S.)

Flat fees have been set for permits to drill or abandon a well or dry hole. (Sec. 377.24 F.S.)

Rates.—Those who sever tertiary and mature field recovery oil in Florida are subject to a tiered tax rate:

    — the first tier tax rate will be 1% levied on the first $60 of gross value (the tiered value per barrel for this tiered tax rate cannot exceed $60);

— the second tier tax rate will be 7% levied on a gross value greater than $60 and less than $80 (the tiered value per barrel for this tiered tax rate will be the total value per barrel minus $60, and cannot exceed $20);.

— the third tier tax rate will be 9% levied on a gross value of $80 or greater (the tiered value per barrel for this tiered tax rate will be the total value per barrel minus $80).

(Sec. 211.02, F.S.)

"Tertiary oil" is defined as the excess of oil produced as a result of the actual use of tertiary recovery methods in a qualified tertiary recovery project, over the oil which could have been produced by continued maximum feasible production methods in use before the tertiary methods. (Sec. 211.02, F.S.)

"Mature field recovery oil" is defined as oil that is recovered from new wells that went into production after July 1, 2012, in oil fields that were discovered prior to 1981. (Sec. 211.02, F.S.)

Small well oil is taxed at 5% of gross value. Ordinary oil production is taxed at 8% of gross value. (Sec. 211.02(1), F.S.)

An additional excise tax of 12.5% of gross value is imposed on oil that has escaped from wells and been recovered from streams and lakes. (Sec. 211.04(1), F.S. Code)

There is a fee required for a permit to drill each well. (Sec. 377.24(1), F.S.) A fee, as set by the Department of Environmental Protection, is imposed when an owner files the required notice of intention to abandon a well or plug a dry hole. (Sec. 377.24(3), F.S.)

Payment.—Payment of tax is due on the 25th day of the month following the month production occurred (Sec. 211.075, F.S.)

The Comptroller holds an assessment collected on escaped oil in a special escrow account for a period of 12 months, at which time the rightful owner of the royalty interest may claim the assessment. (Sec. 211.04, F.S.)

Reports.—Producers of oil are required to file on or before the 25th day of the month following the month production occurred. (Sec. 211.075, F.S.)

•*Gas*

An excise tax is imposed on each person who severs native gas in the state for commercial purposes. The tax is imposed on the basis of the entire production of gas in the state, including royalty interest. (Sec. 211.025, F.S.; Sec. 377.19, F.S.)

The tax is imposed on the producer of the product in proportion to the producer's ownership of the taxable product at the time of the severance. The operator is required to collect the tax by deducting the proportionate amount of tax due from amounts due each producer and withholding the amount deducted from any payments made to producers. Any operator selling taxable products on the open market is required to deduct the amount of tax imposed from any amounts due interest owners and to withhold the amount deducted from any payments made to interest owners. If taxable products have been sold under a contract that requires the purchaser to pay the owners directly, the operator is not required to deduct tax. The purchaser is required to collect the tax by deducting it from the amount due the owners and withholding it from payments made to each of the owners. (Sec. 211.09, F.S.)

A person wishing to drill a well or before storing gas in or recovering gas from a natural gas storage reservoir is required to apply for *a permit before any drilling/ storage begins. (Sec. 377.24(1), F.S.) A fee of $2,000 must be paid with each application. (Reg. Sec. 16C-26.003(9)) The owner of an abandoned well or a dry hole is required to pay a fee, as set by the Department of Environmental Protection, and plug each hole. (Sec. 377.24(3), F.S.)

Exemptions.—Other than the severance tax, no other excise or license taxes will be imposed upon the production of gas by removal from the earth or water in Florida. (Sec. 211.13, F.S.)

An exemption is provided for

— gas production used for lease operations on the lease or unit where produced;

— gas that is returned to a horizon or horizons in the field where they were produced; and

— gas vented or flared directly into the atmosphere.

(Sec. 211.027(1)—(3), F.S.; Rule 12B-7.006, F.A.C.)

Basis of tax.—The tax imposed on gas is determined by volume, in mcf, of gas produced and sold or used by a producer during the month. It is measured at the point where the gas is identifiable as to quality and type and can be transported for further use or processing. (Sec. 211.025, F.S.)

Flat fees have been set for permits to drill or abandon a well or dry hole. (Sec. 377.24, F.S.)

Rates.—Effective July 1, 2022, through June 30, 2023, the production of gas is taxed at the rate of $0.280 per MCF. (*Tax Information Publication, No. 22B07-02*, Florida Department of Revenue, May 10, 2022)

Effective July 1, 2021 through June 30, 2022, the production of gas is taxed at the rate of $0.125 per MCF. (*Tax Information Publication, No. 21B07-01*, Florida Department of Revenue, May 20, 2021)

Payment.—Payment of tax is due by the 25th day of the second month following the end of each calendar quarter. Declarations of estimated tax are due by the 25th day of the month following production, and 90% of the tax is then due. (Sec. 211.075, F.S.)

Reports.—Producers of gas or sulfur are required to file a report on or before the 25th day of the second month following the end of each calendar quarter. (Sec. 211.075 F.S.)

• *Sulfur*

An excise tax is imposed on each person who severs sulfur in the state for commercial use. The tax is imposed on the basis of the entire production of the sulfur in the state, including royalty interest. (Sec. 211.026, F.S.)

The tax is imposed on the producer of the product in proportion to the producer's ownership of the taxable product at the time of the severance. The operator is required to collect the tax by deducting the proportionate amount of tax due from amounts due each producer and withholding the amount deducted from any payments made to producers. Any operator selling taxable products on the open market is required to deduct the amount of tax imposed from any amounts due interest owners and to withhold the amount deducted from any payments made to interest owners. If taxable products have been sold under a contract that requires the purchaser to pay the owners directly, the operator is not required to deduct tax. The purchaser is required to collect the tax by deducting it from the amount due the owners and withholding it from payments made to each of the owners. (Sec. 211.09, F.S.)

Exemptions.—Other than the severance tax, no other excise or license taxes will be imposed upon the production of sulfur by removal from the earth or water in Florida. (Sec. 211.13, F.S.)

¶37-301

Basis of tax.—The tax imposed is determined by the long tons of sulfur produced or recovered by a producer during the month from the hydrogen sulfide gas contained in oil or gas production from a well. It is measured when the sulfur is in its molten, elemental state, and can be sold, delivered, transported, or stored. (Sec. 211.026, F.S.)

Rates.—Effective July 1, 2022, through June 30, 2022, sulfur production is taxed at the rate of $6.54 per ton. (*Tax Information Publication, No. 22B07-02*, Florida Department of Revenue, May 10, 2022)

Effective July 1, 2021, through June 30, 2022, sulfur production is taxed at the rate of $4.78 per ton. (*Tax Information Publication, No. 21B07-01*, Florida Department of Revenue, May 20, 2021)

Payment.—Payment of tax is due by the 25th day of the second month following the end of each calendar quarter. Declarations of estimated tax are due by the 25th day of the month following production, and 90% of the tax is then due. (Sec. 211.075, F.S.)

Reports.—Producers of gas or sulfur are required to file a report on or before the 25th day of the second month following the end of each calendar quarter. (Sec. 211.075 F.S.)

• *Minerals*

An excise tax is imposed on every individual who severs solid minerals for commercial use. Separate excise taxes on the producers of phosphate rock or heavy minerals are imposed under sections 211.325 and 211.326 respectively. (Sec. 211.31, F.S.)

Exemptions.—Those solid minerals not subject to tax include solid minerals sold to governmental agencies in the state, minerals extracted for the purpose of improving the site of severance, minerals severed solely for direct use in agriculture, and minerals upon which the tax is ultimately paid by the state. (Sec. 211.3108, F.S.)

Purchases of machinery and equipment used by new or expanding businesses that mine or process solid minerals or phosphate are exempt. (Sec. 212.08(5)(b)5., F.S.)

Basis of tax.—The imposition of tax on solid minerals severed from water or soil is determined by the value of the identifiable solid minerals at the point of severance. (Sec. 211.31 F.S.)

The tax on phosphate rock is based on the bone dry tons produced at the point of severance. (Sec. 211.3103, F.S.) The tax on heavy minerals is measured on the basis of bone dry tons severed for commercial use at the point of severance. (Sec. 211.3106 F.S.)

Rates.—Tax rates are as follows.

Solid minerals.—The excise tax on the severance of solid minerals other than phosphate rock and heavy minerals for 2022 is 8% of the taxable value of the minerals produced. (Sec. 211.31, F.S.; *Tax Information Publication 22B07-01*, Florida Department of Revenue, March 21, 2022)

Phosphate rock.—For tax years January 1, 2015 to December 31, 2022, the tax rate is $1.80 per ton. (Sec. 211.3103, F.S.; *Tax Information Publication 22B07-01*, Florida Department of Revenue, March 21, 2022)

For information regarding the sales and use tax exemption for equipment used in severance, mining or production of phosphate, see Manufacturing, Processing, Assembling, or Refining.

Lake Belt Area limerock and sand.—The per-ton fees on the extraction of limerock and sand within the Miami-Dade County Lake Belt Area are as follows: the mitigation fee rate is $0.05, effective January 1, 2018, and thereafter. The water treatment plant upgrade fee rate is $0.06, effective July 1, 2015, to June 30, 2018. These fee rates are published by the Florida Department of Revenue and must be used when completing Form DR-146, Miami-Dade County Lake Belt Mitigation and Water Treatment Plant Upgrade Fees Tax Return. These rates should be used indefinitely until a statutory change is enacted by law. Filing of the return and payment are due on the 1st and are considered late after the 20th day of the month following each collection period. If the 20th falls on a Saturday, Sunday, or state or federal holiday, a timely return must be postmarked or hand-delivered on the first business day following the 20th. A return must be filed for each collection period, even if no tax is due or the fees were paid electronically. (*Tax Information Publication, No. 15B07-03*, Florida Department of Revenue, June 19, 2015)

The requirement to collect the water treatment fee will end once the total amount of proceeds collected reaches the amount necessary to design and construct the upgrade. (Sec. 373.41492(2), F.S.)

Heavy minerals.—For tax year 2022, the severance tax rate applicable to heavy minerals in Florida is $3.80 per ton. (*Tax Information Publication 22B07-01*, Florida Department of Revenue, March 21, 2022)

The tax rate is calculated by multiplying the base rate for heavy minerals by the base rate adjustment for the tax year, as determined by the Department of Revenue. The base rate adjustment, if any, is based on the change in the five-year moving average of the annual producer price indexes for titanium dioxide in relation to the base period. The Department of Revenue can make appropriate adjustments to compute the base rate adjustment if the producer price index for titanium dioxide is substantially revised or if the base year used at an index of 100 is changed. The department will select a comparable index in the event the producer price index for titanium is discontinued. Information such as base rate, adjustment and resulting tax rate will be furnished by April 15th of the current year. (Sec. 211.3106, F.S.)

A credit against severance taxes due is available for sales taxes paid on equipment used in the mining or processing of heavy minerals.

Returns.—Sales invoices must separately state the limerock and sand mitigation fee. Miners and producers must report the fee on Form DR-146, Miami-Dade County Lake Belt Mitigation Fee Monthly Return, by the 20th day of the month following the month of the taxable transaction. Returns must be filed and payments must be made electronically when required by the Department of Revenue or when no fee is due with a return for reporting fees. (Sec. 373.41492, F.S.; Rule 12B-7.030, F.A.C.)

The fee is not considered in determining general estimated sales tax payment, and no dealer's credit applies to fee collections. Limerock or sand used within a mine from which it is extracted is not subject to the fee. Authority to audit and assess mitigation fees, to adopt rules, and to prescribe and publish forms for administration purposes, rests with the Department, which must collect, administer, and enforce fees in accordance with general sales tax procedures. (Sec. 373.41492, F.S.)

A declaration of estimated tax must be filed on or before the first day of the fifth month of the taxable year. The tax must be paid in four equal installments. The first installment must be paid at the time of the required filing of the declaration; the second and third installments must be paid before the second day of the 7th and 10th months of the taxable year, respectively; and the fourth installment must be paid before the second day of the next taxable year. (Sec. 211.33, F.S.)

Reports.—Producers of solid minerals must file annual returns on or before April 1. (Sec. 211.33(2)(a), F.S.)

¶37-301

• *Forms*

The Department of Revenue prescribes the following forms to be used in the administration of Florida severance taxes. (Sec. 211.125, F.S.; Sec. 12B-7.008, F.A.C.; Rule 12B-7.026, F.A.C.)

DR-142 . . . . Solid Mineral Severance Tax Return

DR-142ES . . . . Declaration/Installment Payment of Estimated Solid Mineral Severance Tax

DR-144 . . . . Gas and Sulfur Production Quarterly Tax Return

DR-144ES . . . . Declaration of Estimated Gas and Sulfur Production Tax

DR-145 . . . . Oil Production Monthly Tax Return

DR-145X . . . . Oil Production Monthly Amended Tax Return

DR-146 . . . . . Miami-Dade County Lake Belt Mitigation Fee Monthly Return

For conservation purposes, the Florida Department of Environmental Protection prescribes the forms needed to be filed.

• *Assessment, revision, and appeal*

Review from an assessing official is permitted according to Article V, State Constitution, Florida Appellate Rules. (Sec. 377.35, F.S.)

The tax constitutes a first lien on production until it is paid, whether or not the taxable product is in the possession of the producer or any purchaser. (Sec. 211.09, F.S.)

In the event of a deficiency, the Department of Revenue will issue its written notice to the taxpayer or the tax, penalties and interest due. Full payment of the total amount assessed must be made in the manner prescribed by the department. (Sec. 211.125, F.S.)

Taxable oil shown in a required monthly report to have escaped from wells and to have been recovered from streams, lakes, ravines, or other natural depressions is subject to an additional assessment by the Department of Revenue if the monthly report does not disclose the actual source of the oil. (Sec. 211.04(1), F.S.)

Estimated tax paid will be considered assessed on the due date for the taxpayer's return for the taxable year. (Sec. 211.33(l)(e), F.S.)

Electronic funds transfer.—The Executive Director of the Florida Department of Revenue is authorized to require a taxpayer to file returns and remit payments electronically when the amount of taxes paid in the prior state fiscal year reached a certain threshold. (Sec. 213.755, F.S.; Rule 12-24.003, F.A.C.)

• *Penalties and interest*

Florida provides a number of penalties for failure to abide by severance reporting and payment requirements. For information on Florida interest rates on underpayments and overpayments of tax, including oil, gas and sulfur production tax, see Interest Rates.

Oil, gas, and sulfur production.—Failure to file a return will result in a delinquency penalty of 10% for each month, not to exceed 50%. If no tax is due with the return, the delinquency penalty imposed is $50 per month, not to exceed $300 in the aggregate. (Sec. 211.076(2), F.S.)

The failure to pay any part of the tax imposed by the due date will result in the addition of interest at a rate of 12% per year from the due date until the time of payment. (Sec. 211.076(1), F.S.)

A taxpayer making a substantial underpayment of tax is required to pay a penalty of 30% of the underpayment in addition to the delinquency penalty. (Sec.

211.076(3), F.S.) No penalty is assessed for underpayment of estimated tax if the total amount of estimated tax paid on or before the due date equals or exceeds the lesser of:

(1) 90% of the tax finally due for the month, or

(2) the amount of tax determined by the tax rate applicable for the month multiplied by the taxable production for the previous month.

(Sec. 211.076(4), F.S.)

Solid minerals.—The taxpayer is liable for interest at the rate of 12% per year and for a penalty at the rate of 20% per year upon any underpayment of estimated tax.

The amount of any underpayment of estimated tax is the excess of the amount of the installment which would be required to be paid if the estimated tax were equal to 80% of the tax shown on the return, or, if no return were filed, 80% of the tax for the year over the amount of the installment paid on or before the last date prescribed for payment.

The period of underpayment for which interest and penalties will be imposed will begin on the date payment was due and will end on the date that the underpayment is paid.

No penalty or interest will be imposed if the total amount of all payments made on the final day prescribed for payment of the installment equals or exceeds the amount that would have been required to be paid on or before that date if the estimated tax were the lesser of

(1) an amount equal to 80% of the tax finally due for the taxable year, or

(2) an amount equal to the tax shown on the taxpayer's return for the preceding taxable year, if a return showing a liability for tax was filed by the taxpayer for the preceding year.

(Sec. 211.33(1)(f), F.S.)

A delinquency penalty of 10% per month up to 50% of the total tax will be imposed if a tax return is not filed by April 1st for the preceding year due to negligence or intentional disregard of the rules. Additionally, interest will be imposed on the unpaid balance of any such tax that has become delinquent at 12% per year, from April 1st to the date of the payment. Interest will be collected and paid in the same manner. (Sec. 211.33(2), F.S.)

• *Refunds and credits*

Florida has provisions for severance tax refunds and credits.

Strong Families Tax Credit.—Beginning January 1, 2022, a credit of 100% of an eligible contribution made to an eligible charitable organization under the Strong Families Tax Credit Program is authorized against the severance tax on oil and gas production. However, the combined credit under this provision and the tax credit for contributions to nonprofit scholarship funding organizations may not exceed 50% of the tax due on the return on which the credit is taken. If the combined credit exceeds 50% of the tax due on the return, the credit must first be taken under the credit for contributions to nonprofit scholarship funding organizations. (Sec. 211.0253, F.S.; Sec. 402.62, F.S.)

Oil, gas, and sulfur.—The Department of Revenue may refund or credit overpayments of tax revealed by audit or for which a timely claim for refund has been made. Claims for refund must be filed within five years after the date the tax was paid. (Sec. 211.125(6), F.S.)

When a claimant has established ownership of escaped oil, the claimant will be paid the proportionate part of the additional collection in escrow. The Attorney General must approve all such distributions. (Sec. 211.04, F.S.)

Solid minerals.—The Department of Revenue is required to provide by rule for a credit against estimated tax for any amount determined to be an overpayment of the tax for the preceding tax year. (Sec. 211.33(1)(d), F.S.)

A reclamation and restoration program must be instituted upon each site of severance subject to tax. (Sec. 211.32(1)(a), F.S.) Such a program may include qualified sites other than the site of severance as part of the program of reclamation. (Sec. 211.32(1)(b), F.S.)

The Comptroller will issue refunds upon verification in an amount equal to 100% of the costs incurred in mandatory reclamation of land subject to the tax on severance of solid minerals, or 100% of the fair market value of land transferred to the state as part of accomplishing reclamation.

No refund is allowed exceeding the amount of taxes paid into the Land Reclamation Trust Fund. The general fund should not exceed 50% for phosphate rock and the refund should not exceed 25%. A portion of the trust fund can be held back until reclamation is complete, and the department is authorized to establish time schedules for the completion of programs.

A claim for refund must be filed annually within 60 days after the taxpayer has paid the tax for the preceding taxable year. The date for determining the portion of the land reclamation trust fund for which refund claims have not been timely filed and allowed is July 1st of each year. (Sec. 211.32(1)(d), F.S.)

Florida Tax Credit Scholarship Program.—Taxpayers who pay tax on oil production or gas production in Florida may apply to the department for a credit allocation for contributions made to nonprofit scholarship funding organization. Taxpayers must submit an Application for Tax Credit for Contributions to Nonprofit Scholarship Funding Organizations (Form DR-116000) to the department. (Sec. 211.0251; Rule 12-29.002)

[¶37-350]

UNCLAIMED PROPERTY

[¶37-351] Unclaimed Property

Generally, property that is unclaimed by its rightful owner is presumed abandoned after a specified period of years following the date upon which the owner may demand the property or the date upon which the obligation to pay or distribute the property arises, whichever comes first.

What is unclaimed property?

Generally, all intangible property, including any income or increment thereon less any lawful charges, that is held, issued, or owing in the ordinary course of the holder's business and that the owner fails to claim for more than five years after the property becomes payable or distributable is presumed unclaimed.

COMMENT: Escheat is an area of potential federal/state conflict. A federal statute may preempt state escheat provisions, as for instance Sec. 514(a) of the Employee Retirement Income Security Act of 1974 (ERISA). Pursuant to this provision, the Department of Labor and Workforce Development has been of the opinion that funds of missing participants in a qualified employee benefit plan must stay in the plan despite a state escheat provision because ERISA preempts application of the state escheat laws with respect to such funds (Advisory Opinion 94-41A, Department of Labor, Pension and Welfare Benefit Administration, Dec. 7, 1994). Some states have challenged the federal position on this and similar narrowly delineated situations. In the case of federal tax refunds, IRC Sec. 6408 disallows refunds if the refund would escheat to a state.

Practitioners are thus advised that a specific situation where federal and state policy cross on the issue of escheat may, at this time, be an area of unsettled law.

What are the dormancy periods for unclaimed property?

General rule. Generally, intangible property, including income or increment derived from the property, less lawful charges, that is held, issued or owing in the ordinary course of a holder's business and that has remained unclaimed by the owner for more than five years after becoming payable or distributable is presumed abandoned. Other presumptive periods for abandonment apply to certain types of property.

Checks and drafts. Any sum payable on a check, draft, or similar instrument (but not including traveler's checks and money orders) on which a banking or financial organization is directly liable which has been outstanding for more than five years after it was payable (or after its issuance, if an instrument is payable on demand) is presumed unclaimed, unless within the five-year period the owner has communicated with the bank or otherwise indicated an interest.

Bank accounts. Any demand, savings, or matured time deposit with a bank or financial institution is presumed unclaimed after five years unless, within the five-year period, the owner has increased or decreased the balance of his account, established a relationship with the bank, communicated in writing or by documented telephone contact with the bank or otherwise indicated interest concerning the property.

Property distributable in the course of demutualization or related reorganization of an insurance company. Unclaimed property payable or distributable in the course of a demutualization of an insurance company is presumed unclaimed five years after the earlier of the date of last contact with the policyholder or the date the property became payable or distributable.

Gift certificates, gift cards and credit memos. A gift certificate or credit memo issued by a qualifying financial institution or money transmitter that is redeemable by multiple unaffiliated merchants is presumed abandoned after five years and must be reported. However, generally, an unredeemed gift certificate or credit memo is not required to be reported as unclaimed property.

Stock and other intangibles. Stock or other intangible ownership interest in a business association is presumed abandoned three years after the earliest of the date:

— of the most recent dividend, stock split, or other distribution unclaimed by the apparent owner;

— of a statement of account or other notification or communication that was returned as undeliverable; or

— the holder discontinued mailings, notifications, or communications to the apparent owner.

Other dormancy periods. Most states also have specified dormancy periods for:

Business association dissolutions/refunds,

Insurance policies,

IRAs/retirement funds,

Money orders,

Proceeds from class action suits,

Property held by fiduciaries,

Safe deposit boxes,

Shares in a financial institution,

Traveler's checks,

Utilities,

Wages/salaries, and

Property held by courts/public agencies.

Is there a business-to-business exemption for unclaimed property?

Florida does not have a general unclaimed property business-to-business exemption. However, certain business-to-business transactions of transportation companies and healthcare providers are exempt.

What are the notice requirements for unclaimed property?

Within 180 days after an account with a value of at least $50 becomes inactive, the holder must conduct a search to locate the apparent owner of the property. Not more than 120 days and not less than 60 days prior to filing the annual report of unclaimed property, the holder of property presumed unclaimed shall send written notice to the apparent owner's last known address informing the apparent owner that the holder is in possession of the property.

What are the reporting requirements for unclaimed property?

General requirements. A holder of unclaimed property must file a verified annual report containing such information concerning the property as is required by the Department of Banking and Finance (department). The reporting period is based on the calendar year. Thus, the report covering the previous year ending December 31 is due on April 30. The department may postpone the report due date upon a written request and a showing of good cause by the holder.

Negative reporting. Florida requires unclaimed property negative reports if the holder previously has filed an unclaimed property report, but a negative report is not required for holders who have never filed an unclaimed property report. (Florida Division of Unclaimed Property Reporting Instructions Manual, Florida Department of Financial Services)

Minimum reporting. Florida has no minimum reporting amount.

Aggregate reporting. Generally, reportable items under $50 may be reported in an aggregate to simplify reporting. However, securities related property cannot be reported in the aggregate.

Electronic reporting. An unclaimed property report containing 25 or more different apparent owners must be in an electronic format as prescribed by the department. The electronic report is required to be in the National Association of Unclaimed Property Administrators (NAUPA) standard file format, submitted as a NAUPA format text file. All other reports must be manually entered through the Holder Reporting Online System.

Recordkeeping. A holder of unclaimed property must maintain a record of the name and last known address of the apparent owner for five years (three years in the case of traveler's checks and money orders) after the property becomes reportable.

MOTOR FUELS

[¶40-000]
MOTOR FUELS

[¶40-001] Gasoline Taxes

Florida taxes several types of motor fuels. Discussed here are motor fuel or gasoline taxes. The state also taxes diesel fuel, aviation fuel, and miscellaneous fuels. In addition, Florida is a member of the International Fuel Tax Agreement (IFTA).

"Motor fuel" or "fuel" means all gasoline products or any product blended with gasoline or any fuel placed in the storage supply tank of a gasoline-powered motor vehicle. (Sec. 206.01, F.S.)

Specific topics discussed below are:
- persons subject to tax,
- point of taxation,
- license requirements,
- basis of tax,
- rate of tax,
- exemptions,
- reports and payments,
- credits, refunds, and reimbursements, and
- local taxes.

• *Persons subject to tax*

Terminal suppliers, importers, and wholesalers must collect and remit an excise tax upon the first sale or transfer of title, or use within the state of previously untaxed motor fuel. (Sec. 206.41(1), F.S.)

Every position holder must pay taxes on the removal of motor fuel from a terminal. In an exchange agreement between two licensed terminal suppliers the receiving party is the position holder if identified to the terminal operator by the delivering party. (Sec. 206.413(1)(a), F.S.)

A terminal operator is not liable for taxes at the time of removal of the motor fuel if the operator is a terminal supplier, has an unexpired notification certificate from the position holder, and has no reason to believe that any information in the certificate is false. (Sec. 206.413(1)(h), F.S.)

• *Point of taxation*

The person liable for payment of the motor fuel taxes is as follows:

— Position holder shall pay taxes on the removal of motor fuel from a terminal. In an exchange agreement between two licensed terminal suppliers, the receiving party shall be liable as the position holder if the receiving party is identified to the terminal operator by the delivering party.

— Terminal suppliers shall pay taxes on the removal of motor fuel from a refiner.

— Importers shall pay taxes on the entry into this state.

— Any person that produces blended motor fuel outside the bulk transfer or terminal system shall pay all applicable motor fuel taxes.

— Any person using motor fuel upon which the required motor fuel tax has not been paid and which is not exempted from tax is liable for the backup tax.

— The seller of motor fuel is jointly and severally liable for the backup tax if the seller knows or has reason to know that the motor fuel will be used in any nonexempt use.

— Terminal operators are jointly and severally liable for the motor fuel if the position holder with respect to the motor fuel is a person other than the terminal operator and is not a terminal supplier; or the terminal operator has not met the conditions specified in (Sec. 206.41(h), F.S.

— A terminal operator is not liable for motor fuel taxes if at the time of the removal all the following apply: the terminal operator is a terminal supplier, the terminal operator has an unexpired notification certificate from the position holder as required by the Internal Revenue Service, and the terminal operator has no reason to believe that any information in the certificate is false.

(Sec. 206.41(1), F.S. and Sec. 206.873, F.S.)

• *License requirements*

Terminal suppliers, importers, exporters, blenders, biodiesel manufacturers, or wholesalers of motor fuel must have a license to operate in the state. To obtain a license, prospective applicants must apply to the Department of Revenue and pay an annual license tax of $30. The $30 fee is discontinued effective January 1, 2018. (Sec. 206.02, F.S.)

Municipalities, counties, or school districts that manufacture biodiesel fuel solely for its own use are exempt from the general reporting, bonding, and licensing requirements for wholesalers. (Sec. 206.02(2)(d), F.S.) However, these municipalities are required to register with the Department of Revenue and pay the taxes outlined in Sec. 206.874(4)(b), F.S..

Persons engaging in the business of selling motor fuel at retail or engaging in business as a reseller must register with the Department prior to engaging in business. (Sec. 206.404(1)(c), F.S.) If a wholesaler or exporter diverts to Florida, within three consecutive months, more than six loads of fuel which were originally destined for allocation outside the state, the wholesaler or exporter must register as an importer within 30 days after the diversion. (Sec. 206.416(1)(c), F.S.) The diversion registration system is Web-based. (*Tax Information Publication, No. 06B05-03*, Florida Department of Revenue, September 11, 2006)

Temporary fuel tax license issued during a disaster or declared state of emergency.—A person may request a temporary importer/pollutant, exporter, or carrier fuel tax license when the Governor of Florida has declared a state of emergency, or when the President of the United States has declared a major disaster in Florida or in any other state or territory of the United States. A temporary license allows that person to conduct the following activities in Florida:

— Carrier: This license allows a railroad company, pipeline company, water transportation company, or a private or common carrier to transport gasoline or diesel to points within Florida or from a point in Florida to a point outside of Florida.

— Exporter: This license allows a fuel dealer to export taxable motor or diesel fuels from sub storage at a bulk facility or direct from a terminal rack to a destination outside the state. The licensed exporter may apply for a refund of all applicable Florida fuel taxes if the other state's tax has been paid.

— Importer/Pollutant: These licenses allow a fuel dealer to import, other than by bulk transfer, motor or diesel fuel into Florida upon which no pre-collection of tax has occurred.

¶40-001

(*Florida Fuel Tax*, Florida Department of Revenue, September 2019)

To qualify for a temporary license, the applicant must have a:

— business location in Florida or in another state; and

— sales tax registration if located in Florida; or

— Florida fuel tax license; or

— fuel license issued in a state other than Florida.

(*Florida Fuel Tax*, Florida Department of Revenue, September 2019)

A temporary fuel license may be obtained by submitting a completed Florida Temporary Fuel Tax Application (Form DR-156T) to the Florida Department of Revenue.

To receive a temporary fuel license, the applicant must:

— complete the application in its entirety; and

— FAX a copy of the application to (850) 488-5997; or

— scan and email a completed copy of the application to motor_fuel@floridarevenue.com.

(*Florida Fuel Tax*, Florida Department of Revenue, September 2019)

An original signed application should later be mailed to: Florida Department of Revenue, Account Management—Fuel Unit, MS 1-5730, 5050 W. Tennessee St., Tallahassee, FL 32399-0160. (*Florida Fuel Tax*, Florida Department of Revenue, September 2019)

Upon approval of the application, the Department will provide the temporary license via the contact method selected by the licensee on question seven of the DR-156T. The effective date of the temporary license is the date the application is received by the Department. The temporary license is valid until the last day of the month following the month in which the temporary license is issued. (*Florida Fuel Tax*, Florida Department of Revenue, September 2019)

A temporary license may be extended for the duration of a declared emergency or major disaster when the licensee makes a written request for such extension by email or facsimile. Include the license number, name of the licensee, license type, and reason for the extension in the written request. A temporary license may not be extended past the duration of the declared emergency or major disaster. (*Florida Fuel Tax*, Florida Department of Revenue, September 2019)

Any person granted a temporary license will be mailed one or more of the following return(s). Licensees must remit the return and payment, if applicable, to the Department before the 20th day of the month following the month in which the product was imported, exported, or carried in Florida.

— Wholesaler/Importer Fuel Tax Return (Form DR-309632);

— Petroleum Carrier Information Return (Form DR-309637);

— Exporter Fuel Tax Return (Form DR-309638);

— Pollutants Tax Return (Form DR-904).

(*Florida Fuel Tax*, Florida Department of Revenue, September 2019)

• *Basis of tax*

The state tax rate on motor fuel is based on a per gallon rate. The total tax rate on motor fuel is computed by combining the state motor fuel tax rate, the fuel sales tax rate, and all applicable local fuel tax rates. (Sec. 206.41, F.S.)

• *Rate of tax*

Effective January 1, 2022:

— the motor fuel tax rate is increased from 18.5 to 19 cents per gallon;

— the local option rate varies by county and the ninth cent remains the same;

— the State Comprehensive Enhanced Transportation System (SCETS) rate is increased from 8 to 8.3 cents per gallon; and

— the inspection fee on motor fuel remains the same at 0.125 cents per gallon.

(*Tax Information Publication, No. 21B05-02*, Florida Department of Revenue, November 17, 2021)

COMPLIANCE NOTE: Florida Motor Fuel Tax Relief Act of 2022 enacted. From October 1, 2022, through October 31, 2022, the following tax reductions apply:

— the $0.01 county fuel tax is reduced by 1 cent per gallon;

— the $0.01 municipal fuel tax is reduced by 1 cent per gallon;

— the $0.083 State Comprehensive Enhanced Transportation System Tax (SCETS) is reduced by 8.3 cents per gallon; and

— the $0.15 fuel sales tax is reduced by 15 cents per gallon.

During this time period, licensed terminal suppliers, wholesalers, and importers of motor fuel are required to charge and collect the reduced rate of tax on sales of motor fuel to retail dealers located in Florida. (Ch. 97 (H.B. 7071), Laws 2022, effective July 1, 2022, and applicable as noted)

A retail dealer of motor fuel may, at the dealer's option, manage its motor fuel inventory to benefit Florida residents and to maximize the tax reduction during the month. The Attorney General may investigate violations of the act. It is unlawful for a terminal supplier, wholesaler, importer, reseller, or retail dealer of motor fuel to retain any part of the tax reduction or to interfere with providing the full benefit of the tax reduction to the retail purchaser of motor fuel. (Ch. 97 (H.B. 7071), Laws 2022, effective July 1, 2022, and applicable as noted)

These provisions expire effective July 1, 2023. (Ch. 97 (H.B. 7071), Laws 2022, effective July 1, 2022, and applicable as noted)

COMPLIANCE NOTE: Guidance provided on Florida Motor Fuel Tax Relief Act of 2022 for wholesalers, importers, local governments, mass transit system operators, retail dealers, and terminal suppliers. The Florida Department of Revenue has provided guidance regarding the Florida Motor Fuel Tax Relief Act of 2022 for:

— local governments and mass transit system operators (*Tax Information Publication, No. 22B05-01*, Florida Department of Revenue, June 14, 2022);

— retail dealers (*Tax Information Publication, No. 22B05-02*, Florida Department of Revenue, June 14, 2022);

— terminal suppliers (*Tax Information Publication, No. 22B05-03*, Florida Department of Revenue, June 14, 2022); and

— wholesalers and importers (*Tax Information Publication, No. 22B05-04*, Florida Department of Revenue, June 14, 2022).

The guidance includes information regarding filing requirements, rate adjustments, inventory management, tax reduction, and inventory reconciliation.

COMPLIANCE NOTE: Emergency Rule regarding Florida Motor Fuel Tax Relief Act of 2022 adopted. An emergency rule is adopted that implements the Florida Motor Fuel Tax Relief Act of 2022. The rule provides guidance regarding the reduction of the motor fuel tax rate to:

— terminal suppliers, wholesalers, importers, and retail dealers of gasoline;

— local government users of diesel fuel; and

— motor fuel quarterly refund filers.

From October 1, 2022, through October 31, 2022, the Florida motor fuel tax rate is reduced from 33.425 cents to 8.125 cents, which does not include the additional local option tax. (Emergency Rule 12BER22-12, Florida Department of Revenue, effective August 1, 2022)

Minimum local option tax on motor fuel collected at fuel terminals.—Effective January 1, 2022, in addition to the 19 cents per gallon state fuel tax collected at the loading rack, terminal suppliers must collect:

— a minimum local option fuel tax of 14.3 cents per gallon;

— a pollutants tax of 2.071 cents per gallon; and

— an inspection fee of 0.125 cents per gallon on each gallon of motor fuel sold to licensed wholesalers.

Total fuel taxes collected by terminal suppliers on sales of motor fuel to licensed wholesalers is 35.496 cents per gallon. (*Tax Information Publication, No. 21B05-02,* Florida Department of Revenue, November 17, 2021)

Oil inspection fee.—The oil inspection fee is $1/8$¢ per gallon on all gasoline, kerosene (except when used as aviation turbine fuel), and #1 fuel oils. (Sec. 525.09, F.S.)

• *Exemptions*

Motor fuel that is contained in the fuel tank of any motor vehicle that is used to propel the vehicle into Florida from another state or that is supplied by a vehicle manufacturer and contained in the fuel tank of a new and untitled motor vehicle is exempt from the tax. (Sec. 206.41(3), F.S.) Aviation gasoline is exempt. (Sec. 206.42, F.S.) Rocket fuel is exempt, provided the fuel is produced for, sold, and used exclusively for space flight. Motor fuel distributors are exempt from tax on fuel sold to the U.S. government in bulk lots of not less than 500 gallons. (Sec. 206.62(1), F.S.)

Exemption for licensed exporters.—A licensed exporter may purchase from a terminal supplier at a terminal taxable motor fuels for export from Florida without paying the motor fuels tax provided:

— the exporter has designated to the terminal supplier the destination for delivery of the fuel to a location outside the state;

— the exporter is licensed in the state of destination and has supplied the terminal supplier with that license number;

— the exporter has not been barred from making tax-free exports by the Florida Department of Revenue for filing a false refund claim or claiming a false credit; and

— the terminal supplier collects and remits to the state of destination all taxes imposed on said fuel by the destination state

(Sec. 206.052, F.S.)

Exemption for terminal suppliers.—A terminal supplier may purchase motor fuel from another terminal supplier at a terminal without paying Florida motor fuels tax provided:

— the purchasing terminal supplier sells the fuel to a licensed exporter for immediate export;

— the purchasing terminal supplier must designate the out-of-state destination of the fuel to the selling terminal supplier;

— the purchasing terminal supplier is licensed in the state of destination and has supplied the selling terminal supplier with that license number;

— the licensed exporter has not been barred from making tax-free exports by the Florida Department of Revenue for filing a false refund claim or claiming a false credit; and

— the selling terminal supplier collects and remits to the state of destination all taxes imposed by the destination state.

(Sec. 206.052, F.S.; *Tax Information Publication, No. 18B05-01*, Florida Department of Revenue, May 9, 2018)

• *Reports and payments*

Each terminal supplier, importer, blender, and wholesaler must file a report with the Department of Revenue at the time the tax is due and payable. (Sec. 206.48, F.S.) Reports from persons who do not purchase tax-free motor fuel and from carriers are due within 20 days after the month covered by the report. (Sec. 206.08(1), F.S.; Sec. 206.09(1), F.S.) Reports of inspection fees must be filed with the Commissioner of Agriculture on or before the 25th of each month. (Sec. 525.09, F.S.)

The Department of Revenue may suspend the monthly Florida motor fuel tax reporting requirements imposed on terminal operators and bulk carriers that store, handle, or transfer motor fuels and similar products within Florida if substantially the same data is filed with the Internal Revenue Service and provided to the Department through a national information reporting system. (Sec. 206.09(4), F.S.; Sec. 206.095, F.S.)

Taxes are due on the first day of the succeeding month and must be paid on or before the 20th day of each month. (Sec. 206.43(1), F.S.) Oil inspection fees must be paid on or before the 25th of each month. (Sec. 525.09, F.S.)

The Executive Director of the Florida Department of Revenue is authorized to require a taxpayer to file returns and remit payments electronically when the amount of taxes paid in the prior state fiscal year reached a certain threshold. (Sec. 213.755, F.S.; Rule 12-24.003, F.A.C.)

• *Credits, refunds, and reimbursements*

Any person who uses any motor fuel for agricultural, aquacultural, commercial fishing, or commercial aviation purposes on which taxes have been paid are entitled to a refund of such tax. (Sec. 206.41, F.S.)

Persons using fuel for agricultural or commercial fishing purposes on which the tax has been paid are entitled to a refund of 1¢ per gallon. (Sec. 206.64, F.S.)

Terminal suppliers and importers of motor fuel are allowed to deduct 0.2% of the excise tax, county and municipal fuel tax, and fuel sales tax, as well as 1.1% of the voted fuel tax and the first 6¢ of the local option fuel tax in compensation for the services and expenses of compliance. (Sec. 206.43(1), F.S.)

Refund of fuel taxes used for agricultural shipment or hurricane debris removal after Hurricane Michael.—A state and local motor fuels tax exemption is available for fuel purchased and used in Florida from October 10, 2018 through June 30, 2019, in any motor vehicle driven or operated in Florida for agricultural shipment or hurri-

¶40-001

cane debris removal. The exemption is only available through a refund from the Florida Department of Revenue. (Sec. 22, Ch. 42 (H.B. 7123), Laws 2019, effective May 15, 2019, applicable retroactively to October 10, 2018)

The Florida Department of Revenue provides guidance regarding this exemption in the form of a refund. The exemption excludes the 2¢ constitutional fuel tax and the 0.125¢ inspection fee paid on fuel placed in the storage supply tank of a gasoline powered motor vehicle. Taxpayers seeking a refund must submit Form DR-26HF, Fuel Used for Agricultural Shipments or Hurricane Debris Removal, to the department by December 31, 2019. This application is available on the department's website at DR-26HF, Fuel Used for Agricultural Shipments or Hurricane Debris Removal. (*Tax Information Publication, No. 19B05-01*, Florida Department of Revenue, June 6, 2019)

Emergency Rule 12BER19-02 incorporates Form DR-26HF, Application for Refund—Fuel Used for Agricultural Shipments or Hurricane Debris Removal, to allow taxpayers to seek a refund of tax on qualifying purchases. (Emergency Rule 12BER19-02)

"Agricultural shipment" is defined as the transport of any agricultural product from a farm, nursery, forest, grove, orchard, vineyard, garden, or apiary located in Okaloosa, Walton, Holmes, Washington, Bay, Jackson, Calhoun, Gulf, Gadsden, Liberty, Franklin, Leon, or Wakulla County to an agricultural processing or storage facility. (Sec. 22, Ch. 42 (H.B. 7123), Laws 2019, effective May 15, 2019, applicable retroactively to October 10, 2018)

"Hurricane debris removal" is defined as the transport of Hurricane Michael debris from a farm, nursery, forest, grove, orchard, vineyard, or apiary located in Okaloosa, Walton, Holmes, Washington, Bay, Jackson, Calhoun, Gulf, Gadsden, Liberty, Franklin, Leon, or Wakulla County. (Sec. 22, Ch. 42 (H.B. 7123), Laws 2019, effective May 15, 2019, applicable retroactively to October 10, 2018)

To receive a refund pursuant to this section, the fuel purchaser must apply to the Department of Revenue by December 31, 2019. The refund application must include the following information:

— the name and address of the person claiming the refund;

— the names and addresses of up to three owners of farms, nurseries, forests, groves, orchards, vineyards, gardens, or apiaries whose agricultural products were shipped or hurricane debris was removed by the person seeking the refund pursuant to this section;

— the sales invoice or other proof of purchase of the fuel, showing the number of gallons of fuel purchased, the type of fuel purchased, the date of purchase, and the name and place of business of the dealer from whom the fuel was purchased;

— the license number or other identification number of the motor vehicle that used the exempt fuel; and

— an affidavit executed by the person seeking the refund pursuant to this section, including a statement that he or she purchased and used the fuel for which the refund is being claimed during the period from October 10, 2018, through June 30, 2019, for an agricultural shipment or hurricane debris removal.

(Sec. 22, Ch. 42 (H.B. 7123), Laws 2019, effective May 15, 2019, applicable retroactively to October 10, 2018)

This provision is retroactively applicable to October 10, 2018. (Sec. 22, Ch. 42 (H.B. 7123), Laws 2019, effective May 15, 2019, applicable retroactively to October 10, 2018)

Refund of taxes paid on fuel used for agricultural shipments after Hurricane Irma.—Certain purchases of motor or undyed diesel fuels are exempt from state and county Florida motor fuels taxes. The exemption excludes the 2-cent constitutional fuel tax and the 0.125 cent inspection fee paid on fuel placed in the storage supply tank of a gasoline powered motor vehicle. To qualify for the exemption, the fuel must be purchased and used in Florida between September 10, 2017, and June 30, 2018, and the fuel must be used in a motor vehicle driven or operated on public highways for agricultural shipment. (Sec. 59 (H.B. 7087), Laws 2018; *Tax Information Publication, No. 18B05-02*, Florida Department of Revenue, May 18, 2018)

The term "agricultural shipment" means the transportation of any agricultural product from a farm, nursery, forest, grove, orchard, vineyard, garden, or apiary to an agricultural processing or storage facility. The exemption is only available through a refund of tax from the Florida Department of Revenue. Taxpayers who wish to apply for a refund must, by December 31, 2018, submit Form DR-26IF—Application for Refund—Fuel Used for Agricultural Shipments to the department. (Sec. 59 (H.B. 7087), Laws 2018; Emergency Rule 12BER18-03; *Tax Information Publication, No. 18B05-02*, Florida Department of Revenue, May 18, 2018)

• *Local taxes*

Counties may levy several local taxes on fuel.

Voter approval gas and fuel taxes.—Florida counties may impose taxes of 1¢ per gallon on fuels subject to the state taxes, subject to voter approval. (Sec. 336.021(1), F.S.) This tax, known as the Ninth-Cent Tax, may be imposed by an ordinance adopted by the county if it receives an extraordinary vote of the membership of the governing body. The 1¢ per gallon tax must be levied on diesel fuel in every county. The voted gas and fuel taxes are incorporated into the motor fuel and diesel fuel tax provisions. (Sec. 336.021(6), F.S.)

Local option additional gas and fuel taxes.—Counties may impose an additional 1¢, 2¢, 3¢, 4¢, 5¢, or 6¢ per gallon local option tax on motor fuel sold in the county and subject to the state fuel taxes. (Sec. 336.025(1), F.S.) The tax cannot be imposed for more than 30 years and will be collected in the same manner as the state fuel taxes. Counties also may impose another additional 1¢, 2¢, 3¢, 4¢, or 5¢ per gallon local option tax on motor fuel sold in the county and subject to the state fuel taxes. All counties must levy the tax on diesel fuel at the rate of 6¢ per net gallon. (Sec. 336.025(9), F.S.) The local option gas tax is incorporated into the motor fuel and diesel fuel tax provisions.

State Comprehensive Enhanced Transportation System (SCETS) Tax.—In addition to other taxes, in each county, a State Comprehensive Enhanced Transportation System (SCETS) tax is imposed on every gallon of motor fuel sold in that county and taxed under the motor fuel tax. The rate of tax in each county is equal to two-thirds of the lesser of the sum of the voted gas tax and local option gas tax imposed on motor fuels in the county or 6¢, rounded to the nearest tenth of a cent. The tax rate is adjusted on January 1 of each year by the percentage change rounded to the nearest tenth of a cent, except that the base year for the calculation must be the average for the 12-month period ending September 30, 1990. An additional tax is imposed on every gallon of diesel fuel sold in each county and taxed under the diesel fuels tax at the maximum rate. The tax must be collected and remitted by persons selling motor fuel or using or selling diesel fuel within a county in which the tax is imposed. The comprehensive enhanced transportation system tax is incorporated into the motor fuel and diesel fuel tax provisions. (Sec. 336.025, F.S.)

[¶40-003] Diesel Fuel Taxes

An excise tax is imposed on diesel fuel in Florida. "Diesel fuel" is all petroleum distillates commonly known as diesel #2, biodiesel, or any other product blended with diesel or any product placed into the storage supply tank of a diesel-powered motor vehicle. (Sec. 206.86, F.S.)

Licensing.—A person may not act as a retailer of alternative fuel unless that person holds a valid retailer of alternative fuel license issued by the Department. However, a person who has no facilities for placing diesel fuel into the supply system of a motor vehicle and who sells into containers of five gallons or less is not required to be licensed as a retailer of alternative fuel. (Sec. 206.89(1)(a), F.S.)

Specific topics discussed below are:

— persons subject to tax,

— license requirements,

— basis of tax,

— rate of tax,

— exemptions,

— reports and payments, and

— credits, refunds, and reimbursements.

• *Persons subject to tax*

Liability for the tax is imposed on position holders that remove diesel fuel from a terminal, terminal suppliers that remove diesel fuel from a refinery, importers, and producers of blended diesel fuel outside a bulk transfer or terminal system. (Sec. 206.872, F.S.)

• *License requirements*

A person may not act as a retailer of alternative fuel unless he or she holds a valid retailer of alternative fuel license issued by the Department of Revenue. Moreover, a person who has no facilities for placing diesel fuel into the supply system of a motor vehicle and who sells into containers of 5 gallons or less is not required to be licensed as a retailer of alternative fuel.(Sec. 206.89, F.S.)

• *Basis of tax*

"Taxable diesel fuel" is any diesel fuel not held in bulk storage at a terminal and which has not been dyed for exempt use in accordance with Internal Revenue Code requirements. (Sec. 206.86, F.S.)

An excise tax is imposed on each net gallon of diesel fuel that:

(a) is removed from a terminal at the rack;

(b) is removed from a refinery at the refinery rack or by bulk transfer if the owner of the fuel prior to the removal is not a licensed terminal supplier;

(c) enters into Florida for sale, consumption, use, or warehousing by bulk transfer, when the enterer is not a licensed terminal supplier, or other than by bulk transfer;

(d) is removed to an unregistered person, absent prior taxable removal, entry, or sale of such fuel; or

(e) is removed by the blender, to the extent of the difference between the total number of gallons of blended diesel fuel removed or sold and the number of gallons of previously taxed diesel fuel used to produce the blended fuel.

(Sec. 206.87, F.S.)

Diesel fuel use tax.—Diesel fuel purchased for use in a trade or business is subject to a special use tax on the cost price of the fuel consumed. (Sec. 212.0501, F.S.) Diesel fuel subject to the fuel taxes imposed pursuant to Ch. 206 is exempt from this use tax. Also exempt is diesel fuel used for residential or agricultural purposes, diesel fuel purchased or stored for resale, and liquefied petroleum gas or other fuel used exclusively to heat a structure in which started pullets or broilers are raised. A licensed sales tax dealer may elect to collect the tax. If the dealer does not collect the tax, the purchaser or ultimate consumer must pay the use tax due directly to the state.

• *Rate of tax*

Effective January 1, 2022:

• the state diesel fuel tax rate is increased from 18.5 to 19 cents per gallon

• the county tax rate (ninth cent, SCETS, and local option tax rates) on diesel fuel is increased from 15 to 15.3 cents per gallon statewide; and

• the total state and county rates on diesel fuel is increased from 33.5 to 34.3 cents per gallon statewide.

(*Tax Information Publication, No. 21B05-02*, Florida Department of Revenue, November 17, 2021)

Use tax.—The tax rate on diesel fuel purchased for consumption, use, or storage by a trade or business is 6% of the total cost price of diesel fuel consumed. (Sec. 212.0501, F.S.)

• *Exemptions*

The diesel fuel tax does not apply to the following:

(1) The removal from a terminal or refinery of, or the entry or sale of, any diesel fuel when the person otherwise liable for tax is a diesel fuel registrant and the diesel fuel satisfies the dyeing and marking requirements. In the case of a removal from a terminal, the terminal must also be an approved terminal.

(2) Any entry by a licensed importer into Florida of diesel fuel on which taxes have been imposed on a diesel fuel registrant under an agreement with the Department.

(3) The removal of diesel fuel if it is removed by rail car from an approved refinery or terminal and is received at an approved refinery or terminal, when the refinery and terminal are operated by the same diesel fuel registrant.

(4) Diesel fuel that, by contract, must be shipped and is shipped to a point outside Florida by a supplier by means of facilities operated by the supplier, delivery by the supplier to a carrier, customs broker, or forwarding agent for shipment to the out-of-state point, or delivery by the supplier to any vessel clearing from a Florida port for a port outside the state and actually exported from Florida in the vessel.

(5) Diesel fuel which is destined for delivery to a location outside Florida on which the diesel fuel registrant is required to collect the taxes of the destination state.

(6) Public or private secondary schools if the school produces less than 1,000 gallons annually of biodiesel fuel for the sole use at the school by its employees or students.

(Sec. 206.874, F.S.)

• *Reports and payments*

Dealers and diesel fuel registrants must file reports with the Department of Highway Safety and Motor Vehicles on or before the 20th of each month. (Sec. 206.91, F.S.) Quarterly returns and payments may be permitted when the tax remitted for the preceding quarter did not exceed $100. Semiannual returns and payments may be permitted when the tax remitted for the preceding six months did not exceed $200.

Payment of the tax accompanies the report. (Sec. 206.91, F.S.)

¶40-003

The Executive Director of the Florida Department of Revenue is authorized to require a taxpayer to file returns and remit payments electronically when the amount of taxes paid in the prior state fiscal year reached a certain threshold. (Sec. 213.755, F.S.; Rule 12-24.003, F.A.C.)

Use tax.—A licensed sales tax dealer may elect to collect tax on all sales to each person who purchases diesel fuel for consumption, use, or storage by a trade or business. When the licensed sales tax dealer has not elected to collect such tax, the purchaser or ultimate consumer is liable for paying the use tax due directly to the state. (Sec. 212.0501(4), F.S.)

• *Credits, refunds, and reimbursements*

Depending on the type and use of certain diesel fuels, taxpayers may qualify for tax refunds or credits for various motor or diesel fuel local option taxes. (Sec. 206.8745, F.S.; Rule 12B-5.130, F.A.C.)

The following types of refunds or credits are available:

— See Gasoline Taxes for discussion of a refund of fuel taxes used for agricultural shipment or hurricane debris removal after Hurricane Michael. (Sec. 22, Ch. 42 (H.B. 7123), Laws 2019, effective May 15, 2019, and applicable retroactively to October 10, 2018)

— A purchaser of undyed, tax-paid diesel fuel which has paid the motor fuel tax may file a claim for refund or credit of the motor fuel tax if the taxes were paid in error if the fuel was used for the following exempt purposes: (1) the exclusive use of a local government, (2) use in an aircraft museum vehicle, (3) use by the American Red Cross, (4) use in a vessel employed in the business of commercial transportation or commercial fishing, (5) use in a school bus, (6) use in a local public bus service, (7) exclusive use of a nonprofit education facility, (8) use in a U.S. Government vehicle not used on a highway, (9) use in a war vessel, (10) use of diesel fuel for home heating, and (11) use in a self-propelled off-road equipment. (Sec. 206.8745, F.S.; Sec. 206.874(3), F.S.)

— A purchaser of motor fuel used for agricultural, aquacultural, commercial fishing, and commercial aviation purposes. (Rule 12B-5.130, F.A.C.)

— A licensed terminal supplier, importer, or wholesaler who holds title to undyed diesel fuel which has been mixed with dyed diesel fuel in storage may claim a refund or credit for any state and local option tax paid on the undyed diesel fuel. (Sec. 206.8745(3), F.S.)

— A licensed wholesaler which has paid the motor fuel tax and any applicable local option tax on undyed diesel fuel sold tax-free may take a credit on its monthly consolidated fuel tax return in lieu of applying for a refund. (Sec. 206.8745(4), F.S.)

— A terminal supplier or position holder which removes undyed diesel fuel from a terminal and subsequently places the fuel back in the same or another terminal may claim a refund or credit for all state and local option tax paid on the first removal of the fuel. (Sec. 206.8745(5), F.S.)

— Undyed, tax-paid diesel fuel consumed by a power takeoff or engine exhaust for the purpose of unloading bulk cargo by pumping or turning a concrete mixer drum used in the manufacturing process, or for the purpose of compacting solid waste, which is mounted on a motor vehicle and which has no separate fuel tank or power unit, is subject to a refund. (Sec. 206.8745(6), F.S.; Rule 12B-5.130(2), F.A.C.)

— A purchaser of undyed diesel fuel for use by a noncommercial vehicle which has paid the motor fuel tax to the seller may claim a refund if the purchaser:

— makes one claim per year,

— submits the claim prior to April 1 of the year subsequent to the year in which the tax was paid,

— purchased more than 2,500 gallons per year,

— submits the original purchase invoices, and

— remits as an offset to the refund the sales tax due based on the purchase price of the fuel net the state tax refunded.

— Undyed, tax-paid diesel fuel is subject to a refund of motor fuel tax if the fuel is purchased in Florida and consumed by the engine of an idling qualified motor coach for the purpose of running climate control systems and maintaining electrical systems for the motor coach. A qualified motor coach is one that:

— is a privately owned vehicle,

— is designed to carry nine or more passengers,

— has a gross vehicle weight of at least 33,000 pounds,

— is used exclusively in the commercial application of transporting passengers for compensation, and

— has the capacity to measure diesel fuel consumed in Florida during idling, separate from diesel fuel consumed to propel the vehicle in this state, by way of an on-board computer.

(Sec. 206.8745(8), F.S.; *E-mail Correspondence*, Florida Department of Revenue)

Deductions.—Diesel fuel registrants are allowed to deduct an amount equivalent to 0.67% of the excise tax on diesel fuel and fuel sales tax, plus 1.1% of the voted fuel tax and local option fuel tax in compensation for the services and expenses of compliance. (Sec. 206.91, F.S.)

[¶40-005] Aviation Fuel Taxes

Aviation fuel is subject to taxes in Florida. "Aviation fuel" is fuel for use in aircraft. It includes aviation gasoline and aviation turbine fuels and kerosene. (Sec. 206.9815(1), F.S.)

Specific topics discussed below are:

— persons subject to tax,

— basis of tax,

— rate of tax,

— exemptions,

— reports and payments, and

— credits, refunds, and reimbursements.

• *Persons subject to tax*

Licensed wholesalers and terminal suppliers are subject to tax. (Sec. 206.9825, F.S.)

The Florida Department of Revenue provides guidance regarding the application of motor fuels tax to aviation gasoline that has an octane rating greater than 75 or a lead content greater than .05 grams per gallon. Applicable tax treatment is determined by the type of sale and the end use of the aviation gasoline. The tax treatment of terminal suppliers, wholesalers, fixed base operators (FBOs), blenders, and retail dealers is discussed. (*Tax Information Publication No. 12B05-04*, Florida Department of Revenue, August 10, 2012)

¶40-005

Terminal suppliers.—Tax treatment is as follows:

— On sales to wholesalers, a terminal supplier will collect aviation fuel tax of 4.27 cents per gallon.

— On sales to fixed base operators (FBOs), a terminal supplier will get written certification from the FBO that shows the number of gallons purchased for use in an aircraft and for use other than in an aircraft. A terminal supplier will collect aviation fuel tax of 4.27 cents per gallon on fuel identified for use in an aircraft. If any of the aviation gasoline is not purchased for use in an aircraft, it should be taxed as a sale of tangible personal property under Ch. 212 at the general sales and use tax rate plus any applicable discretionary sales surtax. If the FBO underestimates the tax liability on the use of the fuel, the FBO must notify and pay any additional tax to the supplier.

— On sales to retail dealers, a terminal supplier will collect the applicable sales and use tax plus any applicable discretionary sales surtax.

— On sales directly to end users, a terminal supplier will collect the applicable sales and use tax plus any applicable discretionary sales surtax, unless the fuel is for use in an aircraft. If the fuel is for use in an aircraft, the end user must pay the terminal supplier aviation fuel tax of 4.27 cents per gallon, if it provides the terminal supplier with a signed affidavit.

(Sec. 206.41, F.S.; Sec. 206.9825, F.S.; Sec. 212.05, F.S.; *Tax Information Publication, No. 12B05-04,* Florida Department of Revenue, August 10, 2012)

Wholesalers.—Tax treatment is as follows:

— On sales to FBOs, a wholesaler will get written certification from the FBO that indicates the number of gallons purchased for use in an aircraft and for use other than in an aircraft. A wholesaler will collect aviation fuel tax of 4.27 cents per gallon on the fuel identified for use in an aircraft. Any aviation gasoline that is not purchased for use in an aircraft should be taxed as a sale of tangible personal property under Ch. 212 at the general sales and use tax rate plus any applicable discretionary sales surtax. Should the FBO underestimate the tax liability on the use of the fuel, the FBO must notify and pay any additional tax to the wholesaler.

— On sales to retail dealers, a wholesaler will collect the applicable sales and use tax plus any applicable discretionary sales surtax.

— On sales directly to end users, a wholesaler will the applicable collect sales and use tax plus any applicable discretionary sales surtax unless the fuel is for use in an aircraft, in which case the end user is required to pay the wholesaler aviation fuel tax of 4.27 cents per gallon if it provides the wholesaler with a signed affidavit.

(Sec. 206.41, F.S.; Sec. 206.9825, F.S.; Sec. 212.05, F.S.; *Tax Information Publication No. 15B05-02,* Florida Department of Revenue, December 3, 2015)

A wholesaler may take an ultimate vendor credit on its return for the 4.27 cents motor fuels tax paid to its supplier on aviation gasoline if the fuel is sold for use other than in an aircraft. If the fuel is sold for use in a motor vehicle, the wholesaler will collect the applicable motor fuel tax under Ch. 206. If the aviation fuel is sold for use other than in an aircraft but not for use in a motor vehicle, the wholesaler will collect the applicable sales and use tax plus any applicable discretionary sales surtax. (Sec. 206.41, F.S.; Sec. 206.9825, F.S.; Sec. 212.05, F.S.; *Tax Information Publication No. 15B05-02,* Florida Department of Revenue, December 3, 2015)

Fixed base operators (FBOs).—Tax treatment is as follows:

— On sales to licensed air carriers, FBOs will collect aviation fuel tax of 4.27 cents per gallon. Air carriers are not required to provide an affidavit and tail-wing numbers.

— On sales directly to end users, FBOs will collect the applicable sales and use tax plus any applicable discretionary sales surtax unless the fuel is for use in an aircraft, in which case the end user must pay the FBO aviation fuel tax of 4.27 cents per gallon and provide the FBO with a signed affidavit.

(Sec. 206.41, F.S.; Sec. 206.9825, F.S.; Sec. 212.05, F.S.; *Tax Information Publication No. 15B05-02*, Florida Department of Revenue, December 3, 2015)

Blenders.—Blenders who purchase aviation gasoline for use other than in a motor vehicle will pay the applicable sales and use tax plus any applicable discretionary sales surtax on the cost price of the fuel to its supplier. A blender who purchases aviation gasoline for sale must be licensed as a wholesaler. (Sec. 206.41, F.S.; Sec. 206.9825, F.S.; Sec. 212.05, F.S.; *Tax Information Publication No. 15B05-02*, Florida Department of Revenue, December 3, 2015)

Retail dealers.—On all sales of aviation gasoline, retailers will collect the applicable sales and use tax plus any applicable discretionary sales surtax. End users that purchase aviation gasoline from a retail dealer for use in an aircraft may apply to the Florida Department of Revenue for a refund of the sales and use tax and discretionary sales surtax paid. The 4.27 cents per gallon aviation fuel tax will be deducted from the refund. No refund will be granted unless the purchase submits a signed affidavit and an invoice that indicates that sales and use tax was paid on the aviation fuel. Sec. 206.41, F.S.; Sec. 206.9825, F.S.; Sec. 212.05, F.S.; *Tax Information Publication No. 15B05-02*, Florida Department of Revenue, December 3, 2015)

Affidavit requirements.—Affidavits must include the following information:

— the purchaser's name;

— the purchaser's address;

— a statement that the fuel will be or was used in an aircraft; and

— the tail-wing number of the aircraft the fuel will be or was placed in for use.

(*Tax Information Publication, No. 12B05-04*, Florida Department of Revenue, August 10, 2012)

• *Basis of tax*

An excise tax is imposed upon every gallon of aviation fuel sold in Florida, or brought into the state for use, upon which the tax has not been paid. (*Tax Information Publication No. 11B05-01*, Florida Department of Revenue, November 18, 2011; Sec. 206.9825, F.S.)

• *Rate of tax*

Effective January 1, 2022, the aviation fuel tax rate remains at 4.27 cents per gallon. (*Tax Information Publication, No. 21B05-02*, Florida Department of Revenue, November 17, 2021; Sec. 206.9825, F.S.)

The motor fuels tax provisions govern the administration and enforcement of the tax. (Sec. 206.9835, F.S.)

• *Exemptions*

Aviation fuel purchased by the United States or any department or agency of the United States is exempt from the tax imposed by this part when used in governmental aircraft. Any dealer of aviation fuel is entitled to a refund of any tax he or she has paid upon any aviation fuel purchased under such exemption. (Sec. 206.9875, F.S.)

Certain universities or colleges offering a graduate program in aeronautical or aerospace engineering, or flight training through a school of aeronautics or college of aviation, are exempt from aviation fuel tax. The exemption is limited to schools that are:

¶40-005

(1) tax exempt organizations under s. 501(c)(3) of the Internal Revenue Code,

(2) based in the state of Florida, and

(3) accredited by or have applied for accreditation by the Aviation Accreditation Board International.

The exemption is limited to purchases of aviation fuel used exclusively for flight training, which includes instruction on building, repairing, or maintaining aircraft engines or flying an aircraft. (Sec. 206.9825(1)(e), F.S.; *Tax Information Publication No. 15B05-01*, Florida Department of Revenue, June 30, 2015)

• *Reports and payments*

Each terminal supplier, importer, blender, and wholesaler must file a report with the Department of Revenue at the time the tax is due and payable. (Sec. 206.48, F.S.) Reports from persons who do not purchase tax-free motor fuel and from carriers are due within 20 days after the month covered by the report. (Sec. 206.08(1), F.S.; Sec. 206.09(1), F.S.) Reports of inspection fees must be filed with the Commissioner of Agriculture on or before the 25th of each month. (Sec. 525.09, F.S.)

The Department of Revenue may suspend the monthly Florida motor fuel tax reporting requirements imposed on terminal operators and bulk carriers that store, handle, or transfer motor fuels and similar products within Florida if substantially the same data is filed with the Internal Revenue Service and provided to the Department through a national information reporting system. (Sec. 206.09(4), F.S.; Sec. 206.095, F.S.)

Taxes are due on the first day of the succeeding month and must be paid on or before the 20th day of each month. (Sec. 206.43(1), F.S.)

• *Credits, refunds, and reimbursements*

Florida provides a number of refunds and/or credits against the aviation fuel tax.

See Gasoline Taxes for discussion of a refund of fuel taxes used for agricultural shipment or hurricane debris removal after Hurricane Michael. (Sec. 22, Ch. 42 (H.B. 7123), Laws 2019, effective May 15, 2019, and applicable retroactively to October 10, 2018)

Refund for air carriers conducting scheduled or all-cargo operations.—Effective July 1, 2019, an air carrier conducting scheduled operations or all-cargo operations is entitled to receive a refund of 1.42 cents per gallon of the aviation fuel tax purchased by that air carrier. This refund plus the refund for carriers in the business of transporting persons or property may not exceed 4.27 cents per gallon of aviation fuel purchased by an air carrier. (Sec. 206.9826, F.S.)

Refund for carriers in the business of transporting persons or property.—A carrier that is in the business of transporting persons or property for compensation or hire by air is entitled to receive a refund of the aviation fuel tax on fuel purchased by the carrier. The refund cannot exceed 0.6% of the wages paid by the carrier to employees located or based within the state and who are covered by unemployment compensation provisions. (Sec. 206.9855(1), F.S.)

Refund or credit for certain licensed wholesalers and terminal suppliers.—Until July 1, 2019, licensed wholesalers and terminal suppliers that, before July 1, 2016, deliver aviation fuel to an air carrier offering transcontinental jet service and that increase the air carrier's Florida workforce by more than 1000% and by 250 or more full-time employee positions are entitled, as the ultimate vendors, to a refund or credit of the aviation fuel tax paid. The refund or credit applies only if the air carrier has no facility for fueling highway vehicles from the tank in which the aviation fuel is stored. (Sec. 206.9825, F.S.)

[¶40-007] Other Fuel Taxes

Florida imposes tax on various types of fuels at the following rates.

Effective January 1, 2019, alternative fuels are taxed pursuant to a motor fuel equivalent gallon ratio and governed by the statutes beginning at Sec. 206.9951, F.S.. Until December 31, 2018, alternative fuels are exempt from the annual decal fee as well as any sales and use taxes. "Alternative fuels" include butane gas, propane gas, or any other form of liquefied petroleum gas or compressed natural gas. (Sec. 206.86(11), F.S.; *Tax Information Publication, No. 13B05-04*, Florida Department of Revenue, November 8, 2013)

Class	Vehicle License Category	State Fee	Local Fee for Each 1¢ of Local Option Gas Tax
A	Motorcycles, private use automobiles, trucks having a net weight not over 5,000 lbs., antique trucks, for-hire motor vehicles of less than 9 passenger capacity, and motor homes of less than 4,500 lbs. net wt.	$44	$11
B	Trucks having a net weight over 5,000 lbs., motor vehicles equipped with machinery and used exclusively for well drilling, excavation, construction, or spraying, school buses, wreckers, hearses, ambulances, for-hire motor vehicles of more than 8 passenger capacity, motor homes with a net weight of 4,500 lbs. or more, and locally operated motor vehicles for hire.	$60	$15
C	Truck-tractors.	$84	$21

Specific motor fuel types discussed below are:

— A55 / A-21,

— biodiesel,

— compressed natural gas (CNG),

— E-85,

— ethanol,

— gasohol,

— liquefied natural gas (LNG),

— liquefied petroleum gas (LPG),

— M-85,

— methanol,

— natural gas fuel, and

— propane.

• *A55 / A-21*

As a fuel mixed with gasoline, A55/A-21 is taxed as a motor fuel. (Sec. 206.01, F.S.) For 2020, the state tax rate on motor fuel in Florida is 18.3 cents per gallon. (*Tax Information Publication, No. 19B05-03*, Florida Department of Revenue, November 22, 2019)

• *Biodiesel*

Biodiesel is taxed a diesel fuel. For 2020, the state tax rate on motor fuel in Florida is 18.3 cents per gallon. (*Tax Information Publication, No. 19B05-03*, Florida Department of Revenue, November 22, 2019) Biodiesel fuel manufacturers also must meet the reporting, binding, and licensing requirements prescribed for wholesalers. (Sec. 206.02(5), F.S.) "Biodiesel" means any product made from nonpetroleum-base oils or fats which is suitable for use in diesel- powered engines. "Biodiesel manufacturer" means industrial plants, regardless of capacity, where organic products are used in the production of biodiesel and includes businesses that process or blend organic products that are marketed as biodiesel. (Sec. 206.86(14), F.S.)

• *Compressed natural gas (CNG)*

Effective January 1, 2019, alternative fuels will be taxed pursuant to a motor fuel equivalent gallon ratio and governed by the statutes beginning at Sec. 206.9951, F.S.. Effective January 1, 2014, through December 31, 2018, alternative fuels are exempt from the annual decal fee as well as any sales and use taxes. (*Tax Information Publication, No. 13B05-04*, Florida Department of Revenue, November 8, 2013) Prior to January 1, 2014, in lieu of the excise tax, an annual decal fee was required. The fee rates based on vehicle type are outlined above. (Sec. 206.877, F.S.)

• *E-85*

As a fuel mixed with gasoline, E-85 is taxed as a motor fuel. (Sec. 206.01, F.S.) For 2020, the state tax rate on motor fuel in Florida is 18.3 cents per gallon. (*Tax Information Publication, No. 19B05-03*, Florida Department of Revenue, November 22, 2019)

• *Ethanol*

If ethanol is placed in the supply tank of a gasoline-powered motor vehicle, then ethanol is taxed as a motor fuel. (Sec. 206.01, F.S.) For 2020, the state tax rate on motor fuel in Florida is 18.3 cents per gallon. (*Tax Information Publication, No. 19B05-03*, Florida Department of Revenue, November 22, 2019) If ethanol is placed in the supply tank of a diesel-powered motor vehicle, then ethanol is taxed as diesel. (Sec. 206.86, F.S.) For 2020, the state tax rate on diesel fuel in Florida is 18.3 cents per gallon. (*Tax Information Publication, No. 19B05-03*, Florida Department of Revenue, November 22, 2019)

• *Gasohol*

As a fuel mixed with gasoline, gasohol is taxed as a motor fuel. (Sec. 206.01, F.S.) For 2020, the state tax rate on motor fuel in Florida is 18.3 cents per gallon. (*Tax Information Publication, No. 19B05-03*, Florida Department of Revenue, November 22, 2019)

• *Liquefied natural gas (LNG)*

Effective January 1, 2019, alternative fuels will be taxed pursuant to a motor fuel equivalent gallon ratio and governed by the statutes beginning at Sec. 206.9951, F.S. Effective January 1, 2014, through December 31, 2018, alternative fuels are exempt from the annual decal fee as well as any sales and use taxes. (*Tax Information Publication, No. 13B05-04*, Florida Department of Revenue, November 8, 2013)

• *Liquefied petroleum gas (LPG)*

Effective January 1, 2019, alternative fuels will be taxed pursuant to a motor fuel equivalent gallon ratio and governed by the statutes beginning at Sec. 206.9951, F.S. Effective January 1, 2014, through December 31, 2018, alternative fuels are exempt from the annual decal fee as well as any sales and use taxes. (*Tax Information Publication, No. 13B05-04*, Florida Department of Revenue, November 8, 2013) Prior to January 1, 2014, in lieu of the excise tax, an annual decal fee was required. The fee rates based on vehicle type are outlined above. (Sec. 206.877, F.S.)

• *M-85*

As a fuel mixed with gasoline, M-85 is taxed as a motor fuel. (Sec. 206.01, F.S.) For 2020, the state tax rate on motor fuel in Florida is 18.3 cents per gallon. (*Tax Information Publication, No. 19B05-03*, Florida Department of Revenue, November 22, 2019)

• *Methanol*

If ethanol is placed in the supply tank of a gasoline-powered motor vehicle, then ethanol is taxed as a motor fuel. (Sec. 206.01, F.S.) For 2020, the state tax rate on motor fuel in Florida is 18.3 cents per gallon. (*Tax Information Publication, No. 19B05-03*, Florida Department of Revenue, November 22, 2019) If ethanol is placed in the supply tank of a diesel-powered motor vehicle, then ethanol is taxed as diesel. (Sec. 206.86, F.S.) For 2020, the state tax rate on diesel fuel in Florida is 18.3 cents per gallon. (*Tax Information Publication, No. 19B05-03*, Florida Department of Revenue, November 22, 2019)

• *Natural gas fuel*

"Natural gas fuel" means any LPG product, CNG product, or combination thereof used in a motor vehicle, and includes all forms of fuel known or sold as natural gasoline, butane gas, propane gas, or any other form of LPG, CNG, or LNG. Through December 31, 2023, natural gas fuel is exempt from motor and other fuel taxes and sales tax. (Sec. 206.9951, F.S.; Sec. 206.9955, F.S.)

Effective January 1, 2024, the following taxes are imposed:

— an excise tax of 4 cents on each motor fuel equivalent gallon of natural gas fuel;

— an additional tax of 1 cent on each motor fuel equivalent gallon of natural gas fuel (designated as the "ninth-cent fuel tax");

— an additional tax of 1 cent on each motor fuel equivalent gallon of natural gas fuel by each county (designated as the "local option fuel tax");

— an additional tax on each motor fuel equivalent gallon of natural gas fuel (designated as the "State Comprehensive Enhanced Transportation System Tax") (before January 1, 2024, and each year thereafter, the department will determine the tax rate applicable to the sale of natural gas fuel);

— an additional tax on each motor fuel equivalent gallon of natural gas fuel for the privilege of selling natural gas fuel (before January 1, 2024, and each year thereafter, the department will determine the tax rate applicable to the sale of natural gas fuel).

(Sec. 206.9955, F.S.)

Each natural gas fuel retailer is required to electronically file, beginning with February 2024, and each month thereafter, no later than the 20th day of each month, monthly reports with the department showing information on inventory, purchases, nontaxable disposals, taxable uses, and taxable sales in gallons of natural gas fuel for the preceding month. (Sec. 206.996, F.S.)

• *Propane*

Effective January 1, 2019, alternative fuels will be taxed pursuant to a motor fuel equivalent gallon ratio and governed by the statutes beginning at Sec. 206.9951, F.S. Effective January 1, 2014, through December 31, 2018, alternative fuels are exempt from the annual decal fee as well as any sales and use taxes. (*Tax Information Publication, No. 13B05-04*, Florida Department of Revenue, November 8, 2013

[¶40-009] Motor Carriers, International Fuel Tax Agreement

Florida is a participant in the International Fuel Tax Agreement (IFTA).

Specific topics discussed below are:

— Motor carriers, and

— International Fuel Tax Agreement.

• *Motor carriers*

A tax is imposed upon each motor carrier on each gallon of motor fuel or diesel fuel used for the propulsion of a commercial motor vehicle by the carrier within Florida. (Sec. 207.003, F.S.) The rate of tax includes the motor and special fuel tax rates (incorporating the voted fuel tax, local option gas tax, and state comprehensive enhanced transportation system tax) and the sales and use tax. (Sec. 207.003, F.S.)

A tax credit equal to the amount of the motor fuel, diesel fuel, and fuel sales taxes per gallon, and the voted, local option, and enhanced transportation system fuel tax provisions is allowed for each gallon of fuel purchased during the reporting period when the motor fuel or diesel fuel tax was paid at the time of purchase. (Sec. 207.005(3), F.S.) If those taxes exceed this tax, the excess may be allowed as a credit against the future tax payments. A refund may be made for the credit provided it exceeds $10. Excess credits may be carried forward for no longer than eight calendar quarters after the end of the calendar quarter in which the credit accrued.

All commercial motor vehicles, other than Florida-based commercial motor vehicles which travel Florida interstate mileage only, are issued a special fuel and motor fuel use tax identifying device upon payment of an $4 annual fee. (Sec. 207.004, F.S.) Motor carriers are also authorized to operate commercial motor vehicles in Florida if registered under a cooperative reciprocal agreement. Alternatively, motor carriers may secure an emergency or trip permit, valid for 10 days, at a cost of $45.

Registered motor carriers engaged in driveaway transportation may secure an annual driveaway permit upon payment of a $4 fee.

Reports are due on July 1, when annual filing is required; January 1 and July 1, when semiannual filing is required; and January 1, April 1, July 1, and October 1, when quarterly filing is required. (Sec. 207.005(1), F.S.) Taxes due are payable annually on the first day of the month following the last month of the reporting period.

• *International Fuel Tax Agreement*

Citations (e.g., R212) in this discussion of IFTA are to the IFTA Articles of Agreement (e.g., R212), Audit Manual (e.g., A310), or Procedures Manual (e.g., P410), each of which can be reviewed on the International Fuel Tax Association Web site. IFTA does not apply in the states of Alaska or Hawaii; the District of Columbia; or the Canadian provinces of Yukon Territory, Northwest Territory, or Nunavut.

The IFTA is a tax collection agreement among the 48 contiguous states and member Canadian provinces. The agreement is intended to provide uniform administration of motor fuels use taxation laws with respect to qualified motor vehicles operated in more than one member jurisdiction. Concepts at the core of the agreement include:

— base jurisdiction,

— retention of sovereign authority to exercise substantive tax authority over matters such as tax rates and exemptions, and

— uniform definition of vehicles to which the agreement applies.

(R130.100)

Definitions.—For purposes of IFTA, "base jurisdiction" means the member jurisdiction where qualified motor vehicles are based for vehicle registration purposes and where:

— operational control and operational records of a licensee's qualified motor vehicles are maintained or can be made available, and

— some travel is accrued by qualified motor vehicles within the licensee's fleet.

(R212)

The commissioners of two or more affected jurisdictions may allow a person to consolidate several fleets that otherwise would be based in two or more jurisdictions.

A "qualified motor vehicle" is a motor vehicle used, designed, or maintained for transportation of persons or property, and either:

— having two axles with a gross vehicle or registered gross vehicle weight over 26,000 pounds or 11,797 kilograms;

— having three or more axles, regardless of weight; or

— used in combination and the gross vehicle or the registered vehicle weight of the combined vehicle weight exceeds 26,000 pounds or 11,797 kilograms.

(R245)

"Qualified motor vehicle" does not include recreational vehicles.

"Motor fuel" means all fuels placed in the supply tank of qualified motor vehicles. (R239)

Licensing requirements, alternative.—Generally, persons based in a member jurisdiction operating a qualified motor vehicle in two or more member jurisdictions are required to be licensed under this Agreement. (R305) In lieu of such motor fuel tax licensing, persons may elect to satisfy motor fuels use tax obligations on a trip-by-trip basis. (R310) Persons required to register must file an application for licensing with their base jurisdiction and annually must renew their licenses, which expire December 31. (R610)

Recordkeeping requirements.—Generally, licensees must preserve records related to quarterly tax returns for four years from the later of the tax return due date or filing date. (IFTA Procedure Manual, P510.100) The records must be made available to any member jurisdiction upon request. (IFTA Procedure Manual, P520.100)

Reporting periods, due dates, requirements.—Generally, licensees must file a quarterly report on or before the last day of the month immediately following the close of each calendar quarter, even if no operations were conducted or no taxable fuel was used during the reporting period. (R930.100, R960.100) However, a licensee whose operations total less than 5,000 miles or 8,000 kilometers in all member jurisdictions other than the base jurisdiction during 12 consecutive months may ask to report on an annual basis. The request must be approved by the base jurisdiction. (R930.200) If the request is approved, the licensee's annual return will be due on January 31 following the close of the annual tax reporting period. (R960.100)

Payment.—Licensees must pay all taxes due to all member jurisdictions with the remittances payable to the base jurisdictions on the same dates that reports are due. (R910) Payments may be made by hand delivery, postal service delivery, or by electronic means approved by the base jurisdiction. (R960)

Licensee responsibility.—The timely filing of the tax return and the payment of taxes due to the base jurisdiction for all member jurisdiction discharges the responsibility of the licensee for filing of tax returns and payment of individual taxes to all member jurisdictions. (R920)

Refunds.—Licensees can claim a tax-paid credit on the IFTA tax return for fuel purchased at retail only when the fuel is placed into the fuel tank of a qualified motor vehicle and the purchase price includes fuel tax paid to a member jurisdiction. (R1010) For storage fuel purchased in bulk, a credit can be claimed on the IFTA return only when:

— the fuel is placed into the fuel tank of a qualified motor vehicle;

— the bulk storage tank is owned, leased, or controlled by the licensee; and either

— the purchase price of the fuel includes fuel tax paid to the member jurisdiction where the bulk fuel storage tan is located; or

¶40-009

— the licensee has paid fuel tax to the member jurisdiction where the bulk fuel storage tank is located.

(R1020.200)

Licensees can receive full credit or refund for tax-paid fuel used outside the jurisdiction where the fuel was purchased. The base jurisdiction must allow credits and issue refunds for all of its licensees on behalf of all member jurisdictions, as long as the licensee has satisfied all tax liability, including audit assessments, to all member jurisdictions. (R1100) If a credit is not refunded, it shall be carried over to offset the licensee's liabilities for the earlier of:

(1) the time at which the credit is fully offset; or

(2) eight calendar quarters.

(R1120.100)

A licensee may apply an overpayment generated in one jurisdiction to taxes owed to another jurisdiction. (R1120.200)

If a refund is paid more than 90 days after an application was made, the refund is subject to interest at the rate of 1% per month or part of a month calculated from the date the refund was due. (R1150)

Assessment and collection.—A base jurisdiction may, among other things, assess tax against any licensee that:

— fails, neglects, or refuses to file a tax return when due;

— fails to make records available upon written request; or

— fails to maintain records from which the licensee's true liability can be determined.

(R1200)

The assessment made by the base jurisdiction will be presumed correct.

Penalties, interest.—For failing to file a tax return, filing a late tax return, or underpaying taxes due, a licensee may be assessed a penalty equaling the greater of $50.00 or 10% of delinquent taxes. Nothing in the IFTA limits the authority of a base jurisdiction to impose any other penalties provided by the laws of the base jurisdiction. (R1220)

The base jurisdiction shall assess interest on qualifying delinquent taxes at the rate of 1% per month. (R1230.100) Interest will be calculated separately for each jurisdiction from the date tax was due for each month or fraction of a month. (R1230.300) All interest collected shall be remitted to the appropriate jurisdiction. (R1230.400)

A base jurisdiction may waive penalties for reasonable cause. If the base jurisdiction's laws permit waiver of interest and a licensee demonstrates that a tax return was filed late due to misinformation given by the base jurisdiction, the base jurisdiction may waive interest, also. However, to waive interest for another jurisdiction, the base jurisdiction must receive written approval from that jurisdiction. (R1260)

Audits.—While each base jurisdiction must audit its licensees on behalf of all member jurisdictions, other jurisdictions are not precluded from also auditing those licensees. (R1310) Audits conducted by member jurisdictions must be in compliance with IFTA Articles of Agreement, Procedures Manual, and Audit Manual. (R1330)

Appeal Procedures.—While IFTA has appeal procedures for licensees, those procedures only apply if the base jurisdiction does not have provisions for appeals of actions or audit findings. (R1400)

In order to appeal an action or audit finding, a licensee must make a written request for a hearing within 30 days after service of notice of the original action or finding. (R1410) The hearing must be held "expeditiously," and the base jurisdiction must give at least 20 days' notice of the time and place of the hearing. (R1420)

The licensee may appear in person and/or be represented by counsel and may produce witnesses, documents, or other pertinent material. (R1430.100) If the licensee appeals an assessment for one or more jurisdictions, the base jurisdiction will be responsible for participating in the appeal on behalf of the other jurisdictions. (R1430.200) The base jurisdiction will notify the licensee of the findings of fact and the ruling on the appeal. (R1440)

An appeal of any jurisdiction's findings will proceed in accordance with that jurisdiction's laws. (R1450.100) In the case of an audit, the licensee may request any or every jurisdiction to audit the licensee's records. Each jurisdiction can accept or deny the request, and those electing to audit the record will audit only for its own portion of the licensee's operations. (R1450.200)

[¶40-011] Fuel Taxes Practice and Procedure

Discussed here are general topics and administrative matters relative to Florida fuel tax types.

Specific topics discussed below are:

— administration,

— penalties,

— refunds,

— recordkeeping,

— assessment and collection,

— audits,

— appeal procedures,

— forms, and

— federal constitutional issues.

• *Administration*

The Florida Department of Revenue administers the motor fuel tax. (Sec. 206.01, F.S.)

• *Penalties*

If someone fails to pay the tax as required, a penalty in the amount of 10% of any unpaid tax during the first month with an additional 10% of any unpaid tax for each additional month or fraction. However, the penalty may not exceed 50% in the aggregate of any unpaid tax. (Sec. 206.44, F.S.) Taxpayer will be penalized if any false or fraudulent statements of reports are submitted. Additionally, penalties also exist if any person who willfully refuses or neglects to make a statement, report, or return, who knowingly makes or assists in making, a false statement, who knowingly collects or attempts to collect or causes to be paid any refund without being entitled to it, or who violates any other provisions under the motor fuel or diesel fuel tax provisions. (Sec. 206.10, F.S.) A penalty will also be incurred if licensing requirements are not met. (Sec. 206.404, F.S.)

Motor carriers.—Motor carriers who fail to file a return and pay any tax liability on the operation of commercial motor vehicles in Florida are subject to a penalty equal to the greater of: $50 or 10% of the delinquent taxes due, when the failure is for not more than 30 days. An additional 10% penalty is imposed for each additional 30 days during the time which the failure continues, not to exceed a total penalty of 100% in the aggregate. (Sec. 207.007(1), F.S.) Delinquent tax bears interest at the rate of 1% per month (or fraction thereof), calculated from the date the tax was due. (Sec.

207.007(2), F.S.) However, if the Department of Highway Safety and Motor Vehicles enters into a cooperative reciprocal agreement, it must collect and distribute all interest due to other jurisdictions at the same rate as if the interest were due to the state.

• *Refunds*

A refund is available for a tax erroneously paid or legally collected on motor fuel or diesel fuel. (Sec, 206.13, F.S.)

Ethanol.—A ethanol dealer is entitled to a refund if the dealer paid tax on purchases of motor fuel used for denaturing from a duly licensed terminal supplier, importer, or wholesaler. (Sec. 206.626, F.S.)

• *Record keeping*

Each person must maintain records of motor fuel received, used, transferred, sold, and elivered within Florida. (Sec. 206.12, F.S.)

• *Assessment and collection*

The methods and means of effecting and enforcing the collection of fuel taxes are in addition to, and not in lieu of, the methods and means of effecting and enforcing collection set out in the fuel tax laws of Florida. (Sec. 206.25, F.S.)

• *Audits*

The Department of Revenue is authorized to audit and examine the records, books, papers, and equipment of terminal suppliers, importers, exporters, or whole-salers, retail dealers, terminal operators, or all private and common carriers to verify any statement or report. (Sec. 206.14, F.S.)

• *Appeal procedures*

Florida does not provide any specific appeal procedures for motor fuel tax purposes.

• *Federal constitutional issues*

The constitutionality of state motor fuels tax laws is governed, to an extent, by an assortment of U.S. Supreme Court decisions. While an individual state may generally impose a tax on the use, sale, or delivery of gasoline and other motor fuels within its borders, the state is subject to certain federal constitutional limitations. Primary among these restrictions are the U.S. Constitution's provisions that prohibit a state from:

— taxing the federal government,

— violating either the Due Process Clause or the Equal Protection Clause of the federal Constitution's Fourteenth Amendment,

— imposing an undue burden on interstate commercial transactions,

— interfering with an Indian Nation's sovereignty, and

— bypassing the limitations generally placed on the taxation of property.

A select number of U.S. Supreme Court decisions addressing these federal constitutional limitations are briefly summarized below:

General parameters of federal and state authority.—The regulation of all inter-state commerce is within the exclusive power of the federal government under the Commerce Clause of the U.S. Constitution. A state may, however, tax a motor fuel as long as the free flow of interstate commerce is not impeded and the federal Due Process Clause or Equal Protection Clause is not violated. (*National Private Truck Council, Inc. v. Oklahoma Tax Commission* (1995), 515 U.S. 582, 115 S.Ct. 2351)

Taxation of the federal government.—Tennessee could impose a storage tax on gasoline owned by the federal government that was stored by a private company. The applicable tax was not based on the worth of the government's property but was imposed on the privilege of storing such property. The federal Constitution did not extend sovereign immunity from state taxation to a corporation or an individual contracting with the United States merely because the activities of such parties were useful to the federal government. Therefore, federal sovereign immunity did not prohibit this tax. Although the final tax burden was borne by the federal government, federal ownership alone did not immunize a private person. (*Esso Standard Oil Co. v. Evans* (1953), 345 U.S. 495, 73 S. Ct. 800) See, also, *Panhandle Oil Co. v. Mississippi* (1928), 277 U.S. 218, 48 S. Ct. 45, and *Graves v. Texas Co.* (1936), 298 U.S. 393, 56 S. Ct. 818.

Due Process Clause.—A state statute requiring a seller of gasoline to file a motor fuels tax report and to remit to the state any tax collected from the purchaser of such gasoline, and that also assessed a penalty for a seller's failure to do so, did not involve a deprivation of property and did not violate the federal Constitution's Due Process Clause. It was proper for a state to pass these reporting and collection responsibilities to a seller, even though such efforts entailed both an inconvenience and an expense to the seller. (*Pierce Oil Corp. v. Hopkins* (1924), 264 U.S. 137, 44 S. Ct. 251)

A foreign corporation that was a licensed Idaho dealer in motor fuels that sold and transferred gasoline in Utah for importation into Idaho by a federal agency could not be constitutionally taxed by Idaho on the theory that the dealer constructively "received" the gasoline in Idaho upon its importation. The fact that a foreign corporation had an Idaho gasoline dealer's license and engaged in business in Idaho did not permit Idaho to tax the corporation's out-of-state sale of gasoline to a federal agency for use in Idaho. The Utah sale was not related to the corporation's business activity in Idaho. In the absence of any indication that the taxpayer's activity in Idaho contributed to the procurement or performance of its out-of-state contract with the federal government, the federal Due Process Clause did not permit the imposition of a tax on the out-of-state sale. (*American Oil Co. v. Neill* (1965), 380 U.S. 451)

Equal Protection Clause.—A Montana motor fuels tax did not violate the federal Equal Protection Clause where the basis of the tax was the sale of gasoline within the state by a distributor or dealer refining or importing gasoline, and the tax was only applied to an in-state refiner. The tax was not extended to include gasoline shipped in from other states. (*Hart Refineries v. Harmon* (1929), 278 U.S. 499, 49 S. Ct. 188)

Burden on interstate commerce.—A Kentucky tax on gasoline sold within the state at wholesale ("wholesale" being defined to include gasoline obtained from outside the state and used within the state) was unconstitutional as a direct burden on interstate commerce when applied to gasoline purchased in Illinois and consumed in a ferry boat operating mostly in Kentucky. (*Helson v. Kentucky* (1929), 279 U.S. 245, 49 S. Ct. 279)

A South Carolina tax on the privilege of selling gasoline within the state was upheld when applied to an air transport company doing business mainly interstate but purchasing its gasoline within South Carolina. The mere purchase of supplies or equipment for use in conducting an interstate business was not so identified with that commerce as to make the purchase immune from a nondiscriminatory state tax. A nondiscriminatory tax upon a local sale was not regarded as imposing a direct burden upon interstate commerce. (*Eastern Air Transport, Inc. v. South Carolina Tax Commission* (1932), 285 U.S. 147, 52 S. Ct. 340; See, also, *Gregg Dyeing Co. v. Query* (1932), 286 U.S. 472, 52 S. Ct. 631)

A tax imposed on the storage or withdrawal from storage of gasoline for sale or use within the state was constitutionally applied to gasoline shipped into the state by a railroad for storage and subsequent consumption in the operation of its equipment in interstate commerce. This tax was not a direct burden on interstate commerce. (*Nashville, C & St. L. Ry. v. Wallace* (1933), 288 U.S. 249, 53 S. Ct. 345)

A Pennsylvania tax imposed upon a distributor of liquid motor fuels used or sold within the state was constitutional as applied to a Pittsburgh corporation that sold fuel at wholesale as a distributor throughout Pennsylvania. Since the applicable sales contracts were made in Pennsylvania, and interstate transportation was not required or contemplated, any resulting interstate transport was deemed to be merely incidental. Accordingly, interstate commerce was not burdened by this tax. (*Wiloil Corp. v. Pennsylvania* (1935), 294 U.S. 169, 55 S. Ct. 358)

An Arkansas tax imposed on the gasoline in the fuel and storage tanks of a bus entering the state was a federally unconstitutional burden on interstate commerce. While a state may charge reasonable compensation for the use of its highways, this gasoline tax, without regard to the amount actually used within the state, had no reasonable relationship to compensation for highway use. (*McCarroll v. Dixie Greyhound Lines, Inc.* (1940), 309 U.S. 176, 60 S. Ct. 504) See, also, *Bingaman v. Golden Eagle Western Lines, Inc.* (1936), 297 U.S. 626, 56 S. Ct. 624.

A Pennsylvania motor fuels identification marker fee was an unconstitutional burden on interstate commerce. (*American Trucking Association, Inc. v. Scheiner* (1987), 483 U.S. 266)

An Ohio motor vehicle fuels sales tax credit that was available to an in-state producer of ethanol and also to an out-of-state producer whose home state granted a reciprocal credit for ethanol produced in Ohio clearly discriminated against interstate commerce and was not justified by a valid purpose unrelated to economic protectionism. The purpose of the credit was not to promote health or commerce, but rather to provide favorable tax treatment for ethanol produced in Ohio. Furthermore, even if there was neither a widespread advantage to in-state interests nor a widespread disadvantage to out-of-state competitors, when such discrimination was patent, the Court was required to invalidate such a law. (*New Energy Co. of Indiana v. Limbach, Tax Commissioner of Ohio* (1988), 486 U.S. 269, 108 S. Ct. 1803)

Indian Nation's sovereignty.—An Oklahoma motor fuels excise tax imposed on fuel sold by an Indian retail store on an Indian tribe's trust land was prohibited under the doctrine of Indian sovereignty because the legal incidence of the tax ultimately rested on the tribe as the retailer. Although the state's excise tax law did not expressly provide that the tax was imposed on the retailer, the legal incidence of the tax rested upon the retailer, rather than on the distributor or consumer, because:

(1) the tax had to be remitted on behalf of a licensed retailer,

(2) a retailer was liable for any tax not paid by the consumer,

(3) a retailer was not compensated for collecting the tax, and

(4) the tax was imposed when the fuel was sold by a distributor to a retailer without regard to whether the fuel was later purchased by a consumer.

(*Oklahoma Tax Commission v. Chickasaw Nation* (1995), 515 U.S. 450, 115 S. Ct. 2214)

A Kansas tax on motor fuels received by a non-Indian distributor, but subsequently delivered to an Indian reservation's gas station, was constitutionally valid and did not affront a tribe's sovereignty. The distributor paid the tax on its initial receipt of the fuel and then merely passed the tax cost onto its customers, including a retailer located on an Indian reservation. The implementation of this tax did not adversely impact Indian sovereignty because this nondiscriminatory tax was imposed on an off-reservation transaction between non-Indians. The legal incidence of the tax was on the non-Indian distributor and it was the distributor's off-reservation receipt of the fuel that established the tax liability. (*Wagnon v. Prairie Band Potawatomi Nation* (2005), 546 U.S. 95, 126 S. Ct. 676)

Property tax limitations.—A New Mexico motor fuels tax that was measured by the number of gallons of gasoline bought, sold, or used in the state was not unconstitutional. The tax, applicable to a distributor, was an excise tax that was not subject to the federal constitutional limitations generally placed on the taxation of property. While an excise tax could not be imposed upon interstate commerce, it was valid as applied to intrastate commerce. However, gasoline brought from outside the state and sold in its original containers could not be subject to such a tax since any enforcement would be a direct burden on interstate commerce. But gasoline brought from outside the state and sold from broken packages in quantities to suit customers or used by a distributor in the operation of its stations was validly subject to the excise tax, since it had gone beyond interstate commerce. (*Bowman v. Continental Oil Co.* (1921), 256 U.S. 642, 41 S. Ct. 606)

CIGARETTES, TOBACCO PRODUCTS

[¶55-000]
CIGARETTES, TOBACCO PRODUCTS

[¶55-001] Cigarettes

The term "cigarette" is defined to be any roll for smoking, except one of which the tobacco is fully naturally fermented, without regard to the kind of tobacco or other substances used in the inner roll or the nature or composition of the material in which the roll is wrapped, which is made wholly or in part of tobacco irrespective of size or shape and whether such tobacco is flavored, adulterated or mixed with any other ingredient. (Sec. 210.01, F. S.)

An excise tax is imposed upon the sale, receipts, purchase, possession, consumption, handling, distribution, and use of cigarettes in the state. (Sec. 210.02, F. S.)

Cigarettes also are subject to sales tax in the state. See Tobacco Products.

In additional to all other taxes, a surcharge is levied upon the sale, receipt, purchase, possession, consumption, handling, distribution, and use of cigarettes in Florida. The additional surcharge is levied upon existing inventory. (Sec. 210.011)

For a discussion of the tax on tobacco products, see Tobacco Products. Administrative and procedural provisions are discussed at Cigarette, Tobacco Products Tax Practice and Procedure.

Discussed here in relation to the cigarette tax are:

— Persons and products subject to tax,

— Exemptions,

— Basis of tax,

— Rate of tax,

— Reports,

— Payment,

— Credits, refunds, discounts,

— Licenses and permits, and

— Local taxes.

• *Persons and products subject to tax*

The tax is collected only once on the same package of cigarettes. (Sec. 210.04(2), F. S.)

Master Settlement Agreement.—Florida is not bound to the Master Settlement Agreement (MSA) because it is one of four states that settled with the original participating manufacturers prior to the adoption of the MSA. (*Int'l Tobacco Partners, Ltd. v. Kline*, 475 F. Supp. 2d 1078, 1081-1082 (D. Kan. 2007))

Mail order, Internet, remote and delivery sales.—Each person accepting a purchase order for any sale of tobacco products, including cigarettes, to a consumer in Florida for which the consumer submitted the order for the sale by telephone, mail, delivery service, or the Internet, or the products were delivered by use of mail or delivery service must collect and remit cigarette and tobacco product tax. For cigarettes, the collection and remission is not required if the person has obtained proof that taxes have already been paid to Florida. Such proof includes applicable tax stamps or tax exempt stamps. (Sec. 210.095)

Sales on Indian nation or tribal reservations.—Sales to a member of an Indian tribe recognized in Florida who purchases cigarettes on an Indian reservation for a personal use is exempt from paying a cigarette tax and surcharge. However, the tax and surcharge will apply if a member purchases cigarettes outside of the reservation or if a nonmember purchases cigarettes on the reservations. (Sec. 210.1801)

- *Exemptions*

Exemptions apply to sales made:

— in interstate commerce (Sec. 210.04(3), F.S.)

— to or by Army, Navy, Air Force, and effective July 1, 2022, Space Force post exchanges, ship service stores, ship stores, slop chests, or base exchanges (Sec. 210.04(4)(a), F.S.)

— by charitable organizations to patients in government veterans' hospitals or inmates of a federal prison. (Sec. 210.04(4)(b), F.S.; Rule 61A-10.005)

— to a member of an Indian tribe recognized in Florida who purchases cigarettes on an Indian reservation for a personal use is exempt from paying a cigarette tax and surcharge. However, the tax and surcharge will apply if a member purchases cigarettes outside of the reservation or if a nonmember purchases cigarettes on the reservations. (Sec. 210.1801, F.S.)

- *Basis of tax*

The tax on cigarettes is imposed upon the sale, receipt, purchase, possession, consumption, handling, distribution, and use of cigarettes. (Sec. 210.02, F. S.) The tax is added to the sales price of cigarettes sold or distributed, which amount may be stated separately from the price of the cigarettes. (Sec. 210.04(1), F. S.)

- *Rate of tax*

Rates are as follows (Sec. 210.02, F. S.; Sec. 210.011) :

Cigarettes weighing not more than 3 lbs. per thousand	16.95 mills per cigarette (plus a 5 cent surcharge on each cigarette)
Same packed in varying quantities of 20 cigarettes or less:	
Packages containing 10 cigarettes or less	16.95¢ per package (plus a surcharge of 50 cents)
Packages containing more than 10 cigarettes and not more than 20	33.9¢ per package (plus a surcharge of $1)
Cigarettes weighing more than 3 lbs. per thousand, not more than six inches long	33.9 mills per cigarette (plus a surcharge of 10 cents each cigarette)
Same packed in varying quantities of 20 cigarettes or less:	
Packages containing 10 cigarettes or less	33.9¢ per package (plus a surcharge $1)
Packages containing more than 10 cigarettes and not more than 20	67.8¢ per package (plus a surcharge of $2)
Cigarettes weighing more than 3 lbs. per thousand, more than six inches long	67.8 mills per cigarette (plus a surcharge of 20 cents on each cigarette)
Same packed in varying quantities of 20 cigarettes or less:	
Packages containing 10 cigarettes or less	67.8¢ per package (plus a surcharge of $2)
Packages containing more than 10 cigarettes but not more than 20	135.6¢ per package (plus a surcharge of $4)

• *Reports*

Reports are due by the 10th of each month from wholesale dealers, cigarette distributing agents, and exporters (Sec. 210.09(2), F. S.; Rule 61A-10.011) , and from companies operating railroads, passenger vessels, and airlines. (Rule 61A-10.010)

Jenkins Act registration and reporting.—The federal Jenkins Act (15 U.S.C. §§ 375-378), as amended in 2010 by the Prevent All Cigarette Trafficking Act of 2009 (PACT Act), Pub. L. No. 111-154, imposes certain registration and reporting requirements on those who sell, transfer, or ship (or who advertise or offer to do so) cigarettes, roll-your-own tobacco, and smokeless tobacco for profit in interstate commerce to a state, locality, or Indian country of an Indian tribe that taxes the sale or use of such products.

Registration requirement: A statement must be filed with the U.S. Attorney General and with the tobacco tax administrators of the state and place into which the products are shipped (or where advertisements or offers are directed). The statement must provide the name and trade name (if any) of the seller, transferor, or shipper, and the address of its principal place of business and of any other place of business. (15 U.S.C. § 376(a)) Additionally, the statement must include telephone numbers for each place of business, a principal e-mail address, any website addresses, and the name, address, and telephone number of an agent in the state authorized to accept service on behalf of the seller, transferor, or shipper. (15 U.S.C. § 376(a))

As an alternative to filing a statement with the U.S. Attorney General, Form 5070.1 can be filed with the Bureau of Alcohol, Tobacco, Firearms and Explosives (ATF). This federal form is available on the ATF's website at http://www.atf.gov/.

Reporting requirement: The Jenkins Act also imposes a duty to file on the 10th of each month with the relevant state tobacco tax administrator a report of the names and addresses of all of the seller's in-state cigarette and smokeless tobacco purchasers, the brand and quantity of cigarettes or smokeless tobacco, and the name, address, and phone number of the person delivering the shipment. (15 U.S.C. § 376(a)) A copy of the report must be filed with the chief law enforcement officer of the local government and any Indian tribe that applies its own local or tribal taxes on the cigarettes or smokeless tobacco purchased. (15 U.S.C. § 376(a)) These reports can be used by the state tobacco tax administrators and the local chief law enforcement officers that receive them to enforce the collection of any taxes owed on the sales. (15 U.S.C. § 376(c))

• *Payment*

The tax is collected by means of cash paid to the Department of Business Regulation for stamps to be affixed to cigarette packages. Payment for each month's liability is due on or before the 10th of the month following the month in which the stamps were sold and is in lieu of payment by cash on delivery or its equivalent. (Sec. 210.05(1), F. S.) After that date, the tax will bear interest at the rate of 1% per month. If the amount of tax due for a given period is assessed without allocating it to any particular month, the interest will begin with the date of the assessment. (Sec. 210.02(6), F.S.)

The Secretary of the Department of Business Regulation may require a cigarette dealer to remit taxes by electronic funds transfer if the total of taxes paid in the previous year amounted to $50,000 or more. (Sec. 210.021, F.S.) For rules detailing the payment of tax through electronic funds transfer, see Rule 61-15.001, et seq.

• *Credits, refunds, discounts*

Persons affixing stamps are allowed a discount of 2% of the par value of stamps purchased during a fiscal year. However, the discount is computed on the basis of a 24¢ per pack tax. (Sec. 210.05(3)(a), F. S.)

• *Licenses and permits*

Annual permit fees, due July 1, are $5 for distributing agents, and $100 for wholesale dealers and exporters. (Sec. 210.15, F. S.) Each applicant for a temporary initial cigarette permit must pay a $10 fee for the permit (Sec. 1, Ch. 91-131, Laws 1991) Each applicant seeking a temporary initial permit for other tobacco products must pay a fee of $25 for the permit. (Sec. 1, Ch. 91-131, Laws 1991) Retail tobacco products dealer permits are required for each place of business where tobacco products are sold at retail. The annual fee, set by the Division of Alcoholic Beverages and Tobacco, may not exceed $50. (Sec. 3, Ch. 92-285, Laws 1992)

• *Local taxes*

Municipalities may not levy cigarette taxes. (Sec. 210.03, F. S.)

[¶55-005] Tobacco Products

The term "tobacco products" means loose tobacco suitable for smoking; snuff; snuff flour; cavendish; plug and twist tobacco; fine cuts and other chewing tobaccos; shorts; refuse scraps; clippings, cuttings, and sweepings of tobacco, and other kinds and forms of tobacco prepared in such manner as to be suitable for chewing; but "tobacco products" does not include cigarettes or cigars. (Sec. 210.25, F. S.)

A tax is imposed upon all tobacco products in Florida and upon any distributor of tobacco products. A tax is imposed upon the use or storage by consumers of tobacco products (in quantities weighing more than a pound) in the state. (Sec. 210.30, F.S.)

Tobacco products also are subject to sales tax in the state.

A surcharge is levied upon all tobacco products. The surcharge will be levied at the time the distributor:

— brings or causes to be brought into Florida tobacco products for sale;

— makes, manufactures, or fabricates tobacco products in Florida for sale in the state; or

— ships or transports tobacco products to retailers in Florida to be sold by those retailers.

(Sec. 210.276)

A surcharge is also imposed upon the use or storage by consumers of tobacco products in Florida. (Sec. 210.276)

For a discussion of the cigarette tax, see Cigarettes. Administrative and procedural provisions are discussed at Cigarette, Tobacco Products Tax Practice and Procedure.

Discussed here in relation to the tobacco products tax are:

— Persons and products subject to tax,

— Exemptions,

— Basis of tax,

— Rate of tax,

— Reports,

— Payment,

— Credits, refunds, discounts,

— Licenses and permits, and

— Local taxes.

• *Persons and products subject to tax*

A tax is imposed upon all tobacco products and any person engaged in business as a distributor of tobacco products. Moreover, the tax is also applicable to consumers that use or consume tobacco products weighing more than one pound. Moreover, consumers are exempt from the tax if the tax has already been paid by a distributor. (Sec. 210.30, F.S.)

The tax on distributors is imposed when the following events take place:

— imports tobacco products into the state for sale;

— makes, manufactures, or fabricates tobacco products in this state for sale in this state; or

— ships or transports tobacco products to retailers in this state, to be sold by those retailers.

(Sec. 210.30, F.S.)

Mail order, Internet, remote and delivery sales.—Each person accepting a purchase order for any sale of tobacco products to a consumer in Florida for which the consumer submitted the order for the sale by telephone, mail, delivery service, or the Internet, or the products were delivered by use of mail or delivery service must collect and remit the excise tax. (Sec. 210.095)

Sales on Indian nation or tribal reservations.—A member of an Indian tribe recognized in Florida who purchases tobacco products on an Indian reservation for a personal use is exempt from paying a tobacco products tax and surcharge. However, the tax and surcharge will apply if a member purchases tobacco products outside of the reservation or if a nonmember purchases tobacco products on the reservation. (Sec. 210.1801)

• *Exemptions*

Exemptions apply to sales made:

— in interstate commerce (Sec. 210.04(3), F.S.) ;

— to or by Army, Navy, Air Force, and effective July 1, 2022, Space Force post exchanges, ship service stores, ship stores, slop chests, or base exchanges (Sec. 210.04(4)(a), F.S.) ;

— by charitable organizations to patients in government veterans' hospitals or inmates of a federal prison (Sec. 210.04(4)(b), F. S.; Rule 61A-10.005) ;

— to a member of an Indian tribe recognized in Florida who purchases tobacco products on an Indian reservation for a personal use is exempt from paying a tobacco products tax and surcharge. However, the tax and surcharge will apply if a member purchases tobacco products outside of the reservation or if a nonmember purchases tobacco products on the reservation (Sec. 210.1801, F.S.) ; and

— of any tobacco product that has already been taxed. (Sec. 210.30, F.S.)

(Sec. 210.30, F. S.)

• *Basis of tax*

For distributors subject to the tax, the tax is based on the wholesale price of the tobacco products. For consumers subject to the tax, the tax is based on the cost of the tobacco products. (Sec. 210.30, F.S.)

• *Rate of tax*

The tax on distributors is 25% of the wholesale sales price. The tax on consumers is 25% of the cost of the tobacco products. (Sec. 210.30, F.S.)

The surcharge levied upon all tobacco products in Florida and upon any distributor at a rate of 60% of the wholesale price. A surcharge is imposed upon the use or storage by consumers of tobacco products at the rate of 60% of the wholesale sales price. (Sec. 210.276)

The "wholesale sales price" is the full price paid by the distributor to acquire the tobacco products, including charges by the seller for the cost of materials, the cost of labor and service, charges for transportation and delivery, the federal excise tax, and any other charge, even if the charge is listed as a separate item on the invoice paid by the distributor, exclusive of any diminution by volume or other discounts, including a discount provided to a distributor by an affiliate, plus the federal excise tax paid by the distributor on the tobacco products if the tax is not included in the full price. (Sec. 210.25, F. S.)

For the current cigarette tax rate, see Cigarettes.

• *Reports*

Reports are to be made to the Division of Alcoholic Beverages and Tobacco of the Department of Business and Professional Regulation on or before the 10th of each month for the preceding month. (Sec. 210.55(1), F.S.)

• *Payment*

Payments are to be made to the Division of Alcoholic Beverages and Tobacco of the Department of Business and Professional Regulation on or before the 10th of each month for the preceding month. (Sec. 210.55(1), F.S.) The Secretary of the Department of Business and Professional Regulation may require a distributor of tobacco products to remit taxes by electronic funds transfer if the total of taxes paid in the previous year amounted to $50,000 or more (Sec. 210.31, F.S.) For rules detailing the payment of tax through electronic funds transfer, see Rule 61-15.001, et seq.

• *Credits, refunds, discounts*

Distributors are allowed a collection discount of 1% of the amount of tax due. (Sec. 210.55(7), F.S.)

• *Licenses and permits*

Distributors are required to have a license; the license fee is $25. (Sec. 210.40, F.S.) Distributors' licenses expire on June 30 following the date of issue. (Sec. 210.45, F.S.)

• *Local taxes*

Unlike cigarettes, there is not an express ban on municipalities levying a tax on tobacco products.

[¶55-010] Cigarette, Tobacco Products Tax Practice and Procedure

Discussed here are the administrative and procedural issues involved in compliance and enforcement of the tax. Specific topics covered include:

— Administration,

— Penalties,

— Record keeping,

— Assessment and collection,

— Audits,

— Appeal procedures, and

— Forms.

•Administration

Administration of the tax is vested with the Division of Alcoholic Beverages and Tobacco, within the Department of Business and Professional Regulation. (Sec. 210.75, F.S.)

•Penalties

Cigarettes.—Anyone who knowingly omits, neglects, or refuses to comply with any duty imposed upon that person by the Florida laws imposing a tax on cigarettes is subject to, in addition to any other applicable penalties, a fine equalling the greater of $1,000 or five times the retail value of the cigarettes involved. In addition, anyone who fails to pay any tax on a timely basis shall, in addition to any other applicable penalty, be liable for a penalty of five times the unpaid tax due. (Sec. 210.181, F.S.)

Tobacco products.—Late payments shall bear interest at the annual rate of 12 percent. In issuing its final assessment, the division shall add a 10% penalty on unpaid taxes. Taxpayers filing false returns to evade taxes will face a 50% penalty of the tax shown on the corrected return. If the taxpayer fails to file and the division issues a notice, the penalty is 25% of the assessed amount. (Sec. 210.55, F.S.)

•Record keeping

Cigarettes.—All manufacturers, importers, distributing agents, wholesale dealers, agents, or retail dealers are required to keep and maintain records regarding cigarettes received, sold, or delivered within the state for 3 years. Moreover, the division or its duly authorized representative is authorized to examine the books, papers, invoices, and other records pertaining to the sale and delivery of cigarettes subject to tax. (Sec. 210.09, F.S.)

Additionally, all cigarette manufacturers, importers, wholesalers, or distributing agents, and agents and employees of the same, are required to keep daily sales tickets or invoices of cigarette sales. The division shall suspend or revoke the license of any person who is either a cigarette wholesaler, vending machine operator or distributing agent upon sufficient cause appearing that the said persons, their agents or employees have failed to keep daily sales tickets or invoices. (Sec. 210.09, F.S.)

Tobacco products.—Every distributor shall keep in each licensed place of business complete and accurate records for that place of business, including itemized invoices of tobacco products held, purchased, manufactured, brought in or caused to be brought in from without the state, or shipped or transported to retailers in this state, and of all sales of tobacco products made, except sales to an ultimate consumer. All books, records and other papers, shall be preserved for a period of at least 3 years. Duly authorized agents or employees of the division may enter any place of business of a distributor and inspect the premises, the records required to be kept, and the tobacco products contained therein to determine whether the distributor is in compliance the statutory record keeping requirements. (Sec. 210.60, F.S.)

•Assessment and collection

Cigarettes.—In the event a dealer fails to file a return, or files an incorrect/insufficient return (without notifying the division of a forthcoming correction within ten days), the division shall determine the amount of tax due and notify the dealer in writing. The dealer can request a hearing regarding the determination within 30 days of receiving the notice. (Sec. 210.13, F.S.)

When determining an assessment, the division can look to sales within 3 years of the earliest sale. (Sec. 210.13, F.S.)

The division has authority to issue warrants to collect unpaid taxes. (Sec. 210.14, F.S.)

Tobacco products.—There are no specific assessment and collection provisions under Florida tobacco products laws. See the discussion for all statutory provisions at ¶ 89-162 Collection Procedures.

• *Forms*

Forms may be downloaded from the division's website (http://www.myfloridalicense.com/dbpr/abt/forms.html).

SALES AND USE

[¶60-000]

INTRODUCTION

[¶60-020] Application of Sales and Use Taxes

Florida sales tax is a privilege tax imposed on each taxable transaction made by a dealer located in Florida and delivered to the purchaser or the purchaser's representative in Florida. Every person engaged in the business of selling tangible personal property for use, consumption, or storage for use in Florida is exercising a taxable privilege. (Sec. 212.02(2), F.S.; Sec. 212.054(3), F.S.)

The use tax is imposed on all persons that use, consume, distribute, or store tangible personal property in Florida and applies to tangible personal property purchased outside Florida that would have been subject to sales tax if purchased from a Florida dealer. (Sec. 212.05, F.S.; Rule 12A-1.091)

Which transactions are generally subject to sales tax in Florida?

Florida sales tax is imposed on all dealers engaged in the retail sale, lease, or rental of tangible personal property or taxable services in the state. (Sec. 212.05, F.S.) Florida sales tax is imposed at a percentage of the gross receipts and must be remitted to the state by the dealer after it is collected from the purchaser or consumer. The tax is added to the sale price and must be separately stated. The tax is a debt from the consumer to the dealer until paid. (Sec. 212.07, F.S.)

Imposition of tax. The tax is imposed on every person who does any of the following:

— engages in the business of renting or leasing living quarters;

— leases or rents parking or storage spaces for motor vehicles, docking or storage space for boats, or tie-down or storage space for aircraft;

— leases or rents real property;

— sells admissions;

— engages in the business of selling tangible personal property in the state, including the business of making mail remote sales;

— rents or furnishes any taxable things or services;

— leases or rents tangible personal property in the state; or

— engages in the state in the business of soliciting or issuing any service warranty.

Effective July 1, 2021, the definition of "retail sale" is expanded to include a sale facilitated through a marketplace. (Sec. 212.02(14)(e), (f), F.S.) A "marketplace" is any physical place or electronic medium through which tangible personal property is offered for sale. (Sec. 212.05965, F.S.)

Presumption of taxability. Every sale, lease, or rental is presumed taxable, unless it is specifically exempt. The exempt nature of the transaction must be established by the selling dealer.

Sales tax definitions.

Business. A "business" is any activity engaged in by any person for private or public gain, benefit, or advantage, either direct or indirect, except for occasional sales or leases to affiliates.

Dealer. A "dealer" is a person who:

— manufactures or produces tangible personal property for sale at retail, use, consumption, distribution, or storage for consumption in the state;

— imports goods for sale at retail, use, consumption, distribution, or storage for consumption in the state;

— has tangible personal property for sale at retail, use, consumption, distribution, or storage for consumption in the state, including remote sales;

—. cannot prove that the tax was paid on a sale at retail, use, consumption, distribution, or storage for consumption in the state of tangible personal property;

— leases or rents tangible personal property;

— maintains in the state, directly or by subsidiary, an office, distributing house, salesroom, warehouse, or other place of business;

— receives orders as a result of solicitations of business, directly or through representatives or advertising;

— receives orders as a result of solicitations of business as an agent for a principal that refuses to register as a dealer;

— leases out lodging, parking, boat storage, or aircraft storage;

— cannot prove that the tax was paid on the lease of lodging, parking, boat storage, or aircraft storage;

— cannot prove that the tax was paid on the purchase of communication services or electric power or energy;

— provides a taxable service;

— cannot prove that the tax was paid on the purchase, use, or consumption of a taxable service; or

— provides a taxable service warranty.

Retail sale. A "retail sale" or "sale at retail" means a sale to a consumer or to any person for any purpose other than for resale in the form of tangible personal property or taxable services.

Retailer. A "retailer" is a person engaged in the business of making sales at retail or for distribution, use, consumption, or storage for consumption in the state.

Sale. The term "sale" refers to any transfer of title or possession, exchange, barter, license, lease, or rental by any means of tangible personal property for consideration. Included are rentals of lodging; production of tangible personal property for consideration for consumers who furnish the materials used; furnishing food for consumption on or off the premises, including the sale of meals by an employer to employees; and transfer of property where title is retained as security for payment.

Tangible personal property. "Tangible personal property" means personal property that can be seen, weighed, measured, touched, or is perceptible to the senses and includes electric power or energy, boats, motor vehicles, mobile homes, and aircraft, but not including stocks, bonds, notes, insurance, other obligations or securities, intangibles, or pari-mutuel tickets.

Which transactions are generally subject to use tax in Florida?

The use tax is imposed on all persons that use, consume, distribute, or store tangible personal property in the state and applies to tangible personal property purchased outside the state that would have been subject to the sales tax if purchased from a Florida dealer. The use tax complements the sales tax and is imposed only when sufficient sales tax has not been collected. For example, the use tax is not imposed when a like tax equal to or greater than Florida use tax was paid in another state. However, if the amount paid in another state is less than the amount due in Florida, the taxpayer must pay the difference.

Whether use tax applies to transactions involving out-of-state parties implicates federal constitutional and state statutory provisions. For a discussion of these issues see Nexus–Doing Business in Florida. For any other constitutional issues relating to Florida sales and use taxes, see U.S. Constitution and State Constitution.

Transactions subject to use tax. The following transactions are specifically subject to the use tax:

— out-of-state purchases that would have been subject to sales tax if purchased from a Florida vendor, provided that it is presumed that property used in another state for six months or longer before being imported into Florida was not purchased for use in Florida;

— the rental or lease of tangible personal property used or stored in Florida, without regard to its prior use or to tax paid on the purchase of the property outside Florida;

— the solicitation of business by dealers, either directly or through representatives, and the reception of orders for property from consumers in Florida for use, consumption, distribution, or storage;

— the repair of items sent out of Florida and later returned, but not the repair of items shipped into Florida and later shipped back to their owners in other states;

— the importing of property for use, consumption, distribution, or storage for consumption in the state, after it has come to rest and become a part of the general mass of property in the state;

— the purchase from a sales office in Florida of goods shipped to a Florida customer by a factory in another state;

— the sale of goods by a Florida manufacturer to an unregistered out-of-state dealer, and delivery to the customer in Florida;

— the delivery to Florida customers by an out-of-state supplier of law and medical books, accounting manuals, tax service books, and similar publications;

— the importing of a fabricated building built in the owner's plant in another state; and

— the failure to prove that tax has been paid on the use, consumption, distribution, or storage for consumption in the state of tangible personal property, admissions, communication services, or leases of property.

Use tax definitions.

Storage. "Storage" means that items are kept in Florida for use or consumption in Florida, or for any purpose other than the sale at retail in the regular course of business.

Use. "Use" means the exercise of any right of ownership over tangible personal property except a sale at retail in the regular course of business.

Does Florida follow destination or origin based sourcing for general retail sales?

Florida follows destination based sourcing of general interstate and intrastate retail sales. For purposes of the local discretionary sales surtax levied by Florida counties on most transactions that are subject to sales and use tax, a transaction is deemed to have occurred in a county imposing the surtax if the item of tangible personal property or service is delivered within the county. If there is no reasonable evidence of delivery of a service, the sale of a service is deemed to occur in the county in which the purchaser accepts the bill of sale.

Does Florida provide any other information concerning the general applicability of sales and use taxes?

Yes, Florida does provide other general information regarding sales and use taxes.

Rates. Florida has a standard sales and use tax rate, with certain exceptions, as well as various local sales and use tax rates.

Due dates. For a discussion of due dates, see Returns, Payments, and Due Dates.

Filing and payment requirements. For a discussion of filing and payment requirements, see Returns, Payments, and Due Dates.

Services. Services are generally exempt from sales and use tax in Florida unless specifically identified as taxable.

Tax holidays. Florida has a tax holiday for certain back to school items (i.e., clothing and school supplies).

Credits. Florida provides a credit for taxes paid to another state, as well as other credits.

Local taxes. Some counties impose one or more local option taxes on taxable transactions within the county and on the lease or rental of living, sleeping or housekeeping accommodations (i.e., transient rentals) within the county. Many counties self-administer the local transient rental taxes. Counties who self-administer the transient rental taxes are not required by law to notify the Florida Department of Revenue of local tax rate changes. For a discussion of local taxes, see Local Taxes and Administration.

[¶60-025] Nexus--Doing Business in State

Whether an obligation to collect Florida sales or use tax attaches to a sale by an out-of-seller is determined by a combination of federal and state restrictions. At the federal level, the determination revolves around whether a nexus (or connection) between the sale and Florida can be established. If there is sufficient nexus, it then must be determined whether the seller qualifies as a "retailer engaged in business" in the state.

What is sales and use tax nexus?

In the state tax area, nexus is an important concern for companies that have a multistate presence because it is a threshold issue that must be evaluated to determine whether a business has tax registration, filing, collection, and remittance obligations in a particular jurisdiction. "Sales and use tax nexus" refers to the amount and type of business activity that must be present before the business is subject to the state's taxing authority.

State tax nexus considerations differ by tax type and jurisdiction, and there has been limited guidance from tax authorities as to when nexus conclusively exists. State nexus statutes are subject to federal constitutional restrictions.

In a series of cases, the U.S. Supreme Court established a general rule of "substantial nexus" which required an out-of-state seller to have a physical presence in a state before that state could require the seller to register and collect and remit sales or use taxes. Physical presence can be created by employees or other agents, property owned or leased in the state, or other factors. There are many gray areas when it comes to determining whether nexus conclusively exists, particularly for ecommerce.

Timeline of Important U.S. Supreme Court Nexus Cases

However, in *South Dakota v. Wayfair, Inc.*, 585 U.S. ___ (2018), the U.S. Supreme Court held that physical presence is no longer required to establish substantial nexus. Rather, economic and virtual contacts in a state and minimum in-state sales thresholds can establish sales and use tax nexus.

PLANNING NOTE: Nexus determinations are based on a taxpayer's specific set of facts. Taxpayers must carefully evaluate whether specific activities or types of contact create/establish nexus in each state in which they do business, as well as how frequently such contacts must occur in order to create tax nexus. A certain combination of business activities or a specific aspect of an activity may result in a different conclusion. To have a complete picture of all tax reporting requirements, multistate businesses should conduct a nexus review. A nexus review helps businesses understand their exposure and avoid audit situations.

South Dakota v. Wayfair. In a 5 to 4 decision, the U.S. Supreme Court held that *Quill Corp. v. North Dakota*, 504 U.S. 298 (1992), and *National Bellas Hess, Inc. v. Department of Revenue of Ill.*, 386 U.S. 753 (1967), are overruled because *Quill's* physical presence rule is unsound and incorrect. As a result, physical presence is no longer required to establish sales and use tax nexus.

The Court held that the *Complete Auto* (*Complete Auto Transit v. Brady*, 430 U.S. 274 (1977)) substantial nexus requirement with the taxing state is satisfied based on both the economic and virtual contacts the respondents have with the state. As a result of this decision, states are now free to levy taxes on sales of goods and services regardless of whether the seller has a physical presence in the state. Due process requirements, unrelated to those required by the "Commerce Clause" of the Constitution still apply, as do other nexus tests of the Commerce Clause. Since the *Wayfair* decision was issued, many states have enacted economic nexus and/or marketplace nexus thresholds. (*South Dakota v. Wayfair, Inc.*, 585 U.S. ___ (2018))

How is nexus established in Florida?

Florida sales or use tax is imposed on all dealers engaged in the sale, lease, or rental of tangible personal property sold at retail in the state or all persons that use, consume, distribute, or store tangible personal property in the state. (Sec. 212.05, F.S.; Rule 12A-1.091, F.A.C.)

Every person who engages in the business of selling tangible personal property at retail in Florida is exercising a taxable privilege, including the business of making or facilitating remote sales, or who rents or furnishes any items or services that are subject to sales and use tax, or who stores any item or article of tangible personal property for use or consumption in Florida and who leases or rents such property within Florida. (Sec. 212.05, F.S.)

Sales for use within Florida. Every dealer making sales, whether within or outside Florida, of tangible personal property for distribution, storage, or use or other consumption in Florida is required, at the time of making sales, to collect the tax. (Sec. 212.06, F.S.)

Trade shows. Exhibitors who enter into agreements authorizing the display of tangible personal property or services at a convention or trade show are required to register and collect sales and use tax if the agreement authorizes the retail sale of tangible personal property or services subject to tax. Exhibitors who sell at wholesale only must obtain a resale certificate from the purchasing dealer, but are not required to register as dealers. (Sec. 212.18, F.S.; Rule 12A-1.060, F.A.C.)

Does Florida have economic nexus?

Yes. Florida enacted economic nexus provisions effective July 1, 2021. (Sec. 212.0596, F.S.; Sec. 212.05965, F.S.)

Overview. Florida has enacted economic nexus for sales and use tax purposes. Out-of-state retailers and marketplace providers with no physical presence in Florida are required to collect Florida's sales and use tax on sales of taxable items delivered to purchasers in Florida if the out-of-state retailer or marketplace provider makes a substantial number of remote sales into Florida. A "substantial number of remote sales" is defined as any number of taxable remote sales in the previous calendar year in which the sum of the sales prices exceeded $100,000. The legislation is entitled the "Park Randall 'Randy' Miller Act." (Sec. 212.0596, F.S.; Sec. 212.05965, F.S.)

Effective July 1, 2021, Florida sales and use tax must be collected and remitted on remote sales and sales made through a marketplace to be transported into the state. Such persons are required to register with the Florida Department of Revenue and collect, report, and remit state sales and use tax and discretionary sales surtax. (*Tax Information Publication, No. 21A01-03*, Florida Department of Revenue, May 14, 2021)

Remote sales. Beginning July 1, 2021, persons not located in Florida who make a substantial number of remote sales for delivery in Florida are required to register with the Department and collect and remit tax. (*Tax Information Publication, No. 21A01-03*, Florida Department of Revenue, May 14, 2021)

A "substantial number of remote sales" is any number of taxable remote sales in the previous calendar year in which the sum of the total sales exceeds $100,000. (*Tax Information Publication, No. 21A01-03*, Florida Department of Revenue, May 14, 2021)

A "remote sale" is the retail sale of tangible personal property ordered by mail, telephone, the Internet, or other communication, from a person who receives the order outside Florida and causes the property to be transported into Florida. (*Tax Information Publication, No. 21A01-03*, Florida Department of Revenue, May 14, 2021)

Taxation of marketplace sales. A marketplace provider that has a physical presence in Florida or who is making or facilitating a substantial number of remote sales through a marketplace is a sales and use tax dealer.

A marketplace provider that is a sales and use tax dealer or a person who is required to collect and remit sales tax on remote sales is required to collect discretionary sales surtax when the taxable item of tangible personal property is delivered within a county that imposes a surtax. (Sec. 212.0596, F.S.; Sec. 212.05965, F.S.)

Beginning July 1, 2021, marketplace providers who have a physical presence in Florida or who make or facilitate a substantial number of remote sales through a marketplace are required to register with the Department and collect and remit tax. (*Tax Information Publication, No. 21A01-03*, Florida Department of Revenue, May 14, 2021)

A "marketplace" is any physical place or electronic medium through which tangible personal property is offered for sale. (*Tax Information Publication, No. 21A01-03*, Florida Department of Revenue, May 14, 2021)

A "marketplace provider" is a person who:

- facilitates a retail sale by a marketplace seller by listing or advertising for sale by the marketplace seller tangible personal property in a marketplace; and

- directly or indirectly, through agreements or arrangements with third parties, collects payment from the customer and transmits all or part of the payment to the marketplace seller, regardless of whether the marketplace provider receives compensation or other consideration in exchange for its services.

(*Tax Information Publication, No. 21A01-03*, Florida Department of Revenue, May 14, 2021)

In addition, a marketplace provider that is a dealer must certify to its marketplace sellers that it will collect and remit sales and use tax on taxable retail sales made through the marketplace. Such certification may be included in the agreement between the marketplace provider and the marketplace seller.

A marketplace seller may not collect and remit sales and use tax on a taxable retail sale when the sale is made through the marketplace and the marketplace provider certifies that it will collect and remit the tax. A marketplace seller must exclude such sales made through the marketplace from the marketplace seller's tax return. (Sec. 212.0596, F.S.; Sec. 212.05965, F.S.)

Moreover, a marketplace seller who has a physical presence in Florida must register and collect and remit sales and use tax on all taxable retail sales made outside the marketplace. A marketplace seller who does not have a physical presence in Florida but who makes a substantial number of remote sales must register and collect and remit sales and use tax on all taxable retail sales made outside the marketplace. For the purpose of determining whether a marketplace seller made a substantial number of remote sales, the marketplace seller can consider only those sales made outside a marketplace. (Sec. 212.0596, F.S.; Sec. 212.05965, F.S.)

Marketplace providers do not include persons:

- who solely provide travel agency services;

- who are delivery network companies and not registered as sales and use tax dealers; or

- whose sole activity is to process payment transactions between two or more parties.

(*Tax Information Publication, No. 21A01-03*, Florida Department of Revenue, May 14, 2021)

A "marketplace seller" is a person who has an agreement with a marketplace provider that is a sales and use tax dealer and who makes retail sales of tangible personal property through a marketplace owned, operated, or controlled by the marketplace provider. (*Tax Information Publication, No. 21A01-03*, Florida Department of Revenue, May 14, 2021)

A marketplace provider that is required to register must also certify to its marketplace sellers that it will collect and remit the applicable Florida tax on the taxable retail sales made through the marketplace. The certification may be included in the agreement between the marketplace provider and the marketplace seller. When the marketplace provider certifies to the marketplace seller that it will collect and remit the tax, the marketplace seller may not collect the tax and must exclude sales made through the marketplace from the marketplace seller's tax return, if applicable. (*Tax Information Publication, No. 21A01-03*, Florida Department of Revenue, May 14, 2021)

Marketplace sellers who have a physical presence in Florida or who make a substantial number of remote sales to Florida customers outside of the marketplace must register as dealers and collect and remit tax on those taxable Florida retail sales made outside of the marketplace. (*Tax Information Publication, No. 21A01-03*, Florida Department of Revenue, May 14, 2021)

Applicable definitions. A "marketplace" is any physical place or electronic medium through which tangible personal property is offered for sale.

A "marketplace provider" is a person who:

- facilitates a retail sale by a marketplace seller by listing or advertising for sale by the marketplace seller tangible personal property in a marketplace; and
- directly, or indirectly through agreements or arrangements with third parties, collects payment from the customer and transmits all or part of the payment to the marketplace seller, regardless of whether the marketplace provider receives compensation or other consideration in exchange for its services.

(Sec. 212.0596, F.S.; Sec. 212.05965, F.S.)

The term "marketplace provider" does not include a person who is:

- a person who solely provides travel agency services;
- a delivery network company unless the delivery network company is a registered dealer for sales and use tax purposes and the delivery network company notifies all local merchants that sell through the delivery network company's website or mobile application that the delivery network company is subject to the requirements of a marketplace provider; or
- a payment processor business that processes payment transactions from various channels, such as charge cards, credit cards, or debit cards, and whose sole activity with respect to marketplace sales is to process payment.

(Sec. 212.0596, F.S.; Sec. 212.05965, F.S.)

A "delivery network company" is defined as a person who maintains a website or mobile application used to facilitate:

- delivery services;
- the sale of local products; or
- both.

(Sec. 212.0596, F.S.; Sec. 212.05965, F.S.)

A "marketplace seller" is a person who has an agreement with a marketplace provider that is a sales and use tax dealer and who makes retail sales of tangible personal property through a marketplace owned, operated, or controlled by the marketplace provider.

The term "retail sale" is amended to include:

- a remote sale; and
- a sale facilitated through a marketplace.

(Sec. 212.0596, F.S.; Sec. 212.05965, F.S.)

A "remote sale" is defined as a retail sale of tangible personal property ordered by mail, telephone, the Internet, or other means of communication from a person who receives the order outside Florida and transports the property or causes the property to be transported from any jurisdiction, including the state of Florida, to a location in Florida. For these purposes, tangible personal property delivered to a location within Florida is presumed to be used, consumed, distributed, or stored to be used or consumed in Florida. (Sec. 212.0596, F.S.; Sec. 212.05965, F.S.)

Discretionary sales surtax. In addition to the collection and remittance of Florida state sales and use tax, marketplace providers and persons making remote sales are required to collect and remit discretionary sales surtax when delivering tangible personal property to counties imposing a surtax. These surtaxes are levied by individual counties and vary in rate. Some counties do not impose a discretionary sales surtax. *Tax Information Publication, No. 21A01-03*, Florida Department of Revenue, May 14, 2021)

See 61-735 Local Tax Rates, for current discretionary sales surtax rates.

Audit of marketplace provider's books and records. A marketplace provider must allow the department to examine and audit its books and records. If the department audits a marketplace provider, the department may not propose a tax assessment on the marketplace seller for the same retail sales unless the marketplace seller provides incorrect or incomplete information to the marketplace provider. However, the relief provided to a marketplace seller does not apply if:

- it has been assessed;

- is under audit;

- has received a bill; or

- is in court before July 1, 2021.

(Sec. 212.05965, F.S.)

The marketplace provider is relieved of liability for the tax on the retail sale, and the marketplace seller or customer is liable for the sales and use tax if the marketplace provider demonstrates to the department's satisfaction that:

- the marketplace provider made a reasonable effort to obtain accurate information related to the retail sales facilitated through the marketplace from the marketplace seller; but

- the failure to collect and remit the correct amount of tax was due to the incorrect or incomplete information provided to the marketplace provider by the marketplace seller.

(Sec. 212.05965, F.S.)

This provision does not apply to a retail sale for which the marketplace provider is the seller if:

- the marketplace provider and the marketplace seller are related parties; or

- transactions between a marketplace seller and marketplace buyer are not conducted at arm's length.

(Sec. 212.05965, F.S.)

Marketplace seller may contract to collect and remit taxes for marketplace. Effective April 1, 2022, a marketplace provider and a qualifying marketplace seller may contractually agree to have the marketplace seller collect and remit the taxes for sales on the marketplace. This applies to marketplace sellers with annual U.S. gross sales of more than $1 billion, including the gross sales of any related entities. In the case of franchised entities that meet the $1 billion threshold, including the combined sales of all franchisees of a single franchisor. (Sec. 212.05965, F.S.)

Also effective April 1, 2022, a marketplace provider must, at the time of sale, collect and remit the following fees on applicable sales:

- prepaid wireless E911 fee;

- waste tire fee; and

- lead-acid battery fee.

(Sec. 212.05965, F.S.)

Electronic filing. Out-of-state retailers and marketplace providers are required to file returns and remit tax electronically. (Sec. 212.11(4)(f), F.S.)

Moreover, a marketplace provider that is a sales and use tax dealer or a person who is required to collect and remit sales or use tax on remote sales must file with the department an application for a certificate of registration electronically. (Sec. 212.18(3)(c), F.S.)

Department to establish rules. The Florida Department of Revenue may establish, by rule, procedures for collecting use tax from unregistered persons who but for their remote purchases would not be required to remit sales or use tax directly to the department. The procedures may provide for:

- the waiver of registration;
- the irregular remittance of tax;
- the elimination of the collection allowance; and
- the non-application of local option surtaxes.

(Sec. 212.0596, F.S.)

Application and tax relief. The act first applies to remote sales made or facilitated on or after July 1, 2021, by a person who made or facilitated a substantial number of remote sales in calendar year 2020. Further, a marketplace seller should only consider those sales made outside of a marketplace to determine whether it made a substantial number of remote sales in calendar year 2020. (Sec. 25, Ch. 2 (S.B. 50), Laws 2021, effective July 1, 2021)

Relief of liability for tax, penalty, and interest is granted to the following upon registration with the department by October 1, 2021:

- any person who conducted remote sales prior to July 1, 2021;
- a marketplace seller for remote sales made before July 1, 2021; and
- a marketplace provider with a physical presence in Florida on sales the marketplace provider facilitated on behalf of marketplace sellers.

(Sec. 25, Ch. 2 (S.B. 50), Laws 2021, effective July 1, 2021)

This tax relief does not apply to a person who:

- is under audit;
- has been issued a bill, notice, or demand for payment; or
- is under an administrative or judicial proceeding as of July 1, 2021.

(Sec. 25, Ch. 2 (S.B. 50), Laws 2021, effective July 1, 2021)

Additionally, the department may not use data received from registered marketplace providers or persons making remote sales to identify use tax liabilities if the person with the use tax liability:

- is not registered with the department;
- is not required to register with the department; and
- his or her use tax liability was created before July 1, 2021.

(Sec. 25, Ch. 2 (S.B. 50), Laws 2021, effective July 1, 2021)

Does Florida have click-through nexus?

No. Florida does not have click-through nexus provisions.

Does Florida have affiliate nexus?

Yes. Every dealer who makes a remote sale is subject to Florida's power to levy and collect tax when the dealer does not have nexus but is a member of an affiliated group, as defined in IRC §1504(a), whose members are includable under IRC

¶60-025

§ 1504(b) and are eligible to file a consolidated federal income tax return, and any parent or subsidiary corporation in the affiliated group has nexus. (Sec, 212,9596, F.S.)

[¶60-100]

RATES

[¶60-110] Rate of Tax

The rate of tax in Florida is generally 6%. (Sec. 212.05(1)(a), F.S.)

• *Transactions taxed at the 6% rate*

The 6% tax rate is imposed on the following Florida transactions:

— the retail sale of items of tangible personal property (Sec. 212.05(1)(a), F.S.) ;

— the retail sale of motor fuel and special fuel (Sec. 206.41, F.S.; Sec. 212.05(1)(l), F.S.) ;

— the provision of service warranties (Sec. 212.0506(2), F.S.) ;

— admissions charges (Sec. 212.04(1)(b), F.S.) ;

— the lease or rental of tangible personal property (Sec. 212.05(1)(j), F.S.) ;

— living quarters and sleeping or housekeeping accommodations (Sec. 212.03(1), F.S.) ;

— the lease or rental of parking spaces for motor vehicles, docking for boats, and tie-downs for aircraft (Sec. 212.03(6), F.S.) ;

— the installation of telecommunications and telegraphic equipment (Sec. 212.05(1)(e), F.S.) ;

— television system program services (Sec. 212.05(1)(e), F.S.) ;

— the sale, rental, use, consumption, or storage of machines, equipment, parts, and accessories used in manufacturing, processing, compounding, producing, mining, or quarrying personal property for sale or to be used in furnishing communications, transportation, or public utility services (Sec. 212.05(1)(f), F.S.) ;

— the use, consumption, distribution, or storage of tangible personal property in Florida (Sec. 212.05(1)(b), F.S.) ;

— detective, burglar protection, and other protection services (Sec. 212.05(1)(k) 1, F.S.) ;

— nonresidential cleaning and nonresidential pest control services (Sec. 212.05(1)(k) 2, F.S.) ;

— coins or currency (whether in circulation or not) when not legal tender or, if legal tender, when sold, exchanged, or traded at higher than face value or based on the precious metal content (Sec. 212.05(1)(l) 1, F.S.) ; and

— effective January 1, 2022, the lease or rental of a motor vehicle by a peer-to-peer car-sharing program. (Sec. 212.05(1)(c) 1, F.S.)

• *Transactions taxed at other rates*

There are transactions that are taxed at a rate different than the general state sales and use tax rate.

Asphalt used in public works projects.—Manufactured asphalt used in federal, state, and local government public works projects is exempt from the indexed tax effective July 1, 2018. (Sec. 212.06(1)(c), F.S.; Tax Information Publication, No. 18A01-11, Florida Department of Revenue, June 19, 2018)

2022-2023 indexed tax rate on asphalt for a contractor's own use.—Effective July 1, 2022, through June 30, 2023, the per-ton indexed tax rate for the calculation of Florida use tax due on asphalt manufactured by a contractor for the contractor's own use is $0.98 (formerly, $0.84) per ton. The indexed tax is adjusted on July 1 of each year using a producer price index published by the U.S. Department of Labor, Bureau of Labor Statistics. (*Tax Information Publication, No. 22A01-10*, Florida Department of Revenue, June 9, 2022)

A use tax is due on asphalt manufactured for a contractor's own use. This tax is adjusted annually by adding the indexed tax to the cost of the materials that become a component part or an ingredient of the finished asphalt, multiplied by 6%, and the cost of transporting the components and ingredients to the plant site, multiplied by 6%. (Sec. 212.06(1)(c), F.S.)

To calculate use tax on asphalt manufactured by a contractor for the contractor's own use:

— multiply the cost of all materials that become ingredients of the finished asphalt by 6 percent plus applicable discretionary sales surtax; plus

— multiply the cost of transporting such ingredients to the plant site by 6 percent plus the applicable discretionary sales surtax; plus

— multiply each ton of asphalt manufactured by the indexed tax (the indexed tax is in addition to all taxes paid on purchases of overhead items, including boiler fuels).

(*Tax Information Publication, No. 22A01-10*, Florida Department of Revenue, June 9, 2022)

The new indexed tax is in addition to all taxes paid on purchases of overhead items, including boiler fuels. If tax is paid to a third party on the cost or transportation of materials, those costs should not be included in the calculation of the total tax due. Tax is due in the month the asphalt is manufactured for use by the contractor, and must be paid using Form DR-15, Sales and Use Tax Return. (*Tax Information Publication, No. 21A01-07*, Florida Department of Revenue, June 9, 2021)

Coin-operated amusement machines.—A 4% tax is imposed on charges for the use of coin-operated amusement machines. The method used to calculate the charges is detailed under the subhead "Industry Tax Rate" below. (Sec. 212.05(1)(j), F.S.)

Dealer license plates.—A motor vehicle dealer must pay an annual use tax of $27 for each dealer license plate purchased in addition to the license tax. No additional use tax is imposed if a dealer use tax has been paid. (Sec. 212.0601, F.S.)

Electrical power or energy.—The sales and use tax rate applicable to charges for electrical power or energy is 4.35%. (Sec. 212.05(1)(e), F.S.; Emergency Rule 12AER14-4; *Tax Information Publication, No. 14A01-07*, Florida Department of Revenue, June 20, 2014)

An additional communications services tax (utility tax) is imposed on electric power already subject to sales and use tax. (*Tax Information Publication, No. 14A01-07*, Florida Department of Revenue, June 20, 2014)

A seller of electrical power or energy may collect a combined rate of 6.95%, which consists of 4.35% sales and use tax and 2.6% tax on gross receipts from utility services required under Sec. 212.05(1)(e) and Sec. 203.01, respectively, if the provider properly reflects the tax collected with respect to the two provisions as required in the return to the Florida Department of Revenue. (Sec. 6, Ch. 38 (H.B. 5601), Laws 2014; Emergency Rule 12AER14-4; *Tax Information Publication, No. 14A01-07*, Florida Department of Revenue, June 20, 2014)

Dealers selling electricity may collect tax at the combined rate of 6.95% or dealers may separately state each tax on their customers' billings. Dealers that elect to use the combined rate are not required to label the rate in a particular way, provided the tax is clearly identified as a Florida state tax or sales tax. (*Tax Information Publication, No. 14A01-07*, Florida Department of Revenue, June 20, 2014)

Regarding the local option discretionary sales surtaxes imposed on charges for electricity, if the 4.35% sales and use tax is separately stated, the local option discretionary sales surtax should be added to the 4.35% tax rate. The 2.5% gross receipts tax is reported on the Gross Receipts Tax Return (Form DR-133). The combined 6.95% tax rate and any applicable local discretionary sales surtax is reported on the Sales and Use Tax Return (Form DR-15). (*Tax Information Publication, No. 14A01-07*, Florida Department of Revenue, June 20, 2014)

Power farm equipment.—The sale, rental, lease, use, consumption, or storage of power farm equipment is exempt. (Sec. 212.08(3), F.S.)

Rental car surcharge.—A surcharge of $2 per day is imposed for the first 30 days of the term upon the lease or rental of a motor vehicle licensed for hire and designed to carry less than nine passengers. (Sec. 212.0606(1), F.S.)

A member of a car-sharing service who uses a motor vehicle for less than 24 hours under an agreement with a car-sharing service is required to pay a Florida surcharge of $1 per usage. A member of a car-sharing service who uses the same motor vehicle for 24 hours or more must pay a surcharge of $2 per day or any part of a day, as provided. (Sec. 212.0606, F.S.; *Tax Information Publication No. 14A01-10*, Florida Department of Revenue, November 5, 2014)

Rental car surcharge on peer-to-peer car-sharing program agreements.—Effective January 1, 2022, a $1 per day rental car surcharge applies to a peer-to-peer car-sharing program agreement involving a shared vehicle that is registered in Florida and is designed to carry fewer than nine passengers, for financial consideration, and without transfer of the title of the shared vehicle. The surcharge applies to the first 30 days only of a car-sharing period for any peer-to-peer car-sharing program agreement and must be collected by the program. The rental car surcharge should be separately stated on the sales invoice, and is subject to all applicable sales and use taxes. (Sec. 212.0606, F.S.; *Tax Information Publication, No. 21A01-14*, Florida Department of Revenue, December 21, 2021)

When a motor vehicle is rented through a peer-to-peer car sharing program, the peer-to-peer car-sharing program must collect and remit the applicable tax and rental car surcharge due in connection with the rental. A "peer-to-peer car-sharing program" is a business platform that enables peer-to-peer car sharing by connecting motor vehicle owners with drivers for financial consideration. (*Tax Information Publication, No. 21A01-14*, Florida Department of Revenue, December 21, 2021)

A peer-to-peer car sharing program is required to register to collect sales tax, discretionary sales surtax, and the rental car surcharge applicable to motor vehicles rented through the peer-to-peer car sharing program. Peer-to-peer car-sharing programs are required to submit a registration application for each county in which business is located. (*Tax Information Publication, No. 21A01-14*, Florida Department of Revenue, December 21, 2021)

Rental of commercial real estate.—The state sales tax rate on the total rent or license fee charged under a commercial lease of real property (i.e., "business rent tax" or "commercial rentals") is 5.5%. (Sec. 212.031(1)(c), F.S.)

The state sales tax rate, plus any applicable discretionary sales surtax, is due on the total rent charged for renting, leasing, or granting a license to use commercial real property in Florida, unless the rent is specifically exempt. Some examples of taxable commercial real property rentals include commercial office or retail space, warehouses, convention and meeting rooms, and self-storage units or mini-warehouses. (Sec. 212.031(1)(c), F.S.; *Form GT-800016*, Florida Department of Revenue, revised

October 2021; *Tax Information Publication, No. 19A01-11*, Florida Department of Revenue, October 30, 2019; *Tax Information Publication, No. 18A01-14*, Florida Department of Revenue, August 27, 2018)

> *COMPLIANCE NOTE:* **Reduction of the rate applied to the rental of commercial real estate.** Sec. 13 of S.B. 50, Laws 2021 amends Sec. 212.20(6)(d)6.h., regarding funds collected and other powers of the Florida Department of Revenue. As amended, Sec. 212.20(6)(d)6.h.(III) provides: "If the ending balance of the Unemployment Compensation Trust Fund exceeds $4,071,519,600 on the last day of any month, as determined from United States Department of the Treasury data, the Office of Economic and Demographic Research shall certify to the department that the ending balance of the trust fund exceeds such amount." (Ch. 2 (S.B. 50), Laws 2021; Ch. 31 (H.B. 7061), Laws 2021)
>
> Sec. 13 of S.B. 50, Laws 2021, amends Sec. 212.20(6)(d)6.h.(IV) and provides: "This sub-subparagraph is repealed, and the department shall end monthly distributions under sub-sub-subparagraph (II), on the date the department receives certification under sub-sub-subparagraph (III)." (Ch. 2 (S.B. 50), Laws 2021; Ch. 31 (H.B. 7061), Laws 2021)
>
> Sec. 14 of S.B. 50, Laws 2021, provides that effective on the first day of the second month following the repeal of Sec. 212.20(6)(d)6.h., by its own terms, Sec. 212.031, the statute that sets the state sales tax rate on the total rent or license fee charged under a commercial lease of real property (i.e., "business rent tax" or "commercial rentals") is amended to reduce that rate from 5.5% to 2%. (Ch. 2 (S.B. 50), Laws 2021; Ch. 31 (H.B. 7061), Laws 2021)
>
> As a result, once the ending balance of the Unemployment Compensation Trust Fund reaches that specified level, the rate imposed on the total rent or license fee charged under a commercial lease of real property is reduced from 5.5% to 2%. Presumably, the Florida Department of Revenue will issue a notice advising of same if and when this occurs. (Ch. 2 (S.B. 50), Laws 2021; Ch. 31 (H.B. 7061), Laws 2021)

The tax rate in effect at the time that a tenant or person occupies, uses, or is entitled to occupy or use the real property is the tax rate applicable to the transaction regardless of when a rent or license fee payment is due or paid. The applicable tax rate may not be avoided by the delay or acceleration of rent or license fee payments. (Sec. 212.031(1)(c), F.S.; *Tax Information Publication, No. 19A01-11*, Florida Department of Revenue, October 30, 2019)

The local option discretionary sales surtax imposed by the county where the real property is located continues to apply to the total rent charged. (*Tax Information Publication, No. 19A01-11*, Florida Department of Revenue, October 30, 2019)

• *Industry tax rate*

Where it is impracticable, due to the nature of the business practice within an industry, to separately state Florida tax on the bill of sale, the Department of Revenue may establish an effective tax rate for the industry. The Department may amend this effective tax rate as industry's pricing or practices change. (Sec. 212.07(2), F.S.)

Carnival vendors.—Vendors at carnivals, for example, are taxed at 6.59% of gross sales. To compute the tax, the vendor must divide the total receipts by 1.0659 and subtract the quotient from total receipts. (Rule 12A-1.080)

Coin-operated amusement machines.—The generally applicable rate of sales tax to be paid on the charges for the use of coin-operated amusement machines is 4%;

however, there are different divisors applicable depending upon whether a county imposes a discretionary surtax, and if it does, at what rate. (Sec. 212.05(1)(h), F.S.)

Vending machines.—The generally applicable rate of sales tax to be paid on items sold in vending machines is 6.45% for beverages and food, and 6.59% for other items of tangible personal property; however, the rate must reflect any local option tax component as follows:

— for counties imposing a 0.5% sales surtax, the rate is 6.86% for beverage and food items, and 7.07% for other items of tangible personal property;

— for counties imposing a 0.75% sales surtax, the rate is 7.07% for beverage and food items and 7.27% for other items of tangible personal property;

— for counties imposing a 1% sales surtax, the rate is 7.26% for beverage and food items, and 7.49% for other items of tangible personal property; and

— for counties imposing a 1.5% sales surtax, the rate is 7.67% for beverage and food items, and 7.91% for other items of tangible personal property.

(Sec. 212.0515, F.S.)

Milk.—Sales of natural fluid milk, homogenized milk, pasteurized milk, whole milk, chocolate milk, or similar milk products and natural fruit or vegetable juices sold in vending machines are taxable at the rate for food. (Sec. 212.0515, F.S.)

Concession stands.—Dealers operating concession stands who cannot separately state tax must remit tax at the rate of 6.59% of the total taxable sales of food and drink items, unless the records of the dealer clearly demonstrate a lesser rate. To compute the correct amount of tax due, the dealer should divide the total receipts by 1.0659 to compute the taxable sales and then subtract this amount from total receipts to arrive at the amount of tax due. The 6.59% rate takes into account the variations that may result from multiple sales transactions. Such dealers must maintain accurate records of the tax collected, and the exact amount of tax due must be remitted to the state. (Rule 12A-1.011(4)(a) and (4)(b))

Alcoholic beverages.—For the privilege of deviating from the standard taxing procedures, a dealer of alcoholic beverages must remit tax according to the following method:

— if the dealer does not put the public on notice that the tax is included in the total charge, a dealer who sells packages must remit 6.35% of total receipts, and a dealer who sells mixed drinks must remit 6.59% of total receipts; or

— if a dealer does put the public on notice that the tax is included in the total charge, a dealer who sells packages would divide total receipts by 1.0635 and subtract the quotient from the total receipts to figure the amount of tax to be remitted, and a dealer who sells mixed drinks would divide total receipts by 1.0659 and subtract the quotient from the total receipts to figure the amount of tax to be remitted.

(Rule 12A-1.057)

• *Local taxes*

Florida counties are authorized to impose local sales surtaxes and local option taxes in addition to any state sales tax already imposed. Local rates imposed by each county are listed in ¶ 61-735 Local Rates.

[¶60-200]
TAXABILITY OF PERSONS AND TRANSACTIONS

[¶60-230] Admissions, Entertainment, and Dues

Every dealer who sells or receives anything of value by way of admissions is exercising a taxable privilege. (Sec. 212.04(1)(a), F.S.)

"Admissions" are defined as the net sum of money after deduction of any federal taxes for admitting a person or vehicle to any place of amusement, sport, or recreation, or for dues to private clubs and membership clubs providing recreational or physical fitness facilities. (Sec. 212.02(1), F.S.; Rule 12A-1.005)

Places of amusement.—Places of amusement include:

— theaters, mini-theaters, and outdoor theaters;

— shows and exhibitions;

— games; and

— races.

(Rule 12A-1.005)

Also considered a place of amusement is any other place at which there is any exhibition, amusement, sport or recreation, for which a charge is made by way of the sale of tickets, gate charges, seat charges, box charges, season pass charges, cover charges, greens fees, participation fees or entrance fees or the receipt of anything else of value, measured on an admission, entrance or length of stay or seat. (Rule 12A-1.005)

Each ticket must show on its face the actual sales price of the admission and the tax to be collected. Charging admissions is included in the definition of a "business". (Sec. 212.02(2), F.S.) Each admission is a single sale. (Rule 12A-1.005)

Operators of game concessions who customarily award tangible personal property as prizes are the ultimate consumers of the property and are liable for the sales and use tax on their purchases. (Rule 12A-1.080)

• *Admissions related to air commerce*

Although sales and use tax applies to admissions that include charges for many types of sightseeing rides that use boats, buses, trolleys, trains, and other vehicles, federal law prohibits the state from taxing individuals that travel in air commerce. Air commerce relates to activities operated within a federal airway or activities that directly affect safety in interstate or foreign air commerce. As a result, certain sightseeing rides sold to individuals traveling in air commerce, such as helicopter, airplane, and hot air balloon rides, and skydiving, are not subject to sales tax on admissions. (Rule 12A-1.005; *Tax Information Publication, No. 12A01-10*, Florida Department of Revenue, June 4, 2012)

Examples of various taxable and nontaxable activities include the following:

— A company that operates helicopter sightseeing tours in an FAA federal airway that are regulated by the FAA is not required to collect sales tax on the sales price of the tours.

— A company that provides skydiving training and transportation for skydiving jumps that operates the jumps in a federal airway designated by the FAA is not required to collect sales tax on its sale of skydiving jumps. For customers who do not have their own equipment, the company should separately state the charge for the rental or sale of equipment and collect sales tax on the rental charge or sales price collected. The company is required to collect sales tax on the portion of the sales price attributable to the rental of equipment if the company bundled both charges into one lump sum.

— The same company in the above example sells admissions to view its World War II aircraft and makes a separate charge for a videotape while skydiving. The company should separately state the admission charge and videotape charge and collect sales tax on the price paid to view the aircraft and the sales price of the videotape.

— A company that operates a hot air balloon in a federal airway is not required to collect sales tax on the sales price charged for rides.

— A company that sells hot air balloon rides where the balloon is tethered or moored to the ground that does not operate in a federal airway is required to collect sales tax on the sales price charged for the rides because the operations are not within a federal airway.

(*Tax Information Publication, No. 12A01-10*, Florida Department of Revenue, June 4, 2012)

• *Due date for tax on exhibition center admissions*

Florida sales tax on an admissions fee for an event at an exhibition center must be collected when the fee is paid, but is not due or payable to the Florida Department of Revenue until the first day of the month that follows the date of the event. The tax liability becomes delinquent on the 21st day of that month. Exhibition centers include convention halls, auditoriums, stadiums, theaters, arenas, civic centers, performing arts centers, or publicly owned recreational facilities. (Sec. 212.04(3), F.S.)

• *Events sponsored by governmental entities, sports authorities, or sports commissions*

Admissions charges to an event sponsored by a governmental entity, sports authority, or sports commission when the event is held in a convention hall, exhibition hall, auditorium, stadium, theater, arena, civic center, performing arts center, or publicly-owned recreational facility, are exempt. The exemption applies only if:

— 100% of the funds at risk belong to the sponsor;

— 100% of the risk of success or failure lies with the sponsor; and

— student or faculty talent is not exclusively used at the event.

(Sec. 212.04(2), F.S.; *Tax Information Publication 10A01-06*, Florida Department of Reveue, June 18, 2010)

• *Exemptions*

The following charges are exempt:

— *Athletic events.*—Admissions to: (1) a Pro Bowl; (2) National Basketball Association (NBA) and National Hockey League (NHL) all star games; (3) the Major League Baseball Home Run Derby held before the Major League Baseball All-Star Game; (4) Major League Soccer all star games; and (5) all star events produced by the NBA and held at a facility such as an arena, convention center, or municipal facility (Sec. 212.04(2), F.S.; *Tax Information Publication 10A01-06*, Florida Department of Reveue, June 18, 2010)

— Admissions to athletic or other events sponsored by elementary schools, junior high schools, middle schools, community colleges, public or private colleges and universities (other than admissions to athletic events sponsored by an institution within the State University System), schools for the blind or deaf, facilities of the youth services programs of the Department of Children and Families, and state correctional institutions when only student, faculty, or inmate talent is used. (Sec. 212.04(2)(a) 1, F.S.)

— Admissions paid by a student participating in a sport or recreational activity if the student's participation is required by the student's educational institution. (Sec. 212.04(2)(a) 3, F.S.)

— Admissions to a National Football League (NFL) championship game or Pro Bowl, any semifinal or championship game of a national collegiate tournament, or a major league baseball all-star game. (Sec. 212.04(2)(a) 4, F.S.)

— Admissions to any postseason collegiate football game sanctioned by the National Collegiate Athletic Association. (Sec. 212.04(2)(a) 7, F.S.)

— Admissions to a National Basketball Association (NBA) or National Hockey League (NHL) all star game. (Sec. 212.04(2)(a) 4, F.S.)

— Admissions to a Major League Baseball Home Run Derby held before the Major League Baseball All Star Game. (Sec. 212.04(2)(a) 4, F.S.)

— Admissions to th NBA Rookie Challenge, Celebrity Game, 3-Point Shooting Contest, or Slam Bunk Challenge. (Sec. 212.04(2)(a) 4, F.S.)

— Admissions to any FIFA World Cup match sanctioned by the Fédération Internationale de Football Association (FIFA), including any qualifying match held up to 12 months before the FIFA World Cup matches. (Sec. 212.04(2)(a) 5, F.S.; (Tax Information Publication, No. 22A01-13, Florida Department of Revenue, May 24, 2022))

— Admissions to any Formula One Grand Prix race sanctioned by Fédération Internationale de l'Automobile, including any qualifying or support races held at the circuit up to 72 hours before the grand prix race. (Sec. 212.04(2)(a) 5, F.S.; (Tax Information Publication, No. 22A01-13, Florida Department of Revenue, May 24, 2022))

— Admissions to the Daytona 500 sanctioned by the National Association for Stock Car Auto Racing, including any qualifying or support races held at the same track up to 72 hours before the race. (Sec. 212.04(2)(a) 5, F.S.; (Tax Information Publication, No. 22A01-13, Florida Department of Revenue, May 24, 2022))

— *Athletic events sponsored by governmental entities.*—A participation or sponsorship fee imposed by a governmental entity for admission to an athletic or recreational program when the governmental entity, by itself or in conjunction with an organization exempt under IRC 501(c)(3), sponsors, administers, plans, supervises, directs, and controls the program. (Sec. 212.04(2)(a) 5, F.S.; Rule 12A-1.005)

— *Events sponsored by charitable organizations.*—Admissions to live theater, opera, or ballet sponsored by certain tax-exempt charitable organizations. (Sec. 212.04(2)(a) 6, F.S.; Rule 12A-1.005)

— *Fishing boat.*—Charges to charter a boat with a crew for fishing, but not charges to stay upon a "head-boat," party boat, or other boat. Also exempt are entry fees for participation in fresh water fishing tournaments. (Sec. 212.08(7)(y), F.S.; Sec. 212.04(2)(a) 6, F.S.; Rule 12A-1.005)

— *Football games sponsored by nonprofits.*—Amounts charged for the rental, lease, sublease, or license of luxury boxes, skyboxes, or other box seats for high school or college football games sponsored by qualified nonprofit organizations. Taxes imposed prior to the effective date, but not paid or collected, are no longer due from the sponsor. (Sec. 212.031(9), F.S.)

— *Gun clubs.*—Admissions to and membership fees for gun clubs are exempt from the sales and use tax on admissions. For purposes of the exemption, "gun club" is defined as an organization whose primary purpose is to offer its members access to one or more shooting ranges for target or skeet shooting. (Sec. 212.04(2)(a)10, F.S.; Tax Information Publication, No. 15A01-08, Florida Department of Revenue, June 26, 2015)

— *Museums.*—Admissions to any museum or historic building owned by any political subdivision of the state. (Sec. 212.04(2)(a) 2, F.S.)

— *Nonprofits.*—Dues, membership fees, and admissions charges imposed by nonprofit sponsoring organizations exempt from income tax under IRC Sec. 501(c)(3). (Sec. 212.04(2)(a) 2, F.S.)

Admissions to charity-sponsored live theater, opera, or ballet.—The exemption for admissions to live theater, opera, or ballet sponsored by certain exempt charitable organizations applies to governmentally sponsored events. Examples of the exemption's application are provided in the governing regulation. (Rule 12A-1.005)

Foreign vessels carrying passengers to international waters.—Charges made by foreign vessels carrying passengers to international waters are taxable if passengers cannot disembark from the vessel at points other than the origination point ("cruises to nowhere"). However, if the vessel docks and passengers can disembark, the charge is considered to be for transportation and is exempt from tax. (Rule 12A-1.005)

Guidance on expansion of exempt admissions.—Effective July 1, 2022, admissions to certain FIFA World Cup matches, Formula One Grand Prix races, and Daytona 500 races are exempt from Florida sales and use tax. Admissions to the following are exempt from tax:

— any FIFA World Cup match sanctioned by the Fédération Internationale de Football Association (FIFA), including any World Cup qualifying match held up to 12 months before the FIFA World Cup matches;

— any Formula One Grand Prix race sanctioned by the Fédération Internationale de l'Automobile, including any qualifying or support races held at the circuit up to 72 hours before the Grand Prix race; and

— any Daytona 500 race sanctioned by the National Association for Stock Car Auto Racing (NASCAR), including any qualifying or support races held at the same track up to 72 hours before the race.

(*Tax Information Publication, No. 22A01-13,* Florida Department of Revenue, May 24, 2022)

Resales of admission to exempt entity (credit or refund).—A who has purchased a taxable admission and resells that admission to an exempt entity is allowed to seek from the Florida Department of Revenue (DOR) a refund or credit of the tax paid on its purchase of the admission. The exempt entity, however, may not resell the admission. (Sec. 212.04(1)(c) 2, F.S.; *Tax Information Publication, No. 17A01-13,* Florida Department of Revenue, December 11, 2017)

A dealer entitled to a credit or refund may claim the credit on Line 6 of the Sales and Use Tax Return (Form DR-15) or file an Application for Refund—Sales and Use Tax (Form DR-26S). When submitting the refund application, the dealer must provide a copy of the exempt entity's Consumer's Certificate of Exemption or other proof of the entity's exempt status, along with a copy of the ticket, invoice, or other document that verifies the tax paid on the admission. (*Tax Information Publication, No. 17A01-13,* Florida Department of Revenue, December 11, 2017)

In addition, if a purchaser of a taxable admission resells that admission to an entity that is exempt from sales and use tax, and that purchaser is a member of the same controlled group of corporations for federal income tax purposes as the dealer that sold it the admission, the purchaser may then seek a refund or credit of the tax from the vendor who may then seek a credit or refund from the DOR. In such a case, the related purchaser must provide the related selling dealer proof of the purchaser's exempt status. (Sec. 212.04(1)(c) 2, F.S.; *Tax Information Publication, No. 17A01-13,* Florida Department of Revenue, December 11, 2017)

The selling dealer should get and keep:

— a copy of the proof of the purchaser's exempt status (e.g., Consumer's Certificate of Exemption); and

— proof of tax paid for the original purchase of the resold admission.

(*Tax Information Publication, No. 17A01-13*, Florida Department of Revenue, December 11, 2017)

• *Local taxes*

When an event for which a taxable admission is charged is held within a county that imposes a local sales surtax, the surtax is due at the rate imposed by the county where the event occurs. The seller of the admission to an event is required to collect the surtax on the sales price or actual value of the admission. (Rule 12A-15.003(3), F.A.C.)

• *Pari-mutuel wagering*

A pari-mutuel wagering tax is charged on admissions to horse races, dog races, and jai alai games. The admissions tax applicable under sales and use tax law is in addition to the parti-mutuel wagering tax. However, the pari-mutuel wagering tax itself is not subject to the admissions tax. (Sec. 212.04(2)(c), F.S.; Sec. 550.0951, F.S.)

Admission tax.—An admission tax equal to 15% of the admission charge for entrance to the permit holder's facility and grandstand area, or 10¢, whichever is greater, is imposed on each person attending a:

— horse race;

— dog race; or

— jai alai game.

It is the permit holder responsibility to collect the admission tax. The admission tax is not imposed on any free passes or complimentary cards issued to persons for which there is no cost to the person for admission to pari-mutuel events. (Sec. 550.0951, F.S.)

Breaks tax.—Each permit holder conducting jai alai performances mustl pay a tax equal to the breaks. The term "breaks" is defined as that portion of each pari-mutuel pool that is not redistributed to the contributors or withheld by the permit holder as commission. (Sec. 550.0951, F.S.)

Tax on handle.—Each permit holder must pay a tax on contributions to pari-mutuel pools, the aggregate of which is referred to as "handle," on races or games conducted by the permit holder. The tax is imposed daily and is based on the total contributions to all pari-mutuel pools conducted during the daily performance. If a permit holder conducts more than one performance daily, the tax is imposed on each performance separately. (Sec. 550.0951, F.S.)

The tax on handle is as follows:

— for quarter horse racing, 1% of the handle;

— for dogracing, 5.5% of the handle, except that for live charity performances, and for intertrack wagering on such charity performances at a guest greyhound track within the market area of the host, the tax is 7.6% of the handle;

— for jai alai, 7.1% of the handle;

— for intertrack wagering, 2% of the handle if the host track is a horse track, 3.3% if the host track is a harness track, 5.5% if the host track is a dog track, and 7.1% if the host track is a jai alai fronton; and

— for intertrack wagers accepted by certain dog tracks, 3.9% if the host facility is a greyhound permit holder and, 6.1% if the host facility is a jai alai permit holder (exceptions apply).

(Sec. 550.0951, F.S.)

¶60-230

Wagering on live jai alai performances.—Wagering on live jai alai performances is subject to tax on handle per performance for live jai alai performances is 4.25% of handle per performance (however, when the live handle of a permit holder during the preceding state fiscal year was less than $15 million, the tax must be paid on the handle in excess of $30,000 per performance per day). In addition, when the total of admissions tax, daily license fee, and tax on handle for live jai alai performances paid to the commission by a permit holder during the current state fiscal year exceeds the total state tax revenues from wagering on live jai alai performances paid or due by the permit holder in fiscal year 1991-1992, the permit holder must pay tax on handle for live jai alai performances at a rate of 2.55% of the handle per performance for the remainder of the current state fiscal year. Other rates apply depending on certain circumstances. (Sec. 550.09511, F.S.)

Harness horse taxes.—The tax on handle for live harness horse performances is 0.5% of handle per performance. (Sec. 550.09512, F.S.)

The permit of a harness horse permit holder who is conducting live harness horse performances and who does not pay tax on handle for any such performances conducted during any two consecutive state fiscal years is void and may not be reissued unless that failure to operate and pay tax on handle was the direct result of fire, strike, war, hurricane, pandemic, or other disaster or event beyond the ability of the permit holder to control. Financial hardship to the permit holder does not, in and of itself, constitute just cause for failure to operate and pay tax on handle. (Sec. 550.09512, F.S.)

Greyhound dog racing taxes.—The tax on handle for greyhound dogracing is 5.5% of the handle, except that for live charity performances, and for intertrack wagering on such charity performances at a guest greyhound track within the market area of the host, the tax is 7.6% of the handle. (Sec. 550.0951, F.S.; Sec. 550.09514, F.S.)

Thoroughbred horse taxes.—The tax on handle for live thoroughbred horserace performances is 0.5%. (Sec. 550.09515, F.S.)

The permit of a thoroughbred horse permi tholder who does not pay tax on handle for live thoroughbred horse performances for a full schedule of live races during any two consecutive state fiscal years is void and will escheat to and become the property of the state unless that failure to operate and pay tax on handle was the direct result of fire, strike, war, or other disaster or event beyond the ability of the permit holder to control. Financial hardship to the permit holder does not, in and of itself, constitute just cause for failure to operate and pay tax on handle. (Sec. 550.09515, F.S.)

Payment of taxes.—Payment of taxes is made to the Florida Gaming Control Commission. Payment must be remitted by 3 p.m. on the 5th day of each calendar month for taxes imposed and collected for the preceding calendar month. If the 5th day of the calendar month falls on a weekend, payments must be remitted by 3 p.m. the first Monday following the weekend. (Sec. 550.0951, F.S.)

Filing of report.—Permit holders must file a report under oath by the 5th day of each calendar month for all taxes remitted during the preceding calendar month. Such payments must be accompanied by a report under oath showing:

— the total of all admissions;

— the pari-mutuel wagering activities for the preceding calendar month; and

— other information that the commission may require.

(Sec. 550.0951, F.S.)

[¶60-240] Advertising

Sales of advertising services by an advertising agency to a client are exempt from sales and use tax. The exemption also applies to items of tangible personal property such as photographic negatives and positives, videos, films, galleys, mechanicals, veloxes, illustrations, digital audiotapes, analog tapes, printed advertisement, compact discs for the purpose of recording, digital equipment, artwork, and the services to produce those items if the items are:

— sold to an advertising agency acting as an agent for its clients, and are created for the performance of advertising services for the clients;

— produced, fabricated, manufactured, or otherwise created by an advertising agency for its clients, and are used for advertising services for the clients; or

— sold by an advertising agency to its clients in the performance of advertising services for the clients, whether or not the charges are marked up or separately stated.

(Sec. 212.08(7)(vv), F.S.)

The exemption does not apply to film, paper, and videotapes that are purchased to create items such as photographic negatives and positives, videos, films, galleys, mechanicals, veloxes, illustrations, and artwork that are sold to an advertising agency or produced in-house by an advertising agency on behalf of its clients. (Sec. 212.08(7)(vv), F.S.)

Items and creative services used by an advertising agency to design the advertising for promotional goods such as displays, exhibits, newspaper inserts, brochures, catalogues, direct mail letters, shirts, hats, pens, pencils, key chains, or other printed goods are not subject to tax, unless the promotional goods are produced for distribution; then tax applies to the sales price charged to the client. (Sec. 212.08(7)(vv), F.S.)

• *Tangible advertising pieces*

A dealer must collect sales tax on the selling price from the purchaser upon final sales to ultimate consumers resulting from direct-mail advertising pieces, circulars, handouts, throw-aways, and similar advertising matter. (Sec. 212.06(2)(g), F.S.; Rule 12A-1.034) The advertisement itself is exempt if it is a free, circulated publication that is published on a regular basis, contains primarily advertising, and is distributed through the mail, home delivery, or newsstands. (Sec. 212.08(7)(w), F.S.) Advertising materials distributed free of charge by mail in an envelope for 10 or more persons on a monthly, bimonthly, or other regular basis are also exempt. (Sec. 212.08(7)(ccc), F.S.).

A purchaser of printed materials, rather than the printer, must collect and remit Florida sales and use tax on those materials if the printer delivers the materials to the U.S. Postal Service for mailing to persons, other than the purchaser, both within and outside the state. (Sec. 212.06(2)(g), F.S.)

Promotional materials, including printed advertising material, direct-mail literature, correspondence, written solicitations, and renewal notices, that are distributed to promote the sale of a subscription to a publication are exempt if they are imported, purchased, sold, used, manufactured, fabricated, processed, printed, imprinted, assembled, distributed, or stored in Florida, provided the promotional materials are subsequently exported outside Florida. This exemption takes the form of a refund of previously paid taxes or by self-accruing taxes and applies only if the seller of subscriptions to publications sold is registered with the Department of Revenue and remits taxes on the publications. (Sec. 212.06(11), F.S.)

The sale, use, storage, or consumption of all tangible advertising materials imported into the state are retail sales. Tangible advertising material includes displays, display containers, brochures, catalogs, price lists, point-of-sale advertising, technical manuals, and any tangible personal property that does not accompany the product to the ultimate consumer. (Sec. 212.02(14)(b), F.S.)

Handbills, circulars, flyers, advertising supplements and other printed materials furnished with a newspaper are subject to use tax. Copies of these items that are given away are taxable at the retail price, or on the cost price, whichever is less. (Rule 12A-1.008)

Inserts distributed with a newspaper or magazine are exempt with a resale certificate if they are a component part of the newspaper or magazine. Otherwise, their purchase is subject to tax. (Rule 12A-1.008(4))

Advertising materials distributed free of charge by mail in an envelope.—The types of advertisements to which the exemption for certain advertising materials distributed free of charge by mail in an envelope is applicable are individual coupons or other individual cards, sheets or pages of printed advertising. The envelope must contain advertisements from 10 or more persons (advertisers). Sales and use tax is not due on the purchase of materials (i.e., paper, ink, envelopes, glue or replenisher) that are incorporated into and become a component part of the exempt advertising materials. Moreover, no use tax is imposed on the cost of manufacturing, producing, processing, or fabricating the exempt advertising materials. (Sec. 212.08(7)(ddd), F.S.; Rule 12A-1.008(5))

• *Property used to promote magazine subscriptions*

There is a sales tax exemption for promotional materials that are imported, purchased, sold, used, manufactured, fabricated, processed, printed, imprinted, assembled, distributed, or stored in Florida and that are subsequently exported outside the state. The exemption applies regardless of whether the exportation process is continuous and unbroken, whether a separate consideration is charged for the exported material, or whether the taxpayer keeps, retains, or exercises any right, power, dominion, or control over the promotional materials before (or for the purpose of) subsequently transporting them outside Florida. (Sec. 212.06(11), F.S.; Rule 12A-1.034)

The term "promotional materials" means:

— tangible personal property that is given away or otherwise distributed to promote the sale of a subscription to a publication;

— written or printed advertising material, direct mail literature, correspondence, written solicitations, renewal notices, and billings for sales connected with, or promoting, the sale of a subscription to a publication; and

— the component parts of the promotional materials described above.

(Sec. 212.06(11), F.S.)

The exemption inures to the taxpayer only through refund of previously paid taxes or by self-accrual of taxes as provided by Sec. 212.183. In addition, the exemption applies only if the seller of subscriptions to publications sold in Florida (1) is registered with the Department to collect the tax and (2) remits the tax on Florida sales of their publications. (Sec. 212.06(11), F.S.)

[¶60-250] Agriculture

Agricultural products (other than ornamental nursery stock) sold directly from the farm by the producers or produced by the farmer and used by the farmer's family or employees on the farm are exempt from sales and use tax. Sales of agricultural products made to any person who purchases them for the purpose of acquiring raw products not for direct consumption but for use or for sale in the process of preparing, finishing, or manufacturing agricultural products for the ultimate retail consumer trade are also exempt. (Sec. 212.07(5), (6), and (7), F.S.; Rule 12A-1.048)

Applicable definitions.—The term "agricultural commodity" means horticultural, aquacultural, poultry and farm products, and livestock and livestock products. (Sec. 212.02(27), F.S.) The term "farmer" means a person who is directly engaged in the business of producing crops, livestock, or other agricultural commodities; it includes, but is not limited to, horse breeders, nurserymen, dairymen, poultry men, cattle ranchers, apiarists, and persons raising fish. The term "livestock" includes all animals of the equine, bovine, or swine class, including goats, sheep, mules, horses, hogs, cattle, ostriches, and other grazing animals raised for commercial purposes; it also includes fish raised for commercial purposes. (Sec. 212.02(28), F.S.; Sec. 212.02(29), F.S.)

Additional exemptions for items in agricultural use and certain nets.—Further exemptions from sales tax include feed used for poultry, ostriches, and livestock, including race horses and dairy cows, but not including pets; disinfectants; fertilizers (including peat, topsoil and manure); insecticides; pesticides; herbicides; fungicides and weed killers applied to crops and groves; seeds and plants for growing fruits and vegetables for human consumption; portable containers or movable receptacles in which portable containers are placed that are used for processing farm products; field and garden seeds; nursery stock; seedlings; cuttings, or other propagative material purchased from growing stock; water for irrigation; cloth, plastic, and other materials used by farmers for shade, mulch, or protection from frost or insects found on a farm; generators used on poultry farms, and effective July 1, 2022, hog wire and barbed wire fencing, including gates and materials used to construct or repair such fencing, used in agricultural production on lands classified as agricultural. An exemption certificate is required for each transaction. (Sec. 212.08(4), (5)(a), and (7)(d), F.S.; Rule 12A-1.048; Rule 12A-1.001(5), (16), and (22); *Tax Information Publication, No. 22A01-15,* Florida Department of Revenue, June 29, 2022) Feed for livestock is exempt whether the livestock is raised for commercial or domestic purposes. (*Technical Assistance Advisement, No. 05A-025,* Florida Department of Revenue, June 3, 2005)

The sale of performance-enhancing or growth-enhancing products for cattle is exempt. (Sec. 212.08(5)(l), F.S.)

Leasing agricultural property is also exempt. (Sec. 212.031, F.S.)

• *Animal and aquaculture health products*

An exemption is provided for animal health products that are applied to, administered to, or consumed by livestock or poultry for the alleviation of pain or the cure or prevention of sickness, disease, or suffering, including:

— antiseptics;

— absorbent cotton;

— gauze for bandages;

— lotions;

— vaccines;

— vitamins; and

— worm remedies.

(Sec. 212.08(5)(a), F.S.; *Tax Information Publication, No. 17A01-08,* Florida Department of Revenue, July 21, 2017)

"Livestock" means all animals of the equine, bovine, or swine class, including goats, sheep, mules, horses, hogs, cattle, ostriches, and other grazing animals raised for commercial purposes. "Poultry" means domesticated food birds, such as chickens, turkeys, ducks, guineas, geese, pigeons raised as domesticated food birds, and quail. (*Tax Information Publication, No. 17A01-08,* Florida Department of Revenue, July 21, 2017)

¶60-250

The exemption also includes aquaculture health products used by aquaculture producers to prevent or treat fungi, bacteria, and parasitic diseases (e.g., water disinfectants, conditioners, and filters). In order to qualify for the exemption, the purchaser must be an aquaculture producer (i.e., a person engaged in the production of aquaculture products and certified, as provided).(Sec. 212.08(5)(a), F.S.; *Tax Information Publication, No. 17A01-08*, Florida Department of Revenue, July 21, 2017)

The term "aquaculture products" means aquatic organisms, including products derived from aquatic organisms, that are owned and propagated, grown, or produced under controlled conditions. Aquaculture products do not include organisms harvested from the wild for depuration, wet storage, or relay for purification. Some examples of aquaculture products raised for commercial purposes as identified by the Department of Agriculture and Consumer Services include fish, shrimp, crabs, mollusks, and reptiles. (*Tax Information Publication, No. 17A01-08*, Florida Department of Revenue, July 21, 2017)

To be eligible for this exemption, the purchaser must furnish the seller with a certificate stating that the item exempted is for the exclusive use authorized by law. The Florida Department of Revenue recommends that a purchaser present the Suggested Purchaser's Exemption Certificate: Items for Agricultural Use or for Agricultural Purpose and Power Farm Equipment, provided in Rule 12A-1.087(10)(f) and check the category titled "other" and include the following description:

— For an animal health product: "Animal health product in accordance with Sec. 212.08(5)(a), F.S."

— For an aquaculture health product, the purchaser may either use the Suggested Purchaser's Exemption Certificate and include the following language: "Aquaculture health product in accordance with Sec. 212.08(5)(a), F.S. I certify that I am engaged in the production of aquaculture products and certified under s. 597.004, F.S.," or provide a copy of the aquaculture producer's Aquaculture Certification from the Florida Department of Agriculture and Consumer Services to the selling dealer.

The selling dealer must retain the documentation in its books and records for as long as applicable under Florida law. (*Tax Information Publication, No. 17A01-08*, Florida Department of Revenue, July 21, 2017)

• *Aquaculture and fishing*

Equipment and supplies used for the breeding and raising of fish are treated in the same manner as any other agricultural activity. (Rule 12A-1.087) Bait purchased by commercial fishers used solely for the entrapment of stone and blue crabs is specifically exempt. Nets and materials, including parts and labor used to repair them, are exempt when used exclusively by commercial fisheries. (Sec. 212.08(5) and (7)(c), F.S.; Rule 12A-1.001(6))

The charge for chartering a boat with the crew furnished solely for the purpose of fishing, but not the charge for a head boat or party boat, is exempt. Rule 12A-1.001(6)(c) does not reflect this exemption. (Sec. 212.08(7)(y), F.S.)

• *Building materials for nonresidential farm building damaged by Hurricane Michael*

A sales and use tax exemption is enacted for the purchase of certain building materials used to repair or replacement nonresidential farm buildings damaged as a direct result of Hurricane Michael. The exemption is available through a refund of previously paid taxes and applies to purchases made between October 10, 2018, and June 30, 2019. (Sec. 21, Ch. 42 (H.B. 7123), Laws 2019, effective May 15, 2019, applicable retroactively to October 10, 2018)

The Florida Department of Revenue has issued guidance regarding this exemption. The exemption is available only through a refund of tax and is limited to purchases made between October 10, 2018, and June 30, 2019. The owner of the fencing or building materials or owner of the real property where the fence or building is located must submit Form DR-26S-HAG, Application for Refund—Certain Farming Materials Damaged by Hurricane Michael, to the department by December 31, 2019. This application is available on the department's website at DR-26S-HAG Application for Refund—Certain Farming Materials Damaged by Hurricane Michael. (*Tax Information Publication, No. 19A01-04*, Florida Department of Revenue, June 6, 2019)

Emergency Rule 12AER19-03 also incorporates Form DR-26S-HAG, Application for Refund—Certain Farming Materials Damaged by Hurricane Michael, to allow taxpayers to seek a refund of tax on qualifying purchases. (Emergency Rule 12AER19-03)

"Building materials" are defined as tangible personal property that becomes a component part of a nonresidential farm building. (Sec. 21, Ch. 42 (H.B. 7123), Laws 2019, effective May 15, 2019, applicable retroactively to October 10, 2018)

To receive a refund, the owner of the fencing materials must apply to the Florida Department of Revenue by December 31, 2019. The application must include the following information:

— the name and address of the person claiming the refund;

— the address and assessment roll parcel number of the real property where the building materials will be or were used;

— the sales invoice or other proof of purchase of the building materials, showing the amount of sales tax paid, the date of purchase, and the name and address of the sales tax dealer from whom the materials were purchased; and

— an affidavit executed by the owner of the building materials including a statement that the building materials were or will be used to repair the nonresidential farm building damaged as a direct result of the impact of Hurricane Michael.

(Sec. 21, Ch. 42 (H.B. 7123), Laws 2019, effective May 15, 2019, applicable retroactively to October 10, 2018)

This provision is applicable retroactively to October 10, 2018. (Sec. 21, Ch. 42 (H.B. 7123), Laws 2019, effective May 15, 2019, applicable retroactively to October 10, 2018)

• *Electricity used in the production or processing of agricultural products*

Electricity used for the production or processing of agricultural products on a farm is exempt from Florida sales tax. The exemption currently applies to electricity used for indirect purposes in the production or processing of farm products on a farm, including electricity used to:

— supply power to facilities located on a farm used to repair farm equipment;

— supply power to administrative offices located on a farm; and

— supply power for restroom facilities located on a farm.

(Sec. 212.08(5)(e)2, F.S.; Rule 12A-1.087; *Tax Information Publication, No. 07A01-05*, Florida Department of Revenue, July 1, 2007)

The exemption only applies if the electricity is separately metered from any electricity used for non-production or non-processing purposes. If the electricity is centrally metered and the electricity is used for both tax-exempt and taxable purposes, the purchase of the electricity is taxable. Electricity that is separately metered and used to supply power to greenhouses, poultry houses, dairy barns, horse stables, and processing facilities located on a farm is also exempt. To qualify for the exemption, the purchaser must furnish the utility provider with an exemption certificate stating that the electricity will be used for the production or processing of agricultural farm products on a farm or in a packinghouse. (Sec. 212.08(5)(e)2, F.S.; Rule 12A-1.087; *Tax Information Publication, No. 07A01-05*, Florida Department of Revenue, July 1, 2007)

The exemption provided for electricity used for production, packing, or processing of agricultural products on the farm includes electricity used directly or indirectly in a "packinghouse" (defined as any building or structure where fruits, vegetables, or meat from cattle, hogs, or fish is packed or otherwise prepared for market or shipment in fresh form for wholesale distribution). (Sec. 212.08(5)(e)2, F.S.; Rule 12A-1.087)

The exemption for electricity used in a packinghouse includes buildings or structures where fish are packed or prepared for market or shipment. "Fish" are any cold-blooded aquatic vertebrates of the superclass Pisces, which characteristically have fins, gills, and a streamlined body, that are raised through aquaculture. (Sec. 212.08(5)(e)2, F.S.)

The exemption does not apply to electricity used in buildings or structures where agricultural products are sold at retail. *Tax Information Publication, No. 12A01-07* provides a suggested format of an exemption certificate. In instances where the utility provider accepts an exemption certificate in good faith, the Florida Department of Revenue will look to the purchaser for any applicable tax, penalty, or interest due. Utility providers that currently have on record an exemption certificate from the purchaser for electricity used in the production or processing of agricultural products on a farm are not required to obtain a new certificate from the purchaser. (*Tax Information Publication, No. 12A01-07*, Florida Department of Revenue, June 1, 2012)

• *Farm-related materials damaged by Hurricane Irma*

A Florida sales tax exemption is available for certain purchases used to repair farm fences and nonresidential farm buildings damaged as a direct result of Hurricane Irma. The exemption is available only through a refund of tax and is limited to purchases made between September 10, 2017, and May 31, 2018. (Secs. 57 and 58 (H.B. 7087), Laws 2018; *Tax Information Publication, No. 18A01-08*, Florida Department of Revenue, May 18, 2018)

Fencing materials.—The refund is available for sales tax paid on eligible purchases of fencing materials used to repair farm fences damaged by Hurricane Irma. The fences must be located on real property classified as agricultural land for property tax purposes. (Secs. 57 and 58 (H.B. 7087), Laws 2018; *Tax Information Publication, No. 18A01-08*, Florida Department of Revenue, May 18, 2018)

Building materials used to repair nonresidential farm buildings.—The refund is also available for sales tax paid on eligible purchases of building materials used to repair nonresidential farm buildings damaged by Hurricane Irma. A "nonresidential farm building" is defined as any temporary or permanent building or support structure that is classified as a nonresidential farm building on a farm and is not intended to be used as a residence. The term may include a barn, greenhouse, shade house, farm office, storage building, or poultry house. (Secs. 57 and 58 (H.B. 7087), Laws 2018; *Tax Information Publication, No. 18A01-08*, Florida Department of Revenue, May 18, 2018)

Applying for the refund.—The owner of the fencing or building materials or owner of the real property where the fence or building is located must, by December 31, 2018, submit to the Florida Department of Revenue Form DR-26SIAG, Application for Refund—Certain Farming Materials Damaged by Hurricane Irma. (Emergency Rule 12AER18-01; *Tax Information Publication, No. 18A01-08*, Florida Department of Revenue, May 18, 2018)

• *Farm trailers*

Florida sales and use tax may not be imposed on the sales price for a trailer purchased by a farmer for exclusive use in agricultural production or to transport farm products from his or her farm to the place where the farmer transfers ownership of the farm products to another. The exemption: (1) is not forfeited by using a trailer to transport the farmer's farm equipment; (2) is inapplicable to the lease or rental of a trailer; and (3) applies regardless of whether the trailer is licensed, as provided, for highway use. (Sec. 212.08(3), F.S.; *Tax Information Publication, No. 22A01-15*, Florida Department of Revenue, June 29, 2022)

The exemption will not be allowed unless the purchaser furnishes the seller a written certificate that the purchased items qualify for the exemption. (*Tax Information Publication, No. 22A01-15*, Florida Department of Revenue, June 29, 2022)

• *Fencing materials damaged by Hurricane Michael*

A sales and use tax exemption is available for the purchase of fencing materials used in the repair or replacement of agricultural fencing damaged as a direct result of Hurricane Michael. The exemption is available through a refund of previously paid taxes and applies to purchases made between October 10, 2018, and June 30, 2019. (Sec. 20, Ch. 42 (H.B. 7123), Laws 2019, effective May 15, 2019, applicable retroactively to October 10, 2018)

Emergency Rule 12AER19-03 incorporates Form DR-26S-HAG, Application for Refund—Certain Farming Materials Damaged by Hurricane Michael, to allow taxpayers to seek a refund of tax on qualifying purchases. (Emergency Rule 12AER19-03)

To receive a refund, the owner of the fencing materials must apply to the Florida Department of Revenue by December 31, 2019. The application must include the following information:

— the name and address of the person claiming the refund;

— the address and assessment roll parcel number of the agricultural land where the fencing materials will be or were used;

— the sales invoice or other proof of purchase of the fencing materials, showing the amount of sales tax paid, the date of purchase, and the name and address of the sales tax dealer from whom the materials were purchased; and

— an affidavit executed by the owner of the fencing materials including a statement that the fencing materials were or will be used to repair fencing damaged as a direct result of the impact of Hurricane Michael.

(Sec. 20, Ch. 42 (H.B. 7123), Laws 2019, effective May 15, 2019, applicable retroactively to October 10, 2018)

This provision is applicable retroactively to October 10, 2018. (Sec. 20, Ch. 42 (H.B. 7123), Laws 2019, effective May 15, 2019, applicable retroactively to October 10, 2018)

• *Industrial machinery and equipment used in aquacultural activities*

Industrial machinery and equipment purchased for use in aquacultural activities at fixed locations is exempt from sales and use tax. "Aquacultural activities" are defined as the business of the cultivation of aquatic organisms and certification. Aquacultural activities must produce an aquaculture product (e.g. aquatic organisms and any product derived from aquatic organisms that are owned and propagated, grown, or produced under controlled conditions). Such products do not include organisms harvested from the wild for depuration, wet storage, or relay for purification. (Sec. 212.08(5)(t), F.S.)

"Industrial machinery and equipment" is tangible personal property or other property that has a depreciable life of 3 years or more and that is used as an integral part in the manufacturing, processing, compounding, or production of tangible personal property for sale. The term includes a building and its structural components, including heating and air-conditioning systems. The term includes parts and accessories only to the extent that the exemption is consistent with these parameters. (Sec. 212.08(5)(t), F.S.)

• *Livestock, poultry, and other farm products*

Tax does not apply to the sale of livestock, poultry, and other farm products direct from the farm, or to livestock, poultry, and other farm products used by the farmer's family and employees on the farm. The producers are entitled to the exemption even though the livestock sold may have been registered with a breeders' or registry association prior to the sale and even if the sale takes place at a livestock show or race meeting as long as the sale is made by the original producer and within this state. When sales of livestock, poultry, or other farm products are made to consumers by any person other than a producer, they are not exempt from the sales and use tax. (Sec. 212.07(5) and (6), F.S.; Rule 12A-1.049)

The sale of livestock for breeding purposes is exempt. The sale of race horses or race dogs is taxable unless the animal is being sold by the breeder. (Rule 12A-1.049)

Aquaculture.—The definition of "livestock" includes aquaculture products. Feed for livestock is exempt, and in order to qualify as livestock for purposes of this exemption, the aquaculture species must be defined and identified by the Department of Agriculture and Consumer Services. "Aquaculture" products are defined as aquatic organisms and any product derived from aquatic organisms that are owned and propagated, grown, or produced under controlled conditions. Examples of aquaculture products which could qualify as livestock under the revised definition include but are not limited to: fresh, brackish, and saltwater fish; shrimp; stone, mud, and swimming crabs; mollusks including conchs, mussels, oysters, and scallops; and reptiles including turtles, alligators, and crocodiles. (Sec. 212.08(7)(d), F.S.; *Tax Information Publication, No. 15A01-09*, Florida Department of Revenue, June 30, 2015)

To document an exempt purchase of livestock feed, the Florida Department of Revenue suggests that a purchaser provide the selling dealer with a signed copy of the suggested exemption certificate provided in *Tax Information Publication, No. 15A01-09*. Alternatively, the purchaser may provide a copy of their Aquaculture Certification from the Florida Department of Agriculture and Consumer Services if they are purchasing livestock feed for aquaculture products. (*Tax Information Publication, No. 15A01-09*, Florida Department of Revenue, June 30, 2015)

• *Motor fuel*

Motor fuel, including butane gas, propane gas, natural gas, and all other forms of liquefied petroleum gas used for agricultural, aquacultural, or commercial fishing purposes is exempt. (Sec. 212.08(5)(e), F.S.)

This exemption includes tractors, vehicles, or other farm equipment used directly or indirectly for the production, packing, or processing of aquacultural products, whether used on or off the premises of a farm. (Sec. 212.08(5)(e), F.S.)

The Florida Department of Revenue provides a suggested exemption certificate form. (*Tax Information Publication, No. 18A01-10*, Florida Department of Revenue, May 30, 2018, 206-369)

"Agricultural purposes" include use in any tractor, vehicle, or other farm equipment used exclusively on a farm or for processing farm products, including operating equipment for apiaries. None of these vehicles or equipment may be driven or operated on Florida public highways; however, the restriction does not apply to the movement of farm vehicles or equipment between farms or to the transportation of bees. (Sec. 212.08(5)(f) and (5)(k), F.S.)

In addition, the storage, use, or consumption of diesel fuel used in any tractor, vehicle, or other equipment used exclusively on a farm or for processing farm products on the farm is exempt from use tax as long as no part of the fuel is used in any licensed motor vehicle on the public highways of Florida. (Sec. 212.0501, F.S.)

• *Power farm equipment*

Qualifying purchases of power farm equipment are exempt from tax. "Qualifying purchases" are the sale, rental, lease, use, consumption, or storage for use in Florida of power farm equipment used exclusively on a farm or in a forest in the agricultural production of crops or products, or for fire prevention and suppression work with respect to the crops or products. "Power farm equipment" means moving or stationary equipment that contains within itself the means for its own propulsion or power and moving or stationary equipment that is dependent upon an external power source to perform its functions. "Power farm equipment" includes augers, combines, conveyors, disks, dozers, feeding systems, harrows, hay balers, irrigation motors, mowers, plows, pumps, skidders, and tractors. In addition, the exemption includes generators and power units used for a qualifying purpose. In general, "agricultural production" means the production of plants and animals useful to humans. (Sec. 212.08(3), F.S.; *Tax Information Publication, No. 05A01-03*, Florida Department of Revenue, June 15, 2005)

Replacement parts and accessories for power farm or irrigation equipment.— The sale, rental, lease, use, consumption, repair, and storage for use in Florida of power farm equipment or irrigation equipment, including replacement parts and accessories for such equipment, is exempt from sales and use tax. The exemption includes power farm equipment used in the storage of raw products on a farm. Examples of qualifying "power farm equipment" include but are not limited to: augers; combines; conveyors; disks; dozers; feeding systems; forklifts; generators; harrows; hay balers; irrigation motors; mowers; plows; power units; pumps; refrigeration equipment; skidders; and tractors. Examples of qualifying parts and accessories include but are not limited to: tires; batteries; radios; global positioning systems; replacement parts; blades; disks; hoses; pumps; sprinkler heads; conveyor belts; lubricants; and gauges. (Sec. 212.08(3), F.S.; *Tax Information Publication, No. 15A01-11*, Florida Department of Revenue, June 25, 2015)

The exemption is only allowed when the purchaser furnishes the seller with a written statement certifying that the equipment is purchased exclusively for qualified use. Repairs of power farm equipment and purchases of parts to repair power farm equipment remain subject to tax. The sale, rental or purchase of qualifying power farm equipment should be recorded on Line 1, under the category "Exempt Sales" on the applicable sales tax return for the period when the sale occurs. (*Tax Information Publication, No. 05A01-03*, Florida Department of Revenue, June 15, 2005)

• *Stakes used to support plants during agricultural production*

Sales of stakes used by a farmer to support plants during agricultural production are exempt from Florida sales and use tax. "Agricultural production" is defined as the production of plants and animals useful to humans, including the preparation, planting, cultivating, and harvesting of these products, or any other practices necessary to accomplish production of these products through the harvest phase, including storage of raw products on a farm. The term includes aquaculture, horticulture, floriculture, viticulture, forestry, dairy, livestock, poultry, bees, and all forms of farm products and farm production. The exemption is not allowed unless the purchaser signs a certificate stating that the stakes are purchased to support plants during agricultural production. (Sec. 212.08(5)(a), F.S.; *Tax Information Publication, No. 15A01-15*, Florida Department of Revenue, June 26, 2015)

[¶60-260] Alcoholic Beverages

All alcoholic beverages are subject to sales and use tax, (Sec. 212.08(4)(b), F.S.) except vinous and alcoholic beverages provided by distributors or vendors for tasting purposes. (Sec. 212.08(7)(s), F.S.; Rule 12A-1.057) Charges imposed upon the general public for such tastings are subject to tax. (Rule 12A-1.057) The term "alcoholic beverages" includes all alcoholic and malt beverages, including beer, ale, and wine. (Sec. 212.02(9), F.S.; Rule 12A-1.057)

Dealers must add the tax to the sale price of the beverages, but may set prices in such a manner as to avoid the handling of pennies. (Rule 12A-1.057)

Information reports.—Every seller of alcoholic beverages is required to file an information report of any sales to any retailer in Florida. The information report must be filed electronically by using the e-filing website of the Florida Department of Revenue, or secure file transfer protocol or electronic data interchange files with the department's e-filing provider. The information report is due annually on July 1 for the preceding reporting period and is delinquent if not received by the department by September 30. The report must contain the following information for the period from July 1 through June 30:

— the seller's name;

— the seller's beverage license number;

— the retailer's name;

— the retailer's beverage license number;

— the retailer's address, including street address, municipality, state, and five-digit zip code;

— the general item type, such as beer, wine, spirits, or any combination of such items; and

— the net monthly sales total in dollars sold to each retailer.

(Sec. 212.133, F.S.; *Tax Information Publication, No. 11A01-04*, Florida Department of Revenue, June 27, 2011)

"Seller" is defined as any manufacturer, wholesaler, or distributor of alcoholic beverages who sellers to a retailer in Florida. "Retailer" is defined as a person engaged in the business of making sales at retail and who holds a license, as provided. (Sec. 212.133, F.S.; *Tax Information Publication, No. 11A01-04*, Florida Department of Revenue, June 27, 2011)

Any seller who fails to provide the information report by September 30 is subject to a penalty of $1,000 for every month, or part of a month, that the report is not provided, up to a maximum amount of $10,000. The penalty must be settled or compromised if it is determined by the department that the noncompliance is due to reasonable cause and not to wilful negligence, neglect, or fraud. (Sec. 212.133, F.S.)

[¶60-290] Clothing

Sales or rentals of articles of clothing are subject to sales and use tax. Sales and use tax also applies to clothing accessories, repairs, and alterations; tailoring charges for making suits from goods provided by the customer; and sales of military insignia and uniforms. (Rule 12A-1.076)

• *Shoe repairs*

Shoe repair shops must collect tax on the total charges for the repairs and may purchase materials used in repairs tax free. Machinery, equipment, and other supplies purchased and used by shoe repair dealers are taxable to them. (Rule 12A-1.076)

[¶60-310] Computers, Software, and Services

In general, computer hardware and canned software are taxable, but custom software and computer services are exempt. (Sec. 212.08(7)(v), F.S.; Rule 12A-1.032)

Is computer hardware subject to sales tax in Florida?

The sale to a consumer of a computer and its related components is taxable when delivered to the customer in Florida. The rental of a computer and related equipment, including hardware, that is physically located in Florida, is also taxable. "Hardware" is defined as the machine and all of its components. (Rule 12A-1.032)

Computer maintenance contracts. Computer maintenance contracts covering the cost of labor only to repair or maintain computer hardware are taxable as service warranties. (Rule 12A-1.105)

Data centers. A sales and use tax exemption is provided for data center property purchased, rented, or leased by a data center's owners and tenants when used to construct, maintain, and operate computer server equipment at a data center. The data center's owners and tenants must make a cumulative capital investment of $150 million and the data center must have at least 15 megawatts of total power capacity and at least 1 megawatt of power capacity dedicated to each individual owner and tenant of the data center. These requirements must be satisfied no later than five years after the commencement of construction of the data center. In addition, a data center must meet the requisite investment requirements no later than June 30, 2027, must submit to subsequent periodic review by the DOR to assure continued qualification, and is subject to revenue clawback provisions if it utilizes the tax exemption and is not qualified. (Sec. 212.08(5)(s), F.S.; Rule 12AER17-03, F.A.C.)

Exemption eligibility requirements, definitions of data center property, a discussion of the application process, and procedures to document purchases of exempt data center property are included within the rule, which also incorporates Form DR-1214DCP, Application for Data Center Property Temporary Tax Exemption Certificate. (Rule 12AER17-03, F.A.C.)

Is computer software subject to sales tax in Florida?

Canned software is taxable, but custom software is exempt.

Canned software. The sale of pre-packaged software for use with audio-visual equipment or other computer equipment is subject to sales tax when the software, as purchased by the customer, is fully usable without modifications by the vendor and when the vendor does not perform a detailed analysis of the customer's requirements in selecting or preparing the programs. (Rule 12A-1.032)

Custom software. The sale of software is exempt as a service transaction if the vendor, at the customer's request, modifies or alters the pre-packaged program to the customer's specification and charges the customer for a single transaction (including both the sale of the software and the fee for the customization). (Rule 12A-1.032)

However, if the sale to the customer includes hardware, software, and software customization services, then the whole sale is taxable regardless of whether the items are billed separately, because the sale of the software and the software customization are considered part of the sale of the tangible personal property (i.e., the hardware). (*Technical Assistance Advisement 00A-082*, Florida Department of Revenue, December 14, 2000)

Are computer services taxable?

Since services generally are exempt from tax and general computer services are not specifically identified as being taxable, they are not subject to tax. (Sec. 212.05, F.S.; Sec. 212.08(7)(v), F.S.)

¶60-310

Computer technicians. Charges imposed by a computer technician for surveying a customer's needs and making recommendations are exempt as charges for professional services. The charge that a computer technician makes for a customized software package that includes items such as instructional material, pre-punched cards, or programmed tapes is exempt as a service charge. (Rule 12A-1.032)

Key-punch cards. The sale of blank key-punch cards and blank magnetic tape are taxable if purchased by a computer technician or service bureau that uses the items to develop a software package for a customer. The cards and tape are also taxable as tangible personal property when purchased and used to program the customer's own computer. (Rule 12A-1.032)

Is cloud computing taxable?

The taxability of cloud computing depends on the category under which the activity is classified. Cloud computing is a term used to describe the delivery of computing resources, including software applications, development tools, storage, and servers over the Internet. Rather than purchasing hardware or software, a consumer may purchase access to a cloud computing provider's hardware or software. Cloud computing offerings are generally divided into three categories: software as a service (SaaS), infrastructure as a service (IaaS), and platform as a service (PaaS).

Although Florida has not enacted any statutes or adopted any regulations specifically regarding cloud computing, the Florida Department of Revenue has issued a ruling on the issue. The department held that the sale of subscriptions to customized computer software, which are delivered to clients electronically, and sales of cloud computing services sold by the taxpayer to its clients were not subject to Florida sales and use tax. The taxpayer did not deliver any tangible products to its clients. A sale that solely involves software, canned or customized, electronically downloaded by the customer, is exempt since there is no conveyance of tangible personal property. Moreover, the taxpayer did not receive the software in a tangible format from the software provider. The software was hosted at data centers that are owned and operated by the software provider, and the taxpayer and its customers were only able to access the server and the software remotely. The software was never made available to the taxpayer's customers by disk or any other tangible medium, and the taxpayer did not provide any hardware to its customers. As such, the sales of the software subscriptions and the cloud computing services were not subject to tax. (*Technical Assistance Advisement, No. 16A-014*, Florida Department of Revenue, August 8, 2016)

Software as a service. Under the SaaS model, a consumer purchases access to a software application that is owned, operated, and maintained by a SaaS provider. The consumer accesses the application over the Internet. The software is located on a server that is owned or leased by the SaaS provider. The software is not transferred to the customer, and the customer does not have the right to download, copy, or modify the software.

Sales tax authority on SaaS transactions is still evolving. Some states have taken the position that SaaS transactions are a sale of software, reasoning that using software by electronically accessing it is no different than downloading it. Other states have deemed it a service based on the fact that no software is transferred. In some states, the taxability may depend on the specific facts and whether the object of the transaction is the use of software or some other purpose.

Florida has no specific statutory or regulatory authority on the taxability of SaaS.

Infrastructure as a service. IaaS providers sell access to storage, networks, equipment, and other computing resources that the provider operates and maintains. A consumer purchases the ability to store data or deploy and run software using the provider's equipment. The consumer does not manage or control the cloud infrastructure but has control over its applications and data.

Florida has no specific statutory or regulatory authority on the taxability of IaaS.

However, the Florida Department of Revenue held that the taxpayer's sales of simple storage services, elastic cloud computing service (i.e., Infrastructure as a Service or IaaS), and data transfer fees charged in conjunction with either of those two services are information services and are not subject to Florida sales and use tax or communications services tax (CST). The term "communications services" does not include information services. The simple storage service allows the customer to utilize the storage capacity within the taxpayer's server/computer equipment, but the taxpayer does not actually provide access or license to use that equipment or the real property facilities where the servers are located. As such, this service is not a communications service. Moreover, the customer is not purchasing or being granted a license to use tangible personal property or real property, and, as such, the service is also not a sale subject to sales tax. (*Technical Assistance Advisement, No. 14A19-001*, Florida Department of Revenue, March 13, 2014)

Platform as a service. Under the PaaS model, the provider sells access to a platform and software development tools that a consumer uses to create its own applications. A consumer deploys the applications it creates onto the provider's infrastructure. The consumer has control over its deployed applications but does not control the underlying infrastructure.

Florida has no specific statutory or regulatory authority on the taxability of PaaS.

Does a sales tax holiday apply to computer items in Florida?

Florida has not enacted an annual sales tax holiday. However, the state legislature did enact a back-to-school tax holiday in 2017 that applied to personal computers or personal computer-related accessories purchased for noncommercial home or personal use with a sales price of $750 or less per item.

[¶60-330] Construction

In general, construction materials and supplies are taxable, but the treatment of construction related services varies depending on the nature of the transaction. (Sec. 212.06, F.S.; Rule 12A-1.051)

Are construction materials and supplies taxable in Florida?

Contractors are the ultimate consumers of materials and supplies they use to perform real property contracts and must pay sales and use tax on their costs of those materials and supplies, unless the contractor has entered a retail sale plus installation contract.

Real property contracts. Real property contractors determine the taxability of purchases and sales of materials and supplies used in performing real property contracts by the pricing arrangement in the contract. Generally, transactions that involve items that are permanently installed into a structure, where the items cannot be removed without being destroyed, are classified as real property improvements (i.e., real property contracts). "Improvements to real property" are building, erecting, constructing, altering, improving, repairing, or maintaining real property. The purchase of materials and supplies to improve, alter, or repair land, buildings, homes, or other real property is subject to sales and use tax and applicable discretionary sales surtax.

> **EXAMPLE:** Real property improvements include: carpeting (permanent); carpentry; dock, pier, seawall; driveway; electrical system; elevator, escalator; landscaping; masonry work; roofing; and tile work.

Pricing arrangements in contracts. Real property contractors determine the taxability of purchases and sales of materials and supplies used in performing real property contracts by the pricing arrangement in the contract.

Lump sum, cost plus or fixed fee, guaranteed price, or time and materials contracts. Contractors who perform lump sum, cost plus or fixed fee, guaranteed price, or time and materials contracts do not sell tangible personal property to the real property owner, and under these types of real property contracts, the contractor is the final consumer of materials and supplies used in performing the contract, and must pay sales and use tax on the materials and supplies. No sales tax should be collected from the real property owner under these contract types. When the items are delivered to a county that imposes a surtax, the surtax is due at the rate imposed by that county.

Contractors who purchase materials and supplies outside Florida for use in performing these types of contracts must pay use tax and surtax to the Florida Department of Revenue. Surtax is due at the rate imposed by the county where the items are delivered. Contractors not required to register with the department must pay use tax on the materials and supplies purchased outside Florida, but no surtax is due.

Contractors who manufacture, produce, compound, process, or fabricate items used in performing lump sum, cost plus or fixed fee, guaranteed price, or time and materials contracts must pay use tax and surtax on the fabrication cost of the items used in fabrication. When the item is fabricated for use at a manufacturing plant site located within a surtax county, the surtax is due at the rate where the plant is located. Fabrication costs include the cost of direct materials on which Florida sales tax and surtax has not been paid, labor or service costs, and transportation charges. When a contractor fabricates an item at the job site, fabrication labor is not included in the fabrication cost of the item.

Retail sale plus installation contracts. Contractors who enter into retail sale plus installation contracts are not considered the ultimate consumers of tangible personal property and are not responsible for sales and use tax. Retail sale plus installation contracts are for improvements to real property under which the contractor agrees to: (1) sell specifically described and itemized materials and supplies for an agreed price or at the regular retail price; and (2) complete the work for an additional agreed price or on the basis of time spent. All materials that will be incorporated into the work must be itemized and priced in the contract before work begins. The purchaser must assume title to, and risk of loss of, the materials and supplies as they are delivered, rather than accepting title only to the completed work.

Contractors who sell materials that are specifically described and itemized in a retail sale plus installation contract must collect sales tax and surtax on the sales price of the materials. Surtax is due at the rate imposed by the county where the items are delivered.

A retail sale plus installation contract is a real property improvement or construction contract that calls for the contractor to sell specifically described and itemized materials and supplies at an agreed price, and provides for payment for labor either at a separate agreed price or on the basis of time consumed. All the material that will be incorporated into the work must be itemized and priced before work begins. If a contract itemizes some materials but does not itemize other materials that will be incorporated into the work, the contractor will be liable for sales tax on all of the personal property sold.

Contractors who perform retail sales plus installation contracts should register as dealers and provide a copy of their resale certificate to the selling dealer to purchase exempt materials that are itemized and resold. They should not provide the certificate for items that they use themselves rather than reselling such as hand tools, shop equipment, or office supplies. They must charge their customers tax on the price paid for tangible personal property, but not on the charges for installation labor.

Fixture installation contracts. When installing fixtures, a contractor must pay sales tax and surtax on the purchase of the fixtures and installation materials. No sales tax is collected from the customer. When deciding whether an item is a fixture, consider the:

— installation agreement;

— method of attachment;

— intent of the parties; and

— permits and licensing.

EXAMPLE: Fixtures include: built-in cabinets, counters, or lockers; central air-conditioning units; elevators and escalators; furnaces; kitchen and bathroom sinks; and wired lighting.

Items that remain tangible personal property. Contractors who install tangible personal property that remains tangible personal property must collect sales tax and surtax on the total charge. The method of installation is a factor in determining taxability.

EXAMPLE: A mailbox that is bricked into a post beside the road is an improvement to real property; however, when the mailbox is attached to the house or screwed into a wooden post in the ground, it remains tangible personal property.

EXAMPLE: Items that remain tangible personal property after installation include: carpets (except those that become real property) and rugs; drapes, curtains, blinds, shades, or slipcovers; equipment used to provide communications services installed on a customer's premises; garbage can receptacles; household appliances (except built-in appliances); lawn markers; mirrors (except those that become real property); portable ice machines and refrigerators; precast clothesline poles; radio and television antennas; stepping stones; and window air-conditioning units.

Mixed contracts. A mixed contract is one that includes both real property work and tangible personal property that remains tangible personal property and does not become part of the real property. In mixed contracts, taxability depends upon the predominant nature of the work performed under the contract and upon the contract terms. The determination of the predominant nature of a contract depends on the facts and circumstances of each case, and consideration is given to the description of the project and the responsibilities of the contractor under the contract as well as the relative cost of performance of the real property and tangible personal property components of the contract.

If the predominant nature of a mixed contract is for real property improvements, the contractor will be liable for the sales and use tax. However, if the predominant nature of a mixed contract is a contract for tangible personal property, the consumer is liable for the sales and use tax.

If a mixed contract clearly allocates the contract price among the various elements of the contract, and such allocation is bona fide and reasonable in terms of the costs of materials and nature of the work to be performed, taxation will be in accordance with the allocation.

EXAMPLE: A residential developer builds and sells a home, but the contract provides separately stated prices for the sale and installation of certain optional free standing appliances that are tangible personal property and are not classified as real property fixtures. The contractor may purchase those appliances using a resale certificate and charge sales tax on the price paid for the appliances, including installation, to the home buyer. The contractor is responsible for paying tax on all the materials that are included in the price of the home, other than the separately itemized appliances.

EXAMPLE: A manufacturer who sells and installs a mechanical conveyor system in a warehouse could state a separate charge in the contract for providing reinforced concrete with embedded steel plates in the warehouse floor to support the conveyor. The concrete and plates would be considered a real property improvement. The contractor should pay tax on the materials used for the real property part of the contract and not charge tax to the customer on the related charge. The customer should pay tax on the rest of the contract price allocable to the conveyor machinery itself.

EXAMPLE: A residential developer routinely provides some items of tangible personal property, such as free standing appliances, with new homes sold. The predominant nature of the contract is for a dwelling. The developer should pay sales or use tax on the appliances. No tax is collected from the property owner.

EXAMPLE: A contractor constructs a factory under a turnkey contract that includes providing and installing machinery and equipment that is not exempt from sales and use tax. The contract is predominantly for a factory, a real property improvement, and the contractor should pay use tax on the cost of the machinery and equipment. No tax is collected from the property owner.

EXAMPLE: A vendor of a mechanical conveyor system for a warehouse provides reinforced concrete foundations and embeds steel plates in the concrete to permit installation of the equipment by bolting it to the plates. The contract is predominantly for the sale of equipment. The contractor should buy the equipment, concrete, and steel plates using a resale certificate and charge tax on the full price to the customer.

Defense Department and NASA contracts. Sales of tangible personal property other than electricity to a government prime contractor or subcontractor that uses the property to fulfill a contract with the U.S. Department of Defense or NASA (National Aeronautics and Space Administration) are excluded from Florida sales tax as sales to a contractor for resale to the government and are excluded from Florida use tax as property not used by a contractor in Florida.

Overhead materials used by contractors to fulfill a Defense Department or NASA contract are exempt from Florida sales and use tax.

The exemption for overhead materials applies to all tangible personal property other than electricity that is not excluded from sales or use tax as part of a sale for resale. Tangible personal property excluded from taxation as a sale for resale must be a direct cost of performing a contract and identified as a direct cost.

To qualify for an exclusion or exemption, title to property must pass to the U.S. Defense Department or NASA.

Sales of materials and fabrication. Contractors may sell equipment or materials without paying tax as isolated or occasional sales provided they are not engaged in the business of selling tangible personal property of a similar type. For a complete discussion, see Occasional Sales, Including Mergers.

See Manufacturing, Processing, Assembling, or Refining, for a discussion of manufacturing, including fabrication, machinery, and equipment.

¶60-330

Contractors who use and resell materials. Some contractors both use materials themselves in the performance of contracts and resell materials. Those contractors should register as dealers. When they purchase materials that they may either use themselves or that they may resell, they may issue a resale certificate. Florida tax should be remitted when a subsequent event determines the appropriate taxation of the materials. If the materials are subsequently resold, tax should be collected from the buyer and remitted to the state. If the materials are used by the contractor, use tax should be paid to the state instead.

Contractors who manufacture, produce, compound, process, or fabricate items for their own use. Contractors that maintain shops, plants, or similar facilities where they manufacture, produce, compound, process, or fabricate items for their own use in performing contracts are required to pay use tax on the fabricated cost of those items. In the case of real property contracts, the taxable cost of an item manufactured, produced, compounded, processed or fabricated for use in performing a contract does not include labor that occurs at the job site where the item will be incorporated into a real property improvement or transportation from the plant where an item was fabricated to the job site. Examples of such real property contractors that are subject to tax under this subsection include cabinet contractors who build custom cabinets in their shops, roofing contractors who operate tile plants, and heating/air conditioning/ventilation contractors who maintain sheet metal shops for making ductwork. Real property contractors that are required to remit use tax on fabricated items must register as dealers for purposes of remitting tax.

Public works owner-direct purchase programs. The direct purchase of materials by a government entity for use in a public works construction project is commonly referred to as an "owner-direct purchase program" which government entities use to take advantage of their Florida sales and use tax exempt status to directly purchase materials for public works construction projects. When a contractor or subcontractor, as opposed to the government entity, buys materials for use in a public works construction contract, the contractor or subcontractor is required to pay sales tax. Real property contractors and subcontractors are the ultimate consumers of materials they use in the performance of real property construction contracts and, as such, purchases of materials by such contractors are subject to sales tax, including contractors who buy materials for public works construction contracts. However, government entities can buy goods and services tax-free when the government entity makes payment directly to the vendor.

When a government entity directly buys materials for use in a public works construction contract, these purchases are exempt from sales tax provided the entity follows certain procedures. Government entities, contractors, and subcontractors who enter into public works construction projects must meet certain requirements to qualify for the sales tax exemption available for direct purchases by a government entity, especially when a contractor or subcontractor engaged in a public works construction contract provides the materials in an owner-direct purchase program or other similar arrangement.

Proof that government entity is purchaser of materials. Purchases made by the government entity for a public works construction contract without a Certificate of Entitlement are subject to tax. In order to prove that the government entity rather than the contractor or the subcontractor is the purchaser of the materials:

— the government entity must issue its purchase order directly to the vendor supplying the materials the contractor will use and provide the vendor with a copy of the government entity's Florida Consumer's Certificate of Exemption;

— the vendor's invoice must be issued to the government entity, rather than to the contractor;

— the government entity must make payment directly to the vendor from public funds;

— the government entity must take title to the tangible personal property from the vendor at the time of purchase or delivery by the vendor;

— assumption of the risk of damage or loss by the government entity at the time of purchase (a government entity will be deemed to have assumed the risk of loss if it bears the economic burden of obtaining insurance covering damage or loss or directly enjoys the economic benefit of the proceeds of such insurance); and

— to be entitled to purchase materials tax exempt for a public works project, a government entity is required to issue a Certificate of Entitlement to each vendor and to the government entity's contractor to affirm that the tangible personal property purchased from that vendor will go into or become a part of a public work (this requirement does not apply to any agency or branch of the U.S. government).

(Rule 12A-1.094; Tax Information Publication, No. 13A01-01)

Governmental entities (excluding the federal government) must issue a Certificate of Entitlement to each vendor and contractor to purchase materials and supplies tax exempt for use in public works contracts. The Certificate of Entitlement certifies that: the materials and supplies purchased will become part of a public facility; the governmental entity will be liable for any tax, penalty, or interest due if the department later determines that the items purchased do not qualify for exemption; and the regulatory criteria are being followed.

Exclusions. In some cases, the government entity is not able to use its tax exempt status on the purchase of materials. For instance, when the contractor or subcontractor installing the materials is also selling the materials to the government entity, the purchases are taxable, even if the government entity has established an owner-direct purchase program. A government entity cannot, after the fact, prepare or change the documentation to appear to have properly followed the procedures. Other instances in which the government entity is not able to use its tax exempt status and owner-direct purchase program include but are not limited to:

— when the contractor or subcontractor is the manufacturer of the materials;

— when the contractor or subcontractor has exclusive rights from the manufacturer of the materials to furnish and install the materials; and

— when the contractor or subcontractor has already purchased the materials.

Qualified homes, housing projects, and mixed-use projects. The sale, rental, use, consumption, distribution and storage of building materials to be used in the construction of a qualified home, housing project or mixed-use project are exempt from Florida sales and use tax. The costs of labor associated with the construction of a qualified home are also exempt. The exemptions inure to the owner through a refund of previously paid taxes. The owner has six months from the date the qualified home, housing project, or mixed-use project is deemed to be substantially completed by the local building inspector to apply for the refund.

Qualified homes. "Qualified home" means a single-family home that is: constructed and occupied by the owner; located in an enterprise zone, empowerment zone, or a Front Porch Florida Community; and appraised at no more than $160,000.

Housing projects. "Housing project" is defined as the conversion of an existing manufacturing or industrial building to a housing unit in an urban high-crime area, enterprise zone, empowerment zone, a Front Porch Florida Community, a designated brownfield site for which a rehabilitation agreement with the Department of Environmental Protection or a local government delegated by the department has been executed and any abutting real property parcel within a brownfield area, or an urban infill area. The developer must agree to set aside at least 20% of the housing units in the project for low-income and moderate-income persons.

Mixed-use projects. "Mixed-use project" is defined as the conversion of an existing manufacturing or industrial building to mixed-use units that include artists' studios, art and entertainment services, or other compatible uses. A mixed-use project must be located in an urban high-crime area, enterprise zone, empowerment zone, a Front Porch Florida Community, a designated brownfield site for which a rehabilitation agreement with the Department of Environmental Protection or a local government delegated by the department has been executed and any abutting real property parcel within a brownfield area, or an urban infill area and the developer must agree to set aside at least 20% of the square footage of the project for low-income and moderate-income housing.

Brownfield areas. Each "brownfield area" in which housing projects or mixed-use projects are constructed must be a brownfield site for which a rehabilitation agreement with the Department of Environmental Protection has been executed, or any abutting real property parcel within a brownfield area.

Subdivisions and similar improvements. Subdivision owners and developers or their contractors are taxed on their purchases of materials for use in the construction of streets, roadways, water distribution systems, sewers, and similar property that is subsequently transferred to a municipality or other governmental unit. If, however, the municipality or governmental unit purchases and installs water mains and distribution pipes for a property owner, including a subdivision developer under an arrangement whereby the municipality retains ownership, possession and control of the mains and pipes, but recovers all or part of its cost from the property owner through the collection of an installation charge, the installation charge is equal to an assessment for benefits and is not taxable to the property owner.

How does Florida tax construction related services?

In general, since services are exempt from sales and use tax in Florida unless specifically identified as taxable, and construction related services are not specifically identified as taxable, they are not subject to tax. (Sec. 212.02(15)(a), F.S.; Sec. 212.04(14)(a), F.S.; Sec. 212.05, F.S.; Sec. 212.08(7)(v), F.S.)

Asphalt. Contractors that manufacture asphalt for their own use in the performance of improving real property must calculate the tax on that asphalt based on the sum of the following: (1) multiply the cost of all materials that become ingredients of the finished asphalt by 6%; plus (2) multiply the cost of transporting such ingredients to the plant site by 6%; plus (3) apply the indexed tax rate to all other costs associated with the manufacture of asphalt. The indexed tax is in addition to all taxes paid on purchases of overhead items, including boiler fuels. If tax is paid to a third party on the cost or transportation of materials, those costs should not be included in the calculation of the total tax due. Tax is due in the month the asphalt is manufactured for use by the contractor, and must be paid using Form DR-15, Sales and Use Tax Return. (Rule 12A-1.051; Sec. 212.06, F.S.; Rule 12A-1.094(7); Tax Information Publication, No. 12A01-12)

See Rate of Tax, for the current indexed tax rate on asphalt.

Mobile homes. A contractor who makes improvements or repairs to a mobile home is required to ascertain the status of that home as real property or as tangible personal property to determine how tax should be paid. If the mobile home has a real property decal, the contract should be treated as a real property contract. In that case, the contractor generally will be subject to tax on the materials used and the customer will pay no tax.

If the mobile home does not have a real property decal, improvements or repairs are generally treated as contracts to improve or repair tangible personal property. The contractor should charge tax on the full price paid by the customer, including charges for labor. The contractor is not subject to tax on the materials that are incorporated into and become a part of the improvement or repair of the mobile home.

Repairs to machinery and equipment. Any owner or lessee that engages another to make repairs to or perform maintenance services on machinery and equipment that has the appearance of real property, must inform the service provider that the machinery or equipment is tangible personal property. The owner or lessee should pay sales tax on the full price of the repair or maintenance to any service provider that is registered as a dealer. If the service provider is not a registered dealer, the owner or lessee must remit tax on the full price of the repair or maintenance directly to the state.

Contracts for the sale and for the sale and installation of machinery and equipment are not considered real property contracts.

"Machinery and equipment" means any property that may be attached to the real property but which does not lose its identity and is intended to be used in manufacturing, producing, compounding, processing, fabricating, packaging, moving or otherwise handling personal property for sale or other commercial use, in the performance of commercial services, or for other purposes not related to a building or other fixed real property improvements.

EXAMPLE: Machinery and equipment includes conveyer systems, printing presses, drill presses, and lathes.

Machinery and equipment generally does not include junction boxes, switches, conduits, wiring, valves, pipes, and tubing incorporated into the electrical, cabling, plumbing, or other structural systems of fixed works, buildings, or other structures, whether or not such items are used solely or partially in connection with the operation of machinery and equipment.

Are labor charges taxable in Florida?

Yes. In general, repair charges and installation charges are taxable. (Sec. 212.06, F.S.; Rule 12A-1.016, F.A.C.)

What incentives or credits are available for contractors in Florida?

Florida does not provide any incentives or credits for contractors.

What certificate or form must a contractor use to claim an exemption in Florida?

Forms that may be of interest to contractors include:

DR-13 Florida Annual Resale Certificate for Sales Tax; and

Form DR-15, Sales and Use Tax Return.

For a discussion of exemption certificates or forms that may be related to contractors, see Exemption Certificates.

Does Florida have special rules concerning subcontractors?

No. Florida does not have any special rules concerning subcontractors.

Does Florida have other provisions related to construction?

No. Florida does not have any additional general guidance related to the taxability of construction.

[¶60-340] Drop Shipments

A drop shipment is a shipment of tangible personal property from a seller directly to the purchaser's customer, at the direction of the purchaser. These sales are also known as third-party sales because they require that there be, at arm's length, three parties and two separate sales transactions. Generally, a retailer accepts an order from an end purchaser/consumer, places this order with a third party, usually a manufacturer or wholesale distributor, and directs the third party to ship the goods directly to the end purchaser/consumer. Drop shipments are examined as two transactions: (1) the sale from the primary seller to the purchaser and (2) the sale from the purchaser to the purchaser's customer. (Rule 12A-1.091)

• *Florida treatment of drop-shipment sales*

When all the parties are located in the state, the retailer furnishes a resale certificate to the primary seller, rendering the first sale a nontaxable transaction. The retailer then collects sales tax on behalf of the state on the secondary sale to its customer. However, different considerations arise when one or more of the parties are not within the state. If the seller and the consumer are both in Florida, and the retailer is an unregistered out-of-state dealer, the seller must collect the sales tax from the retailer. (Rule 12A-1.091)

A registered nonresident dealer's sales of tangible personal property to an unregistered nonresident purchaser that are drop shipped into Florida are not subject to Florida sales and use tax unless one of the following conditions is met: 1) the taxpayer ships the property to the Florida customer from the taxpayer's facility in Florida; 2) the taxpayer ships the property to the Florida customer from the tax-payer's facility located outside Florida, but uses transportation owned or leased by the taxpayer; or 3) the taxpayer ships the property to the Florida customer from the taxpayer's facility located outside Florida, but the terms of the delivery require the taxpayer to collect the sales price, in whole or in part, from the Florida customer at the time of delivery of the property to the customer. (*Technical Assistance Advisement, No. 09A-010*, Florida Department of Revenue, March 2, 2009)

• *Local taxes*

No general excise tax on sales can be levied by the governing body of any county unless specifically authorized. (Sec. 212.054, F.S.)

[¶60-360] Enterprise Zones and Similar Tax Incentives

Florida authorizes a number of enterprise zone incentives. The Florida Enterprise Zone Program, however, expired effective December 31, 2015.

CAUTION NOTE: Expiration of Florida Enterprise Zone Program.—Except for certain extensions, as provided, the Florida Enterprise Zone Program expires on December 31, 2015. For businesses that do not qualify for extension, enterprise zone credits or refunds will be approved after December 31, 2015, only if the business applying for the credit or refund meets the statutory eligibility requirements for the incentive on or before December 31, 2015. Information is provided in *Tax Information Publication, No. 15ADM-04* regarding each specific incentive. (*Tax Information Publication, No. 15ADM-04*, Florida Department of Revenue, September 8, 2015)

● *Energy economic zones*

The Energy Economic Zone Pilot Program, created to develop a model area that incorporates energy-efficient land-use patterns, encourages the generation of renewable electricity and promotes green manufacturing. According to the Florida Department of Economic Opportunity, the city of Miami Beach (urban service area "city redevelopment program" model) and Sarasota County (urban service area "greenfield" model and landfill energy conversion model) are designated energy economic zone pilot program communities. (*Energy Economic Zone Pilot Program*, Florida Department of Economic Opportunity, March 2014)

The program models include strategies to reduce greenhouse gas emissions, cultivate green economic development, encourage renewable electric energy generation, and promote product manufacturing that contributes energy conservation and green jobs. Once designated, a community receives technical assistance from the Department of Economic Opportunity, Division of Strategic Business Development, the Office of Energy, and the Florida Department of Transportation. (*Energy Economic Zone Pilot Program*, Florida Department of Economic Opportunity, March 2014)

Beginning July 1, 2012, all the incentives and benefits provided for enterprise zones are available to the energy economic zones designated on or before July 1, 2010. In order to provide incentives, by March 1, 2012, each local governing body that has jurisdiction over an energy economic zone must, by local ordinance, establish the boundary of the zone, specify applicable energy-efficiency standards, and determine eligibility criteria for the application of state and local incentives and benefits in the energy economic zone. (Sec. 377.809(5)(a), F.S.)

Effective July 1, 2012, the total amount of state credits, refunds, and exemptions that may be provide by the governing body of each energy economic zone to eligible businesses for energy economic zone incentives is $300,000 per designated energy economic zone in any state fiscal year. The local governing body that has jurisdiction over the energy economic zone is responsible for allocating the incentives, verifying that businesses receiving such incentives are eligible for those incentives, and ensuring that the incentives provided do not exceed the cap for the state fiscal year. (Sec. 377.809(5)(b), F.S.)

Upon approving an incentive for an eligible business, the governing body that has jurisdiction over the energy economic zone is required to provide the taxpayer with a certificate that indicates the name and federal identification number of the eligible business, the date the incentive is provided, the name of the energy economic zone, the incentive type, and the incentive amount. (Sec. 377.809(5)(c), F.S.)

● *Electrical energy used in a designated enterprise zone*

Charges for electrical energy used by a qualified business at a fixed location in an enterprise zone in a municipality that has enacted an ordinance that provides for exemption of municipal utility taxes on such businesses or in an enterprise zone jointly authorized by a county and a municipality that has enacted such an ordinance will receive an exemption equal to 50% of the sales and use taxes imposed on the electrical energy charges. A full exemption for sales and use taxes imposed on electrical energy charges is available when at least 20% of the full-time employees of the business are residents of an enterprise zone. (Sec. 212.08(15)(a), F.S.; Rule 12A-1.107(5), F.A.C.)

CAUTION NOTE: Expiration of Florida Enterprise Zone Program.—Businesses granted a sales tax exemption on electrical energy used in an enterprise zone prior to the expiration of the program (i.e., December 31, 2015) will continue to receive the exemption for the same period of time it would have been available had the Enterprise Zone Program not expired. No new exemptions for electrical energy used in an enterprise zone will be granted after December 31, 2015. (*Tax Information Publication, No. 15ADM-04*, Florida Department of Revenue, September 8, 2015)

A qualified business may receive the exemption for a period of five years from the billing period beginning not more than 30 days following notification to the applicable utility company that an exemption has been allowed. (Sec. 212.08(15)(a), F.S.)

Qualified business.—A "qualified business" is a business that is:

— first occupying a new structure to which electrical service, other than that used for construction purposes, has not been previously provided or furnished;

— newly occupying an existing, remodeled, renovated, or rehabilitated structure to which electrical service, other than that used for remodeling, renovation, or rehabilitation of the structure, has not been provided or furnished in the three preceding billing periods; or

— occupying a new, remodeled, rebuilt, renovated, or rehabilitated structure for which a refund has been granted, as provided.

(Sec. 212.08(15)(f), F.S.)

Filing requirements.—To receive this exemption, a business must file an application, with the enterprise zone development agency having jurisdiction over the enterprise zone where the business is located, on a form provided by the Department of Revenue. The application must include the following information:

— the name and location of the business;

— the identifying number assigned to the enterprise zone in which the business is located;

— the date on which electrical service is to be first initiated to the business;

— the name and mailing address of the entity from which electrical energy is to be purchased;

— the date of the application;

— the name of the city in which the business is located;

— if applicable, the name and address of each permanent employee of the business, including, for each employee who is a resident of an enterprise zone, the identifying number assigned to the enterprise zone in which the employee resides; and

— whether the business is a small business, as defined.

(Sec. 212.08(15)(b), F.S.)

Forms.—Taxpayers claiming the exemption must file Form DR-15JEZ, Application for the Exemption of Electrical Energy Used in an Enterprise Zone, with the Department of Revenue. Form DR-15JEZ must be certified by the Enterprise Zone Coordinator of the enterprise zone where the business is located. Once the application is certified and returned to the applicant, it must be delivered directly to the Department, or postmarked, by the applicant within 6 months after qualifying for the exemption. (Sec. 212.08(15)(c), F.S.; Rule 12A-1.107(5) (b), F.A.C.)

Location of enterprise zones.—A map of local Florida enterprise zones is available at www.floridaenterprisezone.com.

Sunset.—The electrical energy exemption expires on December 31, 2015. Any business that is granted the exemption prior to December 31, 2015, is allowed the full benefit for the unused duration of the five-year period for which it may claim the exemption. (Sec. 212.08(15)(g), F.S.)

• *Incentives to encourage the revitalization of enterprise zones*

The following sales and use tax incentives are provided to encourage the revitalization of enterprise zones:

— a community contribution tax credit;

— an exemption for building materials used in the rehabilitation of real property in enterprise zones;

— an exemption for business equipment used in an enterprise zone;

— an exemption for electrical energy used in an enterprise zone (discussed above); and

— an enterprise zone jobs credit against the sales tax.

(Sec. 290.007, F.S.)

CAUTION NOTE: *Expiration of Florida Enterprise Zone Program.*—Except for certain extensions, as provided, the Florida Enterprise Zone Program expires on December 31, 2015. For businesses that do not qualify for extension, enterprise zone credits or refunds will be approved after December 31, 2015, only if the business applying for the credit or refund meets the statutory eligibility requirements for the incentive on or before December 31, 2015. Information is provided in *Tax Information Publication, No. 15ADM-04* regarding each specific incentive. (*Tax Information Publication, No. 15ADM-04*, Florida Department of Revenue, September 8, 2015)

Various cities and counties may apply to the Florida Department of Economic Opportunity for designation of an enterprise zone within their borders. Upon designation, the jurisdictions become eligible for the sales and use tax incentives detailed above. Among the jurisdictions that have been granted authority to apply are the following:

— the city of Lakeland (Sec. 290.00710, F.S.) ;

— the city of Winterhaven (Sec. 290.0072, F.S.) ;

— the city of Palm Bay (Sec. 290.00727, F.S.) ;

— the city of Vero Beach (Sec. 290.0073, F.S.) ;

— the city of Sebastian (Sec. 290.0073, F.S.) ;

— the city of Apopka (Sec. 290.0077, F.S.) ;

— Martin County (Sec. 290.00726, F.S.) ;

— Lake County (Sec. 290.00728, F.S.) ;

— Indian River County (Sec. 290.0073, F.S.) ;

— Sumter County (Sec. 290.0074, F.S.) ;

— Orange County (Sec. 290.0077, F.S.) ;

— Charlotte County (Sec. 290.00729, F.S.) ; and

— Citrus County (Sec. 290.00731, F.S.).

(Sec. 290.007, F.S.)

[¶60-390] Food and Grocery Items

Food products for human consumption are generally exempt from tax. However, tax does apply to other food items.

Packages that contain exempt food and taxable nonfood.—The application of sales and use tax on a package that contains exempt food products and taxable nonfood products depends upon the essential character of the complete package. If the taxable items represent more than 25% of the cost of the complete package and a single charge is made, the entire sales price of the package is taxable. If the taxable items are separately stated, the separate charge for the taxable items is subject to tax. If the taxable items represent 25% or less of the cost of the complete package and a single charge is made, the entire sales price of the package is exempt. The person who prepares the package is liable for the tax on the cost of the taxable items going into the complete package. If the taxable items are separately stated, the separate charge is subject to tax. (Sec. 212.08, F.S.)

• *Food products provided by restaurants, lunch counters, cafeterias, caterers, hotels, taverns, and other like places*

A rule clarifies the application of sales and use tax on the following:

— food products generally served, prepared, or sold in or by restaurants, lunch counters, cafeterias, caterers, hotels, taverns, or other like places of business;

— food products when sold by such establishments that also maintain a separate department that includes groceries;

— when tax is due on the purchase of, or the cost of furnishing, food products consumed in places where an admission is charged for entrance;

— when sales tax is to be collected on food products separately itemized and priced from the admission charge to a patron;

— sales of meal tickets or coupon books and coupons or discounts for food products

— the exemption provided for donated food products;

— when tax is due on complimentary food products;

— food products sold or furnished by employers to employees;

— food products sold by airlines, railroads (except Amtrak), vessels, or other transportation companies to their passengers while in Florida;

— food products served, prepared, or sold by caterers and event planners;

— purchases, leases, and rentals by caterers or event planners;

— gratuities consistent with the guidelines established as provided;

— fees for preparing or serving food products;

— food products when furnished with living or sleeping accommodations at colleges or other institutions of higher learning;

— the exemption provided for certain complimentary food and drinks provided by public lodging establishments;

— food products when furnished with housing at labor camps or public housing quarters;

— food products furnished at day care facilities, day camps, or other custodial camps;

— the exemption provided to hospital patients and inmates or to residents of homes for the aged;

— food products sold to or prepared and served by social clubs, civic clubs, or fraternal organizations;

— food products sold to or by nonprofit organizations, religious institutions, and organizations sponsoring a fundraising event; and

— the exclusion from tax for items and materials used one time only for packaging or serving food products.

(Rule 12A-1.0115)

Caterers.—Food products that are furnished, prepared, or served for consumption at tables, chairs, or counters or from trays, glasses, dishes, or other tableware, are taxable. This is so even though the tables, chairs, or counters and trays, glasses, dishes, and other tableware may be provided by a person with whom a dealer has contracted to furnish, prepare, or serve the food to others. (Rule 12A-1.0115(2))

Food furnished by an employer to its employees.—Food furnished by an employer to its employees is not subject to tax provided no cash changes hands as payment and the assigned value of the food is not required to be reported as income to the employee for federal income tax purposes. (Rule 12A-1.0115(5))

Food sold by a restaurant to its employees.—Food sold by a restaurant to its employees is taxable. (Rule 12A-1.0115(5))

Food served at hospitals and homes for the aged.—Food served at hospitals and homes for the aged are exempt. An exemption is also provided to residents of a home for the aged with respect to meals provided through the facility. A "home for the aged" means licensed and certified nursing homes or related health care facilities, continuing care facilities, facilities financed by a mortgage loan made or insured by the U.S. Department of Housing and Urban Development under the National Housing Act, and other similar facilities designed and operated primarily for the care of the aged. (Sec. 212.08(7)(i), F.S.; Rule 12A-1.0115(3))

Vending machines and mobile vendors.—Food sold through a vending machine or push cart, motor vehicle, or any other form of vehicle, are taxable. However, drinking water in bottles, can, or other containers sold through a vending machine, push cart, motor vehicle, or any other form of vehicle, is exempt. (Sec. 212.08(1), F.S.; Rule 12A-1.0115(3))

• *Food products sold by grocery stores, convenience stores, supermarkets, bakeries, fish markets, and produce markets*

A rule clarifies the application of sales and use tax on the sale of food products by grocery stores, convenience stores, supermarkets, bakeries, fish markets, produce markets, and other like places of business. (Rule 12A-1.011)

Exempt food products.—These items include, but are not limited to, cereal and cereal products, baked goods, oleomargarine, meat and meat products, fish and seafood products, frozen foods and dinners, poultry, eggs and egg products, vegetables and vegetable products, fruit and fruit products, spices, salt, sugar and sugar products, milk and dairy products, and products intended to be mixed with milk. Also included is natural fruit or vegetable juices or their concentrates or reconstituted natural concentrated fruit or vegetable juices; coffee, coffee substitutes, or cocoa; tea, unless it is sold in a liquid form; and bakery products sold by bakeries, pastry shops, or like establishments that do not have eating facilities. (Sec. 212.08(1), F.S.; Rule 12A-1.011; Rule 12A-1.0115)

Taxable food products.—The tax exemption does not apply to food products sold as meals for consumption on or off the premises of the dealer; hot prepared food products; soft drinks or any noncarbonated drink made from milk derivatives or tea, when sold in cans or similar containers; ice cream, frozen yogurt, and similar frozen products in cones, small cups, or pints; food sold for immediate consumption or through a vending machine, pushcart, or other vehicle; candy and similar products; bakery products sold by bakeries, pastry shops, or like establishments that have eating facilities, except when sold for consumption off the premises; and food products served, prepared, or sold in or by restaurants, lunch counters, cafeterias, hotels, taverns, or other like places of business. (Sec. 212.08(1), F.S.; Rule 12A-1.011(4))

Ice cream, frozen yogurt, and sherbet.—Ice cream, frozen yogurt, or sherbet (and any similar frozen dairy or nondairy products) sold in units larger than one pint is exempt. Water sold in containers, including water that contains minerals or carbonation in its natural state or water to which minerals have been added at a water treatment facility, is exempt. Water sold in bottles, cans, or other containers that has been enhanced by the addition of minerals and that does not contain any added carbonation or flavorings is exempt. (Rule 12A-1.011(2); Rule 12A-1.040)

Water.—Drinking water, including water enhanced by the addition of minerals, sold in bottles, can, or other containers is exempt, except when carbonation or flavorings have been added to the water in the manufacturing process. (Rule 12A-1.011(7))

Bakery products sold by bakeries, pastry shops, or similar establishments.— Bakery products sold by bakeries, pastry shops, or similar establishments as hot prepared food products are taxable. (Rule 12A-1.011(3))

Bakery products are taxable when they are:

— sold for intended consumption on the premises (bakery products sold in quantities of five or less are assumed to be sold for consumption on the premises);

— packaged in a manner consistent with consumption on the premises; or

— sold as hot prepared food products regardless of where or how they are sold (bakery products sold while still warm from the initial baking are not hot prepared food products and bakery products that are kept warm by a heat source used to maintain them in a heated state, or to reheat them, are hot prepared food products).

(*Tax Information Publication, No. 10A01-22*, Florida Department of Revenue, December 21, 2010)

Bakery products are exempt when they are:

— sold for intended consumption off the premises and packaged in a manner consistent with such consumption (examples include packaging that is glued, stapled, wrapped, or sealed); or

— sold by bakeries, pastry shops, and other like establishments that do not have eating facilities.

(*Tax Information Publication, No. 10A01-22*, Florida Department of Revenue, December 21, 2010)

An example of such an exempt bakery product sale includes a bagel shop that operates an establishment with eating facilities that makes a single sale of three bagels. The bagels are exempt provided the seller can establish that they were packaged in a manner consistent with an intent by the customer to consume the products off the seller's premises. (*Tax Information Publication, No. 10A01-22*, Florida Department of Revenue, December 21, 2010)

Exempt sales of bakery products for consumption off of the premises are required to be separately accounted from taxable sales. Examples of such sales include:

— using sales invoices which contain documentation that the sale of the bakery product is for consumption off of the premises;

— using a separate key on a cash register to record tax-exempt sales of bakery products;

— using a separate cash register to record tax-exempt sales of bakery products.

(*Tax Information Publication, No. 10A01-22*, Florida Department of Revenue, December 21, 2010)

Dietary supplements.—Dietary supplements, including herbal supplements, and meal replacements, including liquid food supplements and nutrition bars, including those that are candy-coated or chocolate-coated, are exempt. (Rule 12A-1.011(2)(12))

Food stamps and vouchers.—Food products are exempt when purchased with food stamps issued by the U.S. Department of Agriculture or with vouchers supplied by the Special Supplemental Food Program for Women, Infants, and Children (WIC). Where a purchase of items of food is made partly with food stamps or vouchers and partly with cash, the stamps or vouchers are applied first against the cost of any otherwise taxable food and beverages that can be purchased with them. (Sec. 212.08(1)(e), F.S.; Rule 12A-1.011(9))

• *Food service companies*

Florida does not currently provide any specific guidance regarding food service companies, food service management companies, food management entities, or other such companies. Florida sales tax is imposed on all dealers engaged in the sale, lease, or rental of tangible personal property sold at retail in the state. The use tax is imposed on all persons that use, consume, distribute, or store tangible personal property in the state and applies to tangible personal property purchased outside the state that would have been subject to the sales tax if purchased from a Florida dealer.

There are specific Florida provisions regarding caterers, restaurants, and clubs. See above.

• *Organizations and schools*

Tax is not due on the sale of food and beverages served as part of a school lunch to students, teachers, school employees, or guests in public, parochial, or nonprofit schools attended by kindergarten through grade 12. (Sec. 212.08(7)(q), F.S.)

Meals served by nonprofit organizations to handicapped, elderly, or indigent people in their residence are exempt. (Sec. 212.08(7)(k), F.S.).

• *Hotels*

Room service charges made by hotels for serving meals in guests' rooms are taxable. (Rule 12A-1.011(11))

• *Transient accommodations*

Meals furnished as part of a packaged room rate at rented or leased transient living accommodations are exempt from sales tax if there is no separate charge or specific amount for the food or drinks shown. Such meals are considered as being sold at retail as part of the total charge for the accommodations. (Sec. 212.08(7)(ll), F.S.; Rule 12A-1.0115)

[¶60-420] Government Transactions

Generally, sales to the government of the United States are exempt from the sales and use taxes both by Florida statute and the constitutional constraints discussed below. (Sec. 212.08(6), F.S.)

Sales to state or local governmental units are also not subject to the tax. The discussion below, and the annotations that follow, are separated into United States government transactions, state and local transactions, and public school transactions. Government financial institutions are discussed at Financial Institutions.

• *U.S. Government transactions*

Sales to the U.S. government are exempt by statute. (Sec. 212.08(6), F.S.) In addition, the Supremacy Clause (Article VI) of the U.S. Constitution declares that the U.S. Constitution and laws are the supreme law of the land, and the U.S. Supreme Court held early that this clause invalidated a state tax imposed directly on a federal instrumentality. (*McCulloch v. Maryland* (1819, SCt) 17 US 316)

See U.S. Constitution, for a discussion of limitations on state taxation under the Supremacy Clause of the U.S. Constitution.

Federal areas.—The federal Buck Act provides that state sales tax can be collected in federal areas, such as military reservations, although not from the government itself. (4 U.S.C. Sec. 105—110) Motor fuel sold on military or other federal reservations is also subject to state tax. (4 U.S.C. Sec. 104)

Government contractors.—In general, contractors purchasing tangible personal property or taxable services pursuant to contracts with the United States government are the consumers of the property or services and must pay the sales and use tax when they purchase the property or services. (Sec. 212.08(6), F.S.) However, when a contractor was merely acting as a purchasing agent for the federal government and the latter took title to the property, the contractor was held not subject to a gross receipts tax. (*Kern-Limerick, Inc. v. Scurlock* (1954, SCt) 347 US 110, 74 SCt 403)

The purchase or manufacture of tangible personal property for resale to a governmental entity is exempt from tax, provided the exemption does not include sales of tangible personal property made to, or the manufacture of tangible personal property by, public works contractors when the tangible personal property goes into or becomes a part of public works. This is a general exemption for sales made to the government. A determination of whether a transaction is an exempt sale to a governmental entity or a taxable sale to or use by a contractor is based on the substance of the transaction. (Sec. 212.08(6), F.S.; Rule 12A-1.094(3) and (4))

See Construction, regarding owner-direct purchase program public works contracts, which government entities use to take advantage of their Florida sales and use tax exempt status to directly purchase materials for public works construction projects.

The exemption for sales of tangible personal property made to contractors employed directly to or as agents of any government or political subdivision, as provided, also provides that, for sales of tangible personal property that go into or become a part of public works owned by a governmental entity, other than the federal government, a governmental entity claiming the exemption is required to certify to the dealer and the contractor the entity's claim to the exemption by providing a Certificate of Entitlement to the exemption for such sales. (Sec. 212.08(6), F.S.)

The Florida Department of Revenue discusses the requirement that governmental entities (excluding the federal government) issue a Certificate of Entitlement to each vendor and contractor so that they may purchase supplies and materials for use in public works contracts that are exempt from sales and use taxes. Such a certificate certifies that:

— the materials and supplies purchased will become part of a public facility;

— the governmental entity will be liable for any tax, penalty, or interest due should the department later determine that the items purchased do not qualify for exemption; and

— applicable regulatory criteria are being followed.

(*Tax Information Publication, No. 10A01-18*, Florida Department of Revenue, August 16, 2010)

¶60-420

In addition, the Florida Department of Revenue provides the format of the Certificate of Entitlement to be issued by the govermental entity. The format is provided in *Tax Information Publication, No. 10A01-27.* (*Tax Information Publication, No. 10A01-27*, Florida Department of Revenue, December 30, 2010)

The purchase of industrial equipment and machinery for use in a federal procurement contract is discussed at Manufacturing, Processing, Assembling, or Refining.

Sales of tangible personal property other than electricity to a government prime contractor or subcontractor that uses the property to fulfill a contract with the U.S. Department of Defense or NASA (National Aeronautics and Space Administration) are excluded from Florida sales tax as sales to a contractor for resale to the government and excluded from Florida use tax as property not used by a contractor in Florida. (Sec. 288.106, F.S.) Overhead materials used by contractors to fulfill a Defense Department or NASA contract are exempt from Florida sales and use tax. (Sec. 212.08(17), F.S.)

The exemption for overhead materials applies to all tangible personal property other than electricity that is not excluded from sales or use tax as part of a sale for resale. Tangible personal property excluded from taxation as a sale for resale must be a direct cost of performing a contract and identified as a direct cost under 48 C.F.R. 9904.418-30(a)(2). To qualify for an exclusion or exemption, title to property must pass to the U.S. Defense Department or NASA. The exclusion and exemption do not apply to contracts for repairing, altering, improving, or constructing real property. (Sec. 212.02(14)(a) and (20), F.S.; Sec. 212.08(17), F.S.)

Manufactured asphalt used in federal, state, or local government public works project is taxed at the rate of 60% of the standard sales and use tax rate applied to asphalt. Effective July 1, 2016, the indexed tax rate on manufactured asphalt used in public works projects of the federal, state, and local governments is phased out over three years with the tax being fully eliminated beginning July 1, 2018. (Sec. 212.06(2), F.S.) See Rate of Tax, for the current indexed tax rate on asphalt.

Government employees.—The exemption does not apply to any transaction otherwise taxable when payment is made by a government employee by any means, including but not limited to, cash, check, or credit card, when that employee is subsequently reimbursed by the government entity. (Sec. 212.08(6), F.S.)

People-mover systems.—People-mover systems and their component parts that are purchased or manufactured by a contractor employed by a federal government office or the public operator of a public-use airport are exempt if the systems or parts go into, or become part of, a publicly owned facility. (Sec. 212.08(7)(zz), F.S.; Rule 12A-1.038; Rule 12A-1.094)

Space and spaceport activities.—The sale, lease, use, storage, consumption, or distribution in Florida of any orbital space facility, space propulsion system or space vehicle, satellite, or station of any kind possessing space flight capacity, including components, is exempt from tax. Property placed on or used aboard any facility, system, vehicle, satellite, or station is also exempt even if such property is returned to Florida for subsequent use, storage, or consumption. The exemption is not affected by a failure of a launch to occur, or by the destruction of a launch vehicle or its components. (Sec. 212.08(16), F.S.)

Fuels produced and sold exclusively for space flight are not subject to sales tax; nor are machinery and equipment purchased by new and expanding businesses for exclusive use in spaceport activities. (Sec. 206.42(4), F.S.; Sec. 212.08(5)(b), F.S.)

"Spaceport activities" are defined as those that are directed or sponsored by Space Florida on spaceport territory. "Space flight" means any flight designed for suborbital, orbital, or interplanetary travel of a space vehicle, satellite, or station of any kind. (Sec. 212.02(22) and (23), F.S.)

The following property constitutes spaceport territory:

— certain real property located in Brevard County that is included within the 1998 boundaries of Patrick Air Force Base, Cape Canaveral Air Force Station, or John F. Kennedy Space Center (The territory consisting of areas within the John F. Kennedy Space Center and the Cape Canaveral Air Force Station may be referred to as the "Cape Canaveral Spaceport.");

— certain real property located in Santa Rosa, Okaloosa, Gulf, and Walton Counties that is included within the 1997 boundaries of Eglin Air Force Base

— certain real property located in Duval County that is included within the boundaries of Cecil Airport and Cecil Commerce Center;

— real property within Florida that is a spaceport licensed by the Federal Aviation Administration, as designated by the board of directors of Space Florida; and

— effective May 30, 2013, certain real property located in Brevard County that is included within the boundaries of Space Coast Regional Airport, Space Coast Regional Airport Industrial Park, and Spaceport Commerce Park.

Machinery and equipment purchased by new and expanding businesses for exclusive use in spaceport activities at those designated properties may qualify for exemption. (Sec. 331.304, F.S.; Sec. 212.08(5)(b), F.S.)

U.S. diplomatic tax exemption cards.—The Florida Department of Revenue provides guidance to sales and use tax dealers about the new format for United States Diplomatic Tax Exemption Cards. The U.S. Department of State issues Diplomatic Tax Exemption Cards to foreign diplomats, consular missions, and their employees in the United States. The cards are used for exempt purchases of tangible personal property, transient accommodations, services, meals, and other eligible purchases. (*Tax Information Publication, No. 11A01-05*, Florida Department of Revenue, July 15, 2011)

Exemptions or limitations are determined by the U.S. Department of State, Office of Foreign Missions, in Washington, D.C. Exemptions or limitations are granted to foreign missions and consular personnel strictly on the basis of reciprocity with the foreign nation. The Department of State expects to replace all existing tax exemption cards with new cards by August 31, 2011. Vendors should continue to accept the existing cards until that time. (*Tax Information Publication, No. 11A01-05*, Florida Department of Revenue, July 15, 2011)

Previously, the Department of State used a blue or yellow stripe on the tax exemption card to convey to vendors and revenue agencies the level of tax exemption privilege a cardholder was authorized to receive. The new tax exemption cards replace the color-coding with images of animals. The images are an owl, buffalo, eagle, and deer. Each image provides a visual cue of the general level of exemption privileges enjoyed by the cardholder and whether the card is intended for official or personal purchases. (*Tax Information Publication, No. 11A01-05*, Florida Department of Revenue, July 15, 2011)

General information about each animal image is as follows:

— a card with an image of an owl can only be used for official purchases and the cardholder/mission is eligible for an exemption on sales, occupancy, restaurant/meal, and other taxes without restriction;

— a card with an image of a buffalo can only be used for official purchases and the cardholder/mission's eligibility for exemption from sales, occupancy, restaurant/meal, and other taxes is restricted;

— a card with an image of an eagle can only be used for personal purchases and the cardholder is eligible for exemption from sales, occupancy, restaurant/meal, and other taxes without restriction; and

— a card with an image of a deer can only be used for personal purchases and the cardholder's eligibility for exemption from sales, occupancy, restaurant/meal, and other similar taxes is restricted.

(*Tax Information Publication, No. 11A01-05*, Florida Department of Revenue, July 15, 2011)

In addition to the animal images, the new cards have security features including a description of the cardholder's level of entitlement to exemption privileges on both the front and back sides of the card, laser-engraved personalized data, optically variable device/Kinegram, and tactile microtext (small, raised text). (*Tax Information Publication, No. 11A01-05*, Florida Department of Revenue, July 15, 2011)

Vendors can check the validity of individual Diplomatic Tax Exemption Cards on the U.S. Department of State's website at https://ofmapps.state.gov/tecv/. Cardholders are not required to get or present a *Florida Consumer's Certificate of Exemption (Form DR-14)* when making authorized exempt purchases. Payment for purchases made with mission tax exemption cards must be paid for by mission check or mission credit card, and purchases made with cash or personal checks are prohibited. Payment for purchases made with personal exemption cards may be in any form, including cash, check, or credit card. (*Tax Information Publication, No. 11A01-05*, Florida Department of Revenue, July 15, 2011)

These cards are not transferable and are not valid for exemption of taxes on fuel, utilities, communications services (such as telephone, cellular telephone, cable television, and satellite television), or motor vehicles. Exemptions on the purchase of fuel, utilities, communications services, and motor vehicles are subject to approval of a special application to the Office of Foreign Missions, Miami Regional Office. (*Tax Information Publication, No. 11A01-05*, Florida Department of Revenue, July 15, 2011)

• *State and local government transactions*

The sales and use tax exemption for sales made to state or county governments does not include the sale, rental, use, consumption, or storage for use in any political subdivision or municipality of machines and equipment, parts, and accessories used in the generation, transmission, or distribution of electrical energy by systems owned and operated by a political subdivision in Florida. Those sales, rentals, uses, consumption, or storages for which bonds or revenue certificates are validated for transmission or distribution expansion are exempt. (Sec. 212.08(6), F.S.)

With exceptions for public-use airports and public hospitals, there is no tax exemption for governmental entities' sale, rental, use, consumption, or storage of equipment and parts and accessories used in providing two-way telecommunications services to the public for hire. (Sec. 212.08(6), F.S.)

Admissions charges.—An exemption for admissions to certain government-sponsored athletic and recreational programs is discussed at Admissions, Entertainment, and Dues.

Government employees.—The exemption does not apply to any transaction otherwise taxable when payment is made by a government employee by any means, including but not limited to, cash, check, or credit card, when that employee is subsequently reimbursed by the government entity. (Sec. 212.08(6), F.S.)

Museums.—An exemption from the admissions tax for museums and historic buildings owned by political subdivisions of the state is discussed at Admissions, Entertainment, and Dues.

People-mover systems.—People-mover systems and their component parts that are purchased or manufactured by a contractor employed by a state or local government office or the public operator of a public-use airport are exempt if the systems or parts go into, or become part of, a publicly owned facility. (Sec. 212.08(7)(zz), F.S.; Rule 12A-1.038; Rule 12A-1.094)

Public school transactions.—School districts are expected to purchase necessary goods and services requested by parent-teacher organizations. (Sec. 212.0821, F.S.) School lunches are discussed at Food and Grocery Items. Public and private schools are generally allowed the same exemptions from tax. Private schools are discussed at Nonprofit Organizations, Private Schools, and Churches.

Purchases by municipal golf courses.—Sales made to the U.S. government, the state, or any county, municipality, or political subdivision of the state are exempt from sales tax when payment is made directly to the dealer by the governmental entity. When payment is made by another who is subsequently reimbursed by the government, the sale is generally not exempt. Effective July 1, 2017, the phrase "when payment is made directly to the dealer by the governmental entity" includes a situation in which an entity under contract with a municipality to maintain and operate a municipally owned golf course pays for a purchase or lease for the operation or maintenance of that golf course using the golf course revenues or other funds provided by the municipality for use by that entity. This provision applies to a municipally owned golf course that is located in a county with a population of at least 2 million residents and is the site upon which youth education programs are delivered on an ongoing basis by a nonprofit organization that is exempt from federal income tax under IRC § 501(c)(3). (Sec. 212.08(6)(d), F.S.; *Tax Information Publication, No. 17A01-09*, Florida Department of Revenue, August 30, 2017)

Selling dealers must:

— document exempt sales and maintain documentation in their records; and

— obtain a copy of the government entity's Consumer's Certificate of Exemption when making exempt sales to government entities.

A suggested certificate format to be issued by a qualifying entity under contract with a municipality to maintain or operate a municipally-owned golf course to the selling dealer to make exempt purchases or rentals is provided. (*Tax Information Publication, No. 17A01-09*, Florida Department of Revenue, August 30, 2017)

Unclaimed tangible personal property.—Sales of unclaimed tangible personal property by an agency of the state are not subject to tax. (Rule 12A-1.037(11))

• *Consular officers and employees*

Sales of tangible personal property to career consular officers, consular employees, and members of their families forming part of their households who are not nationals or permanent residents of the United States may be entitled to sales tax exemptions. Exemption will be allowed if the foreign nation they represent has a treaty with the United States that exempts them from federal and local taxes and the nation maintains a consulate-general with Florida. Foreign diplomats and consular personnel seeking an exemption, except an exemption on the purchase or lease of a motor vehicle, must present a tax exemption card to the vendor at the time of purchase. Procedures for obtaining motor vehicle exemptions are discussed below. (Rule 12A-1.0015(4), F.A.C.; *Tax Information Publication, No. 04A01-08*, Florida Department of Revenue, August 6, 2004)

¶60-420

Exemption cards.—There are two different types of tax exemption cards: personal and mission/official. The level and kinds of exemptions noted on the cards are designed to match the levels of exemption encountered by U.S. embassies in foreign countries. The level of tax exemption is indicated by the color of the card and the written explanation in the colored box. Cards with a blue stripe exempt the bearer from all state and local taxes nationwide, including those imposed on hotel stays and restaurants. Cards with a yellow stripe require the bearer to purchase a minimum amount of goods or services before the bearer is entitled to a tax exemption and may specify other requirements. Mission tax exemption cards are issued in the name of individual foreign officials to embassies, consulates, and international organizations for official purchases only and for the sole benefit of the mission identified on the face of the card. Personal tax exemption cards are used for exemption from state and local sales, restaurant, lodging, and similar taxes normally charged to a customer. The cards are not transferable and are not valid for exemption of taxes on gasoline, utilities, or communications services. (*Tax Information Publication, No. 04A01-08*, Florida Department of Revenue, August 6, 2004)

Foreign mission construction projects.—Contractors and subcontractors who procure goods and services as agents for and on behalf of a tax-exempt foreign mission for a mission construction project are permitted to use the mission's tax exemption card to exempt payment of tax on the goods and services. Diplomatic missions that wish to take advantage of this provision should contact OFM's Miami Regional Office at 305-442-4943 as early in the construction process as possible. (*Tax Information Publication, No. 04A01-08*, Florida Department of Revenue, August 6, 2004)

Motor vehicles.—Dealers making sales or leases of motor vehicles to foreign diplomats and consular employees that are exempt from tax must contact the U.S. Department of State, Office of Foreign Missions (OFM), for verification of the purchaser's exempt status. In addition, the purchaser must present valid photo identification from the Department of State. The OFM will provide a letter to the dealer stating whether the purchaser is eligible for exemption. The dealer must keep a copy of the letter issued by the OFM, along with a copy of the Department of State photo identification, in order to document the exempt status of the transaction. Dealers can contact the OFM's Miami Regional Office at 305-442-4943. (Tax Information Publication, No. 03A01-18, Florida Department of Revenue, November 5, 2003; *Tax Information Publication, No. 04A01-08*, Florida Department of Revenue, August 6, 2004)

[¶60-445] Internet/Electronic Commerce

Sales or use tax may apply to a variety of transactions in an electronic commerce environment. Such transactions include (1) purchases over the Internet of taxable services and property that are delivered in a nonelectronic form and (2) purchases of services or property that are delivered electronically and that may or may not be the equivalent of services or property that also can be delivered by nonelectronic means. General principles concerning the taxability of such transactions are discussed below.

If a transaction in an electronic commerce environment is taxable, the seller may or may not have a sufficient taxable connection, or nexus, with the taxing jurisdiction to be required to collect and remit tax on that transaction. Nexus issues in an electronic commerce environment are discussed below.

Under the federal Internet Tax Freedom Act (ITFA) and its amendments (P.L. 105-277, 112 Stat. 2681, 47 U.S.C. Sec. 151 note, amended by P.L. 107-75, P.L. 108-435, P.L. 110-108, P.L. 113-164, P.L. 113-235, P.L. 114-53, P.L. 114-113, and P.L. 114-125), state and local governments are barred from imposing multiple or discriminatory taxes on electronic commerce and taxes on Internet access, except for Internet access taxes allowed under grandfather clauses. The Internet Tax Freedom Act and its amendments are discussed below.

• *Taxability of transactions in electronic commerce*

The federal Internet Tax Freedom Act (ITFA) defines "electronic commerce" as any transaction conducted over the Internet or through Internet access, comprising the sale, lease, license, offer, or delivery of property, goods, services, or information, whether or not for consideration, and includes the provision of Internet access.

Transactions involving nonelectronic delivery.—Sales over the Internet may include the purchase of services that are delivered in a nonelectronic form, tangible personal property that is commonly delivered by mail or common carrier, or property in an electronic form capable of being processed by a computer ("digital property") that is stored on tangible storage media that is commonly delivered by mail or common carrier.

The taxability of such sales over the Internet generally is governed by the same rules as the purchase of such services or property in a traditional Main Street environment. However, the obligation of the seller to collect tax on such remote sales depends on whether the seller has nexus with the taxing jurisdiction, which is discussed below. If a sale is taxable and the seller does not collect tax, then the buyer generally is responsible for remitting use tax on the transaction.

Transactions involving electronic delivery.—Sales over the Internet may also include the purchase of digital property, services, or information delivered electronically.

While most states impose sales and use tax generally on all sales of tangible personal property, the taxability of sales of digital property delivered electronically varies among the states. In some states, a sale of certain types of digital property delivered electronically is considered a taxable sale of tangible personal property. In other states, such a sale is treated as not involving the transfer of tangible personal property and, therefore, is nontaxable. In yet other states, sales of some software delivered electronically are taxable while sales of other items delivered electronically are nontaxable.

In Florida, the charge for furnishing information by way of electronic images appearing on a subscriber's video display screen is neither a sale of tangible personal property nor a sale of a taxable information service. (Rule 12A-1.062(4), F.A.C.)

Some states may also draw a distinction based on whether the digital property delivered electronically would be considered tangible personal property if the same content were transferred on tangible storage media. That is, some states may only tax sales involving the electronic delivery of property if the property is the digital equivalent of tangible personal property.

Most states apply a true object of the transaction test in making taxability determinations. For example, if a state does not tax legal services, the delivery of a will electronically would not be taxable even if the state taxes the digital equivalent of tangible personal property, just as delivery of a will prepared on paper would not be taxable as the sale of tangible personal property.

The taxability of services varies among the states. Florida taxes some services, but not professional services. Charges imposed for services performed by computer technicians are considered professional services and are not subject to tax. (Rule 12A-1.032(5), F.A.C.; Sec. 212.08(7)(v), F.S.).

The taxability of information services and information databases also varies among the states. While information services are subject to tax in Florida, electronic information services are not taxable because they do not constitute a sale of tangible personal property. (Rule 12A-1.062(4), F.A.C.).

¶60-445

• *Nexus and collection responsibility*

Once it is determined that a taxable transaction is involved, it must be determined whether nexus is sufficient to trigger tax liability and on whom tax collection responsibility rests.

In the absence of specific statutes or other defined policy governing taxation of sales of personal property that are made over the Internet, the law and issues applicable to remote sales may provide a basis for determining sales and use tax treatment of sales made by electronic commerce.

As with remote sales, a transaction involving an electronic sale to a purchaser by a vendor that has no physical presence in the purchaser's state raises nexus issues. Under *Quill Corp. v. North Dakota*, 504 US 298 (1992), unless a vendor has substantial nexus with the purchaser's state, the state has no constitutional basis for the imposition of sales and use tax collection responsibility on that vendor.

• *Federal Internet Tax Freedom Act*

The federal Internet Tax Freedom Act (ITFA) (P.L. 105-277, 112 Stat. 2681, 47 U.S.C. Sec. 151 note, amended by P.L. 107-75, P.L. 108-435, P.L. 110-108, P.L. 113-164, P.L. 113-235, P.L. 114-53, P.L. 114-113, and P.L. 114-125) bars state and local governments from imposing multiple or discriminatory taxes on electronic commerce and taxes on Internet access.

Tax on Internet access.—The term "tax on Internet access" applies regardless of whether such a tax is imposed on a provider of Internet access or a buyer of Internet access and regardless of the terminology used to describe the tax. However, the term "tax on Internet access" does not include taxes on or measured by net income, capital stock, net worth, or property value, or other state general business taxes, such as gross receipts taxes, that are structured in such a way as to be a substitute for or supplement the state corporate income tax.

Grandfather provision.—A state or local government may continue to tax Internet access if the tax was generally imposed and actually enforced prior to October 1, 1998. However, this grandfather clause does not apply to any state that, prior to November 1, 2005, repealed its tax on Internet access or issued a rule that it no longer applies such a tax.

Internet access definition.—"Internet access" means a service that enables users to connect to the Internet to access content, information, or other services. The definition includes the purchase, use, or sale of telecommunications by an Internet service provider to provide the service or otherwise enable users to access content, information, or other services offered over the Internet. It also includes incidental services such as home pages, electronic mail, instant messaging, video clips, and personal electronic storage capacity, whether or not packaged with service to access the Internet. However, "Internet access" does not include voice, audio or video programming, or other products and services using Internet protocol for which there is a charge, regardless of whether the charge is bundled with charges for "Internet access."

Telecommunications services.—Under the latest amendments to the Act in 2007, state and local governments that continue to impose tax on telecommunications service purchased, used, or sold by a provider of Internet access have until June 30, 2008, to end these disputed taxes. However, this provision only operates if a public ruling applying such a tax was issued prior to July 1, 2007, or such a tax is the subject of litigation that was begun prior to July 1, 2007.

CCH COMMENT: *Disputed taxes on telecommunications.*—Some states dispute the assertion that taxes they impose on telecommunications service purchased by Internet service providers to connect their customers to the Internet (so-called "backbone" services) were prohibited by Congress in the 2004 renewal of the moratorium. The 2007 amendment and the revised definition of "Internet access" (discussed above) are intended to resolve this issue and end state and local taxation of Internet "backbone" service. According to the Congressional Budget Office, as many as eight states (Alabama, Florida, Illinois, Minnesota, Missouri, New Hampshire, Pennsylvania, and Washington) and several local governments in those states were collecting such taxes in 2007.

Bundled services.—The Act allows the taxation of otherwise exempt Internet access service charges that are aggregated (i.e. bundled) with and not separately stated from charges for telecommunications or other taxable services, unless the Internet access provider can reasonably identify the charges for Internet access from its books and records kept in the regular course of business.

Discriminatory taxes.—Under the Act, prohibited discriminatory taxes are defined as:

—taxes imposed on electronic commerce transactions that are not generally imposed and legally collectible on other transactions that involve similar property, goods, services or information;

—taxes imposed on electronic commerce transactions at a different rate from that imposed on other transactions involving similar property, goods, services or information, unless the rate is lower as part of a phase-out of the tax over a five-year or lesser period;

—collection or payment obligations imposed upon a different person or entity than would apply if the transaction were not transacted via electronic commerce;

—classification of Internet access service providers or online service providers for purposes of imposing on such providers a higher rate of tax than is imposed on providers of similar information delivered through other means;

—collection obligations imposed on a remote seller on the basis of the in-state accessibility of the seller's out-of-state computer server; and

—collection obligations imposed on a remote seller solely because the Internet access service or online service provider is deemed to be the remote seller's agent on the basis of the remote seller's display of information or content on the out-of-state server or because orders are processed through the out-of-state server.

Multiple taxes.—Prohibited multiple taxes are taxes imposed by a state or local government on the same, or essentially the same, transactions in electronic commerce that are also subject to a tax imposed by another state or local government without a corresponding credit or resale exemption certificate for taxes paid in other jurisdictions.

The moratorium against multiple taxes does not include taxes imposed within a state by the state or by one or more local governments within the state on the same electronic commerce.

The moratorium against multiple taxes does not prohibit other taxes from being imposed on persons who are engaged in electronic commerce even though that commerce has been subject to a sales or use tax.

State Internet access taxes.—Florida does not impose a tax on Internet access. (Sec. 212.02(16), F.S.)

• *Related topics*

¶60-445

[¶60-460] Leases and Rentals

Leases and rentals of certain real property and tangible personal property are subject to sales and use tax in Florida. (Sec. 212.02, F.S.)

Are leases and rentals taxable in Florida?

Yes. The lease or rental, including the commercial lease, of certain real property and tangible personal property is subject to Florida sales or use tax. (Sec. 212.02, F.S.; Sec. 212.031, F.S.)

Leases and rentals of motor vehicles and hotel rooms and other accommodations and to nonprofit organizations are discussed separately.

Charges for food, drinks, or services required or available with a lease to use real property. Separately stated charges that are required by a lease or license to use real property are subject to sales tax when imposed by a convention hall, exhibition hall, auditorium, stadium, theater, arena, civic center, performing arts center, or publicly-owned recreational facility. (Sec. 212.031, F.S.)

> *EXAMPLE:* Examples of these separately stated charges include charges for laborers, stagehands, ticket takers, event staff, security personnel, cleaning staff, and other event-related personnel, advertising, and credit card processing.

Convention or industry trade show. A sponsor of a convention or industry trade show who holds the prime lease to the convention hall, exhibition hall, or auditorium, whether publicly or privately owned, is subject to tax on the prime lease, and the sublessee is exempt. (Sec. 212.031, F.S.; Rule 12A-1.070, F.A.C.)

Show promoters and operators of carnivals. The lease or rental of land, hall, or other facilities by a fair association to a show promoter or prime operator of a carnival is exempt from tax, but the sublease of land, hall, or other facility by the show promoter or prime operator is subject to tax. (Sec. 212.031, F.S.; Rule 12A-1.070, F.A.C.)

Commercial real estate rental.—Effective January 1, 2020, the sales tax rate on the total rent or license fee charged under a commercial lease of real property (i.e., business rent tax) is reduced. (Sec. 212.031, F.S.) See Rate of Tax for the current rate.

Concessionaires. Real property is subject to sales tax when rented, leased, subleased, or licensed to a concessionaire by a convention hall, exhibition hall, auditorium, stadium, theater, arena, civic center, performing arts center, or publicly-owned recreational facility, during an event at the facility, to be used by the concessionaire to sell souvenirs, novelties, or other event-related products. (Sec. 212.031, F.S.; Rule 12A-1.070, F.A.C.)

Retail concessionaire services in airports. A person providing retail concessionaire services involving the sale of food and drink or other tangible personal property within the premises of an airport is subject to tax on the rental of real property used for that purpose, but is not subject to the tax on any license to use the property. (Sec. 212.031, F.S.; Rule 12A-1.070, F.A.C.)

Privilege, franchise, or concession fees, and fees for a license to do business, paid to an airport, are not considered payments for leasing, letting, renting, or granting a license for the use of real property. (Sec. 212.02, F.S.)

Exhibition centers. Florida sales tax on the lease or license of an exhibition center used for an event lasting more than seven consecutive days must be collected by the lessor when rent or a license fee is paid, but is not due or payable to the

Florida Department of Revenue until the first day of the month that follows the event's last day. (Sec. 212.031, F.S.)

Leases of parking lots, boat docks, and aircraft hangars. Florida provides guidance on the application of sales and use tax on the rental or leasing of parking lots, boat docks, and aircraft hangars. Florida state sales and use tax, plus any applicable discretionary sales surtax, applies to the rental or leasing of: parking or storage spaces for motor vehicles in parking lots or garages; storage facilities for towed vehicles; docking or storage spaces for boats in docks or marinas; and tie-down or storage space for aircraft. (Sec. 212.03(6), F.S.; *Form GT-800031*, Florida Department of Revenue, February 2018)

Local taxes. When real property that is leased, rented, or upon which a license for use is granted is located within a county imposing a local sales surtax, the rental or license payment is subject to the tax at the rate imposed within the county. (Rule 12A-15.003, F.A.C.)

Parking or storage spaces. Sales and use tax applies to leases or rentals of parking or storage spaces for motor vehicles in parking lots or garages, including storage spaces for towed vehicles, docking or storage spaces for boats in boat docks or marinas, and tie-down or storage spaces for aircraft at airports. (Sec. 212.03, F.S.; Rule 12A-1.070, F.A.C.; Rule 12A-1.073, F.A.C.; *Form GT-800031*, Florida Department of Revenue, February 2018)

Real property. Rental charges or room rates for the use or possession, or the right to the use or possession, of transient accommodations are subject to tax. (Sec. 212.03, F.S.) Transient accommodation rentals subject to written lease agreements stipulating more than six months of continuous residence are exempt from tax. To be exempt, a lease agreement beginning on a certain day of the first month must be in effect through the day after the corresponding day of the seventh month. The terms "lease, let, or rental" are defined as the leasing or renting of living quarters or sleeping or housekeeping accommodations in hotels, apartment houses, rooming houses, tourist or trailer camps and real property. (Sec. 212.02, F.S.) See Lodging.

Lease, sublease, or licensing of real property that is not a business. The lease, sublease, or licensing of real property is not a "business" and is, consequently, not subject to tax if all of these conditions apply to the transaction:

— if the transaction is between two corporations and the stock of both corporations is owned by a common parent corporation;

— if the corporation's sales subject to sales and use tax are not less than $667 million during the most recent twelve-month period ended June 30;

— if the transaction involved property that was already in use, that was transferred between July 2, 1988, and June 30, 1989, and that did not change in use after the transfer; and

— if the transaction is required by an unrelated lender as a condition of providing financing to one or more members of the affiliated group.

(Sec. 212.02, F.S.)

Nontaxable rental or lease of real property. A person who rents or leases real property or who grants a license to use, occupy, or enter any real property is exercising a taxable privilege unless the property is:

— agricultural property;

— property used as a dwelling unit;

— property already subject to tax on parking, docking or storage space;

— a public or private street or right-of-way, including poles, conduits, fixtures, and similar improvements located thereon, used by a utility, provider of communications services, or franchised cable television company for utility, communications, or television purposes;

— a public street or road used for transportation purposes;

— airport or port authority property;

— property used as an integral part of the performance of qualified (motion picture) production services;

— property leased, subleased, or rented to people providing food and drink concessionaire services;

— property leased to licensed educational institutions that hold regular classes and have enrollments of 500 or students;

— property used or occupied predominantly for space flight business purposes.

(Sec. 212.031, F.S.; Rule 12A-1.070, F.A.C.)

Rentals of mobile homes. Special rules apply to rentals of mobile homes, trailers, or recreational vehicle parks requiring owners to certify each year that their camp or park continues to qualify for exemption. (Rule 12A-1.061, F.A.C.)

Total rent or license fee charged. The total rent or license fee charged includes payments for the privilege of using or occupying real property for any purposes and specifically lists, as includable, base rent, percentage rents, and similar charges. These charges must be included in the total rent or license fee taxable, regardless of whether they can be attributed to the ability of the lessor's or licenser's property as used or operated to attract customers. (Sec. 212.031, F.S.)

Registration requirements. Lessors subject to Florida sales tax are required to register as sales tax dealers.

Out-of-state lessors. Leases of property used or stored in Florida are taxable without regard to prior use or tax paid on the purchase outside Florida. An out-of-state owner or lessor of equipment is considered to be doing business in Florida if its tangible personal property is located in Florida in the possession of a lessee.

Tangible personal property. Any rental or lease of tangible personal property as part of a regularly established business is taxable.

Dealers. A person who leases or rents tangible personal property is considered a dealer for sales and use tax purposes and is required to collect tax.

Intrinsically valuable personal property. Payments for intrinsically valuable personal property such as franchises, trademarks, service marks, logos, and patents are not subject to tax. When a contractual arrangement provides for both payments taxable as total rent or license fee and nontaxable payments, the tax is based on a reasonable allocation of those payments and does not apply to the portion which is for the nontaxable payments.

Transfer of possession. All transactions in which there is a transfer of possession of tangible personal property for a consideration without a transfer of title and that are not bailments are taxable lease transactions.

Transfer of possession of property includes the actual or constructive transfer of custody or possession of the property, the transfer of the right to custody or possession, or the transfer of the right to use and control or direct the use of the property.

Types of leases. There are different types of leases in Florida.

Capital leases. When a contract designated as a lease transfers substantially all of the benefits, including depreciation, and risks inherent in the ownership of tangible personal property to the lessee and ownership of the property transfers to the lessee at the end of the lease term, or the contract contains a purchase option for a nominal amount, the contract will be regarded from its inception as a taxable sale under a security agreement. A purchase option amount will be considered nominal if it does not exceed the lesser of $100 or 1% of the total contract price.

Equipment leases. A transaction involving the use of equipment with an operator supplied by the owner is a lease if control or direction over the equipment passes to the customer. If the operator of the equipment is on the payroll of the lessee, the contract becomes a rental of tangible personal property and is taxable. However, if the owner of the equipment furnishes the operator and all supplies and contracts for its use under the owner's direction but according to the customer's specifications and the customer does not take possession or have any control, the contract is a nontaxable service transaction.

Operating leases. Under an operating lease, tax applies to the gross proceeds derived from the lease of tangible personal property for the entire term of the lease when the lessor is an established business. In addition to the amount attributable to the rental of the property, gross proceeds include:

— any interest charges, whether or not separately stated, unless the interest charges are clearly imposed for late payment or other defaults under the lease;

— freight charges incurred as part of the lease transaction;

— ad valorem taxes paid to the lessor or to any other person on behalf of the lessor; and

— any portion of an insurance premium paid to the lessor, or to any other person on behalf of the lessor, if the policy names the lessor as the beneficiary and the amount is separately stated and itemized.

When a lessee pays insurance for the lessee's own protection, however, the premium is not regarded as part of the gross proceeds subject to tax, even if the lessor is also protected by the coverage. If an operating lease is assigned, whether or not title to the property transfers, the rental or lease payments are subject to tax.

Gross proceeds of operating leases also include charges for services required to be provided or performed under the contract by the lessor. For example, the entire charge for the lease or license for use of chemical toilet units is taxable, including charges for cleaning services provided or performed by the lessor or licenser.

Are there any special exemptions for leases or rentals in Florida?

Yes. There are a number of exemptions for certain leases or rentals in Florida.

Capital improvements by those renting real property from Florida Turnpike Enterprise. The Florida Turnpike Enterprise and any nongovernment lessee or licensee renting, leasing, or licensing real property from the Florida Turnpike Enterprise are exempt from paying any commercial rent tax on the value of any capital improvements constructed, improved, acquired, installed, or used. Other types of capital improvements are subject to commercial rent tax. The privilege of being in the business of renting commercial real property, traditional forms of "rent," and other forms of "rental consideration" are subject to sales tax.

Condominium property. Recreational property or other common elements of a condominium that are leased by the condominium association from the developer or owner are exempt. The exemption applies only to the lease payments of the property, and any other use of the property is taxable.

Fair associations. Certain transactions involving fair associations are exempt, including:

— the sale, use, lease, rental, or grant of a license to use, made directly to or by a fair association, of real or tangible personal property;

— any charge made by a fair association, or its agents, for parking, including temporary parking by vehicles used as sleeping quarters, and admissions;

— rentals, subleases, and sublicenses of real or tangible personal property between the central amusement attraction owner and the owner of an amusement devise or attraction for furnishing such amusement device or attraction at a public fair or exposition; and

— other transactions which are directly incurred by the fair association in financing, constructing, or operating a fair, exposition, or other authorized event or facility.

Taxable fair association transactions. Taxable fair association transactions are:

— the sale of tangible personal property by a fair association through an agent or independent contractor;

— the sale of admissions or tangible personal property by a concessionaire, vendor, exhibitor, or licensee; and

— the rental or sublease of real or tangible personal property, except for the furnishing of an amusement device or attraction, between the central amusement attraction owner and a concessionaire, vendor, exhibitor, or licensee.

Full-time students and military personnel. Relief from taxation is provided for people who rent or lease living accommodations rather than own their homes. Full-time students enrolled in a postsecondary educational institution and military personnel currently on active duty are exempt from tax.

Lawful impoundment. Charges for parking, docking, tie-down, or storage arising from a lawful impoundment are not subject to tax. "Lawful impoundment" is defined as the storing of or having custody over an aircraft, boat, or motor vehicle by, or at the direction of, a local, state, or federal law enforcement agency that the owner or owner's representative is not authorized to enter upon, have access to, or remove without the consent of the law enforcement agency.

Multiple use rentals. Leases involving multiple uses of real property are partially exempt if one of the uses is for agriculture, for dwelling units, or for parking, docking, or storage already subject to tax.

Power farm equipment. The rental of power farm equipment is exempt. See Agriculture.

Purchase of property for leasing purposes. Tangible personal property purchased exclusively for leasing purposes may be purchased on an exempt basis if the lessor is registered with the Florida Department of Revenue as a dealer at the time of purchase and it issues the vendor a valid resale certificate in lieu of the tax. Lease payments on property leased solely for the purpose of leasing to a third party are exempt.

Dual purpose. Persons who purchase property with the dual purpose of leasing it to others and keeping it for their own use, or who purchase property with the intention only of leasing it but who in fact also use the property, must pay the tax on the cost of the property and collect and remit the tax on all leases of the property. The subsequent conversion to one's own use of tangible personal property that was purchased tax exempt for exclusive lease is subject to use tax at the time of conversion.

Taxicabs. The lease of, or license to use, a taxicab or taxicab-related equipment and services provided by a taxicab company to an independent taxicab operator is exempt from sales and use tax, provided sales or use tax was paid on the acquisition of the taxicab and its related equipment.

Telecommunications property. Florida sales and use tax on the rental or license fee for use of real property is inapplicable to any real property that is rented, leased, subleased, or licensed to a person who provides telecommunications, data systems management, or Internet services at a publicly or privately owned convention hall, civic center, or meeting space at a public lodging establishment. This is applicable only to that portion of the rental, lease, or license payment that is based upon a percentage of sales, revenue sharing, or royalty payments and not based upon a fixed price.

[¶60-480] Lodging

The lease, let, or rental of living quarters or sleeping or housekeeping accommodations in hotels, apartment houses, multiple unit structures, roominghouses, tourist or trailer camps, mobile home courts, single family dwellings, garage apartments, beach houses or cottages, cooperatively owned apartments, condominium parcels or mobile homes, and real property is a taxable rental of real property. (Sec. 212.02(2) and (10). F.S.; Sec. 212.03(1), F.S.; Rule 12A-1.061(1), F.A.C.)

The granting of a license to use living quarters or accommodations for sleeping or housekeeping also constitutes the exercise of a taxable privilege. However, persons renting, leasing, letting, or granting a license to use any living quarters or sleeping or housekeeping accommodations in apartment houses, roominghouses, and tourist camps, are exercising a taxable privilege unless a written lease agreement stipulates the tenant's continuous possession of the property as a residence for a period that exceeds six months. (Rule 12A-1.061, F.A.C.) To be exempt, a written lease agreement beginning on a certain day of the first month must be in effect through the day after the corresponding day of the seventh month. However, if the rental is intended to be used as the tenant's permanent place of residence, the exemption does not require a written lease exceeding six months. (*Hale et al.*, Florida District Court of Appeal, No. 1D00-4450, January 18, 2002)

A person who leases or rents "transient accommodations", as defined under regulatory provisions, (Rule 12A-1.061(1), F.A.C.) is a dealer who must collect the tax from the lessee or renter at the time of the lease or rental payment. (Sec. 212.03(2), F.S.; Sec. 212.06(2)(j), (3), F.S.)

Furniture, fixtures, supplies, instruments, and tools used in the operation of a business establishment, including hotels, apartment houses, and motels, and not bought for resale, are taxable. (Rule 12A-1.025, F.A.C.).

• *Transient accommodations*

Facilities that cater primarily to the traveling public are taxable. All transient facilities, such as roominghouses, that provide one or more rooms for transients must be registered as dealers. Public housing facilities and migrant labor camps are exempt. (Sec. 212.02(2), F.S.; Sec. 212.03(7), F.S.; Rule 12A-1.061(1), F.A.C.)

Hotel reward points programs.—A rule governs the taxation of transactions between program administrators of hotel reward points programs and hotels that provide transient lodging accommodations that participate in such programs. (Rule 12A-1.0615, F.A.C.)

In transactions between a hotel and a guest using reward points, the hotel is not required to collect transient rental tax from the member of a hotel reward points program when the member uses a certificate or confirmation number that entitles the member to transient accommodations at a participating hotel at no charge. However, the member is required to pay the hotel transient rental tax on the amount of the room rate or rental charged paid using any form of payment other than reward points when the member uses a certificate or confirmation number that entitles the member to transient accommodations and pays the hotel any room rate or rental charges using any form of payment other than reward points. (Rule 12A-1.0615, F.A.C.)

In transactions between a hotel and a reward points program, transient rental tax is due on a hotel's reimbursements when the hotel receives more in reimbursements than it paid in contributions in the prior calendar year. The rule provides the method to calculate taxable reimbursements for periods other than a hotel's initial year of participation and for a hotel's initial 12 months of participation in a reward points program. (Rule 12A-1.0615, F.A.C.)

A member of a hotel rewards points program is not required to pay Florida transient rental tax on the points redeemed for a room or a room upgrade. The member is only required to pay tax on any charges not covered by the redemption of points. When a participating hotel receives more in reimbursements from the reward points program fund than it was required to contribute, taxes have not been paid on the funds the hotel receives in excess of the contributions. As such, the hotel owes tax on the excess amount. (*Tax Information Publication, No. 11A01-11*, Florida Department of Revenue, December 13, 2011)

The determination of whether the hotel received more in reimbursements from the fund than it paid in contributions is required to be made each January using the preceding calendar year's total contributions and reimbursements. The calculation is determined by taking the total reimbursements received in the prior calendar year and subtracting the total contributions paid in the prior calendar year, divided by the total reimbursements received in the prior calendar year. The resulting percentage is then applied to the total reimbursements received in each reporting period in the current calendar year to determine what amount, if any, of the current reimbursements are subject to tax. No "true-up" is required at any point. (*Tax Information Publication, No. 11A01-11*, Florida Department of Revenue, December 13, 2011)

When a hotel first begins participating in a reward points program, it must determine what percentage, if any, of its reimbursements are subject to tax. This determination must be made at the end of the hotel's first 12 months of participation in the program. The calculation is the same as above, except that the totals to be used are for the first 12 months instead of the prior calendar year. The resulting percentage is then applied to the total reimbursements received in the first 12 months, as well as any reimbursements received during any remaining reporting periods in the calendar year in which the calculation is made. Any reimbursements subject to tax should be included in the hotel's gross transient rentals and taxable transient rentals on its sales and use tax return. (*Tax Information Publication, No. 11A01-11*, Florida Department of Revenue, December 13, 2011)

A hotel must maintain records received from or sent to the program administrators indicating reimbursements and contributions, as well as records that indicate the calculations required to determine the amount of transient rentals tax due. (Rule 12A-1.0615, F.A.C.)

Land leased from the federal government.—Anyone who operates transient rental facilities on land leased from the federal government is required to collect sales tax on the rental charged for the use of the facilities. (Rule 12A-1.061, F.A.C.)

Recreational resorts.—Sales of memberships in recreational resorts that provide transient rental accommodations and other recreational facilities are subject to tax. A membership agreement is fully taxable even if the agreement allows the member to use a resort's facility located outside of Florida for a nominal charge or free of charge. Membership agreements with resort facilities located outside the state that allow the member to use facilities located in Florida at a nominal charge or free of charge are not subject to tax. However, the membership charges paid to an out-of-state resort facility are taxable to the extent the out-of-state facility allocates or distributes proceeds to a Florida resort. (Rule 12A-1.061, F.A.C.)

Exempt organizations.—Transient rental accommodations billed to and paid for by an individual representing an exempt organization or governmental entity are taxable, but accommodations billed to and paid directly by the entity are exempt. (Rule 12A-1.061(14), F.A.C.)

Units leased for employee use.—Units leased for the use of employees in a facility that does not qualify as an exempt facility are exempt from sales tax after six months if the rent is paid continuously. It does not matter that the unit is actually unoccupied or that it is occupied by different personnel at different times. (Rule 12A-1.061, F.A.C.)

Trailer lots, mobile home parks, and recreational vehicle parks.—Trailer lots, mobile home parks, and recreational vehicle parks intended for rental as principal places of residence are exempt from tax so long as 50% or more of the total rental units available are occupied by tenants who have continuously resided there for more than three months. The tax-exempt status of the camp or park must be redetermined each year at the end of the owner's accounting year, using a consecutive three-month period with at least one month in the accounting year. With respect to new facilities, all rental charges at a camp or park are presumed taxable until the facility has met the requirements set forth above and the owner or representative has declared to the Department that the rental of transient accomodations at the camp or park is no longer subject to tax. (Sec. 212.03(7)(c), F.S.; Rule 12A-1.061, F.A.C.)

Timeshare resort products.—Florida local option tourist development tax, tourist impact tax, transient rentals tax, and convention development tax is imposed on certain timeshare resort products. The occupancy of an accommodation of a timeshare resort pursuant to a timeshare plan, a multi-site timeshare plan, or an exchange transaction in an exchange program, as defined, by the owner of a timeshare interest or such owner's guest, where the guest is not paying monetary consideration to the owner or to a third party for the benefit of the owner, is not a privilege subject to taxation under these provisions. A membership or transaction fee paid by a timeshare owner that does not provide the timeshare owner with the right to occupy any specific timeshare unit, but only provides the timeshare owner with the opportunity to exchange a timeshare interest through an exchange program, is a service charge and is not subject to taxation. The legislation that enacted these provisions is intended to be clarifying and remedial in nature and does not provide a basis for assessments of tax or refunds of tax for periods prior to July 1, 2009. (Sec. 212.03(1), F.S.; Rule 12A-1.061, F.A.C.)

The following transactions are not subject to tax:

— the exchange of a timeshare unit for the use of another timeshare unit; and

— any membership fee or transaction fee paid by the time'share owner to an exchange program for a timeshare exchange.

(*Tax Information Publication 09A01-04*, Florida Department of Revenue, June 18, 2009)

A timeshare inspection package purchased in Florida is subject to tax, unless the consideration is applied to the purchase of a timeshare estate. Tax is due on the last day of occupancy. A "timeshare inspection package" is defined as a situation in which the purchaser receives the right to use a timeshare unit after attending a sales presentation but has not yet purchased a timeshare interest. (*Tax Information Publication 09A01-04*, Florida Department of Revenue, June 18, 2009)

These provisions apply to vacation clubs only if the club meets the definition of a "multisite timeshare plan," as specified. Vacation clubs that do not meet this definition are unaffected by these provisions. (*Tax Information Publication 09A01-04*, Florida Department of Revenue, June 18, 2009)

Rooms at health care facilities are generally exempt (Sec. 212.08(7)(i); Rule 12A-1.001, F.A.C.).

• *Living accommodations*

The lease or rental of property used as a dwelling unit that is not a "transient accommodation" (Rule 12A-1.061(1), F.A.C.) is not the exercise of a taxable privilege. (Sec. 212.031, F.S.; Rule 12A-1.070(1), F.A.C.)

People who have continuously resided at any one taxable place of residence for six months or longer and have paid the tax due are exempt from further payment as long as they continuously reside at the location. People who have entered into a bona fide written lease for longer than six months for continuous residence at a particular location are exempt, as are those who reside at facilities that are exempt from tax even if they have resided there for less than six months. (Sec. 212.03(4), F.S.; Rule 12A-1.061, F.A.C.)

Rentals of single-family dwellings are taxable. (Rule 12A-1.061, F.A.C.) Owners of duplexes may reside in one unit and rent the other unit. The rent is taxable on the unit not occupied by the owners, unless the renter has continuously resided at the residence for at least six months or has entered into a bona fide written lease for longer than six months. (Rule 12A-1.061, F.A.C.)

Monthly service charges paid by owners of apartments in cooperatively owned apartment houses are not rentals and are exempt from sales taxation. When either the agent for or the owner of a single-family dwelling in a condominium apartment house or the prime leaseholder of a single-family dwelling in a cooperatively owned apartment house rents the unit, the rental is taxable unless it otherwise qualifies for an exemption. (Rule 12A-1.061, F.A.C.)

Full-time students enrolled in post-secondary institutions and military personnel and federal civil service employees on active duty are exempt from the sales and use tax imposed on transient rentals (Sec. 212.03(7)(a), F.S.; Rule 12A-1.061, F.A.C.) However, students at private flying schools operating under contract with the federal government are taxable on their rental of private living quarters that are not furnished by the government. (Rule 12A-1.061, F.A.C.)

Migrant labor camps established to provide living quarters for seasonal, temporary, or migrant workers are exempt. (Sec. 212.03(7), F.S.; Rule 12A-1.061, F.A.C.)

• *Local taxes*

When any transient accommodation is located within a county imposing a local sales surtax, the tax is due at the rate imposed within the county. (Rule 12A-15.003(9), F.A.C.).

[¶60-510] Manufacturing, Processing, Assembling, or Refining

In general, a manufacturer's purchases are exempt, but its sales are taxable.

Are purchases by manufacturers, processors, assemblers, or refiners taxable in Florida?

Yes, certain purchases by manufacturers are exempt, but some are taxable.

Exempt purchases. Many purchases made by manufacturers are exempt.

Aquacultural activities. Industrial machinery and equipment, including parts and accessories, purchased for use in aquacultural activities at fixed locations are exempt from sales tax. "Industrial machinery and equipment" is tangible personal property or other property that has a depreciable life of three years or more and that is used as an integral part in the manufacturing, processing, compounding, or production of tangible personal property for sale. A building and its structural components, including heating and air-conditioning equipment, are included within the definition. (Sec. 212.08(7)(ooo), F.S.; *Tax Information Publication, No. 18A01-10*, Florida Department of Revenue, May 30, 2018)

The term "aquacultural activities" means the business of cultivating aquatic organisms. Such businesses must be certified by the Department of Agriculture and Consumer Services. In addition, aquacultural activities must produce an aquaculture product (i.e., aquatic organisms and any product derived from aquatic organisms that are owned and propagated, grown, or produced under controlled conditions). Such products do not include organisms harvested from the wild for depuration, wet storage, or relay for purification. (Sec. 212.08(7)(ooo), F.S.; *Tax Information Publication, No. 18A01-10*, Florida Department of Revenue, May 30, 2018)

The Florida Department of Revenue provides a suggested exemption certificate form. (*Tax Information Publication, No. 18A01-10*, Florida Department of Revenue, May 30, 2018)

Combustible fuels. Purchases of natural gas, residual oil, recycled oil, waste oil, solid waste material, coal, sulfur, or wood for use as a combustible fuel in an industrial manufacturing, processing, compounding, or production process at a fixed location in Florida are exempt from sales and use tax. (Sec. 212.08(7)(b), F.S.)

Effective July 1, 2022, hydrogen purchased for use as a combustible fuel in manufacturing, processing, compounding, or producing tangible personal property for sale is exempt from Florida sales and use tax. This exemption does not apply to any firm subject to regulation by the Division of Hotels and Restaurants of the Department of Business and Professional Regulation. Purchasers of boiler fuels qualifying for this exemption must provide the seller a signed certificate that states that the boiler fuel is purchased for exempt use. (Sec. 212.08(7)(b), F.S.; *Tax Information Publication, No. 22A01-14*, Florida Department of Revenue, June 30, 2022)

Purchases of alternative fuels such as liquefied petroleum gas, compressed natural gas, natural gasoline, butane gas, and propane gas also are subject to tax. (Rule 12A-1.059(5))

Dyed diesel fuel used in a trade or business is subject to use tax unless the fuel is specifically exempt from sales tax or the dealer selling the fuel has elected to collect sales tax on sales to persons who use or consume the diesel fuel in a trade or business. (Rule 12A-1.059(3))

Fuels (other than those specifically exempt), electric power, any kind of energy or industrial gases used in fabricating, processing, or converting materials into tangible personal property for resale are taxable, unless they become a component of the finished product. (Rule 12A-1.059,; Rule 12A-1.063(1)(b); Rule 12A-1.015)

Defense or space technology. Industrial machinery and equipment used in defense or space technology facilities certified to design, manufacture, assemble, process, compound, or produce defense technology products or space technology products for sale or for use by these facilities are exempt. (Sec. 212.08(5)(j), F.S.) Defense technology products include but are not limited to, weapons, weapons systems, guidance systems, surveillance systems, communications or information systems, munitions, aircraft, vessels, or boats, or components thereof, which are intended for military use and manufactured in performance of a contract or subcontract with the United States Department of Defense or the military branch of a recognized foreign government. (Sec. 212.08(5)(j), F.S.) Space technology products include, but are not limited to, space launch vehicles, space flight vehicles, missiles, satellites or research payloads, avionics, associated control systems and processing systems, and any components of any of these above items. (Sec. 212.08(5)(j), F.S.)

To receive the exemption, qualifying businesses must initially apply to the Division of Strategic Business Development of the Florida Department of Economic Opportunity. The original certification will be valid for a period of two years. In lieu of submitting a new application, the original certification may be renewed biennially by submitting to the Florida Department of Economic Opportunity a certified statement that there has been no material change in the circumstances entitling the business to the original certification. (Sec. 212.08(5)(j), F.S.)

Electrical power or steam manufacturers. The purchase of machinery and equipment for use at a fixed location to produce electrical or steam energy resulting from the burning of hydrogen (effective July 1, 2022) and boiler fuels other than residual oil is exempt. The use of a "de minimis" amount of residual fuel to facilitate the burning of the nonresidual fuel does not reduce the exemption. In facilities where machinery and equipment are necessary to burn hydrogen (effective July 1, 2022), or both residual and nonresidual fuel, the exemption will be prorated. However, if 15% or less of all electrical or steam energy generated was produced by burning residual fuel, the full exemption applies. Purchasers qualifying for the exemption must furnish the Department with an affidavit stating that the items purchased are exempt. Purchasers with self-accrual authority must maintain all documentation necessary to prove the exempt status of their purchases. (Sec. 212.08(5)(c), F.S.; *Tax Information Publication, No. 22A01-11*, Florida Department of Revenue, June 30, 2022)

Tax is not imposed on any person for the manufacture or production of electrical power or energy, steam energy, or other energy at a single location when the power or energy is used directly and exclusively at that location or other locations when the energy is transferred through facilities of the owner. To qualify for the exemption, the energy must be used by machinery or equipment that manufacturers, processes, compounds, produces, fabricates, or prepares for shipment the tangible personal property for sale or for purposes of operating pollution control equipment, maintenance equipment, or monitoring or control equipment that is used in such operations. (Sec. 212.06(1)(b), F.S.; Rule 12A-1.043(5)(a))

Electricity and steam used by specified industries. Charges for electricity used by specified industries at fixed locations in Florida to operate machinery and equipment for qualified purposes are exempt. The exemption also applies to charges for steam used for qualified purposes. Uses of electricity and steam qualified for the exemption include manufacturing, processing, compounding, production, or preparation for the shipment of tangible personal property for sale. The operation of pollution control, recycling, maintenance, or monitoring or control equipment used for such purposes is also eligible for the exemption. (Sec. 212.08(7)(ff), F.S.)

The specified industries to which the exemption applies include several metal industries, textile industries, wood and paper products industries, petroleum and coal industries, mineral and natural products industries, manufacturing industries, electronic industries, rubber and plastic industries, transportation equipment industries, chemical products industries and food products industries. (Sec. 212.08(7)(ff), F.S.)

Electricity and steam used for exempt purposes need not be separately metered to qualify for the exemption. (Sec. 212.08(7)(ff), F.S.)

Recyclable material merchant wholesalers are added to the list specified industries eligible for the exemption. These types of businesses primarily engage in the merchant wholesale distribution of automotive scrap, industrial scrap, and other recyclable materials, and include auto wreckers primarily engaged in dismantling motor vehicles for wholesale scrap. (Sec. 212.08(7)(ff), F.S.)

Equipment used in severance, mining or production of solid minerals and phosphate. Machinery and equipment purchased by new and expanding businesses that mine or process solid minerals or phosphate are exempt from tax. (Sec. 212.08(5)(b) 5., F.S.)

Expanding businesses. Industrial machinery and equipment purchased for use in expanding manufacturing facilities or plant units that manufacture, process, compound, or produce for sales items of tangible personal property at fixed locations in Florida are exempt. (Sec. 212.08(5)(b)2, F.S.)

To qualify, the taxpayer must make an affirmative showing that the items purchased are used to increase the productive output of the expanded business by not less than 5%. Industrial machinery and equipment that is an integral part of the production process or post-production process qualifies for the exemption. (Sec. 212.08(5)(b)2, F.S.Rule 12A-1.096(8))

The increase in productive output is generally measured by comparing the number of physical units produced for 12 continuous months immediately after completion of the installation of qualifying machinery and equipment to the number of physical units produced over the 12 continuous months immediately preceding such installation. (*Tax Information Publication, No. 12A01-05*, Florida Department of Revenue, June 1, 2012)

Federal procurement contracts. Industrial machinery and equipment purchased by an expanding business that manufactures tangible personal property under federal procurement regulations at a fixed location in Florida is exempt from tax. To qualify, the taxpayer must show that the items purchased are used to increase the implicit productive output of the expanded business by at least 10%. (Sec. 212.08(5)(d), F.S.)

Items used in manufacturing and fabricating aircraft and gas turbine engines. An exemption is available for the purchase of certain chemicals, machinery, parts, and equipment used and consumed in the manufacture or fabrication of aircraft engines and gas turbine engines, including cores, electrical discharge machining supplies, brass electrodes, ceramic guides, reamers, grinding and deburring wheels, Norton vortex wheels, argon, nitrogen, helium, fluid abrasive cutters, solvents and soaps, boroscopes, penetrants, patterns, dies, and molds consumed in the production of castings. (Sec. 212.08(7)(hhh), F.S.)

Chemicals, machinery, parts, and equipment used and consumed in the production of castings that are used and consumed in the manufacturing and fabricating of aircraft engines and other gas turbine engines that are exempt from sales and use tax include: cores; fluid abrasive cutters; electrical discharge machining supplies; solvents and soaps; brass electrodes; boroscopes; ceramic guides; penetrants; reamers; patterns; grinding and deburring wheels; dies; Norton vortex wheels; molds; and argon, nitrogen, and helium gases. Sellers of these items are required to document exempt sales. *Tax Information Publication, No. 12A01-06* provides a suggested certificate to be completed by the purchaser and maintained in the seller's books and records. (*Tax Information Publication, No. 12A01-06*, Florida Department of Revenue, June 1, 2012)

New businesses. Industrial machinery and equipment purchased for use in new businesses that manufacture, process, compound, or produce for sale items of tangible personal property at a fixed location are exempt from tax upon an affirmative showing by the taxpayer, to the satisfaction of the Department of Revenue, that the items are used in a new business in the state. (Sec. 212.08(5)(b) 1, F.S.) Industrial machinery and equipment that is an integral part of the production process or postproduction process qualifies for the exemption. (Rule 12A-1.096(8))

The new and expanding business exemptions do not apply to machinery or equipment purchased or used by electric utility companies, communications companies, oil or gas exploration or production operations, publishing firms that do not export at least one-half of their finished product outside Florida, hotels, or restaurants. (Sec. 212.08(5)(b) 5, F.S.; Rule 12A-1.096(7))

Materials used in the construction of railroad spurs that are on the property of an expanding business and that belong to that business for purposes of transporting raw materials are exempt from Florida sales and use tax. However, materials used in the construction of railroad spurs used exclusively for the transport of finished products are subject to tax. (Rule 12A-1.096(9)(f))

Recycling roll off containers. Recycling roll off containers are exempt from sales and use tax when the container:

— is purchased by a business whose primary business activity is within NAICS code 423930 (2007); and

— is used exclusively for business activities classified under that code.

(Sec. 212.08(7)(ooo) 5, F.S.; *Tax Information Publication, No. 18A01-06*, Florida Department of Revenue, May 30, 2018)

Business activities under NAICS code 423930 include merchant wholesale distribution of automotive scrap, industrial scrap, and other recyclable materials. Purchasers of qualifying containers should provide the seller with a signed certificate certifying the purchaser's entitlement to the exemption. This certificate relieves the seller of any potential tax liability on the sale. (*Tax Information Publication, No. 18A01-06*, Florida Department of Revenue, May 30, 2018)

Research and development. Tangible personal property manufactured, produced, compounded, processed, or fabricated for a person's own use in research and development is exempt.

Machinery and equipment used predominantly for research and development are exempt.

Semiconductor technology. Industrial machinery and equipment purchased for use in certified semiconductor technology facilities to manufacture, process, compound, or produce semiconductor technology products for sale or for use by these facilities are exempt. Building materials purchased for use in manufacturing or expanding clean rooms in semiconductor manufacturing facilities are also exempt. Machinery and equipment includes molds, dies, machine tooling, other appurtenances or accessories to machinery and equipment, testing equipment, test beds, computers, and software, whether purchased or self-fabricated, and, if self-fabricated, includes materials and labor for design, fabrication, and assembly. (Sec. 212.08(5)(j), F.S.)

To receive the exemption, qualifying businesses must initially apply to the Division of Strategic Business Development of the Florida Department of Economic Opportunity. The original certification will be valid for a period of two years. In lieu of submitting a new application, the original certification may be renewed biennially by submitting to the Florida Department of Economic Opportunity a certified statement that there has been no material change in the circumstances entitling the business to the original certification. (Sec. 212.08(5)(j), F.S.)

A business that is certified to receive this exemption may elect to designate one or more state universities or community colleges as recipients of up to 100% of the amount of the exemption for which they may qualify. The institution must agree to match the funds with cash, programs, services, or other in-kind support on a one-to-one basis in research and development projects requested by the business to receive the funds, and the rights to any patents, royalties, or real or intellectual property must vest in the business. (Sec. 212.08(5)(j), F.S.)

Spaceport activities. Industrial machinery and equipment purchased for exclusive use in spaceport activities are exempt. (Sec. Sec. 212.08(5)(b), F.S.) For a further discussion of the space program, see Government Transactions.

Industrial machinery and equipment exemption. Industrial machinery and equipment purchased by eligible manufacturing businesses that is used at a fixed location within Florida is exempt from sales and use tax. (Sec. 212.08(7)(jjj), F.S.; *Tax Information Publication No. 13A01-06*, Florida Department of Revenue, June 10, 2013)

Those whose primary activity at the location where the industrial machinery and equipment is located is classified under NAICS code 423930 (metals recyclers) is included in the list of eligible manufacturing businesses. (Sec. 212.08(7)(jjj), F.S.)

An exemption is also available for certain "postharvest machinery and equipment" for eligible businesses whose primary business activity at the location where the postharvest machinery and equipment is located is within NAICS code 115114. "Postharvest machinery" is defined as tangible personal property or other property that has a depreciable life of three years or more and that is used primarily for postharvest activities, and includes repair parts, materials, and labor. (Sec. 212.08(7)(jjj), F.S.)

The exemption for machinery and equipment includes: (1) recycling industries classified under code 423930 of the North American Industry Classification System (NAICS) (2007); and (2) postharvest machinery and equipment purchased by an eligible postharvest activity business to be used at a fixed location in Florida for postharvest activities. Included within the exemption are all labor charges for the repair of such machinery and equipment, as well as parts and materials used in the repair and incorporated into the machinery and equipment. Purchasers of qualifying machinery and equipment are instructed to continue to provide the seller with a signed certificate certifying the purchaser's entitlement to the exemption, which will relieve the seller of any potential tax liability on the sale. (Tax Information Publication, No. 16A01-07)

Provided the purchaser furnishes the seller with a signed certificate certifying the purchaser's entitlement to this exemption at the time of purchase, the seller is relieved of the responsibility of collecting the tax on such a sale and the department will look only to the purchaser for recovery of the tax if it determines the purchaser was not entitled to the exemption. (Sec. 212.08(7)(jjj), F.S.; *Tax Information Publication No. 13A01-06*, Florida Department of Revenue, June 10, 2013)

The selling dealer (vendor) should obtain a signed certificate from the purchaser certifying the purchaser's entitlement to tax exemption. The signed certificate relieves the selling dealer of any potential tax liability on nonqualifying purchases. The Florida Department of Revenue provides a suggested certificate the selling dealer can have the purchaser complete to document the exempt nature of the sales transaction. (*Tax Information Publication No. 13A01-06*, Florida Department of Revenue, June 10, 2013)

"Eligible manufacturing business" is defined, for these purposes, as any business whose primary business activity at the location where the industrial machinery and equipment is located is within the industries classified under NAICS codes 31, 32, 33, 112511, and 423930. Examples of types of manufacturing establishments represented by the applicable NAICS codes include, but are not limited to, food, apparel, wood, paper, printing, chemical, pharmaceutical, plastic, rubber, metal, transportation, and furniture. (Sec. 212.08(7)(jjj), F.S.; *Tax Information Publication No. 13A01-06*, Florida Department of Revenue, June 10, 2013)

"Primary business activity" is defined as an activity that represents more than 50% of the activities conducted at the location where the industrial machinery and equipment is located. (Sec. 212.08(7)(jjj), F.S.)

"Industrial machinery and equipment" is defined as tangible personal property or other property that has a depreciable life of three years or more and that is used as an integral part in the manufacturing, processing, compounding, or production of tangible personal property for sale. However, a building and its structural components do not come within this definition unless the building or structural component is so closely related to the industrial machinery and equipment that it houses or supports that the building or structural component can be expected to be replaced when the machinery and equipment are replaced. The term includes parts and accessories for industrial machinery and equipment only to the extent that the parts and accessories are purchased prior to the date the machinery and equipment are placed in service. (Sec. 212.08(7)(jjj), F.S.)

Heating and air conditioning systems are not industrial machinery and equipment unless the sole justification for their installation is to meet the requirements of the production process, even though the system may provide incidental comfort to employees or serve, to an insubstantial degree, nonproduction activities. (Sec. 212.08(7)(jjj), F.S.)

Recycling roll off containers purchased by a business whose primary business activity is within the industry classified under NAICS code 423930 and that are used exclusively for business activities within that NAICS code are exempt from sales and use tax. (Sec. 212.08(7)(jjj), F.S.)

Taxable purchases. The sale, rental, use, consumption, or storage of machines, equipment, parts, and accessories used in manufacturing, processing, compounding, producing, mining, or quarrying personal property for sale or for use in furnishing communications, transportation, or public utility services is taxable. (Sec. 212.05(1)(f), F.S.)

Are sales by manufacturers, processors, assemblers, or refiners taxable in Florida?

There are no specific provisions for sales by manufacturers, processors, assemblers, or refiners, so it is presumable that they are taxable as retail sales of tangible personal property.

Are self-produced goods used in manufacturing, processing, assembling, or refining taxable in Florida?

Yes, any manufacture, production, compounding, processing, or fabrication of tangible personal property for a person's own use is taxable on the cost of the product manufactured, produced, compounded, processed, or fabricated, without any deduction for the cost of the materials used, labor or service costs, or transportation charges. (Sec. 212.06(1)(b), F.S.; Rule 12A-1.043(1)(a))

Elements of the cost of a product include materials, labor, service, and transportation costs that are attributable to the manufacturing of the product for one's own use and that are properly chargeable to the cost of the product under generally acceptable cost accounting standards. (Rule 12A-1.043(1)(b))

Material costs include:

— all direct materials and related freight costs that are physically observable as being identified with the finished tangible personal property, that are consumed in producing the property, or that become a component or ingredient of the finished property;

— the material handling and warehousing costs of direct materials and goods in process; and

— manufacturer's excise taxes on materials.

(Rule 12A-1.043(1)(b))

Labor costs include:

— all direct labor costs for employees or contract labor that are allocable to the production of the finished property;

— compensation of officers, to the extent the compensation is allocated to production and not administrative functions; and

— costs of service, engineering, design, or other support employees that are allocated to production (service costs include the costs of non-employee services that are allocated to the production of the tangible personal property).

(Rule 12A-1.043(1)(b))

Tax is due at the time the article of property is manufactured, produced, compounded, processed, or fabricated for use or consumption. (Rule 12A-1.043(1)(e))

In the case of asphalt manufactured for one's own use, the tax will apply only to the cost of materials that are an ingredient or component part of the finished asphalt, and to the cost of transporting these materials. (Sec. 212.06(1)(c), F.S.) In addition, there is an indexed tax per ton of manufactured asphalt.

Contractors who manufacture factory-built buildings for their own use in the performance of contracts for the construction or improvement of real property must pay a tax upon the cost price of items used. (Sec. 212.06(1)(b), F.S.; Sec. 212.02(7), F.S.; Rule 12A-1.043(3))

Are labor and services related to manufacturers, processors, assemblers, or refiners taxable in Florida?

Labor and services, including fabrication, may be taxable or exempt, depending on the circumstances.

Fabrication. The producing, fabricating, processing, printing or imprinting of tangible personal property is taxable. In addition, material that is cut, threaded, shaped, bent, polished, welded, sheared, punched, drilled, machined or in some way has work performed on it which changed its original state is considered to have been fabricated and is taxable. Charges for labor, replacement parts, materials and supplies used by dealers to adjust, apply, alter, install, maintain, remodel or repair tangible personal property belonging to others are fully taxable. The term "sale" includes the producing, fabricating, processing, printing, or imprinting of tangible personal property for a consideration for consumers who furnish the materials used in the fabrication process. (Sec. 212.02(15), F.S.; Rule 12A-1.024)

Fabrication labor incurred at the job site in the performance of repairing, altering, improving, or constructing real property is not subject to tax. (Rule 12A-1.051(5)(f))

¶60-510

Fabrication labor is not taxable for those who use their own equipment and personnel for their own account and act as producer of a qualified motion picture. (Sec. 212.06(1)(b), F.S.; Rule 12A-1.043(2)).

Repairing machinery and equipment. The cost of labor, parts, and materials required for repairing industrial machinery and equipment used in the manufacturing or preparation for shipping of tangible personal property at a fixed location in Florida is exempt. Manufacturers are eligible for the exemption if they are among the following industrial classifications: SIC Industry Major Group Numbers 10, 12-14, 20, 22-35, and 36-39 and Industry Group Number 212. (Sec. 212.08(7)(xx), F.S.)

Are there refunds and/or credit provisions for manufacturers, processors, assemblers, or refiners in Florida?

No, Florida does not currently have sales and use tax provisions specifically concerning refunds and credits for manufacturing, processing, assembling, or refining.

[¶60-520] Medical, Dental, and Optical Supplies and Drugs

Sales of hypodermic needles, syringes, chemical compounds, and test kits used for the diagnosis or treatment of human disease, illness, or injury are exempt from the sales tax. Prosthetic and orthopedic appliances are exempt when dispensed according to an individual prescription written by a licensed physician or according to a list prescribed and approved by the Department of Business and Professional Regulation, which is included in the sales and use tax rules. The list includes artificial eyes and limbs, orthopedic shoes, prescription eyeglasses, incidental items, dentures, hearing aids, crutches, and prosthetic and orthopedic appliances. Cosmetics and toilet articles are nonexempt, even though they may contain medicinal ingredients. (Sec. 212.08(2), F.S.; Rule 12A-1.020; Rule 12A-1.021)

Medical products and supplies used in the cure, mitigation, alleviation, prevention, or treatment of injury, illness, disease, or incapacity are taxable unless they are:

— temporarily or permanently incorporated into the patient by a practitioner of the healing arts;

— ordered and dispensed by or on the prescription of a licensed practitioner; or

— ordered and dispensed by a pharmacist.

(Sec. 212.08(2), F.S.; Rule 12A-1.020)

The sale of medical products or supplies to physicians, dentists, veterinarians and hospitals is taxable even though the medical products or supplies may be used in connection with medical treatment, unless the products and supplies are specifically exempt from tax under either Rule 12A-1.020 or Rule 12A-1.021. (Rule 12A-1.020)

Guide dogs for the blind and the sale of food and other items for the dogs are exempt. (Sec. 212.08(7), F.S.; Rule 12A-1.001(3))

Any items intended for one-time use that transfer essential optical characteristics to contact lenses are exempt. The exemption applies after $100,000 of the tax imposed on such items has been paid in any calendar year by the taxpayer who claims the exemption. (Sec. 212.08(2), F.S.)

•*Drugs*

Products, supplies, or medicines dispensed according to a prescription in a retail establishment by a pharmacist licensed in Florida are exempt from sales and use tax. Sales of drugs to or by physicians, dentists, veterinarians, and hospitals in connection with medical treatment are also exempt. (Sec. 212.08(2), F.S.; Rule 12A-1.001(4); Rule 12A-1.020)

The term "prescription" includes any order written or transmitted by a practitioner licensed to practice in a jurisdiction other than Florida, but only if the pharmacist dispensing the order determines that the order is valid and necessary for the treatment of a chronic or recurrent illness. (Sec. 212.08(2), F.S.; Rule 12A-1.020)

Medicines dispensed or administered directly to a patient by a practitioner of the healing arts licensed by Florida or a nurse, intern practitioner, or veterinary technician under the practitioner's supervision are exempt. Any medicines dispensed or administered to a patient by a hospital or institution licensed by Florida for use by or in the institution are also exempt. (Rule 12A-1.020)

Because a veterinarian is a practitioner of the healing arts, medicine, antiseptics, cotton, gauze, lotions, vitamins, and worm remedies used by a veterinarian to treat animals are exempt. (Sec. 212.08(2), F.S.)

Common household remedies recommended and generally sold for internal or external use in the cure, mitigation, treatment, or prevention of illness or disease are exempt if included on a list prescribed and approved by the Department of Health and Rehabilitative Services. (Sec. 212.08(2),F.S.; Rule 12A-1.020)

• *Health care facilities*

Meals provided to patients and inmates of any hospital or other facility for the care of the ill, aged, infirm, mentally or physically incapacitated, or those otherwise dependent on special care are exempt from the sales and use tax. The lease, rental and license to use rooms exclusively as dwelling units by patients in hospitals and other qualifying health care facilities are also exempt from tax. (Sec. 212.08(7), F.S.; Sec. 212.031(1)(a)2, F.S.; Rule 12A-1.001)

Admissions to physical fitness facilities owned or operated by a hospital are not taxed. (Sec. 212.02(1), F.S.)

• *Independent living items*

Effective January 1, 2022, a sales and use tax exemption applies to the following items when purchased for noncommercial home or personal use:

- bed transfer handles selling for $60 or less;
- bed rails selling for $110 or less;
- grab bars selling for $100 or less; and
- shower seats selling for $100 or less.

(Sec. 212.08(5)(u), F.S.; *Tax Information Publication, No. 21A01-11*, Florida Department of Revenue, October 18, 2021)

The exemption does not apply to purchases made by a business, including but not limited to:

- a medical institution; or
- an assisted living facility.

(Sec. 212.08(5)(u), F.S.; *Tax Information Publication, No. 21A01-11*, Florida Department of Revenue, October 18, 2021)

• *Medical marijuana and marijuana delivery devices*

Marijuana and marijuana delivery devices are exempt from Florida sales and use tax. "Marijuana" is defined as all parts of any plant of the genus Cannabis, whether growing or not, the seeds of that, the resin extracted from any part of the plant, and every compound, manufacture, salt, derivative, mixture, or preparation of the plant or its seeds or resin, including low-THC cannabis, that is dispensed from a medical marijuana treatment center for medical use by a qualified patient. A "marijuana delivery device" is an object used, intended for use, or designed for use in preparing, storing, ingesting, inhaling, or otherwise introducing marijuana into the human body that is dispensed from a medical marijuana treatment center for medical use by a qualified patient. (Sec. 212.08(2)(l), F.S.)

• *Menstrual products*

Effective January 1, 2018, products used to absorb menstrual flow are exempt from sales and use tax. "Products used to absorb menstrual flow" include tampons, sanitary napkins, pantiliners, and menstrual cups. (Sec. 212.08(7)(ooo), F.S.; *Tax Information Publication, No. 17A01-15*, Florida Department of Revenue, November 9, 2017)

• *Practitioners of the healing arts*

Fees for the professional services of a practitioner of the healing arts are exempt. Practitioners are taxed as the consumers of taxable tangible personal property purchased by them for use in rendering their services, and are required to register as dealers if they sell tangible personal property subject to tax. (Sec. 212.08(2), F.S.)

• *Therapeutic veterinary diets*

Sales of therapeutic veterinary diets, defined as those animal foods that are specifically formulated to aid in the management of illness and disease of a diagnosed health disorder in an animal that are only available from a licensed veterinarian, are exempt from sales and use tax. (Sec. 212.08(2), F.S.)

The Florida Department of Revenue provides examples of such therapeutic veterinary diets:

— A cat food is marketed as specifically formulated to manage bladder health in cats, and it is only available through a licensed veterinarian. This cat food is exempt as a therapeutic veterinary diet because it is specifically formulated to aid in the management of bladder health in cats and is sold only through a licensed veterinarian.

— A dog food is marketed as specifically formulated for dogs over 10 years of age, and it is available through various retailers and licensed veterinarians. This dog food is subject to sales and use tax because it is not available exclusively from licensed veterinarians, and it is not an exempt therapeutic veterinary diet.

(*Tax Information Publication, No. 15A01-02*, Florida Department of Revenue, February 6, 2015)

Sales of the following animal foods are exempt:

— those that are required by state or federal law to be dispensed only by a prescription (this applies to animal foods that are required to carry a label that states: "Caution: Federal law restricts this drug to sale by or on the order of a licensed veterinarian");

— feed for poultry, ostriches, livestock, racehorses, and dairy cows; and

— food for guide dogs for the blind (i.e., seeing-eye dogs).

(Sec. 212.08, F.S.; *Tax Information Publication, No. 15A01-02*, Florida Department of Revenue, February 6, 2015)

• *Veterinarians*

See ¶ 60-665 Services.

[¶60-560] Motor Fuels

Motor fuel and diesel fuel, unless used by railroad locomotives or vessels to transport persons or property in interstate or foreign commerce, are not taxed under the Sales and Use Tax law (Ch. 212, Tax on Sales, Use, and Other Transactions) but are taxed under the Motor and Other Fuel Tax provisions in Ch. 206.

Fuel other than motor fuel and diesel fuel is subject to sales and use tax with the exception of fuel that is expressly exempt. (Sec. 212.08(4)(a)(2), F.S.)

Dyed diesel fuel exemption.—Dyed diesel fuel used in vessels for commercial fishing and aquacultural purposes is exempt from sales and use tax. (Sec. 212.05(1)(k), F.S.; Sec. 212.0501(4), F.S.; Sec. 212.08(4)(a), F.S.)

The exemption is applicable to sales of dyed diesel fuel placed into the storage tank of boats, vessels, or equipment used exclusively for the taking of fish, crayfish, oysters, shrimp, or sponges from Florida salt or fresh waters for resale to the public. To qualify for this exemption, the purchaser must provide the seller with a certificate at the time of purchase stating that the dyed diesel fuel placed into the storage tank of the vessel or equipment will be used exclusively for commercial fishing and for aquacultural purposes. *Tax Information Publication No. 13A01-09R* provides a suggested certificate to be completed by the purchaser and maintained in the vendor's books and records. The exemption is inapplicable to dyed diesel fuel used for sport or pleasure fishing. In addition, dyed diesel fuel should never be used in a vehicle driven or operated on Florida highways unless authorized, as provided. (*Tax Information Publication No. 13A01-09R*, Florida Department of Revenue, December 20, 2013, 205-895)

• *Aviation gasoline*

Aviation gasoline that has an octane rating greater than 75 or a lead content greater than .05 grams per gallon (i.e., D-910) is subject to motor fuels tax under Ch. 206 or sales tax under Ch. 212. The applicable tax treatment is determined by the type of sale and the end use of the aviation gasoline. (Sec. 206.41, F.S.; Sec. 206.9825, F.S.; Sec. 212.05, F.S.; *Tax Information Publication, No. 12B05-04*, Florida Department of Revenue, August 10, 2012)

Terminal suppliers.—Tax treatment is as follows:

— On sales to wholesalers, a terminal supplier will collect aviation fuel tax of 6.9 cents (4.27 cents effective July 1, 2019) per gallon.

— On sales to fixed base operators (FBOs), a terminal supplier will get written certification from the FBO that shows the number of gallons purchased for use in an aircraft and for use other than in an aircraft. A terminal supplier will collect aviation fuel tax of 6.9 cents per gallon on fuel identified for use in an aircraft. If any of the aviation gasoline is not purchased for use in an aircraft, it should be taxed as a sale of tangible personal property under Ch. 212 at the sales and use tax rate of 6% plus any applicable discretionary sales surtax. If the FBO underestimates the tax liability on the use of the fuel, the FBO must notify and pay any additional tax to the supplier.

— On sales to retail dealers, a terminal supplier will collect sales and use tax of 6% plus any applicable discretionary sales surtax.

— On sales directly to end users, a terminal supplier will collect sales and use tax of 6% plus any applicable discretionary sales surtax, unless the fuel is for use in an aircraft. If the fuel is for use in an aircraft, the end user must pay the terminal supplier aviation fuel tax of 6.9 cents (4.27 cents effective July 1, 2019) per gallon, if it provides the terminal supplier with a signed affidavit.

(Sec. 206.41, F.S.; Sec. 206.9825, F.S.; Sec. 212.05, F.S.; *Tax Information Publication, No. 12B05-04*, Florida Department of Revenue, August 10, 2012)

Wholesalers.—Tax treatment is as follows:

— On sales to FBOs, a wholesaler will get written certification from the FBO that indicates the number of gallons purchased for use in an aircraft and for use other than in an aircraft. A wholesaler will collect aviation fuel tax of 6.9 cents (4.27 cents effective July 1, 2019) per gallon on the fuel identified for use in an aircraft. Any aviation gasoline that is not purchased for use in an aircraft should be taxed as a sale of tangible personal property under Ch. 212 at the sales and use tax rate of 6% plus any applicable discretionary sales surtax. Should the FBO underestimate the tax liability on the use of the fuel, the FBO must notify and pay any additional tax to the wholesaler.

— On sales to retail dealers, a wholesaler will collect sales and use tax of 6% plus any applicable discretionary sales surtax.

— On sales directly to end users, a wholesaler will collect sales and use tax of 6% plus any applicable discretionary sales surtax unless the fuel is for use in an aircraft, in which case the end user is required to pay the wholesaler aviation fuel tax of 6.9 cents (4.27 cents effective July 1, 2019) per gallon if it provides the wholesaler with a signed affidavit.

(Sec. 206.41, F.S.; Sec. 206.9825, F.S.; Sec. 212.05, F.S.; *Tax Information Publication, No. 12B05-04*, Florida Department of Revenue, August 10, 2012)

A wholesaler may take an ultimate vendor credit on its return for the 6.9 cents (4.27 cents effective July 1, 2019) motor fuels tax paid to its supplier on aviation gasoline if the fuel is sold for use other than in an aircraft. If the fuel is sold for use in a motor vehicle, the wholesaler will collect the applicable motor fuel tax under Ch. 206. If the aviation fuel is sold for use other than in an aircraft but not for use in a motor vehicle, the wholesaler will collect 6% sales and use tax plus any applicable discretionary sales surtax. (Sec. 206.41, F.S.; Sec. 206.9825, F.S.; Sec. 212.05, F.S.; *Tax Information Publication, No. 12B05-04*, Florida Department of Revenue, August 10, 2012)

Fixed base operators (FBOs).—Tax treatment is as follows:

— On sales to licensed air carriers, FBOs will collect aviation fuel tax of 6.9 cents (4.27 cents effective July 1, 2019) per gallon. Air carriers are not required to provide an affidavit and tail-wing numbers.

— On sales directly to end users, FBOs will collect sales and use tax of 6% plus any applicable discretionary sales surtax unless the fuel is for use in an aircraft, in which case the end user must pay the FBO aviation fuel tax of 6.9 cents (4.27 cents effective July 1, 2019) per gallon and provide the FBO with a signed affidavit.

(Sec. 206.41, F.S.; Sec. 206.9825, F.S.; Sec. 212.05, F.S.; *Tax Information Publication, No. 12B05-04*, Florida Department of Revenue, August 10, 2012)

Blenders.—Blenders who purchase aviation gasoline for use other than in a motor vehicle will pay 6% sales and use tax plus any applicable discretionary sales surtax on the cost price of the fuel to its supplier. A blender who purchases aviation gasoline for sale must be licensed as a wholesaler. (Sec. 206.41, F.S.; Sec. 206.9825, F.S.; Sec. 212.05, F.S.; *Tax Information Publication, No. 12B05-04*, Florida Department of Revenue, August 10, 2012)

Retail dealers.—On all sales of aviation gasoline, retailers will collect 6% sales and use tax plus any applicable discretionary sales surtax. End users that purchase aviation gasoline from a retail dealer for use in an aircraft may apply to the Florida Department of Revenue for a refund of the sales and use tax and discretionary sales surtax paid. The 6.9 cents (4.27 cents effective July 1, 2019) per gallon aviation fuel tax will be deducted from the refund. No refund will be granted unless the purchase submits a signed affidavit and an invoice that indicates that sales and use tax was paid on the aviation fuel. Sec. 206.41, F.S.; Sec. 206.9825, F.S.; Sec. 212.05, F.S.; *Tax Information Publication, No. 12B05-04*, Florida Department of Revenue, August 10, 2012)

Affidavit requirements.—Affidavits must include the following information:

— the purchaser's name;

— the purchaser's address;

— a statement that the fuel will be or was used in an aircraft; and

— the tail-wing number of the aircraft the fuel will be or was placed in for use.

(*Tax Information Publication, No. 12B05-04*, Florida Department of Revenue, August 10, 2012)

• *Sales tax on fuel used by railroad locomotives and certain vessels*

Sales tax does apply to motor fuel and diesel fuel used by railroad locomotives and vessels that transport persons or property in interstate or foreign commerce. The tax is based on the ratio of intrastate mileage to interstate or foreign mileage traveled by those of the carrier's railroad locomotives or vessels that were used in Florida during the previous fiscal year, as well as in interstate or foreign commerce. Fuel used exclusively in intrastate commerce does not qualify for proration. (Sec. 212.08(4), F.S.; Rule 12A-1.064)

• *Fuel sales tax on motor fuel and diesel fuel*

The motor fuel tax provisions of Ch. 206 incorporate a fuel sales tax that is imposed on each net gallon of motor fuel and diesel fuel. This tax is imposed for the privilege of selling such fuel. The Florida Department of Revenue establishes the annual tax rate but the rate cannot be lower than 6.9 cents per gallon. (Sec. 206.41(1)(g), F.S.; Sec. 206.87(1)(e), F.S.)

To receive a refund of the fuel sales taxes paid on gasoline and gasohol used in any tractor, farm vehicle, citrus harvesting equipment, citrus fruit loaders, or other equipment that is used exclusively on a farm for planting, cultivating, harvesting, or processing farm products for sale, taxpayers holding a *Fuel Tax Refund Permit* must file an *Application for Fuel Tax Refund—Agricultural, Aquacultural, Commercial Fishing, and Commercial Aviation Purposes (Form DR-138)*, with the Florida Department of Revenue no later than the last day of the month following the quarter for which the refund is claimed. (Sec. 206.41, F.S.; *Tax Information Publication, No. 12B05-03*, Florida Department of Revenue, June 29, 2012)

• *Use tax on diesel fuel*

A use tax is imposed on diesel fuel purchased for consumption, use, or storage by a trade or business. The tax is imposed at the rate of 6% of the total cost price of the diesel fuel consumed. Diesel fuel subject to the motor and diesel fuel taxes will be exempt from the use tax. Also exempt will be diesel fuel used for residential purposes, diesel fuel purchased or stored for resale, and liquefied petroleum gas or other fuel used exclusively to heat a structure in which started pullets or broilers are raised. The purchaser or ultimate consumer will be liable for paying the use tax due directly to the state. In addition, the storage, use, or consumption of diesel fuel used in any tractor, vehicle, or other equipment used exclusively on a farm or for processing farm products on the farm is exempt from use tax as long as no part of the fuel is used in any licensed motor vehicle on the public highways of Florida. (Sec. 212.0501, F.S.; Rule 12A-1.059)

• *Fuels used by a public or private utility*

All fuels used by a public or private utility, including any municipal corporation or rural electric cooperative association, in the generation of electric power or energy for sale are exempt from sales and use tax. (Sec. 212.08(4)(a)(2), F.S.)

• *Fuel used for certain agricultural purposes*

Butane gas, propane gas, natural gas, and all other forms of liquefied petroleum gases are exempt from sales and use tax provided:

— the fuel is used in any tractor, vehicle, or other farm equipment that is used exclusively on a farm or for processing farm products on the farm; and

— no part of the gas is used in any vehicle or equipment driven or operated on state public highways (this restriction is inapplicable to the movement of farm vehicles or farm equipment between farms).

(Sec. 212.08(5)(e), F.S.)

Transporting bees by water and the operation of equipment used in the apiary of a beekeeper is also exempt. (Sec. 212.08(5)(e), F.S.)

• *Boiler fuels*

When purchased for use as a combustible fuel, purchases of natural gas, residual oil, recycled oil, waste oil, solid waste material, coal, sulfur, wood, wood residues, or wood bark used in an industrial manufacturing, processing, compounding, or production process at a fixed location in Florida are exempt from sales and use tax. This exemption is not allowed unless the purchaser signs a certificate that states that the fuel to be exempted is for the exclusive use outlined above. Also, the exemption is inapplicable to the use of boiler fuels that are not used in manufacturing, processing, compounding, or producing items of tangible personal property for sale, or to the use of boiler fuels used by any firm subject to regulation by the Division of Hotels and Restaurants of the Department of Business and Professional Regulation. (Sec. 212.08(7)(b), F.S.)

• *Household fuels*

The following sales to residential households or owners of residential models are exempt from sales and use tax:

— sales of utilities by utility companies who pay the gross receipts tax imposed under Sec. 203.01; and

— sales of fuel, including oil, kerosene, liquefied petroleum gas, coal, wood, and other fuel products used in the household or residential model for heating, cooking, lighting, and refrigeration.

(Sec. 212.08(7)(j), F.S.)

The exemption is applicable regardless of whether such sales of utilities or fuels are separately metered and billed directly to the residents or to the landlord. If any part of the utility or fuel is used for a nonexempt purpose, the entire sale is taxable. The landlord is required to provide a separate meter for nonexempt utility or fuel consumption. In addition, licensed family day care homes are also exempt. (Sec. 212.08(7)(j), F.S.)

[¶60-570] Motor Vehicles

All retail sales, including occasional or isolated sales, in Florida of motor vehicles required to be registered, licensed, titled, or documented are subject to tax. No title or registration certificate may be issued for a motor vehicle unless the sales tax has been paid. (Sec. 212.02(2), F.S.; 212.05(1)(a), F.S.; Sec. 212.06(10), F.S.; Rule 12A-1.007(1)(a) and (c), F.A.C.)

The Florida Department of Revenue provides guidance on the application of sales and use taxes to motor vehicles. Topics discussed include trade-in allowances, discretaionary sales surtax, and credit for taxes paid in another state. (*GT-800030, Sales and Use Tax on Motor Vehicles*, Florida Department of Revenue, July 2016)

When a manufacturer replaces a motor vehicle under the "Lemon Law," tax is due on the amount of reasonable offset for use paid by the consumer. When the manufacturer repurchases a motor vehicle, the Department of Revenue will refund to the manufacturer the amount of tax that the manufacturer refunded to the consumer. (Rule 12A-1.007(23), F.A.C.)

When a veteran buys a motor vehicle, no tax is due on the portion of the sales price paid directly to the dealer by the Veterans Administration. (Sec. 212.07(ss), F.S.; Rule 12A-1.007(4), F.A.C.)

The transfer of an ownership interest in a motor vehicle is taxable. (Rule 12A-1.007(25)(d), F.A.C.)

The lease or rental of parking or storage space for a motor vehicle is taxable (Sec. 212.02(2), F.S.; 212.03(6), F.S.; Rules 12A-1.070, F.A.C.; 12A-1.073, F.A.C.)

• *Accessible taxicabs for the transportation of the disabled*

An exemption is available for the sale or lease of an "accessible taxicab," defined as a chauffeur-driven taxi, limousine, sedan, van, or other passenger vehicle for which an operator is hired to use for the transportation of persons for compensation that:

— transports eight passengers or less;

— is equipped with a lift or ramp that is specifically designed to transport physically disabled persons or contains any other device designed to permit access to, and enable the transportation of, physically disabled persons, including those who use wheelchairs, motorized wheelchairs, or similar mobility aids;

— complies with the accessibility requirements of the Americans with Disabilities Act of 1990, regardless of whether such requirements would apply under federal law; and

— meets all applicable federal motor vehicle safety standards and regulations adopted under that act.

(Sec. 212.08(7)(iii), F.S.)

If the lift or ramp or any other device is installed through an aftermarket conversion of a stock vehicle, only the value of the conversion is exempt. The motor vehicle itself is taxable. (Sec. 212.08(7)(iii), F.S.; *Tax Information Publication, No. 12A01-11*, Florida Department of Revenue, June 8, 2012)

To be entitled to this exemption, the purchaser must present to the seller, and the seller must retain in its records, a blanket certificate of exemption that indicates in the "other" field that the purchaser is purchasing an accessible taxicab or any aftermarket conversion of a stock motor vehicle for use, as provided. (*Tax Information Publication, No. 12A01-11*, Florida Department of Revenue, June 8, 2012)

• *Car rentals*

The rental or lease or any vehicle used or stored in Florida is taxable without regard to its prior use or tax paid on the purchase outside Florida. (Sec. 212.05(1)(c), F.S.; Rule 12A-1.007(13)(a), F.A.C.)

When a motor vehicle is leased or rented for a period of less than twelve months, the entire amount is taxable if the vehicle is rented in Florida, even if it is dropped off in another state. However, if the vehicle is rented in another state and dropped off in Florida, it is exempt from Florida tax. (Sec. 212.05(1)(c), F.S.; Rule 12A-1.007(13)(e), F.A.C.)

With a resale certificate, a motor vehicle may be purchased exempt from tax for exclusive use as a rental vehicle. (Rule 12A-1.007(13)(b), F.A.C.)

The first lessee of a commercial motor vehicle that is self-propelled or towed and used on the public highways in commerce to transport people or cargo and that has a gross weight of 10,000 pounds or more is exempt from tax when the term of the lease is for a period of 12 months or more and the owner paid tax on the acquisition of the vehicle. (Sec. 212.05(1)(c), F.S.; Rule 12A-1.007(13)(b), F.A.C.)

The sale, lease, or rental of a motor vehicle registered in Florida is exempt from tax if the transaction occurs between two commonly owned and controlled corporations and if the sales tax was paid at the time of acquisition. (Sec. 212.08(7)(aa), F.S.; Rule 12A-1.007(25)(f), F.A.C.)

Fuel charges for rental vehicles are exempt if a tax has already been paid and the charge is separately stated. (Rule 12A-1.007(13)(g)).

• *Dealers*

Motor vehicle dealers that are required to purchase dealer license plates must pay an annual use tax of $27 for each plate purchased in addition to the license tax imposed. No additional tax will be imposed for the use of a dealer license plate for which use tax has been paid. (Sec. 212.0601, F.S.; Rule 12A-1.007(8)(b), F.A.C.)

The following events are taxable:

— a motor vehicle dealer assigns a motor vehicle to a person other than an employee or officer;

— a motor vehicle dealer purchases under a resale certificate a new motor vehicle of a type that it does not ordinarily sell and uses the vehicle for any purpose other than demonstration or display;

— a motor vehicle is capitalized in a fixed asset account and depreciated for income tax purposes, unless it is held exclusively for leasing;

— a motor vehicle manufacturer, distributor, dealer, or lessor retains title to a motor vehicle, but registers it purchased for resale in another name; and

— a rental car agency sells a motor vehicle.

(Rule 12A-1.007(8), F.A.C.)

No tax is due on a motor vehicle titled in the dealer's name that is used exclusively in a high school driver education and safety program. (Rule 12A-1.007(8)(g), F.A.C.)

A motor vehicle dealer who loans a vehicle to any person at no charge accrues use tax based on the annual lease value as determined by the IRS's Automobile Annual Lease Value Table. However, no sales or use tax and no rental car surcharge accrues to the use of a motor vehicle provided at no charge to a person whose own vehicle is being repaired, adjusted or serviced by the entity providing the replacement vehicle. (Sec. 212.0601, F.S.)

• *Exempt transfers of title*

The following transfers of title of a motor vehicle are exempt from sales tax:

— a transfer to an insurance company as part of the settlement of a claim (Rule 12A-1.007(12), F.A.C.) ;

— the repossession of a motor vehicle by a seller or lienholder (Rule 12A-1.007(15), F.A.C.);

— a transfer of a motor vehicle held in trust for a minor to the real owner when there is no consideration (Rule 12A-1.007(25)(a), F.A.C.) ;

— a gift accompanied by a sworn statement describing the motor vehicle and stating that there are no outstanding liens (Rule 12A-1.007(25)(a), F.A.C.) ;

— a transfer by a partnership to a partner as part of the liquidation of the partnership (Rule 12A-1.007(25)(a), F.A.C.);

— a transfer by a dissolved corporation to one of its stockholders as part of the stockholder's ratable portion of the assets of the corporation (Rule 12A-1.007(25)(a), F.A.C.);

— a transfer to a surviving corporation in a reorganization or merger (Rule 12A-1.007(25)(a), F.A.C.);

— a distribution to the heirs of an estate (Rule 12A-1.007(25)(a), F.A.C.) ;

— a transfer between spouses of marital property (Rule 12A-1.007(25)(a), F.A.C.) ;

— a transfer between former spouses as part of the property settlement in a divorce (Rule 12A-1.007(25)(a)(8), F.A.C.) ; and

— an even trade or trade down of a motor vehicle for another registered vehicle accompanied by a sworn statement describing both vehicles. (Rule 12A-1.007(25)(a)(9), F.A.C.)

• *Interstate transactions*

Imported and exported vehicles, as well as interstate commerce, are discussed.

Exported vehicles.—When the purchaser of a motor vehicle gives the dealer a notarized statement stating that the car will be registered in another state within 45 days of the purchase, the dealer will collect tax at the rate imposed in the state in which the vehicle will be registered or the Florida rate, whichever is less. (Sec. 212.08(10), F.S.; Rule 12A-1.007(8)(a), F.A.C.)

However, a vehicle is subject to tax at the Florida state rate when the vehicle is purchased by a nonresident corporation or partnership and:

— an officer of the corporation is a Florida resident;

— a stockholder of the corporation who owns at least 10% of the corporation is a Florida resident; or

— a partner in the partnership who has at least 10% ownership is a Florida resident.

(Sec. 212.08(10), F.S.)

However, if the vehicle is removed from the state within 45 days of the purchase and remains outside the state for at least 180 days, the vehicle may qualify for the partial exemption. (Sec. 212.08(10), F.S.)

A seller of a motor vehicle to a nonregistered out-of-state dealer must either collect the sales tax or obtain a notarized statement from the out-of-state dealer stating that the mobile home is being purchased for resale, and for no other purpose. No sales tax is due on a sale to an out-of-state purchaser that accepts delivery outside of Florida as long as the seller obtains a notarized statement to that effect. (Rule 12A-1.007(6), F.A.C.)

Imported vehicles. —A motor vehicle purchased in another state but registered, licensed, or titled in Florida is presumed to be taxable unless the person owning the vehicle purchased the vehicle six months or more prior to bringing it into Florida. (Rule 12A-1.007(2)(a), F.A.C.)

A motor vehicle imported from another country for use, consumption, distribution, or storage is taxable regardless of the length of time it was owned out of the country. (Rule 12A-1.007(2)(a), F.A.C.)

A credit is allowed for sales tax paid in another state, but not for taxes paid in another country. (Rule 12A-1.007(3), F.A.C.)

Interstate commerce.—Sales of motor vehicles that are licensed as common carriers and that are used in interstate or foreign commerce and parts for the vehicles are taxed on the Florida portion of use based on a ratio of Florida mileage to total mileage for the year. Parts of a motor vehicle include a separate tank not connected to the fuel supply system of the motor vehicle into which diesel fuel is placed to operate a refrigeration unit or other equipment. (Sec. 212.08(9)(b), F.S.)

Motor vehicle sales tax rates by state as of December 29, 2021.—The Florida Department of Revenue provides motor vehicle sales tax rates by state as of December 29, 2021. Florida law allows a partial sales and use tax exemption on a motor vehicle purchased by a resident of another state. The amount of Florida sales tax to be collected is the amount of sales tax that would be imposed by the purchaser's home state if the vehicle were purchased in that state. If the rate imposed in the purchaser's home state is greater than 6%, the rate of Florida tax to be collected is 6%. The tax collected is Florida tax and must be paid to the Florida Department of Revenue.(*Tax Information Publication, No. 21A01-13*, Florida Department of Revenue, December 29, 2021)

Motor vehicles sold in Florida to residents of another state.—Florida law provides a partial exemption for a motor vehicle purchased by a resident of another state. The tax imposed is the amount of sales tax that would be imposed by the purchaser's home state if the vehicle were purchased in that state; however, the tax imposed cannot exceed the Florida 6% tax rate. A nonresident purchaser is required at the time of sale to complete *Form DR-123, Affidavit for Partial Exemption of Motor Vehicle Sold for Licensing in Another State*, declaring the nonresident purchaser's intent to license the vehicle in his or her home state within 45 days of the purchase date. If the nonresident purchaser licenses the motor vehicle in his or her home state within 45 days from the date of purchase, there is no requirement that the motor vehicle be removed from Florida. (Sec. 212.08(10), F.S.; *Tax Information Publication, No. 19A01-13*, Florida Department of Revenue, December 31, 2019)

Motor vehicles purchased in another state and brought into Florida.—Florida use tax of 6% generally applies to motor vehicles purchased in another state, territory of the U.S., or the District of Columbia, and subsequently titled, registered, or licensed in Florida. Florida law provides a credit to be given on motor vehicles brought into Florida where a like tax has been lawfully imposed and paid in another state, territory of the U.S., or the District of Columbia. Credit against Florida use tax and any discretionary sales surtax is provided for a like tax paid in another state, whether the tax has been paid to that state, or to a county or city (local taxes) within that state. If the amount paid is equal to or greater than the amount imposed by Florida, no additional tax is due, and if the amount is less than the amount imposed by Florida, only the difference between the two is due. Also, Florida law provides a presumption that motor vehicles used in another state, territory of the U.S., or the District of Columbia for six months or longer before being brought into Florida were not purchased for use in Florida. No Florida use tax is due if documentary proof establishes such prior use. (Sec. 212.06(7) and (8), F.S.; *Tax Information Publication, No. 19A01-13*, Florida Department of Revenue, December 31, 2019)

• *Lemon law fee*

Every person who sells or leases a new motor vehicle in Florida must collect a two dollar motor vehicle warranty ("lemon law") fee from the purchaser or lessee of the vehicle. The fee must be collected at the time of sale or entry into a lease agreement and remitted to the county tax collector or private tag agency acting as agent for the Department of Revenue. The fee must be sent directly to the Department when the purchaser or lessee removes the vehicle from the state and titles or registers it in another state. (Sec. 681.117, F.S.; *Tax Information Publication, No. 02A01-06*, Florida Department of Revenue, June 25, 2002)

• *Local taxes*

Motor vehicle sales are subject to local option taxes and discretionary surtaxes. For purposes of the local taxes, the sale of a motor vehicle is presumed to have occurred in the county identified as the residence address of the purchaser on the registration or title document. (Sec. 212.054(3)(a), F.S.)

• *Motor vehicle child restraint*

The sale of a child restraint system or booster seat for use in a motor vehicle is exempt from sales and use tax. (Sec. 212.08(7)(lll), F.S.)

Separately sold components or accessories are subject to tax. The Florida Department of Revenue provides an example: A customer purchases a travel system stroller that includes a stroller, an infant car seat, and an infant car seat base. At the same time, the customer purchases a car seat mirror, so that the driver will be able to see the child while driving. The infant car seat and car seat base are designed and approved to be used in a motor vehicle as a child restraint system. The sale of the travel system is exempt but the sale of the optional mirror is subject to sales tax. (*Tax Information Publication, No. 14A01-05*, Florida Department of Revenue, May 23, 2014)

• *Motor vehicles as secondhand goods*

Motor vehicle dealers are not considered secondhand dealers, and are therefore not required to comply with the requirements imposed on secondhand dealers. (Rule 12A-17.003, F.A.C.)

• *Motor vehicles imported from foreign country by active armed forces personnel*

The importation of a motor vehicle purchased and used for six months or more in a foreign country by an active member of the United States Armed Forces or his or her spouse is exempt from sales and use tax when the vehicle is imported, registered, or titled in Florida for personal use by the member or his or her spouse. Proof of the active status of the member, and, when applicable, proof of the spouse's relationship to the member, must be provided when the vehicle is titled and registered in Florida. (Sec. 212.08(7)(nnn), F.S.; *Tax Information Publication, No. 15A01-14*, Florida Department of Revenue, June 26, 2015)

• *Off-highway vehicles*

All off-highway vehicles, including two-rider ATV's, are taxable at the state rate plus any applicable discretionary sales surtax. However, effective July 1, 2005, off-highway vehicles that are to be used exclusively on a farm or in a forest for agricultural production of plants and animals useful to humans, including the preparation, planting, cultivating, or harvesting of these products or any other practices necessary to accomplish production through the harvest phase, are exempt from tax (they were previously subject to tax at a rate of 2.5%). To qualify for this exemption, the purchaser must furnish the seller with a written statement certifying that the vehicle is for this use only and will not be used for any other purpose. (*Tax Information Publication, No. 05A01-04*, Florida Department of Revenue, June 23, 2005; *Tax Information Publication, No. 02A01-11*, Florida Department of Revenue, August 8, 2002)

An "off-highway vehicle" is any all-terrain vehicle (ATV) or off-highway motorcycle (OHM) that is used off the roads or highways for recreational purposes and that is not registered and licensed for highway use. An "ATV" is any motorized off-highway or all-terrain vehicle that (1) is 50 inches or less in width, (2) has a dry weight of 900 pounds or less, (3) is designed to travel on three or more low-pressure tires, (4) has a seat designed to be straddled by the operator and handlebars for steering control, and (5) is intended for use by a single operator and with no passenger. A "two-rider ATV" is any ATV that is specifically designed by the manufacturer for a single operator and one passenger. An "OHM" is any motor vehicle used off the roads or highways that has a seat or saddle for the use of the rider and that is designed to travel with not more than two wheels in contact with the ground, but excludes a tractor or a moped. (*Tax Information Publication, No. 05A01-04*,

Florida Department of Revenue, June 23, 2005; *Tax Information Publication, No. 02A01-11*, Florida Department of Revenue, August 8, 2002)

Sales of off-highway vehicles between individuals are subject to tax at the time the title is transferred because all off-highway vehicles must be titled in the state if they are purchased by a Florida resident on or after July 1, 2002, or if they were purchased by a Florida resident before July 1, 2002, and are operated on unrestricted public lands in the state. Sales by dealers also are taxable. (*Tax Information Publication, No. 05A01-04*, Florida Department of Revenue, June 23, 2005; *Tax Information Publication, No. 02A01-11*, Florida Department of Revenue, August 8, 2002)

• *Rental car surcharge*

A taxable surcharge of $2 per day or any part of a day is imposed upon the lease or rental of a motor vehicle licensed for hire and designed to carry fewer than nine passengers regardless of whether such motor vehicle is licensed in Florida. The surcharge applies only to the first 30 days of the term of any lease or rental. (Sec. 212.0606, F.S.; Rule 12A-16.002, F.A.C.; *Tax Information Publication No. 14A01-10*, Florida Department of Revenue, November 5, 2014)

A member of a car-sharing service who uses a motor vehicle for less than 24 hours under an agreement with a car-sharing service is required to pay a Florida surcharge of $1 per usage. A member of a car-sharing service who uses the same motor vehicle for 24 hours or more must pay a surcharge of $2 per day or any part of a day, as provided. (Sec. 212.0606, F.S.; *Tax Information Publication No. 14A01-10*, Florida Department of Revenue, November 5, 2014)

A "car-sharing service" is defined as a membership-based organization or business, or a division of either, that requires the payment of an application or membership fee and provides member access to motor vehicles:

— only at locations that are not staffed by car-sharing service personnel employed solely for the purpose of interacting with car-sharing service members;

— 24 hours a day, seven days a week;

— only through automated means, including but not limited to smartphone applications or electronic membership cards;

— on an hourly basis or for a shorter increment of time;

— without a separate fee for refueling the motor vehicle;

— without a separate fee for minimum financial responsibility liability insurance; and

— owned or controlled by the car-sharing service or its affiliates.

(Sec. 212.0606, F.S.)

This surcharge is inapplicable to the lease, rental, or use of a motor vehicle from a location owned, operated, or leased by or for the benefit of an airport or airport authority. (Sec. 212.0606, F.S.)

Automobile dealers that file returns using an out-of-state sales tax certificate number and dealers located in two or more counties that file consolidated returns are required to report to the Department of Revenue all surcharge collections according to the county to which the surcharge is attributed. The surcharge is attributed to the county where the lessee picks up the motor vehicle. (*Tax Information Publication, No. 04A01-02*, Florida Department of Revenue, February 27, 2004; *Tax Information Publication, No. 03A01-08*, Florida Department of Revenue, October 15, 2003)

The lease of a vehicle used in interstate and foreign commerce is exempt from the surcharge to the extent of the proportion of out-of-state mileage to Florida mileage. The surcharge does not apply to a motor vehicle provided at no charge to a person whose motor vehicle is being repaired, adjusted, or serviced by the entity providing the replacement motor vehicle. (Sec. 212.0606, F.S.) Rules administering the surcharge can be found at Rule 12A-16.001, F.A.C.—Rule 12A-16.008, F.A.C.).

Rental car surcharge on peer-to-peer car-sharing program agreements.—Effective January 1, 2022, a $1 per day rental car surcharge applies to a peer-to-peer car-sharing program agreement involving a shared vehicle that is registered in Florida and is designed to carry fewer than nine passengers, for financial consideration, and without transfer of the title of the shared vehicle. The surcharge applies to the first 30 days only of a car-sharing period for any peer-to-peer car-sharing program agreement and must be collected by the program. The surcharge is subject to all applicable sales and use taxes. (Sec. 212.0606, F.S.)

When a motor vehicle is rented through a peer-to-peer car sharing program, the peer-to-peer car-sharing program must collect and remit the applicable tax and rental car surcharge due in connection with the rental. A "peer-to-peer car-sharing program" is a business platform that enables peer-to-peer car sharing by connecting motor vehicle owners with drivers for financial consideration. (*Tax Information Publication, No. 21A01-14,* Florida Department of Revenue, December 21, 2021)

A peer-to-peer car sharing program is required to register to collect sales tax, discretionary sales surtax, and the rental car surcharge applicable to motor vehicles rented through the peer-to-peer car sharing program. Peer-to-peer car-sharing programs are required to submit a registration application for each county in which business is located. (*Tax Information Publication, No. 21A01-14,* Florida Department of Revenue, December 21, 2021)

• *Youth bicycle helmets*

Effective July 1, 2014, the sale of a bicycle helmet marketed for use by youth is exempt from sales and use tax. (Sec. 212.08(7)(mmm), F.S.)

To qualify for the exemption, a helmet must state on a label, packaging, or in its general instructions for use, that it is intended for use as a bicycle helmet for youth. The exemption is inapplicable to bicycle helmets marketed for adults. (*Tax Information Publication, No. 14A01-05,* Florida Department of Revenue, May 23, 2014)

[¶60-580] Nonprofit Organizations, Private Schools, and Churches

Nonprofit, educational, and religious organizations are exempt from Florida sales and use tax in many instances as described below.

"Veterans' organizations" are defined as nationally recognized veterans' organizations and their local chapters that are exempt under IRC Sec. 501(c)(4) or (19). (Sec. 212.08(7)(n), F.S.)

For purposes of making exempt purchases, qualifying organizations must hold a consumer's certificate of exemption. (Rules 12A-1.038)

See Exemption Certificates.

• *Educational organizations*

Sales or leases to state tax-supported educational institutions of tangible personal property used in carrying out their customary activities are exempt. However, tangible personal property sold or rented through the school to students and sales or leases by the educational institution are taxable. (Sec. 212.08(7)(o), F.S.) Sales or leases to parent-teacher organizations and associations, the purpose of which is to raise funds for schools that teach grades K through 12 and that are associated with grades K through 12, are exempt. (Sec. 212.08(7)(nn), F.S.)

Bookstore operations at postsecondary educational institutions.—An exemption from Florida sales and use taxes is available for payments made to a postsecondary educational institution by any person pursuant to a grant of the right to conduct bookstore operations on real property owned or leased by a postsecondary educational institution. The term "bookstore operations" is defined as activities that consist predominantly of sales, distribution, and the provision of textbooks, merchandise, and services traditionally offered in college and university bookstores for the benefit of the institution's students, faculty, and staff. (Sec. 212.08(7)(fff), F.S.; *Tax Information Publication 07A01-06*, Florida Department of Revenue, July 1, 2007)

Credit for contributions to eligible nonprofit scholarship-funding organizations (formerly known as the "Hope Scholarship Program".—This program provides a Florida sales and use tax credit for use by a person that makes an eligible contribution. (Sec. 212.1832, F.S.; Rule 12A-1.110; *Tax Information Publication, No. 18A01-16*, Florida Department of Revenue, September 7, 2018)

The program is:

- funded by taxpayers who make an eligible contribution;
- limited to a single $105 payment;
- at the time of a vehicle purchase or registration in Florida.

(Sec. 212.1832, F.S.)

A credit of 100% of the amount of such eligible contribution by the taxpayer is authorized against the sales and use tax on the vehicle purchase or registration. (Sec. 212.1832, F.S.)

The credit provides the parent of a public school student subjected to a certain incident the opportunity to:

- transfer the student to a public school within the school district;
- receive a scholarship to transport the student to a public school in another school district; or
- receive a scholarship for the student to attend a private school.

(Sec. 212.1832, F.S.)

An "incident," for these purposes, includes:

- harassment;
- hazing;
- bullying;
- kidnapping;
- physical attack;
- robbery;
- sexual offense;
- harassment;
- assault;
- battery;
- threat;
- intimidation; or
- fighting at school.

(Sec. 212.1832, F.S.)

Florida has adopted an emergency sales and use tax rule regarding the credit for contributions to eligible nonprofit scholarship-funding organizations. The rule outlines:

- how a contribution can be made to the program;

- how dealers, designated agents, and private tag agents are to remit and report contributions; and

- how organizations who receive contributions are to report those monies to the Florida Department of Revenue.

(Emergency Rule 12AER19-01)

Qualified motion pictures.—An exemption is allowed for the purchase and lease of material, equipment, and other items used for education or demonstration of the curriculum at schools teaching production of qualified motion pictures. A taxpayer that meets the requirements for this exemption also qualifies for three other specific sales tax exemptions. (Sec. 212.0602, F.S.)

— The first exemption applies to property used as an integral part of performing services in connection with the production of a qualified motion picture. (Sec. 212.031(1)(a), F.S.)

— The second exemption is a refund of sales tax previously paid with respect to the purchase or lease of equipment used for motion picture, video or sound recording activities, and is available upon application. (Sec. 212.08(5)(f), F.S.)

— The third exemption applies to the sale, lease, storage and use of master films, master videotapes, master audio tapes, master records, and other devices used by the motion picture, television and recording industries in the making of visual and audio recordings for reproduction. (Sec. 212.08(12), F.S.)

A limited tax exemption is available to any licensed educational institution that holds regular classes and has an enrollment of 500 or more students, with respect to (1) licensing or leasing real property, (2) materials and equipment used for education, (3) demonstrating its curriculum, and (4) supporting operations. (Sec. 212.0602, F.S.)

• *IRC Sec. 501(c)(3) organizations*

Sales or leases to organizations currently exempt from federal income tax pursuant to IRC Sec. 501(c)(3), including sales of motor vehicles, are exempt from Florida sales and use tax when the leases or purchases are used in carrying out the organizations' customary nonprofit activity. (Sec. 212.08(7)(p), F.S.)

Tangible personal property purchased tax exempt for resale by a dealer and subsequently donated to a tax-exempt entity is exempt from sales and use tax. (Sec. 212.08(7)(p), F.S.; *Tax Information Publication, No. 19A01-08*, Florida Department of Revenue, August 16, 2019)

• *Prepaid meal plans purchased from a college or other institution of higher learning*

Prepaid meal plans purchased from a college or other institution of higher learning by students currently enrolled at that college or other institution of higher learning are exempt from sales and use tax. "Prepaid meal plans" are defined as advance payment to a college or institution of higher learning for the provision of a defined quantity of units that must expire at the end of an academic term, cannot be refunded to the student upon expiration, and that may only be exchanged for food. (Sec. 212.08(7)(r), F.S.)

To qualify for the exemption, the meal plan must meet all of the following requirements:

— the meal plan must be prepaid (for these purposes, this means either purchased in advance of use or purchased using financial aid once disbursed);

— the meal plan must be purchased from the college or other institution of higher learning or from an authorized third-party vendor licensed with the college or institution to provide such meal plans;

— the meal plan must be purchased by, or on behalf of, a student currently enrolled or preparing to enroll at the school (a student taking any number of credit hours qualifies);

— the meal plan must be for a defined quantity of units, such as a number of meals per week, month, year, or term; a set monetary amount; or an unlimited number of meals for a defined number of days;

— the balance of unused units must expire at the end of an academic term (the expiration can be at the end of any academic term, not just the academic term in which they are purchased, and units can rollover from term to term, provided they will eventually expire at the end of an academic term); and

— the units cannot be refunded to the student at expiration (refunds due to withdrawal from school, changing from a school meal plan to a meal plan provided by a sorority or fraternity, or other changes in circumstance do not disqualify a meal plan from the exemption, and refunds at graduation are considered the refund of units at expiration, and would disqualify a meal plan from the exemption).

(*Tax Information Publication, No. 15A01-13,* Florida Department of Revenue, June 26, 2015)

The exemption for prepaid meal plans purchased from a college or other institution of higher learning by students currently enrolled at that college or other institution of higher learning specifies that prepaid meal plans that contain a defined number of meals or a defined number of dollar equivalencies qualify for the exemption. However, the taxability of the dollar equivalencies of the prepaid meal plans is determined on the plan's use, and tax is due when the dollar equivalencies are used to make a purchase if that purchase is otherwise subject to sales and use tax. For these purposes, "dollar equivalencies" include university-specific dollars on a declining balance, such as "flex bucks" or "dining bucks." (Sec. 212.08(7)(r), F.S.; *Tax Information Publication, No. 15A01-13,* Florida Department of Revenue, June 26, 2015)

Hybrid meal plans and flex dollars.—Many colleges offer "flex dollars" as a meal plan option. These flex dollars are treated like other cash equivalents (such as gift cards, which are not taxable upon purchase, but instead, the taxability of the transaction is determined when the gift card is used), that entitle a person to redeem them in the future to receive tangible personal property or services. Most gift cards. Some colleges have hybrid meal plans, which have both a defined quantity of meals and also provide a set amount of flex dollars that can be used at designated dining establishments. These meal plans can be partially or completely eligible for the exemption, depending on the type of plan. (*Tax Information Publication, No. 15A01-13,* Florida Department of Revenue, June 26, 2015)

For hybrid meal plans, the portion of the plan that provides a defined number of meals and otherwise meets the requirements of a prepaid meal plan is exempt regardless of whether the flex dollars qualify. (*Tax Information Publication, No. 15A01-13,* Florida Department of Revenue, June 26, 2015)

Flex dollars are cash equivalents and the taxability is generally not determined until use. If the flex dollars meet the requirements of a prepaid meal plan, the entire meal plan can be exempt, including the use of flex dollars to purchase food or beverages. (*Tax Information Publication, No. 15A01-13,* Florida Department of Revenue, June 26, 2015)

For flex dollars that do not meet the requirements of a prepaid meal plan, taxability depends on the taxable nature of the items purchased. Items that are normally exempt under other provisions (e.g., certain groceries or bottles of water) continue to be exempt, while taxable items (e.g., soft drinks) continue to be taxable when purchased using flex dollars. (*Tax Information Publication, No. 15A01-13*, Florida Department of Revenue, June 26, 2015)

• *Religious institutions*

Sales or leases directly to religious institutions of tangible personal property, including motor vehicles, used in carrying on their customary activities are exempt. Sales or leases of tangible personal property, including motor vehicles, by religious institutions having an established place of worship at which nonprofit religious activities are regularly conducted also are exempt. (Sec. 212.08(7)(m), F.S.)

• *Scholarship-funding organization tax credits*

Florida offers a dollar-for-dollar credit against specific Florida taxes to businesses making voluntary contributions to eligible nonprofit scholarship-funding organizations. The purpose of these tax credits is to:

— allow private, voluntary contributions to nonprofit scholarship-funding organizations;

— expand education opportunities for children from families that have limited financial resources; and

— enable children to achieve a greater level of excellence in their education.

(*scholarship-funding Organization Tax Credits*, Florida Department of Revenue)

Credit for contributions to eligible nonprofit scholarship-funding organizations.—Tenants of commercial rental properties are eligible to apply to the Florida Department of Revenue for an allocation of funds available under the credit for contributions to eligible nonprofit scholarship-funding organizations program each state fiscal year, which is July 1 through June 30. The program authorizes the tenant to receive a credit against the state sales tax due on rent or license fee payments for contributions paid to an eligible nonprofit scholarship-funding organization. These credits may be taken against sales tax on rent or license fee payments beginning October 1, 2018. The Florida Department of Education establishes the eligibility of nonprofit scholarship-funding organizations to participate in the program. (Sec. 212.099, F.S.; Rule 12A-1.109)

Tax credit scholarship program.—A credit is available of 100% of an eligible contribution made to an eligible nonprofit scholarship-funding organization (SFO), as provided, against any sales and use tax imposed by Florida and due from a direct pay permit holder as a result of the direct pay permit held. (Sec. 212.1831, F.S.; Sec. 1002.395, F.S.; Rule 12ER10-04; Rule 12ER11-01; *Tax Information Publication, No. 18A01-15*, Florida Department of Revenue, August 27, 2018)

The Florida Tax Credit Scholarship Program tax credit cap amount is increased to $1,091,957,093 for the 2022-2023 state fiscal year. (*Tax Information Publication, No. 22ADM-05*, Florida Department of Revenue, June 6, 2022)

The Florida Tax Credit Scholarship Program is funded with contributions to private nonprofit scholarship-funding organizations from taxpayers who receive a tax credit for use against self-accrued sales and use tax liabilities of direct pay permit holders. The program provides private school scholarships to students from families that meet specified income levels. (Sec. 212.1831, F.S.; Sec. 1002.395, F.S.; Rule 12ER10-04; Rule 12ER11-01)

Eligible taxpayers must file an *Application for Tax Credit Allocation for Contributions to Nonprofit Scholarship-Funding Organizations* with the Florida Department of Revenue to receive a credit allocation from the tax cap authorized by law for that state fiscal year. (*Tax Information Publication No. 15ADM-02*, Florida Department of Revenue, June 15, 2015) A contribution to an eligible nonprofit scholarship-funding organization must be made by an eligible taxpayer prior to taking a tax credit on a tax return. (Rule 12-29.002; Rule 12ER11-01)

Tax credits earned in a taxable year beginning on or after January 1, 2018, may be carried forward up to 10 years when a taxpayer's tax liability is insufficient to use the entire credit. However, any unused credits earned in a taxable year beginning before January 1, 2018, may be carried forward for a period not to exceed five years. Unused tax credits automatically carry forward. Applications to carry forward an unused tax credit into a specific tax year are no longer required. (*Tax Information Publication, No. 18ADM-03*, Florida Department of Revenue, June 22, 2018)

Taxpayers who are unable to use a credit allocation may submit an *Application for Rescindment of Tax Credit Allocation for Contributions to Nonprofit Scholarship-Funding Organizations*. (Rule 12-29.002; Rule 12ER11-01)

Taxpayers must apply online or submit an application to the department to receive a credit allocation. The department will approve credit allocations on a first-come, first-served basis. (Rule 12-29.001; Rule 12-29.003)

The collection allowance for a direct pay permit holder claiming a Florida Tax Credit Scholarship Program credit under sales and use tax provisions will be calculated based on the amount due on Line 10, plus the amount of the tax credit reported on Line 21(a) of the Sales and Use Tax Return (Form DR-15). Direct pay permit holders must electronically file a return and electronically pay tax timely to receive a collection allowance. (*Tax Information Publication, No. 18ADM-03*, Florida Department of Revenue, June 22, 2018)

Florida has adopted an emergency rule regarding the Tax Credit Scholarship Program. The rule outlines:

- how to apply for an allocation;
- how to claim a credit following approval of the allocation application and donation to the organization;
- how to transfer an unused allocation or credit;
- how to report a change in the property or the lessor;
- how to rescind an unused allocation; and
- how organizations who receive donations are to report those donations to the Department, as required by statute.

(Emergency Rule 12AER18-06; *Tax Information Publication, No. 18ADM-03*, Florida Department of Revenue, June 22, 2018)

The rule also incorporates four forms to be used in the program:

- Form DR-117000, Florida Sales Tax Credit Scholarship Program Application for a Credit Allocation;
- Form DR-117100, Florida Sales Tax Credit Scholarship Program Application to Change a Credit Allocation;
- Form DR-117200, Florida Sales Tax Credit Scholarship Program Application for Rescindment of a Credit Allocation; and
- Form DR-117300, Florida Sales Tax Credit Scholarship Program Application Contributions Received by an Eligible Nonprofit Scholarship-Funding Organization.

(Emergency Rule 12AER18-06; *Tax Information Publication, No. 18ADM-03*, Florida Department of Revenue, June 22, 2018)

• *School books and lunches*

School books used in regularly prescribed courses of study, and lunches served in public, parochial, or nonprofit schools operated for and attended by pupils in grades K through 12 are exempt. School books and food sold or served at community colleges and other institutions of higher learning are taxable, except for prepaid meal plans, as provided. (Sec. 212.08(7)(r), F.S.)

See "prepaid meal plans purchased from a college or other institution of higher learning" discussed above.

• *School support organizations*

In lieu of collecting sales and use tax from the purchaser, school support organizations may pay tax to their suppliers on the cost price of food, drink, and supplies necessary to serve such food and drink when the food, drink, and supplies are purchased for resale. "School support organization" is defined as an organization whose sole purpose is to raise funds to support extracurricular activities at public, parochial, or nonprofit schools that teach students in grades K through 12. (Sec. 212.08(7)(ll), F.S.; *Tax Information Publication, No. 15A01-12R*, Florida Department of Revenue, October 8, 2015)

The sale of food and drinks prepared for immediate consumption is generally subject to sales tax, including the sale of food and drinks at school fundraisers. Unless an exemption applies, organizations that conduct such fundraisers are required to be registered as dealers with the department in order to collect and remit sales tax. Beginning July 1, 2015, school support organizations may pay tax to their suppliers on the cost price of taxable food, drinks, and supplies necessary to serve such food and drinks, instead of having to collect and remit tax to the department. In order to take advantage of this option, the school support organization must pay sales tax when purchasing taxable food, drinks, and serving supplies that will be used or resold as a part of fundraising activities. The final sale of those items for school fundraising is then exempt from sales tax. The school support organization is not required to pay sales tax when making purchases of exempt items in order to qualify for this option. (*Tax Information Publication, No. 15A01-12R*, Florida Department of Revenue, October 8, 2015)

• *Specific provisions*

The following charges are exempt:

— admissions to school events when only student or faculty talent is utilized, except athletic events sponsored by a state university;

— admissions for a student to a recreational facility, if student participation in the activity is under the jurisdiction of the educational institution;

— dues and admissions imposed by nonprofit sponsoring organizations exempt under IRC Sec. 501(c)(3); and

— admissions to live theater, opera, or ballet productions sponsored by a nonprofit organization with more than 10,000 members.

(Sec. 212.04(2)(a), F.S.)

Art sold to or used by educational institutions .— A "work of art" that is sold to or used by an educational institution is exempt from tax. The term includes pictorial representations, sculptures, jewelry, antiques, stamp and coin collections, and other tangible personal property whose value is attributable predominantly to its artistic, historical, political, cultural, or social importance. (Sec. 212.08(7)(cc) 6, F.S.)

The exemption also applies to the sale to, or use in, Florida of any work of art that is purchased or imported exclusively for the purpose of being donated or loaned to and made available for display by any educational institution, provided that the term of the loan agreement is for at least 10 years. (Sec. 212.08(7)(cc) 2, F.S.; Rule 12A-1.001)

The sale or use of works of art purchased or imported exclusively for the purpose of being donated to an educational institution is exempt. The work of art may remain in the possession of the donor or purchaser as long as title is transferred to the educational institution. The Department of Revenue must be provided with an affidavit to establish proof of transfer. (Sec. 212.08(7)(cc) 2, F.S.)

The exemption for artwork loans only applies during the period the work of art is in the possession of the educational institution or is in storage before transfer of possession. Once the exempt work of art ceases to be so possessed or stored, tax is payable by the owner on the basis of the sale price paid for the art. Within 60 days of transferring from its possession a work of art with respect to which the exemption was claimed, an educational institution must notify the Department of Revenue of the transfer. (Sec. 212.08(7)(cc) 5, F.S.)

The exemption provided to the purchaser of the work of art is not terminated if the educational institution to which the purchaser loaned the work of art loans the work to another educational institution so long as the physical custody of the work is returned to the original educational institution at the conclusion of the loan agreement. However, an educational institution that loans out exempt works of art to other educational institutions must notify the Department within 60 days of such transfers. (Rule 12A-1.001)

A work of art is presumed to have been purchased in or imported into Florida exclusively for loan if it is actually loaned, or placed in storage in preparation for a loan, within 90 days after purchase or importation, whichever is later. A work is not deemed to be placed in storage for purposes of the exemption if is displayed at any place other than an educational institution. (Sec. 212.08(7)(cc) 4, F.S.)

To claim the exemption, the purchaser of the work of art must supply the vendor and the Department of Revenue an affidavit that documents the purchaser's entitlement to the exemption. (Sec. 212.08(7)(cc) 4, F.S.; Rule 12A-1.001)

Bibles .—The use, sale, or distribution of religious publications, bibles, hymn books, vestments, altar paraphernalia, and other church service and ceremonial raiments and equipment is exempt. (Sec. 212.06(9), F.S.).

Coin-operated machines .—Charges for the use of coin-operated amusement machines and vending machines owned and operated by churches are exempt. (Sec. 212.05(1), F.S.; Sec. 212.0515(6), F.S.) Sales for 25¢ or less through a vending machine sponsored by a nonprofit corporation exempt under IRC Sec. 501(c)(3) or (4) are also exempt. (Sec. 212.08(7)(z), F.S.; Rule 12A-1.011) School grades 1 through 12 are not taxed on vending machine sales in the lunchroom. Sales at other locations and at institutions of higher learning are taxable. (Rule 12A-1.044(11)(a))

Commemorative flowers .—The sale of artificial commemorative flowers by a veterans' organization is exempt. (Sec. 212.08(7)(a), F.S.)

Donations .—If the donor of tangible personal property paid any tax due as the consumer on acquisition of the property, donations to any person, religious, educational, or charitable institution are exempt. (Rule 12A-1.077(1))

Florida Fire and Emergency Services Foundation.—Sales or leases to the Florida Fire and Emergency Services Foundation are exempt. (Sec. 212.08(7)(aaa), F.S.)

Good character in minors .—Nonprofit organizations whose primary purpose is to provide activities that contribute to the development of good character or the educational or cultural development of minors are exempt from tax. Counties and municipalities are expected to use their exemption certificates to purchase necessary goods and services requested by these organizations. (Sec. 212.08(7)(l), F.S.; Sec. 212.0821(2), F.S.)

Library cooperatives .—Sales or leases of books, supplies and materials to library cooperatives are exempt. (Sec. 212.08(7)(uu), F.S.)

Meals .—The sale by a nonprofit volunteer organization of prepared meals delivered to the residence of handicapped, elderly, or indigent people is exempt. An exemption is also provided to residents of a home for the aged with respect to meals provided through the facility. (Sec. 212.08(7)(k), F.S.)

A "home for the aged" means licensed and certified nursing homes or related health care facilities, continuing care facilities, facilities financed by a mortgage loan made or insured by the U.S. Department of Housing and Urban Development under the National Housing Act, and other similar facilities designed and operated primarily for the care of the aged. (Sec. 212.08(7)(i), F.S.)

Neighborhood crime watch .—Counties and municipalities are expected to use their exemption certificates to purchase necessary goods and services requested by neighborhood crime watch groups. (Sec. 212.0821(2), F.S.)

Nonprofit cooperative hospital laundries .—A nonprofit organization whose sole purpose is to offer laundry supplies and services to its members is exempt from tax if it is incorporated, is treated as cooperative under subchapter T of the Internal Revenue Code, and its members are all exempt pursuant to IRC 501(c)(3) from federal income tax. (Sec. 212.08(7)(ii), F.S.)

A member of a nonprofit cooperative hospital laundry whose Internal Revenue Code status changes is required, within 90 days after such change, to divest all participation in the cooperative. In addition, the provision of laundry supplies and services to a nonmember business pursuant to a declaration of emergency, as specified, and a written emergency plan of operation executed by the members of the cooperative does not invalidate or cause the denial of a cooperative's certificate of exemption. (Sec. 212.08(7)(ii), F.S.)

Occasional sales .—Sales by nonprofit charitable, civic, educational, neighborhood, religious, volunteer firefighter organizations, and other nonprofit organizations are exempt occasional sales under the following circumstances:

— the sales occur twice or less during any 12-month period provided the organization is not a registered dealer;

— the organization pays any applicable tax on the property purchased exclusively for resale;

— the organization is not making the sales on commercial premises where other businesses are making similar taxable sales; and

— the sale does not involve an aircraft, boat, mobile home, motor vehicle, or other licensed vehicle.

(Rule 12A-1.037)

Parent-teacher organizations .—School districts are expected to use their sales tax exemption certificates to purchase goods and services requested by parent-teacher organizations. (Sec. 212.0821, F.S.)

Public library .—Public libraries are expected to use their sales tax exemption certificates to purchase goods and services requested by groups engaged solely in fundraising activities for the libraries. (Sec. 212.0821, F.S.)

Retired educators .—Purchases of office supplies, equipment, and publications by the Florida Retired Educators Association are exempt. (Sec. 212.08(7)(g), F.S.)

Veterans' organizations.—An exemption is provided for sales or leases of tangible personal property to qualified veterans' organizations and their auxiliaries when used in carrying on their customary veteran's organization activities. "Veterans' organizations" are defined as nationally chartered organizations that hold certain exemptions from federal income tax, including but not limited to Florida chapters of the Paralyzed Veterans of America, Catholic War Veterans of the U.S.A., Jewish War Veterans of the U.S.A., and the Disabled American Veterans, Department of Florida, Inc. (Sec. 212.08(7)(n), F.S.)

Sales of food or drinks by qualified veterans' organizations in connection with customary veterans' organization activities to members of qualified veterans' organizations are added to the exemption. In addition, the American Legion and Veterans of Foreign Wars of the United States, are added to the list of qualified veterans' organizations. (Sec. 212.08(7)(n), F.S.)

To qualify for the exemption, the veterans' organization must hold a current Florida Consumer's Certificate of Exemption (Form DR-14) as a nationally chartered or recognized veterans' organization exempt from federal income tax under IRC § 501(c)(4) or (19). Qualified veterans' organizations may apply for an exemption certificate by filing an Application for a Consumer's Certificate of Exemption (Form DR-5) with the Florida Department of Revenue. On or after July 1, 2016, a qualified veterans' organization that is registered as a sales and use tax dealer may cancel its Sales and Use Tax Certificate of Registration (Form DR-11) if the only reason for holding the certificate is for the sole purpose of collecting and remitting sales tax on sales of food or drink to members of veterans' organizations. To cancel a certificate of registration, go to the department's website, click on "Taxes" and then click on "Update Account Information Online." (*Tax Information Publication, No. 16A01-08*, Florida Department of Revenue, June 24, 2016)

Volunteer fire department.—Fire fighting and rescue service equipment and supplies purchased by nonprofit, volunteer fire departments are exempt. (Sec. 212.08(7)(u), F.S.)

Water systems.—Sales and leases to nonprofit water systems, qualified under IRC Sec. 501 are exempt, provided the primary function of the entity is to construct, maintain, or operate a water system in Florida. (Sec. 212.08(7)(tt), F.S.)

• *Strong Families Tax Credit Program*

Beginning January 1, 2022, a credit of 100% of an eligible contribution made to an eligible charitable organization under the Strong Families Tax Credit Program is authorized against any state sales and use tax due from a direct pay permit holder as a result of the direct pay permit held. The credit is enacted for businesses that make monetary donations to certain eligible charitable organizations that provide services focused on child welfare and well-being. (Sec. 212.1834, F.S.; Rule 12ER21-17, F.A.C.; Rule 12ER21-18, F.A.C.)

• *New Worlds Reading Initiative*

Beginning October 1, 2021, a taxpayer may submit an application to the Florida Department of Revenue for a tax credit under the New Worlds Reading Initiative. Under the New Worlds Reading Initiative, businesses that make monetary donations to the administrator may receive a dollar-for-dollar credit against the following tax liabilities: (1) corporate income tax; (2) insurance premium tax; (3) severance taxes on oil and gas production; (4) alcoholic beverage tax on beer, wine, and spirits; or (5) self-accrued sales tax liability of direct pay permit holders. (Sec. 212.1833, F.S.; Sec. 1003.485, F.S.; Rule 12ER21-19, F.A.C.; Rule 12ER21-20, F.A.C.)

[¶60-650] Resales

A "sale at retail" means a sale to a consumer or to any person for any purpose other than the resale of tangible personal property. Therefore, resales are exempt. (Sec. 212.02(14), F.S.; Sec. 212.07(1)(b), F.S.; Rule 12A-1.039)

The Florida Department of Revenue provides guidance regarding annual resale certificates. (*GT—800060*, Florida Department of Revenue, July 2015)

The provisions that authorize an exempt sale for resale do not apply to sales of admissions. However, if an admission is purchased and subsequently resold for a higher price, tax must be collected and a credit will be given for tax already paid. If the admission is resold for a lower price, no tax must be collected and no credit will be given for taxes already paid. (Sec. 212.04(1)(c), F.S.)

A sale will be considered as being a taxable retail sale unless the dealer obtains a certificate stating that the property or service was purchased for resale. The certificate must bear the name and address of the purchaser, the effective date and the number of the dealer's certificate of registration, and the dealer's signature. Resale certificates must be renewed annually. (Sec. 212.07(1)(b), F.S.; Rule 12A-1.039)

Sales for resale include, but are not limited to, the following sales, leases, or rentals when made to a person who is an active registered dealer:

— the sale of tangible personal property to a dealer when such property is resold to the dealer's customers;

— the sale, lease, or rental of tangible personal property to a dealer when such property is held exclusively for leasing or rental purposes;

— the sale of taxable services to a dealer when such services are being resold to the dealer's customers under certain conditions;

— the lease or rental of real property to a dealer when such property is subsequently leased, rented, or licensed by the dealer's tenants;

— the sale of tangible personal property to a dealer when such property is incorporated as a material, ingredient, or component part of tangible personal property that is being produced for sale by manufacturing, processing, or compounding;

— the sale of inserts of printed materials that are distributed as a component part of a newspaper or magazine;

— the sale of tangible personal property to a repair dealer when such property is incorporated into and sold as part of a repair of tangible personal property by the dealer; and

— the alteration, remodeling, maintenance, adjustment, or repair of tangible personal property, when labor and materials are provided, that is held in inventory for resale or exclusively for leasing purposes by a dealer.

(Sec. 212.07(1)(b), F.S.; Rule 12A-1.039)

If a resale certificate is not presented when required, the dealer must collect and remit sales and use tax. A dealer may refuse to accept a resale certificate (except in cases in which delivery of tangible personal property is made in Florida to a nonresident dealer who does not hold a Florida certificate of registration) if the purchaser has not obtained a dealer's certificate of registration. (Rule 12A-1.039)

When every purchase made by a person from a particular dealer is for resale or is to be incorporated as a material part of other tangible personal property to be produced for sale, the dealer is authorized to take a blanket certificate for resale from the purchaser stating that all of the purchases are for either of the above purposes. Each subsequent order must contain the certificate of registration number of the purchaser. (Rule 12A-1.039)

• *Second-hand dealers*

Rules specific to second-hand dealers or secondary metals recyclers have been adopted to clarify the existing statutory sections. The rules explain registration procedures; the denial, suspension, or revocation of registration; and the forms used for registration. (Rule 12A-17.003; Rule 12A-17.005)

• *Defense Department and NASA contracts*

Sales of tangible personal property other than electricity to a government prime contractor or subcontractor that uses the property to fulfill a contract with the U.S. Department of Defense or NASA (National Aeronautics and Space Administration) are excluded from Florida sales tax as sales to the contractor for resale to the government. The property must be a direct cost of performing a contract and identified as a direct cost under 48 C.F.R. 9904.418-30(a)(2). Title to the property must pass to the U.S. Defense Department or NASA. The exclusion does not apply to contracts for repairing, altering, improving, or constructing real property. (Secs. 212.02(14)(a) and (20), F.S.)

• *Withdrawals from inventory*

A person who purchases tangible personal property for resale but who then uses, consumes, distributes, or stores the property for use or consumption in Florida in a manner that is inconsistent with the resale provisions must pay use tax on the property. The tax is due at the rate of 6% of the cost price of each item or article of tangible personal property. However, for property originally purchased exempt from tax for use exclusively for lease that is converted to the owner's own use, tax may be paid on the fair market value of the property at the time of conversion. If the fair market value of the property cannot be determined, use tax at the time of conversion is based on the owner's acquisition cost. Under no circumstances may the aggregate amount of sales tax from leasing the property and use tax due at the time of conversion be less than the total sales tax that would have been due on the original acquisition cost paid by the owner. (Sec. 212.05(1)(b), F.S.; Rule 12A-1.039(7)(g))

The distribution or sale of inventory originally purchased for resale does not qualify for an exemption as an isolated or occasional sale. (Rule 12A-1.037(2)(a))

[¶60-665] Services

Services are generally exempt from sales and use tax in Florida unless specifically identified as taxable. (Sec. 212.02(15)(a), F.S.; Sec. 212.04(14)(a), F.S.; Sec. 212.05, F.S.; Sec. 212.08(7)(v), F.S.)

What services are taxable in Florida?

Taxable services include:

    detective and other protection services;

    fingerprinting services;

    nonresidential cleaning services; and

    nonresidential building pest control services. (Sec. 212.05, F.S.)

What about transactions that also involve tangible personal property?

Services that involve sales of tangible personal property as inconsequential elements for which no separate charges are made are exempt. (Sec. 212.08(7)(v), F.S.)

If a transaction involves both the sale of a taxable service and the sale of a nontaxable service, then the consideration paid must be separately stated or the entire transaction is presumed taxable. The burden is on the seller of the service or the purchaser of the service, whichever applies, to overcome the presumption by providing appropriate documentary evidence. (Sec. 212.05, F.S.)

How is tangible personal property purchased by the service provider treated?

Tangible personal property purchased and used or consumed by a service provider is subject to tax. If property is purchased by a service provider for sale to customers, however, then the purchase would be exempt and sales tax would be collected on the sale of that property. (Rule 12A-1.0161, F.A.C.)

Does Florida provide any detailed guidance on specific services?

Yes, the Florida Department of Revenue provides detailed guidance on certain services.

Beauty salons and barber shops. Charges for services provided by beauty salons and barber shops are not subject to tax. They are the consumers of the tangible personal property they use in rendering such services. Beauty salons and barber shops must, however, collect tax on items they sell, such as cosmetics, hair products, nail kits, polishes, ornamental nails, and other items of tangible personal property. (Rule 12A-1.010, F.A.C.)

Bookkeeping services. When a service bureau performs a bookkeeping service for a client, the charges imposed are exempt as professional services. The various statements furnished are construed to be sales of inconsequential elements for which no separate charges are made. (Rule 12A-1.032(6))

Cleaning services. Nonresidential cleaning services, including North American Industry Classification System, (NAICS) National Number 561720, are subject to state sales tax, plus any applicable local discretionary sales surtax. (Sec. 212.05, F.S.; Rule 12A-1.0091, F.A.C.)

The Florida Department of Revenue provides guidance regarding nonresidential cleaning services. (*GT-800015, Sales and Use Tax on Cleaning Services*, Florida Department of Revenue, September 2015)

> **Nonresidential buildings.** Nonresidential buildings include commercial buildings, industrial buildings, public lodging establishments, and any other facilities rented as living or sleeping accommodations (also called "transient accommodations"). (*GT-800015, Sales and Use Tax on Cleaning Services*, Florida Department of Revenue, September 2015)

> Examples of taxable cleaning services for nonresidential buildings include: acoustical tile cleaning; building cleaning (interior); custodial services; deodorant servicing of restrooms; disinfecting; floor waxing; housekeeping (cleaning services); janitorial services; maid services; maintenance of buildings (except repairs); office cleaning; restroom cleaning; service station cleaning and degreasing; venetian blind cleaning; washroom sanitation; and window cleaning (interior or exterior). (Rule 12A-1.0091, F.A.C.; *GT-800015, Sales and Use Tax on Cleaning Services*, Florida Department of Revenue, September 2015)

> **Purchases by service providers.** Cleaning service providers must pay tax on items used in providing the services, such as equipment or cleaning supplies. (*GT-800015, Sales and Use Tax on Cleaning Services*, Florida Department of Revenue, September 2015)

> **Nontaxable services.** Nontaxable services include: carpet cleaning; pressure cleaning the exterior of a building; cleaning of the interiors of transportation equipment; residential and transient rental cleaning services; (charges for cleaning services required to be paid by a guest for the right to use a transient rental are subject to sales tax, surtax, and the local option transient rental tax); sales to nonprofit organizations that hold a current Florida Consumer's Certificate of Exemption (Form DR-14); and sales of services for resale. (*GT-800015, Sales and Use Tax on Cleaning Services*, Florida Department of Revenue, September 2015)

Consulting services. Consulting services are not subject to tax provided there has been no exchange of tangible personal property. (*Technical Assistance Advisement, No. 06A-011*, Florida Department of Revenue, May 22, 2006)

¶60-665

Decorators. Fees charged by an interior decorator or interior designer are not subject to sales tax or applicable local discretionary sales surtax when the fee is charged only for advice and is not contingent on the sale of tangible personal property. Paint color card samples, flooring and wall samples, fabric swatch samples, window covering samples, and similar samples that are provided at no charge and serve no useful purpose other than as a comparison of color, texture, or design, are exempt.(Rule 12A-1.001(2)(a)(1), F.A.C.; *GT-800052, Sales and Use Tax on Interior Decorators and Interior Designers*, Florida Department of Revenue, March 2015)

> *EXAMPLE:* Examples of fees charged solely for services rendered include designing a decorative scheme, advising clients, or recommending colors, paints, wallpaper, fabrics, brands, or supply sources. (*GT-800052, Sales and Use Tax on Interior Decorators and Interior Designers*, Florida Department of Revenue, March 2015)

Fees charged by an interior decorator or interior designer in conjunction with the sale of tangible personal property are subject to sales tax and applicable local discretionary sales surtax. Decorators and designers are required to collect tax on the total amount billed to the client. (Sec. 212.02(16), F.S.; *GT-800052, Sales and Use Tax on Interior Decorators and Interior Designers*, Florida Department of Revenue, March 2015)

Detective and protection services. Detective, burglar protection, and other protection services listed under NAICS National Numbers 561611, 561612, 561613, and 561621 are subject to sales tax and applicable local discretionary sales surtax. Taxable services include: armored car services; bodyguard (personal protection) services; burglar alarm monitoring and maintenance; detective agency services; fingerprinting services (except fingerprinting services required by law to obtain a license to carry a concealed weapon or firearm, which are exempt); fire alarm monitoring and maintenance; guard dogs, detection dogs, and other dogs for protection or investigative services (not including training), with or without a handler; guard, patrol, and parking or other facility services; investigation services (except credit); lie detection or polygraph services; missing person tracing services; passenger screening services; and skip tracing services. (Sec. 212.05(1)(i)1.a, F.S.; Rule 12A-1.0092, F.A.C.; *GT-800018, Sales and Use Tax on Detective, Burglar Protection, and Other Protection Services*, Florida Department of Revenue, September 2015)

If a transaction involves both taxable and nontaxable charges, then the charges must be separately stated or the entire charge is presumed taxable. Sellers of detective or protection services are required to maintain monthly logs that disclose every transaction for which tax was not collected and identify the purchasers of the services. (Sec. 212.05(1)(i)1.a, F.S.; Rule 12A-1.0092, F.A.C.)

Detective, burglar protection, and other protection service providers are deemed the consumers of tangible personal property sold them and used by them in connection with the performance of their services, (Rule 12A-1.0092(7), F.A.C.) and are required to pay sales tax on such sales. (Sec. 212.05(1)(i)1.a, F.S.; Rule 12A-1.0092, F.A.C.)

Nontaxable services. Examples of nontaxable services include: (1) investigative services performed within Florida but used outside Florida by the purchaser, or investigative services performed when the purchaser's primary benefit of the services is outside Florida; (2) investigative or security services provided directly to a government entity that is exempt from sales and use tax, if payment is made directly by the government entity; and (3) sales of services to nonprofit organizations that hold a current Florida Consumer's Certificate of Exemption, Form DR-14, (the seller must have a copy of the purchaser's Consumer's Certificate of Exemption or a transaction authorization number issued by the Florida Department of Revenue). (*GT-800018, Sales and Use Tax on Detective, Burglar Protection, and Other Protection Services*, Florida Department of Revenue, September 2015)

Protection services provided by employees for their employers. Protection services are taxable for all persons, businesses, residences, or nonresidential properties, except when provided by employees for their employers. Services are taxable if the seller's primary cost of performance is within Florida or if the purchaser has tax nexus with Florida and the primary benefit of the services is used or consumed in this state. Generally, detective agency services and investigative services that require a license are taxable. Services, such as process serving, that do not require a license are generally nontaxable unless performed in furtherance of a taxable service. (Sec. 212.05(1)(i)1.a, F.S.; Rule 12A-1.0092, F.A.C.)

Purchases by service providers. Detective protection service providers are the consumers of any tangible personal property used in providing their services, so service providers are liable for the tax on any purchase used in providing these services. (*GT-800018, Sales and Use Tax on Detective, Burglar Protection, and Other Protection Services*, Florida Department of Revenue, September 2015)

Law enforcement officers. The tax does not apply to law enforcement officers who: (1) perform approved duties in their capacity as law enforcement officers under the direct and immediate command of a law enforcement agency; and (2) perform, in authorized uniform, law enforcement and public safety services (not detective, burglar protection, or other protective services), if the law enforcement officer is performing approved duties in geographical areas where the officer has arrest jurisdiction. (Sec. 212.05(1)(i)1.a, F.S.; Rule 12A-1.0092, F.A.C.)

The above services are not subject to tax regardless of whether they are performed as "extra duty," "off-duty" or "secondary employment," and regardless of whether the law enforcement officer is a full-time or part-time law enforcement officer, or an auxiliary law enforcement officer working under the direct supervision of a full-time or part-time law enforcement officer. (Sec. 212.05(1)(i)1.a, F.S.; Rule 12A-1.0092, F.A.C.)

Although Florida sales and use tax is imposed on all charges for detective, burglar protection, and other protection services, there is an exclusion for law enforcement officers, as defined. A law enforcement officer does not perform taxable detective, burglar protection, or other protection services but instead provides law enforcement and public safety services when the following conditions are met by the officer and the authorizing law enforcement agency: (1) the officer performs approved duties as determined by his or her local law enforcement agency in his or her capacity as a law enforcement officer; (2) the officer is subject to the direct and immediate command of his or her agency; and (3) the officer is in uniform, which could include plain clothes, as authorized by his or her agency; and (4) the officer performs the approved duties in a geographical area in which the officer has arrest jurisdiction. (*Tax Information Publication, No. 12A01-13*, Florida Department of Revenue, August 23, 2012)

If these conditions are met, the duties will not be deemed a taxable service even if they are characterized as "extra duty," "off-duty," or "secondary employment." (*Tax Information Publication, No. 12A01-13*, Florida Department of Revenue, August 23, 2012)

It is also immaterial if the officer is paid directly or through the officer's agency by an outside source for the completed duty detail. In addition, when performing the described law enforcement and public safety services, it will not be considered a taxable rental if the law enforcement officer uses agency issued equipment (patrol car, gun, uniform, etc.), since there is no transfer of control or possession to the hiring party for the duty detail. The term "law enforcement officer" includes full-time or part-time law enforcement officers, and any auxiliary law enforcement officer, when the auxiliary law enforcement officer is working under the direct supervision of a full-time or part-time law enforcement officer. (*Tax Information Publication, No. 12A01-13*, Florida Department of Revenue, August 23, 2012)

Service of process and skip-tracing services. Separately stated freestanding service of process charges are not subject to Florida sales and use tax. However, skip-tracing services performed by a taxpayer who is in the business of providing service of process for law firms, that are in turn billed to the taxpayer's customers are subject to sales and use tax. Every person that charges for detective, burglar protection, and other protection services exercises a taxable privilege. Taxable services include skip tracing services, but process serving services performed by detectives, private investigators, or others are not subject to tax when freestanding, or when separately stated on an invoice given to a purchaser that includes taxable services. (Sec. 212.05(1)(i), F.S.; Rule 12A-1.0092(2)(a), F.A.C.; *Technical Assistance Advisement No. 13A-008*, Florida Department of Revenue, April 11, 2013)

"Skip tracing," for these purposes, is the process of locating a person for any number of reasons. Skip tracing is accomplished by collecting information about the person to determine the person's location. Information sources used to locate the person may include a phone number database, credit reports, job application information, and a criminal background check. Skip tracing services are specifically listed as a taxable service and as an investigation service under NAICS National Number 561611. Skip tracing includes any services performed to locate a person by the collection and analysis of information, such as telephone directories, credit reports, and criminal background checks. Consequently, charges for skip tracing or locating services are subject to sales tax regardless of whether the service is performed by a licensed private detective agency of some other person. When a person performs skip tracing services and process serving services, the transaction involves both taxable and nontaxable services. The person who provides the services must separately state the taxable and nontaxable charges in order for the process serving services to remain nontaxable; otherwise, the entire transaction is subject to tax. (Sec. 212.05(1)(i), F.S.; Rule 12A-1.0092(2)(a) and (3)(a), F.A.C.; *Technical Assistance Advisement No. 13A-008*, Florida Department of Revenue, April 11, 2013)

Fingerprinting services. Businesses that capture and transmit fingerprints, whether transmitting digitalized fingerprints (i.e., live scan) or traditional ink fingerprints (i.e., cardscan), are providing a service subject to sales and use tax. Live scan fingerprinting captures fingerprints digitally, so that they may then be sent electronically to law enforcement agencies for identification and screening. Cardscan fingerprinting captures fingerprints using paper and ink. The fingerprints are scanned and sent electronically to law enforcement agencies. (Sec. 212.05(1)(i), F.S.; *Tax Information Publication, No. 16A01-02*, Florida Department of Revenue, March 2, 2016)

Florida law imposes sales and use tax on services listed under NAICS National Numbers 561611, 561612, 561613, and 561621. Fingerprint services are specifically included under NAICS National Number 561611 and, as such, this service is taxable. A business that charges for fingerprint services must register as a Florida dealer to collect and remit sales tax to the department. Other mandatory fees, such as fees imposed by the Florida Department of Law Enforcement (FDLE) or the Federal Bureau of Investigation (FBI), are not subject to sales tax when separately stated from the charges for fingerprinting services. (Sec. 212.05(1)(i), F.S.; *Tax Information Publication, No. 16A01-02*, Florida Department of Revenue, March 2, 2016)

Fingerprinting services required to get concealed carry license. Effective July 1, 2017, fingerprinting services required by law to obtain a license to carry a concealed weapon or firearm are not subject to sales tax. (Sec. 212.05(1)(i), F.S.)

Home service contracts. Premiums paid by customers to home service contract providers are not subject to Florida sales tax as service warranties, but are instead subject to the 2% insurance premiums tax. Home service contract providers sell contracts that cover the service, repair, or replacement of a home's systems and appliances, such as interior plumbing, heating systems, electrical systems, water heaters, duct work, dishwashers, ovens, ranges, cook-tops, garbage disposals, garage door openers, air conditioning units, refrigerators, washers, dryers, and pool and spa equipment. (Sec. 212.056, F.S.; *Technical Assistance Advisement, No. 13A-022*, Florida Department of Revenue, October 1, 2013)

If a repair made by a local contractor is a repair to real property, then the amount the local contractor charges the providers for the repairs is not subject to sales tax, but the local contractor owes sales and use tax on the materials and supplies. The local contractor may pass on this cost to the provider, as long as it is not separately stated on the invoice as sales tax. However, if a local contractor repairs tangible personal property, then sales tax is due by the provider on the total charge, including any charges for labor that the local contractor bills for the repair of tangible personal property. Such tax must be separately stated on the invoice. Generally: (1) for tangible personal property repairs, sales tax is due from the provider as the person being billed for the repairs; and (2) for real property repairs, sales tax is due from the local contractor. No sales tax is due from the customer on the service charge paid to the local contractor. (Rule 12A-1.006, F.A.C.; Rule 12A-1.051, F.A.C.; *Technical Assistance Advisement, No. 13A-022*, Florida Department of Revenue, October 1, 2013)

Key-punching. The charge made for key-punching cards furnished by a customer is an exempt service charge. Blank key-punch cards and blank magnetic tape are considered to be taxable tangible personal property when purchased and used to program the customer's own computer. The sale of the cards and tape are also taxable if purchased by a computer technician or service bureau that uses the items to develop a software package for a customer. (Rule 12A-1.032(7))

Local taxes. When a dealer sells a taxable service and delivery of the service, or tangible personal property representing a taxable service, is made to a location within a county imposing a local sales option tax or surtax, the dealer is required to collect the tax at the rate imposed in the county where the services are provided or where the tangible personal property representing the services is delivered. If there is no reasonable evidence of delivery of a service, the sale of a service occurs in the county in which the purchaser accepts the invoice for services rendered. (Rule 12A-15.003(6), F.A.C.)

Moving, storing, packing, and shipping services. Charges by warehousemen solely for moving, storing, packing, or shipping tangible personal property belonging to other persons are not subject to tax. Warehouse workers must pay tax on their purchases of the crating, boxing, packaging, and packing materials used. Sales at auction made by warehouse workers to satisfy a lien for a claim on account of moving, storing, or other service charge are deemed exempt occasional sales. (Rule 12A-1.036, F.A.C.)

Pest control services. Nonresidential pest control services are subject to state sales tax plus any applicable local discretionary sales surtax. Nonresidential pest control services are services (not involving repair) enumerated in NAICS National Number 561710 and 561720 that are performed to reduce or eliminate any infestation of nonresidential buildings by vermin, insects, and other pests. Nonresidential pest control service providers must charge tax on the total sales price of such services. (Rule 12A-1.009, F.A.C.; *GT-800026, Sales and Use Tax on Insect or Pest Exterminator Services*, Florida Department of Revenue, March 2015)

Examples of taxable pest control services. Examples of taxable nonresidential pest control services include: annual or periodic pest inspections; bird control or proofing; exterminating services; fumigating services; pest control; termite control; soil treatment for termites or other pests performed before constructing a nonresidential building; charges to a lessor of a nonresidential building for pest control services, even if the tenant or lessee is a tax-exempt entity. (Rule 12A-1.009, F.A.C.; *GT-800026, Sales and Use Tax on Insect or Pest Exterminator Services*, Florida Department of Revenue, March 2015)

Purchases by pest control service providers. Pest control service providers are the users or consumers of items purchased and used in connection with their service, such as chemicals, insecticides, equipment, or motor vehicles. Sales and use tax is due on the purchase of such items. (Rule 12A-1.009, F.A.C.; *GT-800026, Sales and Use Tax on Insect or Pest Exterminator Services*, Florida Department of Revenue, March 2015)

Examples of nontaxable services. Examples of nontaxable services include: residential pest control services; spraying of lawns, whether residential or nonresidential; charges for pest control services provided at residential facilities that offer temporary or permanent residences, even though the rental, lease, letting, or licensing of such living accommodations may be subject to tax; pest control services provided by employees to their employers; pest control services provided to a utility shed located on the same property as a residential building, providing that no commercial activity goes on at the utility shed and the services are part of the pest control services provided to the residential building; pest control services provided to aircraft, boats, motor vehicles, and other vehicles; sales to nonprofit organizations that hold a current and valid Florida Consumer's Certificate of Exemption (Form DR-14) and provide a copy of their certificate to the seller at the time of purchase. (Rule 12A-1.009, F.A.C.; *GT-800026, Sales and Use Tax on Insect or Pest Exterminator Services*, Florida Department of Revenue, March 2015)

Stenographers. The taking of dictation by a public stenographer and the resulting transcriptions are exempt as professional services. Charges by a court reporter are also exempt, except for charges for transcripts provided to people who are not parties to the proceedings, as are fees for the videotaping or distribution of recordings of legal proceedings such as depositions or independent medical examinations when the videotape is provided to a party of the proceedings. (Rule 12A-1.001(2)(c), F.A.C.; *Technical Assistance Advisement No. 01A-077*, Florida Department of Revenue, December 27, 2001)

Travel agent services. Services provided by travel agents are exempt. If however, the travel agent itemizes the taxable components of a vacation package, the services are taxable. (Sec. 212.04, F.S.; Rule 12A-1.005, F.A.C.)

Veterinary services. Professional services provided by a veterinarian are exempt. In addition, charges for the hospitalization of animals and boarding and grooming charges are likewise not subject to tax, although items consumed in providing boarding and grooming services are subject to tax. (Sec. 212.08(7)(v) 4, F.S.; Rule 12A-1.0215, F.A.C.)

Items sold by veterinarians. The sale, lease, or rental of tangible personal property by veterinarians and veterinary clinics, such as the following items, are subject to sales tax and discretionary sales surtax: animal foods that are not specifically exempt; bedding; bowls; cages; chains; clothing; collars; crates; deter-

Guidebook to Florida Taxes

gents; dishes; doors; feeders; gates; houses; kennels; leads; leashes; pet carriers; soaps; tie-outs; and toys. In addition, substances that possess curative or remedial properties that are not required by federal or state law to be dispensed only by a prescription are subject to tax. (*GT—800045*, Florida Department of Revenue, July 2015)

Items purchased by veterinarians. Florida sales tax applies to taxable supplies or items purchased tax-exempt and then used by veterinarians and veterinary clinics in providing their professional services. Some examples of common taxable items used by veterinarians are: disposable medical restraint collars and muzzles; identification chips; and rubber gloves. (*GT—800045*, Florida Department of Revenue, July 2015)

Laboratory supplies used in making diagnoses, such as diagnostic kits, chemical compounds, and x-ray films and developing solutions are taxable. Instruments and equipment purchased by a veterinarian or veterinary clinic for use in the business are also taxable. Items initially purchased exempt for resale to customers (such as pet products and supplies) that are used in the business are subject to Florida use tax. (*GT—800045*, Florida Department of Revenue, July 2015)

Exemptions. Sales tax is inapplicable to: professional services provided by veterinarians; boarding charges for animals; drugs, medicinal drugs, and veterinary prescription drugs sold or used in connection with the medical treatment of animals; antiseptics, absorbent cotton, gauze for bandages, lotions, hypodermic needles and syringes, vitamins, and worm remedies purchased by veterinarians; germicides used directly on bodies of animals; x-ray opaques (radiopaques) such as opaque dyes and barium sulfate; purchases of medical products, supplies, or devices by a licensed veterinarian that must be dispensed under federal or state law only by the prescription or order of a licensed practitioner and are intended for a single use; purchases of medical products, supplies, or devices by a licensed veterinarian used in the cure, mitigation, alleviation, prevention, or treatment of injury, disease, or incapacity of an animal that are temporarily or permanently incorporated into an animal; and commonly recognized substances possessing curative or remedial properties that are ordered and dispensed as treatment for a diagnosed health disorder of an animal (examples: transdermal medications, sprays, or powders that prevent or treat flea or tick infestation when purchased, ordered, and dispensed by a licensed veterinarian). (Rule 12A-1.0215, F.A.C.; *GT—800045*, Florida Department of Revenue, July 2015)

[¶60-740] Transportation

In general, transportation equipment and supplies are subject to sales and use tax in Florida, but transportation services are exempt from tax.

How does Florida tax transportation equipment and supplies?

The sale (including occasional sales or isolated sales), use, consumption, or storage of transportation supplies such as a vehicle, vessel, or aircraft in Florida is generally taxable.

Aircraft. The state 6% use tax, plus any discretionary sales surtax, must be paid on aircraft used or stored in Florida when:

— the aircraft is purchased from a person who is not a registered aircraft dealer and the sale or delivery of the aircraft occurs in Florida;

— the aircraft is purchased in another state, territory of the United States, or District of Columbia and is brought into Florida within six months of the purchase date; or

— the aircraft is purchased in a foreign country and is brought into Florida at any time.

Florida use tax is due when the aircraft is brought into Florida for use or storage.

Aircraft exported out of U.S. The sale of an aircraft being exported out of the United States under its own power and the installation of parts and equipment on an aircraft of foreign registry are exempt.

Aircraft modification services. Charges for aircraft modification services, including parts and equipment, performed under authority of a supplemental certificate issued by the Federal Aviation Administration, are exempt from sales and use tax.

Aircraft sold by manufacturers. The sale of flyable aircraft by a manufacturer, including necessary equipment and modifications, is taxed in an amount equal to tax imposed under the laws of the state in which the aircraft will be domiciled. No tax is imposed if the aircraft will be domiciled in a state that does not allow credit against sales or use tax for taxes paid in Florida. This exemption applies only if the purchaser is a resident of another state who will not use the aircraft in Florida, if the purchaser is a resident of another state and uses the aircraft in interstate or foreign commerce, or if the purchaser is a resident of a foreign country.

An air carrier using mileage apportionment for corporate income tax purposes may elect to be taxed in Florida on a reduced tax base.

Aircraft temporarily in state. An aircraft owned by a nonresident is exempt from use tax provided the aircraft enters or remains in Florida for less than a total of 21 days during the six-month period after the date of purchase. The temporary use of the aircraft and subsequent removal from Florida can be proven by invoices for fuel, tie-down, or hangar charges issued by out-of-state vendors or suppliers or similar documentation that clearly and specifically identifies the aircraft.

An aircraft owned by a nonresident is exempt from use tax provided the aircraft enters or remains in Florida exclusively for the purpose of flight training, repairs, alterations, refitting, or modification. Such purposes must be supported by written documentation issued by in-state vendors or suppliers that clearly and specifically identifies the aircraft.

The Florida Department of Revenue provides guidance regarding aircraft that is temporarily in the state, as well as flight training, repairs, alterations, refitting, or modification of aircraft.

Compliance. Form DR-15AIR, Sales and Use Tax Return for Aircraft should be used to report sales and use tax on purchases of aircraft when the purchaser does not pay Florida sales tax to the seller. No title certificate, license, or registration may be issued on an aircraft unless sales and use taxes have been paid.

Tax returns and payments are due on the 1st day (and are late after the 20th day), of the month following the month that:

— the aircraft was purchased in Florida;

— the aircraft was delivered to a Florida location; or

— the aircraft enters Florida for use or storage.

If the 20th falls on a Saturday, Sunday, or state or federal holiday, the tax return and check or money order must be postmarked or hand-delivered on the first business day following the 20th. Registered sales and use tax dealers are required to file and pay Florida's 6% sales and use tax, plus any discretionary sales surtax, on their *DR-15* or *DR-15EZ* sales and use tax return.

Fractional aircraft ownership programs. The sale or use of aircraft primarily used in a fractional aircraft ownership program or of any parts or labor used in the completion, maintenance, repair, or overhaul of such aircraft is exempt from sales and use tax. The exemption is disallowed, however, unless the program manager of the fractional aircraft ownership program furnishes the dealer with a certificate that states that the lease, purchase, repair, or maintenance is for aircraft primarily used in a fractional aircraft ownership program and that the program manager qualifies for the exemption. If a program manager makes exempt purchases on a continual basis, the program manager may allow the dealer to keep the certificate on file. In addition, the program manager is required to inform a dealer that keeps the certificate on file if the program manager no longer qualifies for the exemption.

The maximum sales and use tax that may be imposed, including any discretionary sales surtax, is limited to $300 on the sale or use in Florida of a fractional ownership interest in aircraft pursuant to a fractional aircraft ownership program. The tax applies to the total consideration paid for the fractional ownership interest, including any amounts paid by the fractional owner as monthly management or maintenance fees. Moreover, the tax applies only if the fractional ownership interest is sold by or to the program manager of the fractional aircraft ownership program, or if the fractional ownership interest is transferred upon the approval of the program manager of the fractional aircraft ownership program. A "fractional aircraft ownership program" is defined as a program that meets certain requirements that relate to fractional ownership operations, as provided, except that the program must include a minimum of 25 aircraft owned or leased by the program manager and used in the program.

The Florida Department of Revenue provides guidance regarding fractional aircraft ownership programs.

Nonresident purchase of aircraft in Florida for use in other locations. Nonresidents who purchase a boat or aircraft in Florida for use in other locations are not required to pay Florida sales tax on their purchase if the item is removed from Florida within a statutory time frame and documentation is provided to the Florida Department of Revenue to show that the boat or aircraft was removed and titled or registered in another jurisdiction. This exemption is not allowed unless:

— the purchaser removes a qualifying boat from Florida within 90 days after the date of purchase or extension, or the purchaser removes a nonqualifying boat or an aircraft from Florida within 10 days after the date of purchase or, when the boat or aircraft is repaired or altered, within 20 days after completion of the repairs or alterations; or if the aircraft will be registered in a foreign jurisdiction; and

— application for the aircraft's registration is properly filed with a civil airworthiness authority of a foreign jurisdiction within 10 days after the date of purchase;

— the purchaser removes the aircraft from Florida to a foreign jurisdiction within 10 days after the date the aircraft is registered by the applicable foreign airworthiness authority; and

— the aircraft is operated in Florida solely to remove it from Florida to a foreign jurisdiction.

Sec. 212.05(1)(a)2.a., F.S.

Qualified aircraft sold by common carrier. The sale or lease of a qualified aircraft or an aircraft of more than 15,000 pounds maximum certified takeoff weight for use by a common carrier is exempt from tax. (Sec. 212.08, F.S.) "Qualified aircraft" means any aircraft that (1) has a maximum certified takeoff weight of less than 10,000 pounds, (2) is equipped with twin turbofan engines that meet Stage IV noise requirements, and (3) is used by a business that operates as an on-demand air carrier under a Federal Aviation Administration Regulation, as specified, that owns or leases and operates a fleet of at least 25 of such aircraft in Florida. (Sec. 212.02, F.S.) To be eligible to receive the exemption for "qualified aircraft," a purchaser or lessee must offer, in writing, to participate in a flight training and research program with at least two Florida universities that offer graduate programs in aeronautical or aerospace engineering and offer flight training through a school of aeronautics or college of aviation. (Sec. 212.0801, F.S.)

See Government Transactions, for information about space vehicles.

Resales. Registered aircraft dealers who purchase aircraft exclusively for resale are exempt from tax at the time of purchase, but must pay tax computed on 1% of the value of the aircraft each calendar month the aircraft is used by the dealer.

Boats and vessels. No title certificate, license, or registration may be issued on a boat unless the sales and use taxes have been paid. (Sec. 212.06, F.S.)

The Florida Department of Revenue provides guidance to owners and purchasers of boats.

Bare boat exemption. Tax is not due on the purchase or use of a vessel that is used exclusively for bare boat chartering purposes both inside and outside Florida waters. To qualify for the exemption, the vessel may not be used for any reason other than for rental on a bare boat basis or for some other activity reasonably designed to further the boat's use for bare boat chartering.

Bare boat rentals. When a boat or vessel is leased or rented on a "bare boat" basis, the sales tax applies to the gross proceeds derived from the lease or rental. The lease or rental is considered to be on a bare boat basis when (1) the lessor does not provide a crew, or (2) the lessor does provide a crew but it is hired by the lessee under a separate employment contract.

Boats temporarily docked in state. A boat upon which the state sales or use tax has not been paid is exempt from the use tax for 20 days or less use in Florida per calendar year, calculated from the date of first dockage or slippage at a registered facility. The 20-day period is tolled the first time per year that the boat is temporarily brought into Florida for repairs, alterations, refitting or modifications are physically in the care, custody, and control of the repair facility, including the time spent on sea trials conducted by the facility. The owner may request an additional tolling of the 20-day period for purposes of repairs that arise from a written guarantee given by the registered repair facility and covering only those repairs or modifications made during the first tolled period.

The owner must provide the registered repair facility, within 72 hours after the date upon which the facility takes possession of the boat, with an affidavit stating that the boat is under its care, custody, and control and that the owner does not use the boat while in the facility. The affidavit must be maintained by the registered repair facility as part of its records for the prescribed period. Upon completion of the repairs, the registered repair facility must, within 72 hours after the date of release, have in its possession a copy of the release form which shows the date of release and any other information required by the Department. The repair facility is required to maintain a log that documents all alterations, additions, repairs, and sea trials during the time such boats are under their care, custody, and control.

The 6-month period for use in the state of property purchased outside the state is tolled for boats that are temporarily brought into Florida for such purposes within six months after the date of purchase.

The term "sea trial" is defined as a voyage for the purpose of testing repair or modification work, which is in length and scope reasonably necessary to test repairs or modifications, or a voyage for the purpose of ascertaining the seaworthiness of a vessel. If the sea trial is to test repair or modification work, the owner or repair facility must certify what repairs have been tested. The owner and the repair facility may also be required to certify that the length and scope of the voyage were reasonably necessary to test the repairs or modifications.

Tax is not imposed on any vessel imported into Florida for the sole purpose of being offered for sale at retail by a yacht broker or yacht dealer registered in Florida. To be exempt, the vessel must remain under the care, custody, and control of the registered broker or dealer and the owner of the vessel may not make personal use of the vessel during that time.

Nonresident purchase of boat in Florida for use in other locations. See above under "Aircraft."

Presumption that vessel used outside of Florida for six months before being imported was not purchased for use in Florida. Use tax applies on tangible personal property imported or caused to be imported into Florida for use, consumption, distribution, or storage to be used or consumed in Florida. However, it is presumed that tangible personal property used in another state, territory of the U.S., or the District of Columbia for six months or longer before being imported into Florida was not purchased for use in Florida. The rental or lease of tangible personal property that is used or stored in Florida is subject to sales and use tax regardless of its prior use or tax paid on the purchase outside Florida. This presumption does not apply to any boat for which a saltwater fishing license fee is required.

Tax caps. The maximum amount of sales and use tax that may be imposed and collected on each sale or use of a boat or vessel in Florida is capped at $18,000.

The Florida Department of Revenue provides guidance regarding the $18,000 tax cap on boats and vessels.

The maximum Florida sales and use tax due on each boat repair transaction in Florida is capped at $60,000. Subsequent and separate repairs are each subject to their own $60,000 cap. As a result, a dealer should not collect tax in excess of $60,000 on a single repair, and is required to maintain records to substantiate the application of the cap to the transaction. Taxpayers who make their own repairs to a boat in Florida will owe a maximum of $60,000 of use tax. The $60,000 cap includes both the state sales or use tax and any applicable discretionary sales surtax.

> *EXAMPLE: $60,000 cap on each boat repair.* A boat or vessel is repaired for $1,500,000 in Indian River County, a 1% county surtax jurisdiction. The total maximum tax due is $60,000. For purposes of reporting, the dealer subtracts the surtax from the maximum tax amount to determine the maximum state sales tax. The county surtax is due on only the first $5,000 of the taxable sales amount. The total county surtax would be $50 ($5,000 X .01). So the maximum state sales tax is $59,950.
>
> $60,000 maximum tax — $50 county surtax = $59,950 maximum state sales tax.
>
> The dealer should then divide the maximum state sales tax by the 6% state sales tax rate to determine the taxable sales amount.
>
> $59,950 / .06 = $999,166.66 taxable sales (repair) amount.

The dealer should then subtract the taxable sales amount from the gross sales amount to determine the exempt sales amount.

$1,500,000 gross sales amount — $999,166.66 taxable sales amount = $500,833.34 exempt sales amount.

$59,950 tax collected at 6%. $50 county surtax at 1%. $60,000 tax due (Lines 5, 7, and 10 of *Form DR-15, Sales and Use Tax Return*). $50 amount reported as county surtax on back of return on Line 15(d).

To calculate the Line 15(a) amount (sales exempt from the county discretionary sales surtax) subtract $5,000 (amount of the sale that was subject to the surtax) from the taxable sales amount.

$999,166.66 taxable sales amount — $5,000 amount of sale subject to the county surtax = $994,166.66 amount reported on Line 15(a).

This example is based on a surtax rate of 1%. The amount of surtax will vary if the applicable county has a different surtax rate.

Vessels used for demonstration, promotional, or testing purposes. A vessel used solely for demonstration, sales promotional, or testing purposes is not subject to tax. "Promotional purposes" means the entry of a vessel in a marine-related event where prospective purchasers would be in attendance, where the vessel is entered in the name of the dealer or the manufacturer, where the vessel is clearly marked as for sale, and which vessel has never been transferred from an inventory item to a capital asset for depreciation purposes. The term includes participation in fishing tournaments.

However, this exemption does not apply to any vessel when used for transporting persons or goods for compensation; when lent to another for consideration; when offered for rent or hire as a means of transportation for compensation; or when offered or used to provide transportation for persons solicited on a share expenses basis.

Vessels used to transport people or property in interstate or foreign commerce. The sale or use of vessels, parts of vessels, and fuels used by vessels that are used to transport people or property in interstate or foreign commerce is taxed only on the Florida portion of use. Parts of the vessel include any items appropriate to carry out the purpose for which a vessel is designed and used. See Tax Base.

Boats and aircraft sold through dealers. Sales and use tax is not imposed on boats or airplanes sold through a registered dealer to a purchaser who, at the time of taking delivery, is a nonresident of Florida, does not make his or her permanent place of abode in the state, and is not engaged in carrying on in Florida any employment, trade, business, or profession in which the boat will be used in Florida, or is a corporation none of the officers or directors of which is a resident of, or makes his or her permanent place of abode in, Florida. For the exemption to apply, the purchaser must remove a boat or airplane from Florida within 10 days after the date of purchase or, when the boat or airplane is repaired or altered, within 20 days after completion of the repairs or alterations. However, nonresident purchasers of boats weighing more than five net tons may obtain from the selling dealer a decal authorizing the removal of a boat or airplane within 90 days after the date of purchase.

The Florida Department of Revenue provides guidance for boat dealers and brokers.

A purchaser that meets the qualifications for this exemption is exempt from use tax if the aircraft enters and remains in Florida for no more than a total of 20 days during the six-month period after the date of purchase.

A boat or aircraft sold to an unregistered, out-of-state dealer delivered in Florida is taxable unless the dealer furnishes the seller a notarized statement that the boat or aircraft is being purchased solely for resale outside of Florida. The sale of a boat or aircraft is exempt if delivery is accepted outside of Florida.

A nonresident purchaser may purchase a boat of 5 net tons of admeasurement or larger (i.e., a qualified boat) exempt from Florida sales and use tax and keep the qualified boat in Florida for a period of 180 days under certain conditions.

Aircraft registered in a foreign jurisdiction. Aircraft being exported under their own power to a destination outside the continental limits of the United States are subject to tax, unless the purchaser furnishes the dealer a duly signed and validated United States Customs declaration, showing the departure of the aircraft from the continental United States and the canceled United States registry of said aircraft. The burden of obtaining the evidential matter to establish the exemption rests with the selling dealer, who must retain the proper documentation to support the exemption.

The exemption applies on the purchase of an aircraft in Florida that will be registered in a foreign jurisdiction provided:

— application for the aircraft's registration is properly filed with a civil airworthiness authority of a foreign jurisdiction within 10 days from the date of purchase;

— the purchaser removes the aircraft from Florida to a foreign jurisdiction within 10 days from the date the aircraft is registered by the applicable foreign airworthiness authority; and

— the aircraft is operated in Florida solely for the removal from the state to a foreign jurisdiction.

Decals. Those who wish to order the 90-day extension decal may request *Form DR-42E, Application for Extension of 90-Day Decal to 180 Days* by calling the Department's Boat Enforcement Unit at 904-488-3821. The extension decal sheets cost $425.00, and there are two decals per sheet, one for each side of the boat.

Purchaser's criteria for extended exemption. The following criteria must be met in order for the purchaser to request extended exemption:

— within 10 days of removal of the boat, the nonresident purchaser must provide the Department proof of removal which includes copies of out-of-state fuel receipts, dockage charges, or repair bills; and

— within 30 days of removal of the boat, the nonresident purchaser must provide the Department written proof that it was licensed, titled, registered, or documented outside Florida (if such proof is not available within 30 days, the purchaser must provide written proof to the Department that he or she has applied for a license, title, registration, or documentation of the boat outside Florida within the 30-day period).

A copy of the license, title, registration, or documentation of the boat outside Florida must be provided to the Department when issued.

Purchaser's failure to comply. The Department will pursue collection of the tax, penalty, and interest from the nonresident purchaser of a qualified boat if any of the following conditions occur:

— the boat is not removed from Florida within the maximum 180 days after the date of purchase (the authorized extension period cannot be interrupted or extended for any purpose, including repairs);

— the required documentation is not provided to the Department within the specified time frames;

— the boat returns to Florida within six months of departure except for repairs, alterations, refitting, or modifications by a registered repair facility (the penalty is an amount equal to the tax and is mandatory; or

— the decal is removed, defaced, changed, modified, or altered in any way that affects its expiration date before it expires.

A 200% penalty will apply in addition to the tax. Further, the nonresident purchaser may be subject to imprisonment of up to one year and a fine of up to $1,000.

Seller's criteria for extended exemption. The following criteria must be met in order to qualify for exemption:

— the selling dealer must be registered with the Florida Department of Revenue;

— the qualifying boat must be sold to a nonresident purchaser;

— the nonresident purchaser must apply to the selling dealer at the time of sale for a decal that authorizes the boat to remain in Florida for 90 days;

— within 60 days after the date of purchase, the nonresident purchaser must apply to the selling dealer for an extension decal that authorizes the boat to remain in Florida for an additional 90 days, but not more than a total of 180 days;

— the selling dealer is obligated to purchase the 90-day decal from the Department, validate the decal, and affix it to the boat; and

— the selling dealer is obligated to purchase the extension decal from the Department and affix it to the boat.

Seller's failure to comply. The Department will pursue collection of the tax, penalty, and interest from the selling dealer if any of the following conditions occur:

— the required documentation is not submitted and maintained; or

— the decals are issued falsely, are not affixed to the boat, are incorrectly marked for expiration, or are not properly accounted for.

A 200% penalty will apply in addition to the tax and the dealer may be subject to imprisonment of up to one year and a fine of up to $1,000.

Miscellaneous exemptions. The following transactions related to transportation equipment are exempt:

— the amount paid directly to the dealer by the Veterans Administration when a veteran purchases an aircraft or boat;

— the transfer of title of any aircraft or boat from the insured to an insurance company as part of the settlement of a claim, though repairs and replacements of boats and aircraft paid for by an insurance company in settlement of claims are fully taxable;

— repairs under a warranty contract;

— claims paid by a common carrier to a dealer for damage suffered by merchandise in transit, unless the carrier reimburses the dealer for repair or replacement of the damaged merchandise;

— repossession of a boat or aircraft (see Returned Goods and Possessions) ;

— a transfer of a boat or aircraft held in trust for a minor to the real owner when there is no consideration;

— a gift accompanied by a sworn statement describing the boat or aircraft and stating that there are no outstanding liens;

¶60-740

— a transfer by a partnership to a partner as part of a liquidation of the partnership;

— a transfer by a dissolved corporation to one of its stockholders as part of the stockholder's ratable portion of the assets of the corporation (see Liquidation Sales and Foreclosures) ;

— a transfer to a surviving corporation in a reorganization or merger;

— a distribution to the heirs of an estate;

— a transfer between spouses of marital property;

— a transfer between former spouses as part of the property settlement in a divorce;

— an even trade or trade down of a boat or aircraft for another registered vehicle accompanied by a sworn statement describing both vehicles; and

— materials for use in repairing a motor vehicle, airplane, or boat when such materials are incorporated into the repaired vehicle, airplane or boat.

Military personnel. A member of the United States military residing in Florida who registers a boat or aircraft must pay sales or use tax (see Government Transactions). Foreign military personnel must pay sales or use tax on boats or aircraft purchased or brought into Florida. NATO personnel are exempt from the use tax.

Leases and rentals. The rental or lease of a boat or aircraft is taxable without regard to prior use or tax paid on the purchase outside the state. A boat or aircraft may be purchased tax free on a resale certificate if it will be used exclusively for rental purposes.

Garage, docking, and tie-down space. The lease or rental of garage space, docking for boats, and tie-down space for aircraft is taxable.

Public streets, property used for aircraft landing, and property used at port authorities for docking and loading. The lease or rental of public streets and roads used for transportation, of property used for aircraft landing and loading, or of property used at a port authority for docking and loading is not taxable. There is also no tax to the extent that the amount paid for any property at the port is based on the charge for the amount of tonnage actually imported or exported through the port by the tenant. The amount that the charge for the use of the property exceeds the amount charged for tonnage actually imported or exported remains subject to the tax.

Taxicabs. The lease of, or license to use, a taxicab or taxicab-related equipment and services provided by a taxicab company to an independent taxicab operator is exempt from sales and use tax. The exemption only applies, however, if sales or use tax was paid on the acquisition of the taxicab and its related equipment.

Local taxes. A registered aircraft or boat dealer who makes a sale of an aircraft or boat is required to collect local sales surtax when the aircraft or boat is delivered to a location within a county that imposes the tax. A registered mobile home, motor vehicle, or other vehicle dealer who makes sales of any mobile home or vehicle is required to collect local sales surtax when the residence address of the purchaser identified on the registration or title document for the mobile home or vehicle is located within a county that imposes the tax.

See Local Tax Rates.

Railroads. Railroads that are licensed as common carriers by the U.S. Surface Transportation Board are subject to tax on rolling stock, and parts thereof, used to transport persons or property for hire in interstate or foreign commerce. The tax is imposed only on that portion used in Florida. See Tax Base.

Railroad cars. The lease of railroad cars to a railroad company for use on its tracks is exempt from tax, but the rental of railroad cars to a lessee other than a railroad company is taxable.

Use of a side track. The charge made to its customer by a railroad for the use of a side track located on railroad property is taxable. Railroad roadway materials used in the construction, repair or maintenance of railways are exempt. Railroad roadway materials include: rails, ties, ballasts, communications equipment, signal equipment, power transmission equipment, and any other track materials.

Importing property without certificate of registration. Importing taxable property by means other than common carrier without a certificate of registration is construed as an attempt to evade payment of tax; under these circumstances the property and vehicle are subject to seizure and forfeiture.

See Levy and Sale of Taxpayer's Property.

What is the tax treatment of transportation services in Florida?

In general, transportation services are exempt from sales and use tax in Florida.

Passenger tickets. Federal law prohibits a state and its political subdivisions from collecting or levying a tax, fee, head charge, or other charge on:

— passengers traveling in interstate commerce by motor carrier;

— transport of passengers traveling in interstate commerce by motor carrier;

— the sale of passenger transportation in interstate commerce by motor carrier; or

— the gross receipts derived from such transportation.

(Sec. 14505, Title 49 U.S.C.)

[¶60-750] Utilities

Electric power and energy are tangible personal property subject to sales and use tax. (Sec. 212.02(19), F.S.; Rule 12A-1.053, F.A.C.)

• *Natural gas and natural gas fuel*

Natural gas and natural gas fuel, as defined, is exempt from sales and use tax when placed into the fuel supply system of a motor vehicle. (Sec. 212.08(4)(a), F.S.)

Natural gas and natural gas fuel are exempt from Florida sales tax and gross receipts tax when placed into the fuel supply system of a motor vehicle. To qualify for the exemption from sales tax and gross receipts tax at the time of purchase, the purchaser must give the seller a certificate stating that the natural gas or natural gas fuel is for exclusive use in the fuel supply system of a motor vehicle. (*Tax Information Publication, No. 14B05-02*, Florida Department of Revenue, April 9, 2014)

Any person purchasing natural gas and natural gas fuel, who is not separately metered, for a use that is subject to sales tax and/or gross receipts tax and for use in a motor vehicle (i.e., a dual user) should obtain a natural gas fuel retailer's license, a sales and use tax registration, and a gross receipts tax registration, if applicable. The purchaser will purchase the fuel exempt from tax and will be required to self-accrue and remit the applicable taxes to the Florida Department of Revenue. To qualify for the exemption from sales tax and gross receipts tax at the time of purchase, the purchaser must give the seller a certificate stating that it will self-accrue the applicable taxes and remit them to the department. If the natural gas or natural gas fuel purchased for use in a motor vehicle is separately metered, the purchaser is only required to obtain a license as a retailer of natural gas fuel. Any applicable sales tax and/or gross receipts tax owed by the purchaser will be paid directly to the supplier. (*Tax Information Publication, No. 14B05-02*, Florida Department of Revenue, April 9, 2014)

• *Natural gas used to generate electricity*

Natural gas used to generate electricity in a non-combustion fuel cell used in stationary equipment is exempt from sales and use tax. (Sec. 212.08(4)(a), F.S.)

Sellers of natural gas are required to document exempt sales. A suggested certificate to be completed by the purchaser and maintained in the selling vendor's books and records is provided by the Florida Department of Revenue. (*Tax Information Publication No. 13A01-08*, Florida Department of Revenue, June 17, 2013)

• *Exempt utility purchases*

Fuels used in generation.—All fuels used by a public or private utility in the generation of electric power or energy for sale, except dyed diesel fuel, are exempt. (Sec. 212.08(4)(a) 2, F.S.; Rule 12A-1.053, F.A.C.)

Dyed diesel fuel used in a trade or business is subject to use tax unless the diesel fuel is specifically exempt from sales tax or the dealer selling the fuel has elected to collect sales tax on sales to persons who use or consume the diesel fuel in a trade or business.Rule 12A-1.059(3), F.A.C.)

Lease of right-of-way.—The lease of a public or private street or right-of-way for utility purposes is exempt. (Sec. 212.031(1)(a), F.S.)

• *Exempt vs. nonexempt sales*

Residential.—Sales of utilities to residential households or owners of residential models in Florida by utility companies who pay gross receipts tax are exempt from sales and use tax. Sales of fuel to residential households or owners of residential models, including oil, kerosene, liquefied petroleum gas, coal, wood, and other fuel products used in the household or model to heat, cook, light, or refrigerate are exempt. This exemption applies regardless of whether the sales of utilities and fuels are separately metered and billed directly to the residents or are metered and billed to the landlord. If any part of the utility or fuel is used for a nonexempt purpose, the entire sale is taxable. (Sec. 212.08(7)(j), F.S.; Rule 12A-1.053, F.A.C.; Rule 12A-1.059(1)(a), F.A.C.)

The exemption applies to licensed family day care homes. (Sec. 212.08(7)(j), F.S.; Rule 12A-1.053, F.A.C.; Rule 12A-1.059(1)(a), F.A.C.)

A utility that, in good faith, relies on a customer's affidavit stating that the customer is a residential household and, accordingly, does not charge sales tax, but later learns that the customer was ineligible for the residential exemption, is not responsible for the uncollected tax. Rather, the customer would be responsible for this tax. (*Technical Assistance Advisement 00(A)-064*, Florida Department of Revenue, November 8, 2000)

Pollution control equipment.—Energy or power used to operate pollution control equipment, maintenance equipment, or monitoring or control equipment used in manufacturing and electrical power or energy consumed or dissipated in the transmission or distribution of power or energy for resale are exempt. (Sec. 212.06(1)(b), F.S.)

Charges for the transmission of electricity are also exempt. (Sec. 212.08(4), F.S.)

Enterprise zone.—See ¶60-360 Enterprise Zones and Similar Tax Incentives, regarding an exemption for electrical energy used in an enterprise zone. (Sec. 212.08(15), F.S.) The Florida Enterprise Zone Program expires December 31, 2015. (*Tax Information Publication, No. 15ADM-04*, Florida Department of Revenue, September 8, 2015)

¶60-750

However, electrical power or energy used for space heating, lighting, office equipment, air conditioning, or any other nonmanufacturing, nonprocessing, noncompounding, nonproducing, nonfabricating, or nonshipping activity is taxable. (Sec. 212.06(1)(b), F.S.)

Governmental units.—The exemption from tax for governmental units does not apply to sales, rental, use, consumption, or storage in any political subdivision of machines, equipment, and parts used in the generation, transmission, or distribution of electrical energy by systems owned and operated by the political subdivision, except for those sales, rentals, uses, consumption, or storage for which bonds or revenue certificates were validated on or before January 1, 1973, for transmission or distribution expansion. (Sec. 212.08(6), F.S.)

CCH COMMENT: Distinction between repair and expansion.—A Florida appellate court determined that the purchase of materials by a municipally owned utility is exempt from Florida sales and use tax when those materials will be used to repair, replace or refurbish an existing electric energy transmission or distribution system rather than to expand it. (*Electric Association, Inc. v. Department of Revenue,* Florida District Court of Appeal, No. 1D99-3770, August 16, 2000)

Boiler fuels.—Boiler fuels purchased for use as combustible fuels, purchases of natural gas, residual oil, recycled oil, waste oil, solid waste material, coal, sulfur, wood, wood residues, or wood bark used in an industrial manufacturing, processing, compounding, or production process at a fixed location in Florida are exempt from tax. (Sec. 212.08(7)(b), F.S.)

However, the exemption is inapplicable to:

— sales of boiler fuels that are not used in manufacturing, processing, compounding;

— sales of boiler fuels that are not used in producing items of tangible personal property for sale; and

— the sale of boiler fuels used by any firm subject to regulation by the Division of Hotels and Restaurants of the Department of Business and Professional Regulation.

(Sec. 212.08(7)(b), F.S.)

Charges for the filling of liquefied petroleum in 22-pound gas tanks are exempt if the gas is used by the purchaser for purposes of residential heating, cooking, lighting, or refrigeration. The dealer must document on the customer's invoice or other written evidence of sale that the charge is for filling the tank or that the gas is sold for the purposes of residential household cooking, heating, lighting, or refrigeration. (Rule 12A-1.053, F.A.C.)

The sale, rental, use, consumption, or storage of machines, equipment, and parts used in furnishing public utility services is taxable. (Sec. 212.05(1)(f), F.S.)

However, all fuels used by a public or private utility in the generation of electric power or energy for sale, except dyed diesel fuel, are exempt. (Sec. 212.08(4)(a) 2, F.S.; Rule 12A-1.001(7), F.A.C.)

Dyed diesel fuel used in a trade or business is subject to use tax unless the diesel fuel is specifically exempt from sales tax or the dealer selling the fuel has elected to collect sales tax on sales to persons who use or consume the diesel fuel in a trade or business. Rule 12A-1.059(3), F.A.C.)

Water.—The sale of water delivered to the purchaser through pipes or conduits is exempt. (Sec. 212.08(4)(a) 2, F.S.)

• *Local taxes*

When a dealer sells electricity or natural or manufactured gas to a consumer located within a county that imposes a local sales surtax, the dealer is required to collect the tax at the rate imposed by the county where the consumer is located. In addition, any dealer who provides electricity or natural or manufactured gas to consumers located within a county that imposes a local sales surtax is required to register for sales tax purposes in each county imposing the tax in which its consumers are located. (Rule 12A-15.003(8), F.A.C.)

In the case of a local discretionary surtax, the entire utility tax billed after the effective date of the surtax is subject to the surtax, and the entire utility tax billed after the expiration of the surtax is exempt. (Sec. 212.054, F.S.)

[¶60-770] Sales Tax Holidays

Florida provides sales tax holidays on the following:

- children's books beginning May 14, 2022, and ending August 14, 2022;

- disaster preparedness items and pet evacuation supplies beginning May 28, 2022, and ending June 10, 2022;

- impact-resistant doors, impact-resistant garage doors, and impact-resistant windows purchased for commercial or non-commercial use beginning July 1, 2022, and ending June 30, 2024;

- children's diapers and baby and toddler clothing, apparel, and shoes beginning July 1, 2022, and ending June 30, 2023;

- new Energy Star appliances purchased for noncommercial use beginning July 1, 2022, and ending June 30, 2023;

- admissions and outdoor activity supplies beginning July 1, 2022, and ending July 7, 2022.

- back-to-school items from July 25, 2022, through August 7, 2022; and

- tools commonly used by skilled trade workers from September 3, 2022, through September 9, 2022.

• *Admissions and outdoor activity supplies*

Florida provides a "Freedom Week" sales and use tax holiday on specific admissions and outdoor activity supplies. The holiday begins July 1, 2022 and ends July 7, 2022. During the holiday period, tax is not due on the retail sale of admissions to music events, sporting events, cultural events, specified performances, movies, museums, state parks, and fitness facilities. Also exempt during this holiday period are eligible boating and water activity supplies, camping supplies, fishing supplies, general outdoor supplies, residential pool supplies, and sporting equipment. The holiday is inapplicable to rentals of any eligible items and sales within a theme park, entertainment complex, public lodging establishment, or airport. (Ch. 97 (H.B. 7071), Laws 2022, effective July 1, 2022; Emergency Rule 12AER22-4, *Tax Information Publication, No.22A01-04*, Florida Department of Revenue, May 6, 2022)

• *Back-to-school holiday*

A back-to-school sales tax holiday will be held from July 25 through August 7, 2022. During the holiday, the following items are exempt from state sales and use tax:

— clothing, footwear, and certain accessories with a sales price of $100 or less per item;

— certain school supplies with a sales price of $50 or less per item;

— learning aids and jigsaw puzzles with a sales price of $30 or less; and

— personal computers and certain computer-related accessories with a sales price of $1,500 or less when purchased for noncommercial home or personal use. (Ch. 97 (H.B. 7071), Laws 2022, effective July 1, 2022; Emergency Rule 12AER22-8, *Tax Information Publication, No.22A01-08*, Florida Department of Revenue, May 6, 2022)

Due to the enactment of multiple tax holidays, the retail sale of children's diapers and baby and toddler clothing, apparel, and footwear, regardless of the sales price, is exempt during the period from July 1, 2022 through June 30, 2023. Moreover, the retail sale of children's books (children ages 12 or younger), regardless of the sales price, is exempt during the period from May 14, 2022 through August 14, 2022. (Ch. 97 (H.B. 7071), Laws 2022, effective July 1, 2022; Emergency Rule 12AER22-8, *Tax Information Publication, No.22A01-08*, Florida Department of Revenue, May 6, 2022)

The holiday does not apply to: rentals of any eligible items; repairs or alterations of any eligible items; and sales of any eligible items within a theme park, entertainment complex, public lodging establishment, or airport. (Ch. 97 (H.B. 7071), Laws 2022, effective July 1, 2022; Emergency Rule 12AER22-8, *Tax Information Publication, No.22A01-08*, Florida Department of Revenue, May 6, 2022)

• *Children's books*

Florida' provides a temporary sales and use tax exemption on children's books. The exemption period begins May 14, 2022 and ends August 14, 2022. During the exemption period, tax is not due on the retail sale of children's books. The term "children's books" means any fiction or nonfiction book primarily intended for children ages 12 or younger, including any board book, picture book, beginning reader book, juvenile chapter book, middle grade book, or audiobook on CD or tape. (Ch. 97 (H.B. 7071), Laws 2022, effective July 1, 2022; Emergency Rule 12AER22-2, *Tax Information Publication, No.22A01-02*, Florida Department of Revenue, May 6, 2022)

Books that qualify for the exemption are labeled with an age range that includes 12 years old and younger. The exemption does not apply to books that are primarily intended for, or marketed to, adults, even if the book is purchased for a child 12 years old or younger. Bibles, prayer books, and school books are always exempt. "School books" include printed textbooks and workbooks containing printed instructional material, such as questions and answers, that are used in regularly prescribed courses of study in schools offering grades K through 12. (Ch. 97 (H.B. 7071), Laws 2022, effective July 1, 2022; Emergency Rule 12AER22-2, *Tax Information Publication, No.22A01-02*, Florida Department of Revenue, May 6, 2022)

• *Children's diapers, clothing, and shoes*

Florida provides guidance on the temporary sales and use tax exemption for children's diapers and baby and toddler clothing, apparel, and shoes, which begins July 1, 2022 and ends June 30, 2023. During this exemption period, tax is not due on the retail sale of children's diapers or on baby and toddler clothing, apparel, and shoes primarily intended for children age 5 or younger. (Ch. 97 (H.B. 7071), Laws 2022, effective July 1, 2022; Emergency Rule 12AER22-6, *Tax Information Publication, No.22A01-06*, Florida Department of Revenue, May 6, 2022)

"Clothing" and "apparel" are defined as any article of clothing or wearing apparel intended to be worn on or about the human body. "Children's diapers" include single-use and reusable diapers, including those used for toilet training and diaper inserts. The exemption does not apply to: alterations to any eligible items; clothing, apparel, or shoes primarily intended for children over the age of 5 years; rentals of any eligible items; and watches, watchbands, jewelry, umbrellas, or handkerchiefs. (Ch. 97 (H.B. 7071), Laws 2022, effective July 1, 2022; Emergency Rule 12AER22-6, *Tax Information Publication, No.22A01-06*, Florida Department of Revenue, May 6, 2022)

• *Disaster preparedness*

The Florida 2022 disaster preparedness sales and use tax holiday begins May 28, 2022 and ends June 10, 2022. During the holiday period, tax is not due on the retail sale of eligible disaster preparedness items and pet evacuation supplies. The sales tax holiday does not apply to commercial purchases of eligible pet evacuation supplies, sales within a theme park, entertainment complex, public lodging establishment or airport, and the rental or repair of any qualifying items. (Ch. 97 (H.B. 7071), Laws 2022, effective July 1, 2022; Emergency Rule 12AER22-3, *Tax Information Publication, No.22A01-03*, Florida Department of Revenue, May 6, 2022)

• *Energy Star appliances*

Florida provides a sales and use tax exemption on new Energy Star appliances purchased for noncommercial use beginning July 1, 2022, and ending June 30, 2023. The rental of an eligible new Energy Star appliance does not qualify for the exemption. An "Energy Star appliance" is one of the listed products designated by the United States Environmental Protection Agency and the United States Department of Energy as meeting or exceeding each agency's requirements under the Energy Star program and that is affixed with an Energy Star label. The exemption does not apply when the new Energy Star appliance is purchased for trade, business, or resale. (Ch. 97 (H.B. 7071), Laws 2022, effective July 1, 2022; Emergency Rule 12AER22-5, *Tax Information Publication, No.22A01-05*, Florida Department of Revenue, May 6, 2022)

Eligible items are:

— clothes dryers selling for $1,500 or less;

— refrigerators or combination refrigerator/freezers selling for $3,000 or less;

— washing machines selling for $1,500 or less; and

— water heaters selling for $1,500 or less.

(Ch. 97 (H.B. 7071), Laws 2022, effective July 1, 2022; Emergency Rule 12AER22-5, *Tax Information Publication, No.22A01-05*, Florida Department of Revenue, May 6, 2022)

• *Impact-resistant doors, garage doors, and windows*

A temporary Florida sales and use tax exemption applies to impact-resistant doors, impact-resistant garage doors, and impact-resistant windows purchased for commercial or non-commercial use beginning July 1, 2022, and ending June 30, 2024. "Impact-resistant doors," "impact-resistant garage doors," and "impact-resistant windows" refer to doors, garage doors, or windows that are labeled as impact-resistant or have an impact-resistant rating. (Ch. 97 (H.B. 7071), Laws 2022, effective July 1, 2022; Emergency Rule 12AER22-7, *Tax Information Publication, No.22A01-07*, Florida Department of Revenue, May 6, 2022)

• *Tools commonly used by skilled trade workers*

Florida sales and use tax may not be collected during the period from September 3, 2022 through September 9, 2022, on the retail sale of:

• hand tools selling for $50 or less per item;

• power tools selling for $300 or less per item;

• power tool batteries selling for $150 or less per item;

• work gloves selling for $25 or less per pair;

• safety glasses selling for $50 or less per pair, or the equivalent if sold in sets of more than one pair;

• protective coveralls selling for $50 or less per item;

• work boots selling for $175 or less per pair;

- tool belts selling for $100 or less per item;
- duffle bags or tote bags selling for $50 or less per item;
- tool boxes selling for $75 or less per item;
- tool boxes for vehicles selling for $300 or less per item;
- industry textbooks and code books selling for $125 or less per item;
- electrical voltage and testing equipment selling for $100 or less per item;
- LED flashlights selling for $50 or less per item;
- shop lights selling for $100 or less per item; and
- handheld pipe cutters, drain opening tools, and plumbing inspection equipment selling for $150 or less per item.

The sales tax holiday does not apply to rentals of any eligible items and sales within a theme park, entertainment complex, public lodging establishment, or airport. (Ch. 97 (H.B. 7071), Laws 2022, effective July 1, 2022; Emergency Rule 12AER22-8, Emergency Rule 12AER22-9*Tax Information Publication, No.22A01-09*, Florida Department of Revenue, May 6, 2022)

[¶61-000]
EXEMPTIONS

[¶61-020] Exemption Certificates

Every sale, admission, use, storage, consumption, or rental is taxable, unless such sale, admission, use, storage, consumption, or rental is specifically exempt. The exempt nature of a transaction must be established by the selling dealer. Unless the selling dealer has obtained proper documentation from the purchaser, the sale is deemed taxable. The Florida Department of Revenue issues resale certificates and consumer certificates of exemption to various entities. A regulation provides the suggested format of an exemption certificate at Rule 12A-1.038. (Secs. 212.07(1)(b); 212.08, F.S.; Rule 12A-1.038; Rule 12A-1.039)

• *Exemption certificates*

Every sales tax exemption certificate issued by the Florida Department of Revenue expires five years after it is issued. After expiration, it is subject to a review process. The Department chooses entities for review based on an alphabetical selection procedure in each county. (Sec. 212.084, F.S.)

During a review, an entity may be asked to submit documentation and evidence of its organizational structure, federal tax status, program content, and any other material deemed necessary. After the review is complete and the Department has determined that the entity is actively engaged in a bona fide exempt endeavor, the exemption certificate will be reissued. Each reissued certificate is valid for five consecutive years before it is subject to another review. If the entity no longer qualifies for an exemption, the exemption certificate will be revoked. (Sec. 212.084, F.S.)

A certificate will be revoked if the entity fails to respond to either of two written requests made by the Department for information regarding its taxable status. The two letters are mailed at least four weeks apart to the entity's last known address. An entity may apply for reissuance of a revoked certificate if the revocation occurred because of the failure to respond. (Sec. 212.084(2), F.S.)

Upon request to the Department of Revenue, the name and address of any institution, organization, individual, or other entity possessing a valid sales tax exemption certificate will be furnished. (Sec. 212.084(7), F.S.)

Penalties for misuse.—Fraudulent claims of exemption create liability for the tax, a mandatory 200% penalty, and additional fines and punishment for conviction of a third degree felony. (Sec. 212.085, F.S.; Rule 12A-1.038).

• *Specialized certificates*

A number of specialized exemption certificates are discussed.

Electrical energy used in an enterprise zone.—To receive an exemption on the purchase of electricity in an enterprise zone, a business must file an application under oath that includes the following:

— the name and location of the business;

— the identifying number of the enterprise zone;

— the date on which electrical service is to start;

— the name and mailing address of the electrical energy supplier;

— the date of the application;

— the name of the city in which the business is located;

— a statement of whether the business is a small business; and

— the name and address of each permanent employee, including the identifying number for the enterprise zone of residence, if applicable.

(Sec. 212.08(15)(b), F.S.)

CAUTION NOTE: *Expiration of Florida Enterprise Zone Program.*—Except for certain extensions, as provided, the Florida Enterprise Zone Program expires on December 31, 2015. For businesses that do not qualify for extension, enterprise zone credits or refunds will be approved after December 31, 2015, only if the business applying for the credit or refund meets the statutory eligibility requirements for the incentive on or before December 31, 2015. (*Tax Information Publication, No. 15ADM-04*, Florida Department of Revenue, September 8, 2015)

If the business is subsequently shown to have failed to meet the criteria for a permit, the business must pay the amount of taxes that was exempted plus interest and penalties. (Sec. 212.08(15)(b), F.S.)

Guide dogs for the blind.—A blind person who owns, rents, or contemplates ownership or rental of a seeing-eye dog may apply for a consumer's certificate of exemption, which shall be issued free of charge and shall be wallet-size. (Sec. 212.08(7)(h), F.S.)

Natural gas and natural gas fuel.—To qualify for the exemption from sales tax and gross receipts tax at the time of purchase, the purchaser must give the seller a certificate stating that the natural gas or natural gas fuel is for exclusive use in the fuel supply system of a motor vehicle. (*Tax Information Publication No. 14B05-02*, Florida Department of Revenue, April 9, 2014)

Any person purchasing natural gas and natural gas fuel, who is not separately metered, for a use that is subject to sales tax and/or gross receipts tax and for use in a motor vehicle (i.e., a dual user) should obtain a natural gas fuel retailer's license, a sales and use tax registration, and a gross receipts tax registration, if applicable. The purchaser will purchase the fuel exempt from tax and will be required to self-accrue and remit the applicable taxes to the department. To qualify for the exemption from sales tax and gross receipts tax at the time of purchase, the purchaser must give the seller a certificate stating that it will self-accrue the applicable taxes and remit them to the department. If the natural gas or natural gas fuel purchased for use in a motor vehicle is separately metered, the purchaser is only required to obtain a license as a retailer of natural gas fuel. Any applicable sales tax and/or gross receipts tax owed by the purchaser will be paid directly to the supplier. (*Tax Information Publication No. 14B05-02*, Florida Department of Revenue, April 9, 2014)

The department provides a suggested exemption certificate for this purpose. (*Tax Information Publication No. 14B05-02*, Florida Department of Revenue, April 9, 2014)

Natural gas used to generate electricity.—Sellers of natural gas are required to document exempt sales. A suggested certificate to be completed by the purchaser and maintained in the selling vendor's books and records is provided by the Florida Department of Revenue. (*Tax Information Publication No. 13A01-08*, Florida Department of Revenue, June 17, 2013)

New or expanding businesses.—To receive an exemption on purchases of industrial machinery and equipment, a qualifying business entity must apply for a temporary tax exemption permit. The application must state that a new business exemption or expanded business exemption is being sought. The Department of Revenue will issue the permit upon a tentative affirmative determination. After the purchases have been made, the business must return the permit to the Department of Revenue. (Sec. 212.08(5)(b), F.S.)

If the business is subsequently shown to have failed to meet the criteria for a permit, the business must pay the amount of taxes that was exempted plus interest and penalties. A business that qualifies for a permit, but was denied, may apply for a refund of taxes paid. (Sec. 212.08(5)(b), F.S.)

Nonprofit organizations.—Chartered nonprofit religious, charitable, or educational institutions located in Florida that desire to qualify for an exemption must obtain a consumer's certificate of exemption from the Department of Revenue. The effective date of the certificate is the postmark date of the application if mailed by the taxpayer, or the date the application is received by the Department if delivered by the taxpayer. (Rule 12A-1.038)

The Florida Department of Revenue advises that, for sales and use tax purposes, a new application for a Consumer's Certificate of Exemption (Form DR-5) is now available for use by nonprofit organizations and governmental entities. Information on who qualifies, what is exempt, and how to establish qualification is provided on the new form. Although exemption certificates expire after five years, holders of exemption certificates no longer need to reapply for a new certificate every five years. The department will review each exemption certificate 60 days before the current certificate expires, and for those nonprofit organizations and governmental entities located in Florida, the department will use available public information to determine whether the organization or entity continues to qualify for an exemption certificate. If the organization or entity continues to meet the statutory exemption criteria, a new exemption certificate will be issued. If, however, additional information is needed, a letter requesting documentation will be mailed to the organization or entity. For those nonprofit organizations and governmental entities located outside Florida, the department will mail a letter asking whether the organization or entity wishes to have their certificate renewed. The letter will also provide a list of documentation necessary for the department to renew the exemption certificate. If the organization or entity fails to respond to the written requests for information or documentation, or the department is unable to confirm that the organization or entity continues to qualify for an exemption, a written notice denying the renewal of the exemption certificate will be mailed to the organization or entity. (*Tax Information Publication, No. 16A01-03*, Florida Department of Revenue, April 27, 2016)

An exemption certificate must be presented by the purchaser to the dealer when any purchases are made for use in carrying on the work of the organization. Purchases made prior to the effective date are not exempt from tax. (Rule 12A-1.038)

A consumer's certificate of exemption may be used to purchase tangible personal property and may not be applied to contracts for the construction or improvement of real property. (Rule 12A-1.038)

Political subdivisions and public libraries.—State political subdivisions and public libraries issued exemption certificates are urged to use the certificates to purchase services, supplies, equipment, and items necessary for the operation of specific groups. (Sec. 212.0821, F.S.)

Production companies.—Any production company engaged in the production of motion pictures, made-for-TV motion pictures, television series, commercial advertising, music videos, or sound recordings in Florida may apply to the Department of Revenue and the Office of Film and Entertainment to be approved as a qualified production company eligible to receive a certificate of exemption. (Sec. 288.1258, F.S.; Rule 12A-1.085; Rule 12A-1.097)

• *Electronic exemption certificates*

Sales and use tax dealers can verify the status of a customer's Consumer's Certificate of Exemption online at https://suntax.state.fl.us/irj/portal/anonymous. Dealers may verify one to five certificates instantly or upload a file of up to 50,000 certificate numbers to receive results within 24 hours.

• *Multiple point of use certificates (MPUs)*

Florida does not have any provisions for MPUs.

• *MTC and SST certificates*

MTC.—Under the Multistate Tax Compact, a vendor is relieved of liability for sales or use tax with respect to a transaction for which the vendor accepts in good faith a resale or other exemption certificate, or other authorized written evidence of exemption. The Commission has adopted a Uniform Multijurisdiction Exemption Certificate that is to be filled out by buyers claiming sales tax exemptions and is maintained on file by sellers. In order for the certificate to be accepted in good faith by a seller, the seller must exercise caution that the transaction, or property being sold, is of a type that normally qualifies for exemption in the state. Florida allows sellers to accept the Uniform Multijurisdiction Exemption Certificate for at least some purposes.

SST.—The Streamlined Sales Tax Governing Board has approved a uniform exemption certificate. Florida, as a nonmember state, may but is not required to accept the certificate.

• *Direct payment permit holders*

Florida has no provisions regarding requirements for direct payment permit holders to file exemption certificates.

[¶61-100]
BASIS OF TAX

[¶61-110] Tax Base

Sales tax is levied on the sales price of an item of tangible personal property purchased. (Sec. 212.05(1)(a), F.S.) Real property that is leased, let, or rented is taxed on the total rental charged. (Sec. 212.03(1); Sec. 212.031(1)(c), F.S.) See Rate of Tax for the current rate.

Tangible personal property that is leased or rented is taxed on the gross proceeds or the rental price paid. (Sec. 212.05(1), F.S.) Admissions are taxed on the net sum of money charged after the deduction of any federal taxes paid. (Sec. 212.02(1); Sec. 212.04(1)(b), F.S.)

Use tax is levied on the cost price or fair market value of property that is not sold, but is used, consumed, distributed, or stored for use or consumption in Florida. (Sec. 212.05(4), F.S.) Property manufactured, produced, compounded, processed, or fabricated for a person's own use is also taxed on the cost of the product. Asphalt manufactured for a person's own use is taxed only on the cost of the materials and transportation, in addition to a tax per ton of asphalt. (Sec. 212.06(1), F.S.)

Use tax is also due at the rate of 6% of the cost price of each item or article of tangible personal property purchased as an exempt resale, but then withdrawn from inventory for the purchaser's own use or consumption in the state. However, for property originally purchased exempt from tax for use exclusively for lease that is converted to the owner's own use, tax may be paid on the fair market value of the property at the time of conversion. If the fair market value of the property cannot be determined, use tax at the time of conversion is based on the owner's acquisition cost. Under no circumstances may the aggregate amount of sales tax from leasing the property and use tax due at the time of conversion be less than the total sales tax that would have been due on the original acquisition cost paid by the owner. (Sec. 212.05(1)(b), F.S.).

"Sales price" means the total amount paid for the property, including any services (valued in money) that are a part of the sale. It also may include any amount for which credit is given to the purchaser by the seller, but not the cost of the property sold, the cost of the materials used, labor or service costs, interest charged, losses or any other expenses. "Sales price" also includes the consideration for a transaction which requires both labor and material to alter, remodel, maintain, adjust, or repair tangible personal property. Trade-ins or discounts allowed and taken at the time of sale shall not be included within the purview of this subsection. "Sales price" also includes the full face value of any coupon used by a purchaser to reduce the price paid to a retailer for an item of tangible personal property (1) where the retailer will be reimbursed by the manufacturer for the coupon, or (2) whenever it is not practicable for the retailer to determine, at the time of sale, the extent to which reimbursement for the coupon will be made. "Sales price" does not include federal excise taxes imposed upon the retailer on the sale of tangible personal property. "Sales price" does include federal manufacturers' excise taxes, even if the federal tax is listed as a separate item on the invoice. (Sec. 212.02(16), F.S.)

In addition, To the extent required by federal law, the term "sales price" does not include charges for Internet access services which are not itemized on the customer's bill, but which can be reasonably identified from the selling dealer's books and records kept in the regular course of business. The dealer may support the allocation of charges with books and records kept in the regular course of business covering the dealer's entire service area, including territories outside this state. (Sec. 212.02(16), F.S.)

"Cost price" means the actual cost of articles of tangible personal property, without any deduction for expenses such as materials, labor, services, or transportation charges. (Sec. 212.02(4), F.S.; Rule 12A-1.043(1)(a))

Direct materials on which sales tax has been paid are not included when computing the tax on the cost price of items of tangible personal property manufactured, produced, compounded, processed, or fabricated. People who manufacture, produce, compound, process, or fabricate tangible personal property items for resale or for their own use may make tax-exempt purchases of direct materials, but they must include the cost of the materials when computing tax on the cost of the items created for their own use. (Rule 12A-1.043(1))

"Gross sales" mean the sum total of all sales of tangible personal property or services, without any deduction except as provided by statute. (Sec. 212.02(14)(d), F.S.)

• *Interstate transportation*

Florida taxes the sale or use of vessels, parts of vessels, and fuels used by vessels that are used to transport people or property in interstate or foreign commerce based on the ratio of intrastate mileage to interstate or foreign mileage traveled during the previous fiscal year. "Parts of vessels" includes any items appropriate to carry out the purpose for which a vessel is designed and used. (Sec. 212.08(8), F.S.; Rule 12A-1.0641)

Railroads that are licensed as common carriers by the U.S. Surface Transportation Board are subject to tax on rolling stock, and parts thereof, used to transport persons or property for hire in interstate or foreign commerce on the basis of the ratio of intrastate mileage to interstate or foreign mileage traveled during the previous fiscal year. The ratio is applied each month to total purchases of tangible personal property used in the state and fuel. (Sec. 212.08(9), F.S.; Rule 12A-1.064(3))

For purposes of calculating sales and use tax due on motor fuels and diesel fuels used by railroad locomotives or vessels in interstate or foreign commerce, during the fiscal year in which a carrier begins its initial operations in Florida, the carrier's mileage apportionment factor used to calculate tax due may be determined on the basis of an estimated ratio of anticipated miles in the state to anticipated total miles for that year. The carrier must then request a refund or pay additional tax on the basis of the actual ratio of the carrier's miles in the state to its total miles for that year. (Sec. 212.08(4), F.S.)

An air carrier using mileage apportionment for corporate income tax purposes may elect to be taxed in Florida on the basis of the ratio of intrastate mileage to interstate and foreign mileage. The ratio is applied each month to the carrier's total system wide gross purchases of tangible personal property, taxable services, and lease payment for real property used for large scale aircraft maintenance. (Sec. 212.0598, F.S.)

• *Telecommunications*

Telecommunications services are taxed on the charges made. Interstate interoffice channel mileage charges are taxed on the basis of a ratio of Florida channel mileage to total channel mileage between the last Florida channel termination point and the first channel termination point outside of Florida. (Sec. 212.05(1)(e), F.S.)

• *Boats licensed for saltwater fishing*

A boat imported to Florida requiring a saltwater fishing license for noncommercial fishing must pay use tax. A boat that is first licensed within one year after purchase is subject to use tax on the full amount of the purchase price; a boat that is first licensed in the second year after purchase is taxed on 90% of the purchase price; a boat that is first licensed in the third year after purchase is taxed on 80% of the purchase price; a boat that is first licensed in the fourth year after purchase is taxed on 70% of the purchase price; a boat that is first licensed in the fifth year after purchase is taxed on 60% of the purchase price; and a boat that is first licensed in the sixth year after purchase or later is taxed on 50% of the purchase price. If the owner of the boat does not have an invoice, the fair market value of the boat at the time it is imported into Florida is used to compute the tax. (Rule 12A-1.007(9)(e))

• *Coins and currency*

Sales tax is imposed on coins or currency at the rate of 6% of the price at which it is sold, exchanged, or traded. However, coins or currency which are legal tender of the U.S. and are sold, exchanged, or traded at a rate in excess of its face value are taxed at a rate of 6% of the difference between the price at which they are sold, exchanged, or traded and their face value. (Sec. 212.05(1)(j) 2, F.S.)

¶61-110

• *Carnival prizes*

Prizes given by carnival vendors are taxed on 25% of the vendors' gross receipts. (Rule 12A-1.080)

[¶61-200]
RETURNS, PAYMENTS, AND RECORDS

[¶61-220] Returns, Payments, and Due Dates

All dealers must file a return and remit the tax on or before the 20th day of the month to the Department of Revenue. Returns are accepted as timely if postmarked on or before the 20th day of the month. If the 20th day falls on a Saturday, Sunday, or federal or state legal holiday, returns are accepted if postmarked on the next workday. A "legal holiday" is a legal holiday in the District of Columbia or a Statewide legal holiday at a location outside the District of Columbia but within an Federal Internal Revenue District. (Sec. 212.11(1), F.S.; Rule 12A-1.056(1), F.A.C.)

However, the Department of Revenue may require dealers to make returns and payments based on the amount of tax remitted in the preceding four calendar quarters as follows:

— dealers who remitted $100 or less, annual reports and payments;

— dealers who remitted at least $100 but less than $500, semiannual reports and payments;

— dealers who remitted at least $500 but less than $1,000, quarterly reports and payments;

— dealers who remitted between $1,000 and $12,000, quarterly reports with monthly payments.

(Sec. 212.11(1)(c), F.S.)

Taxpayers who paid more than $1,000 in Florida sales and use tax during the most recent state fiscal year (i.e., July 1—June 30) are required to pay tax and file returns on a monthly basis. If the amount reported over $1,000 was due to non-recurring taxable business activities, the taxpayer may request permission to continue filing paper tax returns by sending a letter to the Department. (Sec. 212.12, F.S.; Rule 12A-1.056, F.A.C.; *Tax Information Publication 08A01-10*, Florida Department of Revenue, November 19, 2008)

A taxpayer whose tax payment history exceeds these thresholds may continue filing and paying tax on a quarterly, semi-annual, or annual basis or file a quarterly return and pay a monthly tax if the taxpayer submits a written request to the Department stating that the tax amount submitted represents nonrecurring business activity. (Sec. 212.11(1)(c), F.S.)

Dealers that are authorized to file quarterly, semiannually or annually must file a return and remit the tax on or before the 20th day of the month following the authorized reporting period. (Rule 12A-1.056(1), F.A.C.)

Dealers newly required to file and pay tax quarterly may file returns and remit the tax for the three-month periods ending in February, May, August, and November. Dealers newly required to file and pay tax semiannually may file returns and remit the tax for the six-month periods ending in May and November. (Sec. 212.11(1)(d), F.S.)

The Department of Revenue may also permit persons to deviate from monthly filing if it determines that the information required for making an accurate return cannot reasonably be compiled by the taxpayer on a monthly basis. (Rule 12A-1.056(4), F.A.C.)

Each dealer must file a return for each tax period even if no tax is due for that period. (Sec. 212.11(1)(e), F.S.)

For discussion of self-accrual, see Direct Payment Permits.

Electronic filing required for out-of-state retailers and marketplace providers. Out-of-state retailers and marketplace providers are required to file returns and remit tax electronically. (Sec. 212.11(4)(f), F.S.)

Moreover, a marketplace provider that is a sales and use tax dealer or a person who is required to collect and remit sales or use tax on remote sales must file with the department an application for a certificate of registration electronically. (Sec. 212.18(3)(c), F.S.)

Guidance for business owners.—Florida has updated sales and use tax guidance for business owners. Topics discussed include tax and surtax rates, discretionary sales surtax, use tax, exemptions, and annual resale certificates. (*Form GT-300015*, Florida Department of Revenue, February 2018)

• *Collection compensation for dealers who file and pay by electronic means*

The sales tax dealer's collection allowance, which is provided as compensation for recordkeeping and collection to taxpayers who timely file returns and pay taxes, is limited to those dealers who file and pay by electronic means. They are allowed a discount of 2.5% of the first $1,200 of tax due for each reporting period for keeping records, filing timely tax returns, and properly accounting and remitting taxes. (Sec. 212.12, F.S.; Rule 12A-1.056(5)(d), F.A.C.)

The same limitation applies on collection discounts for remitting the admissions tax. (Sec. 212.04(5), F.S.) The allowance does not apply to the rental car surcharge. (Sec. 212.0606, F.S.) Vendors may elect to forgo the allowance and instead direct that the amount be transferred into the Educational Enhancement Trust Fund. (Sec. 212.12(1)(c), F.S.)

The Florida Department of Revenue provides guidance regarding the collection allowance dealers may deduct only when they timely file returns and pay tax electronically ("e-file" and "e-pay"). To file and pay sales and use tax electronically, dealers should go to the department's website at: http://www.myflorida.com/dor and use the website to file and pay tax electronically or purchase software. Dealers will not be entitled to a collection allowance if they file a paper tax return or pay tax by cash, check, or money order. (*Tax Information Publication, No. 12A01-03*, Florida Department of Revenue, April 30, 2012)

Also, if a dealer files and pays tax electronically but is late, the dealer cannot deduct a collection allowance from the amount due with the return. Standard banking regulations require one business day to complete an electronic payment, so tax returns and payments must be initiated before 5:00 p.m., Eastern Time, on the last banking day before the 20th of the month to be considered timely. To enroll for e-Services or to electronically file and pay tax without enrolling, a dealer must provide specific information, including the dealer's sales and use tax certificate number and/ or business partner number, the dealer's federal employer identification number (FEIN) or social security number (SSN), contact information, bank routing/transit number, and bank account number. (*Tax Information Publication, No. 12A01-03*, Florida Department of Revenue, April 30, 2012)

Consolidated returns.—A dealer operating more than one place of business and filing a consolidated return that provides the monthly business activity for each location may take the collection allowance for each reporting location that is registered. If a dealer files a combined return for multiple locations using only one registration number, however, the dealer is entitled to the collection allowance based on the total amount reported. (Rule 12A-1.056(5)(e), F.A.C.)

• *Confidentiality*

Nothing contained in the sales and use tax law shall be construed to require the disclosure of privileged information, the confidentiality of which is protected under the Florida Evidence Code. (Sec. 212.184, F.S.)

All information contained in returns, reports, accounts, or declarations received by the Department of Revenue, including investigative reports and letters of technical advice, is confidential except for the following official purposes (the following is only a partial list):

— information relative to the entertainment industry financial incentive program may be provided to the Office of Film and Entertainment and the Florida Department of Economic Opportunity;

— a taxpayer authorizes the Department in writing to divulge specific information;

— the Department releases statistics in a manner that prevents identification of specific accounts;

— the Department makes the information available to the United States Department of the Treasury, the Internal Revenue Service, or the United States Department of the Interior for official purposes;

— the Department makes the information available to the Auditor General, the Comptroller, the Treasurer, or a property appraiser or tax collector for official purposes unless prohibited by federal law;

— the Department makes certain information available to the Division of Alcoholic Beverages and Tobacco, the Division of Hotels and Restaurants, the Department of the Lottery, the Department of Banking and Finance, the Revenue Estimating Conference, and the Division of Condominiums, Timeshares, and Mobile Homes in the conduct of their official duties;

— the Department makes the information available to the Nexus Program of the Multistate Compact pursuant to a formal agreement for the exchange of mutual information;

— a court of competent jurisdiction orders the information, or a properly issued subpoena *duces tecum* requires the information;

— the Department makes the names and addresses of registered dealers available to a municipality or county responsible for issuing an occupational license;

— the Department verifies whether a taxpayer holds a certificate of registration;

— the Department provides the U.S. Bankruptcy Court with information concerning tax liability for official purposes;

— the Department reveals the reason for revocation or cancellation of a sales and use certificate of registration;

— the Department may allow full access to certain documents to the Department of Banking and Finance and the Department of Law Enforcement during joint investigations of large currency transactions, with the information made available for use in civil or criminal investigations and in court proceedings;

— the Department may disclose location information limited to the names and addresses contained in returns, reports, accounts, or declarations filed with the Department by persons subject to a state tax to the child support enforcement program to assist in the location of parents who owe or potentially owe a duty of support pursuant to the Social Security Act;

— the Department may provide to the person against whom transferee liability is being asserted under Sec. 213.758, F.S. information relating to the basis of the claim;

— the Department may disclose to a person entitled to compensation under Sec. 213.30, F.S. the amount of any tax, penalty, or interest collected as a result of information furnished by such person;

— the Department may disclose to the Department of Commerce information concerning a taxpayer's sales and use tax payments for purposes of the qualified defense contractor tax refund program or the qualified target industry business tax refund program, discussed at ¶60-360 Enterprise Zones and Similar Tax Incentives;

— the Department may disclose information relative to the Bill of Lading Program to the Office of Agriculture Law Enforcement of the Department of Agriculture and Consumer Services in the conduct of its official duties;

— the Department may disclose names, addresses and sales tax registration information to the Division of Consumer Services of the Department of Agriculture and Consumer Services in the conduct of its official duties;

— the Department may share information related to returns required by Secs. 175.111 (Municipal Firefighters' Pension Trust Funds) and 185.05 (Municipal Police Officers' Pension Trust Funds) with the Department of Management Services;

— the Department may disclose names, addresses, and federal employer identification numbers to the Department of Highway Safety and Motor Vehicles; and

— information relative to the exemption (provided in the form of a refund of taxes previously paid) for equipment, machinery, and other materials for renewable energy technologies.

(Sec. 213.053, F.S.; Rule 12-22.001, F.A.C.)

In addition, any information received by the Florida Department of Revenue in connection with the administration of taxes, including but not limited to information contained in returns, reports, accounts, or declarations filed by persons subject to tax, will be made available to the following in performance of their official duties:

— the taxpayers' rights advocate; and

— the coordinator of the Office of Economic and Demographic Research.

(Sec. 213.053, F.S.)

Registration and Information Sharing Exchange Program.—The Department may disclose information under a state program called "Registration Information Sharing and Exchange Program (RISE)," which is established to allow tax administration information exchange between state and local government agencies. Information that might be exchanged includes the registrant/licensee/taxpayer's name, mailing address, business location, federal employer identification number or social security number, applicable business type code, any applicable county code, and such other tax registration information as is prescribed by the Department of Revenue. (Sec. 213.053(7)(j), F.S.; Sec. 213.0535, F.S.; Rule 12-22.007, F.A.C.)

The RISE Program permits the sharing of tax administration information between different specified local government entities, including local officials responsible for collecting tourism taxes (i.e., level-two participants). These participants are permitted to share information between each other but not with other related entities. A level-two participant is authorized to publish aggregate statistics on tourism taxes. However, such statistics may not be published if they contain data regarding fewer than three taxpayers or if the statistics are prepared for geographic areas below the county level and contain data regarding fewer than 10 taxpayers. Statistics published may only relate to tourist development taxes, tourist impact taxes, convention development taxes, or the municipal resort tax. (Sec. 213.0535(5), F.S.)

• *Consolidated returns*

A dealer that operates two or more places of business for which returns are required to be filed and maintains records for such places in a central office may file a consolidated return for all such places of business in lieu of separate returns for each place of business. The returns must clearly indicate the amounts collected within each county in Florida. Dealers can apply for consolidated filing by submitting Form DR-1CON, Application for Consolidated Sales and Use Tax Filing Number, to the Department of Revenue. (Sec. 212.11(1)(d), F.S.)

Any dealer who files a consolidated return must calculate the estimated tax liability for each county by the same method used to calculate the estimated tax liability on the consolidated return as a whole (see above discussion of estimated tax payments). Any dealer who is eligible to file a consolidated return and who paid sales and use tax of $100,000 or more for the immediately preceding state fiscal year, or who would have paid such an amount if a consolidated return had been filed, is subject to the estimated tax provisions discussed above, notwithstanding an election by the dealer in any month to file a separate return. (Sec. 212.11(1)(d) and (4)(c), F.S.)

• *Estimated tax payments*

Each dealer who operates one place of business, or who operates two or more places of business and maintains records for those businesses in a central office or place, or who files or was eligible to file a consolidated return (see discussion below), and who paid state sales and use taxes for the preceding state fiscal year of $200,000 or more must calculate the amount of estimated tax due for any month by one of the following methods:

— 60% of the current month's gross tax liability as shown on the tax return or the consolidated tax return;

— 60% of the gross tax reported on the tax return or the consolidated tax return for taxable transactions occurring during the corresponding month of the previous year; or

— 60% of the average gross tax liability for months during the preceding calendar year in which the dealer reported taxable transactions.

(Sec. 212.11(1), F.S.; Sec. 212.11(4), F.S.)

The Florida Department of Revenue provides guidance regarding estimated Florida sales and use tax payments for businesses with multiple locations using the same taxpayer identification number. (*Tax Information Publication, No. 06A01-14*, Florida Department of Revenue, October 6, 2006)

Estimated tax payments are reported on Line 9 of the sales tax return, Form DR-15CS. Taxpayers that calculate their estimated tax due incorrectly or that forget to enter their estimated tax cannot amend their return. The amount of any estimated tax calculated under the above provisions must be remitted by electronic funds transfer. The returns also must be filed electronically. The difference between the amount of estimated tax paid and the actual tax liability is due on the first day of the month following the date of sale and must be remitted by electronic funds transfer by the 20th day of the month. (Sec. 212.11(4)(b), F.S.; *Tax Information Publication, No. 04A01-09*, Florida Department of Revenue, October 13, 2004, 204-585; *Tax Information Publication No. 01A01-12*, Florida Department of Revenue, October 8, 2001; *Tax Information Publication No. 01A01-13*, Florida Department of Revenue, October 8, 2001)

Dealers who paid sales and use tax of $200,000 or more (excluding local option surtax and transient rental taxes) during July 1 through June 30 (the state's fiscal year) must make estimated sales tax payments during the next calendar year. An estimated sales tax payment must be made every month beginning with the December return due January 1st of the next calendar year. (*Business Owner's Guide for Sales and Use Tax, GT-300015,* Florida Department of Revenue, February 2018)

Exclusions from computation.—In computing estimated tax liability, a dealer is not required to include any local option sales tax, the rental car surcharge, the motor vehicle warranty fee, or any solid waste fee. (Rule 12A-1.056(3), F.A.C.)

A dealer who made at least one sale of a boat, motor vehicle, or aircraft with a sales price of $100,000 or greater in the previous state fiscal year is required to make estimated sales tax payments. To qualify a dealer must apply annually to the Department prior to October 1. A qualifying dealer who is granted the option to pay estimated tax must calculate that option as 66% of the average tax liability for all sales excluding those sales that individually are $100,000 or greater. The dealer must remit the sales tax for each individual sale of $100,000 or greater by either electronic funds transfer or on a form prescribed by the department. (Sec. 212.11(4)(d)., F.S.)

• *Exhibition center rentals, admissions*

Florida sales tax on the lease or license of an exhibition center used for an event lasting more than seven consecutive days must be collected by the lessor when rent or a license fee is paid, but is not due or payable to the Florida Department of Revenue until the first day of the month that follows the event's last day. (Sec. 212.031(3), F.S.) The tax liability becomes delinquent on the 21st day of that month. Similarly, sales tax on an admissions fee for an event at an exhibition center also must be collected when the fee is paid and is not due until the first day of the month that follows the date of the event. Tax delinquency also arises as of the 21st day of that month. Exhibition centers include convention halls, auditoriums, stadiums, theaters, arenas, civic centers, performing arts centers, or publicly owned recreational facilities. (Sec. 212.04(3), F.S.)

• *Final returns*

If a dealer that is liable for tax, interest, fee, surcharge, or imposed penalties administered by the Department of Revenue sells its business or its stock of goods, it must make a final return and payment in 15 days after the date of selling or quitting the business. Any person failing to file the final return and make the payment will be denied the right to engage in any business in Florida. All money must be paid in full and all returns filed before business operations may be commenced. (Sec. 213.758, F.S.) See Business Successor Liability.

• *Payment*

The full amount of the tax due, shown on the return, must accompany the return. (Sec. 212.11, F.S.; Rule 12A-1.056(1), F.A.C.) Tokens may not be used to pay the tax. (Sec. 212.18(2), F.S.)

Failure to remit the full amount will cause the taxes to become delinquent. A return filed without payment is considered prima facie evidence of a dealer's intent to convert the money due the state. (Sec. 212.14(3), F.S.)

Interest and penalties are discussed at Penalties and Interest.

Electronic funds transfer and electronic filing.—The Executive Director of the Florida Department of Revenue is authorized to require a taxpayer to file returns and remit payments electronically when the amount of taxes paid in the prior state fiscal year reached a certain threshold. (Sec. 213.755, F.S.; Rule 12-24.003, F.A.C.)

Returns also must be filed electronically. (Sec. 213.755, F.S.; *Tax Information Publication No. O1A01-14,* Florida Department of Revenue, October 8, 2001) All consolidated sales tax, solid waste, and surcharge accounts must submit their tax payments and file their tax returns electronically. (*Tax Information Publication, No.*

¶61-220

02A01-22, Florida Department of Revenue, October 25, 2002) Electronic payments must be initiated no later than 5:00 p.m., Eastern Time, on the last business day before the due date of the return. (*Tax Information Publication, No. 04A01-10*, Florida Department of Revenue, October 18, 2004, 204-586)

Taxpayers required to remit sales and use taxes by electronic funds transfer will be required to make their returns in a form that is initiated through an electronic data interchange. The acceptable method of transfer and the form and content of the electronic data interchange will be prescribed by the Department of Revenue. (Sec. 212.11(1)(f), F.S.) Taxpayers will not be required to purchase equipment or incur a financial hardship to file electronically and the Department of Revenue may waive the electronic filing requirement under certain conditions. Taxpayers that have valid business reasons for not filing returns electronically must submit Form DR-654, Request for Waiver from Electronic Filing, to the Department in order to request a waiver. Taxpayers whose requests are approved must still remit payments by electronic funds transfer. (*Tax Information Publication, No. 04A01-10*, Florida Department of Revenue, October 18, 2004, 204-586)

Stipulated time payment agreements.—A taxpayer who admits liability for taxes, penalties, and interest as determined by the Department of Revenue and who would suffer undue hardship if the entire amount were due at once may enter into a written agreement with the Department that schedules payments over a specified period of time. (Rule 12-17.001, F.A.C., et seq.) Taxpayer remedies are discussed further starting at Application for Refund.

See Prepayment of Taxes and Direct Payment Permits.

• *Vending machines*

Returns by a person who sells food and beverages to an operator for resale through vending machines are due on the 20th day of the month following the close of each calendar quarter. The return must identify by dealer registration number each vending machine operator who has made such purchases and must state the net dollar amount of purchases made by each operator. (Sec. 212.0515(5)(a) and (b), F.S.; Rule 12A-1.044(5), F.A.C.)

In addition, the return must include the purchaser's name, dealer registration number, and sales price for any tax-free sale for resale of canned soft drinks of 25 cases or more. Operators who purchased food or beverages for resale in vending machines must annually provide the dealer from whom their items are purchased a certification affirmatively stating that the purchaser is a vending machine operator. The certificate is to be provided upon the first transaction between the parties and by November 1 of each year thereafter. (Sec. 212.0515(5)(a) and (b), F.S.; Rule 12A-1.044(5), F.A.C.)

• *Voluntary payment and collection procedures*

The Department of Revenue is authorized to enter into a contract with public or private vendors to develop and implement a voluntary system for sales and use tax collection and administration. A taxpayer who utilizes this system for purposes of computing and paying tax is not subject to the general sales and use tax payment and reporting requirements, is not eligible for the accounting discount credit, and may not be subject to audit for transactions handled through the system unless it appears that fraud is involved. (Sec. 213.27(9)(a), F.S.)

[¶61-240] Vendor Registration

Businesses that want to act as dealers, charge admissions, lease or rent tangible personal property or living quarters, or sell taxable services in Florida must file an application for a certificate of registration with the Florida Department of Revenue or a county tax collector authorized to act as the Department's agent for accepting registration applications. Businesses, other than businesses that own and operate vending machines and newspaper rack machines or certain businesses that rent or lease transient accommodations, must apply for a separate dealer's certificate of registration for each place of business. (Sec. 212.18(3), F.S.; Rule 12A-1.060(1)(a), F.A.C.)

The Florida Department of Revenue provides guidance for new dealers (i.e., vendors) in *GT-800054, New Dealer Guide to Working with the Florida Department of Revenue*. (*GT-800054, New Dealer Guide to Working with the Florida Department of Revenue*, Florida Department of Revenue, December 2017)

Dealers include:

— every person who manufactures or produces tangible personal property or who imports tangible personal property or who causes tangible personal property to be imported for sale at retail or who sells taxable services: for use, consumption or distribution; or for storage to be used or consumed in Florida;

— any person who has sold at retail; or used or consumed in Florida, tangible personal property or taxable services and who cannot prove that the appropriate sales and use tax has been paid;

— any person who leases or rents tangible personal property for a consideration;

— any person who maintains an office, distributing house, sales room or house, warehouse or other place of business in Florida;

— any person who solicits business and receives orders for tangible personal property from consumers for use, consumption, distribution, and storage for use or consumption in Florida;

— every person who, as a representative, agent, or solicitor of an out-of-state principal or principals, solicits, receives and accepts orders from consumers in Florida for future delivery and whose principal refuses to register as a dealer;

— the state, county, municipality, any political subdivision, agency, bureau or department, or other state or local government instrumentality;

— any person who leases, or grants a license to use, occupy, or enter upon for a duration of less than six months, living quarters, sleeping or housekeeping accommodations in hotels, apartment houses, rooming houses, tourist or trailer camps, real property, parking spaces for motor vehicles, docking or storage spaces for boats, or tie-down or storage space or spaces for aircraft at airports;

— any person who has leased, occupied, or used, or was entitled to use, any living quarters, sleeping or housekeeping accommodations in hotels, apartment houses, rooming houses, tourist or trailer camps, real property, parking spaces for motor vehicles, or docking or storage spaces for boats; or, who has purchased telecommunication services, electrical power, or energy; and who cannot prove that the sales and use tax has been paid to the vendor or lessor on any such transactions;

— any person who solicits, offers, provides, enters into, issues, or delivers any taxable service warranty or who receives, on behalf of such a person, any consideration from a warranty holder; and

— every person who sells tangible personal property at retail for use, consumption, distribution, or storage to be used or consumed in Florida including a retailer who transacts a substantial number of remote sales or a marketplace provider that has a physical presence in Florida or that makes or facilitates through its marketplace a substantial number of remote sales.

(Sec. 212.06(2), F.S.)

¶61-240

The following taxpayers also must register as dealers with the Department: (1) taxpayers wanting to obtain self-accrual authority or authorization to remit sales tax on behalf of their independent dealers or sellers; (2) air carriers electing to remit tax; and (3) taxpayers who want to pay tax based on a partial exemption directly to the Department. (Rule 12A-1.060(1)(a), F.A.C.)

No registration fee is required to conduct a remote sales business. However, remote exhibitors at trade shows are required to register even though no fee is required. (Sec. 212.06, F.S.)

The applicant will be granted a separate Certificate of Registration for each place of business. Engaging in a business without first obtaining a Certificate of Registration or after the Certificate has been canceled is prohibited. The failure or refusal of any person to register as a dealer is a first degree misdemeanor. (Sec. 212.18(3), F.S.; Rule 12A-1.060(2), F.A.C.) Such failure or refusal subjects the offender to a registration fee of $100. (Sec. 212.18(3), F.S.; Sec. 213.30(1)(b), F.S.)

Failure to register as a dealer.—See ¶ 61-530 Penalties and Interest.

• *Annual resale certificates*

Businesses that register with the Florida Department of Revenue to collect sales and use tax are issued an Annual Resale Certificate (*Form DR-13*). For each calendar year, the Florida Department of Revenue issues to each active registered dealer an Annual Resale Certificate. A newly registered dealer will receive a Sales and Use Tax Certificate of Registration (form DR-11) and an Annual Resale Certificate. The business name and location address, registration effective date, and certificate number will be indicated on the Annual Resale Certificate. (Rule 12A-1.039, F.A.C.)

• *Importation of property*

Tangible personal property subject to sales and use tax may not be imported into Florida by truck, automobile, or by any means other than common carrier or private automobile unless the dealer has obtained a dealer's certificate of registration and an importation permit. There is no fee for the certificate and permit. (Sec. 212.16(1), F.S.)

• *Issues related to registration of specific businesses*

A number of specific businesses are discussed.

Contractors.—A person who is required to obtain a contractor's occupational license before contracting for the repair, alteration, construction, or improvement of realty must also apply for a dealer's certificate of registration, unless the person has held the contractor's occupational license for at least 12 months immediately preceding the date of the contract. The contractor must either file a bond or pay the taxes in advance before receiving the certificate of registration. (Sec. 212.14(5), F.S.)

Dealers using independent sellers.—Dealers that use independent sellers to sell merchandise may remit tax on the retail sales price charged to the ultimate consumer rather than having the independent seller register as a dealer and remit the tax upon the prior authorization of the Department of Revenue. The dealer must apply to the Department of Revenue and agree to report and pay directly to the Department all sales tax liabilities that are transferred from the independent sellers to the dealer applicant as a result of the request. (Sec. 212.18(3), F.S.; Sec. 212.18(3)(a), F.S.; Rule 12A-1.0911, F.A.C.)

Lessors and property management companies.—Owners of living quarters or sleeping or housekeeping accommodations, including owners of time-shares, must file an application for sales and use tax registration. The owner must file a separate application for each property or time-share period rented, leased, let, or in which a license to use has been granted to others. The licensed agent or management company for a time-share resort that rents, leases, lets, or grants licenses to others to use time-share properties is presumed to be the dealer that must comply with sales tax registration requirements. (Rule 12A-1.060(1)(a), F.A.C.)

An agent or management company required to be licensed as a broker under Chapter 475 of the Florida Statutes may collectively register all properties and time-share units in a single county if (a) the agent, representative, or management company is authorized by means of a written agreement with the property owner to collect rental charges or room rates and (b) the agreement contains the following provisions (1) the property owner is ultimately liable for any sales and use tax due to the State of Florida on rentals, leases, lets, or licenses to use owner's property and (2) in the event that the state is unable to collect any taxes, penalties, and interest due from the rentals, leases, etc., a warrant for such uncollected amount will be issued and become a lien against the owner's property until satisfied. (Rule 12A-1.060(1)(a), F.A.C.)

Secondary metals recyclers.—Any person, corporation, or other business entity must apply for and be issued a secondary metals recycler certificate of registration before engaging in business as a secondary metals recycler at any location. (Rule 12A-17.003(1), F.A.C.) A certificate is required for each location, and no property may be disposed of until any holding period required by law has expired. There is a fee of $24 plus $6 for each location. A background check will be completed before a nontemporary certificate will be issued. (Rule 12A-17.003(3), F.A.C.)

A person may not engage in the business as a secondary metals recycler at any location without registering with the department. The department can accept applications only from a fixed business address and may not accept an application that provides an address of a hotel room or motel room, a vehicle, or a post office box. (*Tax Information Publication, No. 12A01-08*, Florida Department of Revenue, June 29, 2012)

The Florida Department of Revenue maintains a statewide registration system for secondhand dealers and secondary metals recyclers that oversees initial and annual registration renewals. Department staff also provide registration reports to law enforcement upon request. (*Tax Information Publication, No. 12A01-08*, Florida Department of Revenue, June 29, 2012)

Before engaging in business in Florida, every person or business entity who purchases or sells secondhand goods, precious metals, or metals for conversion to raw material products must register with the Florida Department of Revenue: (1) as a sales and use tax dealer to collect and report sales tax and any applicable discretionary sales surtax; and (2) as a secondhand dealer or secondary metals recycler. Such dealers or recyclers should complete a Florida Business Tax Application (Form DR-1). A separate application is required for each: (1) county where secondhand goods are purchased, consigned, or traded and at each business location where secondhand goods are sold; (2) county where an automated kiosk is operated; (3) business location where secondary metals are purchased, gathered, or obtained; and (4) secondary metals recycler business location where ferrous and nonferrous metals are converted into raw products. (*GT-800036 Secondhand Dealers and Secondary Metals Recyclers*, Florida Department of Revenue, July 2016)

Secondhand dealers.—Any person, corporation, or other business entity must apply for and be issued a secondhand dealer certificate of registration before purchasing, consigning, or pawning secondhand goods from any location. A certificate is required for each location, and goods must be held at the location for 15 days after the transaction. A background check will be completed before a nontemporary certificate will be issued. (Rule 12A-17.003(1), F.A.C.)

Any person who is in the business of purchasing, consigning, or trading secondhand goods at a flea market must have a Certificate of Registration (DR-11S) issued for the flea market location, unless that person already has a business registered as a secondhand dealer in the same county as the flea market. Any person who purchases, consigns, or trades secondhand goods must register at least one address in that county. In addition, an auction business that buys and sells estates, business inventory, surplus merchandise, or business liquidations, is exempt from secondhand dealer registration requirements. (*Tax Information Publication, No. 12A01-08*, Florida Department of Revenue, June 29, 2012)

Any business purchasing secondhand goods through an automated kiosk is a secondhand dealer. Also effective July 1, 2016, secondhand dealer transaction reports must include digital photographs of secondhand goods acquired. (*Tax Information Publication, No. 16A01-05*, Florida Department of Revenue, June 24, 2016)

Trade shows.—Exhibitors who enter into agreements authorizing the display of tangible personal property or services at a convention or trade show are required to register and collect sales and use tax if the agreement authorizes the retail sale of tangible personal property or services subject to tax. Exhibitors who sell at wholesale only must obtain a resale certificate from the purchasing dealer, but are not required to register as dealers. (Sec. 212.18(3), F.S.; Rule 12A-1.060(4), F.A.C.)

Any exhibitor who displays tangible personal property or services at a convention or trade show must register as a dealer and collect and remit tax on sales of taxable property or services subject to Florida sales tax when:

— the written agreement authorizes an exhibitor to make retail sales in this state of taxable tangible personal property or services; or

— the written agreement authorizes an exhibitor to make remote sales.

(Rule 12A-1.060(4), F.A.C.)

An exhibitor who does not carry on any other activity in Florida that requires registration is not required to register as a dealer to collect sales tax when:

— the written agreement prohibits the sale of taxable tangible personal property or taxable services; or

— the written agreement provides that the exhibitor shall only make sales for the purposes of resale and the exhibitor obtains a copy of the purchaser's annual resale certificate.

(Rule 12A-1.060(4), F.A.C.)

Vending machine operators.—Owners and operators of vending machines or newspaper rack machines are required to obtain only one certificate of registration for each county in which their machines are located. In addition to registering, a vending machine operator must affix a notice containing specified information to each vending machine. (Sec. 212.18(3), F.S.)

• *Revocation of certificate*

The Department may revoke a sales tax certificate of registration for any failure by the dealer to comply with any provision of the sales tax law. The procedures that are to be followed in a revocation action are set forth in the applicable statute. (Sec. 212.18(3), F.S.)

• *Reward for identifying noncompliant taxpayer*

The Department of Revenue is authorized to pay a $100 reward to any person who provides information leading to the identification and registration of a taxpayer who is not in compliance with applicable statutory registration requirements. The reward will be paid only if the noncompliant taxpayer conducts business from a permanent fixed location, is engaged in a bona fide taxable activity, and is found by the Department to have an unpaid tax liability. (Sec. 213.30(1)(b), F.S.)

• *Security required from dealers*

When it is necessary to ensure compliance, a cash deposit, bond, or other security may be required as a condition to a person obtaining or retaining a dealer's certificate of registration. (Sec. 212.18(3)(a), F.S.)

The requirements and procedures the Department of Revenue uses when it requires security in the form of a cash deposit, surety bond, or irrevocable letter of credit as a condition to obtaining or retaining a dealer's certificate of registration are provided by rule. (Rule 12A-1.060(6), F.A.C.)

• *Security requirements for new registrations*

The Florida Department of Revenue is authorized, where necessary to ensure compliance with the Sales and Use Tax, to require a cash deposit, bond, or other security as a condition to a person obtaining or retaining a dealer's certificate of registration. (Sec. 212.14(4), F.S.)

The term "person" includes:

— any individual, firm, copartnership, joint adventure, association, corporation, estate, trust, business trust, receiver, syndicate, or other group or combination acting as a unit and also includes any political subdivision, municipality, state agency, bureau, or department (plural and singular);

— an individual or entity owning a controlling interest in a business;

— an individual or entity that acquired an ownership interest or a controlling interest in a business that would otherwise be liable for posting a cash deposit, bond, or other security, unless the department has determined that the individual or entity is not liable for the taxes, interest, or penalties, as provided; and

— an individual or entity seeking to obtain a dealer's certificate of registration for a business that will be operated at the same location as a previous business that would otherwise have been liable for posting a cash deposit, bond, or other security, if the individual or entity fails to provide evidence that the business was acquired for consideration in an arms-length transaction.

(Sec. 212.14(4), F.S.)

[¶61-270] Credits

Credits for tax paid in another state, resales, and credits for enterprise zone activities are discussed below. The credit allowance for accounting and prompt payment of tax is discussed at Returns, Payments, and Due Dates.

The Florida Department of Revenue may require dealers claiming any credit against Florida sales and use tax to file a report with the claim for the credit. The Department may disallow any credit not accompanied by the report, if required. In addition, a penalty of 25% of the amount of the disallowed credit will be imposed. (Sec. 212.11, F.S.)

See Nonprofit Organizations, Private Schools, and Churches for a discussion of the Florida tax credit scholarship program, which provides a credit of 100% of an eligible contribution made to an eligible nonprofit scholarship funding organization, as provided, against any sales and use tax imposed by Florida and due from a direct pay permit holder as a result of the direct pay permit held.

See Motion Pictures for a discussion of the entertainment industry financial incentive program, which provides a credit against Florida corporate income taxes, sales and use taxes, or a combination of the two against qualified expenditures.

• *Community contribution tax credit*

A community contribution tax credit (Community Contribution Tax Credit Program) is available to taxpayers who make donations to eligible sponsors, such as a sponsor of a community action program or a sponsor of a nonprofit community-based development organization aimed at low-income housing or entrepreneurial development. The contribution must be made in the form of: cash or other liquid assets; real property; goods or inventory; or other physical resources approved by the Florida Department of Economic Opportunity, which approves credit proposals. (Secs. 212.08(5)(p), F.S.)

The donation of real property includes the transfer of 100% ownership of a real property holding company. A "real property holding company" is defined as a Florida entity, such as a Florida limited liability company, that meets the following requirements:

— is wholly owned by the donor;

— is the sole owner of the real property;

— is a disregarded entity for federal income tax purposes; and

— at the time of contribution to an eligible sponsor, has no material assets other than the real property and any other property that qualifies as a community contribution.

(Secs. 212.08(5)(p), F.S.)

The program was established to encourage private sector participation in community revitalization and housing projects. The program offers a corporate income tax credit, an insurance premium tax credit, or a refund against sales and use tax to businesses or persons (donor) that contribute to eligible projects undertaken by approved program sponsors. Eligible program sponsors under the program include a wide variety of community development organizations, housing organizations, and units of state and local government. (Secs. 212.08(5)(p), F.S.)

An eligible project includes activity undertaken by an eligible sponsor that is designed to:

— construct, improve or substantially rehabilitate housing that is affordable to low or very-low income households;

— provide housing opportunities for persons with special needs;

— provide commercial, industrial, or public resources and facilities; or

— improve entrepreneurial and job-development opportunities for low-income persons.

(Secs. 212.08(5)(p), F.S.)

The credit includes donations made to provide housing opportunities for persons with special needs, as defined. Before making a donation for which a credit will be claimed, the Florida Department of Revenue advises taxpayers to be sure the donation will qualify. A list of eligible organizations is available from the Florida Department of Economic Opportunity (DEO). To receive approval, a business donating to an eligible sponsor must submit an application to DEO. In order to claim the credit, taxpayers should attach proof of the approved donation when they file their state tax return. To claim a sales tax refund, taxpayers need to submit a Form DR-26S Sales and Use Tax Application for Refund. Donations to projects that would have qualified previously will continue to be eligible for the credit if the projects are in an area that was located in an enterprise zone, as provided, as of May 1, 2015. (*Tax Information Publication, No. 15ADM-03*, Florida Department of Revenue, June 25, 2015)

Credit amount.—The credit is computed as 50% of the taxpayer's annual community contribution and may be carried over for up to a three-year period without regard to any time limitation that would otherwise apply. However, the annual tax credit for all approved community contributions made by a taxpayer may not exceed $200,000 in any one year. (Secs. 212.08(5)(p), F.S.)

2022-2023 credit amount cap.—The total amount of credits for all approved programs is limited to $14.5 million in the 2022-2023 fiscal year for projects that provide housing opportunities for persons with special needs or homeownership opportunities for low-income households or very-low-income households. The cap is $4.5 million each fiscal year for all other qualifying projects. (Secs. 212.08(5)(p), F.S.)

If credit applications, for projects other than those that provide home ownership opportunities for low-income or very-low-income households, are received during the first 10 business days of the state fiscal year that are less than the credits available for those projects, the remaining credits will be granted on a first-come, first-served basis. (Secs. 212.08(5)(p), F.S.)

Qualification.—Before making a donation for which a taxpayer will claim a credit, taxpayers are encouraged to confirm the donation will qualify. A list of eligible organizations is available from the Florida Department of Economic Opportunity (DEO). To receive approval, a business donating to an eligible sponsor must submit a tax credit application to DEO. To claim the tax credit, a taxpayer should attach proof of the approved donation to their state tax return. To claim a sales tax refund, a taxpayer should submit Form DR-26S, Sales and Use Tax Application for Refund. Donations to projects that would have qualified previously will continue to be eligible for the credit if the projects are in an area that was located in an enterprise zone pursuant to Sec. 290.0065, F.S., as of May 1, 2015. (*Tax Information Publication, No. 15ADM-03*, Florida Department of Revenue, June 25, 2015)

Sunset.—Effective July 1, 2017, the community contribution tax credit is made permanent (formerly, the credit was set to expire June 30, 2018). (Secs. 212.08(5)(p), F.S.; *Tax Information Publication, No. 15ADM-03*, Florida Department of Revenue, June 25, 2015)

• *Credit for tax paid in another state*

Credit is provided in Florida for a like tax paid in another state for the use or consumption of services, or the use, consumption, distribution, or storage of tangible personal property in Florida up to the amount of tax imposed in Florida. The dealer must pay the Florida Department of Revenue the difference between the tax imposed by Florida and any lesser tax imposed in the other state. (Sec. 212.06(7), F.S.; Rule 12A-1.091(3))

Credit for motor vehicles brought into Florida from another state in which sales tax was paid.—A Department of Revenue publication provides information concerning the Florida sales tax credit for motor vehicles brought into Florida from another state in which a like tax was lawfully imposed and paid. The publication provides a state-by-state breakdown of (1) the rate of sales tax charged in other states; (2) whether Florida grants a credit for the other state's tax, and vice versa; and (3) the application of other states' taxes on sales of motor vehicles. The publication also contains information concerning the imposition of Florida use tax on motor vehicles exported to territories or foreign countries. (*Tax Information Publication, No. 04A01-14*, Florida Department of Revenue, December 1, 2004)

• *Entities that do business with Western Hemisphere countries*

Corporations, partnerships, associations and other entities that travel to or do business with any country located in the Western Hemisphere that lacks diplomatic relations with the United States will not be eligible to claim a credit against any tax imposed by the State of Florida. (Sec. 110.1155(1)(c), F.S.)

¶61-270

• *New Worlds Reading Initiative*

The New Worlds Reading Initiative, enacted in 2021, provides at-home literacy support for students reading below grade level. Under the initiative:

— a high quality, hardcopy book is delivered on a monthly basis to eligible students; and

— their parents are provided resources to help improve their student's reading skills and instill a love of reading.

Under this legislation:

— a tax credit program is enacted to provide funding for the initiative; and

— the Department of Education must designate a state university to administer the initiative.

(Sec. 1003.485, F.S.; Rule 12ER21-19, F.A.C.; Rule 12ER21-20, F.A.C.)

Credit for contributions to the New Worlds Reading Initiative.—Beginning January 1, 2022, there is allowed a credit of 100% of an eligible contribution made to the New Worlds Reading Initiative against any state sales tax due from a direct pay permitholder as a result of the direct pay permit held. For purposes of the dealer's credit granted for keeping prescribed records, filing timely tax returns, and properly accounting and remitting taxes, the amount of tax due used to calculate the credit includes any eligible contribution made to the New Worlds Reading Initiative from a direct pay permitholder. A dealer who claims this tax credit must electronically file returns and pay taxes. (Sec. 212.1833, F.S.; Sec. 1003.485, F.S.; Rule 12ER21-19, F.A.C.; Rule 12ER21-20, F.A.C.)

Eligible tax types.—Under the New Worlds Reading Initiative, businesses that make monetary donations to the administrator may receive a dollar-for-dollar credit against the following tax liabilities:

— corporate income tax;

— insurance premium tax;

— severance taxes on oil and gas production;

— alcoholic beverage tax on beer, wine, and spirits; or

— state sales and use tax self-accrued and paid directly to the Florida Department of Revenue in accordance with a valid Sales and Use Tax Direct Pay Permit, issued by the department.

(Sec. 212.1833, F.S.; Sec. 1003.485, F.S.; Rule 12ER21-19, F.A.C.; Rule 12ER21-20, F.A.C.)

Application and approval of tax credits by the Florida Department of Revenue.—Taxpayers who wish to participate in the program by making a donation to the initiative must apply to the department beginning October 1, 2021, for an allocation of tax credit. The taxpayer must specify in the application:

— each tax for which the taxpayer requests a credit;

— the applicable taxable year for a credit relating to the corporate income and insurance premium tax credits; and

— the applicable state fiscal year for a credit relating to oil and gas production, direct pay permit sales, and alcoholic beverage tax credits.

The department will approve the tax credits on a first-come, first-served basis. (Sec. 1003.485, F.S.; Rule 12ER21-19, F.A.C.; Rule 12ER21-20, F.A.C.)

A taxpayer can apply for a credit allocation on the first business day of January of the calendar year preceding the state fiscal year beginning on July 1 of the calendar year. The application must be made by June 30 of the state fiscal year for which the taxpayer is applying. For example, for a credit allocation for the 2022-2023 state fiscal year, taxpayers may apply for a credit allocation beginning on January 3, 2022, and the application must be made on or before June 30, 2023. (Rule 12ER21-19, F.A.C.)

Carryforward of unused credit.—Any unused credit may be carried forward up to 10 years. Taxpayers are not allowed to convey, transfer, or assign the credit to another entity unless all of the assets of the taxpayer are conveyed, transferred, or assigned in the same transaction. Upon approval of the department, transfers can be made between members of an affiliated group of corporations if the credit transferred will be taken against the same tax type. (Sec. 1003.485, F.S.; Rule 12ER21-19, F.A.C.)

Rescindment of unused tax credits.—A taxpayer can apply to the department to rescind all or part of an approved tax credit. The amount rescinded becomes available for that state fiscal year to another eligible taxpayer as approved by the department if the taxpayer receives notice that the rescindment has been accepted. (Sec. 1003.485, F.S.; Rule 12ER21-19, F.A.C.)

Cap on annual tax credit approvals.—The annual tax credit cap for all credits under the initiative increases as follows:

— $10 million for fiscal year 2021-22;

— $30 million for fiscal year 2022-2023; and

— $50 million for each following fiscal year.

(Sec. 1003.485, F.S.; Rule 12ER21-19, F.A.C.)

• *Strong Families Tax Credit Program*

Effective July 1, 2021, the Strong Families Tax Credit Program is available to businesses that make monetary donations to certain eligible charitable organizations that provide services focused on child welfare and well-being. (Sec. 212.1834, F.S.; Rule 12ER21-17, F.A.C.; Rule 12ER21-18, F.A.C.)

Eligible tax types.—The Strong Families Tax Credit Program provides that a taxpayer may receive a credit against the following taxes for making an eligible monetary donation to certain eligible charitable organizations that provide services focused on child welfare and well-being:

— corporate income taxes;

— insurance premium taxes;

— severance taxes on oil and gas production; and

— state sales and use tax self-accrued and paid directly to the Florida Department of Revenue in accordance with a valid Sales and Use Tax Direct Pay Permit, issued by the department.

(Sec. 212.1834, F.S.; Rule 12ER21-17, F.A.C.)

Program qualifications.—To qualify for the program, an eligible charitable organization must be: (1) exempt as an IRC Sec. 501(c)(3) organization; (2) a Florida entity with its principal office in Florida; and (3) must provide services to:

— prevent child abuse, neglect, abandonment, or exploitation;

— assist fathers in learning and improving parenting skills or to engage absent fathers in being more engaged in their children's lives;

— provide books to the homes of children eligible for a free or reduced-price meal program or those testing below grade level in kindergarten through fifth grade;

— assist families who have children with a chronic illness or a physical, intellectual, developmental, or emotional disability; or

— provide workforce development services to families of children eligible for a free or reduced price meal program.

(Sec. 212.1834, F.S.)

An eligible charitable organization cannot:

— provide, pay for, or provide coverage for abortions or financially support any other entity that provides, pays for, or provides coverage for abortions; or

— either directly or indirectly, receive more than 50% of its total annual revenue from the Department of Children and Families.

(Sec. 212.1834, F.S.; Rule 12ER21-17, F.A.C.; Rule 12ER21-18, F.A.C.)

Sales taxes paid by direct pay permit holders.—Beginning January 1, 2022, a credit of 100% of an eligible contribution made to an eligible charitable organization under the Strong Families Tax Credit Program is authorized against any state sales and use tax due from a direct pay permit holder as a result of the direct pay permit held. (Sec. 212.1834, F.S.; Rule 12ER21-17, F.A.C.)

Application and approval of tax credits by the department.—Beginning October 1, 2021, a taxpayer can submit an application to the Florida Department of Revenue for a tax credit. In the application, the taxpayer must specify:

— the eligible charitable organization to which the proposed contribution will be made;

— each tax for which the taxpayer requests a credit; and

— the applicable state fiscal year for a credit relating to oil and gas production and direct pay permit sales.

The department is required to approve the tax credits on a first-come, first-served basis. (Sec. 212.1834, F.S.; Rule 12ER21-17, F.A.C.; Rule 12ER21-18, F.A.C.)

To apply for an allocation of the available program credits, a taxpayer must submit a Strong Families Tax Credit – Application for Tax Credit Allocation for Contributions to Eligible Charitable Organizations (Form DR-226000) to the department. (Rule 12ER21-17, F.A.C.; Rule 12ER21-18, F.A.C.)

A taxpayer may make an application for a credit allocation on the first business day of January of the calendar year preceding the state fiscal year beginning on July 1 of the calendar year. The application must be made by June 30 of the state fiscal year for which the taxpayer is applying. For example, for a credit allocation for the 2022-2023 state fiscal year, taxpayers may apply for a credit allocation beginning on January 3, 2022, and the application must be made on or before June 30, 2023. (Rule 12ER21-17, F.A.C.)

Transfers of unused tax credits.—Any unused credit may be carried forward up to 10 years. A taxpayer may not generally convey, transfer, or assign the credit to another entity unless all of the assets of the taxpayer are conveyed, transferred, or assigned in the same transaction. Upon approval of the department, transfers may be made between members of an affiliated group of corporations if the credit transferred will be taken against the same type of tax. (Sec. 212.1834, F.S.; Rule 12ER21-17, F.A.C.; Rule 12ER21-18, F.A.C.)

Cap on annual tax credit approvals.—The annual tax credit cap for all credits under this program is $5 million per state fiscal year. (Sec. 212.1834, F.S.; Rule 12ER21-17, F.A.C.; Rule 12ER21-18, F.A.C.)

Rescindment of unused tax credits.—Credit allocations that will not be used by the taxpayer may be reallocated to other taxpayers. Taxpayers must apply online or submit Strong Families Tax Credit – Application for Rescindment of Previous Allocation of Tax Credit (Form DR-226100) to the department to rescind all or a portion of an unused credit allocation. (Rule 12ER21-17, F.A.C.; Rule 12ER21-18, F.A.C.)

• *Urban High-Crime Area Jobs Tax Credit Program and Rural Job Tax Credit Program*

Businesses are allowed a credit against their remitted sales and use tax for each qualified job they create in designated and ranked urban high-crime areas and rural areas. (Sec. 212.097, F.S.; Sec. 212.098, F.S.)

Administration.—The Urban High-Crime Area Job Tax Credit Program and the Rural Job Tax Credit Program are administered by the Florida Department of Economic Opportunity. By applying criteria laid out in the law to areas making applications, the Office will designate fifteen areas to participate in each program. The fifteen areas, in turn, will be ranked and divided into three tiers. In each program, credit requirements will be differentiated between qualified new businesses and qualified existing businesses. A qualified high-crime area includes a federal empowerment zone, and a qualified county for purposes of the rural job tax credit program includes a county containing an area that has been designated as a federal enterprise community. (Sec. 212.097, F.S.; Sec. 212.098, F.S.)

Carryforward.—Excess credits against sales and use tax liability can be carried forward for one year. (Sec. 212.097, F.S.; Sec. 212.098, F.S.)

Credit amount.—The credits range from $500 to $1,500 and are in addition to the $500 credit allowed for employees who also are participating in the welfare transition program. (Sec. 212.097, F.S.; Sec. 212.098, F.S.)

Businesses can apply for the credit as a new business once within the first year of operation. New businesses in the first tier with at least 10 qualified employees will be entitled to a credit of $1,500 per employee. New businesses in tier two must have at least 20 qualified employees and will be entitled to a credit of $1,000 for each. Tier three new businesses with at least 30 employees will qualify for a $500 credit for each of them. (Sec. 212.097, F.S.; Sec. 212.098, F.S.)

Existing businesses will be granted credits after they hire a minimum number of qualified new employees within a year of applying for the credit. In tier one, a credit of $1,500 will be given for each new employee beginning with the fifth employee. In a tier two business, the credit will be $1,000 per new employee beginning with the tenth new employee. The $500 credit for a tier three firm will be applied to each qualified new employee beginning with the 15th qualified new employee. (Sec. 212.097, F.S.; Sec. 212.098, F.S.)

Credit limitations.—For each program, there will be a maximum credit amount of $5 million approved for each calendar year. In the high-crime program, at least $1 million of the credit will be reserved for tier one areas. Applications will be considered in the order in which they are received. (Sec. 212.097, F.S.; Sec. 212.098, F.S.)

Corporations can elect to take the credit against their income tax liability. However, the election is exclusive of any credit against sales and use tax liability as it may be taken against only one tax. Excess credits against sales and use tax liability can be carried forward for one year, as compared to a five-year carryforward period for the corporate income tax credit option. Also, firms predominantly engaged in standard industrial classifications SIC 52-57, 59 involving retail will qualify for the sales and use tax credit but not the corporate income tax credit. (Sec. 212.097, F.S.; Sec. 212.098, F.S.)

Eligibility.—To be eligible for the credit, the number of qualified employees employed one year before the application date must be no lower than the number of qualified employees on January 1, 2009, or on the application date on which the credit was based for any previous application. An existing eligible business that filed an application for the credit on or after January 1, 2009, and was denied because of the requirement regarding the number of qualified employees, may refile the application on or before December 31, 2012, if the number of qualified employees employed on the day the denied application is refiled is no lower than the number of qualified employees on the day the denied application was initially filed. Any credit that results from the refiled application is subject to the aggregate limitation for calendar year 2012. For purposes of applying the tax credit eligibility determination to the refiled application, the terms "date of application" and "application date" are defined as the date the denied application was initially filed. (Sec. 212.097, F.S.)

Industry classifications.—The programs are applicable to firms predominantly engaged in the following standard industrial classifications (SIC):

— agriculture, forestry, and fishing (SIC 01-09);

— manufacturing (SIC 20-39);

— retail (SIC 52-57, 59), but available only for sales and use tax urban high-income area job tax credit, not available for sales and use tax rural job tax credit or corporate income tax credit;

— public warehousing and storage (SIC 422);

— research and development (SIC 7391);

— hotels and other lodging places (SIC 70);

— public golf courses (SIC 7992), and

— amusement parks (SIC 7996).

(Sec. 212.097, F.S.; Sec. 212.098, F.S.)

A call center or similar customer service operation that services a multistate market or international market is also an eligible business. Furthermore, the Florida Department of Economic Opportunity may recommend additions to or deletions from the list of standard industrial classifications used to determine eligible businesses and the legislature may implement such recommendations. (Sec. 212.097, F.S.; Sec. 212.098, F.S.)

"Predominantly" engaged in a classification means that more than 50% of the business's gross receipts is generated by activities usually provided for consideration by firms within the SIC. In the first four categories listed above, the credit cannot be applied on receipts from retail sales. (Sec. 212.097, F.S.; Sec. 212.098, F.S.)

Refund on purchases of electricity.—A new or existing eligible business that receives a rural job tax credit is eligible for a tax refund of up to 50% of the amount of Florida sales tax on purchases of electricity paid by the business during the one year period after the date the credit is received. The total amount of tax refunds approved for all eligible businesses may not exceed $600,000 during any calendar year. (Sec. 212.098, F.S.)

[¶61-600]
TAXPAYER REMEDIES

[¶61-610] Application for Refund

An application for refund must be filed within three years after the date on which the tax was paid. (Sec. 215.26(2), F.S.) Taxpayers may contest the denial of a tax refund.

In addition, a taxpayer is entitled, both in connection with an audit and in connection with an application for refund filed independently of any audit, to establish the amount of any refund or deficiency through statistical sampling, or any other sampling method agreed upon by the taxpayer and the Department. The taxpayer's records must be adequate and voluminous and the completed sample must reflect both overpayments and underpayments of taxes due. (Sec. 212.12, F.S.)

The Florida Department of Revenue has issued a tax information publication discussing the requirements for using the sampling method and establishing a refund or deficiency. (*Tax Information Publication, No. 03A01-01*, Florida Department of Revenue, January 22, 2003)

• *Brownfield redevelopment bonus refund*

A bonus refund of property tax, sales and use tax, documentary stamp tax, corporate income tax, intangible personal property tax, emergency excise tax, or insurance premium tax is available to any qualified target industry business or "other eligible business" for each new Florida job created in a brownfield that is claimed on the business's annual tax refund claim. (Sec. 288.107(2), F.S.)

CAUTION NOTE: Expiration of the Florida Enterprise Zone Program.—Except for certain extensions, as provided, the Florida Enterprise Zone Program expires on December 31, 2015. For businesses that do not qualify for extension, enterprise zone credits or refunds will be approved after December 31, 2015, only if the business applying for the credit or refund meets the statutory eligibility requirements for the incentive on or before December 31, 2015.

Extensions approved through December 31, 2018, are for businesses located in an enterprise zone as of May 1, 2015, that entered into contracts between January 1, 2012 and July 1, 2015, with the Florida Department of Economic Opportunity (DEO) for the:

— Qualified Defense Contractor and Space Flight Business Tax Refund Program (Sec. 288.1045, F.S.) ;

— Tax Refund Program for Qualified Target Industry Businesses (Sec. 288.106, F.S.) ; and

— Brownfield Redevelopment Bonus Refunds (Sec. 288.107, F.S.).

These qualified businesses are eligible for the exemptions and credits noted above through December 31, 2018. Effective January 1, 2016, DEO will process and certify Florida enterprise zone tax incentive applications in place of local enterprise zone coordinators. The Florida Department of Revenue will continue to receive and process refund applications for these qualified businesses. (*Tax Information Publication, No. 15ADM-04*, Florida Department of Revenue, September 8, 2015)

• *Defense contractors and space flight businesses refund*

Qualified defense contractor or space flight business applicants may apply by January 31 of each fiscal year to the Florida Department of Economic Opportunity for a refund from the Economic Development Trust Fund for the sales and use tax due and paid by them, beginning with the applicant's first taxable year commencing after entering into a tax refund agreement. Qualified applicants must:

— consolidate Department of Defense contracts;

— obtain new Department of Defense production contracts;

— convert defense production to non-defense production; or

— contract for reuse of a defense-related facility.

(Sec. 288.1045(4), F.S.)

CAUTION NOTE: Expiration of the Florida Enterprise Zone Program.—Except for certain extensions, as provided, the Florida Enterprise Zone Program expires on December 31, 2015. For businesses that do not qualify for extension, enterprise zone credits or refunds will be approved after December 31, 2015, only if the business applying for the credit or refund meets the statutory eligibility requirements for the incentive on or before December 31, 2015.

Extensions approved through December 31, 2018, are for businesses located in an enterprise zone as of May 1, 2015, that entered into contracts between January 1, 2012 and July 1, 2015, with the Florida Department of Economic Opportunity (DEO) for the:

— Qualified Defense Contractor and Space Flight Business Tax Refund Program (Sec. 288.1045, F.S.) ;

— Tax Refund Program for Qualified Target Industry Businesses (Sec. 288.106, F.S.) ; and

— Brownfield Redevelopment Bonus Refunds (Sec. 288.107, F.S.).

These qualified businesses are eligible for the exemptions and credits noted above through December 31, 2018. Effective January 1, 2016, DEO will process and certify Florida enterprise zone tax incentive applications in place of local enterprise zone coordinators. The Florida Department of Revenue will continue to receive and process refund applications for these qualified businesses. (*Tax Information Publication, No. 15ADM-04*, Florida Department of Revenue, September 8, 2015)

Space flight business.—A "space flight business" is defined as the manufacturing, processing, or assembly of space flight technology products, facilities, propulsion systems, or space vehicles, satellites, or stations of any kind that possess the capability for space flight, as defined. The phrase includes vehicle launch activities, flight operations, ground control or ground support, and all administrative activities directly related to such activities. The definition does not include products designed or manufactured for general commercial aviation or other uses even if those products may also serve an incidental use in space flight applications. (Sec. 288.1045, F.S.)

Among the information that must be included in applications for certification based upon a new space flight business contract or the consolidation of such a contract is the following:

— the applicant's federal employer identification number, Florida sales tax registration number, and a signature of an officer of the applicant;

— the permanent location of the space flight business facility in Florida where the project is or will be located;

— the new space flight business contract number, the space flight business contract numbers of the contract to be consolidated, or the request-for-proposal number of a proposed space flight business contract;

— the date the contract was executed and the date the contract is due to expire, is expected to expire, or was canceled;

— the commencement date for project operations under the contract in Florida;

— the number of net new full-time equivalent Florida jobs included in the project as of December 31 of each year and the average wage of such jobs;

— the total number of full-time equivalent employees employed by the applicant in Florida.

(Sec. 288.1045, F.S.)

An "applicant" is defined as any business entity that holds a valid Department of Defense contract or space flight business contract. (Sec. 288.1045(1), F.S.)

Refund eligibility.—Upon approval by the Director of the Florida Department of Economic Opportunity, a qualified applicant is allowed tax refund payments equal to: (1) $3,000 times the number of jobs specified in the tax refund agreement; or (2) $6,000 times the number of jobs if the project is located in a rural county or an enterprise zone. In addition, a qualified applicant is allowed additional tax refund payments equal to: (1) $1,000 times the number of jobs specified in the tax refund agreement if such jobs pay an annual average wage of at least 150% of the average private sector wage in the area; or (2) $2,000 times the number of jobs if such jobs pay an annual average wage of at least 200% of the average private sector wage in the area. In addition, a qualified applicant may not receive refunds of more than 25% of the total tax refunds provided in the tax refund agreement in any fiscal year, provided that no qualified applicant may receive more than $2.5 million in tax refunds in any fiscal year. (Secs. 288.1045(2), (5), F.S.)

In order to be eligible for qualification, an applicant must have derived not less than 60% of its gross receipts in Florida from Department of Defense contracts or space flight business contracts during the previous fiscal year and not less than an average of 60% of its gross receipts in Florida from Department of Defense contracts or space flight business contracts over the five years preceding the submission of the application. An applicant must establish that jobs proposed under the application will pay at least 115% of the average annual wage in the area where the project is to be located, that the consolidation of a Department of Defense contract will result in a net increase of at least 80 jobs or at least 25% of the number of jobs at the defense contractor's facilities in the state, and that the conversion of the defense production jobs will result in net increases in private commercial employment at the applicant's facilities in the state. Certain requirements concerning the structure of the Department of Defense contract are also specified. (Sec. 288.1045(3), F.S.)

Jobs.—A "job," for purposes of the refund program, is defined as a full-time equivalent position, including a position obtained from a temporary employment agency, employee leasing company, or union agreement or co-employment under a professional employer organization agreement, that results directly from a project in Florida. This number does not include temporary construction jobs involved with the construction of facilities for the project. (Sec. 288.1045(1)(j), F.S.)

A new space flight business contract or the consolidation of a space flight business contract must result in net increases in space flight business employment at the applicant's facilities in this state. (Sec. 288.1045(3), F.S.)

Certification requirements.—Requirements for certification based on a contract for reuse of a defense-related facility differ slightly from requirements applicable to defense contractors. To qualify for refund, the reuse of the defense-related facility must result in the creation of at least 100 jobs at the facility. A "contract for reuse of a defense-related facility" is defined as a contract of at least two years' duration for the use of a facility for manufacturing, assembling, fabricating, research, development, or design of tangible personal property, but does not apply to any contract to provide goods, improvements to real or tangible personal property, or services directly to or for a particular military base or installation in Florida. (Sec. 288.1045(1), F.S.)

An applicant must enter into a written agreement with the Office specifying, among other things, the number of jobs dedicated to the project, the average wage of the jobs, the time schedule for filling the jobs, the amount of refund to be received each year, review provisions, and the time for filing a claim. (Sec. 288.1045(3), F.S.)

Funds made available pursuant to this refund program may not be expended in connection with the relocation of a business from one community to another community in the state unless there is a compelling economic rationale for the relocation which creates additional jobs or, without the relocation, the business will move outside the state. For purposes of the refund, a "Department of Defense contract" includes a contract with the U.S. Department of Defense, U.S. Department of State, or the U.S. Department of Homeland Security. (Sec. 288.1045(1)(e), F.S.)

Applicants may not be certified as qualified after June 30, 2014. (Sec. 288.1045(7), F.S.)

Refund limitations.—A qualified defense and space contractor business may not receive refund payments of more than 25% of the total tax refunds specified in the tax refund agreement in any fiscal year. Moreover, such a business may not receive more than $2.5 million in refunds in any single fiscal year. Prior to July 1, 2013, such a business may not receive more than $7 million in refund payments in all fiscal years. Effective July 1, 2013, the limitation on the maximum amount of tax refunds a qualified defense and space contractor business can receive over all fiscal years is eliminated. (Sec. 288.1045(2), F.S.)

• *Local taxes*

Local option taxes are not subject to refund.

• *Qualified target industry businesses refund*

Through June 30, 2020, qualified target industry (QTI) businesses, after entering into a tax refund agreement with the Florida Department of Economic Opportunity, are entitled to apply by January 31 of each fiscal year for refunds from the Economic Development Incentives Account for sales and use taxes due and paid by them after entering into the agreement. The agreement must specify that: (1) the office may conduct a review of the business to evaluate whether the business continues to contribute to the economy of the state or area; and (2) in the event the business does not complete the agreement, the business will provide the office with the reasons the business was unable to do so. (Sec. 288.106, F.S.)

CAUTION NOTE: Expiration of the Florida Enterprise Zone Program.—Except for certain extensions, as provided, the Florida Enterprise Zone Program expires on December 31, 2015. For businesses that do not qualify for extension, enterprise zone credits or refunds will be approved after December 31, 2015, only if the business applying for the credit or refund meets the statutory eligibility requirements for the incentive on or before December 31, 2015.

Extensions approved through December 31, 2018, are for businesses located in an enterprise zone as of May 1, 2015, that entered into contracts between January 1, 2012 and July 1, 2015, with the Florida Department of Economic Opportunity (DEO) for the:

— Qualified Defense Contractor and Space Flight Business Tax Refund Program (Sec. 288.1045, F.S.) ;

— Tax Refund Program for Qualified Target Industry Businesses (Sec. 288.106, F.S.) ; and

— Brownfield Redevelopment Bonus Refunds (Sec. 288.107, F.S.).

These qualified businesses are eligible for the exemptions and credits noted above through December 31, 2018. Effective January 1, 2016, DEO will process and certify Florida enterprise zone tax incentive applications in place of local enterprise zone coordinators. The Florida Department of Revenue will continue to receive and process refund applications for these qualified businesses. (*Tax Information Publication, No. 15ADM-04*, Florida Department of Revenue, September 8, 2015)

The term "target industry business" is defined as a corporate headquarters business or any business that is engaged in one of the target industries identified pursuant to criteria developed by the Department of Commerce through rulemaking in consultation with Enterprise Florida, Inc. (Sec. 288.106, F.S.)

Identification of target industries.—Six criteria are established for identifying target industries:

— future growth (special consideration should be given to businesses that export goods to, or provide services in international markets and businesses that replace domestic and international imports of goods or services);

— stability;

— high wages;

— market and resource independence (the location of industry businesses should not be dependent on Florida markets or resources as indicated by industry analysis, except for businesses in the renewable energy industry);

— industrial base diversification and strengthening (special consideration should be given to industries that strengthen regional economies by adding value to basic products or building regional industrial clusters and to the development of strong industrial clusters that include defense and homeland security businesses); and

— positive economic impact (special consideration should be given to industries that facilitate the development of the state as a hub for domestic and global trade and logistics).

(Sec. 288.106, F.S.)

The following businesses are not considered target industry businesses:

— industries engaged in retail activities;

— electrical utility companies;

— phosphate or other solid minerals severance, mining or processing operations;

— oil or gas exploration or production operations; or

— firms subject to regulation by the Division of Hotels and Restaurants of the Department of Business and Professional Regulation.

(Sec. 288.106, F.S.)

The amount requested as a tax refund may not exceed the amount specified for that fiscal year in the agreement. (Sec. 288.106, F.S.)

Special consideration granted.—Special consideration is given to businesses that export goods or services to international markets or to businesses that replace domestic and international imports of goods or services. Moreover, the location of industry businesses should not be dependent on Florida markets or resources as indicated by industry analysis except for businesses in the renewable energy industry. In addition, any business within NAICS code 5611 or 5614, office administrative services and business support services, respectively, may be considered a target industry business only after the local governing body and Enterprise Florida, Inc., make a determination that the community where the business may locate has conditions affecting the fiscal and economic viability of the local community or area, including but not limited to factors such as low per capita income, high unemployment, high underemployment, and a lack of year-round stable employment opportunities, and such conditions may be improved by the location of such a business to the community. By January 1 of every third year, beginning January 1, 2011, the office, in consultation with Enterprise Florida, Inc., economic development organizations, the State University System, local governments, employee and employer organizations, market analysts, and economists, is required to review and revise the list of such target industries and submit the list to the Governor, the President of the Senate, and the Speaker of the House of Representatives. (Sec. 288.106, F.S.)

Local financial support.—A QTI business is allowed sales and use tax refund payments, in addition to other payments authorized, equal to $1,000 multiplied by the number of jobs specified in the tax refund agreement if the local financial support is equal to that of the state's incentive award. In addition to the other tax refund payments authorized, a QTI business is allowed a tax refund payment equal to $2,000 multiplied by the number of jobs specified in the tax refund agreement if the business:

— falls within one of the high-impact sectors; or

— increases exports of its goods through a seaport or airport in Florida by at least 10% in value or tonnage in each of the years that the business receives a tax refund (for these purposes, seaports in Florida are limited to the ports of Jacksonville, Tampa, Port Everglades, Miami, Port Canaveral, Ft. Pierce, Palm Beach, Port Manatee, Port St. Joe, Panama City, St. Petersburg, Pensacola, Fernandina, and Key West).

(Sec. 288.106, F.S.)

Jobs.—A "job," for purposes of the refund program, is defined as a full-time equivalent position, including a position obtained from a temporary employment agency, employee leasing company, or union agreement or co-employment under a professional employer organization agreement, that results directly from a project in Florida. This number does not include temporary construction jobs involved with the construction of facilities for the project. (Sec. 288.1045(1)(j), F.S.)

Refund limitations.—QTI businesses are entitled to refunds equal to $3,000 times the number of jobs specified in the tax refund agreement or equal to $6,000 times the number of jobs if the project is located in a rural county or an enterprise zone, plus an additional refund equal to $1,000 times the number of jobs specified in the tax refund agreement if such jobs pay an annual average wage of at least 150% of the average private-sector wage in the area or equal to $2,000 times the number of jobs if such jobs pay an annual average wage of at least 200% of the average private-sector wage in the area. (Sec. 288.106, F.S.)

A QTI business may not receive refund payments of more than 25% of the total tax refunds specified in the tax refund agreement in any fiscal year. Moreover, a QTI business may not receive more than $1.5 million in refunds in any single fiscal year, or more than $2.5 million in any single fiscal year if the project is located in an enterprise zone. Prior to July 1, 2013, a QTI business may not receive more than $7 million in refund payments in all fiscal years, or more than $7.5 million if the project is located in an enterprise zone. Effective July 1, 2013, the limitation on the maximum amount of tax refunds a QTI business can receive over all fiscal years is eliminated. (Sec. 288.106(3)(c), F.S.)

Application for certification.—To apply for certification as a qualified target industry business, an application must be filed with the Florida Department of Economic Opportunity before the business has made the decision to locate a new business in Florida or to expand an existing business in Florida. (Sec. 288.106, F.S.)

To qualify for review, the application must establish the following to the department's satisfaction:

— the proposed jobs pay an estimated 115% of the average private sector wage in the area where the business is to be located or the statewide private-sector average wage;

— the target industry business's project results in the creation of at least 10 jobs at the project or, if the project is an expansion of an existing business, must result in a net increase in employment of at least 10% at such business; and

— the business activity or product for the applicant's project is within an industry that the Department of Commerce has identified as a high-value-added industry that contributes to the area and to the economic growth of Florida and that produces a higher standard of living for Florida citizens or makes an equivalent contribution.

(Sec. 288.106, F.S.)

The average wage requirement may be waived at the request of the local governing body recommending the project and Enterprise Florida, Inc. Target businesses that achieve at least 80% of projected employment will receive a prorated refund, less a 5% penalty, provided the business had met all other requirements. (Sec. 288.106, F.S.)

The Governor may designate up to three rural areas of critical economic concern and, acting through the Rural Economic Development Initiative within the Florida Department of Economic Opportunity, may waive criteria, requirements, or similar provisions of any economic development incentive, including but not limited to the Qualified Target Industry Tax Refund Program and brownfield redevelopment bonus refunds. (Sec. 288.0656 F.S.)

Brownfield redevelopment bonus refund.—A bonus refund of property tax, sales and use tax, documentary stamp tax, corporate income tax, intangible personal property tax, emergency excise tax, or insurance premium tax is available to any qualified target industry business or "other eligible business" for each new Florida job created in a brownfield that is claimed on the business's annual tax refund claim. (Sec. 288.107(2), F.S.).

Eligibility restrictions.—No refund application may be approved for any project located outside an enterprise zone in a county having a designated enterprise zone absent a specific finding by the Secretary of the Department of Commerce that within a jurisdiction a similar amount of local financial support was also made available to the project for location within an enterprise zone. The Secretary may waive the requirement, however, where he or she determines that, due to the particular nature of the business or the location of an existing business that is being expanded, it is impractical to locate or expand the project in an enterprise zone. (Sec. 288.106, F.S.)

The tax refund must be reduced by the appraised market value of municipal or county land conveyed or provided at a discount to the business and the limitations on such refunds must also be reduced by that amount. (Sec. 288.106, F.S.)

• *Rural areas of opportunity refund*

Effective July 1, 2017, a sales and use tax exemption is provided for the purchase of building materials, pest control services, and the rental of tangible personal property used in new construction in rural areas of opportunity. A "rural area of opportunity" (RAO), is a rural community or a region comprised of rural communities, designated by the Governor, that has been adversely affected by an extraordinary economic event, a natural disaster, or severe or chronic distress. (Sec. 212.08(5)(r), F.S.)

The area may also be classified as a RAO if it presents a unique economic development opportunity of regional impact. The exemption is provided in the form of a refund of taxes paid, and is capped at $10,000 per parcel. Taxpayers must submit an application to Florida's Rural Economic Development Initiative (REDI). Within 10 days of receipt of a completed application, REDI must review the application and, if it meets the requirements, certify to the DOR that a refund is to be issued. (Sec. 212.08(5)(r), F.S.)

The exemption is inapplicable to improvements for which construction began before July 1, 2017. (Sec. 212.08(5)(r), F.S.)

[¶61-620] Administrative Remedies

A taxpayer may contest the legality of any assessment or denial of refund of tax, fee, surcharge, permit, interest, or penalty under the applicable provisions of the Florida Administrative Procedures Act. (Sec. 72.011(1)(a), F.S.; Rule 12-3.007) However, a taxpayer may not file such an action until the taxpayer complies with the registration requirements applicable to the tax for which the action is filed. (Sec. 72.011(1)(b), F.S.)

• *Technical assistance advisements*

The Department of Revenue may issue informal technical assistance advisements to taxpayers, upon written request, as to the position of the Department on the tax consequences of a stated transaction or event. No technical assistance advisement will be issued on a matter on which an assessment has been made, except that one may be issued to a taxpayer who requests one relating to the exemptions for groceries or medical products at any time. Technical assistance advisements have no precedential value except to the taxpayer who requests the advisement for the specific transaction addressed. (Sec. 213.22, F.S.)

• *Conferences*

Once it has completed an audit, the Department of Revenue issues a Notice of Intent to Make Audit Changes, unless the case at hand involves a jeopardy assessment, an estimated assessment, a refund denial, or is a case where review of the taxpayer's books and records results in no liability due to the state or no refundable amount due to the taxpayer. (Rule 12-6.002(1), F.A.C.)

Taxpayers may request a conference concerning the Notice of Intent to Make Audit Changes. However, they must do so within 30 consecutive calendar days after the receipt of the notice. Requests must be submitted directly to the local office of the Department that issued the notice. (Rule 12-6.002(1), F.A.C.)

Conferences, when requested, must be held at the earliest convenience of both the taxpayer and the Department. However, the conferences may not be held later than 90 consecutive calendar days after the date on which the Notice of Intent to Make Audit Changes or the Revised Notice of Intent to Make Audit Changes was issued. (Rule 12-6.002(3), F.A.C.)

A taxpayer that fails to timely request a conference waives its rights to the conference. However, even taxpayers that fail to timely request the conference may use the protest procedures for obtaining review of proposed assessments. (Rule 12-6.002(4), F.A.C.; Rule 12-6.003, F.A.C.)

The 30-day period required for filing the request may be waived by the taxpayer to expedite resolution of issues if the Department's representative and the taxpayer jointly determine that the issues cannot be resolved at the local level. (Rule 12-6.002(5))

A Notice of Proposed Assessment will be issued by the Department if: (1) an agreement is not reached after the conference; (2) the taxpayer has not timely filed a written request for a conference; (3) the taxpayer has not timely filed a written request for an extension of time for requesting a conference; or (4) the taxpayer has waived his or her right to a conference pursuant to this section. (Rule 12-6.002(6), F.A.C.) Protests of Notices of Proposed Assessments are discussed below.

• *Jeopardy conferences*

When the Department issues a jeopardy assessment, it must notify the taxpayer that the taxpayer has the opportunity to appear at a conference within 10 days to make an oral or written statement explaining why no jeopardy exists or why a lien or warrant should be released if one was recorded. (Sec. 213.732(3), F.S.) If the taxpayer so requests, the Department must meet with the taxpayer within 10 days after the issuance of the assessment. If the taxpayer provides a statement, the Department must determine within 20 days whether the jeopardy lien, warrant, or other detainer should be released and must send written notice of its finding to the taxpayer. (Sec. 213.732(5), F.S.) If the Department proceeds to seize or freeze the taxpayer's assets upon a determination of jeopardy, the taxpayer has further rights to meet with the

Department and, subsequently, to request a hearing before the circuit court to review the finding of jeopardy. (Sec. 213.732(7), F.S.)

• *Protests of Notices of Proposed Assessment*

A taxpayer may secure review of a Notice of Proposed Assessment resulting from an audit by filing a protest with the Department of Revenue within 60 consecutive calendar days of the issuance of the assessment. The protest must be delivered to the address, or faxed to the number, designated on the Notice of Proposed Assessment. (Rule 12-6.003(1), F.A.C.)

Upon receipt of a complete, timely filed written protest, the Compliance Support Process will review the protest and initiate an attempt to resolve the issues. If a resolution is not achieved, the protest will be forwarded to Technical Assistance and Dispute Resolution for review. If requested by the taxpayer, an opportunity for submission of additional information and an oral conference will be provided. If the taxpayer and the Department are still unable to resolve the disputed issues, a Notice of Decision (NOD) will be issued and the assessment will become final as of the date of issuance on the NOD, unless the taxpayer files a petition for reconsideration of the NOD within 30 days. If a petition for reconsideration is timely filed and the taxpayer and the Department are unable to resolve the disputed issues, a Notice of Reconsideration (NOR) will be issued and the assessment will become a final as of the date of issuance on the NOR. (Rule 12-6.003, F.A.C.)

• *Final assessment*

An assessment becomes final as follows: (1) 60 days after issuance, unless the taxpayer is not the U.S., then 150 days after issuance, unless the taxpayer has filed a protest, or secured a written extension of time from the Department; (2) if a protest is timely filed and the taxpayer and the Department are unable to resolve the disputed issues, the assessment will become a final assessment as of the date of the issuance of the Notice of Decision, unless the taxpayer timely files a petition for reconsideration; and (3) if such a petition is timely filed, the written denial or issuance of a reconsidered Notice of Decision shall constitute a final assessment on the date of its issuance. (Rule 12-3.006, F.A.C.; Rule 12-3.007, F.A.C.)

• *Compromise and settlement*

The Department of Revenue may enter into a written closing agreement with the taxpayer settling or compromising the taxpayer's liability for any tax, interest, or penalty. (Sec. 213.21, F.S.)

The Department may compromise a taxpayer's liability for tax or interest upon grounds of doubt as to the taxpayer's liability or upon grounds of doubt as to the collectibility of the tax or interest. (Sec. 213.21(2) and (3), F.S.)

The Department may also compromise a taxpayer's liability for tax or interest based on the taxpayer's reasonable reliance on a written determination issued by the Department (i.e., audit workpapers show that issue was settled in a former audit, notice of decision withdrawing the issue was filed during a prior audit, technical assistance advisement was received by the taxpayer regarding the issue). The taxpayer's reliance on a written determination is not reasonable if: (1) the taxpayer misrepresented material facts or did not fully disclose material facts at the time the written determination was issued; (2) the specific facts and circumstances have changed in such a material manner that the written determination no longer applies; (3) the statutes or regulations on which the determination was based have been materially revised or a published judicial opinion constituting precedent has overruled the Department's determination; or (4) the Department has informed the taxpayer in writing that its previous written determination has been revised and should no longer be relied upon. (Sec. 213.21(2) and (3), F.S.)

The Department may also settle or compromise a taxpayer's liability for penalties if it determines that the noncompliance is due to reasonable cause rather than willful negligence, willful neglect, or fraud. The Department's authority to settle or compromise a taxpayer's liability extends to liability for the service fee imposed on an erroneously dishonored check or draft. In addition, a taxpayer's liability for penalties in excess of 25% of the tax must be settled or compromised if the Department determines that the noncompliance is due to reasonable cause. For discussion of penalties and interest. (Sec. 213.21(3), F.S.)

In addition, a penalty for failing to collect Florida sales and use tax will be settled or compromised if a taxpayer failed to collect the tax due to a good faith belief that tax was not due on the transaction and, because of that good faith belief, the taxpayer is now unable to charge and collect the tax from the taxpayer's purchaser. (Sec. 213.21(9), F.S.)

The Department will settle or compromise a taxpayer's Florida sales and use tax liability for penalty without requiring the taxpayer to submit a written request for compromise or settlement if (1) for monthly taxpayers, the taxpayer has no noncompliant filing event in the immediately preceding 12-month period and no unresolved sales and use tax liability resulting from a noncompliant filing event, or if the taxpayer has a noncompliant filing event, resolution of the event through payment of tax and interest, the filing of a return within 30 days after notification by the Department, and no unresolved sales and use tax liability resulting from a noncompliant filing event; or (2) for quarterly taxpayers, the taxpayer has no noncompliant filing event in the immediately preceding 12-month period and no unresolved sales and use tax liability resulting from a noncompliant filing event. (Sec. 213.21(10), F.S.)

During compromise or settlement procedures, a taxpayer has the right to be represented at the taxpayer's cost and to record procedures electronically or manually at the taxpayer's cost. (Sec. 213.21(1)(c), F.S.)

The Department is authorized, under certain circumstances, to modify applicable filing and reporting periods to facilitate the calculation of penalty and interest due as a result of a taxpayer's voluntary self-disclosure or the Department's selection of a taxpayer for self-analysis. (Sec. 213.21(6), F.S.)

• *Taxpayers' Bill of Rights*

The Florida Taxpayers' Bill of Rights lists and explains the rights and obligations of taxpayers and the Department of Revenue. However, the rights afforded taxpayers to protect their privacy and property during tax assessment and collection are available only insofar as they are implemented in other parts of the Florida statutes or in the Department's rules. (Sec. 213.015, F.S.)

The following protections are guaranteed:

— the right to available information and prompt, accurate responses to questions and requests for tax assistance;

— the right to request assistance from a taxpayers' rights advocate;

— the right to be represented or advised by counsel or other qualified representatives in administrative interactions with the Department, to procedural safeguards with respect to the recording of interviews conducted by the Department, to be treated in a professional manner by Department personnel, and to have audits, inspections, and interviews conducted at a reasonable time and place (except in criminal and internal investigations);

— the right to freedom from penalty, freedom from payment of uncollected sales and use taxes, and abatement of interest when the taxpayer reasonably relies upon binding written advice furnished by the Department in response to a specific written request that provided adequate and accurate information;

— the right to obtain simple explanations of the procedures, remedies, and rights available during audit, appeals, and collection proceedings and to be provided with a narrative description that explains the basis of audit changes, assessments, and refund denials, that identifies any amount of tax, interest, or penalty due, and that states the consequences of the taxpayer's failure to comply with the notice;

— the right to be informed of impending collection actions that require the sale or seizure of property or freezing of assets, except jeopardy assessments, and to at least 30 days' notice in which to pay the liability or seek further review;

— the right to have all other collection actions attempted before a jeopardy assessment, unless delay will endanger collection, and to have an immediate review of a jeopardy assessment;

— the right to seek review of any adverse decision and to seek a reasonable administrative stay of enforcement while the taxpayer pursues other administrative remedies;

— the right to have the taxpayer's tax information kept confidential unless otherwise specified by law;

— the right to procedures for retirement of tax obligations by installment payment agreements;

— the right to procedures for requesting cancellation, release, or modification of liens filed by the Department and for requesting that any lien filed in error be so noted;

— the right to procedures assuring that employees of the Department are not paid, evaluated, or promoted on the basis of the amount of assessments or collections from taxpayers;

— the right to an action at law, within the limitations of the state's waiver of sovereign immunity, to recover damages against the state or the Department for injury caused by the wrongful or negligent act or omission of a Department officer or employee;

— the right of the taxpayer or the Department, as the prevailing party in a judicial or administrative action brought or maintained without the support of justiciable issues, to recover all costs of the action, including reasonable attorney's fees, and of the Department and taxpayer to settle such claims through negotiations;

— the right to have the Department begin and complete its audit in a timely and expeditious manner after notification of intent to audit;

— the right to have the department actively identify and review multistate proposals that offer more efficient and effective methods for administering the revenue sources of this state;

— the right to have the department actively investigate and, where appropriate, implement automated or electronic business methods that enable the department to more efficiently and effectively administer the revenue sources of this state at less cost and effort for taxpayers;

— the right to waiver of interest that accrues as the result of errors or delays caused by a department employee;

— the right to participate in free educational activities that help the taxpayer successfully comply with the revenue laws of this state;

— the right to pay a reasonable fine or percentage of tax, whichever is less, to reinstate an exemption from any tax which a taxpayer would have been entitled to receive but which was lost because the taxpayer failed to properly register as a tax dealer in this state or obtain the necessary certificates entitling the taxpayer to the exemption; and

— the right to fair and consistent application of the tax laws of this state by the Department of Revenue.

(Sec. 213.015, F.S.)

• *Taxpayers' Rights Advocate*

A Taxpayers' Rights Advocate from the Department of Revenue is available to facilitate the resolution of taxpayer complaints and problems that have not been resolved through the Department's normal administrative channels and to assure that taxpayers' rights are protected during tax determination and collection processes. (Sec. 213.018(1), F.S.)

Taxpayer assistance orders .—The advocate may, with or without a formal written request from the taxpayer, issue a taxpayer assistance order that suspends or stays actions by the Department when the taxpayer suffers or is about to suffer a significant hardship as a result of a tax determination, collection, or enforcement process. The advocate may grant such relief only as an extraordinary measure, however, and the process may not be used to contest the merits of a tax liability. When a taxpayer requests such an order, the running of the limitations period on assessment is tolled from the date of the request until either the date the request is denied or the date specified in the taxpayer assistance order. (Sec. 213.018(2), F.S.)

[¶61-700]
LOCAL TAXES

[¶61-735] Local Tax Rates

Below are charts of discretionary sales surtaxes as well as total sales and use tax rates imposed by each county. For a general discussion of local sales and use taxes, see Local Taxes and Administration.

• *Recent local tax rate changes*

Recent local tax rate changes include the following.

Madison County tourist development rate increased effective February 1, 2022.— The Madison County Board of County Commissioners adopted Ordinance No. 2021-246 increasing the tourist development tax rate from 3% to 5% on transient rental transactions occurring in Madison County. Beginning February 1, 2022, dealers must collect a combined tax rate of 12.5% on transient rental transactions in Madison County. The combined tax rate of 12.5% is composed of the 6% state sales tax, the 5% tourist development tax, the 1% small county surtax, and the 0.5% indigent care surtax. (*Tax Information Publication, No. 22A01-01*, Florida Department of Revenue, January 6, 2022)

Glades County small county surtax effective January 1, 2022.—The Glades County Board of County Commissioners adopted a 1% small county surtax effective January 1, 2022, for Florida sales and use tax purposes. The small county surtax will sunset December 31, 2031. The combined state and local sales and use tax rate for Glades County will continue to be 7%. The new combined rate for Glades County beginning January 1, 2022, will be composed of the 6% state sales tax plus the recently adopted 1% small county surtax. The current 1% local government infrastructure surtax is set to expire on December 31, 2021. (*Tax Information Publication, No. 21A01-10*, Florida Department of Revenue, October 1, 2021)

Santa Rosa County local government infrastructure surtax.—The Santa Rosa county local government infrastructure surtax continues at 0.5% rate for Florida sales and use tax purposes. The Santa Rosa County Board of County Commissioners adopted an ordinance that extended the expiration date of the local government infrastructure surtax from December 31, 2021, to December 31, 2026. As a result, the combined Florida state and local sales and use tax rate for Santa Rosa County will continue to be 7%. The combined rate is composed of the 6% state sales tax plus the 0.5% local government infrastructure surtax and the 0.5% school capital outlay surtax. All state sales and use tax and local surtaxes collected must be reported and remitted to the Florida Department of Revenue. (*Tax Information Publication, No. 21A01-09*, Florida Department of Revenue, July 15, 2021)

Franklin County tourist development tax rate hike effective July 1 2021.— Effective July 1, 2021, the tourist development tax rate on transient rental transactions occurring within Franklin County increases from 2% to 3%. The combined tax rate for Franklin County transient rentals will be 10%, composed of the 6% state sales tax, the 3% tourist development tax, and the 1% small county surtax. The Franklin County Board of County Commissioners adopted Ordinance No. 2021-06 increasing the tourist development tax. (*Tax Information Publication, No. 21A01-06*, Florida Department of Revenue, June 8, 2021)

Hillsborough County 1% transportation discretionary sales surtax held unconstitutional.—The Florida Supreme Court has held that the amendment to the Hillsborough County Charter that imposed a 1% transportation discretionary sales surtax for transportation improvements and was codified as article 11, is unconstitutional in its entirety. As a result, and effective immediately, the combined state and local sales and use tax rate for Hillsborough County is 7.5%. Dealers should collect only the combined 7.5% rate. The revised combined 7.5% rate is composed of the 6% state sales tax plus the 0.5% school capital outlay surtax, the 0.5% indigent care surtax, and the 0.5% local government infrastructure surtax. All state sales and use tax and local surtaxes collected must be reported and remitted to the Florida Department of Revenue. (*Tax Information Publication, No. 21A01-01*, Florida Department of Revenue, March 16, 2021; *Tax Information Publication, No. 21A19-01*, Florida Department of Revenue, March 16, 2021)

COMPLIANCE NOTE: *Florida Supreme Court holds that Hillsborough County charter amendment that enacted a 1% surtax is unconstitutional.* An amendment to the Hillsborough County Charter that enacted a 1% transportation discretionary sales surtax along with elaborate provisions regarding the distribution and use of the Florida local surtax proceeds was unconstitutional. The amendment conflicted with a state law that authorizes the county commission to allocate such funds. The Florida Supreme Court ruled that the charter amendment had to be struck down in its entirety because it could not reasonably be said that the voters would have approved the tax without the accompanying spending plan. No portion of the amendment could be severed.

A state statute authorizes charter counties in Florida to levy a discretionary sales surtax at a rate of up to 1%, the proceeds of which may be applied to as many or as few of the uses enumerated specifically in the statute in whatever combination the county commission deems appropriate. There are a wide range of permitted transportation-related uses of the surtax proceeds. However, the legislature has authority over taxation as provided for in Art. VII of the Florida Constitution. The surtax at issue in this case, codified as article 11 of the Hillsborough County Charter, was adopted in a referendum conducted in the 2018 general election based on a citizens' initiative proposal. The purpose of the surtax, as stated in article 11, was to fund transportation improvements in the county. Moreover, article 11 provided a complicated scheme governing the distribution of surtax proceeds to various entities.

A local ordinance or charter provision that interferes with the operation of a state statute cannot coexist with that statute. The Florida Constitution prohibits any charter county from supplanting or overriding state law through either an ordinance or a charter provision. Core provisions of article 11 directly clash with the surtax statute's assignment to county commissions of authority to direct the application of surtax revenues to various permitted uses. All the provisions of article 11 that establish a detailed scheme governing and enforcing the distribution and use of surtax proceeds cannot coexist in the face of the commission's statutory authority. As such, the charter provisions are unconstitutional because they are inconsistent with general law. If the charter provisions of article 11 were given effect, they would supplant the authority of the county commission established by the state statute.

Lastly, the 1% sales surtax could not be severed and preserved from the provisions regarding the distribution and use of the tax proceeds. The severability of a statutory provision is determined by its relation to the overall legislative intent of the statute of which it is a part, and whether the statute, less the invalid provisions, can still accomplish this intent. The portions of article 11 that violate the authority of the county commission under the surtax statute are not functionally independent from the portion of article 11 imposing the sales surtax. The legislative purpose expressed in the valid provisions cannot be accomplished independently of those provisions that are void. The valid and invalid elements of article 11 are so inseparable in substance that, according to the Court, it cannot be said that the voters would have adopted the one without the other. As a result, the Florida Supreme Court held that article 11 is unconstitutional in its entirety. (*Emerson v. Hillsborough County, Florida*, Florida Supreme Court, No. SC19-1343, February 25, 2021)

• *Discretionary sales surtaxes*

The following are the discretionary sales surtax rates for 2022:
— Alachua 1%;
— Baker 1%;
— Bay 1%;
— Bradford 1%;
— Brevard 1%;
— Broward 1%;
— Calhoun 1.5%;
— Charlotte 1%;
— Citrus 0%;
— Clay 1.5%;
— Collier 1%;
— Columbia 1%;
— Dade 1%;
— DeSoto 1.5%;
— Dixie 1%;
— Duval 1.5%;
— Escambia 1.5%;
— Flagler 1%;
— Franklin 1%;
— Gadsden 1.5%;
— Gilchrist 1%;

— Glades 1%;
— Gulf 1%;
— Hamilton 1%;
— Hardee 1%;
— Hendry 1%;
— Hernando 0.5%;
— Highlands 1.5%;
— Hillsborough 1.5%;
— Holmes 1.5%;
— Indian River 1%;
— Jackson 1.5%;
— Jefferson 1%;
— Lafayette 1%;
— Lake 1%;
— Lee 0.5%;
— Leon 1.5%;
— Levy 1%;
— Liberty 1.5%;
— Madison 1.5%;
— Manatee 1%;
— Marion 1%;
— Martin 0.5%;
— Miami-Dade 1%;
— Monroe 1.5%;
— Nassau 1%;
— Okaloosa 1%;
— Okeechobee 1%;
— Orange 0.5%;
— Osceola 1.5%;
— Palm Beach 1%;
— Pasco 1%;
— Pinellas 1%;
— Polk 1%;
— Putnam 1%;
— St. Johns 0.5%;
— St. Lucie 1%;
— Santa Rosa 1%;
— Sarasota 1%;
— Seminole 1%;
— Sumter 1%;
— Suwannee 1%;
— Taylor 1%;
— Union 1%;

— Volusia 0.5%;

— Wakulla 1%;

— Walton 1%; and

— Washington 1.5%.

(*Form DR-15DSS, Discretionary Sales Surtax Information For Calendar Year 2022*, Florida Department of Revenue, January 2022)

• *Local tax rates by county*

Some counties impose one or more local option taxes on taxable transactions within the county and on the lease or rental of living or sleeping or housekeeping accommodations ("transient rentals") within the county, and many counties self-administer the local transient rental taxes.

Current local option transient rental tax rates.—Taxpayers may find current local option transient rental tax rates at: Local Option Transient Rental Tax Rates (Tourist Development Tax Rates)

Some counties impose one or more local option taxes on taxable transactions within the county and on the lease or rental of living, sleeping, or housekeeping accommodations (i.e., transient rentals) within the county. Counties that self-administer the local transient rental taxes are not required by law to notify the Florida Department of Revenue of local tax rate changes. Consequently, the tax rates in this chart may not be current. Taxpayers are advised to contact local county taxing authorities to verify tax rates and obtain information regarding the collection and remittance of locally administered taxes. (*Sales and Use Tax and Discretionary Sales Surtax Rates*, Florida Department of Revenue)

History of local sales tax and current rates.—Taxpayers may find a history of local sales tax and current rates at: History of Local Sales Tax and Current Rates.

UTILITIES

[¶80-100]
UTILITY SERVICES

[¶80-101] Gross Receipts Tax on Utility Services

Florida utility gross receipts tax is imposed on gross receipts from utility services that are delivered to a retail consumer in Florida. (Sec. 203.01(1)(a)1., F. S.) "Utility service" means electricity for light, heat, or power and natural or manufactured gas for light, heat, or power, including transportation, delivery, transmission, and distribution of electricity or natural or manufactured gas. The definition of "utility service" is not intended to include separately stated charges for tangible personal property or services that are not charges for electricity or natural or manufactured gas or the transportation, delivery, transmission, or distribution of electricity or natural or manufactured gas. (Sec. 203.012(3), F. S.; Rule 12B-6.001, F.A.C.)

The utility gross receipts tax does not apply to:

— the sale or transportation of natural or manufactured gas to a public or private utility;

— qualifying sale or delivery of electricity to a public or private utility for resale within the state or as part of a qualifying electrical interchange agreement (Rule 12B-6.0015(5), F.A.C.);

— wholesale sales of electric transmission services;

— the use of natural gas (1) in the production of oil or gas or (2) by a person transporting natural or manufactured gas, when used and consumed in providing such services; or

— qualified sales or transportation to, or use of natural or manufactured gas by, a person eligible for an exemption under Sec. 212.08(7)(ff)2, F.S., for use as an energy source or a raw material.

(Sec. 203.01(3), F.S.)

• *Communications services*

Florida also imposes a gross receipts tax on communications services. However, that tax is administered and collected pursuant to the provisions of the state's communications services tax, and it is discussed along with that tax at ¶80-115. (Sec. 203.01(1)(a)2., F. S.)

• *Rates*

The gross receipts tax rate is 2.5% for utility services. (Sec. 203.011(2)(b), F. S.; Rule 12B-6.0015, F.A.C)

An additional tax on gross receipts from utility services is imposed on electrical power or energy already subject to sales and use tax. The additional tax is not imposed on transactions that are exempt from sales and use tax. A seller of electric power may collect a combined rate of 6.95% to account for the 4.35% sales and use tax rate and the 2.6% utility tax rate, provided that the seller distinguishes the two amounts collected when submitting a return to the Florida Department of Revenue.

(Sec. 203.01(1)(b), F.S.; *Tax Information Publication, No. 14A01-07*, Florida Department of Revenue, June 20, 2014)

Dealers selling electricity may collect tax at the combined rate of 6.95% or dealers may separately state each tax on their customers' billings. Dealers that elect to use the combined rate are not required to label the rate in a particular way, provided the tax is clearly identified as a Florida state tax or sales tax. (*Tax Information Publication, No. 14A01-07*, Florida Department of Revenue, June 20, 2014)

• *Basis of tax*

The term "gross receipts" does not include gross receipts derived from the sale of natural or manufactured gas to a public or private utility or the sale of electricity to a public and private utility for resale within the state or as part of an electrical interchange agreement. (Sec. 203.01(3), F. S.)

Taxable receipts are determined based on, among other things, the type of service provided and who the provider is. In the immediately following discussions of the tax basis for electricity, natural or manufactured gas, or any of those services imported for the importer's own use, the resulting tax would be reduced by any amount of qualifying taxes the consumer paid to the person from whom the service was purchased. (Sec. 203.01(1)(d), F. S.)

Electricity.—For distribution companies that deliver utility services to retail consumers who, in turn, pay a charge for the service that includes a charge for both the electricity and the transportation of the electricity, the tax is levied on the total amount of the distribution companies' gross receipts. (Sec. 203.01(1)(c), F. S.; Rule 12B-6.0015(2), F.A.C) If a distribution company charges for the delivery of electricity separately from the sale of electricity itself, the company is subject to a tax in an amount determined by multiplying the number of kilowatt hours delivered by an annually determined index price and applying the tax rate to the result. (Sec. 203.01(1)(d), F. S.)

Natural or manufactured gas.—A distribution company that receives payment for the sale or transportation of natural or manufactured gas is subject to the tax in an amount determined by:

— dividing the number of cubic feet delivered by 1,000,

— multiplying the resulting number by an annually determined index price, and

— applying the tax rate to that result.

(Sec. 203.01(1)(e), F. S.; Rule 12B-6.0015, F.A.C)

Importation for own use.—Any person who imports electricity, natural gas, or manufactured gas into Florida for that person's own use or consumption as a substitute for purchasing utility services and who cannot demonstrate payment of the utility gross receipts tax must register with the Department of Revenue and pay the tax on a monthly basis. The tax shall be equal to the cost price of the electricity, natural gas, or manufactured gas times the tax rate. "Cost price" has the same meaning as it does under the Florida sales and use tax statute. (Sec. 203.01(1)(f), F. S.; Sec. 212.02(4), F. S.)

• *Collections, Remittances, Reports*

For sales of utility services other than to importers of the service for their own use, the gross receipts tax on utility services is levied by distribution companies against the total amount of gross receipts or, for qualifying sales of services, to an amount determined by multiplying the gross receipts by an index. Distribution companies must report and remit to the Department of Revenue by the 20th day of each month the taxes levied during the preceding month. (Sec. 203.01(1)(c), (d)3, and (e)3, F. S.; Rule 12B-6.005, F.A.C.)

Any person, other than a distribution company, that engages in the transportation of natural or manufactured gas must furnish to the Department of Revenue an annual list of customers for whom transportation services were provided in the prior year. The reports are subject to confidentiality provisions. Any person required to furnish a customer list may comply by maintaining a publicly accessible customer list on its Internet website; such a list must be updated at least annually. (Sec. 203.01(9), F. S.; Rule 12B-6.005, F.A.C.)

The Department of Revenue may require taxpayers to file returns and pay tax as follows:

— on a quarterly basis if the tax remitted for the preceding four calendar quarters did not exceed $1,000;

— on a semiannual basis if the tax remitted for the preceding four calendar quarters did not exceed $500; or

— on an annual basis if the tax remitted for the preceding four calendar quarters did not exceed $100.

(Sec. 203.01(1)(j), F.S.)

Florida requires electronic filing of returns and electronic payment for the gross receipts tax if the tax paid in the previous state fiscal year exceeds a threshold. (Sec. 213.755, F.S.)

• *Penalties and Interest*

Under the gross receipts statute, it is a misdemeanor of the first degree for anyone to

— receive payment for the furnishing things or services without first complying with the provisions of the law, and

— willfully violate or fail to comply with any of the provisions of the law.

(Sec. 203.03, F.S.) Penalties for misdemeanors of the first degree include up to one year's imprisonment and a maximum fine of $1,000. (Sec. 775.082, F.S.; Sec. 775.083, F.S.)

Interest on delinquent gross receipts tax for utility services is assessed at the rate of 1% per month, accruing from the date due until paid. (Sec. 203.06, F.S.) For information on Florida interest rates on underpayments and overpayments of tax, including gross receipts tax, see ¶ 89-204.

• *Local public service tax*

Municipalities may levy a public service tax on the purchase of electricity, metered or bottled gas, and water service. The tax is levied only upon purchases within the municipality and cannot exceed 10% of the payments received by the seller of the taxable item from the purchaser for the purchase of the service. However, the tax may be applied to water service provided to property in a qualified development outside a municipality if agreed to in writing by the development and the municipality prior to March 31, 2000. The purchase of natural gas, manufactured gas, or fuel oil by a private or public utility, either for resale or for use as fuel in the generation of electricity is exempt from this tax. (Sec. 166.231(1), F.S.)

Municipalities must notify the Department of any subsequent adoption or repeal of public service tax levies at least 120 days prior to the effective date of the levies and provide other pertinent information on request. (Sec. 166.233, F.S.)

Municipalities can audit sellers to ascertain that the services have been provided and that returns are correct. Proposed assessments can be issued within three years of the due date of the taxes. Municipalities also can assess interest up to 1% a month on past due taxes and can assess penalties in cases of willful neglect, willful negligence, or fraud. (Sec. 166.234, F.S.)

Consumers in enterprise zones.—Through December 31, 2015, municipalities may exempt not less than 50% of the tax imposed on purchasers of electrical energy if such purchasers are eligible for the sales tax exemption for the use of electrical energy in an enterprise zone. Businesses must qualify for the exemption prior to 1995. (Sec. 166.231(8)(a), F.S.)

Industrial consumers.—Municipalities may provide full or partial exemptions from local utilities tax or a reduced tax rate for electricity or gas purchased by an industrial consumer that uses the electricity or gas directly in an industrial manufacturing, processing, compounding, or production process at a fixed location in that municipality. The municipality must establish the requirements to qualify for the exemption in the manner prescribed by ordinance. Effective July 1, 2009, the exemption must be granted to all companies classified in the same five-digit North American Industry Classification System ("NAICS") Industry Number. Previously, the SIC Industry Major Group Number was used. (Sec. 166.231(6), F.S.)

Sellers who possess a written document from the purchaser certifying the purchaser's entitlement to the exemption will be relieved of their responsibility to collect tax on the nontaxable amounts. The municipality must look solely to the purchaser for recovery of the tax if it determines that the purchaser was not entitled to the exemption. (Sec. 166.231(6), F.S.)

[¶80-110]

COMMUNICATIONS SERVICES

[¶80-115] Communications Services Tax

Florida imposes two state taxes on the retail sale of communications services in the state. (Sec. 202.12, F.S.) In addition, a separate gross receipts tax (GRT) is imposed on each communications services tax (CST) and a second GRT is imposed on one of the CSTs. The gross receipts taxes apply to the same services and transactions that are subject to the CST, and the two taxes are administered and collected pursuant to the provisions of the CST. (Sec. 203.01(1)(a)2, F.S.)

CCH COMMENT: Streaming video service and sales of electronic books.—The Florida Department of Revenue has held, in an advisement that is binding on the department only under the facts and circumstances described, that the portion of a membership program that provides a streaming video service to its subscribers that is attributable to that service is subject to Florida communications services tax (CST) but is not subject to sales and use tax. If that portion is not separately allocable in the taxpayer's books and records, then the entire membership fee is subject to the CST. Streaming video services are not subject to sales and use tax because such services are neither tangible personal property nor any of the enumerated taxable services. As a result, the portion of membership fees attributable to streaming video services is also not subject to sales and use tax.

In addition, Florida law does not currently impose sales or use tax on the sale of electronic books, and as such, the portion of membership fees attributable to the lending or permanent download of electronic books is not subject to sales and use tax. The temporary or permanent download of electronic books is the acquisition or retrieval of information; specifically, it is access to electronic publishing products. Such access is specifically listed as "information services," and information services are specifically excluded from communications services, these services are not subject to the CST. Consequently, the portion of the membership fees attributable to the lending or permanent downloading of electronic books is not subject to the CST.

The definition of "communications services" includes video services. Streaming video services are video services, and consequently, they are communications services. The retail sale of streaming video services is the retail sale of communications services and when such services originate and/or terminate in Florida and are charged to a Florida service address, the sale is subject to the CST. The sale of a membership includes streaming video services, and as a result, the portion of the membership fees attributable to such services is subject to the CST. (*Technical Assistance Advisement, No. 14A-010*, Florida Department of Revenue, April 7, 2014)

CCH COMMENT: Streaming video and music service membership program.— The Florida Department of Revenue advises taxpayers that the benefit of a membership program under which members can stream or download digitized versions (i.e., digital content) of movies, television shows, sporting events, news events, and other video content and play or download music content is a "communications service" and, specifically, a video service. Consequently, the portion of the membership charge attributable to that service is subject to Florida communications services tax when charged to a Florida service address.

The video service allows a member to:

— select and view digital video content on compatible devices; and

— download digital video content to a compatible device when that option is available.

The member can view the content by streaming or downloading it provided the membership subscription has been paid. If the subscription lapses or is cancelled, the member is no longer able to view the digital video content, even if the digital video content was downloaded.

In addition, the music service benefit is a music service that falls within the definition of a "video service" under Florida law. The music service provided by membership under which members can play or download music content is likewise a video service under Florida law, and the portion of the membership charge attributable to the music service is also subject to the CST when charged to a Florida service address. The music service can be played on a compatible device, like a computer or tablet, and the digital music content may be downloaded or streamed. The member can play the content by streaming or downloading it provided the member's subscription is paid. Once the subscription lapses or is cancelled, the member is no longer able to play the digital music content, even if the digital audio content was downloaded. The transmission or routing of audio or voice to a point, or between or among points, by any medium or method is a communications service. The definition of "video service" includes music services.

Lastly, the video and music service benefits are not sales of tangible personal property or other taxable services and, as such, are not subject to Florida sales tax. The video service benefit is comprised of electronic images that appear on a video display screen. The music benefit is also not an information service for sales tax purposes. The taxpayer does not furnish any tangible personal property for sale or rental to the customer for either service benefit. (*Technical Assistance Advisement, No. 14A19-006*, Florida Department of Revenue, December 19, 2014)

CCH COMMENT: Digital video content.—The Florida Department of Revenue has held, in an advisement that is binding on the department only under the facts and circumstances described, that the taxpayer's sales and rentals of digital video content are not subject to Florida sales tax as they are not the sale of tangible personal property or taxable services. The taxpayer provides digital video content, which includes television shows, movies, sporting events, and news events, for sale or rental. Florida law imposes sales tax on retail sales in the state of tangible personal property. A regulation provides that furnishing information by way of electronic images that appear on a subscriber's video display screen does not constitute the sale of tangible personal property or a taxable information service. Since the taxpayer does not furnish any tangible personal property for sale or rental to the customer, such sales are not subject to sales tax.

The taxpayer's rental of digital video content is a video service and, as such, charges made to customers for the rental of digital video content to a Florida service address are subject to communications services tax (CST) on the sales price. The Florida CST is imposed on the retail sale of communications services in Florida. Communications services include video services, and video services include pay-per-view and digital video services.

The taxpayer's sales of digital video content, whether stored online or downloaded to a customer's device, are sales of information services. Such sales are not the sale of a communications service subject to the CST. Information services are excluded from the definition of "communications services." Information services do not include video services. The CST is imposed on the retail sale of communications services when the services: (1) originate and terminate in Florida; or (2) originate or terminate in Florida and are charged to a Florida service address. (*Technical Assistance Advisement, No. 14A19-005*, Florida Department of Revenue, December 18, 2014)

• *Definitions*

"Communication services" means the transmission, conveyance or routing of information or signals including video services, to or between points by any medium. The term also includes such transmission, conveyance, or routing in which computer processing applications are used to act on the form, code, or protocol of the content without regard to whether such service is referred to as voice-over-Internet-protocol

(VOIP) services or is classified by the Federal Communications Commission as enhanced or value-added. Communication services do not include:

— information services;

— installation or maintenance of wiring or equipment on a customer's premises;

— the sale or rental of tangible personal property;

— the sale of advertising (including directory advertising);

— bad check charges;

— late payment charges;

— billing and collection services; or

— Internet access service, electronic mail service, electronic bulletin board service, or similar on-line services.

(Sec. 202.11(1), F.S.)

"Service address" means the location of the communications equipment from which communications services originate or at which communications services are received by the customer. In the case of a communications service paid through a credit or payment mechanism that does not relate to a service address, such as a bank, travel, debit, or credit card, and in the case of third-number and calling-card calls, the service address is the address of the central office for the originating phone number. If the location of the communications equipment is not known and payment is not through a credit or payment mechanism that does not relate to a service address, "service address" means the location of the customer's primary use of the communications service, which is the residential or business street address of the customer. (Sec. 202.11(14), F.S.)

• *Sale of services originating and/or terminating in state*

There is a tax applied to the sale price of communications services that originate and terminate in the state, or that originates or terminates in Florida and is charged to a Florida address. (Sec., 202.12(1)(a), F.S.) In addition, this tax applies to charges with respect to a channel termination point located within Florida:

— with respect to a channel termination point located within this state;

— for the use of a channel between two channel termination points located in this state; and

— in certain situations where channel termination points are located both within and outside of this state.

(Sec. 202.12(1)(c), F.S.)

Finally, that CST also applies to the sales price of all mobile communications services deemed to be provided to a customer by a home service provider pursuant to the federal Mobile Telecommunications Sourcing Act, Pub. L. No. 106-252. The customer's address must be in Florida. (Sec. 202.12(1)(d), F.S.)

• *Sale of direct-to-home satellite service*

The CST is imposed at a different rate on the retail sales price of any direct-to-home satellite service received in the state.

• *Gross receipts tax*

There are two GRTs that apply to one or both CSTs.

The gross receipts tax on communications services applies to the same services and transactions that are subject to the state communications services tax, as well as to one class of services that are exempt from the communications services tax. The gross receipts tax

— applies to the sales price of communications services when sold at retail,

— is due and payable at the same time as the communications services tax, and

— is administered and collected pursuant to the provisions of the communications services tax statute.

(Sec. 203.01(1)(b)2, F. S.)

The other GRT applies to the CST on sales of services originating and/or terminating within the state. (Sec. 203.01(1)(b)3, F. S.)

• *Rate of tax*

The CST on communications services originating or terminating within the state is imposed together with two GRTs. The satellite services CST is imposed with one GRT.

Services originating, terminating within state.—The tax rates applicable to the sale of services originating or terminating within the states are as follows:

— CST, 4.92%

— GRT on CST, 2.37%

— second GRT, 0.15%

(Sec. 202.12(1)(a), (c), (d), F.S.; Sec. 203.01(1)(b)2, 3, F. S.) The combined rate is 7.44%.

Satellite services.—The tax rates applicable to the sale of satellite services are as follows:

— CST, 9.07%

— GRT on CST, 2.37%

(Sec. 202.12(1)(b), F.S.; Sec. 203.01(1)(b)2, 3, F. S.) The combined rate is 11.44%.

Local communications services tax rates are discussed at ¶ 80-310.

• *Exemptions*

There are several exemptions from the CST. (Sec. 202.125, F.S.) However, the first of those items as listed immediately below is not exempt from the gross receipts tax on communications services. (Sec. 203.01(1)(a)2, F.S.)

Sales specifically exempt from the communications services tax are for:

— separately stated communications services (excluding mobile communications service, video service, and direct-to-home satellite service) to residential households that are not all or part of a public lodging establishment (unlike the other exemptions from the communications services tax, this item is not exempt from the gross receipts tax on communications services) (Sec. 203.01(1)(a)2, F.S.);

¶80-115

— communications services to the federal government or any agency or instrumentality of the federal government;

— communications services to any entity that is exempt form state taxes under federal law;

— communications services to Florida, any Florida county, municipality, or political subdivision when payment is made directly to the dealer by the governmental entity;

— communications services to a home for the aged; and

— communications services to a religious institution or educational institution that is exempt from federal income tax under IRC 501(c)(3).

(Sec. 202.125, F.S.; Rule 12A-19.041, F.A.C.—Rule 12A-19.043, F.A.C.)

Purchases of communications services for resale are also exempt from tax if the purchaser has registered with the Department prior to making the purchase. The dealer must document the sale by obtaining either:

— a signed copy of the annual resale certificates obtained by the selling dealer;

— the transaction resale authorization number issued prior to or at the point of sale, which is valid for a single transaction; or

— the vendor resale authorization number for regular customers who have previously submitted documentation to the selling dealer.

(Rule 12A-19.060, F.A.C.)

• *Registration and collection*

Taxpayers engaged in providing communications services are required to register with the Department on Form DR-700014, *Communications Services Tax Certificate of Registration*. Persons who must register include those who provide the transmission, conveyance, or routing of voice, data, audio, video, or any other information or signals, including video services, to a point or between or among points through electronic, radio, satellite, cable, optical, microwave, or other mediums. (Rule 12A-19.010, F.A.C.)

However, taxpayers engaged only in the following activities are not required to register:

— information services;

— installation or maintenance of wiring or equipment on a customer's premises;

— sale or rental of tangible personal property;

— sale of advertising services, such as directory advertising;

— bad check services;

— late payment services;

— billing and collection services;

— Internet access services, electronic mail services, electronic bulletin board services, or similar on-line computer services;

— communications services provided through coin-operated communications devices;

— sale or recharge of prepaid calling arrangements;

— air-to-ground communications services; and

— professional or advertising services, such as facsimile charges.

(Rule 12A-19.010(3)(c), F.A.C.)

Generally, persons registering for the communications services tax must notify the Department of the methods that will be employed to determine the local taxing jurisdiction in which service addresses are located. The form, Form DR-700020, *Notification of Method Employed to Determine Taxing Jurisdiction (Communications Services Tax)*, is not required with respect to the following persons:

— direct-to-home satellite providers;

— substitute communications system operators;

— resellers of prepaid calling arrangements;

— direct pay permit applicants with no obligations to collect and remit local communications services taxes;

— pay telephone operators; and

— persons who will make no sales of communications services except to qualifying purchasers for resale.

(Rule 12A-19.010(3)(a), F.A.C.)

To obtain a communications tax certificate, taxpayers must file a Form DR-1, "Florida Business Tax Application."

The communications services tax is collected on the same taxable transactions and remitted to the Department of Revenue in the same manner as the gross receipts (utilities) tax. The full amount of the taxes on a credit sale, installment sale, or sale made on any kind of deferred payment plan is due at the moment of the transaction in the same manner as a cash sale. (Sec. 202.16, F.S.) Each dealer of communications services, except public lodging establishments, must separately state the communications services tax on the bill or invoice. Instead of separately stating the tax, public lodging establishments may notify purchasers of the taxes in a notice posted in the guest rooms. (Sec. 202.16, F.S.) Effective July 1, 2011, the dealer must compute the tax due based on a rounding algorithm. (Sec. 202.16(3)(a), F.S.

• *Return and payment deadline*

Taxpayers must file Form DR-700016 along with a tax payment by the 20th day of the month following each reporting period. (Sec. 202.27(1), F.S.; Instructions, Form DR-700016, Florida Communications Services Tax Return) Florida requires electronic filing of returns and electronic payment if the tax paid in the previous state fiscal year exceeds a threshold. (Sec. 213.755, F.S.)

• *Use tax*

Any person who purchases communications services that are otherwise subject to the Florida communications services tax, or a local communications services tax, at retail from a seller in another state, territory, the District of Columbia, or any foreign country must pay a use tax on the communications services purchased and used, the same as if the services had been purchased at retail from a dealer in the state. However, use tax is not due if the out-of-state seller registers as a dealer in the state and collects the required taxes from the purchaser. (Sec. 202.151, F.S.)

Communications services providers that are not registered with the Department should report communications services use tax on Form DR-700019, Communications Services Use Tax Return. However, registered communications services providers should use Form DR-700016, Communications Services Tax Return, to report use tax. Use tax is due semiannually on July 1 and January 1. (*Tax Information Publication, No. 02A19-09*, Florida Department of Revenue, December 5, 2002; Rule 12A-19.020, F.A.C.)

• *Confidentiality requirements*

Information received by the Florida Department of Revenue relating to the Florida communications services tax and the gross receipts tax on communications services is exempt from public record disclosure requirements, with an exception for the release of information to local governments. Disclosure of this information would adversely affect the business interests of communications services companies, compromise the security of the communications network, and impair competition in the communications industry. Thus, as of October 1, 2001, communications services returns, reports, accounts, or declarations received by the Department, including investigative reports and letters of technical advice, are confidential. Any Department officer, employee, or former employee who divulges such information for non-official purposes commits a first degree misdemeanor. (Sec. 213.053, F.S.)

• *Penalties and interest*

There is a variety of penalties for violations of the communications services tax law.

Failure to timely file or pay.—Any person who fails to make a required return or to pay any required communications services tax is subject to the following fines in relation to the amount of unpaid tax:

— 10% if the failure is for not more than 30 days;

— 10% for each additional 30 days or fraction thereof;

— up to a maximum of 50%.

(Sec. 202.28(2)(a), F.S.)

Failure to report appropriately.—If a communications services dealer fails to separately report and identify local communications services taxes on the appropriate return schedule, the dealer will be subject to a penalty of $5,000 per return. If the department is unable to obtain appropriate return schedules, any penalty imposed will be allocated in the same manner as provided in Sec. 202.18(2), F.S.. (Sec. 202.28(2), F.S.)

Willful evasion of taxes.—Anyone convicted of failing to file six consecutive returns commits a felony of the third degree and is subject to a maximum fine of $5,000 or a maximum prison year of five years. (Sec. 775.082, F.S.) For anyone who makes a false or fraudulent return to evade communications services tax, penalties are graduated based on the amount of tax involved and the number of offenses. Anyone convicted of the crime is liable for fines ranging from $500 to $10,000. (Sec. 775.083, F.S.) Alternatively, that person could be liable for imprisonment for terms ranging from 60 days to 30 years. (Sec. 775.082, F.S.)

Failure to keep proper records.—If a dealer keeps records in both machine-readable and hardcopy formats, the dealer must make the records available to the Department of Revenue upon request in the machine-readable format. Any dealer who fails or refuses to provide the required records within 60 days after the Department's request or any applicable extension will, in addition to all other penalties, be subject to a specific penalty of $5,000 per audit. (Sec. 202.34(5), F.S.)

Interest.—For information on Florida interest rates on underpayments and overpayments of tax, including communications services tax and gross receipts tax, see ¶89-204.

• *Forms*

For a complete list of forms, see Rule 12AER20-15, F.A.C.

• *Tax refunds*

Though not characterized as credits, taxpayers that create new jobs under specific conditions are eligible for tax refunds from multiple tax types (including the communication services tax, but not the gross receipts tax). The refunds are available to qualified defense contractors/space flight businesses, qualified target industry businesses, and qualified target industry businesses redeveloping a brownfield. See below for general information and ¶89-224, Refunds for additional details.

Taxpayers are allowed a credit against the communications services tax equal to the amount of similar tax paid to another state or local jurisdiction. (Sec. 202.14, F.S.)

Economic Development Trust Fund refunds to qualified defense contractors and space flight business.—Qualified applicants may apply by January 31 of each fiscal year to the Department of Economic Opportunity for a refund from the Economic Development Trust Fund for the corporate income, sales and use, excise, property, documentary stamp, and communications services taxes due and paid by them, beginning with the applicant's first taxable year commencing after entering into a tax refund agreement. The amount of the refund is based on the number of jobs created by the taxpayer's activities. (Sec. 288.1045, F.S.) For further details, see ¶89-224, Refunds.

Refunds for qualified target industry businesses.—Qualified target industry businesses, after entering into tax refund agreements with the Department of Economic Opportunity, are entitled to apply by January 31 of each fiscal year for refunds from the Economic Development Incentives Account for the corporate income, insurance premium, sales and use, intangible personal property, excise, communication services, and property taxes due and paid by them after entering into the agreement. The amount of the refund is based on the number of jobs created by the taxpayer's activities. (Sec. 288.106, F.S.) For further details, see ¶89-224, Refunds.

Brownfield redevelopment bonus refund.—A bonus refund of property tax, sales and use tax, documentary stamp tax, corporate income tax, intangible personal property tax, emergency excise tax, communication services, or insurance premium tax is available to any qualified target industry business or "other eligible business" for each new Florida job created in a brownfield that is claimed on the business's annual tax refund claim. The amount of the refund is based on the number of jobs created by the taxpayer's activities. (Sec. 288.107, F.S.) For further details, see ¶89-224, Refunds.

[¶80-150] Emergency Telephone Users Surcharge

All Florida wireless telephone service subscribers are subject to a monthly emergency telephone (E911) users fee of 50¢. State and local taxes do not apply to the fee, and state and local governments are not authorized to levy additional fees on wireless providers or subscribers for E911 service. (Sec. 365.172, F.S.)

Collection of fee.—Voice communications service providers are required to collect the fee from their subscribers and to remit them to the Wireless 911 Board, which was created to assume responsibility for E911 fee administration and related duties, subject to the oversight of the Department of Management Services; for purposes of this provision, state and local governments are not customers. (Sec. 365.172, F.S.)

Remittance of fee.—For prepaid wireless telephone service, the 50¢ fee must be remitted based upon each prepaid wireless telephone associated with Florida for each wireless service customer that has a balance as of the last day of each month that is equal to or greater than the monthly fee. The fee amount or an equivalent number of minutes may be reduced from the prepaid subscriber's account in lieu of direct billing, but the reduction would not constitute a reduction in the sales price for Florida sales and use tax purposes. (Sec. 365.172, F.S.)

Adjustment of allocation percentages.—The board may adjust allocation percentages, as provided in Sec. 365.173, or reduce the fee amount, or both, to ensure full 911 system cost recovery or to prevent over recovery. Fee reduction or new allocation percentages may not be adjusted for one year, and the monthly fee may not exceed 50¢ per each service number. (Sec. 365.172, F.S.)

Text-to-911 services.—Effective July 1, 2019, each county must develop a county-wide implementation plan addressing text-to-911 services and, by January 1, 2022, enact a system to allow text-to-911 services. (Sec. 365.172, F.S.)

INSURANCE

[¶88-000]

INSURANCE

[¶88-010] Companies Subject to Tax

All insurers doing business in the state, including wet marine and transportation companies and reciprocal insurers, are subject to premiums tax. (Sec. 624.509(1), F.S.; Sec. 624.510, F.S.; Sec. 629.5011, F.S.) Regulatory provisions further elaborate the insurance and surety policies subject to premium taxation to include those issued by risk retention groups, legal expense insurance corporations, captive and industrial captive insurers, surety companies, and joint underwriting associations and plans. (Rule 12B-8.001, F.A.C.) Insurers are also subject to a state fire marshal regulatory assessment. (Sec. 624.515, F. S.; Rule 12B-8.006, F.A.C.)

However, premium taxation and state fire marshal regulatory assessments do not apply to recoupment of joint underwriting association and assigned risk plan deficit assessments paid by insurers, net of earnings returned to insurers by such plans. (Rule 12B-8.001, F.A.C.) Generally, insurance premium taxation also excludes certain crop insurance premiums, orphan insurers that do not hold a Florida certificate of authority, and service warranty and motor vehicle service agreement insurers. (Rule 12B-8.001, F.A.C.)

The premiums, contributions and assessments received by prepaid limited health service organizations are subject to tax. (Sec. 624.509(1), F.S.)

A nonprofit self-insurance corporation organized for the purpose of providing property insurance to group members is subject to tax on premiums, contributions, and assessments received by the corporation. (Sec. 624.4625, F.S.)

A self-insurance fund formed by two or more public housing authorities for the purpose of pooling and spreading liabilities of its members as to any one or combination of casualty risk or self-insuring real or personal property risk of every kind and every interest in such property against loss or damage from any hazard or cause and against any loss consequential to such loss or damage is subject to tax on premiums, contributions, and assessments received by the corporation. (Sec. 624.46226, F.S.)

• *Retaliatory taxes*

Whenever the laws of any state or country require insurance companies organized under the laws of Florida to pay higher taxes or fees or to comply with rules, regulations and prohibitions in excess of those required by Florida, foreign insurance companies incorporated in that state or country are required to comply with the same rules, regulations and prohibitions in Florida.

Generally, net premium tax is used as a starting point in computing retaliatory taxes, with exclusions for various taxes and assessments. (Sec. 624.5091, F.S.; Rule 12B-8.016, F.A.C.) Retaliatory calculations include real and personal property tax deductions from premium taxes and Florida Insurance Guarantee Association property insurance policy assessments. Foreign insurers' taxable income for a prior year and resulting corporate income tax liability are used to calculate aggregate Florida taxes. Sales and use taxes and reimbursement premiums and emergency assessments paid to the Florida Hurricane Catastrophe Fund are excluded from the calculation of the amount of retaliatory taxes imposed on foreign insurance companies. Allowable deductions against premium taxes claimed for Florida workers' compensation premium assessments paid must be added back to net premium taxes. In addition, comparable deductions allowed in other states must also be added back to net premium taxes.

No additional retaliatory tax is required if the insurer claims to capital investment, community contribution, scholarship contribution, new market, or former CAPCO credits. In addition, a percentage of the salary credit is disregarded for purposes of the retaliatory tax.

In calculating the retaliatory tax, 80%, and a portion of the remaining 20%, of the salary credits is disregarded. The "portion of the remaining 20%" is calculated by multiplying the remaining 20% by a fraction, the numerator of which is the sum of salaries qualifying for either salary credit of employees whose place of employment is located in an enterprise zone and the denominator of which is the sum of all salaries qualifying for the credits. (Sec. 624.5091, F.S.)

If another state imposes any requirement, including a tax, upon a Florida resident insurance adjuster in connection with the issuance of, and activities under, a nonresident adjuster's license, then the same requirements are imposed upon every insurance adjuster of that state doing business in Florida under such a license. (Sec. 626.8737, F.S.)

• *Captive insurance companies*

Captive and industrial captive insurers are subject to tax. (Rule 12B-8.001, F.A.C.) Florida has no special provisions related to captive insurance companies.

• *Surplus line brokers and nonadmitted insurance*

Under the federal Nonadmitted and Reinsurance Reform Act of 2010 (NRRA), only an insured's home state can require the payment of a premiums tax on nonadmitted insurance, which includes both surplus lines and independently procured insurance. However, the NRRA authorizes the states to enter into an agreement to allocate the taxes among the states. Information on the Nonadmitted Insurance Multistate Agreement (NIMA) is available at http://www.floir.com/Sections/PandC/NIMA.aspx and information on the Surplus Lines Insurance Multistate Compliance Compact (SLIMPACT) is available at http://www.csg.org/NCIC/SLIMPACT.aspx.

Surplus lines agents are subject to a tax. Effective May 26, 2011, if a surplus lines policy or an independently procured coverage policy covers risks or exposures only partially in Florida and Florida is the "home state", as defined in the federal NRRA, the tax payable is computed on the gross premium. (Sec. 626.932, F. S.)

A service fee is imposed upon insureds, at a rate of up to 0.3% of the total gross premium of each surplus lines policy. (Sec. 626.921, F.S.) The Florida Surplus Lines Service Office will determine the exact rate of the service fee, which is collected and remitted by surplus lines agents. Premiums, contributions and assessments received by an assessable mutual insurer are subject to tax. (Sec. 628.6015, F.S.)

• *Reimbursement premiums paid to hurricane fund*

Insurers writing covered policies, defined as any insurance policy covering residential property in Florida or any other policy covering a residential structure issued by any authorized insurer, but not including any policy excluding wind coverage or any reinsurance agreement, must pay a reimbursement premium into the Florida Hurricane Catastrophe Fund. (Sec. 215.555, F.S.) Applicable to reimbursement contracts entered into in 1996 and thereafter, policies that exclude hurricane coverage are not considered to be "covered policies." In exchange, each such insurer is entitled to receive reimbursement of a percentage of its losses from hurricanes.

¶88-010

[¶88-015] Exemptions

A beneficial, relief, or mutual aid society, formed by a religious organization under IRC Sec. 501 for the purpose of aiding members who sustain property losses, and in which the coverages, privileges, and memberships in the society are confined to members of the religious organization, is exempt from the insurance code. (Sec. 624.126, F.S.)

Insurance premium taxation also excludes crop insurance premiums received by insurers in accordance with the Federal Crop Insurance Act after January 1, 1994, orphan insurers that do not hold a Florida certificate of authority, and service warranty and motor vehicle service agreement insurers. (Rule 12B-8.001, F.A.C.)

The Residential Property and Casualty Joint Underwriting Association is no longer exempt from the insurance premium tax, but retains its exemption from the corporate income tax. (Sec. 627.351, F.S.)

The property, revenues, and other assets of the Special Disability Trust Fund Financing Corporation are exempt from taxation by Florida and its political subdivisions. Also exempt are the corporation's transactions and operations and the income these generate, and the bonds issued by the corporation and the interest on these bonds. (Sec. 440.49(14)(e)2, F.S.)

Before 2011, minority owned property and casualty insurers that were initially issued a certificate of authority in Florida after May 1, 1998, but before January 1, 2002, were exempt from the premium tax, the firefighters' pension trust fund excise tax and the police officers' retirement trust fund excise tax. They were also exempt from non-emergency assessments by the Florida Residential Property and Casualty Joint Underwriting Association or by the Florida Windstorm Underwriting Association. These provisions only applied to personal lines and commercial lines residential property insurance policies and only to an insurer that had employees and a home or regional office in Florida. Furthermore, the exemptions applied only if during the year an average of at least 10% of the insurer's Florida residential property policies in force covered properties located in designated enterprise zones. The exemptions applied for a period not to exceed ten years from the date the insurer received its certificate of authority and they terminated on the expiration of the statute on December 31, 2010. (Former Sec. 624.4072, F.S.)

• *Reimbursement premiums paid to hurricane fund*

Applicable to reimbursement contracts entered into in 1996 and thereafter, the State Board of Administration may, by rule, exempt from payment of a reimbursement premium to the hurricane fund those insurers that have less than $500,000 in aggregate exposure for covered policies and whose exposure would result in a de minimum reimbursement premium, provided the actuarial soundness of the fund would not be harmed by such exemption. (Sec. 215.555, F.S.)

• *Insurers domiciled outside the U.S.*

Insurance and annuity contracts sold to nonresidents of the United States by an insurer domiciled outside of the United States are exempt from the Florida gross premiums tax, provided the insurer meets specified requirements of financial condition and contract disclosure. Such insurers are also exempt from the requirement to obtain a certificate of authority.

• *Hospital alliances*

An alliance formed by hospitals for the purpose of pooling and spreading liabilities of its members relative to property exposure, implementing self-insurance coverage for its members, or securing such property insurance coverage for the benefit of its members, is not subject to insurance premium tax or other premium assessments and may issue tax exempt bonds or other debt obligations to finance insurance coverage. The tax exemption does not apply to corporate income tax on interest income or profits on debt obligations owned by corporations. (Sec. 395.106, F.S.)

[¶88-020] Basis of Tax

Taxes are based on gross premiums from policies covering risks resident or to be performed in Florida, less reinsurance and return premiums or assessments. (Sec. 624.509(1), F.S.) The fire marshal tax is based on gross premiums from fire insurance on property in Florida. (Sec. 624.515, F.S.) The tax on surplus lines coverage is based on all gross premiums charged for such insurance. Effective May 26, 2011, if a surplus lines policy or an independently procured coverage policy covers risks or exposures only partially in Florida and Florida is the "home state", as defined in the federal Nonadmitted and Reinsurance Reform Act of 2010 (NRRA), the tax payable is computed on the gross premium. The tax cannot exceed the tax rate where the risk or exposure is located. (Sec. 626.932, F.S.)

Amounts recouped from policyholders as a result of a Florida Insurance Guaranty Association's assessment under Sec. 631.57(3)(a), F.S. relating to an insolvency that occurs after June 30, 2010, are considered taxable premiums. However, amounts recouped from policyholders as a result of an emergency assessment under Sec. 631.57(3)(e), F.S. are not considered taxable premiums. (*Tax Information Publication, No. 10B8-02R*, issued June 17, 2010, revised June 28, 2010)

Receipts of annuity premiums or considerations paid by holders in Florida are exempt from premium tax if the tax savings derived are credited to the annuity holders. (Sec. 624.509(8), F.S.)

[¶88-030] Rates

Florida imposes the insurance premiums tax at a rate of:

- 1.75% on life, property, casualty, accident and most other insurance; (Sec. 624.509(1)(a), F.S.)

- 1.75% on health insurance (Sec. 624.509(1), F.S.) and prepaid limited health service organizations; (Sec. 636.066, F.S.)

- 1.6% on commercial, (Sec. 624.475, F.S.) group, (Sec. 624.4621(7), F.S.) nonprofit, (Sec. 624.4625(4), F.S.) and public housing authority self-insurance funds; (Sec. 624.46226, F.S.)

- 1.6% on medical malpractice self-insurance; (Sec. 627.357(9), F.S.)

- 1.6% on assessable mutual insurers; (Sec. 628.6015, F.S.)

- 1% on annuities; (Sec. 624.509(1), F.S.)

- .75% on wet marine and transportation insurance; (Sec. 624.510(1), F.S.) and

- 4.94% (5% before July 1, 2020) on surplus lines insurance. (Sec. 626.932(1), F.S.)

It also has a fire marshal assessment of 1%. (Sec. 624.515(1), F.S.)

[¶88-035] Credits

Can insurers claim credits against Florida insurance premiums tax?

Insurers computing Florida insurance premiums tax liability can claim credits for:

- workers' compensation administrative assessments paid by the insurer; (Sec. 440.51(5), F.S.; Rule 12B-8.001(3)(c), F.A.C.)

- firefighters' pension trust fund assessments paid by the insurer; (Sec. 175.141, F.S.)
- municipal police officers' retirement trust fund assessments paid by the insurer; (Sec. 185.12, F.S.)
- corporate income tax paid by the insurer for the tax year; (Sec. 624.509(4), F.S.; Rule 12B-8.001(3)(a), F.A.C.)
- 15% of the salary paid by the insurer to employees located and based in the state who are covered by state unemployment tax assistance; Sec. 624.509(5), F.S.; Rule 12B-8.001(3)(b), F.A.C.; *Tax Information Publication, No. 04B8-02*) and
- 5% of Florida Life and Health Insurance Guaranty Association (FLAHIGA) assessments paid by the insurer; (Sec. 631.72(1), F.S.)

Florida corporate income tax credits that also apply to the insurance premiums tax, include:

- the community contributions credit; (Sec. 624.5105, F.S.)
- the capital investment credit; (Sec. 220.191, F.S.; Rule 12C-1.0191(4), F.A.C.)
- the new markets credit; (Sec. 288.9912, F.S.; Sec. 288.9916(1), F.S.)
- the tax credit scholarship program credit; (Sec. 624.51055, F.S.; Rule 12-29.002(2), F.A.C.)
- the strong families credit program, effective for tax years beginning on or after January 1, 2021; (Sec. 624.51057, F.S.) and
- the new worlds reading initiative credit, effective for tax years beginning on or after January 1, 2021. (Sec. 624.51056, F.S.)

COMPLIANCE ALERT: To receive strong families and new worlds reading initiative credits for the 2021 tax year, taxpayers must contribute money to the program by June 1, 2022. Eligible taxpayers then have 14 days after credit approval to file a refund for taxes paid. The refund cannot exceed the amount indicated on the certificate of contribution. Taxpayers can also apply credits against estimated tax liability for the tax year indicated on the credit approval letter. (Uncodified Sec. 40, Ch. 2022-97 (H.B. 7071), Laws 2022)

Does Florida require insurers to claim credits in a specific order?

Yes, Florida requires insurers to claim premium tax credits in the following order:

- the workers' compensation administrative assessments credit;
- the firefighters' pension trust fund credit;
- the municipal police officers' retirement trust fund credit;
- the corporate income tax credit;
- the salary tax credit;
- the strong families credit; and
- all other credits. (Sec. 624.509(7), F.S.; Rule 12B-8.001(6), F.A.C.)

Do other limits or special rules apply?

Florida limits the corporate income and salary tax credit to 65% of the insurer's premiums tax liability after deducting:

- the workers' compensation administrative assessment credit;
- the firefighters' pension trust fund credit; and
- the municipal police officers' retirement trust fund credit. (Sec. 624.509(6), F.S.)

Special computation rules also apply to affiliated groups claiming the salary tax credit. An insurer that made an irrevocable election on or before August 1, 2005, can use an alternative formula to compute the credit. The formula allocates the eligible salaries of the affiliated group to the members of the affiliated group that are covered by the election. (Sec. 624.509(5)(a), F.S.) The alternative calculation is limited to:

- the combined salary tax credits for all insurance companies that were members of the affiliated group for the tax year ending December 31, 2002 divided by

- the combined taxable premiums written by all insurance companies that were members of the affiliated for the tax year ending December 31, 2002 multiplied by

- the combined taxable premiums of the affiliated group for the current year. (Sec. 624.509(5)(a), F.S.)

An affiliated group that created a service company within its affiliated group on July 30, 2002 can allocate the salary of each service company employee covered by contracts with affiliated group members to the companies for which the employees perform services. The salary allocation is based on the amount of time during the tax year that the individual employee spends performing services or otherwise working for each company over the total amount of time the employee spends performing services or otherwise working for all companies. (Sec. 624.509(5)(b), F.S.)

How do insurers claim the credits?

Insurers claim premium tax credits on Form DR-908. (Instructions, Form DR-908, Insurance Premium Taxes and Fees Return)

[¶88-040] Practice and Procedure

• *Annual returns and payments*

The annual premium tax report (DR 908, Insurance Premium Taxes and Fees) is due with the Department of Revenue on or before March 1 of each year. (Sec. 624.5092, F.S.) Tax is due with the filing of each report. (Sec. 624.5092, F.S.) Form DR 908 may be filed electronically.

Reports covering gross underwriting profits on wet marine and transportation insurance must be filed on or before March 1 with the Department of Revenue. (Sec. 624.510, F.S.) The report is made on Form DR-908.

Reports covering the fire marshal assessment are due with the Department of Revenue on or before March 1. (Sec. 624.515, F.S.) The report is made on Form DR-908.

Amended returns.—A taxpayer must file an amended insurance premium tax return within 60 days of being required to amend its corporate income tax return or receiving a refund of its workers' compensation administrative assessment. (Sec. 624.50921, F.S.) Insurers should only file amended corporate income tax returns and corresponding insurance premium tax returns when the adjustments result in a net change to their total combined Florida corporate income and insurance premium tax liability. (*Tax Information Publication, No. 05B8-01*, Florida Department of Revenue, July 11, 2005) If an amended insurance premium tax return is required, a deficiency notice may be issued by the Department within three years after the date the amended return is filed. If a taxpayer fails to file a required amended return, a notice of deficiency may be issued at any time (i.e., no statute of limitations applies).

¶88-040

• *Estimated returns and payments*

Insurance premium tax reports and payments are due with the Department of Revenue on or before April 15, June 15, and October 15 with a final return for the year due on or before March 1 of each year. (Sec. 624.5092, F.S.; Form DR-907, Insurance Premium Installment Payment) In order to avoid a penalty, the installments must total 90% of the amount finally determined to be due. Form DR 907 may be filed electronically.

Surplus lines agents must pay premiums tax by:

• May 15 for Q1 transactions;

• August 15 for Q2 transactions;

• November 15 for Q3 transactions; and

• February 15 for Q4 transactions. (*Suplus Lines Payment Requirements*, Florida Surplus Lines Service Office)

Surplus lines agents must file reports by:

• June 30 for Q1 transactions;

• September 30 for Q2 transactions;

• December 31 for Q3 transactions; and

• March 31 for Q4 transactions. (*Suplus Lines Filing Requirements*, Florida Surplus Lines Service Office)

• *Additional practice and procedure information*

Additional practice and procedure information on Florida premiums tax is discussed in

payment methods;

assessment of delinquent tax; and

refunds.

[¶88-050] Special Assessments

Florida imposes special assessments on insurance companies, as discussed below.

Administrative expense assessment.—In order to provide funds for the Life and Health Insurance Guaranty Association, member insurers are subject to an assessment payable not less than 30 days after written notification. (Sec. 631.718, F.S.)

To secure the necessary funds for the payment of covered claims of the Self-Insurers Guaranty Association and to pay administrative costs, the Department of Insurance will levy assessments based on the annual written premium each employer would have paid had he not been self-insured. Every assessment will be made as a uniform percentage of the figure applicable to all individual self-insurers, provided that the assessment levied against any self-insurer in any one year cannot exceed 1% of the annual written premium during the calendar year preceding the date of the assessment. (Sec. 440.385(3), F.S.)

Members of the Florida Life and Health Insurance Guaranty Association are permitted an offset against their Florida corporate income or insurance premiums tax liabilities any assessments charged due to impaired or insolvent insurers. (Sec. 631.72, F.S.)

Insurers are allowed to offset 5% of the amount addressed, less any refund received, for 20 calendar years following the year in which the assessment was paid.

Insurers may only offset their tax liability for one tax, whether corporate or insurance premiums tax. Allowable deductions against premium taxes claimed for

Florida workers' compensation premium assessments paid must be added back to net premium taxes. (Rule 12B-8.016, F.A.C.) In addition, comparable deductions allowed in other states must also be added back to net premium taxes.

Emergency assessment for Hurricane Fund.—When the amount of revenue produced by the reimbursement premium imposed on insurers writing covered policies is insufficient to fund the obligations, costs, and expenses of the Florida Hurricane Catastrophe Fund (Fund) and the State Board of Administration Finance Corporation (Corporation), including repayment of revenue bonds at the promised levels, the State Board of Administration (SBA) will direct the Department of Insurance to levy an emergency assessment on all such insurers. (Sec. 215.555, F.S.)

The emergency assessment imposed on insurers writing covered policies generally is set by the Board but may not exceed 2% of their gross direct written premium for the prior year from all covered policies, except for workers' compensation. However, if the Governor declares a state of emergency due to the occurrence of a hurricane, the amount of the assessment for the contract year may be increased to a maximum of 4% of such premium. Any assessment authority not used for the contract year may be used for a subsequent contract year. If, for a subsequent contract year, the SBA determines that revenues are insufficient to meet expenses, including repayment of revenue bonds for that contract year, the SBA will direct the Department of Insurance to levy an emergency assessment up to an amount of unused assessment authority from a previous contract year or years, plus an additional 2% if the Governor declares a state of emergency due to a hurricane. The maximum aggregate annual assessments that may be imposed is limited to 6% of premium. However, no more than 4% may be assessed for any one contract year.

The emergency assessment is payable to the Corporation by July 1 of each year. (Sec. 215.555, F.S.) However, the payments must be made to the Fund, rather than the Corporation, until the Department of Insurance receives notice from the Corporation and the Fund, that the Corporation has issued bonds and the Fund as no bond revenue agreements in effect with local governments.

Unless adequate provision has been made to pay the revenue bonds that are responsible for the imposition of an emergency assessment, the emergency assessment will continue for each subsequent year for as long as the revenue bonds are outstanding. (Sec. 215.555, F.S.)

Additional emergency assessment.—An additional administrative assessment is imposed, upon certification of the Board of Directors of the Florida Insurance Guaranty Association (FIGA) and as an emergency measure related to insolvencies caused by hurricanes, on insurers holding a certificate of authority. The assessment imposed on any insurer cannot exceed, in any one year, more than 2% of that insurer's direct written premiums, net of refunds, in Florida during the preceding calendar year for all insurance covered by the FIGA, other than auto liability insurance, and auto physical damage insurance. (Sec. 631.57, F.S.)

Emergency assessments may be payable in a single payment or, at the option of the FIGA, may be payable in 12 monthly installments, with the first installment due and payable at the end of the month after an assessment is levied. Subsequent installments would be due not later than the end of each succeeding month. (Sec. 631.57, F.S.)

The emergency assessments are not considered premiums and are not subject to the insurance premiums tax, or to any fees or commissions. An insurer is liable for any emergency assessment collected from an insured and the failure of an insured to pay the assessment will be treated as a failure to pay the premium. Insurers will not be held liable for uncollectible emergency assessments. (Sec. 631.57, F.S.)

¶88-050

PRACTICE AND PROCEDURE

[¶89-010]
TAX CALENDARS

[¶89-012] Annual Tax Calendar

Several Florida taxes are reported or paid once a year or on a periodic basis other than quarterly or monthly. The following calendar, arranged by month, lists the principal dates concerning tax assessments, returns, statements, reports, applications, declarations, and payments. The following calendar pertains to taxpayers that operate on a calendar-year basis. Dates will need to be adjusted for corporate taxpayers operating on a fiscal-year basis. For a calendar with respect to property tax.

March

1st—Insurance premium tax return

Fire marshal insurance assessment

April

1st—Partnership information return

May

1st—Corporate income tax return

[¶89-014] Quarterly Tax Calendar

Some Florida taxes are reported or paid on a quarterly basis. Unless otherwise noted, payments are due March, June, September, and December. The principal due dates for tax returns, reports, or payments are:

20th—Sales and use, admission, and rental tax return and payment

31st day of May, 30th day of Jun., Sept., 31st day of Dec.—Estimated corporate income tax payments

15th day (Apr., Jun., Oct.)—Estimated insurance premium tax payments

15th day (May, Aug., Nov., Feb.)—Surplus lines agents' tax payment

Last day (Jun., Sept., Dec., Mar.)—Surplus lines agents' report

[¶89-016] Monthly Tax Calendar

Each month, there are deadlines for some Florida reports and taxes. Many of them relate to specific industries, such as alcohol and tobacco, while others revolve around tax type, notably sales and use, admission, and rental tax. The following lists the principal monthly dates:

10th—Alcoholic beverage tax reports and payments (manufacturers, distributors, importers, exporters, and agents)

Cigarette and tobacco product tax reports and payments

15th—Alcoholic beverage tax reports and payments (common carriers and railroad, steamship, bus, and airplane operators)

20th—Sales and use, admission, and rental tax return and payment

Motor and special fuel tax reports and payments

Perchloroethylene tax report and payment

Utility gross receipts tax report

[¶89-050]

ADMINISTRATION OF TAXES

[¶89-060] State Taxing Authority

The Department of Revenue is part of the state's executive branch and has the primary responsibility for taxation in Florida. Specifically, the Department administers and collects taxes on:

— corporate income;

— diesel fuel;

— documentary stamp;

— dry cleaning facilities;

— electric, gas, light, heat and power company gross receipts;

— telecommunication services;

— water and sewer companies;

— estates;

— insurance company gross premiums (with State Treasurer);

— intangible personal property and personal property (with local officers);

— motor fuel, oil, gas and sulfur production;

— perchloroethylene;

— petroleum pollutants;

— railroad, express and Pullman companies;

— sales and use of goods and specific services;

— solid minerals; and

— unemployment compensation.

(Sec. 213.05, F.S.)

• *Scope of authority*

The Department can act on:

— Assessment, collection, enforcement, audit, adjustment, and refund of all taxes, fees, and assessments for which the Department has been given control and administrative responsibility. These functions include:

(a) Taxation of intangible personal property;

(b) Audit planning, organization, administration, and control;

(c) Tax collection and enforcement;

(d) Development, maintenance, and management of the information services for tax return processing and taxpayer registration;

(e) Rendering of advice to Department personnel and the public on tax matters; and

(f) Receipt processing, tax return processing, license registration, and taxpayer registration; (Sec. 213.05, F.S.)

— Administration of the state's child support enforcement program; and

— Administration of specified ad valorem tax issues.

(Sec. 20.21, F.S.)

• *Department structure*

The Department is headed by the Governor and the Cabinet, who are authorized to delegate to the Executive Director the responsibility of running the day-to-day affairs of the Department, as well as the oversight of the administration of the

¶89-050

Department's statutory mandates. (Sec. 20.03(6), F.S.; Sec. 20.05(1)(b), F.S.; Rule 12-3.007, F.A.C.)

State and departmental organization charts follow:

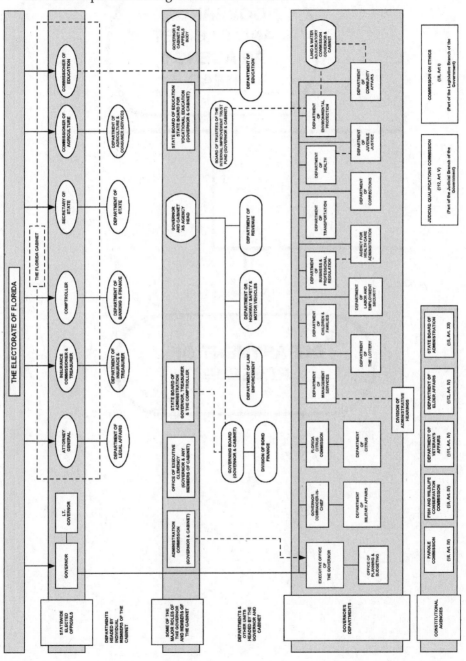

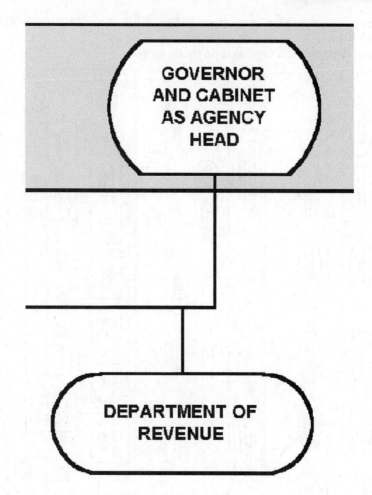

GOVERNOR AND CABINET AS AGENCY HEAD

DEPARTMENT OF REVENUE

Florida Department of Revenue

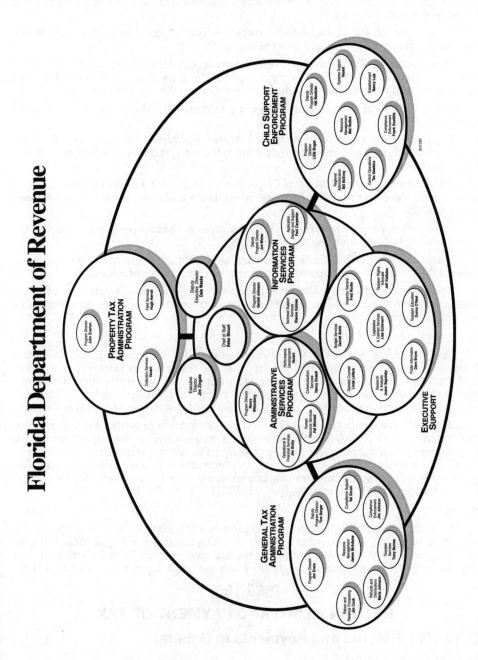

• *Additional state administrative personnel*

The following is a listing bodies that administer some form of tax in Florida, in addition to the Department of Revenue.

Secretary of State.—The Secretary administers and collects filing fees including the annual report filing fee.

Agency for Health Care Administration.—This Agency sets and collects the quarterly assessment for each nursing home.

Department of Business and Professional Regulation.—The Division of Alcoholic Beverages and Tobacco issues licenses for the sale of alcoholic beverages and administers and collects the alcoholic beverage tax and the cigarette tax.

The Division of Pari-Mutuel Wagering administers the various pari-mutuel racing taxes.

Department of Highway Safety and Motor Vehicles.—The Division of Motor Vehicles administers and collects the motor vehicle registration fees and the aircraft registration fee.

Department of Agriculture and Consumer Services.—The Commissioner of Agriculture with the Department of Revenue administers and collects the petroleum fuels inspection tax.

Public Service Commission.—The Commission administers and collects the gross receipts tax on water and sewer utilities.

State Treasurer.—The State Treasurer, as ex-officio Insurance Commissioner, collects the tax on insurance companies (with the Department of Revenue).

Local Taxing Officers.—The local taxing officers, with the Department of Revenue, administers and collects the general property tax and the tax on commercial hazardous waste facilities.

• *Taxpayers' rights advocate*

The Taxpayers' Rights Advocate is appointed by and reports to the Executive Director. The advocate is available to facilitate the resolution of taxpayer complaints and problems that have not been resolved through the Department's normal administrative channels and to ensure that taxpayers' rights are protected during tax determination and collection processes. (Sec. 20.21, F.S.) For a discussion of taxpayers' rights.

Taxpayer assistance orders.—The advocate may, with or without a request from the taxpayer, issue a taxpayer assistance order suspending or staying actions by the Department when the taxpayer suffers or is about to suffer a significant hardship as a result of a tax determination, collection, or enforcement process. The advocate may grant such relief only as an extraordinary measure. The process may not be used to contest the merits of a tax liability. (Sec. 213.018(2), F.S.)

• *Legal services*

Except for paternity or support obligations, legal services for the Department, including litigation, are provided by the Florida Department of Legal Affairs. Pursuant to agreements with other state departments and agencies, the Department may process taxes, fines, or license or regulatory fees for those departments and agencies.

[¶89-100]

RETURN FILING AND PAYMENT OF TAX

[¶89-102] Returns and Payments in General

What returns must be filed in Florida?

Corporate income and franchise tax returns. Every taxpayer must file a Florida corporate income and franchise tax return using Form F-1120 for each taxable year in which the taxpayer is liable for tax under the Florida income tax code or is required to file a federal income tax return. (Sec. 220.22(1), F.S.; Rule 12C-1.022(1), F.A.C.) The filing requirement applies to:

¶89-100

— all corporations doing business, earning income, or existing in Florida;

— every bank and savings association doing business, earning income, or existing in the state;

— all associations or artificial entities doing business, earning income, or existing in the state;

— foreign (out-of-state and non-U.S) corporations that are partners or members in a Florida partnership or joint venture;

— limited liability companies (LLCs) classified as a corporation for Florida and federal income tax purposes;

— homeowner and condominium associations that file federal Form 1120; (*Technical Assistance Advisement No. 01C1-013*, Florida Department of Revenue, November 6, 2001)

— political organizations that file federal Form 1120-POL;

— S corporations that pay federal income tax on excess net passive income, LIFO recapture, or built-in gains;

— tax-exempt organizations that have unrelated trade or business taxable income for federal income tax purposes or that file federal Form 990T; (Rule 12C-1.022(1), F.A.C.; Instructions, Form F-1120, Corporate Income/Franchise Tax Return)

— corporate owners of LLCs classified as a partnership for Florida and federal income tax purposes; (Instructions, Form F-1120, Corporate Income/ Franchise Tax Return)

— real estate investment trusts (REITs) conducting business, earning income, or existing in the state;

— real estate mortgage investment conduits (REMICs) liable for federal tax on income from foreclosure property under IRC Sec. 860G; and

— professional service corporations or associations conducting business, earning income, or existing in the state. (Rule 12C-1.022(1), F.A.C.)

A single member LLC (SMLLC) or qualified subchapter S corporation that is disregarded for Florida and federal tax purposes is not required to file a separate Florida corporate income tax return. However, the income of the SMLLC is not exempt from tax. If it is owned by a corporation, whether directly or indirectly, the corporation is required to file Form F-1120 reporting its own income, together with the income of the SMLLC. (Rule 12C-1.022(1), F.A.C.; Instructions, Form F-1120, Corporate Income/Franchise Tax Return)

A corporation may file a short form Florida corporate income tax return using Form F-1120A if it meets all the following criteria:

— it has Florida net income of $45,000 or less;

— it conducts 100% of its business in Florida;

— it does not report any federal taxable income addition or subtraction adjustments, except an addition for state income taxes and/or net operating loss deduction, if any;

— it is not included in a federal or Florida consolidated corporate income tax return;

— it claims no tax credits other than tentative tax payments or estimated tax payments; and

— it is not required to pay federal alternative minimum tax (AMT). (Instructions, Form F-1120A, Corporate Short Form Income Tax Return)

Federal attachments. A copy of the actual federal income tax return filed with the Internal Revenue Service (IRS) must be attached to a taxpayer's Florida corporate income/franchise tax return. (Instructions, Form F-1120, Corporate Income/Franchise Tax Return) In addition, the following federal forms and schedules must be attached, if applicable:

— Form 4562 (depreciation and amortization);

— Form 851 (affiliations schedule);

— Form 1122 (authorization and consent of subsidiary corporation to be included in a consolidated income tax return);

— Form 1125-A (cost of goods sold);

— Form 4626 (alternative minimum tax);

— Schedule D (capital gains and losses);

— Schedule M-3 (taxpayers with $10 million or more in total assets); and

— Schedules M1 and M2 (foregin corporation reconciliation of income/ loss and analysis of unappropriated retained earnings per books). (Instructions, Form F-1120, Corporate Income/Franchise Tax Return)

Amended returns. An amended Florida corporate income/franchise tax return may be filed on Form F-1120X. Taxpayers must file an amended Florida return if:

— an amended federal return is filed by the taxpayer;

— a redetermination of the taxpayer's federal income is made (e.g., through an audit adjustment); and

— the adjustments would affect the taxpayer's Florida corporate income/franchise tax liability. (Sec. 220.23(2), F.S.; Rule 12C-1.023(1), F.A.C.; Instructions, Form F-1120X, Amended Corporate Income/Franchise Tax Return; Instructions, Form F-1120, Corporate Income/Franchise Tax Return)

The following must be attached to the amended return:

— a copy of the federal amended return and a copy of any schedule, form, or statement filed with the federal form that applies to the taxpayer's Florida amended return; or

— copy of federal Form 4549A (Income Tax Examination Changes), also referred to as a Revenue Agent Report (RAR), or other document evidencing a completed federal audit. (Rule 12C-1.023(1), F.A.C.; Instructions, Form F-1120X, Amended Corporate Income/Franchise Tax Return)

Signature requirements. A Florida corporate income/franchise tax return must be signed by an officer (e.g., president, vice-president, treasurer, assistant treasurer, chief accounting officer, or other authorized officer), fiduciary, (Rule 12C-1.0221(2), F.A.C.) or person authorized to sign for the corporation. (Instructions, Form F-1120, Corporate Income/Franchise Tax Return) A fiduciary includes a receiver, trustee in dissolution, trustee in bankruptcy, or assignee. (Rule 12C-1.0221(2), F.A.C.; Instructions, Form F-1120, Corporate Income/Franchise Tax Return)

The Florida Department of Revenue (DOR) requires an original signature and does not accept a photocopy, facsimile, or stamp. (Instructions, Form F-1120, Corporate Income/Franchise Tax Return) Any person, firm, or corporation who prepares a return for compensation must also sign the return and provide a:

— federal employer identification number (FEIN); and

— preparer tax identification number (PTIN). (Instructions, Form F-1065, Partnership Information Return)

Short period returns. A taxpayer required to file a federal income tax return for a portion of a taxable year must file a Florida corporate income and franchise tax return for the same period. (Sec. 220.03(1)(y), F.S.; Rule 12C-1.022(4), F.A.C.)

Partnership information returns. Every Florida partnership that has any partner subject to the Florida corporate income tax must file an information return using Form F-1065. (Sec. 220.22(2), F.S.; Rule 12C-1.022(6), F.A.C.; Instructions, Form F-1065, Partnership Information Return) A limited liability company with a corporate partner, if classified as a partnership for federal income tax purposes, must also file Form F-1065. (Instructions, Form F-1065, Partnership Information Return) A partnership is not required to file a partnership return if the only partner is an S corporation. Corporations that are members of a Florida partnership or joint venture must file a partnership information return, as well as, a corporate income/franchise tax return. (Rule 12C-1.022(6), F.A.C.)

Federal attachments. A copy of the federal partnership return is not required to be attached to the Florida partnership return. (Instructions, Form F-1065, Partnership Information Return)

Signature requirements. A Florida partnership information return must be signed by any one of the general partners, (Rule 12C-1.0221(2), F.A.C.) an officer, or person authorized to sign for the partnership. (Instructions, Form F-1065, Partnership Information Return) The Florida DOR requires an original signature and does not accept a photocopy, facsimile, or stamp. (Instructions, Form F-1065, Partnership Information Return)

Any person, firm, or corporation who prepares a return for compensation must also sign the return and provide a:

— federal employer identification number (FEIN); and

— preparer tax identification number (PTIN). (Instructions, Form F-1065, Partnership Information Return)

If a partnership is in bankruptcy proceedings, a Florida partnership return must be signed by the receiver, trustee, or assignee. (Rule 12C-1.0221(2), F.A.C.)

Sales and use tax. Dealers must file DR-15, Sales and Use Tax Return.

1099-K information returns. Effective January 1, 2021, credit card companies and third-party settlement organizations (TPSOs) must electronically provide the Florida Department of Revenue with a copy of their federal 1099-K forms. Credit companies and TPSOs that fail to file 1099-Ks are subject to a penalty. (*1099-K Reporting Requirements*, Florida Department of Revenue, February 2021)

When are returns due?

Corporate income and franchise tax returns. Florida corporate income and franchise tax returns are due by the later of::

— May 1 (the 1st day of the 5th month following the close of the taxable year); or

— May 15 (the 15th day following the original due date of the taxpayer's federal return). (Sec. 220.222(1), F.S.; *Tax Information Publication, No. 17C01-02*, Florida Department of Revenue, August 16, 2017; Instructions, Form F-1120, Corporate Income/Franchise Tax Return)

Effective for tax years beginning before January 1, 2026, all June 30 year-end returns must be filed by the 1st day of the 4th month following the close of the taxable year or the 15th day after the federal due date. (Sec. 220.222(1), F.S.; *Tax Information Publication, No. 17C01-02*, Florida Department of Revenue, August 16, 2017; Instructions, Form F-1120, Corporate Income/Franchise Tax Return)

Effective for tax years before 2016, corporate income and franchise tax returns were due by the later of:

— April 1 (the 1st day of the 4th month following the close of the taxable year); or

— April 15 (the 15th day following the original due date of the taxpayer's federal return). (*Tax Information Publication, No. 17C01-02*, Florida Department of Revenue, August 16, 2017;Instructions, Form F-1120, Corporate Income/ Franchise Tax Return)

Extensions. Taxpayers may obtain an automatic extension for filing a Florida corporate income tax and franchise tax return if a federal extension and Form F-7004 are filed by the due date of the original return. A separate state extension may be granted if Form F-7004 is filed by the due date of original return and the taxpayer shows good cause for the extension. (Sec. 220.222(2), F.S.; Rule 12C-1.0222(2), F.A.C.; Instructions, Form F-7004, Tentative Income/Franchise Tax Return and Application for Extension of Time to File Return) A copy of Form F-7004 must be attached to the taxpayer's return when filed and the extension box checked on the front page of the return. (Instructions, Form F-1120, Corporate Income/Franchise Tax Return)

The Florida extension period for filing a Florida corporate income tax and franchise tax return is equal to:

— 6 months for a taxable year that ends other than June 30; or

— 7 months for a taxable year that ends June 30. (Sec. 220.222(2), F.S.; Rule 12C-1.0222(2) and (3), F.A.C.)

Effective for tax years before 2016, the extension period was equal to:

— the earlier of 6 months or 15 days after the expiration of the taxpayer's federal extension; or

— 6 months for a state extension. (Sec. 220.222(2), F.S.)

All outstanding tax liability must be paid with F-7004 by the due date of the original return to avoid penalties. The extension is void if any tax liability is not paid or if the amount paid is underpaid by the greater of $2,000 or 30% of the tax liability shown when the return is filed. (Rule 12C-1.0222(3), F.A.C.; Instructions, Form F-7004, Tentative Income/Franchise Tax Return and Application for Extension of Time to File Return)

Reporting federal changes. If a federal amended income tax return is filed or redetermination of federal taxable income is made and those adjustments would affect Florida corporate income tax liability, the taxpayer must file an amended Florida corporate income and franchise tax return within 60 days after (whichever occurs first):

— the federal adjustment has been finally determined or agreed to by the taxpayer; or

— any resulting federal income tax deficiency or refund has been assessed, paid, or collected. (Sec. 220.23(2), F.S.; Rule 12C-1.023(5), F.A.C.)

Partnership information returns. Florida information returns for partnerships and LLCs classified as partnerships for income tax purposes must be filed by:

— April 1; or

— the 1st day of the 4th month following the close of the partnership's or LLC's fiscal year. (Sec. 220.222(1), F.S.; *Tax Information Publication, No. 17C01-02*, Florida Department of Revenue, August 16, 2017; Instructions, Form F-1065, Partnership Information Return)

Effective for tax years before 2016, partnership information returns were due by:

— May 1; or

— 1st day of the 5th month following the close of the partnership's or LLC's fiscal year. (*Tax Information Publication, No. 17C01-02*, Florida Department of Revenue, August 16, 2017; Instructions, Form F-1065, Partnership Information Return)

An automatic 6-month extension may be obtained for filing a Florida partnership return if a federal extension and Form F-7004 are filed by the due date of the original return. A separate 6-month state extension may be granted if Form F-7004 is filed by the due date of original return and the taxpayer shows good cause for the extension. (Sec. 220.222(2), F.S.; Rule 12C-1.0222(2) and (3), F.A.C.; Instructions, Form F-1065, Partnership Information Return) Effective for tax years before 2016, the extension period was 5 months. (Instructions, Form F-1065, Partnership Information Return)

Sales and use tax. Dealers generally must file a return on or before the 20th day of each month. However, the Department of Revenue may require dealers to make returns and payments based on the amount of tax remitted in the preceding four calendars quarters, as follows:

— dealers who remitted $100 or less, annual reports;

— dealers who remitted at least $100 but less than $500, semiannual reports; and

— dealers who remitted at least $500 but less than $12,000, quarterly reports.

Dealers authorized to file quarterly, semiannually, or annually must file a return and remit the tax before the 21st day of the month following the authorized reporting period. Dealers newly required to file quarterly may file returns for the three-month periods ending in February, May, August, and November. Dealers newly required to file and pay tax semiannually generally may file returns and remit the tax for the six-month periods ending in May and November. Each dealer must file a return for each tax period even if no tax is due for that period.

1099-K information returns. Effective January 1, 2021, credit card companies and third-party settlement organizations (TPSOs) must file a copy of their federal 1099-K forms within 30 days from the federal filing deadline. (*1099-K Reporting Requirements*, Florida Department of Revenue, February 2021)

How and when are tax payments made?

Corporate and franchise income tax payments. Payment of corporate franchise and income tax liability is due at same time as the original return filing deadline.

Sales and use tax. Dealers generally must remit sales and use taxes on or before the 20th day of each month. However, the Department of Revenue may require dealers to make payments based on the amount of tax remitted in the preceding four calendar quarters, as follows:

— dealers who remitted $100 or less, annual payments;

— dealers who remitted at least $100 but less than $500, semiannual payments;

— dealers who remitted at least $500 but less than $1,000, quarterly payments; and

— dealers who remitted between $1,000 and $12,000, monthly payments.

Dealers authorized to file quarterly, semiannually, or annually must remit the tax before the 21st day of the month following the authorized reporting period. Dealers newly required to file and pay tax quarterly may remit the tax for the three-month periods ending in February, May, August, and November. Dealers newly required to file and pay tax semiannually generally may remit the tax for the six-month periods ending in May and November.

Where else can I find information on returns and payments in Florida?

Additional information on Florida returns and payments is provided in the discussions of:

— estimated tax payments and returns;

— electronic filing requirements and options;

— electronic funds transfer (EFT) and other payment methods;

— mailing rules and legal holidays;

— interest rates and penalties;

— limitations periods for audits and assessments; and

— insurance premiums tax returns.

Information on Florida filing and payment deadlines is also available in the annual, quarterly, and monthly tax Calendars.

[¶89-104] Estimated Payments and Returns

Are payments of estimated tax required?

Corporate income tax. Every corporate income taxpayer must declare and pay estimated tax for the taxable year if the amount of income tax liability reasonably can be expected to be more than $2,500. (Sec. 220.24, F.S.; Rule 12C-1.034(2), F.A.C.) There are no special estimated tax requirements for large corporations. (Rule 12C-1.034(7), F.A.C.)

The estimated tax is based on the amount of Florida net income which the taxpayer can reasonably expect to receive or accrue, based on the facts and circumstances existing at the time for filing the declaration, as well as those reasonably anticipated for the taxable year. "Reasonably expect" does not mean that a taxpayer can wait until more than $2,500 of tax is actually due on income already earned. A taxpayer is required to declare and pay estimated tax even though income may not actually be earned until later in the taxable year. (Rule 12C-1.034(3), F.A.C.)

In determining whether a corporation that existed for a full 12 months during the previous year can reasonably expect to owe more than the estimated tax threshold, the Florida Department of Revenue (DOR) will consider the taxpayer's past payment history and circumstances. If the tax due for the corporation's previous taxable year exceeded the threshold, there is a presumption that the taxpayer can reasonably expect to owe more than the threshold amount in the current taxable year. (Rule 12C-1.034(3), F.A.C.) The DOR will consider the following factors in considering a factual determination of a specific taxpayer:

— general economic conditions;

— economic conditions of a specific industry; and

— cause and timing of taxable income. (Rule 12C-1.034(3), F.A.C.)

There is no first year exception from the estimated corporate income tax requirements. (Rule 12C-1.034(3), F.A.C.)

Amended declarations. A taxpayer may amend a declaration of Florida estimated corporate income tax. (Sec. 220.24, F.S.) A declaration must be amended if the taxpayer determines that circumstances have developed that materially change the amount of estimated tax reported in the declaration. The remaining estimated tax payments must be increased or decreased to reflect the adjusted income. (Rule 12C-1.034(7), F.A.C.)

Safe harbor calculation. Interest and penalties may be imposed on corporate income taxpayers if the taxpayer fails to comply with the estimated tax requirements or there is an underpayment of estimated tax, unless the total amount of all payments made before the estimated tax installment due date equals or exceeds the lesser of:

— 90% of the tax liability for the current tax year; or

— 100% of the tax liability shown on the taxpayer's return for the previous tax year computed by applying tax rates for the current taxable year. (Sec. 220.34(d), F.S.; Rule 12C-1.034(9), F.A.C.)

If a corporation merges with another corporation, the prior year safe harbor exception is based on the prior year's return of the surviving corporation. (Rule 12C-1.034(9), F.A.C.)

A contribution to an eligible nonprofit scholarship-funding organization (SFO), which is eligible for a corporate income tax credit, reduces the amount required to meet the prior year safe harbor exception. The certificate of contribution must be issued on or before the estimated tax installment due date. (Rule 12C-1.034(9), F.A.C.)

Affiliated or controlled groups. The manner in which the members of a controlled group of corporations, as defined under IRC Sec. 1563, allocate the corporate income tax exemption amount among members is binding on all the members for estimated tax purposes, including whether a declaration is required and the computation of underpayment penalties and interest. If an affiliated group is not required to file a consolidated declaration of estimated tax for a taxable year because the parent corporation has not elected to file a Florida consolidated tax return, each affiliated group member must file separate declarations and make separate payments of estimated tax. If the members of a group are treated as separate taxpayers for the taxable year, then each member is entitled to a separate estimated tax threshold determination. (Rule 12C-1.034(10), F.A.C.)

After an affiliated group files a Florida consolidated tax return, it must file its declaration of estimated tax on a consolidated basis, until the affiliated group is granted permission to file separate Florida tax returns. Until that time, the group is treated as a single taxpayer for purposes of declaring and paying estimated tax. An affiliated group that files a Florida consolidated tax return for the taxable year is limited to a single estimated tax threshold for purposes of determining estimated tax requirements and cannot use the prior year safe harbor exception to determine whether there is an underpayment of estimated tax. Any estimated tax payments made by individual group members for the year before filing a consolidated return may be credited against the tax liability of the group. (Rule 12C-1.034(11), F.A.C.)

If, after filing Florida consolidated tax returns, the affiliated group is granted permission to file separate Florida tax returns, the amount of any estimated tax payments made with a consolidated declaration of estimated tax will be credited against the separate tax liabilities of the members in the manner designated on a statement from the common parent. This statement must be attached to the Florida corporate income/franchise tax returns of each affiliated group member, setting forth the name, address, and federal employee identification number of each member, and the amount of estimated tax payment that will be allocated to each member. Each member of the group is also entitled to a separate estimated tax threshold determination. (Rule 12C-1.034(11), F.A.C.)

Short taxable years. A separate declaration is required if the taxpayer is required to file an income tax return for a period of less than 12 months, unless the short taxable year is:

— a period of less than 4 months; or

— the estimated tax threshold is first met after the 1st day of the last month in the short taxable year. (Rule 12C-1.034(12), F.A.C.)

A taxpayer may not use the prior year safe harbor exception if the previous tax year was for a short tax year, unless the short period is due to a change in accounting period. (Rule 12C-1.034(9), F.A.C.) If the short period is due to a change in accounting, the taxpayer must annualize net income for the short period to determine estimated tax liability and the underpayment safe harbor exceptions. The short year's income must be multiplied by 12 and the result divided by the number of months in the short period. (Rule 12C-1.034(12), F.A.C.; Instructions, Form F-2220, Underpayment of Estimated Tax on Florida Corporate Income/Franchise Tax)

Sales and use tax. Each dealer who operates one place of business, or who operates two or more places of business and maintains records for those businesses in a central office or place, or who files or was eligible to file a consolidated return, and who paid state sales and use tax for the preceding state fiscal year of $200,000 or more must calculate the amount of estimated tax due each month.

How are payments of estimated tax made?

Corporate income tax. Estimated Florida corporate income tax liability must be paid in four equal installments. (Sec. 220.33(1), F.S.; Rule 12C-1.034, F.A.C.) There are no provisions that allow taxpayers computing estimated tax liability to use the annualization method. (Rule 12C-1.034(6), F.A.C.) Electronic payment of estimated corporate income tax liability is mandatory for certain taxpayers.

Sales and use tax. The amount of any estimated tax calculated must be remitted by electronic funds transfer.

What are the due dates for estimated tax?

Corporate income tax. Installments of 25% of estimated Florida corporate income tax for the taxable year are due by:

— May 31 or before the 1st day of the 6th month of the taxable year for fiscal-year taxpayers;

— June 30 or before the 1st day of the 7th month of the taxable year for fiscal-year taxpayers;

— September 30 or before the 1st day of the 10th month of the taxable year for fiscal-year taxpayers; and

— December 31 or before the 1st day of the following taxable year. (Sec. 220.241(1), F.S.; Sec. 220.33(1), F.S.; Rule 12C-1.034(5), F.A.C.; *Tax Information Publication, No. 16C01-03*, Florida Department of Revenue, October 14, 2016)

Effective for tax years before 2017, the first installment of estimated tax was due April 30 or before the 1st day of the 5th month of the taxable year for fiscal-year taxpayers. (*Tax Information Publication, No. 16C01-03*, Florida Department of Revenue, October 14, 2016)

Effective for tax years beginning on or after January 1, 2017, and before January 1, 2026, the first installment for taxpayers with a June 30 taxable year end is due before the 1st day of 5th month of the taxable year. (Sec. 220.241(2), F.S.; Rule 12C-1.034(5), F.A.C.; *Tax Information Publication, No. 16C01-03*, Florida Department of Revenue, October 14, 2016)

A taxpayer who first meets the estimated tax threshold after the first installment due date must spread the estimated tax payments equally over the remaining installments, depending on the date when the threshold is first met. (Sec. 220.241(1), F.S.; Sec. 220.33, F.S.)

Sales and use tax. The amount of any estimated tax calculated must be remitted by the 20th day of the month for which the tax is estimated.

What forms are required for filing estimated tax?

Corporate income tax. Estimated income tax payments must be made with Form F-1120ES. (Rule 12C-1.034(4), F.A.C.; Instructions, Form F-1120ES, Declaration/Installment of Florida Estimated Income/Franchise Tax) Taxpayers must use Form F-2220 to determine their estimated safe harbor calculation and any underpayment penalty. (Instructions, Form F-2220, Underpayment of Estimated Tax on Florida Corporate Income/Franchise Tax)

Sales and use tax. The estimated tax is filed electronically.

Where can I find other information on estimated payments and returns?

Additional information about Florida estimated tax returns and payments is provided in the discussions of:

— electronic filing;

— electronic funds transfer (EFT) and other payment methods;

— mailing rules and legal holidays; and

— interest rates and penalties.

[¶89-106] Electronic Filing

Effective January 1, 2023, taxpayers must file tax returns electronically if the tax amount paid in the prior state fiscal year (July 1 – June 30) was $5,000 or more. (Sec. 213.755, F.S.; *Tax Information Publication, No. 22ADM-06*, Florida Department of Revenue, June 24, 2022) The reduction in the electronic filing requirement threshold from $20,000 to $5,000 applies to the following tax returns:

— communications services;

— corporate income;

— documentary stamp;

— fuel - local government user, mass transit system provider;

— fuel - pollutants;

— fuel - Florida air carriers;

— gross receipts;

— insurance premium;

— prepaid wireless E911 fee;

— sales and use, including local option sales taxes, surcharges, surtaxes, solid waste fees and surcharges; and

— severance, including oil, gas, and sulphur production, solid minerals, and Miami-Dade Lake Belt Mitigation Fee. (*Tax Information Publication, No. 22ADM-06*, Florida Department of Revenue, June 24, 2022)

If a taxpayer files a return without a payment, the electronic filing deadline is 5:00 p.m. Eastern Time on or before the filing deadline for the particular return. (*Filing and Paying Taxes Electronically*, Florida Department of Revenue) Electronic payment methods are also available or required for a variety of Florida taxes.

This electronic filing requirement applies separately to each tax and is based on the amounts remitted as estimated payments, tentative payments, tax return payments, or any other type of payment made for the specific tax. (*Tax Information Publication, No. 22ADM-06*, Florida Department of Revenue, June 24, 2022, ¶206-582)

A taxpayer can request a waiver from the electronic filing requirement using Form DR-654 if the taxpayer is unable to comply despite good faith efforts or due to circumstances beyond the taxpayer's reasonable control. (Sec. 213.755(9), F.S.; Rule 12-24.010(4), F.A.C.) A waiver is valid for up to two years. (Rule 12-24.010(4), F.A.C.)

All taxpayers are notified of the requirement to pay taxes or file returns electronically by November 1 of each year. Unemployment compensation taxpayers are notified by January 1 of each year. The notification includes:

— Form DR-600, Enrollment and Authorization for e-Services Program, or instructions on how to access the online enrollment form,

— a Florida e-services program calendar of due dates, and

— an explanation of the options available for the electronic payment of tax or filing of returns.

Upon receipt of the notification, the taxpayer must complete the online enrollment form or return Form DR-600 to the Department of Revenue before December 1 (February 1 for unemployment compensation taxpayers). (Rule 12-24.004, F.A.C.)

The department will notify taxpayers and unemployment tax agents who initially meet the requirements to participate on the basis of prior state fiscal year tax payments. Once notified, the taxpayer or unemployment tax agent must transmit by electronic means all payments and/or returns. (Rule 12-24.003, F.A.C.)

Electronic digital signatures.—The Florida Department of Revenue accepts electronic digital signatures for purposes of all taxes administered by the department. Electronic digital signatures have the same force and effect as a written signature under Florida law. Taxpayers and/or their representatives may use established and secured messaging systems to submit documents with electronic digital signatures, such as power of attorney forms or other documents that must be signed. (Sec. 213.053, F.S.; *Tax Information Publication, No. 22ADM-07*, Florida Department of Revenue, August 24, 2022, ¶ 206-600)

An electronic digital signature binds a person or entity to the information included in the document. This affirmation can be verified by the receiver as well as any third party. The department must be able to validate the electronic digital signature and any other electronic signature (eSignature) of the signer(s). Moreover, the department will accept images with signatures (scanned or photographed) in any of the following file types: TIFF, JPG, JPEG, PDF (Adobe Reader), Microsoft Office suite, or ZIP. Accepted electronic digital signatures are those using encryption techniques that provide proof of original and unchanged documentation. (Sec. 213.053, F.S.; *Tax Information Publication, No. 22ADM-07*, Florida Department of Revenue, August 24, 2022, ¶ 206-600)

In addition, department employees may use electronic digital signatures when signing documents sent to taxpayers, authorized representatives, or other authorized entities for tax administration purposes, such as forms, letters, and payment agreements. Forms requiring an electronic digital signature are formatted using a digital certificate. Electronic digital signatures capture the employee's full name, date, and time of the signature. Employees may use an eSignature (fill and sign) on other general forms and correspondence. (Sec. 213.053, F.S.; *Tax Information Publication, No. 22ADM-07*, Florida Department of Revenue, August 24, 2022, ¶ 206-600)

•*Corporation income tax returns*

Florida requires electronic filing of corporate income tax returns if:

— the taxpayer must file its federal income tax return electronically; or

— the taxpayer meets the state's electronic filling threshold. (Sec. 220.21(2), F.S.; Sec. 213.755(1), F.S.; *Tax Information Publication, No. 22ADM-06*, Florida Department of Revenue, June 24, 2022)

Taxpayers can file a return on Form F-1120 electronically through federal Modernized e-File (MeF) program using approved software. (Instructions, Form F-1120, Florida Corporate Income/Franchise Tax Return) Florida also has an online application for filing:

— a short form return on Form F-1120A; and

— extension requests on Form F-7004. (Instructions, Form F-1120, Florida Corporate Income/Franchise Tax Return)

¶89-106a

Florida imposes a penalty for failure to comply with the electronic filing requirement equal to:

— 5% of the outstanding tax liability for the first 30 days of noncompliance; and

— 5% of outstanding tax liability for each additional month, or part of a month, of noncompliance up to $250. (Sec. 220.21(2), F.S.)

• *Partnership, LLP, and LLC returns*

Florida does not require or allow electronic filing for partnership information returns. (Rule 12C-1.022(6), F.A.C.; Instructions, Form F-1065, Florida Partnership Information Return) It has an online application for filing partnership return extension requests on Form F-7004. (Instructions, Form F-7004, Florida Tentative Income / Franchise Tax Return and Application for Extension of Time to File Return)

[¶89-108] Payment Methods

Florida accepts electronic payment of taxes. Taxpayers can use either ACH debit or ACH credit as the method for electronic tax payments. (Rule 12-24.005, F.A.C.; Rule 12-24.008, F.A.C.)

Electronic payment requirements apply if taxes paid for the previous state fiscal year exceed a threshold. The mandatory electronic payment threshold is the same threshold that applies to electronic filing requirements for returns. The taxes subject to electronic payment requirements are also the same as those subject to electronic filing requirements. (Sec. 213.755, F.S.; *Tax Information Publication, No. 22ADM-06,* Florida Department of Revenue, June 24, 2022)

Any taxpayer who operates two or more places of business for which it must file returns must combine the tax payments to determine if it meets the electronic payment threshold. (Sec. 213.755(1), F.S.)

The banking process requires one business day to complete an electronic payment. So, taxpayers must initiate their payment and receive a confirmation number by 5 p.m. Eastern Time on the business day before the deadline for payment. Florida publishes a calendar for electronic payment deadlines on Form DR-659. (Rule 12-24.009(1), F.A.C.; *Filing and Paying Taxes Electronically,* Florida Department of Revenue)

• *Cigarette, alcohol, and pari-mutuel permitholder taxes paid by EFT*

Taxes subject to EFT payments include taxes due from:

— cigarette dealers, under Sec. 210.02, F.S.;

— distributors of tobacco products, under Sec. 210.30, F.S.;

— pari-mutuel permitholders, under Sec. 550.09, F.S. and Sec. 551.06, F.S.;

— manufacturers, distributors, and vendors of malt beverages, under Sec. 563.05, F.S.;

— manufacturers and distributors of wine and beverages, under Sec. 564.06, F.S.;

— manufacturers and distributors of liquor and beverages, under Sec. 565.12, F.S.

(Rule 7-8.002, F.A.C., *et seq.*)

Taxpayers required to remit sales and use taxes by EFT must make their returns in a form that is initiated through an electronic data interchange. Taxpayers experiencing problems with their computer capabilities, data systems changes, or operating procedures may receive a waiver from the electronic data interchange requirement for returns. (Sec. 212.11(1)(f), F.S.)

• *Motor fuel wholesalers*

To obtain an annual license as a wholesaler, a person must file with the department a Florida Fuel Tax Application (Form DR-156), with the required attachments, and enroll in the department's e-Services Program. All wholesalers who sell gasoline, gasohol, diesel, or aviation fuel are required to electronically report all taxes on a Wholesaler/Importer Fuel Tax Return (Form DR-309632) with the department. (Sec. 206.43(5), F.S.)

• *Motor fuel terminal operators*

To obtain an annual license as a terminal operator, a person must file a Florida Fuel Tax Application (Form DR-156), with the department, as provided in the application, and enroll in the department's e-Services Program. All terminal operators who operate terminals in this state are required to file a Terminal Operator Information Return (Form DR-309636), electronically with the department. The electronic return must be submitted by electronic data interchange, as provided in the Florida Department of Revenue Motor Fuels EDI Technical Implementation Guide. The electronic return must be filed on or before the 20th day of each month for transactions occurring during the previous month. A separate return is required for each terminal location. To be timely, the electronic return must be initiated and a confirmation from the Department must be received before 5:00 p.m., Eastern Time, on or before the 20th day of each month. (Rule 12B-5.070, F.A.C.)

[¶89-110] Mailing Rules and Legal Holidays

An official postmark of the U.S. Postal Service is considered the date of filing a return. When the deadline for filing a return falls on Saturday, Sunday, or a legal holiday, the deadline is extended through the next working day immediately following the statutory deadline. A "legal holiday" is a holiday observed by state agencies. (Sec. 192.047, F.S.; Sec. 212.11(1)(e), F.S.; Rule 12C-1.222, F.A.C.)

Property tax. For property tax exemption applications, special assessment classification applications, or returns mailed via a commercial delivery service, the postmark on the commercial parcel will be treated the same as a U.S. Postal Service postmark. (Sec. 192.047, F.S.)

[¶89-130]

AUDITS

[¶89-132] Audits in General

The Department of Revenue must examine tax returns to determine the correct amount of tax as soon as practicable after the returns are filed. (Sec. 220.709, F.S.)

Except in criminal and internal investigations, the Department must conduct its audits, inspections of records, and interviews at reasonable times and places. (Sec. 213.025, F.S.)

Within the appropriate limitations period, the Department may audit and examine the accounts, books, or records of a taxpayer to ascertain that taxpayer's compliance with tax laws. (Sec. 213.34, F.S.; Sec. 95.091(3), F.S.) The audit authority of the Department includes the power to investigate accounts, books, and records of persons who may not be subject to the revenue laws but are otherwise placed under the control and administration of the Department. (Sec. 213.34(1), F.S.)

The Department also has tax-specific authority to audit and investigate a particular tax. For discussion of tax-specific audit and assessment procedures.

A taxpayer who has been given written notice of the Department's intent to audit a specific tax for a specific time period (including managed audits, self-audit requests, self analysis, or written approval from the Department to participate in a certified audit) is considered to be "under audit." (Rule 12-11.002(6), F.A.C.)

If it determines that an adjustment is necessary, the Department issues a Notice of Intent to Make Tax Audit Changes. The taxpayer has 30 consecutive calendar days after receipt of the Notice to mail or fax a written request for a conference. The request is made directly to the local office that issued the Notice. If the Department issues a Revised Notice of Intent to Make Audit Changes, the taxpayer has 30 consecutive calendar days after the date of issuance on each Revised Notice of Intent to Make Audit Changes to mail or fax a written request for a conference to the office address or fax number on the revised notice. (Rule 12-6.002(2), F.A.C.) A taxpayer may request an extension of time in which to request a conference by mailing or faxing a written request to the appropriate office address or fax number prior to the expiration of the period within which a conference must be requested. Each extension of time will be for 30 consecutive calendar days. (Rule 12-6.002(2), F.A.C.)

The conference must be held within 90 consecutive calendar days after the Notice was issued. (Rule 12-6.002(3), F.A.C.) Failure to request a conference does not prevent a taxpayer from obtaining administrative and judicial review of a subsequently issued notice of deficiency. (Rule 12-6.002(4), F.A.C.) If the taxpayer fails to request a conference or if, after the conference, the taxpayer and the Department are unable to agree on the proposed adjustments, the Department issues the taxpayer a notice of deficiency, also known as a notice of proposed assessment. (Sec. 220.709, F.S.; Sec. 220.711, F.S.; Rule 12-6.003, F.A.C.)

After the notice of deficiency has been issued, the taxpayer has 60 consecutive calendar days in which to file a protest. (Sec. 220.713, F.S.). If no protest is filed within 60 days, the deficiency becomes final and is assessed. (Sec. 220.703, F.S.)

If a resolution is not reached in the conference, the protest will be forwarded to Technical Assistance and Dispute Resolution for further review. If requested by the taxpayer, an opportunity for submission of additional information and an oral conference will be provided. If the taxpayer and the Department are still unable to resolve the disputed issues, a Notice of Decision (NOD) will be issued and the assessment will become final as of the date of issuance on the NOD, unless the taxpayer files a petition for reconsideration of the NOD within 30 days. If a petition for reconsideration is timely filed and the taxpayer and the Department are unable to resolve the disputed issues, a Notice of Reconsideration (NOR) will be issued and the assessment will become a final as of the date of issuance on the NOR. (Rule 12-6.003, F.A.C.)

• *Notices of Intent to Make Audit Changes*

The Department of Revenue, once it has completed an audit, issues a Notice of Intent to Make Audit Changes, unless the case at hand involves a jeopardy assessment, an estimated assessment, a refund denial, or is a case where review of the taxpayer's books and records results in no liability due to the state or no refundable amount due to the taxpayer. (Rule 12-6.002(1), F.A.C.)

Taxpayers may request a conference concerning the Notice of Intent to Make Audit Changes. However, they must do so within 30 consecutive calendar days after the receipt of the notice. Requests must be submitted directly to the local office of the Department that issued the notice. (Rule 12-6.002(1), F.A.C.)

Conferences, when requested, must be held at the earliest convenience of both the taxpayer and the Department. However, the conferences may not be held later than 90 consecutive calendar days after the date on which the Notice of Intent to Make Audit Changes or the Revised Notice of Intent to Make Audit Changes was issued. (Rule 12-6.002(3), F.A.C.)

A taxpayer that fails to timely request a conference waives its rights to the conference. However, even taxpayers that fail to timely request the conference may use the protest procedures for obtaining review of proposed assessments. (Rule 12-6.002(4), F.A.C.; Rule 12-6.003, F.A.C.)

The 30-day period required for filing the request may be waived by the taxpayer to expedite resolution of issues if the Department's representative and the taxpayer jointly determine that the issues cannot be resolved at the local level. (Rule 12-6.002(6), F.A.C.)

A Notice of Proposed Assessment will be issued by the Department if:

(1) an agreement is not reached after the conference;

(2) the taxpayer has not timely filed a written request for a conference;

(3) the taxpayer has not timely filed a written request for an extension of time for requesting a conference; or

(4) the taxpayer has waived his or her right to a conference pursuant to this section.

(Rule 12-6.002(6), F.A.C.)

• *Delinquency notices or billings*

Taxpayers that receive delinquency notices or billings from the Department may request a conference if no assessment has been issued. Requests must be made by mailing, telephoning, or faxing the request directly to the address, telephone number, or fax number of the office designated on the delinquency notice or billing. (Rule 12-6.0023(1), F.A.C.)

The taxpayer must request a conference within 20 consecutive calendar days after issuance of the notice. (Rule 12-6.0023(1), F.A.C.) A taxpayer may request an extension of time in which to request a conference if the request for an extension is received by the proper office prior to the expiration of the period within which a conference must be requested. Each extension of time will be for 30 consecutive calendar days. (Rule 12-6.0023(1), F.A.C.)

Conferences must be held at the earliest convenience of both the taxpayer and the Department, but no later than 40 consecutive calendar days after the date of the notice, unless specifically agreed to in writing by the Department. (Rule 12-6.0023(3), F.A.C.) If the taxpayer and the division fail to reach an agreement at the conference, or if a request is not timely made for a conference, an assessment will be issued and the taxpayer may file a protest. (Rule 12-6.0023(3), F.A.C.)

• *Contracts with private auditors*

The Department may contract with certified public accountants to audit taxpayer accounts. (Sec. 213.28(1), F.S.; Rule 12-25.001, F.A.C.; Rule 12-22.002(3), F.A.C.; Rule 12-25.002, F.A.C.)

To qualify for selection, an applicant:

— must be an independent certified public accountant in good standing under the laws of both the state in which the applicant is licensed and the state in which the audit services will be performed;

— must be willing to certify that the applicant and his or her firm have not performed accounting services for any client on which the applicant is asked to perform an audit;

— must be willing to certify that no one in the applicant's firm will perform accounting services for any client for whom the applicant has conducted a tax audit under a contract with the Department, for a period of 36 consecutive calendar months from the date the Department's assessment of tax due, or denial of refund, becomes final;

— cannot have provided private brokering services to the Department;

— cannot use the statutory provisions governing contracts with debt collection agencies (Sec. 213.27, F.S.) or compensation for information relating to a violation of the tax laws (Sec. 213.30, F.S.) while under contract to the Department or with regard to any information obtained during the performance of a contractual obligation with the Department;

— must be willing to file a sworn statement with the Department that no one in the applicant's firm has been convicted of a public entity crime; and

— must be willing to sign a certification regarding the confidentiality of tax information acknowledging the applicant's legal responsibility to not disclose any taxpayer or Departmental records. (Rule 12-25.004, F.A.C.)

Contract auditor selection procedures, training, authority, and compensation are exempt from the competitive bid selection procedures and are governed by administrative rule. (Rule 12-25.005, F.A.C.; Rule 12-25.008, F.A.C.; Rule 12-25.009, F.A.C.; Rule 12-25.010, F.A.C.)

Certified public accountants licensed by other states may participate in the program if they are in good standing in their states and in the states where the work is performed. (Sec. 213.28(4), F.S.; Rule 12-25.004(1), F.A.C.) The department may contract with a private firm to secure the services of qualified out-of-state certified public accountants. (Sec. 213.28(2), F.S.; Rule 12-25.003(1), F.A.C.; Rule 12-25.006, F.A.C.) Contracting accountants who willfully violate confidentiality requirements (Sec. 213.053, F.S.) may be guilty of a felony in the third degree. (Sec. 213.28(4), F.S.; Rule 12-25.011, F.A.C.)

Requests for information regarding the Department's contract auditing program should be directed to:

Contract Manager, Bureau of Audit Standards, Division of Audits, P.O. Box 5139, Tallahassee, Florida 32314-5139. (Rule 12-25.012, F.A.C.)

• *Confidentiality*

All information contained in returns, reports, accounts, or declarations received by the department is confidential except for official purposes. The information is also exempt from the public record disclosure requirements. (Sec. 213.053, F.S.) The department will permit taxpayers, their representatives, or representatives of the estate to inspect the taxpayer's return and may furnish them with an abstract of the return. Additionally, the taxpayer may authorize the department in writing to divulge specific information concerning the taxpayer's account.

The confidentiality requirements apply to income tax, sales and use tax, severance tax, emergency excise tax, tourist impact tax, estate tax, intangible personal property tax, document excise tax, communications services tax, gross receipts tax, and various fees and surcharges. (Sec. 213.053, F.S.)

• *Florida Single Audit Act*

Certain tax credits and refunds have been determined to be "state financial assistance" and, consequently, are subject to the auditing and reporting requirements of the Florida Single Audit Act. A taxpayer receiving a total amount of state financial assistance of $500,000 or more in a fiscal year ending September 30, 2004, or thereafter, must have a state single or project-specific audit for that fiscal year. Taxpayers receiving less than $500,000 are not required to have a state single or project-specific audit. The credits and refunds qualifying as state financial assistance can be found in *Tax Information Publication, No. 05ADM-01*, Florida Department of Revenue, May 9, 2005, which revised *Tax Information Publication, No. 02ADM-02*, Florida Department of Revenue, July 29, 2002.

[¶89-134] Audits by Tax Type

Florida has specific audit provisions applicable to sales and use taxes, intangibles taxes, motor fuel tax, and severance taxes, as discussed below.

• *Sales and use taxes*

Department of Revenue enforcement power includes authority to audit and assess dealers in order to ensure sales and use tax compliance. (Sec. 212.12(6)(a), F.S.) If a dealer or other person refuses to make records available for inspection so that no audit or examination can be made, the Department must make an assessment from an estimate based upon the best information available to it for the taxable period. (Sec. 212.12(6)(b), F.S.) Estimated assessments based on a test or sampling are also authorized if a dealer maintains inadequate records, or if a dealer's records are adequate, but unduly voluminous. (Sec. 212.12(7), F.S.)

In the case of a sale of a business, the seller or buyer of an existing business may request that the Department audit the books and records of the seller to protect the buyer from undisclosed sales tax liability. (Sec. 212.10(1), F.S.)

Notification.—Routine audits commence with a written notification by the Department to the taxpayer informing the taxpayer of the audit. This notification also schedules a date on which the Department will actually begin the audit. The notification must be sent at least 60 days before the date the audit will begin. (Sec. 212.13(5)(a), F.S.)

Extent of audit and inspection.—The Department may audit or inspect the records and accounts of dealers and correct by credit any overpayment of tax. (Sec. 212.12(5)(a), F.S.; Sec. 213.34(1), F.S.) In the event of a deficiency, the Department can issue a proposed assessment. No administrative finding of fact is necessary before the assessment of any tax deficiency. (Sec. 212.12(5)(a), F.S.)

Under the Southeastern U.S. State Tax Compact, Florida must report to other member states when, pursuant to information resulting from audits, it does any of the following:

assesses a company over $100,000 for unpaid sales taxes;

finds that a company has an annual sales volume of over $250,000 in or into a member state;

finds a taxable but untaxed transaction over $3,000; or

finds that use tax accrued to a resident of another state as the result of an interstate transaction.

(FICPA Meeting, Q 26 (January 11, 1990))

Estimated assessments.—The Department can assess tax using an estimate based on the best information available for the taxable period when:

a dealer fails or refuses to make records available for inspection so that no audit or examination of books and records can been made,

a person fails or refuses to register as a dealer as required, or

a dealer fails or refuses to report and pay tax as required, files a grossly incorrect report, or files a report that is false or fraudulent.

(Sec. 212.12(5)(b), F.S.; Rule 12A-1.056(5)(a), F.A.C.)

Under these circumstances, the Department also can collect estimated taxes, interest, and penalties on the basis of that assessment that is considered prima facie correct. Thereafter, the burden is shifted to the dealer, seller, owner, or lessor to show that the assessment is incorrect. (Sec. 212.12(5)(b), F.S.)

Jeopardy assessments.—In jeopardy situations, the Department can act when tax avoidance may result if the Department does not act. (Sec. 212.12, F.S.) When it is clear that the tax is in jeopardy and it is likely that the taxpayer will escape or otherwise avoid payment of the tax, the Department may issue an order to show cause and on 10 days' written notice, compel the taxpayer to present books and records, answer interrogatories, and attend a hearing, at times and places established by the Department. (Sec. 212.14(1), F.S.) The target of the investigation may, by written request, require the hearing to be set at a place within the judicial circuit of Florida where the person's business is located, or within the judicial circuit of Florida where the person's books or records are kept.

If the taxpayer fails to produce books, records, and papers, fails to appear and answer proper questions, or prevents or impedes agents or employees from giving testimony, the Department may estimate any unpaid deficiencies and taxes on the information that is available. (Sec. 212.14(1), F.S.) The estimate in such a situation may be based on information furnished by the taxpayer or, if books and records are unavailable, on prior reports filed by the taxpayer or on reports filed by businesses similar to that of the taxpayer. (Sec. 212.14(1), F.S.) The estimate may also be based on unrefuted deposition testimony from federal proceedings. This mechanism effectively shifts the burden from the state to the taxpayer to come forth with proper books and records to establish that the estimate of the Department was incorrect. However, due process requires that this assessment contain a statement of the factual bases relied on by the Department, or the assessment will be void. (See *Bryant v Grand Union Co*, 189 So 2d 885 (Fla 1966)) The Department then can issue a distress warrant for the collection of estimated taxes, interest, or penalties. (Sec. 212.14(1), F.S.; Sec. 212.15(4), F.S.)

Notice requirements.—Except in the case of jeopardy assessments or distress warrants, the Department must send written notification to the taxpayer at least 60 days before an auditor is scheduled to begin an audit, informing the taxpayer of the audit. The notification requirement warns dealers that the Department is scheduling an audit, advises the dealers that books and records will be necessary for the performance of the audit, and allows a time period within which that material can be obtained. (Sec. 212.13(5), F.S.; Sec. 212.14, F.S.; Sec. 212.15, F.S.)

The notification sent by the Department must contain the following:

the approximate date on which the auditor is scheduled to begin the audit;

a reminder that all of the records, receipts, invoices, resale certificates, and related documentation of the taxpayer should be made available to the auditor; and

any other requests or suggestions the Department may deem necessary for a complete audit.

(Sec. 212.13(5)(b), F.S.)

Emergency audits.—The Department need not give the 60-day notice when the taxpayer requests an emergency audit. Emergency audits are requested occasionally by taxpayers who are anticipating a sale of the business or a sale of the stock of goods found in the business. The seller may request an audit so as to fix the tax liability as of the time of the sale to the satisfaction of the buyer. (Sec. 212.13(5)(a), F.S.)

Audits by sampling.—When a dealer lacks adequate records of retail sales or purchases, the Department may determine the proportion that taxable retail sales bear to total retail sales and the proportion that taxable purchases bear to total purchases. The Department determines this ratio by testing or sampling the dealer's available records or other information. (Sec. 212.12(6)(b), F.S.) In some cases, the Department may assume that all sales are taxable and the taxpayer bears the burden of disproving this presumption in view of the inadequacy of records. (See, e.g., *Benson, dba BI Sub Shop and BI Auto Parts v DOR*, No. 89-2437 (August 15, 1989); *Latin Am Sales Intl, Inc. v DOR*, No. 89-0136 (October 30, 1990) (DOR may not conduct sampling audit when taxpayer has documented retail sales))

Department authority to determine taxable sales or purchases on the basis of a dealer's record for a sample period is limited to the authority granted to the Department to determine the proportion the taxable retail sales or purchases bear to total retail sales or purchases. The law does not provide for the Department to establish or to project an estimated rate based on any such sampling. (Sec. 212.12(6)(b), F.S.)

Generally, in making a test or sampling, the Department only examines the purchase records and invoices for some months. (Rule 12A-1.056(1), F.A.C.) The Department establishes and compares the ratio of taxable to nontaxable sales of tangible personal property with the taxpayer's returns and the sales tax remitted to see if the tax remitted is consistent with the taxable sales as established through the test or sampling and through the projection of the ratio or proportion. (Sec. 212.12(6)(b), F.S.)

It has been the general practice of the Department to establish this ratio by examining purchase records and invoices of the dealer, provided that taxable and nontaxable items of tangible personal property are differentiated therein. The Department assumed that the dealer purchased tangible personal property in the same proportion that the dealer sold it. The Department established a ratio or proportion of purchases of taxable personal property, compared to nontaxable personal property, and assumed sales were in the same proportions or ratios. (Sec. 212.12, F.S.)

The Department's sampling authority encompasses the dealer's records or other information pertaining to purchases made by such dealer. (Sec. 212.12(6)(b), F.S.)

The Department compares the ratio of taxable sales and purchases to nontaxable sales and purchases established by the sampling to the ratio of sales tax in the return. If the tax actually paid by the taxpayer compares favorably to the tax calculated on the basis of the sampling, the Department accepts that which has been returned by the taxpayer as the proper tax. If the actual tax paid does not compare favorably, the taxpayer must justify the difference. Some allowance may be required for breakage and pilferage because large amounts of either one can skew the sampling, and the results of the Department.

The Department may instead of, or in addition to, using purchase records, conduct a sampling for a given time period of current sales in which taxable and nontaxable sales of tangible personal property will be distinguished. This allows the Department to establish a ratio of sales of taxable to nontaxable personal property and use this ratio to compare to the returns previously filed by the taxpayer. The Department can then determine if the tax reported by the dealer in prior months is consistent with the taxable sales as established in the sampling of current sales. As in all such samplings, the period sampled must be fairly representative of the dealer's transactions for the time period to which the results of the sampling are being compared.

Generally, any test or sampling of the dealer's records is considered as an estimated assessment, so that the Department must comply with requirements of Sec. 212.12(5)(b), F.S., and the jurisdictional prerequisites for administrative findings. (Sec. 212.12(5)(b), F.S.; Sec. 212.14(1), F.S.) Such estimates of taxes due and owing to the Department are appropriate only on a finding of the nonproduction of records. If the taxpayer can establish that the sampling is not representative, the audit results can be challenged. (Sec. 212.12(6)(b), F.S.)

In contrast to sampling methods undertaken when a dealer has inadequate records, samplings based on voluminous records are done to save the Department time. Samplings based on voluminous records are considered to be more fairly representative of the actual taxable sales made by the taxpayer and thus are not considered to be an estimate. The Department must make a good-faith effort to reach an agreement with the taxpayer on the means and methods to be employed in the

¶89-134

sampling process. Whenever the taxpayer is unable to conclude an agreement, the taxpayer is entitled to a review by the executive director. (Sec. 212.12(6)(b), F.S.)

The agreement entered into between the dealer and the Department is not required by statute to be reduced to writing. (Sec. 212.12(6)(c), F.S.) However, it is the practice of the Department to do so. This agreement should set forth the method to be used and should include:

the means for developing the ratio of sales or purchases of taxable tangible personal property to sales or purchases of nontaxable tangible personal property;

the periods or months that are to be sampled and tested; and

the basis for the determination and sampling of such months.

• *Intangibles taxes*

For a discussion of audits with respect to property tax.

• *Motor fuel tax*

The Department may verify by audit the accuracy of tax returns to determine whether gasoline taxes have been paid by examining the records, books, papers, and equipment of refiners, importers, wholesalers, jobbers, retail dealers, terminal facilities, and common carriers. (Sec. 206.14(2), F.S.)

The Department also may investigate and audit inventories, receipts, and disposals of motor fuel to ascertain the validity of all taxes collected and remitted to the Department. Any motor fuel that cannot be accounted for by a refiner, importer, or wholesaler is subject to all applicable taxes. (Sec. 206.59(3), F.S.)

• *Severance taxes*

The Department may audit or examine pertinent books and records to determine whether necessary returns and tax payments have been submitted. An audit is commenced by service of a written notice of intent to audit on the taxpayer, in person or by certified mail. The date notice is given determines the period subject to audit. Audits may be commenced for any month for which the Department can make assessments of production taxes due. (Sec. 211.125(4), F.S.)

[¶89-142] Record Maintenance and Production

Anyone performing any act in connection with the administration of any Florida tax must keep adequate books and records, including invoices, bills of lading, and other pertinent records and papers. These books and records must be kept until the expiration of the time within which the Department of Revenue may make an assessment with respect to that tax. (Sec. 213.35, F.S.; Rule 12-24.021, F.A.C.; Rule 12-24.030, F.A.C.; Rule 12-3.0012, F.A.C.).

• *Sales and use taxes*

During the course of an audit and examination, a taxpayer must produce the required books and records so that they may be inspected and examined by the Department agent. In some situations, the taxpayer may need to produce records peculiar to the nature of the taxpayer's business that may be necessary or helpful to the Department in completing the audit. Also, the Department may require records that are not kept at the taxpayer's central business office, but which are necessary for the Department to properly examine the books and records of a taxpayer and complete an audit. Thus, the taxpayer may be asked to obtain additional records in the course of the audit.

One of the most common areas in which taxpayers fail to meet statutory requirements is in failing to obtain proper resale certificates or exemption certificates from purchasers who are buying tangible personal property that would be tax exempt or for resale. If unable to obtain such certificates during the audit or protest period, the seller, rather than the purchaser, must pay the tax. (Sec. 212.07, F.S.; *DOR v Robert N Anderson*, 403 So 2d 397 (Fla 1981); *Pioneer Oil Co v DOR*, 381 So 2d 263 (Fla 1st DCA 1980); affd 401 So 2d 1319 (Fla 1981))

[¶89-144] Limitations Period for Audits

The statute of limitations period for assessment of Florida taxes is generally governed by uniform provisions that apply to all taxes. Florida also has special rules that apply to income and property tax assessments.

• *Uniform provisions*

Generally, a notice of proposed assessment for Florida taxes, including corporation income and personal income taxes, must be mailed to the taxpayer within three years after the date the tax is due, after any return with respect to the tax is due, or after the return is filed, whichever occurs later. However, the Department of Revenue may audit and assess a taxpayer's tax liability at any time while the right to a refund or credit of the tax is available to the taxpayer. (Sec. 95.091(3)(a), F.S.)

Assessments may be allowed after the general time limit under a variety of circumstances, including the failure to file a return or report federal changes, a substantial understatement of tax liability, and the filing of a fraudulent return.

Tax returns filed before the last day prescribed by law, including any extensions, are deemed to have been filed on that last day, and any payments made before the last day prescribed by law are deemed to have been paid on that last day. (Sec. 95.091(3)(b), F.S.)

Tolling of limitations period.—The statute of limitations is tolled for a period of one year if, within the applicable limitation period, the Department has issued a notice of intent to conduct an audit or investigation of the taxpayer's account. (Sec. 213.345, F.S.) The Department must commence an audit within 120 days after it issues a notice of intent to conduct an audit unless the taxpayer requests a delay. If the taxpayer does not request a delay and the Department does not begin the audit within 120 days after issuing the notice, the tolling period terminates. (Sec. 213.345, F.S.) In addition, the running of the limitations period is tolled during the pendency of an administrative or judicial proceeding for review of the tax assessment or collection that is begun within the appropriate limitations period. (Sec. 95.091 (4), F.S.)

The running of the period of limitations on assessment is tolled from the date of a taxpayer's request for a taxpayer assistance order until either the date the request is denied or the date specified in the taxpayer assistance order, whichever is applicable. (Sec. 213.018(2)(b), F.S.)

Fraud or failure to file.—A notice of proposed assessment may be mailed at any time after the taxpayer has failed to make any required payment of the tax, has failed to file a required return, or has filed a fraudulent return, except that for taxes due on or after July 1, 1999, the three-year limitation applies if the taxpayer has disclosed in writing the tax liability to the department before the department has contacted taxpayer. (Sec. 95.091(3)(a), F.S.)

In any case in which there has been a refund of tax erroneously made for any reason, a notice of proposed assessment may be mailed within three years after making the refund, or at any time after making the refund if it appears that any part of the refund was induced by fraud or the misrepresentation of a material fact. (Sec. 95.091(3)(a), F.S.)

Waiver or extension agreements.—The Department of Revenue will enter into a consent agreement extending the time period for an assessment unless the department determines that (1) the taxpayer does not intend to provide the required documentation, books, or records, (2) the taxpayer intends to delay the issuance of an assessment, or (3) there is significant endangerment to the revenues involved.

Effective June 28, 2010, a consent agreement is effective when it has been signed and dated by both the taxpayer or authorized representative and on behalf of the department by a person with the delegated authority. The department will use the later of the date the agreement or extension is signed or dated by the taxpayer or the department to determine whether the agreement is timely.

Previously, a consent agreement was effective when it has been signed and dated by the taxpayer and received by the Department, unless the agreement as originally signed by the department has been subsequently altered by the taxpayer. The Department would use the date the agreement is signed and dated by the taxpayer to determine whether the agreement is timely. A consent agreement will remain in effect until both parties mutually agree to nullify or extend it, or until the consent agreement period has expired.

Additionally, a signed consent agreement may be transmitted by electronic means or facsimile. (Rule 12-16.005, F.A.C.)

• *Income tax*

When a deficiency is the result of a change in the taxpayer's federal income tax return, the Department may assess tax at any time within five years after the taxpayer notifies the Department of the change. If a taxpayer fails to notify the Department of the change, the Department may assess income tax due as a result of the change at any time. (Sec. 220.23(2)(c))

[¶89-160]

COLLECTION OF TAX

[¶89-164] Assessment of Delinquent Tax

The dates on which taxes become delinquent vary according to the tax type. Monthly sales and use tax on tangible personal property is delinquent if not paid by the 21st day, or if not post marked by the 20th day, of the month following the month for which the taxes are due. Quarterly tax payments are delinquent on the 20th day of the month following the period for which the taxes are due. (Sec. 212.15, F.S.; Rule 12A-1.056, F.A.C.) Corporate income and property provisions are discussed below.

The Department of Revenue must provide a taxpayer with notice of the taxes due, delinquent taxes, and any actions it takes to collect the taxes. No collection action may be taken until 30 days after notice of the action is issued to the taxpayer. (Sec. 213.731, F.S.)

Notices of income tax deficiencies must be given to the taxpayer by personal delivery or certified mail and must include the amount of tax due and a computation of, and reasons for, the adjustments giving rise to the tax. (Sec. 220.739, F.S.; Sec. 220.711, F.S.)

• *Corporate income*

Corporate income taxes are delinquent if not paid on or before the due date of the return or the estimated tax payment. (Sec. 220.222, F.S.; Rule 12C-1.034, F.A.C.; Rule 12C-1.0222, F.A.C.)

If the Department of Revenue finds that the amount of tax shown on the return is less than the correct amount and the difference is not solely the result of mathematical error, it must issue a notice of deficiency to the taxpayer setting forth the amount of additional tax and any penalties proposed to be assessed. (Sec. 220.709(1), F.S.) Sixty days after the date on which it was issued (150 days if the taxpayer is outside the United States), a notice of deficiency will constitute an assessment of the tax and penalties specified therein, except any amounts on which the taxpayer has filed a protest with the Department. (Sec. 220.713, F.S.)

• Insurance gross premiums tax

The amount of any deficiency assessment of the insurance gross premiums tax is limited to the amount of any deficiency resulting from recomputation of the taxpayer's insurance premium and retaliatory taxes for the taxable year, giving effect only to the change in the corporate income tax and/or the workers' compensation administrative assessment paid. (Sec. 624.50921, F.S.) Interest on such a deficiency assessment is computed from the date on which the original insurance premium tax return was due until the payment of the deficiency. If an amended insurance premium tax return is required, a deficiency notice may be issued by the Department within three years after the date the amended return is filed. If a taxpayer fails to file a required amended return, a notice of deficiency may be issued at any time (i.e., no statute of limitations applies). (Sec. 624.50921, F.S.)

[¶89-166] Other Liable Parties

A transferee of a taxpayer is liable for any tax in the same manner as the original taxpayer. (Sec. 220.829, F.S.)

A receiver, trustee in bankruptcy, or assignee who has possession of or holds title to all, or substantially all, of the business or property of a taxpayer, must make the returns required of the taxpayer. (Sec. 220.22, F.S.)

The owner, holder, or assignee of any tax lien may be included as a defendant in a proceeding for foreclosure of municipal tax. (Sec. 173.15, F.S.)

Transfer of tax liabilities.—A taxpayer who is liable for any tax, interest, surcharge, penalty, or fee administered by the department, excluding corporate income tax, and who quits a business with the benefit of a purchaser, successor, or assignee, or without transferring the business or stock of goods to a transferee, must file a final return and make full payment within 15 days after quitting the business. Additionally, a taxpayer who transfers a business or stock of goods must make a final return and full payment for any taxes due, excluding corporate income tax, within 15 days of the date of transfer. (Sec. 213.758)

The transferee of more than 50% of a business is liable for the tax, interest, surcharge, fee or penalty owed by the transferor, unless the transferor provides the transferee a receipt or certificate from the department showing that the transferor is not liable for taxes and the department finds that the transferor is not liable for taxes after the audit. (Sec. 213.758)

[¶89-168] Jeopardy Assessments

The Department of Revenue may demand the immediate payment of a tax if it finds that a taxpayer is about to depart from, or conceal property in, the state or do any other act rendering the normal collection procedures ineffective, or if the Department otherwise finds that collection will be jeopardized by delay. The Department must include with that demand notice of the findings of fact supporting the jeopardy assessment. (Sec. 220.719, F.S.) Jeopardy also may exist in the case of estimated tax billings when the taxpayer has stopped making regular payments and the estimated deficiency is substantial. (Rule 12-21.005, F.A.C.)

A warrant, lien, or other detainer of property may be issued and recorded simultaneously with the notice of jeopardy. The Department may immediately proceed with collection actions, but must, upon the taxpayer's request, meet with the taxpayer within 10 days after the issuance of the assessment to hear the taxpayer's written or oral statement of why no jeopardy to the revenue exists or why a jeopardy lien or warrant should be released. The taxpayer must be given notice of this right at the time of the assessment. (Sec. 213.732, F.S.).

In making its determination that delinquent sales and use taxes are in jeopardy, the Department may consider:

the taxpayer's prior history of compliance or noncompliance;

the type of taxpayer's business, including its transient or non-transient nature;

the liquidity of the taxpayer's assets;

the mobility of the assets;

the pending sale or transfer of title of the assets; or

the financial status of the taxpayer.

(Rule 12A-1.090, F.A.C.)

[¶89-172] Tax Liens

Any recorded warrant issued for the full amount of taxes due becomes a lien on the taxpayer's real and personal property. All taxes imposed are a first lien, which remains in effect until the taxes are paid, on any property against which the taxes are assessed. If the taxes due are not paid on time, the Department of Revenue may proceed on the lien through a tax sale to collect the taxes owed. (Sec. 199.262, F.S.; Rule 12A-1.090, F.A.C.) All district taxes constitute liens of equal dignity to the liens for state and county taxes. (Sec. 190.024, F.S.; Sec. 190.025, F.S.)

If no lien exists to secure payment of the tax after five years from the later of the date the tax was assessed or the date it became delinquent, no action to collect the tax may be taken. Tax liens expire either five years after the date the tax is assessed or becomes delinquent, whichever is later, or 20 years after the last date the tax may be assessed, after the tax becomes delinquent, or after the filing of a tax warrant, whichever is later, depending on the tax type for which the lien was issued. A tax lien against the estate of a nonresident who claimed a homestead exemption for property located in Florida is subject to the 20-year limitations period. No action to collect a tax may begin after the expiration of the lien securing the tax. (Sec. 95.091, F.S.)

A tax lien is extinguished when title reverts to the state or its agency, except that the state or its agency must redeem any tax certificate or tax deed in the hands of a person, private firm, or private corporation. (Sec. 270.18, F.S.; Sec. 270.19, F.S.)

Integrated enforcement authority.—Effective July 1, 2010, if the department files a warrant, notice of lien, or judgment lien certificate against the property of a taxpayer, the department may also revoke all certificates of registration, permits, or licenses issued by the department to that taxpayer. Prior to the revocation of the certificate, the department must schedule an informal conference where the taxpayer may present evidence regarding the department's intended action or enter into a compliance agreement. (Sec. 213.692, F.S.)

• *Corporate income*

The state has a lien for all or any portion of the tax, penalty, or interest that may be due upon all of the real and personal property of any taxpayer. If the lien arises from an assessment pursuant to a notice of deficiency, the lien will not attach and a notice of lien will not be filed until all proceedings in court for review of the assessment have terminated or the time for seeking a review of the assessment has expired without the proceedings being instituted.

The lien created by assessment pursuant to a notice of deficiency expires unless a notice of lien is filed within five years from the date all proceedings in court for the review of the assessment have terminated or the time for seeking a review of the assessment has expired without the proceedings being instituted. The lien created by assessment pursuant to the filing of a return without payment of the tax shown to be due or the penalty or interest properly due expires unless a notice of lien is filed within five years from the date on which the return was filed with the department. (Sec. 220.813, F.S.)

[¶89-174] Warrants for Collection of Tax

The Department of Revenue, or any of its offices, may issue a tax warrant to secure payment of any delinquent taxes. (Rule 12-21.002, F.A.C.) Upon recording, the warrant becomes a lien upon the taxpayer's real and personal property located in the county. The property may then be levied upon, seized, and sold to satisfy the taxes. (Sec. 213.69, F.S.) The warrant may be issued in addition to any other collection actions taken by the Department. (Sec. 210.14, F.S.) No warrant, absent jeopardy, may be issued until 30 days after the issuance of a notice to the taxpayer that the action is impending. (Sec. 213.731, F.S.).

A distress warrant may be issued against any person who files a return or pays a tax with the intent to deceive or defraud the state and who fails to appear or present required evidence at a hearing held by the Department. The property of the taxpayer located anywhere in the state will be seized and sold to satisfy the tax deficiencies. (Sec. 212.14, F.S.)

The department can publish a list of taxpayers against whom the department has filed a warrant, notice of lien, or judgment lien certificate for the taxes, surtaxes, surcharges, or fees administered by the department. (Sec. 213.053(20), F.S.; Rule 12-22.008, F.A.C.)

• *Corporate income*

If any tax is not paid within the required time, the department or its designee may cause a demand to be made on the taxpayer for payment of the tax. If the tax remains unpaid for ten days after the demand for payment and no proceedings for review have been instituted, the department may issue a warrant directing any sheriff or other person authorized to serve process to levy upon and sell the real and personal property of the taxpayer found within the jurisdiction for payment of the tax, including penalties, interest, and the cost of executing the warrant. (Sec. 220.827, F.S.)

[¶89-176] Other Collection Methods

The following non-exclusive collection actions are available to the Department of Revenue at any time after taxes become delinquent.

• *Foreclosure*

Any lien on real or personal property may be foreclosed in any court with jurisdiction. A proceeding to foreclose must be filed within 20 years after the filing of the notice of lien. (Sec. 220.825, F.S.) Note, however, that, since liens can expire either five or 20 years after they are issued and no action to collect a tax may begin after the expiration of the lien securing the tax, some foreclosure actions must be brought within five years of the filing of the notice of lien. Suits for foreclosure of tax liens are proceedings in rem against the land upon which the taxes are a lien; it is not material that the ownership of the land be correctly alleged in the proceedings or that the parties with interests in the land be made parties to the proceedings. (Sec. 173.02, F.S.).

• *Offsets*

Whenever a delinquent taxpayer has a refund or credit due from overpayment of other taxes, the Department may use all or part of that refund or credit to pay any unsatisfied tax debt. (Sec. 213.25, F.S.; Rule 12-26.009, F.A.C.)

• *Garnishment*

The Department may give notice of a tax delinquency to all persons who have in their possession or under their control any credits or personal property, excluding wages, of the delinquent taxpayer or who owe a debt to the delinquent taxpayer. This property may not be transferred or disposed of until 60 days after receipt of the notice without consent from the Department. During the last 30 days of the 60-day period, the Department may, after giving notice, levy upon the credits, property, or debts owed. To be discharged from liability, the third party then must either pay the delinquent tax debt or turn over the assets to the Department. (Sec. 213.67, F.S.; Sec. 199.262, F.S.)

PLANNING NOTE: Florida has joined the Multistate Tax Commission's (MTC's) tax shelter voluntary compliance program. The program allows a taxpayer to unwind an abusive tax shelter in exchange for a state benefit, usually the waiver or abatement of a penalty. The program runs from May 1 until October 1, 2007. In consideration for a taxpayer's participation in this program, Florida will waive or abate only the following penalties that could otherwise be assessed against the participating taxpayer with respect to its participation in a tax shelter for the tax years listed on its submitted Forms 8886 and its accompanying state income tax returns:

— the penalty for filing an incomplete return;

— the penalty for underpayment of estimated tax;

— the penalty for failure to timely file; and

— the penalty for failure to pay.

Multistate Tax Shelter Voluntary Compliance Program (Participating States and Benefits, Multistate Tax Commission, June 12, 2007

[¶89-178] Requirement to Post Bond or Security

Agents, county comptrollers, or clerks of the circuit court authorized to collect taxes must post a bond with the Florida Department of Revenue. (Sec. 201.132, F.S.; Sec. 201.11, F.S.)

Average of five or more taxable transactions per month.—All persons who average or will average five or more transactions subject to sales tax a month must post a bond as required by the Department. (Sec. 201.133, F.S.)

Temporary exemption certificate.—An applicant for a temporary exemption certificate may be required to file a cash or surety bond in an amount sufficient to satisfy the Department's estimate of taxes that would be due if the applicant failed to timely qualify for a regular exemption certificate. (Rule 12A-1.038, F.A.C.)

Terminal suppliers and wholesalers.—Every terminal supplier, exporter, wholesaler, or producer/importer of pollutants is required to post a bond in the amount of three times the average monthly diesel fuel tax and local option tax on diesel fuels paid within the preceding 12 months, but not more than $300,000 ($100,000 prior to July 1, 2020). Each license type must get a separate bond for motor fuel, diesel fuel, aviation fuel, and pollutants. No bond is required if the average monthly tax is less than $50. (Sec. 206.05, F.S.; Sec. 206.90, F.S.; Sec. 206.9931, F.S.; Rule 12B-5.060, F.A.C.; *Tax Information Publication, No. 20B05-01,* Florida Department of Revenue, June 15, 2020)

Before being licensed, an importer must post a bond equivalent to 60 days' tax liability, make a cash deposit, or provide a letter of credit to establish credit worthiness with the Department. (Sec. 206.051, F.S.; Rule 12B-5.060, F.A.C.)

[¶89-180] Civil Action

The Department of Revenue may bring an action in court to enforce a collection action, to recover delinquent taxes, or at any time that it levies upon property for the collection of taxes. A certificate of the Department showing the amount of delinquency is prima facie evidence of the correctness and validity of that amount. (Sec. 220.733, F.S.; Sec. 195.092, F.S.; Sec. 120.69, F.S.)

[¶89-182] Civil Action in Another Jurisdiction

The Department of Revenue may, to commence levy proceedings, bring an action in any court with jurisdiction outside the state. (Sec. 220.733, F.S.)

[¶89-184] Intergovernmental Tax Collection Agreements

There are a number of agreements among governmental agencies to provide for assistance in tax collection, both between the Internal Revenue Service and the states, and among the states themselves.

• *Agreement with IRS*

Abusive Tax Avoidance Transactions (ATAT) Memorandum of Understanding.— The Small Business Self-Employed Division of the Internal Revenue Service signed ATAT Memorandums of Understanding with 40 states and the District of Columbia on September 16, 2003, that provide for information sharing on abusive tax avoidance transactions. (*Memorandum of Understanding*, Internal Revenue Service) The Memorandum authorizes the IRS and a state to:

— exchange tax returns and return information,

— share audit results from ATAT participant cases,

— exchange information on identified types of ATAT schemes, and

— share audit technique guides.

The IRS will provide states with a list of participants in a particular ATAT scheme on a semi-annual basis on July 31 and January 31. The IRS generally refers to an abusive tax shelter arrangement as the promise of tax benefits with no meaningful change in the taxpayer's control over or benefit from the taxpayer's income or assets.

Florida has signed the ATAT Memorandum of Understanding with the IRS.

• *Agreements with other states*

Enforcement actions from other states.—Actions to enforce lawfully imposed sales, use, corporate income, and motor and other fuel taxes of other states may be brought in Florida if:

the state seeking the action extends a like courtesy to Florida;

venue for the action is the circuit court in which the defendant resides;

in an action for a tax warrant, the warrant has been obtained as a result of a court judgment or the courts of the other state will enforce warrants issued by the Department of Revenue; and

all tax liabilities in Florida are paid first and shall be prior in right to any tax liability arising under the other state's laws.

(Sec. 72.041, F.S.)

Out-of-state fuel suppliers.—A licensed terminal supplier who is a position holder in a terminal outside Florida, a licensed importer, or a seller transferring outside Florida ownership of motor fuels destined for Florida may enter into an agreement with the state agreeing to be subject to the tax laws of Florida in the same manner as if the fuel were withdrawn, or the transfer of ownership occurred, in Florida. (Sec. 206.413, F.S.; Sec. 206.872, F.S.)

Motor fuel and motor vehicle tax collections.—Although it has not yet done so, the Florida Department of Highway Safety and Motor Vehicles may enter into cooperative reciprocal agreements with another state or group of states for the administration of motor fuels and motor vehicles taxes, including the International Fuel Tax Agreement. (Sec. 207.0281, F.S.)

[¶89-186] Agreements in Compromise of Tax Due

The Executive Director of the Department of Revenue or a designee may enter into written closing agreements settling or compromising a taxpayer's tax liability. These agreements are final except upon a showing of fraud or misrepresentation of a material fact. (Sec. 220.733, F.S.; Rule 12-13.009, F.A.C.; Rule 12-13.004, F.A.C.; Rule 12-13.010, F.A.C.; Rule 12-13.007, F.A.C.)

In order for a tax liability to be settled or compromised, the taxpayer must request it in writing and establish doubt as to the tax liability or the collectibility of the tax. The Department also may compromise or settle tax liabilities that are voluntarily disclosed by the taxpayer for the three years immediately preceding the date that the taxpayer initially contacted the Department concerning the voluntary self-disclosure. (Rule 12-25.038; Sec. 213.21, F.S.) For a penalty to be compromised, the taxpayer must establish that noncompliance was due to a reasonable cause. (Rule 12-13.003, F.A.C.; Rule 12-13.008, F.A.C.)

In determining the amount of compromise when there is doubt as to the taxpayer's liability, the Department will consider:

the likelihood of prevailing in litigation;

ambiguity in the applicable laws or rules; and

whether the tax was collected but not remitted to the state.

In determining the amount of compromise when the collectibility of the tax is at issue, the Department will consider:

whether the taxpayer's financial problems can be addressed through the use of a payment plan;

whether the taxpayer has a pattern of chronic tax delinquencies; and

whether tax was collected but not remitted to the state.

The amount of compromise of a penalty depends on factors including;

the taxpayer's history of delinquency;

the amount of tax assessed as compared to total tax liability;

the taxpayer's audit history; and

the taxpayer's failure to remit tax collected to the state.

(Rule 12-13.0075, F.A.C.)

The Department of Revenue has adopted regulations detailing procedures for agreements for scheduling payments of unpaid tax liabilities. These regulations appear at Rule 12-17.001, F.A.C., et seq.

• *Certified audits project*

The Department will settle or compromise penalty liabilities of taxpayers who participate in the certified audits project. (Sec. 213.21(8), F.S.)

• *Voluntary disclosure*

The Florida Department of Revenue provides guidance regarding its Voluntary Disclosure Program for taxpayers who wish to avoid or alleviate penalties for failure to pay the following taxes: corporate income tax, sales and use tax discretionary sales surtax (county tax), documentary stamp tax, unemployment compensation tax, communications services tax, and gross receipts tax. (*Florida Taxpayer's Voluntary Disclosure of Tax Liability*, Florida Department of Revenue)

Florida is also a participant in the Multistate Tax Commission's *Tax Shelter Voluntary Compliance Program*.

• *Property tax*

Florida has no provisions for the compromise of real property and tangible personal property taxes.

[¶89-188] Installment Payments

For a discussion of installment payments with respect to property tax, see ¶20-756.

[¶89-190] Recovery of Erroneous Refunds

The Department of Revenue must inform a taxpayer by registered mail of any taxes erroneously refunded. If the taxpayer fails to return an erroneous refund of sales and use or motor fuels taxes within 15 days of receiving the letter, the Department may institute an action in court for the recovery of the erroneous refund plus a 25 penalty. (Sec. 206.41, F.S.) An erroneous refund of income tax is considered a deficiency of tax due on the date made and, if the request for refund was not due to reasonable cause, will be assessed interest from the date of the payment until the amount is repaid to the Department. (Sec. 213.255, F.S.; Sec. 220.709, F.S.; Rule 12C-1.343, F.A.C.)

[¶89-200]

INTEREST AND PENALTIES

[¶89-202] Interest and Penalties in General

Rather than general administrative provisions for penalties and interest for all taxes, Florida has separate provisions for each tax. For a discussion of applicable interest rates.

Interest and penalties are reported on Form F1120, Florida Corporate Income, Franchise and Emergency Excise Tax Return, for a corporate taxpayer after calculating the interest and penalties on F-2220, Underpayment of Estimated Tax on Florida Corporate Income, Franchise and Emergency Excise Tax Return.

Administrative collection processing fee.—The Florida Department of Revenue must collect an administrative collection processing fee equal to 10% of the total amount of tax, penalty, and interest which remains unpaid after 90 days, or $10 for each collection event, whichever is greater. The fee will offset payment processing and administrative costs incurred by the state due to late payment of a collection event. A "collection event" is when a taxpayer fails to timely file a complete return, pay the full amount of tax reported on a return, or timely pay the full amount due resulting from an audit after all appeal rights have expired.

The department will collect the fee within 90 days following the initial notification of the collection event. If the taxpayer demonstrates that the failure to pay was due to extraordinary circumstances, the department may waive or reduce the fee. The fee applies retroactively to any remaining unpaid amount of tax, interest, and penalty due from any collection event occurring before May 27, 2009. However, the department may not collect the fee until September 1, 2009, calculated on the amount remaining unpaid on that date. (Sec. 213.24, F.S.)

[¶89-204] Interest Rates

The floating interest rate on Florida underpayments (deficiencies), late payments, and overpayments for January 1, 2021 through December 31, 2022, is 7%, for among other taxes, corporate income, franchise, emergency excise, sales and use, communications services, motor fuel, and documentary stamp taxes. The daily interest rate factor for this period is 0.000191781. (*Tax Information Publication, No. 22ADM-03*, Florida Department of Revenue, May 4, 2022)

Generally, Florida charges or pays a floating interest rate on tax payment deficiencies or overpayments that is determined by the adjusted prime rate charged by banks, rounded to the nearest full percent. (Sec. 213.235, F.S.) The rate for corporate income tax and local communications services tax deficiencies or overpayments is capped at 12%. (Sec. 202.35, F.S.; Sec. 220.807, F.S.)

The Executive Director of the Department of Revenue establishes the interest rate on a semiannual basis. This interest rate applies to all taxes administered by the Department unless a particular tax has a lower statutory interest rate. (Sec. 213.235, F.S.)

The interest rate is applied to underpayments, late payments, and overpayments. Taxes and enactments subject to this rate include:

- Local Option Tourist Development Act;
- communications services tax;
- Miami-Dade County Lake Belt Area mitigation fee;
- tourist impact tax;
- estate taxes;
- excise tax on documents;
- gross receipts tax on utility services;
- gross receipts tax on dry cleaning facilities;
- motor and other fuel taxes;
- tax on production of oil and gas and severance of solid minerals;
- sales and use tax;
- corporate income tax;
- emergency excise tax;
- pollutant spill prevention and control;
- waste tire fees;
- lead-acid battery fees;
- registration of secondhand dealers;
- registration of secondary metals recyclers;
- group self-insurer's fund premium tax;
- retaliatory tax;
- insurance code: administration and general provisions;
- State Fire Marshal regulatory assessment;
- medical malpractice self-insurance premium tax;
- reciprocal insurers premium tax; and
- motor vehicle warranty enforcement.

(Sec. 213.05, F.S.; Sec. 213.235, F.S.)

• *Underpayments*

No interest is applied to any tax amount due if it is paid within 30 days of billing or notice and demand. No billing for deficiency shall be issued in an amount less than the actual cost to the Department to produce the billing.

• *Overpayments*

Interest will be paid on overpayments, payments not due, or erroneous payments if the taxpayer has filed a timely and complete application for refund. The Department has 30 days within which to validate the application, and interest begins accruing 90 days after receiving the completed application if the Department has not refunded the overpayment. (Sec. 213.255, F.S.)

•*Property tax*

For a discussion of interest rates with respect to property tax, see Interest.

[¶89-206] Civil Penalties

The following civil penalties are provided for various tax types in Florida.

•*Corporate income tax*

Failure to file.—A corporation that fails to file an income tax return is liable for a penalty in the amount of $50 for each month or portion of a month, not to exceed $300 in the aggregate. This penalty will only apply if the corporation also is required to file a federal return and no state tax was due. If tax is due, a penalty of 10% of the tax due is assessed per month, up to a total penalty of 50% of the tax due. (Sec. 220.801, F.S.) If an incomplete return is filed (even if no tax is finally determined to be due for the taxable year), a penalty in the amount of $300 or 10% of the tax finally determined to be due, whichever is greater, will be added to any tax, penalty, and interest otherwise due. The penalty for filing an incomplete return may not exceed $10,000. (Sec. 220.211, F.S.)

Failure to pay.—Interest at the rate of 12% per annum and a penalty equal to 12% per year imposed on the amount of the underpayment. Amount of the underpayment is the excess of the amount of the installment over the amount of the installment required to be paid if estimated tax were equal to 90% of current year's liability. (Sec. 220.34, F.S.)

Underpayment of estimated tax.—A penalty equal to 12% each year may be imposed on the amount of any underpayment of estimated Florida corporate income tax. (Sec. 220.34(2), F.S.; Rule 12C-1.034(9), F.A.C.) Interest at the current rate is also imposed from the installment due date to earlier of:

— date the underpayment is actually paid; or

— 1st day of 5th month after the close of the taxpayer's tax year. (Sec. 220.34(2), F.S.; Rule 12C-1.034(9), F.A.C.; Instructions, Form F-2220, Underpayment of Estimated Tax on Corporate Income/Franchise Tax)

The underpayment amount, penalty, and interest is computed on Form F-2220. (Instructions, Form F-2220, Underpayment of Estimated Tax on Corporate Income/Franchise Tax)

A taxpayer will not owe a penalty or interest if the total amount of all payments made by the installment date equals or exceeds the estimated tax safe harbor exception.

Penalties for disclosure of client information.—A penalty of up to $5,000 for each count or separate offense may be imposed by the Florida Board of Accountancy against an accountant that violates client confidentiality provisions. (Sec. 473.16, F.S.; Sec. 473.323, F.S.)

•*Sales and use taxes*

Failure to collect tax.—A dealer who fails to collect the tax from the consumer is liable for payment of the tax. (Sec. 212.07(3), F.S.) In addition to other penalties, a dealer who willfully attempts to evade paying a tax must pay a penalty equal to the total amount of the tax. (Sec. 213.29, F.S.)

Failure to remit estimated tax.—Any person, firm, or corporation that fails to remit the proper estimated tax payment required is subject to a penalty in an amount equal to 10% of any unpaid tax. (Sec. 212.12(2), F.S.)

Failure to file a complete return.—The collection allowance may be reduced by 10% if a taxpayer files an incomplete return. An "incomplete return" is a return that is lacking such uniformity, completeness, and arrangement that the physical handling, verification, or review of the return may not be readily accomplished. (Sec. 212.12(1)(b), F.S.)

Failure to file return or pay tax on time.—Any taxpayer that does not file a return or pay any tax or fee within the time specified or that fails to timely file the return must pay a penalty in the amount of 10% of the unpaid amount. (Sec. 212.12(2), F.S.; Sec. 212.04(4), F.S.) An additional 10% is imposed for each additional 30 days or fraction thereof for which the failure continues, not to exceed a total penalty of 50%. The minimum penalty for failure to file a return is generally $10. However, the minimum penalty for late quarterly and semiannual dealer returns is $5. No collection allowance will be granted if the tax is delinquent at the time of payment. (Sec. 212.12(1)(a), F.S.; Rule 12A-1.056(5)(f), F.A.C.) Further, a taxpayer who knowingly or repeatedly fails to remit taxes in a timely manner may be subject to an escrow requirement.

Effective January 1, 2021, credit card companies and third-party settlement organizations (TPSOs) that fail to file a copy of their federal 1099-K information returns with the Florida Department of Revenue are subject to a penalty of $1,000 each month up to $10,000 annually. (*1099-K Reporting Requirements*, Florida Department of Revenue, February 2021)

Fraudulent return or willful intent to evade payment of tax or fee.—Any taxpayer who files a fraudulent return or willfully intends to evade payment of a tax or fee is liable for a specific penalty of 100% of the tax bill or fee and for fine and punishment as provided by law. (Sec. 212.12(2), F.S.) In addition, the taxpayer must pay a penalty equal to twice the total amount of tax evaded or not accounted for or paid. (Sec. 213.29, F.S.) A corporate officer who refuses to make a return and pay the taxes due is subject to a penalty of 6 per year. (Sec. 212.14(3), F.S.) The officer also must pay a penalty equal to twice the total amount of tax evaded or not accounted for or paid. (Sec. 213.29, F.S.)

Fraudulent claim of exemption.—If a person issues, for the purpose of evading tax, a certificate or statement to a vendor in which there is a claim of exemption from sales tax, that person is subject to payment of the tax plus a mandatory penalty of 200% of the tax. (Sec. 212.085, F.S.)

Fraudulent claim of a credit for job creation in an enterprise zone.—Any person who fraudulently claims a credit for jobs in an enterprise zone is liable for repayment of the credit plus a mandatory penalty of 100% of the credit plus interest. (Sec. 212.096(10), F.S.)

Occasional or isolated sales.—Any party who reports a sales price from an occasional or isolated sale of an aircraft, boat, mobile home, or motor vehicle that is less than the actual sales price must pay any tax due in addition to any penalty and interest assessed, plus a penalty equal to twice the amount of the additional tax owed. (Sec. 212.05(1)(a), F.S.)

• *Other taxes*

Admissions.—Any person who attempts to evade payment of admissions taxes, or who attempts to file a false or misleading return, is subject to a 100% penalty. (Sec. 212.04(4), F.S.)

Oil, gas, and sulfur production tax.—Failure to file a return will result in a delinquency penalty of 10 for each month, not to exceed 50%. If no tax is due with the return, the delinquency penalty imposed is $50 per month, not to exceed $300 in the aggregate. A taxpayer making a substantial underpayment of tax is required to pay a penalty of 30% of the underpayment in addition to the delinquency penalty. (Sec. 211.076(2), F.S.)

Solid mineral severance tax.—A delinquency penalty of 10% per month up to 50% of the total tax will be imposed if a tax return is not filed by April 1st for the preceding year due to negligence or intentional disregard of the rules. (Sec. 211.33(2), F.S.)

Municipal license taxes.—Licenses not renewed when due and payable will be considered delinquent and will be subject to a delinquency penalty of 10% for the month of October, plus an additional 5% penalty for each succeeding delinquent month, up to 25% of the license fee. If the license tax is not paid within 150 days after the initial notice of tax due, and if the required occupational license is not obtained, a penalty of up to $250 may be imposed, along with other civil actions and penalties. (Sec. 205.053, F.S.)

Special and motor fuel use tax.—Motor carriers who fail to file a return and pay any tax liability on the operation of commercial motor vehicles in Florida are subject to a penalty equal to the greater of: $50 or 10% of the delinquent taxes due, when the failure is for not more than 30 days. An additional 10% penalty is imposed for each additional 30 days during the time while the failure continues, not to exceed a total penalty of 100% in the aggregate. (Sec. 207.007, F.S.)

Motor fuel tax.—Any person who willfully evades or attempts to evade payment of the fuel tax will be penalized $10 for every gallon of motor fuel involved or $1,000, whichever is greater, for the first offense. The penalty will increase for subsequent offenses. (Sec. 206.413(3)(a), F.S.)

[¶89-208] Criminal Penalties

Some failures to file returns or pay taxes rise to the level of criminal activity.

• *Sales and use taxes*

Because taxes become state funds at the moment of collection, failure to remit sales and use taxes collected is a theft of state funds classified as follows:

the first offense, if the amount stolen is less than $100, is a second degree misdemeanor;

the second offense within three years, if the amount stolen is less than $100, is a first degree misdemeanor;

the third offense within three years, if the amount stolen is less than $100, is a third degree felony;

the offense, if the amount stolen is $100 or more, is a third degree felony; and

the offense, if the amount stolen is $20,000 or more, is a second degree felony.

(Sec. 212.14, F.S.)

In addition, filing a fraudulent return or evasion of payment is a first degree misdemeanor. (Sec. 212.12(2)(a), F.S.)

Failure to register as a dealer.—A person engaging in business without a valid certificate of registration as a dealer may be convicted of a first degree misdemeanor or may be subject to injunctive proceedings. (Sec. 212.18(3)(a), F.S.)

Fraudulent return or willful intent to evade payment of tax or fee.—Any taxpayer who files a fraudulent return or willfully intends to evade payment of a tax or fee is liable for a specific penalty of 100% of the tax bill or fee and for fine and punishment as provided by law. (Sec. 212.12(2)(a), F.S.)

Corporate officers.—A corporate officer who refuses to make a return and pay the taxes due may be convicted of a first degree misdemeanor. (Sec. 212.14(3), F.S.)

Fraudulent claim of exemption.—If a person issues, for the purpose of evading tax, a certificate or statement to a vendor in which there is a claim of exemption from sales tax, that person is subject to fine and punishment as provided for a conviction of a third degree felony. (Sec. 212.085, F.S.)

Fraudulent claim of a credit for job creation in an enterprise zone.—Any person who fraudulently claims a credit for jobs in an enterprise zone is subject to punishment as provided for a conviction of a second degree misdemeanor. (Sec. 212.096(10), F.S.)

Occasional or isolated sales.—Any party who reports a sales price from an occasional or isolated sale of an aircraft, boat, mobile home, or motor vehicle that is less than the actual sales price is guilty of a first degree misdemeanor. (Sec. 212.05(1)(a), F.S.)

Transient rentals reports.—Failure to report a transaction involving the taxable rental of real property is a second degree misdemeanor for the first offense and a first degree misdemeanor for each subsequent offense. (Sec. 212.12(13), F.S.)

• *Corporate income tax*

Anyone who willfully fails to comply with the statutes governing corporate income tax, including failing to remit taxes or paying with a check that fails to clear, can be guilty of a misdemeanor. Anyone aiding or abetting a taxpayer in that regard is subject to the same penalties as the taxpayer. (Sec. 220.901, F.S.; Sec. 220.903, F.S.; Sec. 220.905, F.S.)

Anyone who fraudulently claims an enterprise zone jobs credit or makes an underpayment of tax as a result of a grossly overstated claim for the credit is guilty of a felony. (Sec. 220.181, F.S.)

• *Documentary stamp tax*

Failure to pay a required documentary stamp tax is a misdemeanor. (Sec. 201.08, F.S.; Sec. 201.11, F.S.; Sec. 201.17, F.S.)

• *Other taxes*

There are criminal penalties for willful failure to file, pay taxes, or make false claims for other tax types, including the following:

Local Option Tourist Development Act; (Sec. 125.0104, F.S.)

estate taxes; (Sec. 198.37, F.S.; Sec. 198.38, F.S.; Sec. 198.39, F.S.; Sec. 198.40, F.S.)

communications tax; (Sec. 202.27, F.S.; Sec. 202.28, F.S.; Sec. 202.33, F.S.; Sec. 202.34, F.S.; Sec. 202.35, F.S.)

tax on gross receipts for utilities services; (Sec. 203.01, F.S.; Sec. 203.03, F.S.)

motor fuel taxes; (Sec. 206.11, F.S.; Sec. 206.18, F.S.; Sec. 206.23, F.S.; Sec. 206.56, F.S.; Sec. 206.8735, F.S.)

tax on operation of commercial motor vehicles; (Sec. 207.007, F.S.)

tax on tobacco products; (Sec. 210.18, F.S.; Sec. 210.65, F.S.)

severance taxes; (Sec. 211.25, F.S.; Sec. 211.335, F.S.)

convention development taxes; (Sec. 212.0305, F.S.)

qualified defense contractor tax refund program; (Sec. 288.1045, F.S.)

tax refund program for qualified target industry businesses; (Sec. 288.106, F.S.)

brownfield redevelopment bonus refunds; (Sec. 288.107, F.S.)

entertainment industry qualified production companies; (Sec. 288.1258, F.S.) and

Employing and Training Our Youth program. (Ch. 97-278, Sec. 58)

[¶89-210] Abatement of Interest, Penalties, or Additions to Tax

The Department of Revenue may enter into a closing agreement with a taxpayer settling or compromising the taxpayer's liability for any tax, interest, or penalty. The agreement must be in writing when the amount compromised exceeds $30,000, or when the Department deems it appropriate, or the taxpayer requests it. (Sec. 213.21, F.S.; Rule 12-13.001, F.A.C., *et seq.*)

The Department may compromise a taxpayer's liability for tax or interest upon grounds of doubt as to the taxpayer's liability for the tax or interest or doubt as to the collectibility of the tax or interest. The Department also may settle or compromise a taxpayer's liability for penalties if it determines that the noncompliance is due to reasonable cause rather than to willful negligence, willful neglect, or fraud. (Sec. 213.21, F.S.)

[¶89-220]
TAXPAYER RIGHTS AND REMEDIES

[¶89-222] Taxpayers' Bill of Rights

The Florida Taxpayers' Bill of Rights lists and explains the rights and obligations of taxpayers and the Department of Revenue. However, the rights afforded taxpayers to protect their privacy and property during tax assessment and collection are available only to the extent they are applied elsewhere in the Florida Statutes or in the Department Rules. Guaranteed protections include the right to:

(1) available information and prompt, accurate responses to questions and requests for tax assistance;

(2) assistance from a taxpayers' rights advocate;

(3) representation in administrative interactions with the Department; procedural safeguards in the recording of interviews conducted by the Department; and the conduct of audits, inspections, and interviews at a reasonable time and place (except in criminal and internal investigations);

(4) freedom from penalty, freedom from payment of uncollected sales and use taxes, and abatement of interest on underpayments that result from reasonable taxpayer reliance upon binding written advice furnished by the Department in response to a specific written request that provided adequate and accurate information;

(5) simple explanations of procedures, remedies, and rights available during audit, appeals, and collection proceedings; and a narrative description that explains the basis of audit changes, assessments, and refund denials, identifying the tax, interest, or penalty amount due, and stating the consequences of the taxpayer's failure to comply with the notice;

(6) notice of impending collection actions that require the sale or seizure of property or freezing of assets, except with respect to jeopardy assessments; and at least 30 days to pay the liability or seek further review;

(7) application of all other available collection actions before a jeopardy assessment is imposed, unless delay will endanger collection; and immediate review of a jeopardy assessment;

(8) seek review of any adverse decision and to seek a reasonable administrative stay of enforcement while the taxpayer pursues other administrative remedies;

(9) confidential treatment of taxpayer information unless otherwise specified by law;

(10) procedures for retirement of tax obligations by installment payment agreements;

(11) procedures for requesting cancellation, release, or modification of liens filed by the Department and for requesting that any lien filed in error be so noted;

(12) procedures assuring that employees of the Department are not paid, evaluated, or promoted based on the volume of taxpayer assessments or collections;

(13) an action at law, subject to limitations of the state's waiver of sovereign immunity, to recover damages against the state or the Department for injury caused by the wrongful or negligent act or omission of a Department officer or employee;

(14) recover all costs of the action, including reasonable attorney's fees, and to settle such claims through negotiations (applicable to the taxpayer or the Department, as the prevailing party in a judicial or administrative action brought or maintained with supporting justiciable issues);

(15) commencement and completion of audit by the Department in a timely and expeditious manner after notification of intent to audit;

(16) active identification and review of multistate proposals that offer more efficient and effective methods for administering the revenue sources of this state;

(17) active investigation and, where appropriate, implementation of automated or electronic business methods that enable the Department to more efficiently and effectively administer the revenue sources of this state at less cost and effort for taxpayers;

(18) waiver of interest that accrues as the result of errors or delays caused by a Department employee;

(19) participation in free educational activities that help the taxpayer successfully comply with the revenue laws of this state;

(20) payment of a reasonable fine or percentage of tax, whichever is less, to reinstate an exemption from any tax which a taxpayer would have been entitled to receive but which was lost because the taxpayer failed to properly register as a tax dealer in the state or obtain the necessary certificates entitling the taxpayer to the exemption;

(21) fair and consistent application of the tax laws of this state by the Department.

(Sec. 24, Art. I, Fla. Const.; Sec. 213.015, F.S.)

• *Taxpayers' Rights Advocate*

A Taxpayers' Rights Advocate facilitates the resolution of taxpayer complaints and problems that have not been resolved through normal Department administrative channels and ensures that taxpayer rights are protected during tax determination and collection procedures. The Advocate can issue a stay order pursuant to irreparable loss sustained by a taxpayer due to an action by the Department. A stay order also is authorized if irreparable taxpayer loss is anticipated because of Department action. (Sec. 213.018(1), F.S.; Sec. 20.21(3), F.S.)

Taxpayer assistance orders.—The Advocate may, without a formal written request from the taxpayer, issue a taxpayer assistance order that suspends or stays actions by the Department when the taxpayer suffers or is about to suffer a significant hardship as a result of a tax determination, collection, or enforcement process. The advocate may grant such relief only as an extraordinary measure, however, and the process may not be used to contest the merits of a tax liability. When a taxpayer requests such an order, the running of the limitations period on assessment is tolled from the date of the request until the date the request is denied or the date specified in the taxpayer assistance order. (Sec. 213.018(1), F.S.)

• *Confidentiality—email address*

A taxpayer's email address is exempt from certain disclosure requirements when held for specific purposes. The exemption applies when the email is held to:

— send a quarterly tax notice for prepayment of estimated taxes;

— obtain the taxpayer's consent to send the tax notice electronically;

— send an additional tax notice or delinquent tax notice to the taxpayer; or

— send a tax notice to a designated third party, mortgagee, or vendee.

(Sec. 197.3225, F.S.)

[¶89-224] Refunds

Statutory and regulatory provisions generally distinguish refund claim requirements and procedures according to tax type.

• *General refund provisions*

The State Comptroller may refund overpayments or erroneous payments of any tax, license, or account. (Sec. 215.26(1), F.S.) Refund applications must generally be filed within three years of the date tax was paid. (Sec. 215.26(2), F.S.) Specific conditions, discussed below, apply to ad valorem property tax refunds.

Taxpayers may contest the legality of any assessment or denial of refund of tax, fee, surcharge, permit, interest, or penalty under Florida Administrative Procedures Act provisions. Taxpayers may not file such an action, however, without first complying with applicable registration requirements. (Sec. 72.011, F.S.)

Offsets.—If a taxpayer is due a refund or credit for overpayment of taxes, the Department may reduce the refund or credit to the extent of any billings not subject to protest for the same tax or other tax owed by the taxpayer. (Sec. 213.25, F.S.)

• *Corporate income tax*

Refund claims for corporate income tax must be filed with the Department of Revenue in writing, stating the amount claimed, the specific grounds upon which the claim is founded, and the taxable years or periods involved. (Sec. 220.725(1), F.S.) After a claim is filed, the Department must examine the claim as soon as practicable, and must issue a notice of refund, abatement or credit to the claimant or issue a notice of denial. (Sec. 220.725(2), F.S.)

Interest on overpayments.—Interest is allowed and paid on any overpayment of tax. However, if any overpayment is refunded or credited within three months after the taxpayer files written notice of the overpayment with the Department, no interest is allowed on the overpayment. (Sec. 220.723, F.S.; Rule 12-3.0015, F.A.C.).

Time limitations.—Refund applications must generally be filed within three years after the date tax was paid. (Sec. 215.26(2), F.S.; Sec. 220.727(1), F.S.)

For purposes of the three-year limitation period, estimated tax payments are considered paid at the time the return was required to be filed, including any extensions of time allowed to the taxpayer to file the return, and not when the estimated tax payments were actually made. (Sec. 220.727(1)(b), F.S.)

A claim for a refund resulting from a change in the taxpayer's federal return must be filed within two years from the date on which notification of the change was due to the Department, regardless of whether the notification was actually given. (Sec. 220.23(2)(d)) Notification is due by the earlier of 60 days after the final determination of the federal adjustment or 60 days after any federal income tax deficiency or refund resulting from the adjustment has been assessed, paid, or collected. (Sec. 220.23(2)(a))

• *Sales and use taxes*

Refund applications must generally be filed within three years of the date tax was paid. (Sec. 215.26(2), F.S.)

• *Insurance gross premiums tax*

If an overpayment of insurance premium tax has been paid, the Florida Department of Revenue (DOR) may refund the amount of the overpayment to the taxpayer by a warrant of the Chief Financial Officer. Although the DOR may refund the overpayment without regard to whether the taxpayer has filed a written claim for a refund, the DOR may request that the taxpayer file a statement affirming that the taxpayer made the overpayment. A refund of the insurance premium tax may not be made, and a taxpayer is not entitled to bring an action for a refund of the insurance premium tax, after three years after the right to the refund has accrued. If an amended insurance premium return is required, a refund may be claimed within two years of the original filing date for the return. If a refund exceeds the amount of refund legally due to the taxpayer, the penalties and interest do not apply if the taxpayer reimburses the DOR for any overpayment within 60 days after the taxpayer is notified that the overpayment was made. (Sec. 624.511(3), F.S.)

• *Multiple tax types*

Economic Development Trust Fund refunds to qualified defense contractors and space flight business.—Qualified applicants may apply by January 31 of each fiscal year to the Department of Economic Opportunity for a refund from the Economic Development Trust Fund for the corporate income, sales and use, excise, property, documentary stamp, and communications services taxes due and paid by them, beginning with the applicant's first taxable year commencing after entering into a tax refund agreement. Qualified applicants are those who:

(1) consolidate Department of Defense contracts,

(2) obtain new Department of Defense production contracts,

(3) convert defense production to non-defense production,

(4) contract for reuse of a defense-related facility,

(5) enter into a valid new space flight business contract, or

(6) consolidate a space flight business contract

(Sec. 288.1045(5), F.S.)

Refunds from the Fund are not allowed for any amount of credit, refund, or exemption granted to the contractor for any of such taxes.

A qualified applicant is allowed tax refund payments equal to $3,000 times the number of jobs specified in the tax refund agreement, or $6,000 times the number of jobs if the project is located in a rural county or an enterprise zone. Additionally, a qualified applicant is allowed additional tax refund payments equal to $1,000 times the number of jobs specified in the tax refund agreement if such jobs pay an annual average wage of at least 150% of the average private sector wage in the areas, or $2,000 times the number of jobs if such jobs pay an annual average wage of at least 200% of the average private sector wage in the area. (Sec. 288.1045(2)(b), F.S.)

An applicant that has achieved at least 80 of its projected employment will be approved for a prorated refund, less a 5 penalty, provided that all other applicable requirements have been satisfied. No qualified applicant may receive refunds of more than 25 of the total tax refunds provided in the tax refund agreement. (Sec. 288.1045(5), F.S.) No qualified applicant may receive more than $2.5 million in such tax refunds in any fiscal year. (Sec. 288.1045(2)(b), F.S.)

Funds made available pursuant to the qualified defense contractor tax refund program may not be expended in connection with the relocation of a business from one community to another community in the state unless there is a compelling economic rationale for the relocation which creates additional jobs or, without the relocation, the business will move outside the state. (Sec. 288.1045(2)(g), F.S.)

For purposes of the refund, a "Department of Defense contract" includes a contract with the U.S. Department of Defense, U.S. Department of State, or the U.S. Department of Homeland Security. (Sec. 288.1045(1)(g), F.S.)

Applicants may not be certified as qualified after June 30, 2014. (Sec. 288.1045(8), F.S.)

Qualified applicants for the Qualified Defense Contractor Refund Agreement who cannot meet the requirements of the tax refund agreement during the year may request an economic-stimulus exemption. The request must be submitted to the Department of Economic Opportunity and must provide evidence demonstrating how negative economic conditions in the applicant's industry, the effects of a named hurricane or tropical storm, or specific acts of terrorism affecting the applicant have prevented the applicant from complying with the terms of the agreement. (Sec. 288.1045(4), F.S.)

Refunds for qualified target industry businesses.—Qualified target industry businesses, after entering into tax refund agreements with the Department of Economic Opportunity, are entitled to apply by January 31 of each fiscal year for refunds from the Economic Development Incentives Account for the corporate income, insurance premium, sales and use, intangible personal property, excise, and property taxes due and paid by them after entering into the agreement. (Sec. 288.106, F.S.) The refund requested may not exceed the amount specified for that fiscal year in the agreement. (Sec. 288.106(6), F.S.) Businesses may not receive a refund for any amount of credit, refund, or exemption granted for taxes for which the refund is permitted. (Sec. 288.106, F.S.)

A "target industry business" is a corporate headquarters business or any business that is engaged in one of the target industries. Six criteria are established for identifying target industries:

(1) future growth;

(2) stability;

(3) high wages;

(4) market and resource independence (special consideration must be given to the development of strong industrial clusters which include defense and homeland security businesses);

(5) industrial base diversification and strengthening; and

(6) positive economic impact.

Special consideration will be given to industries that facilitate the development of the state as a hub for domestic and global trade and logistics.
(Sec. 288.106(2), F.S.)

The following businesses are not considered target industry businesses:

(1) industries engaged in retail activities;

(2) electrical utility companies;

(3) phosphate or other solid minerals severance, mining, or processing operations; or

(4) firms subject to regulation by the Division of Hotels and Restaurants of the Department of Business and Professional Regulation.
(Sec. 288.106(2)(o), F.S.)

An application for certification as a qualified target industry business must be filed with the Department of Economic Opportunity before the applicant locates a new business in Florida or expands an existing business in Florida. (Sec. 288.106(4)(a),

F.S.) Applicants may not be certified as qualified after June 30, 2010. (Sec. 288.106(8), F.S.)

Qualified target industry businesses are entitled to refunds equal to $3,000 times the number of jobs specified in the tax refund agreement or equal to $6,000 times the number of jobs if the project is located in a rural county or an enterprise zone, plus an additional refund equal to $1,000 times the number of jobs specified in the tax refund agreement if such jobs pay an annual average wage of at least 150 of the average private-sector wage in the area or equal to $2,000 times the number of jobs if such jobs pay an annual average wage of at least 200 of the average private-sector wage in the area. A qualified target industry business may not receive refund payments of more than:

(1) 25 of the total tax refunds specified in the tax refund agreement in any fiscal year;

(2) $1.5 million in refunds in any single fiscal year; or,

(3) for projects located in an enterprise zone, $2.5 million. A qualified target industry may not receive more than $5 million ($7 million, effective July 1, 2012) in refund payments in all fiscal years or, for projects located in an enterprise zone, $7.5 million.

To be eligible for refunds as a qualified target industry, the proposed jobs must pay either an estimated annual average wage of at least 115 of the average private sector wage for the area or the statewide private-sector average wage. This average wage requirement may be waived at the request of the local governing body recommending the project and Enterprise Florida, Inc. (Sec. 288.106(4)(b) 1, F.S.)

Qualified target businesses that achieve at least 80 of projected employment will receive a prorated refund, less a 5 penalty, provided the business has met all other requirements. (Sec. 288.106(6), F.S.)

With an exception noted below, the tax refund may not be approved for a qualified target industry business unless the required local financial support has been paid into the account in that fiscal year. The tax refund must be reduced if the local financial support provided is less than 20% of the approved tax refund. The tax refund may not exceed an amount that is equal to five times the amount of the local financial support received. The amount of tax refund, and the limitations on such refunds, must be reduced by the amount of any tax abatement granted to such businesses. The tax refund must also be reduced by the appraised market value of municipal or county land conveyed or provided at a discount to the business and the limitations on such refunds must also be reduced by that amount. (Sec. 288.106(6)(c), F.S.)

A bonus refund of property tax, sales and use tax, documentary stamp tax, corporate income tax, intangible personal property tax, emergency excise tax, or insurance premium tax, in an amount up to $2,500, is available to any qualified target industry business or "other eligible business" for each new Florida job created in a brownfield area eligible for bonus refunds that is claimed on the business's annual tax refund claim. (Sec. 288.107(2), F.S.) Refunds are paid from the Economic Development Incentives Account. The bonus refunds are available on the same schedule as the tax refund payments scheduled in an agreement authorized by the qualified target industry business refund provisions or other similar agreement for "other eligible businesses." (Sec. 288.107(4)(c), F.S.)

The Department of Economic Opportunity will approve all claims for a brownfield redevelopment bonus refund payment if they meet all the requirements. (Sec. 288.107(4)(g), F.S.) Eligible businesses must submit a claim once a year on a form that indicates the location of the brownfield site for which rehabilitation agreement with the Department of Environmental Protection (DEP) or a local government delegated by the DEP has been qualifiedly executed, the address of the business facility's brownfield location, the name of the brownfield in which it is located, the number of jobs created, and the average wage of the jobs created by the business within the brownfield or "other eligible business." (Sec. 288.107(4)(b), F.S.) Requests to waive the average wage requirement for brownfield areas must be granted, unless it is demonstrated that such action is not in the public interest. (Sec. 288.106(6)(c), F.S.) After entering into a tax refund agreement or other similar agreement for "other eligible businesses," an eligible business may receive brownfield redevelopment bonus refunds from the account. (Sec. 288.107(4)(d), F.S.)

"Eligible businesses other than qualified target industry businesses" are businesses that can demonstrate a fixed capital investment of at least $2 million in mixed-use business activities, including multi-unit housing, commercial, retail, and industrial in brownfield areas, or at least $500,000 in brownfield areas that do not require site cleanup, and that provide benefits to their employees. (Sec. 288.107(1)(e), F.S.)

The Governor may designate up to three rural areas of critical economic concern and, acting through the Rural Economic Development Initiative within the Department of Economic Opportunity, may waive criteria, requirements, or similar provisions of any economic development incentive, including but not limited to the Qualified Target Industry Tax Refund Program and brownfield redevelopment bonus refunds. (Sec. 288.0656(7), F.S.)

Qualified applicants for the Qualified Target Industry Tax Refund Program who cannot meet the requirements of the tax refund agreement during the year may request an economic-stimulus exemption. The request must be submitted to the Department of Economic Opportunity (formerly, Office of Tourism, Trade, and Economic Development) and must provide evidence demonstrating how negative economic conditions in the applicant's industry, the effects of a named hurricane or tropical storm, or specific acts of terrorism affecting the applicant have prevented the applicant from complying with the terms of the agreement. (Sec. 288.106(5)(b), F.S.)

• *Protests of refund changes or denial*

Conferences for Notices of Intent to Make Refund Claim Changes.—Upon determining that a refund should be wholly or partially denied, the Department will issue a notice to the taxpayer that will include an explanation of the reason for the denial. The taxpayer will have 30 consecutive calendar days after the date of issuance on the notice to sign the notice agreeing to the proposed changes or to mail or fax a written request for a conference to the address or fax number designated on the notice. (Rule 12-6.030(1), F.A.C.)

If a conference is requested, it will be held at the earliest convenience of both the taxpayer and the Department, but it will not be held more than 40 consecutive calendar days after the date of issuance on the notice, unless specifically agreed to in writing by the Department. (Rule 12-6.030(3), F.A.C.)

The Department will issue a Notice of Proposed Refund Denial (Form DR-832R) if:

    (1) an agreement is not reached after the conference,

    (2) the taxpayer has not timely filed a written request for a conference,

    (3) the taxpayer has not timely filed a written request for an extension of time for requesting a conference, or

    (4) the taxpayer has waived the right to a conference.

(Rule 12-6.030(6), F.A.C.)

Protests of Notices of Proposed Refund Denials.—A taxpayer may secure review of a Notice of Proposed Refund Denial (Form DR-832R), by filing a written protest that is postmarked or faxed within 60 consecutive calendar days from the date of issuance on the notice. (Rule 12-6.032(1), F.A.C.)

Upon receipt of a complete, timely filed written protest, the Refunds and Distribution Process will review the protest and attempt to resolve the issues. If a resolution is not reached, the protest will be forwarded to Technical Assistance and Dispute Resolution. If requested by the taxpayer, an opportunity for submission of additional information and an oral conference will be provided. (Rule 12-6.032(3), F.A.C.)

If a protest is timely filed and the taxpayer and the Department are unable to resolve the disputed issues, the protest will be denied and the proposed refund denial will become final as of the date of issuance on the denial, unless the taxpayer timely files a petition for reconsideration of the denial. (Rule 12-6.032(3), F.A.C.) The taxpayer has 30 consecutive calendar days from the date of issuance on the denial to file a petition for reconsideration. The Department will not grant an extension of time for filing a petition for reconsideration. (Rule 12-6.032(4), F.A.C.)

If a petition for reconsideration is timely filed and the taxpayer and the Department are unable to resolve the disputed issues, the petition will be denied and the proposed refund denial will become final as of the date the petition is denied. (Rule 12-6.032(4), F.A.C.)

[¶89-230] Taxpayer Conferences

Taxpayers may request conferences with the Department of Revenue concerning Notices of Intent to Make Audit Changes or delinquency notices or billings that the taxpayer receives from the Department.

• *Notices of Intent to Make Audit Changes*

The Department of Revenue, once it has completed an audit, issues a Notice of Intent to Make Audit Changes, unless the case at hand involves a jeopardy assessment, an estimated assessment, a refund denial, or is a case where review of the taxpayer's books and records results in no liability due to the state or no refundable amount due to the taxpayer. (Rule 12-6.002(1), F.A.C.)

Taxpayers may request a conference concerning the Notice of Intent to Make Audit Changes. However, they must do so within 30 consecutive calendar days after the receipt of the notice. Requests must be submitted directly to the local office of the Department that issued the notice. (Rule 12-6.002(1), F.A.C.)

Conferences, when requested, must be held at the earliest convenience of both the taxpayer and the Department. However, the conferences may not be held later than 90 consecutive calendar days after the date on which the Notice of Intent to Make Audit Changes or the Revised Notice of Intent to Make Audit Changes was issued. (Rule 12-6.002(3), F.A.C.)

A taxpayer that fails to timely request a conference waives its rights to the conference. However, even taxpayers that fail to timely request the conference may use the protest procedures for obtaining review of proposed assessments. (Rule 12-6.002(4), F.A.C.; Rule 12-6.003, F.A.C.)

The 30-day period required for filing the request may be waived by the taxpayer to expedite resolution of issues if the Department's representative and the taxpayer jointly determine that the issues cannot be resolved at the local level. (Rule 12-6.002(6), F.A.C.)

A Notice of Proposed Assessment will be issued by the Department if: (1) an agreement is not reached after the conference; (2) the taxpayer has not timely filed a written request for a conference; (3) the taxpayer has not timely filed a written request for an extension of time for requesting a conference; or (4) the taxpayer has waived his or her right to a conference pursuant to this section. (Rule 12-6.002(6), F.A.C.).

• *Delinquency notices or billings*

Taxpayers that receive delinquency notices or billings from the Department may request a conference if no assessment has been issued. Requests must be made by mailing, telephoning, or faxing the request directly to the address, telephone number, or fax number of the office designated on the delinquency notice or billing. (Rule 12-6.0023(1), F.A.C.)

The taxpayer must request a conference within 20 consecutive calendar days after issuance of the notice. (Rule 12-6.0023(1), F.A.C.) A taxpayer may request an extension of time in which to request a conference if the request for an extension is received by the proper office prior to the expiration of the period within which a conference must be requested. Each extension of time will be for 30 consecutive calendar days. (Rule 12-6.0023(1), F.A.C.)

Conferences must be held at the earliest convenience of both the taxpayer and the Department, but no later than 40 consecutive calendar days after the date of the notice, unless specifically agreed to in writing by the Department. (Rule 12-6.0023(3), F.A.C.) If the taxpayer and the division fail to reach an agreement at the conference, or if a request is not timely made for a conference, an assessment will be issued and the taxpayer may file a protest. (Rule 12-6.0023(3), F.A.C.).

• *Property tax*

For a discussion of informal conferences with respect to property tax, see ¶ 20-906.

[¶89-234] Administrative Appeals

Taxpayers may challenge any final assessment or denial of refund under any tax within the jurisdiction of the Department of Revenue. However, they must elect whether to appeal to the Department, pursuant to the terms of the Administrative Procedure Act, or to circuit court. In either event, appellate review would be to the appropriate Florida District Court of Appeals. No action may be commenced until the complaining taxpayer complies with all registration requirements relating to the tax type. Further, an action cannot be brought more than 60 days after a refund is denied or an assessment becomes final. (Sec. 72.011, F.S.)

[¶89-236] Judicial Appeals and Remedies

Taxpayers may challenge any final assessment or denial of refund under any tax within the jurisdiction of the Department of Revenue. However, they must elect whether to appeal to the Department, pursuant to the terms of the Administrative Procedure Act, or to circuit court. In either event, appellate review would be to the appropriate Florida District Court of Appeals. No action may be commenced until the complaining taxpayer complies with all registration requirements relating to the tax type. Further, an action cannot be brought more than 60 days after a refund is denied or an assessment becomes final. (Sec. 72.011, F.S.)

Pursuant to actions filed in circuit court, taxpayers must tender to the court contested taxes, penalties, and accrued interest assessed, unless the proper authority waives this requirement. Alternatively, taxpayers must file a cash bond or surety bond, along with uncontested taxes and the complaint, in the amount of the contested assessment. Actions must be filed in the Circuit Court in Leon County for non-residents with no commercial domicile, or in the circuit court in the county where the taxpayer resides, maintains its principal commercial domicile, or, in the ordinary course of business, regularly maintains it books and records in this state. (Sec. 72.011, F.S.)

Appellate judicial review is available to parties adversely affected by final agency action. A preliminary, procedural, or intermediate order of an agency or administrative law judge is immediately reviewable if a final agency decision would not yield an adequate remedy. Adversely affected parties must seek judicial review where the agency maintains its headquarters or where an adversely affected party resides or as otherwise provided. A notice of appeal or petition for review must be filed no later than 30 days after the order being appealed has been rendered. (Sec. 120.68, F.S.)

• *Federal court actions*

An assessment may be appealed to a federal court if there is a question involving the U.S. Constitution or a federal statute. However, the right to bring a federal suit is limited by the Tax Injunction Act and the fundamental principle of comity. The Tax Injunction Act prohibits injunctions in federal district courts against the assessment, levy, or collection of any state tax when there is a "plain, speedy, and efficient remedy" in state courts. (28 U.S.C. 1341) Because this federal provision has been the subject of considerable litigation, the case law interpreting this provision should be researched if a federal action is contemplated.

In addition, any appeal of a state tax case to a federal court would be subject to established principles of federal jurisdiction and abstention.

• *Property tax*

For a discussion of judicial appeals with respect to property tax, see ¶ 20-906.

[¶ 89-238] Representation of Taxpayer

Among the rights enumerated in the Taxpayers' Bill of Rights (TBOR) is the right to be represented or advised by counsel or other qualified representatives at any time in administrative interactions with the Department of Revenue. A Power of Attorney (POA) form, or declaration of representation, must be filed with the Department in order to designate a taxpayer's representative. Among other powers granted, a POA form authorizes representatives to sign documents, receive and inspect confidential tax information, and execute closing agreements. A POA and Declaration of Representative (Form DR-835) may be downloaded directly from the Department's website (http://sun6.dms.state.fl.usdorforms).

Further, TBOR grants taxpayers the right to request assistance from a Taxpayers' Rights Advocate of the Department to help resolve taxpayer complaints and problems not resolved throught normal administrative channels. (Sec. 213.015, F.S.)

• *Corporate income tax*

For corporate income tax purposes, taxpayer representatives must be recognized to practice before the Department. Qualified representatives include:

attorneys and certified public accountants in good standing in their professions in their jurisdictions;

enrolled agents certified to practice before the Internal Revenue Service under Treasury Circular Number 230; and

partnership members; corporate officers; authorized employees, provided adequate identification is furnished to the Department.

In general, taxpayers must execute a power of attorney clearly expressing the taxpayer's intention to empower a representative to:

receive a refund check;

execute a waiver of restriction on an assessment or collection of a tax deficiency; or

execute a consent to extend the statutory period for tax assessment or collection.

Likewise, a tax information authorization signed by the taxpayer is generally required to allow a representative to receive or inspect confidential information. (Rule 12C-1.318, F.A.C.)

[¶89-240] Limitations Period for Appeals

A taxpayer has 60 days from notice of a final assessment or a denial of refund to appeal to either the Department of Revenue or to a circuit court. (Sec. 72.011, F.S.) Taxpayers have 30 days in which to appeal a final action by the Department. (Sec. 120.68, F.S.)

TOPICAL INDEX

⟫⟫→ *References are to paragraph (¶) numbers.*